DIPLOMATIC RELATIONS
BETWEEN THE
UNITED STATES AND JAPAN

1853–1895

DIPLOMATIC RELATIONS

BETWEEN THE

UNITED STATES

AND JAPAN

1853-1895

By PAYSON J. TREAT

Professor of History at Stanford University

VOLUME I
(1853-1875)

GLOUCESTER, MASS.

PETER SMITH

1963

PREFACE

THE PURPOSE of this study is to present, primarily from archive material, an account of the diplomatic relations between the United States and Japan from their inception to the close of the Sino-Japanese War in 1895. For the early years, into 1865, when the Foreign Representatives and their governments understood but vaguely what was stirring in Japan, considerable use has been made of contemporary Japanese materials. The study of this period, which is covered by the first eleven chapters, was presented as the Albert Shaw Lectures on Diplomatic History at Johns Hopkins University in 1917. I am indebted to The Johns Hopkins Press for permission to reprint this material, with corrections and revisions. After 1865 the material has been drawn largely from the archives of the State Department in Washington. How much of it is new may be inferred from the fact that, between 1855 and 1894, 2,080 instructions were sent to the Representatives in Japan, and of these only 202 were printed in any official publication. Some 4,433 dispatches were sent from the Legation, and only 639 were printed. In addition the dispatches from Peking and Seoul were examined, and other collections of diplomatic papers in the archives were explored. After working for more than twenty-five years in the printed source and secondary materials dealing with this period I am confident that the information now drawn from the archives will permit a rewriting of the earlier accounts of many of the incidents and developments covered by these volumes.

The presentation of the subject-matter in chapters covering a single year in most instances was decided upon as a choice of evils. Many of the questions which come into the narrative were under discussion for several years; the most important one, Treaty revision, having been the subject of diplomatic correspondence constantly between 1872 and 1894. While a topical treatment would have had the advantage of bringing the discussion of any subject within a chapter or two it would have lessened the significance of the influence of other issues which from time to time affected the main controversy. In fact, any event of a single year should be carefully studied in the light of developments in connection with other questions. It was finally decided to make use of year periods, grouping the topics in each chapter according to their subject-matter. This also had the advantage of saving a great repetition of dates in the text and in the numerous citations. Unless a contrary year is stated, it may be assumed that all dates refer to the year covered by the chapter.

While it was my first intention to confine the discussion to matters of a diplomatic nature I finally decided to include, very briefly, an account of practically everything which became the subject of correspondence between the Legation and the State Department. Some of these incidents may seem to be of a fugitive nature, but they serve, however, to give the student an idea of the work of an American Legation over a long period, which may prove interesting and helpful.

On such a detailed survey a few generalizations may be based. Among them would be a recognition of the praiseworthy nature of American-Japanese diplomatic relations throughout this period, of the consistent friendliness of the American Government, of the equally eager desire of the Japanese Government to deserve this friendship, of the remarkable aptitude of Japanese diplomats in grasping and following the practices of Western diplomacy; and, I trust, an appreciation of the fact that few governments have been as amenable to kindly and constructive criticism as that of Japan. Where exceptions to these general attitudes have been recorded they simply throw into greater contrast the more usual conditions. The author, at any event, has gained from this study a firmer belief that, in intercourse between nations, honesty, fair play, and a fine appreciation of the rights and sensibilities of one's neighbors are as important as in relations between individuals.

It is with a deep sense of appreciation that I record my obligation to all those who have in any way helped me in the preparation of this study. For the facilities I enjoyed in the State Department I am especially indebted to Dr. Tyler Dennett, then historical adviser, Mrs. Maddin Summers, in charge of archives, and Miss Amy Holland, in charge of treaties. Mr. Robert C. Pruyn, private secretary at the Yedo Legation in 1862–65, placed the private papers of his father at my disposal. The late Mr. Eli T. Sheppard not only permitted me to examine his papers but on many occasions gave me suggestions which helped to interpret the formal correspondence of the period. And the Honorable Frank L. Coombs also gave me an insight into some of the events during his service in Japan. My colleague, Dr. Yamato Ichihashi, gave me much aid in gathering information from Japanese sources. The Consul General of Japan in San Francisco, Mr. Kaname Wakasugi, very kindly examined materials in the Consulate General for my information. In transcribing documents in the State Department, Miss Eileen Berrall rendered accurate service, and in the preparation of the manuscript Miss Bernice Miller and Miss Marion Dwight gave generous assistance. To the staff of the Stanford University Press I am indebted for unfailing consideration and help.

PAYSON J. TREAT

STANFORD UNIVERSITY, CALIFORNIA
March 31, 1932

CONTENTS

CHAPTER I

COMMODORE PERRY: PEACE AND AMITY
1853–54

WHEN the exchange of ratifications of the first American Treaty with Japan took place, almost a year after the Treaty had been signed, the Japanese commissioners sent this message to the American commodore, that "his name would live forever in the history of Japan."[1] Rarely does a prophecy stand the test of half a century, and yet after seventy years the name of Perry is familiar to almost every schoolboy in Japan, although in his own country his fame has not fared so well. From the Japanese standpoint the American Treaty of 1854 was of the deepest significance. It marked the beginning of the end, not only of the old policy of seclusion and exclusion, but of the far older system of dual government, and it was the real commencement of that era of progress and world intercourse which has placed the Island Empire among the great Powers of the world. From the American point of view it was an interesting episode, reflecting honor and glory upon a nation which had hitherto played but a small part in the world's affairs; but so absorbed did the country soon become in the Civil War and in the later problems of reconstruction and internal development that the passing interest in Japan soon waned. The American Government continued to be the unselfish friend of Japan, but leadership in Japanese affairs for a time passed into other hands. That it was American diplomacy which brought Japan into peaceful intercourse with the civilized world remains to the credit of the United States, no matter what efforts were made then and later to minimize the contribution. And there is

---

[1] Hawks, *Narrative of the Expedition of an American Squadron to the China Seas and Japan, etc.*, I, 512.

1

reason to believe that Japan herself has cause to be thankful that her first lessons in international law were learned from American representatives.

For more than two centuries Japan had been closed to all foreign intercourse, save only a strictly regulated commerce with the Dutch and the Chinese at Nagasaki.[2] The adoption of this policy of exclusion and seclusion had come after a century of friendly and liberal relations with several European states. Beginning in 1542 with the discovery of Japan by storm-bound Portuguese, commercial relations developed first with Portugal, carried on through Macao on the China coast; then with Spain, through Manila and even directly through Acapulco; and later with Holland and England, conducted by their great East India companies. The Japanese with their "intelligent curiosity" welcomed the foreign traders with their new wares and, especially, their firearms. In 1613 Iyeyasu, founder of the Tokugawa Shogunate, gave to the English a charter which granted them privileges far more liberal than could have been found in any Western state, including even free trade and extraterritoriality. That the Japanese sought commerce and intercourse with other states during this period is evident from the record. That they sacrificed both in order to free themselves from the political menace of the Western religion is also evident. The story of missionary propaganda in Japan from the time of Francis Xavier is a record in which religious zeal and devotion is intermingled with individual indiscretions and national rivalries. It is difficult today to unravel all the motives from the skein of tangled political, religious, and economic elements, but there is reason to believe that if religious propaganda could have been divorced from commercial intercourse, the doors of Japan might never have been closed. As it was, the English East India Company abandoned its factory in 1623, the Spaniards were excluded in 1624, seclusion was decreed in 1636, and the Portuguese were excluded in 1638. The Dutch, who professed a different brand of Christianity and who were not inter-

[2] Murdoch and Yamagata, *History of Japan,* II (1542–1651).

ested in its propaganda, were transferred to Nagasaki in 1641 and permitted to carry on their trade, under the strictest regulations, at that port. The Chinese also were allowed to trade there under rigid restrictions. Though the English tried in 1673 to re-establish their factory, their request was denied, and seclusion and exclusion remained the firm policy of Japan.

This policy was inaugurated by Iyemitsu, the third of the Tokugawa Shoguns, who administered the country from 1623 until 1651. He was the grandson of the great Iyeyasu, who had retired in 1605 and yet virtually ruled the country until his death in 1616. Seclusion, therefore, was not the work of the founder of the Tokugawa Shogunate, although he is generally credited with its establishment.

The government of Japan throughout this period was unique. At Kyoto resided the Mikado, or Tenno, descendant of the gods and supreme monarch of the land. But from the earliest historic period the Mikado had withdrawn more and more from the actual administration of affairs, intrusting it at first to nobles of his court, represented between 670 and 1156 by the great Fujiwara family, and after that date to great military families who held the title of Sei-i-tai Shogun (Barbarian Subjugating Great General). The first of these leaders was Minamoto Yoritomo, who became Shogun in 1192. From 1199 until 1333, members of the Hojo family served as regents for titular Shoguns. In 1338 the Ashikaga family was established in the Shogunate, holding it until 1573. Then out of thirty years of civil war arose the three great generals, Nobunaga, Hideyoshi, and Iyeyasu, the latter of whom was made Shogun in 1603. His descendants held that office until its abolition in 1868.

Under the dual system of government the Mikado resided at Kyoto, surrounded by his court but under the watchful eye and control of the representative of the Shogun. At Yedo, the Tokugawa capital, resided the Shogun, invested with supreme authority in political affairs. To him the feudal lords, daimyos, swore allegiance, and his power over them was real and during the early years was frequently exercised. The authority of the Mikado was nominal, though present. He invested the Shogun with his office, but the Shogun was not called upon to secure approval for his actions. The momentous decision to close the country was taken by Iyemitsu without Imperial approval, nor at that time, when the Tokugawa Shogunate was at its height, was such deemed necessary. It was easy, therefore, for the early writers on Japan to speak of the Mikado as a spiritual emperor and the Shogun as a temporal ruler, for it was with the Shogun that all foreign affairs were transacted.

During the later Tokugawa period the actual government very largely passed out of the hands of the Shoguns and was exercised by the Rojiu (*Gorogio*), senior ministers or council. These were five in number, chosen from the more important of the fudai dai-myos, and at times one of them was given the office of dairo (tairo), corresponding very nearly to that of regent. It was the Rojiu which handled foreign affairs after the reopening of Japan. Occasionally members of the Waka-doshiyori, or junior council, composed of five junior ministers, were called upon to treat with the Foreign Representatives when the pressure of internal and foreign affairs proved too burdensome on the Rojiu.

In regard to the feudal system it is necessary to note that at the close of the Tokugawa period there were two hundred and fifty-eight daimyos. Of these, twenty-one were related to the Tokugawas, one hundred and thirty-nine were known as fudai (hereditary vassals), or descendants of those who had come to the support of Iyeyasu early in his career, and ninety-eight were tozama lords, descended from the old feudal nobility which had either come reluctantly to the support of the Tokugawas or had been beaten into submission. None of the latter lords was per-mitted to hold office in the Yedo administration, and among them were found the leaders in the anti-Tokugawa movement of the period covered by the early part of this study. Within their fiefs the daimyos exercised almost unlimited power. They could be called upon to maintain troops in the field in time of need. The Shogunate (sometimes spoken of as Bakufu) exercised a measure of control over the feudatories through the law of compulsory residence at Yedo, the exchange of fiefs, and fines disguised as orders to carry out some costly public work.[3]

After 1641 Japan was closed to all foreign intercourse except that with the Dutch and the Chinese at Nagasaki. The Dutch were confined to the artificial fan-shaped islet of Deshima, about six hundred by two hundred and forty feet in size.[4] The whole island was surrounded by a high board fence, and access to the mainland was over a stone bridge, carefully guarded. No Japanese was permitted to visit the island without permission, nor could a Hollander cross the bridge without leave. At first six or seven Dutch ships a year were allowed to visit Nagasaki; later the number was reduced to two, and after 1790 to one. Before that date the head of the factory had to make a visit to Yedo annually with presents, but later the visit was made every four years. Residence at Deshima was permitted under regulations both strict and humiliating, and the annual ships had to observe stringent rules. Yet because of the profit from the trade, which was great down to the nineteenth century, the Dutch accepted this confinement. During the two centuries much information concerning Japan was secured and published by officials at Deshima, and the works of Kaempfer, Thunberg, Titsingh, and Siebold were the great sources of Western knowledge during the period. On the other hand, in spite of official prohibitions, some Japanese gratified their love of learning by studying with the Dutch agents, and thus through Nagasaki there seeped into the country some knowledge of Western history, politics, science, and medicine. It is a great mistake to think that Japan was hermetically sealed during her centuries of seclusion. Nagasaki was a keyhole through which some light entered.

The Chinese trade was governed by similar regulations. Until 1684 seventy junks a year might visit Nagasaki; then the number was reduced to twenty, and after 1740 to ten. To a less extent

---

[3] See Gubbins, *The Progress of Japan, 1853–1871,* pp. 1–39; Brinkley, *History of the Japanese People,* pp. 592–95, 632–37; Gubbins, "The Feudal System in Japan under the Tokugawa Shoguns," in *Transactions of the Asiatic Society of Japan,* Vol. 15, Part II.

[4] Longford, *The Story of Old Japan,* p. 286; Paske-Smith, *Western Barbarians in Japan and Formosa in Tokugawa Days, 1603–1868.*

than in the case of the Dutch, news from the outer world filtered in from China, and some also came through the junks of Satsuma which were allowed to trade with the Loochoo (Ryukyu) Islands, a dependency of that fief, but also in touch with China.

It could hardly be expected that with the development of European commerce in the Far East such states as Japan and Korea would be permitted to maintain their exclusive systems. In the very year that the Portuguese were expelled from Japan (1638) the Russians had carried their standard clear across Siberia to Okhotsk, on the Pacific, and the next two centuries saw the consolidation of their control. In 1792 Lieutenant Laxman was sent to return some Japanese seamen and to endeavor to open friendly relations.[5] This attempt failed, as did a more elaborate one in 1804, under Resanoff. Other Russian expeditions will be mentioned later. The Japanese knew of the growth of Russian power to the north, and this knowledge was one of the influences in arousing interest in foreign affairs during the early nineteenth century.

Other flags were occasionally seen in Japanese waters. French and British explorers visited the northern islands. During the Napoleonic Wars the Dutch trade was carried on under the American flag,[6] and in 1807 an American ship, chartered by the Russian American Company, and under the Russian flag, unsuccessfully sought trade at Nagasaki. The next year a British frigate, the "Phaeton," put in at Nagasaki in search of the Dutch merchantman.[7] This invasion resulted in the suicide of several of the Japanese officials who were responsible for allowing the ship to enter and aroused in Japan an indignation which persisted until Perry's time.[8] While the British held Java, 1811–16, the annual ship was British, but the agent at Deshima refused to surrender his post to the conquerors. A unique attempt was that of the

---

[5] Hawks, *op. cit.*, I, 45.

[6] Dennett, *Americans in Eastern Asia*, pp. 242–44.

[7] Aston, "H.M.S. 'Phaeton' at Nagasaki in 1808," in *Transactions of the Asiatic Society of Japan*, Vol. 7, Part IV, pp. 329–44.

[8] Williams, "Journal of the Perry Expedition to Japan," *ibid.*, Vol. 37, Part II, pp. 149, 220.

American ship "Morrison," in 1837, to return some Japanese
sailors who had been blown clear across the Pacific to Vancouver.
This humanitarian attempt failed; and the result of this and other
efforts to return seamen and open commercial relations was the
edict of 1843 to the effect that shipwrecked Japanese could be returned only in Dutch or Chinese ships.[9]

After the Napoleonic Wars the trade between China and the
West rapidly developed. In this commerce Americans took a
prominent part. With the end of the English East India Company's monopoly of British trade came a great increase in British
shipping, and there began the struggle between the royal representatives and the Chinese officials which, complicated by the
contraband trade in opium, led to the Anglo-Chinese war of
1839–42, which will ever be known in China as the Opium War.
Its great result was the opening of five ports in China to foreign
trade, and America, France, and other countries secured treaties
similar to that of Great Britain.

This development of Chinese commerce led to increased interest in Japan. In the 'forties two British surveying ships and
two French ships of war visited Japanese ports, as well as two
American expeditions. One of the latter, under Commodore
Biddle,[10] went in 1846 to Yedo to ascertain if the ports were open,
and the other, under Commander Glynn,[11] in 1849, visited Nagasaki, to receive some shipwrecked American seamen. It became
evident that Japan's days of seclusion were soon to end.

To two Western countries the opening of Japan was of prime
importance, but for very different reasons. Russia, on the north,
had pushed down into the Kurile Islands, and to round out her
illicit occupation of the Amur Valley sought the possession of
Karafuto (Sakhalin).[12] Her advance was feared by Japan, for
her commercial interests were small. Japan lay beyond the route

---

[9] *32d Cong., 1st Sess., S. Ex. Doc. No. 59,* pp. 78–79. *Serial Number 620,*
and hereafter so cited.

[10] *Ibid.,* pp. 64–66 (2 ships).   [11] *Ibid.,* pp. 1–44 (1 ship).

[12] Takekoshi, *The Economic Aspects of the History of the Civilization of
Japan,* III, 164–69, 177–92, 288–324.

of the usual European commerce of the time; but in the case of the United States, with the development of direct shipping between San Francisco and Shanghai, the Japanese islands lay right in the track. The interests of the United States were primarily commercial, and it had more to gain immediately from the opening of the Japanese ports than had other commercial states. With the development of steam navigation the necessity for coaling stations somewhere between Honolulu and Shanghai became important, and the presence of American whalers in the northern waters of Japan after 1820 made it necessary that ports of refuge and supply be obtained, and that guaranties for the humane treatment of our shipwrecked mariners be secured.

These were the reasons which led to active American interest in Japan in the early 'fifties. Before then, in 1832 and in 1835, Mr. Roberts, our Minister to Siam and Muscat, had borne letters of credence to Japan, but had not gone there; and in 1846 Commodore Biddle had carried the letter of credence which had been given to Mr. Everett, our Minister to China. But in the 'fifties more serious efforts to open intercourse were made. In 1851 Commodore Aulick, who had been placed in command of the East India squadron, was instructed to visit Japan and secure, if possible, a treaty of amity and commerce which was to include the right to obtain coal, the opening of one or more ports for commerce, and protection for shipwrecked seamen and property.[13] After his recall on November 18, 1851, the mission was intrusted to Commodore Matthew Calbraith Perry, brother of the well-known Oliver Hazard Perry, the hero of Lake Erie.

So much has been written concerning the mission of Commodore Perry that only the more important phases of it need be treated here.[14] His instructions, which were drafted by Mr. Con-

---

[13] *Serial Number 620,* pp. 81–82. That Commodore Aulick was not well qualified for such a mission may be inferred from the ill-treatment of some Japanese seamen on the "Susquehanna" at Hong Kong (Heco, *Narrative of a Japanese,* I, 113–21).

[14] For Perry's expedition see: *Serial Number 751;* Hawks, *op. cit.;* Williams, *op. cit.* For a Japanese account of the negotiations in 1854 see "Diary of an Official of the Bakufu," *Transactions of the Asiatic Society of Japan,* 2d Se-

rad, Secretary of War and Acting Secretary of State, set forth that the object of his mission was to secure protection for shipwrecked American seamen and property, permission to secure supplies (especially coal), and the opening of one or more ports for commerce. These objects were to be obtained by argument and persuasion; but if unsuccessful he was to state "in the most unequivocal terms" that American citizens wrecked on the coasts of Japan must be treated with humanity,

and that if any acts of cruelty should hereafter be practised upon citizens of this country, whether by the government or by the inhabitants of Japan, they will be severely chastised.

He was also instructed that,

as the president has no power to declare war, his mission is necessarily of a pacific character, and [he] will not resort to force unless in self defence in the protection of the vessels and crews under his command, or to resent an act of personal violence offered to himself, or one of his crews.[15]

He was, further, to be

courteous and conciliatory, but at the same time, firm and decided. He will therefore, submit with patience and forbearance to acts of discourtesy to which he may be subjected, by a people to [sic] whose usages it will not do to test by our standards of propriety, but, at the same time, will be careful to do nothing that will compromit, in their eyes, his own dignity, or that of the country. He will, on the contrary, do everything to impress them with a just sense of the power and greatness of this country, and to satisfy them that its past forbearance has been the result, not of timidity, but of a desire to be on friendly terms with them.

The history of the expedition shows how perfectly Perry carried out these instructions.

The appointment of a naval diplomat was due to the fact that much depended upon the wise use of the naval force to be sent to Japan. Perry was appointed to the command of the East India squadron, then consisting of three ships of war and two store

ries, Vol. 7, pp. 98–119; Paullin, *Diplomatic Negotiations of American Naval Officers, 1778–1883;* Griffis, *Matthew Calbraith Perry;* Nitobe, *Intercourse between the United States and Japan;* Foster, *American Diplomacy in the Orient;* Dennett, *Americans in Eastern Asia.*

[15] November 5, 1852. See *Serial Number 751,* pp. 4–9.

ships, which was to be reinforced by eight additional vessels.[16] During the nine months which elapsed before any of the new vessels were ready for sea, he spent as much time as possible in working out all the details connected with the expedition, and in gathering books, charts, presents, and all manner of information. To this thorough preparation the success of the expedition was in large part due.

On November 24, 1852, Perry sailed from Norfolk, Virginia, in the steam frigate "Mississippi." His course lay via Madeira, St. Helena, Cape Town, Mauritius, Point de Galle, Singapore, Macao, Hong Kong, to Shanghai. There his squadron of six vessels was assembled. He then visited the Ryukyu (Loochoo) Islands, owing dependence to both Japan and China, and also the Bonin Islands, both of which places he considered suitable for rendezvous and coaling stations. Finally, on July 8, 1853, with only four ships of war, he entered the Bay of Yedo and anchored off the town of Uraga.

The Japanese were not unprepared for his arrival, for in 1844 the king of Holland, William II, had addressed a letter to the Shogun warning him of the impossibility of longer maintaining the seclusion policy and urging him to open friendly commercial relations with the Powers, and the Shogun had replied that Japan would not alter her ancient laws.[17] Again, in 1852, when the news of the proposed American expedition reached the Netherlands, another effort was made, and a draft of a commercial treaty was presented for Japanese consideration.[18] There is reason to believe that the Dutch may have stressed the warlike nature of Perry's enterprise.[19]

[16] Only one of the additional ships arrived in time for the first visit to Japan. Two did not arrive at all.

[17] D. C. Greene, "Correspondence between William II of Holland and the Shogun of Japan, A.D. 1844," in *Transactions of the Asiatic Society of Japan,* Vol. 34, Part IV.

[18] Hawks, *op. cit.,* I, 65.

[19] "The American expedition has not always been represented to be of a wholly friendly and peaceful character" (Governor General Van Twist of the Netherlands Indies to Perry, September 22, 1852, in *Serial Number 751,* pp. 20-21).

On his first visit to Japan, Perry remained for ten days. He succeeded in impressing the Japanese with the strength of his squadron, containing the largest naval force and the first steamers ever seen in Japanese waters, and with his own good will. He refused to go to Nagasaki or to deal through the Dutch; he refused to accept presents unless some were received by the Japanese in exchange; and he insisted upon treatment suitable to his position as the representative of a great Power. His mixture of "firmness, dignity, and fearlessness" made a deep impression on the Japanese.[20] He succeeded, therefore, in having the President's letter[21] received, "in opposition to the Japanese law," by two of the high officials of the Shogun's court, Toda Idzu-no-Kami and Ido Iwami-no-Kami; and he sailed away, promising to return in the spring for an answer. His reasons for leaving were not only his wish to allow the Japanese time to consider so revolutionary a proposal as the amendment of their exclusion laws but also his lack of supplies for a long stay on the coast, the non-arrival of the gifts for the Japanese, and, above all, the desirability of appearing with a larger force when the final negotiations should take place.[22]

The presence of the American squadron had occasioned consternation in the Shogun's court. Its appearance was anticipated; its hostile aspect had been stressed. It was the duty of the Shogunate to deal wisely with this crisis. The well-known laws of the land decreed that the squadron should have been ordered away; if it would not go, the armed forces of the Shogunate and the daimyos should compel it to retire. But among the Shogunate officials were men who were more or less informed concerning world movements, and who knew that it would be foolhardy to

[20] Taylor, *Visit to India, China, and Japan,* p. 417.

[21] This letter, signed by President Fillmore, countersigned by Edward Everett, Secretary of State, and dated November 13, 1852, was a longer document than that intrusted to Commodore Aulick in 1851 (*Serial Number 620,* p. 82). In brief, it asked for "friendship, commerce, a supply of coal and provisions, and protection for our shipwrecked people." It requested that the Emperor appoint a convenient port "in the southern part of the Empire" where the supplies might be obtained. In the earlier letter there was no reference to the protection of shipwrecked seamen.

[22] *Serial Number 751,* pp. 32, 53–54.

precipitate hostilities with a Power represented by four of the greatest vessels ever seen in Japanese waters. It was their knowledge which saved the situation, for the great bulk of the daimyos and their samurai retainers favored the immediate expulsion of the foreigners. And yet it was the weakness of these same officials which complicated matters. Without question the Yedo Government should have dealt with this situation on its own responsibility. But Lord Abe, president of the Rojiu, or Cabinet, was unwilling for the Shogunate to act alone. The weakening of the Tokugawa administration during the past fifty years had sapped the initiative and the fearlessness of the Cabinet. An unprecedented step was taken when the President's letter was transmitted to the Mikado and the daimyos for their consideration, and later when a conference of daimyos was convened.[23]

This action was the beginning of the process which eventually undermined the Shogun's power. Almost to a man the daimyos favored the maintenance of the exclusion laws, and the Imperial court instructed the Shogun to drive away the Americans.[24] From the beginning the opposition was led by the senior prince of Mito, member of one of the Three Families (Sanke)[25] and one of the strongest and ablest daimyos in the land. Only a few of the lords favored a policy of conciliation and intercourse, and among these were the lords of Obama, Tsuyama, Uwajima, Fukuoka, Nakatsu, and Ii Naosuke, Lord of Hikone.[26] One clause in the President's letter strengthened their arguments: "If your imperial majesty is not satisfied that it would be safe altogether to abrogate the ancient laws which forbid foreign trade, they might be suspended for five or ten years, so as to try the experiment. If it does not prove as beneficial as was hoped, the ancient laws can be restored. The United States often limit their treaties with foreign States to a few years, and then renew them or not, as they please."[27]

---

[23] Gubbins, *The Progress of Japan,* p. 91.

[24] Satoh, *Lord Hotta,* p. 26; Gubbins, *op. cit.,* p. 92.

[25] The houses of Mito, Owari, and Kii, from which a Shogun was chosen in case of failure of issue in the direct line.

[26] Satoh, *op. cit.,* p. 27.   [27] Hawks, *op. cit.,* I, 257.

This statement of the President was remembered by the Yedo officials in the troubled days which followed. Ii, Hotta, and others thought that if the experiment did not succeed, at the end of a few years Japan would have become strong enough to close the doors again.[28] In the meantime, although the Shogunate realized that a war could not be successfully maintained, defensive measures were taken.[29]

After leaving Japan, Perry visited Loochoo, and then made his way to Hong Kong and to Macao, which was his headquarters during the winter. The great Taiping Rebellion was raging in China, and it was felt by the American merchants there, and especially by the American commissioner, Humphrey Marshall, that Perry should have used his squadron for the protection of established American interests in China rather than for the opening of relations of doubtful value with Japan.[30] But in this case Perry was right, for during the absence of the squadron in both 1853 and 1854 American interests did not suffer during the civil commotion in China.

The argument of the President and of Perry, that Japan should open her doors to trade because of the changed state of the world, was strengthened by the visits to Nagasaki of a Russian squadron under Admiral Poutiatine in August 1853 and another early in 1854.[31] In November 1853 Poutiatine had suggested "mutual cooperation" to Perry, which the latter courteously declined.[32] It

---

[28] Satoh, *op. cit.*, p. 29; Gubbins, *op. cit.*, p. 287.

[29] "Under the guidance of Abe Masahiro, one of the ablest statesmen that Yedo ever possessed, batteries were built at Shinagawa to guard the approaches to Yedo; defensive preparations were made along the coasts of Musashi, Sagami, Awa, and Kazusa; the veto against the construction of ocean-going ships was rescinded, and the feudatories were invited to build and arm large vessels; a commission was given to the Dutch at Deshima to procure from Europe a library of useful books; cannon were cast; troops were drilled, and everyone who had acquired expert knowledge through the medium of the Dutch was taken into official favour. But all these efforts tended only to expose their own feebleness, and on the 2nd of November, 1853, instructions were issued that if the Americans returned, they were to be dealt with peacefully" (Brinkley, *op. cit.*, p. 666).

[30] Correspondence in *Serial Number 734; Serial Number 751.*

[31] Hawks, *op. cit.*, I, 62, 63.   [32] *Serial Number 751,* pp. 80–82.

was the belief that both the French and Russian squadrons were about to visit Japan and seek treaties which caused Perry to hasten his return,[33] and on January 14, 1854, he sailed again from Hong Kong for Japan.

Once more the squadron rendezvoused at Loochoo. There Perry received a letter from Duymaer Van Twist, Governor-General of Netherlands India, advising him of the death of the Emperor (Shogun) of Japan shortly after he had left Uraga, and transmitting the request of the Japanese authorities that Perry postpone his promised visit because of the impossibility of transacting any important business during the period of mourning.[34] This news did not alter the Commodore's plans. On February 13 the American squadron anchored off Gorihama in the Bay of Yedo. Although two of the promised vessels had not been sent out from home, Perry was able to muster a respectable force of seven, and later nine, ships, three of them being steamships, although three of the sailing craft were only store ships.[35] The enlarged force caused the Japanese at first to question his peaceful intentions.

The first difficulty arose over the place where the conference concerning the President's letter should be held. The Japanese insisted upon either Uraga or Kamakura. Perry objected to both places because of the unfavorable harbors, and declared that Yedo, the capital, was the proper place. Finally both sides yielded, and the village of Yokohama was agreed upon. Then came the conferences, formal and informal, over the terms of the proposed treaty. Three times Perry landed, with all formality, to discuss the matter with the Imperial commissioners. At the first inter-

---

[33] Hawks, *op. cit.,* I, 303.

[34] *Ibid.,* p. 322.

[35] The squadron consisted of the steamships "Susquehanna," "Mississippi," and "Powhatan," the sloops of war "Vandalia," "Macedonian," and "Saratoga," and the armed store ships "Southampton," "Lexington," and "Supply." The "Southampton" arrived on February 10, the "Susquehanna," "Mississippi," "Powhatan," "Vandalia," "Macedonian," and "Lexington" on February 13, the "Saratoga" on March 4, and the "Supply" on March 19. The "Susquehanna" left for China on March 24, one week before the Treaty was signed.

view, Perry alluded to the harsh treatment accorded shipwrecked seamen, and said, according to the Japanese version:

> If your country should persist in its present practices and fail to mend them, and if ships are not helped, it will surely be looked upon with hostility. If your country becomes an enemy, we will exhaust our resources if necessary to wage war. We are fully prepared to engage in a struggle for victory. Our country has just had a war with a neighboring country, Mexico, and we even attacked and captured its capital. Circumstances may lead your country into a similar plight. It would be well for you to reconsider.

To which Hayashi, the Lord Rector of the University, replied:

> If forced by circumstances, we also will go to war; but many of your statements are not true, due, I assume, to the fact that many of your ideas have been created by mistaken reports.[36]

Perry offered as a basis for discussion the American Treaty with China of 1844, but the Japanese replied that they certainly were not ready for the opening of such a trade. The Commissioners then presented a series of propositions, based on Perry's letters. These became the real basis of the Treaty.[37] The negotiations were carried on with the utmost friendliness. During their progress gifts were exchanged, those from the United States including two telegraph instruments, a miniature locomotive, tender, cars, and rails, a number of books, various weapons, quantities of spirits, and many objects of unusual interest to the Japanese.[38] A state dinner was held on the flagship at which the Japanese showed their appreciation of the champagne and other wines and spirits. It must have been a rare sight when "the jovial Matsusaki threw

[36] "Diary of an Official of the Bakufu," in *Transactions of the Asiatic Society of Japan,* 2d Series, Vol. 7, p. 98. The appointment of the Lord Rector as chief negotiator is significant. Hayashi's remark might well have been repeated by later Japanese diplomats.

[37] There is no evidence that the Japanese made use of the draft Treaty submitted by the Dutch in 1852. Commodore Perry had not seen the text, although Dr. Nitobe believes that Perry "availed himself of this draft," and "finds but little in Perry's treaty that is original" (Nitobe, *op. cit.,* pp. 56–57). Williams, *op. cit.,* p. viii; Hawks, *op. cit.,* I, 66.

[38] A complete list in Williams, *op. cit.,* pp. 131–34. The illustrations in Kendall, *War in Mexico,* and Ripley, *History of the Mexican War,* were said to have made a profound impression on Lord Abe and the Rojiu (*Japan Weekly Mail,* August 1, 1914).

his arms about the Commodore's neck, crushing, in his tipsy embrace, a pair of brand new epaulettes, and repeating, in Japanese, with maudlin affection, these words, as interpreted into English: 'Nippon and America, all the same heart.' "[39] On March 31 a treaty of peace and amity was signed, the text being in English and Japanese, with translations in Dutch and Chinese.

This epoch-making treaty consisted of twelve articles.[40] The first article established a "perfect, permanent, and universal peace, and a sincere and cordial amity" between the United States and Japan. The second provided for the opening of the ports of Shimoda at once, and of Hakodate a year later, for supplies. The third, fourth, and fifth articles assured good treatment for shipwrecked Americans in Japan and freedom from the restrictions and the confinement suffered by the Dutch and the Chinese at Nagasaki. The sixth article called for careful deliberation between the parties in case any other goods were wanted or any business had to be arranged.[41] The seventh permitted trade under temporary Japanese regulations. The eighth required the agency of Japanese officers when supplies were required. The ninth was the "most-favored-nation" clause.[42] The tenth limited the visits of American ships to Shimoda and Hakodate except in distress or when forced by bad weather. The eleventh permitted the appointment by the United States of consuls or agents at Shimoda after eighteen months, provided either of the two governments deemed such arrangement necessary.[43] The twelfth dealt with the approval and the exchange of ratifications.[44]

[39] Hawks, *op. cit.*, I, 376.

[40] In this and the other early treaties the Shogun is spoken of as the Taikun. For the Japanese explanation of this term, see Hawks, *op. cit.*, II, 207–8.

[41] This was inserted by Perry to pave the way for a later commercial treaty.

[42] Dr. S. Wells Williams, the first interpreter, is given credit for the inclusion of the "most-favored-nation clause" and the absence of an extraterritorial provision (Williams, *op. cit.*, p. vii). Griffis, *Townsend Harris, First American Envoy in Japan,* p. 258 n. Griffis, *Matthew Calbraith Perry,* p. 366 n., cites letter of Williams, February 8, 1883, as to "most-favored-nation clause."

[43] The Japanese agreed to this as a means of controlling American citizens in Japan.

[44] Additional regulations were signed at Shimoda, June 17, 1854. Article I stated that any Americans "who are found transgressing Japanese laws may be

Such were the terms of Japan's first modern treaty; such was the first breach in her walls of exclusion. In comparison with the ordinary intercourse between Western Powers the Treaty secured very little, and as such was a source of disappointment in certain quarters. But when viewed in the light of Japanese history for two hundred years it was a real achievement. Century-old laws had been set aside. Ports were opened for American shipping. Shipwrecked mariners were no longer to be treated as criminals, and the beginnings of commerce were to be tolerated. Commodore Perry had carried out his instructions well. Without the use of force he had secured all that could have been hoped for, and far more than many dared expect.

This study would be incomplete if some effort were not made to discover the reasons for Perry's success. They lie deeper than the surface. Much credit is certainly due to the Commodore himself. As Dr. Paullin has so excellently said: "Perry's success was in no small measure the result of a rare combination of strong qualities of character—firmness, sagacity, tact, dignity, patience, and determination."[45] It is easy to imagine how such an enterprise might have turned out if its commander had not possessed some or all of these qualities. The story of the contact between Western and Eastern peoples is not always such pleasant reading as is the narrative of Perry's voyage.

Much importance has been placed upon the imposing armament which supported Perry's demands, and a false interpretation has been given to it. Typical of this attitude is Douglas's statement: "At Yedo the consternation was not less than at Uraga; and it was further accentuated by the announcement that, if Commodore Perry's request met with a refusal, he should open hostilities."[46] But Perry had no such instructions or intentions. His instructions stressed the point that he was engaged in a pacific mission, and that he was to resort to force only in self-defense.

apprehended by the police and taken on board their ships." After leaving Japan Perry signed a Treaty with Loochoo on July 11, 1854.

[45] Paullin, *op. cit.*, p. 281.

[46] *Europe and the Far East*, p. 153.

He was to secure concessions by argument and persuasion; but
if no assurance was given for the good treatment of our seamen,
he was to state that for future acts of cruelty the Japanese would
be severely chastised. When, on the way to the East, Perry outlined a plan for seizing one of the Loochoo Islands as a port of
refuge, he was again instructed that he must not use force, except
for defense and self-preservation.[47] On the way to Japan the men
were thoroughly drilled and the ships kept in perfect readiness,
and as they entered the bay "the decks were cleared for action,
the guns placed in position and shotted, the ammunition arranged,
the small arms made ready, sentinels and men at their posts, and,
in short, all the preparations made, usual before meeting an
enemy."[48] But these were measures for defense, and were based
upon the hostile reception of the "Morrison" in 1837 and the
character of the exclusion laws. During the negotiations no threat
of opening hostilities was made. At most, Perry informed the
Japanese that he would land and deliver the President's letter if
it was not properly received, would consider his country insulted
if the letter was not received and duly replied to, and would not
hold himself accountable for the consequences. Perry also let the
Japanese know that he would return with a larger squadron in the
spring.[49]

In his dispatch to the Secretary of the Navy of August 3, 1853,
Perry mentioned the fortifications which had been erected, probably in order to expel the Americans from Japan, but stated that
with his augmented force he could penetrate to within three or
four miles of Yedo. In reply to this the President warned him
"that the great end should be attained, not only with credit to the
United States, but without wrong to Japan"; and the Secretary
of the Navy reminded him that his mission was of a peaceful
character, "and that, although in consideration of the peculiar
character of the Japanese much importance may well be attached

47 *Serial Number 751,* pp. 12–14.

48 Hawks, *op. cit.,* I, 231. For the "Morrison," see Dennett, *op. cit.,*
pp. 246–48.

49 *Serial Number 751,* pp. 47–49.

to the exhibition of impressive evidences of the greatness and power of our country, no violence should be resorted to except for defence."[50]

On his return voyage to Japan, Perry outlined, while at Loochoo, his course of action.[51] He again decided to take the island of "Great Lew-Chew" under the "surveillance of the American flag" if the Japanese refused to assign a port of resort for our merchant and whaling ships. His former visit had convinced him that this could be done without bloodshed, nor would he use force except in self-defense. Happily the successful outcome of the treaty negotiations relieved Perry from taking this step, for his conduct would certainly have been disavowed, as the President replied that he would not act without the authority of Congress.[52]

During the second visit of the expedition there was one episode which contained a suggestion of the use of force at some future time. After receiving, on March 8, the reply to the President's letter which granted the requests for the kind treatment of seamen, the furnishing of provisions, supplies, and coal, and the opening of Nagasaki (which was a port "in the southern part of the Empire"), Perry believed that "something still more advantageous might be gained," and considered it good policy "to hold out for a specific treaty,"[53] as he had been instructed.[54] He therefore replied that, "though the propositions set forth in the communication of your highness furnish strong evidence of the enlightened spirit with which the Imperial commissioners are disposed to meet the suggestions which I have had the honor to submit, they fall far short of my anticipations, and I do not hesitate to say that they would not satisfy the views of the President." His instructions, he said, required him to look "for an intercourse of a more enlarged and liberal character," and he urged the necessity of opening as many ports as were open in China (five) free from any restrictions "not recognized by the usages of free and independent nations." He urged, furthermore, the need of a written compact "that will be binding as well upon the citizens of the United States

[50] *Ibid.*, p. 57.   [51] *Ibid.*, p. 109.
[52] *Ibid.*, pp. 112–13.   [53] *Ibid.*, p. 127.   [54] *Ibid.*, p. 8.

as the subjects of Japan"; and he expressed the sincere desire of his heart to bring these negotiations to an amicable and satisfactory termination, "as well to save time as to prevent the necessity of sending from America more ships and men, and possibly with instructions of more stringent import."[55]

This was a threat, and as such it aroused the indignation of Dr. S. Wells Williams, the missionary-interpreter, who had to translate the letter.[56] But it referred to possible future action, over which the Commodore could have no control; and so well had he estimated the situation that the negotiation of a treaty was soon in process, without further reference to additional ships and men. The five ports were reduced to two, but the matter of unrestricted trade was postponed for an indefinite period.

These facts have been narrated to show that the American Government had no hostile intention in furnishing Perry with a respectable naval force, that the Commodore was repeatedly reminded that his mission was one of peace and that force was to be used only in self-defense, and that he neither threatened the Japanese nor considered using force against them. On this point we have the testimony of the outspoken critic, Dr. S. Wells Williams: "The appointment of a naval man as the envoy was wise, as it secured unity of purpose in the diplomatic and executive chief, and probably Perry is the only man in our navy capable of holding both positions, which has been proved by the general prudence and decision of his proceedings since he anchored at Uraga last July."[57] It was the evidence of force, not in the fleet but in the

[55] *Serial Number 751,* pp. 138–39. The Japanese version reads: "Perry said that he would enter into negotiations, but if his proposals were rejected, he was prepared to make war at once: that in the event of war he would have 50 ships in nearby waters and 50 more in California, and that if he sent word he could summon a command of one hundred warships within twenty days" (*Diary of an Official of the Bakufu,* p. 101). As Perry's remarks on this day were summarized in a few sentences it is probable that only the "gist" was recorded. It is very doubtful if Perry used the exaggerated phrases set down by the Japanese scribe.

[56] Williams, *op. cit.,* p. 129. But he soon realized that Perry was right in trying to secure a treaty.

[57] *Ibid.,* p. 222. "The best friend the Japanese had in the squadron became convinced that they would suffer no evil from a man of Perry's principles, and

modern nation behind the fleet, which worked upon the minds of the Japanese observers.[58]

But back of the Commodore and his "black ships" there lay other causes which entered into the sum total of achievement. Prominent among these must be reckoned the presence of the Dutch at Nagasaki. For two hundred years, while the great gates of Japan were closed, they held open a wicket through which some knowledge of the Western world entered, and out of which passed most of the information concerning Japan which the West obtained. It was the Dutch who called to the attention of the Japanese the changes which were going on in the world at large: the use of steam in navigation, with its shortening of trade routes and its indifference to the formerly all-important monsoons; the increase in world commerce with China, and the insistence of Britain that her merchants be decently treated and that national intercourse be on terms of equality; and finally the news that a single Western Power had opened hostilities with the Middle Kingdom and in a brief campaign humbled the old giant of the East.[59] These were tidings of immense import, and there were some Japanese who were able to appreciate their significance.

The letter of William II to the Shogun in 1844, and the draft Treaty submitted in 1852 by Mr. Curtius, a special agent from Java, indicate the interest taken by Holland in opening Japan to general intercourse on better terms than she herself enjoyed. After Perry's successful mission the Dutch Minister of the Colonies issued an official report[60] pointing out "the persevering and disinterested efforts" which the Dutch Government had made to cause Japan to mitigate her system of exclusion. No one would

he maintained through his life a feeling of profound gratitude that such a man had been providentially designed to perform this difficult mission. If he was one who admitted none to his councils, he at least needed no prompting to be just" (F. W. Williams, editor, in Williams, *op. cit.*, p. v).

[58] Biddle in 1846 had two imposing ships, Perry in 1853 had but four.

[59] While Perry's squadron was at Shimoda in 1854 some of the officers saw a Japanese book describing the Anglo-Chinese war of 1839–42 (Williams, *op. cit.*, p. 182).

[60] Hawks, *op. cit.*, I, 64–69.

deny the influence exerted by the Dutch; and yet the fact remains that it was not Holland, with her centuries of intercourse, which succeeded in breaking down the barriers, but the United States. And it may at least be doubted whether the Dutch, with their long record of subserviency, could have secured so great a change in the Japanese system as Perry, insisting upon the rights and the dignity of his nation, was able to obtain.

Another European factor to be considered is Russia.[61] It was the Russian advance which really alarmed the Japanese in the nineteenth century. By 1713, Russian explorers had passed down the Kurile Islands from Kamchatka almost to Hokkaido. In 1739 and 1768 Russian vessels reached Awa Province, not far from Yedo, and in 1778 they visited Hokkaido.[62] The Japanese now took alarm, and on investigation found that Kamchatka and some of the Kurile Islands, hitherto claimed by Japan, had been occupied by the Russians. This discovery led to the publication of a remarkable book on coast defense (*Kai-koku Hei-dan*) by Hayashi Sihei, who had associated with the Dutch at Deshima, in which he advocated the building of ocean-going vessels and the fortifying and strengthening of the defenses of Yedo Bay. He was imprisoned for his audacity; but when Lieutenant Laxman arrived at Hakodate in 1792, ostensibly to return some shipwrecked Japanese seamen but really to seek the opening of trade between Japan and Russia, his foresight was recognized. Just at this time Commissioners from Yedo were investigating the situation in the North. Their report and the visit of the Russians caused steps to be taken for the establishment of Japanese control over Hokkaido. The western half was intrusted to the Daimyo of Matsumae, and the eastern half was taken under the direct control of the Shogunate.[63] Furthermore the coast daimyos were to re-establish the forces for the defense of the seacoast.[64]

[61] Renewed interest in early Russo-Japanese relations is indicated in an interview with Count Okuma in *Shin-Nippon*, August 1916.

[62] Brinkley, *op. cit.*, p. 658.

[63] *Ibid.*; also Takekoshi, *op. cit.*

[64] Akimoto, *Lord Ii Naosuke and New Japan*, p. 92.

In 1804 came the formal but unsuccessful attempt of Resanoff, sent to Nagasaki as a special ambassador. This was followed by the raid on Sakhalin and some of the Kurile Islands by the Russians in 1806.[65] Annually, between 1811 and 1814, Russian ships visited the northern islands, the first being the ship of Captain Golownin, who was taken prisoner. Efforts were also being made in each country to learn about the other. Catherine II established a Japanese professorship at Irkutsk, and there, in 1805 and 1806, Klaproth, the Orientalist, studied under a Japanese professor who had embraced the Greek religion.[66] In Japan, scholars translated some Russian works.

The Japanese, therefore, knew something of the Russians, and were alarmed at their advance, so that the appearance of Admiral Poutiatine at Nagasaki, on August 22, 1853, with a squadron of four vessels, must have lent weight to the President's letter delivered by Perry the month before. Yet the Russians were unable to secure the treaty they desired. They sailed away and returned to Japan the next spring before Perry arrived, but were again unsuccessful. Commander Adams, who was present at Shimoda in 1855, when Admiral Poutiatine finally negotiated a treaty, records that the Japanese "appeared to entertain no goodwill toward the Russians."[67] The latter, however, served to stimulate thought among the Japanese concerning coast defense and maritime intercourse, and must have contributed to the state of mind which brought success to Perry.

Finally, credit is certainly due to those Japanese who, in spite of the oppressive laws of the time, sought to obtain all available information concerning the West. Such were Watanabe and Takano, who in 1838 advocated foreign intercourse, only to be arrested and punished. Both at length committed suicide.[68]

[65] Aston, "Russian Descents in Saghalien and Itorup in the years 1806–1807," in *Transactions of the Asiatic Society of Japan,* Vol. 1.

[66] Hildreth, *Japan as It Was and Is,* II, 199.

[67] Hawks, *op. cit.,* I, 511.

[68] "That the Restoration should have been combined with the opening of the country and the adoption of a policy of enlightened progress was a surprise to all. . . . . No inconsiderable amount of credit, however, must in this respect be

Others were the early students of Dutch medicine, whose reading led them to a knowledge of other Western subjects;[69] and there were some who strove to master the history, philosophy, military art, and government of the West.[70] Some of these scholars were officials in the various fiefs, and were able to exert a liberal influence upon their lords. In other cases the daimyos themselves encouraged Western studies, in the face of the restrictive laws of the time. For instance, Lord Hotta, who later negotiated the commercial Treaty of 1858, had long encouraged the study of Western science and foreign affairs among his clansmen.[71] In 1841 he sent two physicians to study Dutch medicine at Nagasaki, and the next year opened a medical institution at his capital, Sakura. He also encouraged the study of the Dutch language, science, and military art, and he revised the military regulations of his clan, introducing muskets in the place of flint-locks, and creating cavalry forces. His liberal attitude in 1858 was, therefore, based on long conviction. As Nagasaki was an Imperial city, under the direct rule of the Shogunate, it happened that Tokugawa officials who had gained some knowledge of foreign affairs through their intercourse with the Dutch were frequently transferred to Yedo, and were able to voice their opinions there. It was but natural that among the officials at Yedo there should be a better understanding of the spirit of the age than among many of the daimyos who held no position in the administration and who spent only half their time in the capital.[72]

With these facts in mind it becomes evident that there were favoring agencies at work which Commodore Perry little under-

given to patriots and servants like Sihei Hayashi, Kwazan Watanabe, Choei Takano, Shozan Sakuma and others" (Prince Ito, quoted in S. Ballard, "Sketch of the Life of Watanabe Noboru," in *Transactions of the Asiatic Society of Japan*, Vol. 32, p. 1). See also K. Mitsukuri, "The Early Study of Dutch in Japan," in *ibid.*, Vol. 5, Part I, pp. 207–16.

[69] See Professor Ukita in Okuma, *Fifty Years of New Japan*, II, 134–60.

[70] About 1740 the importation of foreign books was allowed except those relating to Christianity (Brinkley, *op. cit.*, p. 614).

[71] Satoh, *Lord Hotta*, pp. 21–24.

[72] Dr. Williams remarked on the courtesy, decorum, open-mindedness, and general good sense of the officials (Williams, *op. cit.*, p. 226).

stood. And yet this fact should not lead us to underestimate the services of the naval diplomat. Captain Brinkley adopted a dubious tone in his latest work. "Much has been written about Perry's judicious display of force and about his sagacious tact in dealing with the Japanese, but it may be doubted whether the consequences of his exploit did not invest its methods with extravagant lustre."[73] But after due credit is given to Holland and to Russia and to the Japanese pioneers in Western education, the fact remains that neither Holland nor Russia was able to secure a treaty of any sort, nor were the liberals able to persuade the Shogunate to repeal voluntarily the exclusion laws. The treaty was won by America because, at a time when many elements were favorable, she sent out a special mission, well equipped, and led by a man well qualified for the work at hand. It requires little imagination to conceive of some of the errors in judgment which might have brought the expedition to disaster. That he succeeded where others had failed, and that he left behind a reputation for courtesy as well as dignity, and for good will as well as strength, will always remain to the credit of Commodore Matthew Calbraith Perry.

[73] Brinkley, *op. cit.*, p. 666.

CHAPTER II

TOWNSEND HARRIS, FIRST CONSUL GENERAL
1856–57

THE NEWS that Commodore Perry had succeeded in concluding a treaty with Japan was received with mingled feelings among Western people. Those who realized best the situation in Japan appreciated the importance of Perry's work. But there were others who believed that he had not gone far enough, and that a commercial treaty should have been secured. On this point the Commodore had no illusions.

The treaty with Japan professes to be nothing more than a compact, establishing between the United States and that empire certain obligations of friendly intercourse with, and mutual protection to, the citizens and subjects of the contracting powers, and granting to American citizens rights and privileges never before extended to strangers. This treaty, in its concessions on the part of the Japanese, far exceeds the most sanguine expectations, even of those who, from the first, advocated the policy of the Japan expedition. It purports to be a preliminary, and surely a most important step, in advance of a commercial arrangement to be agreed upon when the Japanese government may be better prepared by a more perfect knowledge of the usual requirements of international law and comity to enter upon additional pledges.[1]

The Commodore believed that the reasons advanced by the Japanese for postponing open commerce were good, and he also felt, and rightly too, that if the growth of liberal views were not destroyed by the conduct of merchants who sought to secure advantages not specified by the Treaty, there would soon come commercial treaties and the development of a valuable trade. From every point of view it was desirable to make haste slowly in bringing Japan into intercourse with the world at large.

[1] Hawks, *Narrative of the Expedition of an American Squadron to the China Seas and Japan,* II, 185.

The success of Perry incited the Powers most concerned to renewed efforts to secure treaty rights in Japan. An additional stimulus was present in the breaking out of the Crimean War and the alliance of England and France with Turkey against Russia in March 1854. It was at once planned to carry the war into the East,[2] and an allied expedition against the Russian naval station of Petropavlovsk, in Kamchatka, was considered.[3] This plan made it more desirable than ever that the ships of the warring Powers might take refuge and find supplies in Japanese waters. The Japanese, however, who promptly learned of the war, were anxious to avoid aggression by either party; so that when Admiral Sir James Stirling, with a squadron of four vessels, entered Nagasaki on September 7, 1854, he had little difficulty in obtaining a treaty.[4] This Treaty of October 14 was somewhat less liberal than Perry's, although it contained a "most-favored-nation" clause which secured for the British all that Perry had gained. It opened the ports of Nagasaki and Hakodate to British ships for effecting repairs and for obtaining fresh water, provisions, "and other supplies of any sort they may absolutely want for the use of the ships." Ships in distress might enter other ports.

British ships in Japanese ports shall conform to the laws of Japan. If high officers or commanders of ships shall break any such laws, it will lead to the ports being closed. Should inferior persons break them, they are to be delivered over to the Commanders of their ships for punishment.

This was a crude sort of extraterritoriality, the last sentence being similar to a portion of Article I of the additional regulations to the American Treaty. In the "most-favored-nation" clause an exception was made for "the advantages accruing to the Dutch and Chinese from their existing relations with Japan." The last

---

[2] It is interesting to note that the North American possessions of the Russian American Company and the Hudson's Bay Company were protected by a convention of neutrality (H. H. Bancroft, *History of Alaska*, pp. 570–72).

[3] Petropavlovsk was unsuccessfully attacked in August 1854, and was abandoned by the Russians the next year, before the allied squadron arrived in June.

[4] "Correspondence Relating to the Late Negotiations with Japan," *Parliamentary Papers, 1856, Com. 61 (2077)*; Tronson, *Voyage of the "Barracouta."*

clause contained this remarkable statement: "When this Convention shall be ratified, no high officer coming to Japan shall alter it." Gubbins thinks that "this was evidently intended to place on record the high-water mark of Japanese concessions."[5] The brief and rather informal nature of the document would lead one to believe that the Admiral was primarily interested in the work at hand—the opening of ports to British warships—and that he was willing to allow the question of further concessions to be left to a more suitable time. Thus when the Admiral returned the next year to exchange the ratifications, an exposition of the Treaty was agreed to which considerably broadened its meaning. This exposition will be noted later.

Two months after Stirling had signed this Treaty, his antagonist, Vice-Admiral Poutiatine, appeared at Shimoda with a single vessel, the "Diana." This was his fourth visit to Japan. His earlier visits, with a more imposing force, had been unsuccessful. This time he lost the only ship that he had, and yet, marooned and powerless, he was able to negotiate the wished-for Treaty.[6] This indicates perhaps better than anything else that the Japanese concessions were not based on the presence of force.

The Russian Treaty of February 7, 1855, was more like Perry's Treaty. Three ports were opened to Russian ships, Shimoda, Hakodate, and Nagasaki; shipwrecked men were to receive good treatment; trade was to be permitted at Shimoda and Hakodate; a Consul would be named by Russia at one of the latter ports if she deemed it necessary; and the "most-favored-nation" clause was inserted. New clauses were those which defined the Russo-Japanese boundary in the Kurile Islands but left the boundary in Sakhalin unmarked, and which introduced the full principle of extraterritoriality in these words: *"Tout individu qui aurait com-*

---

[5] Gubbins, *The Progress of Japan, 1853–1871*, pp. 62, 232–35.

[6] The "Diana" was severely damaged in the great earthquake and tidal wave of December 23, 1854. She later foundered while on the way to a harbor, about sixty miles from Shimoda, where she could be heaved down. Captain McCluney, of the "Powhatan," furnished the Russians with such supplies as he could spare, and they finally reached Petropavlovsk in the American schooner "C. E. Foote" (Hawks, *op. cit.*, I, 390, 511).

mis un crime peut être arrêté, mais il ne peut être jugé que selon les lois de son pays." The unrestricted trade at Shimoda and Hakodate, permitted by the fifth article, was reduced to a regulated trade by the explanatory articles which accompanied the Treaty, so that, as under the American Treaty and Regulations, no trade could take place except through the mediation of Japanese officials.[7]

The next statement of foreign rights in Japan came with the exposition of the British Treaty, which was agreed to at Nagasaki on October 18, 1855, when Admiral Stirling returned with the ratified Treaty. This document rounded out the brief terms of the earlier convention. But in connection with the third article it was agreed that,

ships of war have a general right to enter the ports of friendly powers in the unavoidable performance of public duties, which right can neither be waived nor restricted; but her Majesty's ships will not enter any other than open ports without necessity, or without offering proper explanations to the Imperial authorities.

And this proviso was attached to the fourth article:

It is not intended by this Article that any acts of individuals, whether high or low, previously unauthorized or subsequently disapproved by Her Majesty the Queen of Great Britain, can set aside the Convention entered into with Her Majesty alone by His Imperial Highness the Emperor of Japan.

An interesting provision was to the effect that "all official communications will hereafter, when Japanese shall have time to learn English, be made in that language."[8]

While these various negotiations were in progress the Dutch continued to trade under the old regulations at Nagasaki. So irksome were the restrictions there that Commodore Perry had deliberately refused to accept Nagasaki as an open port; and although the port was to be open to British and Russian ships, no provision was made for trade. The Dutch naturally desired to

---

[7] Texts in Gubbins, *The Progress of Japan, 1853–1871*, pp. 235–37.

[8] Article VII of Additional Regulations to the American Treaty, June 17, 1854, provided that the Chinese language should not be employed in official communications except when there was no Dutch interpreter.

improve their status and to be freed from the restraints which they had so long endured. On November 9, 1855, the Netherlands Commissioner in Japan, Mr. J. H. Donker Curtius, signed a preliminary Convention, which was to become void if a treaty were signed soon after, but which would remain in force if ratified by both rulers.[9] The Convention provided, however, that of the twenty-nine articles all but eight were to go into immediate operation, and of those excepted, one was to date from December 1 and the others from January 1. This preliminary Convention was followed by a treaty signed on January 30, 1856,[10] the ratifications being exchanged on October 16, 1857. All the stipulations, however, came into operation on its signature. A comparison between the preliminary Convention and the formal Treaty shows that aside from a few slight changes the only important difference was the withdrawal of the article providing for the sale of dwellings and warehouses and the lease of the ground at Deshima to the Dutch. The change in status of the Dutch really came, therefore, with the signature of the preliminary Convention.

The terms of this Convention indicate the sort of regulations which the Dutch had to endure, and from which they were now freed. From December 1, 1855, the Netherlanders would enjoy full personal freedom and would be allowed to leave Deshima at all times without an escort. Salutes from small arms and even from cannon might be fired at the funeral of Dutch soldiers and seamen. The Dutch ships need no longer give hostages on entering the harbor. The crews might row from ship to ship or to Deshima or around the bay for recreation (when a captain or mate was with them), but they could land at no place but the water gate of Deshima. Building and repairs might be done by Japanese workmen after previous notice to the Governor of Nagasaki. The land gate of Deshima was still to be guarded by Japa-

[9] Gubbins, *The Progress of Japan, 1853–1871*, pp. 245–50. Townsend Harris believed that he saw a copy of the ratified Japanese text in October 1856. The Japanese officials denied that it had been ratified (Griffis, *Townsend Harris, First American Envoy in Japan*, p. 125); Cosenza, *The Complete Journal of Townsend Harris*, p. 318.

[10] Gubbins, *The Progress of Japan, 1853–1871*, pp. 250–55.

nese, and merchant sailors were to be searched there. In matters of courtesy the Japanese would follow Japanese forms, and the Netherlanders their national forms. The Dutch might now send letters by Chinese junks or foreign ships, and they might communicate by letter with the commanders of ships of friendly nations in the bay. Their merchant ships might now retain their gunpowder and arms. The presents to the Emperor (Shogun) and the annual presents to the local officials were to be continued. Finally, no alteration was to be introduced in the manner in which the trade with the factory was carried on. So far these articles were concerned with freeing the Dutch from century-old restrictions, and the work was not finished. Two clauses were of importance. One provided for extraterritoriality, and the other granted the "most-favored-nation" privileges.

Such were the Treaties of 1854 and 1855. By the use of the "most-favored-nation" clause the sum total of foreign rights in Japan was the privilege of resorting to Shimoda, Hakodate, and Nagasaki for supplies; of carrying on trade at these ports under Japanese regulations and through Japanese officials;[11] of residing at Nagasaki, a right which did not apply to women and children; and of appointing consuls at Shimoda and Hakodate.

While Commodore Perry and other observers feared that the foreign merchants would endeavor to take advantage of their status and insist upon commercial rights not conferred by the Treaties, thus stirring up trouble and delaying the negotiation of true treaties of commerce,[12] the Japanese were quite as anxious to grant no more than the letter of the Treaties.

In February 1855 a French ship appeared at Shimoda with the object of returning two Japanese shipwrecked seamen. But the authorities would have nothing to do with the ship, refused to accept the seamen, and ordered the vessel away. They insisted that they had "no treaty with France, and French vessels had no right to come there under any pretext." The seamen were finally

[11] No trade at Nagasaki was attempted under these Treaties by any except the Dutch.

[12] Hawks, *op. cit.,* II, 187.

landed by way of the American ship "Powhatan," thus seeming to come from the ship of a Treaty Power.[13] In March an American merchant ship put into Shimoda, the owner's intention being to proceed to Hakodate as soon as that port was opened and establish there a store for supplying whalers with ship chandlery; but the Japanese protested successfully against the residence of Americans at either port.[14] In August an American schooner, the "Wilmington," visited Shimoda and later Hakodate, but was unable to trade at either place.[15] The American ships of war which visited these ports during this period were hospitably received and well treated.[16]

It would be well now to note the attitude of the Japanese in regard to these changed relations. As far as the foreigners were able to meet the people near the ports they were impressed with their general friendliness. This attitude was evident during the brief excursions about Yokohama and Shimoda, and it was in striking contrast to the attitude of the Chinese about the treaty ports.[17] The officials also made an excellent impression, which was again in contrast to the experience which Western representatives had had in China.[18] Bayard Taylor records that "it was the unanimous opinion of all our officers that they were as perfect

[13] Hawks, *op. cit.,* I, 511.

[14] *Ibid.,* pp. 390–91. Griffis, *Matthew Calbraith Perry,* pp. 133–34. The first American ship to visit Japan after the treaty was the "Lady Pierce," of San Francisco, which visited Yedo Bay and Shimoda in July 1854 (Hildreth, *Japan as It Was and Is,* II, 312–13).

[15] Nitobe, *Intercourse between the United States and Japan,* p. 64; *U.S. Commercial Relations, 1855,* I, 508. The "Wilmington" claim arose from this incident; see Index (Vol. II).

[16] The "Susquehanna" and the "Mississippi" visited Shimoda in September 1854, the "Powhatan," with the ratified Treaty, January–February 1855. The "Vincennes" visited Shimoda and Hakodate, May–June 1855 (Hildreth, *op. cit.,* II, 314).

[17] For the comparison between Japan and China see Hawks, *op. cit.;* Williams, "Journal of the Perry Expedition to Japan," in *Transactions of the Asiatic Society of Japan,* Vol. 37, Part II, and "Lecture on Japan," in *Journal of North-China Branch of Royal Asiatic Society,* No. II, May 1859; Oliphant, *Narrative of the Earl of Elgin's Mission to China and Japan;* De Fonblanque, *Niphon and Pe-che-li;* Griffis, *Townsend Harris, First American Envoy in Japan.*

[18] Williams, *op. cit.,* p. 226.

gentlemen as could be found in any part of the world,"[19] and Wells Williams said that "in no country could more agreeable and kind-hearted men be found than old Yendo and Fuzhiwara at Hakodadi." To be sure, the Americans spoke of the "well known duplicity"[20] of the Japanese, and of their "artful and dissimulating policy"; but suspicion is a natural element of relations between strange peoples, and doubtless the Japanese were quite as suspicious of American cunning, duplicity, and dissimulation.[21] The use of censors or "spies" to report on the conduct of their own officials impressed the Americans,[22] and the surveillance to which they were subjected on shore was the occasion for protest. When Captain Adams visited Shimoda in 1855 he wrote:

I found the Japanese during my visit much more disposed to be friendly and sociable than formerly. Our officers roamed where they pleased over the country and the villages, and were welcomed everywhere. There was no attempt to watch or follow them. . . . . An anxious wish was expressed by these people that trading vessels from America would soon begin to visit them, and the governor of Simoda intimated to me that it would be very agreeable to him personally if a consul from the United States should be appointed to reside at Simoda. They were eager to obtain books on medical or scientific subjects, and many valuable works were presented to them by Dr. Maxwell and others. Indeed, they were glad to receive books on any subject except religion. They told me they had learned how to manage the locomotive engine sent to the Emperor by the United States government, but the magnetic telegraph was too hard for them.[23]

The Americans were impressed on all sides by the eagerness of the Japanese to learn about the new and strange things in use among the foreigners. The visitors to Perry's flagship studied

[19] Taylor, *Visit to India, China, and Japan,* p. 434.

[20] Some of these early statements were revised when Hawks compiled the narrative of Perry's mission.

[21] For early Japanese suspicions see Clement, "British Seamen and Mito Samurai in 1824," in *Transactions of the Asiatic Society of Japan,* Vol. 33, Part I.

[22] Captain Brinkley compares this to the secret-service force employed by all European states (*History of the Japanese People,* p. 635 n.).

[23] Hawks, *op. cit.,* II, 209. The governor of Shimoda sent off to Captain Adams a bundle of religious books left clandestinely by Chaplain Bittinger, of the "Susquehanna," in 1854 (*ibid.,* I, 512).

with interest the weapons, from Colt revolvers to Paixhan cannon; they descended into the engine-room and watched the machinery in motion; and they observed keenly the maneuvers of the crew at general quarters.[24] Many of the Japanese were engaged in sketching the Americans and their belongings and in taking copious notes. In the library of the Imperial University at Tokyo are some of the original drawings, portraying with remarkable exactness ships, sailors, armament, and equipment, down to details of the wearing apparel of the crew. These drawings were prepared for the use of the Yedo officials and certain of the daimyos. On the second visit Wells Williams saw a book of twenty pages giving neat and accurate drawings and diagrams of cannons, guns, revolvers, swords, and other arms.[25] It was printed in Yedo in October, after the first visit, and he believed it was a digest of what was seen aboard the "Susquehanna," "though the author must have had some European work on gunnery to copy his drawings from." Later at Shimoda some of the officers saw a pictorial representation and description of the squadron, and an account of the war between England and China.[26] Nitobe sums up the period as follows:

Immediately after Perry's squadron had left the Japanese waters, the rulers of the country, whether actuated by clear foresight and comprehension of the moment, or whether impelled by that mental confusion which attends sudden awakening from slumber and apprehension of the next moment, were aroused to immediate activity. Schools were opened for the study of foreign languages; academies shot up, where youths could receive instruction in military and naval tactics; raw recruits were drilled; foundaries and smithies sprang into existence, and belfries were molested to furnish metal for arsenals.[27]

Japan was torn between two lines of action. One was respect for

---

[24] Hawks, *op. cit.*, I, 248, 358. Harris was told in 1857 that the Japanese had cast 1,000 brass howitzers like those given them by Perry (Griffis, *Townsend Harris, First American Envoy in Japan*, p. 112).

[25] Williams, *op. cit.*, p. 110.   [26] *Ibid.*, p. 182.

[27] Nitobe, *op. cit.*, p. 62. Two steam vessels were purchased in Holland and shipyards were established at Nagasaki (Griffis, *Townsend Harris, First American Envoy in Japan*, p. 69). See also *Journal of the North-China Branch of the Royal Asiatic Society*, II, 211–21.

the long-standing laws of the realm; the other was obedience to the appeal of new ideas. The first was negative, but the second called for positive action; and although the pressure came from without, yet the Japanese themselves eventually accepted the second course.

The officials at the open ports were by no means representative of the ruling classes at this time. They were acquainted with the foreigners, and could understand the necessity of dealing fairly with them, but in the interior few of the daimyos or their retainers possessed such knowledge, and among them respect for the old laws and hostility to foreign intercourse were strong.

At the capital of the Shogunate the situation was complicated by other questions. The treaties had been concluded without the Mikado's sanction, but that difficulty was removed when in February 1855 the Mikado approved the first treaties with America, Great Britain, and Russia.[28] The influence of the Shogunate at Kyoto was still supreme, although for some sixty years ill-feeling had persisted,[29] and the opponents of the Shogun's foreign policy had not yet realized the importance of causing a breach between the two courts on this question. The majority of the councillors of the Shogunate were convinced of the wisdom of foreign intercourse. The Rojiu, or Cabinet, was presided over by Lord Abe, who had directed the treaty negotiations. A second council, of increasing importance, was the Tamarizume, or lords of the ante-chamber, a majority of whose nine members also favored the treaties, under the influence of Lords Ii and Hotta.[30] But the Sanke, the three noble Tokugawa houses, led by the senior prince of Mito (Lord Nariaki),[31] were bitter opponents of the new policy. It was a serious thing for a small group of officials to oppose not merely the Imperial court and the great mass of the daimyos but also the Three Families, which were supposed to be the strongest supporters of the Tokugawa Shogunate. All the

---

[28] Gubbins, *The Progress of Japan, 1853–1871,* p. 100.

[29] Brinkley, *op. cit.,* p. 630.

[30] *Ibid.,* p. 636; Akimoto, *Lord Ii Naosuke and New Japan,* pp. 125–27.

[31] He had resigned his fief in 1853.

more credit, therefore, is due to Hotta and Ii and their associates for risking their all in order to bring the nation peaceably into contact with the rest of the world.

A struggle now developed between the Sanke and the Tamarizume for the control of the Cabinet, and in August 1855 Lord Nariaki gained the upper hand and succeeded in having two of the pro-foreign ministers dismissed. In November, however, Lord Hotta, one of the leaders of the pro-foreign party, was appointed to the presidency of the Cabinet, and Lord Abe stepped down to the second place.[32] This was a great blow to Lord Nariaki and the exclusion party, and Nariaki could not fathom its meaning, but others realized that Lord Ii and the Tamarizume had been able to wield enough influence to checkmate the Sanke.[33] By this time a well-developed feud was on between Lord Nariaki and his followers and Lord Ii and his. The foreign question was, however, but one of many points of difference, and it could not stand upon its own footing when state decisions had to be made. In addition a bitter controversy was brewing as to the appointment of an heir to the Shogun, Iyesada. Lord Nariaki urged the claims of his son, Lord Hitotsubashi, and a powerful party supported them. But the Shogun and his confidential officials, including Lord Ii, favored the young Lord of Kii (Kishiu). We shall see how this decision became involved with the later treaty negotiations.

Even among daimyos and officials who were reconciled to the necessity of negotiating the first treaties there was a strong feeling that enough concessions had been made, and that it would be possible to hold the foreigners aloof, with only three points of very limited contact. It was the arrival of the first Consul to be appointed under the Treaties which precipitated a new crisis in foreign affairs.[34]

---

[32] Satoh, *Lord Hotta,* p. 30.

[33] Akimoto, *op. cit.,* p. 138.

[34] Although Donker Curtius had resided at Nagasaki since 1852, he was looked upon by the Japanese as a commercial agent in charge of the Dutch post at Deshima. His title of factory superintendent had been raised by his govern-

Once again the United States was most fortunate in the choice of its representative. Townsend Harris[35] was born on October 3, 1804, at Sandy Hill, Washington County, New York.[36] From 1817 until 1848 he was engaged in business in New York, and among other civic duties served for two years as president of the Board of Education. Later he was instrumental in founding the Free Academy, which has developed into the splendid College of the City of New York. In 1848 he embarked upon a trading voyage to California and the Far East, and for the next seven years he was engaged in the Eastern trade, gaining a useful knowledge of the countries and the peoples of Eastern Asia, Malaysia, and the Pacific. While in China he made a study of the resources of Formosa, and advocated the purchase of the island in a letter to the Secretary of State, March 24, 1854. When it was determined to appoint a Consul for Japan, Townsend Harris was selected upon a joint recommendation of Commodore Perry and Senator William H. Seward.[37] He returned to the United States from China, and received his formal appointment on August 4, 1855, later being commissioned to negotiate a commercial treaty with Siam. Harris left New York on October 17 and proceeded by the "overland route" to Penang, where, after a delay of seventy-six days, the United States steam frigate "San Jacinto" arrived, bearing his interpreter, Mr. Henry C. J. Heusken, of New York, and the presents for the rulers of Siam and Japan. Reaching Bangkok on April 13, 1856, Mr. Harris succeeded in signing a

ment to that of Netherlands commissioner in Japan, and he was given full powers to negotiate treaties (Gubbins, *The Progress of Japan, 1853–1871,* p. 65).

[35] His journal was printed in Griffis, *Townsend Harris, First American Envoy in Japan* (1895), but the definitive edition is *The Complete Journal of Townsend Harris, First American Consul General and Minister to Japan,* with introduction and notes by Mario Emilio Cosenza, 1930.

[36] His grandfather's home was burned during Burgoyne's expedition, and his grandmother brought him up " 'to tell the truth, fear God, and hate the British,' and all three things he did all his life" (Griffis, *Townsend Harris, First American Envoy in Japan,* p. 4). This injunction may furnish a partial explanation of his troubled relations later with Rutherford Alcock, the British Minister.

[37] *United States Diplomatic Correspondence, 1862,* p. 816 (cited as *F.R., 1862).* See Cosenza, *op. cit.,* pp. 1–16, for additional details.

new treaty with Siam based on the British Treaty of 1855.[38] It was not until August 21 that the "San Jacinto" entered the harbor of Shimoda.

The instructions which were given by Secretary Marcy and dated September 13, 1855, were as follows:

You are aware that the Treaty with Japan which was negotiated by Commodore Perry on our part, does not expressly provide for any commercial intercourse between the United States and that Empire and, from the notorious jealousy of the Japanese in regard to foreigners, it is at least questionable whether they would assent to such a construction of the instrument, as would permit trade between the two countries. It is true that the Treaty secures privileges and immunities, the want of which has been much felt by our citizens and vessels navigating in the vicinity of the coasts of Japan. It is not improbable, however, that if we could obtain free access to the Japanese Empire upon all occasions or, for trading purposes, to some of the ports of that populous country, an advantageous commerce therewith might ultimately, at least, be carried on. A principal motive of the President in selecting you as Consul General for Japan was the hope that, by your knowledge of eastern character, and your general intelligence and experience in business, you would make such an impression upon the Japanese as would in time induce them to enter into a commercial treaty with us. As it is possible that a juncture favorable for making an overture for this purpose might arise before you could communicate with the Department, upon the subject, after your arrival at Simoda, you are now furnished with a full power to negotiate and conclude such a Treaty. This will enable you to lose no time in availing yourself of a favorable opportunity for the purpose. It is deemed unnecessary to specify the details of such a treaty as would be desirable. If, however, its commercial stipulations were to be similar to those which you are instructed to insert in the treaty with Siam, it is believed that they would be sufficient, at least as a beginning. The intolerance of the Japanese in regard to the Christian religion forbids us to hope that they would consent to any stipulation by which missionaries would be allowed to enter that Empire or christian worship, according to the form of any sect would be permitted.

If you should succeed in concluding such a treaty, you may take the

---

[38] Harris' Treaty with Siam was based almost exactly upon the British Treaty of April 18, 1855. While Harris was at Bangkok Harry Parkes exchanged the ratifications of that Treaty and secured some supplementary articles, May 13, 1856. These treaties included a clear statement of extraterritoriality, the free importation of opium but the confining of its sale to the opium farmer or his agents, open trade at all ports but residence only at Bangkok, freedom of religion and the right to build places of worship, and low import and export duties.

same course in forwarding it to the United States, as is prescribed for the treaty which you are empowered to negotiate with Siam.

You will also, herewith receive, a letter from the President of the United States to the Emperor of Japan and an office copy of the same.[39]

There now began a struggle between the Japanese officials, eager to whittle away the concessions already granted, and the American Consul, anxious to complete the process of opening wide the doors of Japan. Fortunately Harris possessed an open mind and a kindly disposition, so that in spite of early disagreements he was able to retain the opinion formed at his first interview: "We were all much pleased with the appearance and manners of the Japanese. I repeat they are superior to any people east of the Cape of Good Hope." His journal records the steps in his work of enlightenment and shows how he was able to win the confidence of the Japanese, and then, without bluster or threat, to break down the barriers which their suspicions and fears had raised.

First of all, the Japanese did not wish to receive him. They protested that Shimoda had not recovered from the disastrous earthquake of 1855 and there was no place ready for him; that he had better go away and return in about a year. Then they asserted that a Consul was to come if both nations wished it, not merely the United States alone, for so the Japanese text read. Finally, they offered him a temporary residence at Kakizaki, on the outskirts of Shimoda. All the while they assured him that they had no intention of breaking the Treaty or of refusing to receive him.

The question of his reception and place of residence once settled, other difficulties promptly arose. Harris objected to the presence of Japanese officers in his temple residence, and after four months of repeated protests they were removed. He also resented the presence of censors or spies during official conferences, and these also were dispensed with. He found that the

---

[39] Six instructions were given to Harris in September–October 1855, before he left Washington. Only one was sent in 1856 (August 19), directing him to pay a note for $2,000 given by a Mr. Reed to the Governor of Shimoda, and none in 1857. Harris' dispatches for 1856 were numbered 1–21, and for 1857, 1–27.

Japanese were discounting American money heavily; he was unable to secure Japanese servants, and the shopmen were apparently ordered not to deal with his Chinese servants; and the officials would not send written replies to his communications, nor would they return his social visits. All these points were eventually cleared up. Throughout the early entries in his diary Harris frequently complains of the untruthfulness of the officials. On September 11 the journal records:

> Had a *flare up* with the officials, who told me some egregious lies, in answer to some requests I made. I told them plainly I knew they lied; that, if they wished me to have confidence in them, they must always speak the truth; that, if I asked anything they were not authorized to grant, or about which they wished to consult, let them simply say they were not prepared to answer me; but that to tell lies to me was treating me like a child, and that I should consider myself as insulted thereby; that in my country a man who lied was disgraced, and that to call a man a liar was the grossest insult could be given him; that I hoped they would for the future, if they told me anything, simply tell me the truth, and that I should then respect them, which I could not do when they told me falsehoods.[40]

After this time friendly relations steadily increased. On October 30 the two Governors and the Vice-Governor called upon him at his residence, and the process of instruction in Western affairs—beginning with an account of the coast-surveying operations of the maritime powers—commenced. To be sure, the attempts at deception did not entirely cease, and on January 8, 1857, he wrote bitterly: "They are the greatest liars on earth."[41] But this was a "sweeping generalization" which was only "more or less" correct. In certain cases where he believed the Japanese were deceiving him he was himself in error.[42] And when we make allowance for the inexperience of the officials in dealing with a foreign representative, their desire not to give offense, their fear of incurring the displeasure of the Yedo administration, and the difficulties of carrying on communications through the use of three languages,

[40] Cosenza, *op. cit.,* pp. 251–52; Harris to Marcy, No. 15, September 3.

[41] Cosenza, *op. cit.,* p. 300; May 26, "However to *lie* is, for a Japanese, simply to speak" (*ibid.,* p. 366).

[42] Note in re Dutch treaties, *ibid.,* p. 319 n.

it is easy to discount these early observations of one who later became one of the staunchest friends and admirers of the Japanese.[43] As the officials gained more confidence in Harris and found that he spoke the truth and kept faith, their dealings became more straightforward.

Harris had two important missions to perform. One was to present his credentials at Yedo; and the other was to secure, if possible, a real commercial treaty. On the first subject he carried on a correspondence with the Council of State, and engaged in countless interviews with the local officials from October 25, 1856, until September 25 of the next year, when information came that his reception would be granted. As to the second, he received much encouragement from some of the officials: "all agree that it is only a question of time, and Moriyama Yenosky [the interpreter] goes so far as to place it less than three years distant";[44] and later he was told that the first commercial treaty would be negotiated with him.[45] In the meantime he determined to remedy certain defects in the existing Treaty, even though a new and broader one could not be obtained.

The first question was that of the currency. Perry's Treaty contained no provision for exchange of currency, and the Japanese insisted upon receiving silver (Mexican) dollars at their bullion value, which meant a discount of sixty-six and two-thirds per cent on their currency value.[46] When Harris found this rate of exchange still in force, he promptly asked that the coins be exchanged by weight. His arguments were supported by Commodore Possiet, of the Russian corvette "Olivoutsa," who brought the ratified Russian Treaty. On leaving, Commodore Possiet paid

---

[43] Harris' early opinions must be considered in the light of his mature convictions (Griffis, *Townsend Harris, First American Envoy in Japan,* p. 105 n.). See also Oliphant, *op. cit.,* p. 345; De Fonblanque, *op. cit.,* p. 105.

[44] November 14, 1856; Cosenza, *op. cit.,* p. 269.

[45] April 15, 1857; *ibid.,* p. 345.

[46] Harris' No. 16, October 9. The silver dollar was worth 4,800 sen or cash, but was received at only 1,600 (Hawks, *op. cit.,* I, 479 n.). One ichibu worth 34 cents (based on Chinese tael at $1.36) was exchanged for a dollar Mexican (Cosenza, *op. cit.,* p. 234).

only one-third of the Japanese bill for pilotage and boat hire, and left the balance in Harris' hands to await the settlement of the account when a Russian Consul should arrive.[47] In reply to Harris' offer to allow five per cent for recoinage, the Japanese assured him that it cost twenty-five per cent, and of course refused his offer to bring out coiners from America who would do the work for five per cent or even less.[48] As on this point there seemed to be a deadlock, Harris wisely proceeded to the other topics he wished to open.

As the Russians had stipulated for the opening of Nagasaki, Harris asked for this, and promptly obtained it. It will be remembered that Perry distinctly refused to accept Nagasaki as an open port. Harris also asked for extraterritoriality, and "to my great and agreeable surprise this was agreed to without demur."[49] The right to lease ground and to buy, build, and repair buildings was a difficult question. Harris based the demand upon the Dutch Treaty of November 9, 1855.[50] He did not know of the Treaty of January 30, 1856, which withdrew the clause regarding the sale of buildings and the lease of land at Deshima. This was an instance in which the Japanese were not so untruthful as Harris believed, and the Japanese stood by their refusal to grant this new right. He later saw the new Dutch Treaty on November 18, 1857.[51]

The currency question was now reopened, and the Japanese offered to exchange gold and silver coins with a fifteen per cent discount. Harris again stood out for five per cent, and when his three propositions had been rejected he played his last card:

At last I told them I had something of great importance to communicate confidentially, and to them alone. To my great surprise the room was at once cleared of all but the two Governors and Moriama Tatsitsio. I

---

[47] Cosenza, *op. cit.,* pp. 287, 290 n. ; No. 21, December 10.

[48] Cosenza, *op. cit.,* p. 312.

[49] *Ibid.,* p. 317. It had already been granted to the Russians and the Dutch.

[50] *Ibid.,* pp. 317–20. Captain Fabius told Harris the buildings at Deshima had been sold to the Dutch (*ibid.,* p. 333), and one of the Japanese interpreters gave Heusken a similar report (*ibid.,* p. 341).

[51] *Ibid.,* p. 410.

then read to them an extract from a letter to me from the Secretary of State, which was to the effect that, if the Japanese sought to evade the Treaty, the President would not hesitate to ask Congress to give him power to use such arguments as they could not resist. The fluttering was fearful —the effect strong.[52]

Three days later the discount rate was reduced to six per cent, and Harris eventually accepted this, on their plea that if less were taken the Government would lose through the recoinage.[53] It should be clearly borne in mind that this "warning" was concerned with an interpretation of the existing Treaty, not with an attempt to secure some new concession from the Japanese.

The last questions to be settled were those concerning the residence of Americans and the rights of Consuls. For two months these were the subject of frequent conferences. During this period Harris felt the weakness of his isolation. He had received no word from Washington since he had left there in October 1855.[54] The "San Jacinto," which was to have returned in six months, was long overdue. The Russian Consul, who would have supported him in his arguments, had not arrived, nor had any French or British vessels visited the port. Although only nine days distant from Hong Kong, he was "more isolated than any American official in any part of the world." He believed at this time that "the absence of a man-of-war also tends to weaken my influence with the Japanese. They have yielded nothing except from *fear,* and any future ameliorations in our intercourse will only take place after a demonstration of force on our part."[55] In this respect he was wrong, for without the presence of any of the aids which he so much desired, he was able to carry all his points, through friendly argument alone, and on June 8, 1857, he records the agreement of the Japanese to all the material requests.[56] It took some nine days to settle the wording of the articles, because of the poor knowledge of Dutch possessed by the Japanese interpreters

[52] *Ibid.,* p. 325.   [53] *Ibid.,* p. 327.

[54] *Ibid.,* p. 350.   [55] *Ibid.,* pp. 357–58.

[56] *Ibid.,* p. 373. The first ship to visit Shimoda was the "Portsmouth," September 8, 1857, *ibid.,* pp. 387–93. See Captain Foote's account in *Journal of the Shanghai Literary and Scientific Society,* June 1858.

and their desire to have the words in the Dutch version stand in the exact order in which they were found in the Japanese,[57] but on June 17 the Convention was signed with due formality by Harris and the two Governors of Shimoda.

This was a Convention "for the purpose of further regulating the intercourse of American citizens within the Empire of Japan." It contained nine articles. The first article opened the port of Nagasaki for supplies. The second permitted, after July 4, 1858, the residence of Americans at Shimoda and Hakodate.[58] The third dealt with the currency and established the exchange of coins by weight, with a discount of six per cent allowed the Japanese for recoinage. Harris was quite unaware of the disastrous effect of this arrangement in a country where the ratio of gold to silver was so much lower than in the neighboring countries. The fourth established American extraterritoriality. The fifth restated the seventh clause of Perry's Treaty, to the effect that American ships could pay for their supplies and repairs with goods, if they had no money. The sixth and seventh articles dealt with consular rights, recognizing the right of the Consul to travel beyond the Treaty limits of seven ri, coupled with Harris' consent not to exercise it "except in cases of emergency, shipwreck, etc.," and permitting the direct purchase of goods for the Consul's use without the intervention of any Japanese officials and with Japanese money furnished for the purpose. The eighth article established the Dutch as the true version of the Convention, and the ninth declared all the articles to be in effect, except the second.[59]

Thus after nine months of education and persuasion Harris was able to secure some improvement in the status of Americans in Japan. The important clauses were those which dealt with the currency, residence at Shimoda and Hakodate, and consular privileges, for the others were already covered by the Russian and

---

[57] Cosenza, *op. cit.*, p. 375.

[58] As no classes of Americans were named, missionaries could come and reside in Japan, a proceeding which would have occasioned a conflict between the Treaty and Japanese municipal law.

[59] Malloy, *Treaties and Conventions*, I, 998–1000; No. 7, June 18.

Dutch Treaties. But he well realized that he had made only a beginning. He wrote:

> Am I elated by this success? Not a whit. I know my dear countrymen but too well to expect any praise for what I have done, and I shall esteem myself lucky if I am not removed from office; not for what I have done, but because I have not made a commercial treaty that would open Japan as freely as England is open to us.
>
> Besides, it is so easy to criticise, and so agreeable to condemn. It is much more pleasant to write imbecile, ass, or fool, than to say able, discreet, and competent.[60]

Yet in these months he had laid the foundations for his greater successes. He had established a reputation for frankness and fair dealing, for sympathy and understanding, which made him persona grata to the Japanese.

While Harris was negotiating at Shimoda, Mr. Donker Curtius was at work at Nagasaki, and on October 16, 1857, he was able to sign additional articles to the Dutch Treaty of January 30, 1856.[61] This document contained forty articles, and was longer than the original Treaty. It was concerned with removing more of the restrictions which hampered the Dutch trade, but it was by no means a treaty of commerce. Among other things it removed the limit on the number of merchant ships trading in Japan and on the amount of trade; fixed a temporary import duty of thirty-five per cent; made the Treasury the clearing-house for all commercial transactions; prohibited the purchase and exportation of Japanese gold and silver coins; created a government monopoly in the sale of various foodstuffs, coal, books, maps, brass-work, copper, weapons, and silk; and restated the extraterritorial and "most-favored-nation" clauses. Two clauses were especially interesting: one forbade the introduction of opium into Japan, and the other permitted the Netherlanders to practice "their own or the Christian religion" within their buildings or burying-places.

In a supplement to these additional articles the long-established practice of giving presents to the Shogun and the local officials was abolished, "considering that the Company trade ceases from

[60] Cosenza, *op. cit.*, p. 374.
[61] Gubbins, *The Progress of Japan, 1853–1871*, pp. 255–64.

henceforth, and no copper may be exported, except by the Imperial Government alone, in payment of goods required."[62] In written communications the Dutch Commissioner was advised[63] that his countrymen might now have their wives and children reside with them in Japan; that negotiations concerning an audience of the highest Dutch official with the Emperor (Shogun) would take place; that negotiations concerning the exportation of Japanese coins were already in progress; that Japan had no idea of concluding a treaty of friendship and commerce with Portugal; and that while the trampling on images was abolished, the introduction of the Christian worship and the importation of Christian and other foreign religious books, prints, and images would not be allowed.

To the Dutch belongs the credit of inserting in a foreign treaty a prohibition of the introduction of opium. The Japanese did not use opium, and were aware of its evil influence in China, but in none of the earlier treaties was the prohibition found. Dr. Wells Williams in 1853 dreaded the introduction of opium by merchants from the China coast, but could think of no way to prevent it.[64] Harris had an example of the strength of the habit when his Chinese servants seized the opium in two drugshops in Shimoda.[65] If the Japanese had desired to introduce a prohibitory clause, Harris would certainly have accepted it.[66] In fact the introduction of this clause by the Dutch could hardly be credited to humanitarian reasons alone when their attitude toward opium in Java is considered. No doubt a good deal of interest lay in the fact that an anti-opium clause might not only seriously affect the profits but also disturb the balance of the trade which would be established under the British flag in Japan. The Russians; in their Treaty of the next week, accepted this prohibition of the "pernicious trade," and the next year Harris wrote the clause into his great commercial Treaty.

[62] Gubbins, *The Progress of Japan, 1853–1871,* p. 264.

[63] *Ibid.,* pp. 265–66.

[64] Williams, *op. cit.,* p. 5.

[65] Cosenza, *op. cit.,* pp. 272–76.

[66] Note Harris' advice to the Japanese in 1857, in *F.R., 1879,* p. 629.

The Russian Supplementary Treaty[67] was signed at Nagasaki on October 24, 1857, by Vice-Admiral Count Poutiatine. It contained many of the provisions of the Dutch Treaty of 1856 and the supplementary articles just signed, as well as Harris' agreement for the exchange of coins with a discount of six per cent. New clauses provided that the communications between the governments should be exchanged through the hands of the local Governor, and that Russia would respect the neutrality of Japan in case she was involved in a foreign war.

The American, Dutch, and Russian Conventions of 1857, in fact and in name supplementary to the first treaties, mark the second phase of the partial opening of Japan. General trade, without the intervention of Japanese officials, was still forbidden, and in other respects the privileges of foreigners were circumscribed. But some advance had been made in the three years, and the time when a real commercial treaty could be negotiated was at hand.

[67] Gubbins, *The Progress of Japan,* pp. 239–45.

CHAPTER III

THE COMMERCIAL TREATY OF 1858

W<small>HILE</small> Townsend Harris was toilfully working out the details of the Convention of 1857, he also kept in mind the more important object of his mission, which was to secure, if possible, an audience of the Shogun and to open negotiations in Yedo for a real treaty of commerce. He therefore requested an interview in order to present a letter from the President of the United States and to make certain communications, with which he was charged, to the proper Minister. The Japanese insisted that the letter be delivered at Shimoda and the communication made to the Governors there, and even presented an Imperial mandate to that effect, only to be dumbfounded at Harris' refusal to yield.[1] In Yedo there was much opposition. The Lord of Mito led the conservatives, but even Lord Abe, recently head of the Rojiu, was opposed. Lord Hotta favored intercourse and won over the Cabinet.[2] Finally, on September 22, Harris was informed that his request had been granted, and that he was to go to Yedo in the most honorable manner and have an audience of the Shogun.[3] With the memory of the experience of foreign diplomats in China over the "kowtow" in mind, Harris feared that some objectionable proposition would be made. But a "faint request that I would prostrate myself and 'knock-head'" was the only reference to the ceremony, and on Harris' statement that the very mentioning of such a thing was offensive the matter was definitely dropped.

Two months were now occupied in preparing for the visit, and on November 23 the start was made. Harris was accompanied by the Vice-Governor of Shimoda, the Mayor of Kakizaki,

[1] Cosenza, *The Complete Journal of Townsend Harris,* p. 375. The letter was his letter of credence.

[2] Satoh, *Lord Hotta,* pp. 42–47.   [3] Cosenza, *op. cit.,* p. 394.

48

and the private secretary of the Governor. His own train consisted of some eighty men,[4] and the whole party numbered about three hundred and fifty. Three days were spent in crossing the mountain range which isolated Shimoda; but the Tokaido, or highway, beyond it, was wide and good. Most careful preparations had been made for his coming, and he was treated like a lord of the land. On November 30 the journey of one hundred and eighty miles was ended, and Harris was installed in one of the buildings of the "Office for the Examination of Barbarian Books," near the castle and within the aristocratic quarter of the city.[5]

After a week of hospitality and exchange of courtesies, in which Harris was in charge of eight noblemen appointed as "Commissioners of the voyage of the American Ambassador to Yedo," he was received on December 7 in a most dignified manner by the Shogun. While princes of the blood and members of the Great Council were prostrate on their faces in the presence of the Tycoon, Harris alone stood erect, and addressed the ruler.

After a short silence the Tykoon began to jerk his head backward over his left shoulder, at the same time stamping with his right foot. This was repeated three or four times. After this, he spoke audibly and in a pleasant and firm voice, what was interpreted as follows:—

"Pleased with the letter sent with the Ambassador from a far distant country, and likewise pleased with his discourse. Intercourse shall be continued forever."[6]

Mr. Heusken, the interpreter, then stepped forward with the President's letter, which Harris showed to the Tycoon and then handed, in its box, to Lord Hotta, the Minister for Foreign

---

[4] "I shall not take any of my Chinese with me, as the Japanese have a great dislike to the Chinese, and I do not wish to be associated in their minds with the Chinese or any other people" (*ibid.*, p. 396).

[5] Harris has given an account of this trip in his journal, and in two letters reprinted in *Littell's Living Age,* Vol. 60, pp. 567–74. In 1879 a Japanese record of the arrangement for Harris' journey and reception was turned over to Dr. David Murray by the successor of Hotta Bitchiu-no-Kami. The documents were translated and published in *F.R., 1879,* pp. 620–36. They show the careful arrangements for and the honor accorded the American representative. He reported the events in No. 26, December 10.

[6] Cosenza, *op. cit.,* p. 475.

Affairs, who placed it on a lacquered stand before the Shogun. This ended the audience. Harris retreated, made his three bows, and was received by the ministers, who later said that they were filled with admiration to see him stand erect, "look the awful 'Tycoon' in the face, speak plainly to him, hear his reply—and all this without any trepidation, or any 'quivering of the muscles of the side.' "[7] An elaborate banquet was spread before Harris, but he refused to partake of it unless a member of the royal family or the Prime Minister would eat with him. As Harris had already announced this decision at Shimoda, the Japanese were prepared for his refusal, and the orders of the day called for the sending of all the food to his lodging place, where he distributed it among his retainers. But every arrangement for the feast, even the height of the trays and the unvarnished cypress of which they were made, testified to the honor in which Harris was held.

Once again the unexpected had happened. The American flag had been borne through the streets of Yedo and the American Consul General had stood in the presence of the Shogun. Precedents were established which were to govern the reception of other representatives of the Western Powers. But although Harris had obtained the desired audience, yet the "real object" of his mission was not yet attained.[8] The first move in this direction was taken when on December 12 he visited Lord Hotta, to make the communication which accompanied the President's letter. In his journal[9] he has given a summary of this most important two-hour conversation, but fortunately the Japanese records contain a much fuller account.[10] The object which Harris had in view was to impress the Japanese with the wisdom of voluntarily abandoning the remaining features of their exclusive system and of coming into full intercourse with the world at large. Happily Harris was dealing with one of the most enlightened of the Shogun's officials, one who had already determined to place foreign

[7] *Littell's Living Age,* Vol. 60, p. 570.

[8] *Ibid.,* p. 568.

[9] Cosenza, *op. cit.,* pp. 484–87.

[10] *F.R., 1879,* pp. 627–31.

relations on a firm basis,[11] and who considered the communication "the most important matter ever brought before the Government."[12]

Harris began by pointing out the disinterestedness of the United States. It had no possessions in the East and it made no annexations by force of arms. Improved means of communication, the steamship and the electric telegraph, had brought distant countries near at hand. "The nations of the West hope that by means of steam communications all the world will become as one family. Any nation that refuses to hold intercourse with other nations must expect to be excluded from this family. No nation has the right to refuse to hold intercourse with others." Two things were desired in connection with this intercourse: a Minister or Agent resident at the capital, and free commerce between countries. Misfortunes were threatening Japan. England, dissatisfied with Admiral Stirling's Treaty, was ready to make war. She feared Russia's advance to the Amur and Sakhalin, which would threaten Manchuria and China, as well as her own interests in the East. If Russia should take possession of Manchuria and China and attack England's possessions, then England would desire to seize Sakhalin, Yezo, and Hakodate, in order to defend herself. China had been involved in two wars with England, and with France in the latter case, primarily because there was no foreign agent at Peking. France wanted Korea, and England desired Formosa. The United States would not join these Powers in their war; and when the American flag was fired upon at Canton Commodore Armstrong retaliated, but after an explanation had been made the hostilities were stopped. He then pointed out the great danger from the introduction of opium, stated that the English desired to introduce it into Japan, and urged that its importation be prohibited by treaty.[13] After congratulating Japan on its long

---

[11] Satoh, *op. cit.*, p. 32.

[12] Cosenza, *op. cit.*, p. 487.

[13] Harris dwelt at length upon this matter. But the importation of opium had been prohibited by the Dutch and Russian Treaties of 1857. The extract which follows is from *F.R., 1879*, p. 629.

period of peace, he pointed out that one result of it was to leave the country weak and inefficient; therefore war should be avoided until Japan could become strong.

If Japan had been near to either England or France, war would have broken out long ago. The great distance between the countries is the reason why peace has been preserved thus long. In case of war, a treaty would have to be made at the end of the war. The President wants to make a treaty without any war, and with mutual goodwill and respect. . . . .

The President is of opinion that if Japan makes a treaty with the United States, all other foreign countries will make the same kind of a treaty, and Japan will be safe thereafter.

The President wants to make a treaty that will be honorable to Japan, without war, in a peaceful manner, after deliberate consultation. If Japan should make a treaty with the ambassador of the United States, who has come unattended by military force, her honor will not be impaired. There will be a great difference between a treaty made with a single individual, unattended, and one made with a person who should bring fifty men-of-war to these shores. We were sent to this country by the President, who desires to promote the welfare of Japan, and are quite different from the ambassadors of other countries. We do not wish to open your ports to foreign trade all at once. It will be quite satisfactory if you open them gradually, as the circumstances may require; but the President assures you that this will not be the case if you make a treaty with England first. . . . . When the ambassadors of other foreign countries come to Japan to make treaties, they can be told that such and such a treaty has been made with the ambassador of the United States, and they will rest satisfied with this.

Harris then pointed out the religious tolerance existing in the United States and the West. He dwelt upon the desirability of general trade, which increases friendly intercourse and tends toward peace between nations. Then he told of the use of import taxes. He showed how Siam had protected herself from England by making treaties with America and France, and he asserted that the independent states of India were conquered by England because they had no treaties with other Powers. He pledged the good offices of the President in case of any difficulty between Japan and a foreign country, and gave the promise point by saying that Sir John Bowring, Governor of Hong Kong, had told him that he intended to bring a large fleet to Japan and either secure the opening of several ports and the right to have a

Minister-Resident or else declare war.[14] His last letter stated that he would have more than fifty steamers. The Chinese war would soon be over; then the English ambassador would come, and it was to be hoped that matters would be arranged before he came. "If I write in my name to the agents of England and France residing in Asia and inform them that Japan is ready to make a commercial treaty with their countries, the number of steamers will be reduced from fifty to two or three." In closing he said:

I have to-day told you what is the opinion of the President and the intention of the English Government. To-day will be the happiest day of my life if what I have said is attended to so as to secure the welfare of Japan. I hope you will consider what I have advanced and communicated to your associates in office. What I have told you are the unadorned facts acknowledged in all the world.

Such, in brief, were the statements which Harris presented for the consideration of Lord Hotta. Many of them were doubtless already familiar to this enlightened daimyo,[15] but the treatment of the whole subject was bound to be impressive. The effect of this conference upon the whole foreign question cannot be overestimated. Copies of Harris' remarks were later placed before all the daimyos and the Imperial court, and thus his arguments reached all the important personages in the land.[16] Of Harris' good will for Japan and his desire to help her to avoid the evils of foreign complications there can be no doubt. His argument that she could negotiate with better grace with him, alone and unsupported, than with an ambassador at the head of a mighty squadron, was absolutely true. His frequent references to the aggressive designs of Britain, to which exception might be taken, were justified by all too recent events. The conquest of India,[17] the first and second wars with China, and many other episodes in Britain's intercourse

[14] The Dutch at Nagasaki had already given warning of Bowring's proposed expedition (Akimoto, *Lord Ii Naosuke and New Japan*, p. 141).

[15] Satoh, *op. cit.*, pp. 33–35.

[16] *Ibid.*, pp. 64, 73.

[17] During the administration of Lord Dalhousie, 1848–56, more than 200,000 square miles were annexed to British India, including the kingdoms of the Punjab, Nagpur, Oudh, and some smaller states, and the Burmese province of Pegu.

with the East seemed to indicate what might be the fate of Japan.
But the march of events, in this as in so many other cases, proved
how unwise it is to prophesy regarding developments in the Far
East. Russia has not yet overrun China, nor even all of Manchuria. England, instead of seizing Sakhalin and Yezo as defensive measures against Russia, found in her old enemy a staunch
ally in her greatest war. Finally, England and France, instead of
sending large squadrons over to Japan to extort treaties at the
cannon's mouth, actually sent only a few vessels and disavowed
any intention of using force.

It might be well here to point out certain effects which the experience of the West in China had upon the new relations with
Japan. The haughty and unyielding attitude of the Chinese Government toward foreign representatives caused Perry and Harris
to stand on their dignity and to brook no insult, and in turn they
had the greater satisfaction when they received far more liberal
treatment in Japan. At great expense of life and treasure China
had become an object lesson of the inability of an Eastern people
to oppose the armaments of Europe. The Japanese knew of the
two recent wars in China, and those who read their lessons aright
realized that Japan was in no condition to adopt China's attitude
toward the Powers. On the other hand, Britain's share in those
wars had not been altogether a glorious one. Although trade relations had been bettered, a feeling of wrong-doing remained in
many minds. It is very doubtful if any British Cabinet would
have approved the use of force in order to open wider the doors
of Japan. Surely Lord Elgin, who felt so strongly the un-
righteousness of the second Chinese war, would never have
adopted a high-handed attitude at Yedo.

Notwithstanding his friendliness, therefore, Harris felt that
he should base his arguments on fear rather than on expediency.
But instead of making threats in the name of the United States
he used England and France as ogres with which to frighten the
Japanese. In this way he brought the good will of the United
States into stronger relief. Although all the diplomats and naval
officers of the time believed in the efficacy of fear in bringing

about improved relations with Japan, we may at least wonder what would have happened if Harris had emphasized the benefits to be derived from world commerce rather than the dangers which would follow seclusion. Certainly Hotta, Ii, Echizen, Satsuma, and other daimyos could have understood such arguments. Perhaps as many samurai were driven into opposition because of the threats which were from time to time used as were converted to a belief in foreign intercourse through fear.

A few days after this remarkable interview Harris recorded in his journal: "I may be said to be now engaged in teaching the elements of political economy to the Japanese and in giving them information as to the working of commercial regulations in the West."[18] This task was a tedious one, for the ideas were new and it was difficult to find terms in which to translate them. Moreover, Harris had no library to refer to, but could rely only on his well-stored mind and his commercial training. The Japanese records contain a detailed account of an interview between Harris and five of the "Commissioners of the voyage of the American Ambassador to Yedo" on December 21.[19] This interview consisted of questions by the Commissioners and answers by Harris. It was concerned with the two points which he insisted should be covered by a new treaty—a Resident Minister and unrestricted trade—as well as some questions regarding China and her wars. Concerning the first they inquired as to his duties, rank, rights, services, ceremonies, status, and residence, and as to trade they wished to know about customs duties and freedom from restrictions. Harris again used England as an example, saying:

When the English ask for trade, they say they will come with men-of-war and demand that ports be opened at once. If opened, well; if not, war will at once be declared. There will be a great difference between granting their demands and making a treaty with me, who am consulting the advantage of both countries. It will be greatly to the honor of Japan to do as I say.

He closed by quoting from a recent letter from Sir John Bowring to the effect that England could not endure the present manage-

[18] Cosenza, *op. cit.*, p. 490.   [19] *F.R., 1879*, pp. 631–34.

ment of affairs in Japan. In this interview Harris also mentioned the important features of a new treaty.

He now waited for some official notice concerning all he had said. But the Ministers, who agreed with him, were engaged in endeavoring to convert the hostile daimyos and the leaders of the military and literary classes. After almost a month's anxiety Harris brought matters to a head on January 9, 1858, by bluntly telling Shinano-no-Kami "that such treatment could not be submitted to," and that "their treatment of me showed that no negotiations could be carried on with them unless the plenipotentiary was backed by a fleet, and offered them cannonballs for arguments."[20] He closed by threatening to return to Shimoda if nothing were done.

This procedure was successful, and a week later Harris had an interview with Lord Hotta in which he was told that the Shogun had assented to the two major points in a commercial treaty—unrestricted trade and a Resident Minister—and that commissioners would be appointed to arrange the details.[21] These proved to be his "good friends," Inouye, Lord of Shinano, and Iwase, Lord of Higo. They met for the first time on the eighteenth and exchanged their full powers, and Harris offered a draft of a commercial treaty, but it took five days to translate it into Japanese.

A brief account of the subsequent negotiations is given in Harris' journal. The record is prefaced by this statement:

In this *Journal* I shall confine myself to the main leading facts of actual transactions, omitting the interminable discourses of the Japanese where the same proposition may be repeated a dozen times; nor shall I note their positive refusal of points they subsequently grant, and meant to grant all the while; nor many absurd proposals made by them, without the hope, and scarcely the wish, of having them accepted,—for all such proceedings are according to the rule of Japanese diplomacy, and he who shows the greatest absurdity in such matters is most esteemed. They do not know the value of a straightforward and truthful policy, at least they do not practice it. They never hesitate at uttering a falsehood even where the truth would serve the same purpose.[22]

[20] Cosenza, *op. cit.*, pp. 495–96.
[21] *F.R., 1879*, pp. 635–36.
[22] Cosenza, *op. cit.*, p. 505.

This indictment sounds not unlike one of diplomacy in the West, even among representatives far more versed in the intricacies of the game than were the Commissioners who dealt with Harris. But it was a long and wearisome task to thresh out the details of the Treaty of Commerce. Twenty sessions were held, clauses were discussed time and time again, and even those which had been accepted were considered anew. At first the Commissioners wished to open trade, not on an unrestricted basis, but according to the latest Dutch and Russian Treaties. But this Harris successfully opposed. Articles which he thought might cause trouble were readily granted, such as the right to build churches and to export Japanese money; but others, such as opening new ports, caused repeated interviews. Finally, when the Treaty was almost agreed upon, the Commissioners reported that such was the uproar in the castle over the concessions about to be granted that bloodshed would surely follow an immediate signing of the Treaty. A delay was asked in order that an ambassador might proceed to the "Spiritual Emperor" at Kyoto to get his approval, and the statement was made "that the moment that approval was received, the daimyos must withdraw their opposition." Harris naturally asked what they would do if the Mikado refused his assent, and the Commissioners replied, "in a prompt and decided manner, that the Government had *determined not to receive any objections from the Mikado.*"[23] He then asked what was the use of delaying the Treaty "for what appears to be a mere ceremony," and he was told that "it was this solemn ceremony that gave value to it." He proposed, therefore, that they complete the drafting of the Treaty but postpone signing it until the end of sixty days. This proposition was finally accepted, the details were agreed upon, the tariff was worked out, and on February 26 Harris was able to give a clean copy of the Treaty to the Japanese Commissioners.[24] On March 10 he returned to Shimoda on a government steamer to await the outcome of the reference to Kyoto and the promised signing of the Treaty on April 21.

[23] Cosenza, *op. cit.*, p. 539.
[24] *Ibid.*, p. 556; No. 6, March 4, 1858.

Harris had ample reason for satisfaction in this achievement, and, as he wrote,

the pleasure I feel in having made the treaty is enhanced by the reflection that there has been no show of coercion, nor was menace in the least used by me to obtain it. There was no American man-of-war within one thousand miles of me for months before and after the negotiations. I told the Japanese at the outset that my mission was a friendly one; that I was not authorized to use any threats; that all I wished was that they would listen to the truths that I would lay before them.[25]

It was, indeed, a triumph of reason; and yet, in the background, there was fear of the two Western Powers whose record in the East gave force to any misgivings.

The Treaty of Amity and Commerce which was thus completed but not yet signed consisted of fourteen articles. A summary of its terms indicates what a great advance it was over the treaties of the preceding years.

Article I provided for the reciprocal right of residence of a Diplomatic Agent at each capital and of Consuls or Consular Agents at the open ports of Japan or at any or all of the ports of the United States.

Article II stated that "the President of the United States, at the request of the Japanese Government, will act as a friendly mediator in such matters of difference as may arise between the Government of Japan and any European Power," and it also promised the friendly aid of American ships of war and Consuls to Japanese vessels on the high seas or in foreign ports.

Article III, which caused the greatest difficulty in negotiating, opened, in addition to Hakodate, the ports of Kanagawa and Nagasaki, from July 4, 1859, Niigata from January 1, 1860, and Hiogo from January 1, 1863. (Kanagawa was opened in place of Shimoda, which had been found undesirable soon af er it was opened. The harbor was small and ill-protected and the port was on a peninsula, cut off from the mainland by a difficult mountain range.) It was now provided that if Niigata were found unsuitable another port would be chosen. In these open ports the right to lease land and erect buildings was granted. It was also provided that after January 1, 1862, Americans might reside in Yedo and after the first of the next year in Osaka. This article also provided for open trade without the intervention of Japanese officers, with these limitations— that munitions of war should be sold only to the Japanese Government and foreigners, that no rice or wheat should be exported as cargo, and that the Government would sell at public auction any surplus copper.

Article IV provided for customs duties according to the appended tariff, and gave the United States the right to land naval stores at Kanagawa, Hakodate, and Nagasaki, without the payment of duty, and to keep them there in warehouses in the custody of an officer of the American Government.[26] It also forbade the importation of opium, and permitted the Government to seize and destroy any amount over four pounds found on any American trading ship.

Article V permitted foreign coins to pass current in Japan for the corresponding weight of Japanese coins of the same description; until the Japanese became familiar with foreign coins the Japanese Government would exchange, without discount, their coin for American coins. Coins of all descriptions, except copper coins, might be exported from Japan.

Article VI defined the extraterritorial rights of Americans in civil as well as criminal matters.

Article VII defined the limits at the various ports within which Americans might travel.

Article VIII granted to Americans the free exercise of their religion and the right to erect suitable buildings of worship. It also stated that Japan had abolished the practice of trampling on religious emblems.

Article IX promised the assistance of the Japanese authorities in the arrest and imprisonment of offenders on the request of the American Consul.

Article X related to the purchase in the United States by the Japanese Government of ships of war, munitions, and other things, and to the employment of experts.

Article XI stated that the Trade Regulations attached to the Treaty should be considered equally binding with it.

Article XII revoked conflicting provisions of the Treaties of 1854 and 1857.

Article XIII should be quoted in full:

"After the 4th of July, 1872, upon the desire of either the American or Japanese Governments, and on one year's notice given by either party, this Treaty, and such portions of the Treaty of Kanagawa as remain unrevoked by this Treaty, together with the regulations of trade hereunto annexed, or those that may be hereafter introduced, shall be subject to revision by commissioners appointed on both sides for this purpose, who will be empowered to decide on, and insert therein, such amendments as experience shall prove to be desirable."

Article XIV fixed July 4, 1859, as the date when the Treaty should go

---

[26] "By this I have secured the choice of three good harbors for our Naval Depot in the East, in a country that has the most salubrious climate in the world, where the men cannot desert, and with a power that is sufficiently civilized to respect our rights, and above all not a power with whom we might have a rupture, like England. I consider this clause of immense importance, as now the depot can be removed from that wretched place, Hongkong, and the stores out of the power of England" (Cosenza, *op. cit.*, pp. 529–30).

into force, and designated Washington as the place where the ratifications should be exchanged. The Treaty was executed in quadruplicate, each copy being written in the English, Japanese, and Dutch languages, but the Dutch version was considered to be the original.

Accompanying the Treaty were the Regulations under which American trade was to be conducted in Japan. The details are of little interest, except that we may note that the Regulations were more liberal than before, the penalties reduced, and tonnage duties given up. But the tariff provisions were of great importance. Under the Dutch and Russian Conventions of 1857 a temporary import duty of thirty-five per cent was in effect, pending the negotiation of import, export, and transit duties. Harris explained the operation of customs duties to the Commissioners, and eventually was able to write the tariff article into the Regulations. The Japanese had intended to levy a twelve and a half per cent duty on both imports and exports. Harris tried to have them do away with the export duties, but had to accept a reduction in their amount. As accepted, the tariff on imports was levied on goods in four classes. Class 1, which was free of duty, consisted of gold and silver, coined and uncoined, wearing apparel in actual use, household furniture, and printed books not intended for sale. Class 2, consisting of foodstuffs, articles for the building or repairing of ships, coal, timber for building houses, steam machinery, raw silk, and certain metals, paid five per cent. Class 3, including all intoxicating liquors, paid thirty-five per cent; and Class 4, including all other articles, paid twenty per cent. The export duty was fixed at five per cent on all articles except gold and silver coin and copper in bars. Five years after the opening of Kanagawa the import and export duties were subject to revision, if the Japanese Government so desired.

As the terms of this Treaty, with few modifications, governed the international relations of Japan until 1899, it is proper to dwell upon some of its significant provisions. Every important concession which Harris had desired was granted; in only a few minor particulars had he been forced to yield. In China the right to appoint a Minister-Resident was one of the points at issue in the war which was then in progress, and it was conceded only in the Treaties of Tientsin signed in June of that year, five months after Harris had secured the Shogun's approval. In his draft treaty Harris had asked that eight ports and two cities be opened, but the Japanese absolutely refused to open Kyoto. They were certainly right in this step, for the Imperial capital had become the center of the anti-foreign party. After much discussion the ports of Hakodate, Nagasaki, Kanagawa, Niigata, and Hiogo were agreed upon (which was the number asked for by Commodore Perry in 1854), and the cities of Yedo and Osaka were opened for residence. The right to conduct trade without official intervention opened Japan to the fullest commercial development. This was the most important commercial article in the Treaty. The right to lease ground and erect buildings, which Harris had failed to secure in 1857, was now granted. To the eighth article Harris attached too much importance.[27] The Dutch had already secured the right to practice their religion, and the Japanese had given up the practice of trampling on religious emblems. The only new provision was the right to erect suitable places of worship. As we have seen, the prohibition of opium was already found in the Dutch and Russian Treaties.

In after years Harris received undeserved censure for having inserted the extraterritorial clause in this Treaty. But his critics did not realize that this clause had already found its way into the first Russian and Dutch Treaties and into Harris' Convention of 1857. Great Britain also enjoyed this right under the "most-favored-nation" clause. Even if Harris had given it up, as he would have liked to do, it is impossible to believe that any of the European ambassadors would have followed him in this step. Indeed, the feeling of the time is evident from the fact that Mr. Marcy, the Secretary of State, had told Harris that although he considered it an unjust provision, yet no treaty with an Oriental country could secure ratification without its presence.[28] Harris

[27] *Littell's Living Age,* Vol. 60, p. 572.
[28] *Atlantic Monthly,* Vol. 47, p. 610.

always considered it a temporary measure, and asserted that he introduced it "against his conscience."

Although there can be no question of Townsend Harris' desire to serve not only the needs of his countrymen but also the best interests of Japan, weak, ignorant, and at the mercy of all comers, yet three of his stipulations proved, in the event, to be disastrous. The first was that permitting the export of Japanese gold and silver coin, which produced the first ill effects of the new commerce. The second was the conventional tariff; for, although Harris drew up very favorable terms, he could not prevent other diplomats from altering them, as we shall see, and Japan was bound fast by a treaty-made tariff until the revision of 1894. Finally, he provided for the revision of the Treaty, on the desire of either party, after July 4, 1872, and on one year's notice. His intention was that after the Japanese had gained experience in foreign affairs they should take up the question again and work out a new treaty in the light of experience. And this was what the Japanese believed; but they were disillusioned in 1872 when they found that revision could come only with the consent of all the Treaty Powers; and it actually was accomplished, not in 1872, but twenty-two years later. It would have been better had this Treaty expired in 1872 rather than remain subject to revision.[29] But despite these unforseen errors in judgment, the Japanese have ever been grateful to Townsend Harris for framing an honorable treaty on which their enlarged intercourse was to be based.

After his return to Shimoda, in March, Harris passed through a serious nervous breakdown, during which he was the recipient of many tokens of friendship and esteem from the Japanese. The Shogun sent down two of his best physicians from Yedo and daily messages and presents of food and fruit.[30] This solicitude was manifested also on his return to Yedo in April. But instead of being able to sign the Treaty on the twenty-first, as had been promised, Harris was told that Lord Hotta had not returned from Kyoto. For more than a month he waited, anxious and impatient.

[29] *Atlantic Monthly,* Vol. 47, p. 610.
[30] *Littell's Living Age,* Vol. 60, p. 571.

He was disgusted, and, according to a Japanese historian, threatened to go himself to Kyoto and conclude the Treaty there.[31] On June 1 Hotta returned, defeated. The Treaty could not be signed in the face of Imperial and daimyo opposition. Harris finally agreed to a second postponement, until September 4, on condition that the Japanese would sign no Treaty or Convention with any Power until thirty days after the signing of the American Treaty.[32] This delay was insisted upon because of the presence in Yedo of Mr. Curtius seeking a new treaty for Holland. On June 18 Harris returned to Shimoda, bearing a letter from the Grand Council agreeing to his terms, and also a letter from the Shogun to the President, the first sent to any foreign ruler in two hundred and forty years.[33] Mr. Curtius also returned overland to Nagasaki, convinced that no liberal terms could be secured at this time.[34]

[31] Satoh, *op. cit.,* p. 92.

[32] No. 19, July 8; Cosenza, *op. cit.,* p. 561.

[33] The letter addressed to the King of Holland in 1845 had been written by the Council of State (Griffis, *Townsend Harris, First American Envoy in Japan,* p. 316).

[34] Oliphant, *Narrative of the Earl of Elgin's Mission to China and Japan,* p. 307.

CHAPTER IV

JAPANESE POLITICS AND FOREIGN RELATIONS
1858-59

It now becomes necessary to consider the effect of the political situation within the Empire upon the foreign policy of the Shogunate, for, as we have seen, the question of foreign affairs could not stand upon its own footing but was involved in a maze of conflicting interests. The concessions granted in the Treaties of 1854–57 had strengthened the opposition among the daimyos, and the fact that the Shogunate seemed firmly convinced of the wisdom of a pro-foreign policy served to unite in the opposition party all those elements which had reasons for hostility to the Tokugawa rule. Harris was told in February by the Lord of Shinano that

of the 18 great *Daimyo,* 4 were in favor, and 14 opposed to the Treaty; that, of the 300 *Daimyo* created by Iyeyasu, 30 out of every 100 were in favor, and the remainder opposed; that the Government was constantly working on these men and, when they could get them to listen, they frequently convinced them; but many—like the obstinate of more enlightened countries—refused to listen to a word of reason, argument or explanation. This last class will only yield to the opinion of the Mikado when it shall be promulgated.[1]

Although Lord Hotta had taken office as Prime Minister and later as Minister for Foreign Affairs with the intention of settling, once for all, the uncertainty concerning the Shogunate's foreign policy, even he dared not accept the responsibility of signing the new Treaty. First the great daimyos and high officials were consulted, and copies of the Treaty as well as of Harris' statement to Hotta were circulated among them.[2] In the covering letter at-

[1] Cosenza, *The Complete Journal of Townsend Harris,* p. 543.
[2] Gubbins, *The Progress of Japan, 1853–1871,* pp. 289–90.

tention was called to the fact that "the present time offers a new foundation for enhancing the power of the country." Of the memorials presented in reply most were strongly opposed to further concession to the foreigners. Again the leader was Lord Nariaki, the retired daimyo of Mito. A little before this, while the negotiations with Harris were still under way, he had replied to a delegate of the Shogunate: "Let Bitchu and Iga commit hara kiri, and decapitate Harris at once."[3] A few of the daimyos, however, favored the new treaty proposals, notably the powerful lords of Echizen and Satsuma.[4] But among these there was a feeling that the Imperial consent should first be secured.

Thus originated the mission to Kyoto, which it was thought would secure the Mikado's approval as a matter of course, and then the opposition would cease.[5] The first mission, composed of Hayashi Daigaku-no-Kami,[6] with Tsuda Hanzaburo as deputy delegate, arrived in Kyoto on February 5, 1858. Hayashi laid before the Imperial court a letter from Hotta which gave the reasons for the foreign policy of the Shogunate;[7] but instead of winning the Imperial approval his visit served to widen the breach between the two capitals. At Kyoto the opponents of the Shogunate cried out that the mission of such minor officials as Hayashi and Tsuda was an insult to the Throne, and in this way they gained adherents to their party. The first mission, therefore, proved to be a complete failure, and at the same time it weakened the prestige of the Shogunate in Kyoto.

The seriousness of the situation was at once recognized in Yedo, and the Prime Minister himself, Lord Hotta, who was

---

[3] Bitchu, i.e., Hotta (Akimoto, *Lord Ii Naosuke and New Japan*, p. 147).

[4] Satoh, *Lord Hotta*, p. 66.

[5] "It must be remembered in this connection that according to some historians, Lord Abe while in office as the Dean of the Ministerial Council of the Shogunate committed the Yedo Government to an understanding with Prince Sanjo Sanetsumu, a High Councillor of the Court of Kioto, to conduct foreign affairs subject to the Imperial sanction" (*ibid.*, p. 69).

[6] Hayashi was one of the signers of the Perry Treaty, and he had served as one of the commissioners for the reception of Harris in Yedo.

[7] Satoh, *op. cit.*, p. 70; Baba Bunyei, *Japan, 1853-1864, or Genji Yume Monogatari* (Satow, translator), pp. 17-20.

more familiar than anyone else with the general international situation and with the arguments advanced by Harris, determined to proceed to Kyoto to overcome the opposition which was developing there. With Lord Hotta went the Accountant-General, Kawaji, and the Censor, Iwase Higo-no-Kami, the latter of whom had been one of the negotiators of the Treaty under discussion. Arriving in Kyoto on March 19, Lord Hotta first won the support of the Prime Minister of the Imperial court, Prince Kujo Hisatada, and two of the high councillors. He also prepared an address to the Throne which was presented through the Prime Minister. This was a remarkable document.[8] It pointed out the changed conditions in international affairs, the increasing relations between the world Powers, their mutual dependence, and the impossibility of any country's remaining secluded. This statement led to the conclusion that "either a war has to be fought, or amicable relations have to be established." But Japan was threatened from all sides, as she lay in the midst of the ocean routes connecting the different countries. The issue of such a war was obvious, and its evils were portrayed. Then he developed an argument which should have had great weight among the courtiers of Kyoto: "Among the rulers of the world at present, there is none so noble and illustrious as to command universal vassalage, or who can make his virtuous influence felt throughout the length and breadth of the whole world. To have such a Ruler over the whole world is doubtless in conformity with the Will of Heaven." But before such a world empire could be created international relations must be established by treaties of alliance or of amity; reciprocal relations should be encouraged, ministers should be sent and received, no effort should be spared to become thoroughly acquainted with the affairs of the Treaty Powers, "and in establishing relations with foreign countries, the object should always be kept in view of laying a foundation for securing the hegemony over all nations." Shipping should be encouraged, defects remedied, the national resources developed, and military preparations carried out.

[8] Satoh, *op. cit.*, p. 73.

When our power and national standing have come to be recognized, we should take the lead in punishing the nation which may act contrary to the principle of international interests; and in so doing, we should join hands with the nations whose principles may be found identical with those of our country. An alliance thus formed should also be directed towards protecting harmless but powerless nations. Such a policy could be nothing else but the enforcement of the power and authority deputed (to us) by the Spirit of Heaven. Our national prestige and position thus ensured, the nations of the world will come to look up to our Emperor as the Great Ruler of all the nations, and they will come to follow our policy and submit themselves to our judgment.

In conclusion he urged that

now is the opportune moment offered us by the changed condition of the world to throw off the traditional policy three centuries old, and make a united national effort to seize the opportunity for realizing the great destiny awaiting our country, as stated above. For this purpose, speedy permission is respectfully and humbly solicited for opening intercourse with foreign countries.

Such an appeal should have struck the imagination of every loyalist, with its vision of a world empire under the benign sway of the Son of Heaven. And it is probable that if the question of opening intercourse had stood alone the court would have yielded a ready assent, but the issue was now involved with the whole question of the relation between the Mikado and the Shogun. At first Hotta was successful. The Mikado's Prime Minister and the high councillors drafted an Imperial reply which, although desiring that the opinions of the Three Houses of the Tokugawa family and of the daimyos be consulted, still conferred on the Shogunate authority to use its own discretion in dealing with foreign relations.[9] Before this reply could be officially presented, the opposition forces had succeeded in winning over most of the court officials to their views. The first move was for seven of the high officials to present to the Imperial court on April 20 a memorial which denounced friendship with the foreigners as a stain upon the country, and fear of them as an everlasting shame.[10] Here were two arguments which also appealed to conservative patriots, assured, in their ignorance, of the superiority of Japan. This

[9] Satoh, *op. cit.*, p. 79.   [10] Text in *Japan. No. 1 (1865)*, p. 40.

memorial was followed five days later by an address signed by eighty-eight court officials urging the withdrawal of the clause granting discretionary power to the Shogunate. These memorials, as well as threats of personal violence against his two fellow councillors, failed to move Prince Kujo. On the night of the twenty-ninth, however, the eighty-eight signers, armed with swords, appeared in a body at the Prime Minister's house, and insisted that if the clause were not expunged they would go to the temple where Hotta was lodged and compel him to commit seppuku (hara-kiri). Fearing for his own life, Prince Kujo finally yielded, and promised that the reply would be changed as they demanded.[11]

This was another victory for the anti-Tokugawa forces, and it was followed by the formal presentation of quite a different reply, on May 1, which denounced the foreign policy of the Shogunate and demanded that the opinions of the Three Houses and of the daimyos be consulted before asking for Imperial sanction.[12] Lord Hotta, realizing the necessity for action in dealing with the foreign treaties, again urged that the Shogunate be given authority to act in the emergency, but a second reply denied the request and stated that three things should be done:

(1) Permanent safety should be secured whereby the Imperial anxiety could be removed; (2) measures should be taken so as to uphold the national dignity and save the country from future calamities; (3) the national defences should be placed on an efficient footing, lest the refusal to grant any more than the concession made in the Shimoda Treaty be made a cause of war.

If the replies of the daimyos were not sufficiently clear, an Imperial messenger would be sent to the Great Shrine at Ise. Finally, on May 6, a third reply stated that if the American envoy insisted upon his treaty and resorted to any act of violence, war should be declared.

The opponents not only of the pro-foreign policy but of the Shogunate itself were now in control of the situation at Kyoto. Lord Ii, who in the absence of Lord Hotta was the dominant figure in Yedo, learned that the Mito party was urging not only that

---

[11] Satoh, *op. cit.,* p. 83.   [12] *Ibid.,* p. 84.

the court take the strongest position against foreign intercourse but also that it appoint one of the Mito princes, Lord Hitotsubashi, as heir to the Shogun, and confer on the daimyo of Mito the duty of guarding Kyoto.[13] The struggle between Lord Ii and Lord Nariaki had thus been transferred to Kyoto, and the control of the Imperial court was the prize to be won. Lord Hotta returned, baffled, on June 1.

A crisis had now been reached in the affairs of the Shogunate. For the first time since its establishment the Tokugawa Bakufu had failed to secure the approval of the Mikado for one of its desired measures, and the Throne had asserted control over its policies. At Kyoto and in the provinces a strong party had been formed in opposition to its administration. Among its own houses a bitter controversy was raging over the selection of an heir, and at its doors might be expected the great Western Powers prepared to fight for treaty rights if longer denied. In this emergency the Shogun resorted to the old precedents and appointed a tairo, or regent, with full powers to meet the issue at hand. Lord Ii Kamon-no-Kami was selected for this powerful office. The reasons assigned for this appointment differ. Of his loyalty to the Shogun and of his courage there could be no doubt. His family was one of the oldest supporters of the Tokugawas. But the issue which he was especially called upon to meet was the question of the heirship; and whether the Shogun realized for himself the strong character of Lord Ii, or whether the ladies of his court urged the appointment, it meant that a strong opponent of the Mito claims had been designated.[14] On June 4 he was publicly installed, and he at once took over the conduct of affairs.[15]

To him the matter of vital importance was the American Treaty; the question of the heirship might wait. He at once sent Lord Hotta to reason with Harris, as we have seen, and secure his consent to a postponement of the formal signing until Septem-

[13] Akimoto, *op. cit.*, p. 148.

[14] Satoh, *Agitated Japan*, p. 55; Satoh, *Lord Hotta*, p. 91; Brinkley, *History of the Japanese People*, p. 668.

[15] Akimoto, *op. cit.*, p. 152.

ber 4. He next convened a meeting of the heads of the Three
Houses and of the daimyos resident in Yedo, and informed them
of the Imperial reply, stating that although the Shogun was convinced that the new foreign policy was the only possible one, yet
in obedience to the Imperial commands he now laid the matter
before the lords for their most careful and prudent consideration.
Finally, he sent a representative to explain the situation anew to
the court at Kyoto.[16]

Then came the question of the heirship. The Shogun, Iyesada,
who had succeeded in 1853, just after Perry's first visit, was now
dying, without an heir. Two claimants were presented for the
office, Iyemochi, son of Nariyuki, Lord of Kii, and Yoshinobu[17]
(Keiki), son of Lord Nariaki of Mito, but adopted into the
Hitotsubashi family. The former was a boy of twelve, while
Hitotsubashi was a man of twenty-one. In support of Hitotsubashi were found many of the great feudatories, including Satsuma and Echizen, as well as Lord Hotta, recently the Prime
Minister. Some favored him because of his maturity, others because he belonged to the great house of Mito, and still others
because he was believed to be anti-foreign, as was his father. But
the Shogun was opposed to his appointment, for it meant his own
virtual abdication, and the Prince of Kii represented the nearer
line of descent. Lord Ii agreed with his master, but stressed the
fact that Hitotsubashi would support the opponents of the Shogun's foreign policy. The controversy had also been carried up
to the Imperial court, where the claims of Hitotsubashi were
popular but where the Kii party was able to have the words "full-
grown and enlightened" expunged from the formal Imperial
order for the appointment of an heir.[18] The preliminary announcement of the appointment of Iyemochi was made in Yedo
on July 11, and the formal approval of the Throne was sought.[19]

[16] Satoh, *Lord Hotta,* pp. 93–94; Akimoto, *op. cit.,* p. 153.

[17] The Hitotsubashi family was one of the Sankyo, or branch families, from
which a Shogun might be chosen. Although often spoken of as Keiki, the name
Hitotsubashi will be used throughout this study, as it was generally employed
by the Foreign Ministers at this time.

[18] May 8. Satoh, *Lord Hotta,* p. 100.   [19] Satoh, *Agitated Japan,* p. 63.

Thus matters stood when, on July 23, the U.S.S. "Mississippi" arrived at Shimoda with news of the success of the British and the French in China and of the Tientsin Treaties between China and Russia, the United States, England, and France, signed, respectively, on June 13, 18, 26, and 27. Two days later Commodore Tatnall arrived in the "Powhatan."[20] The news brought by these ships was of great significance. China had again been beaten to her knees; greater concessions than ever before had been demanded and granted; and it was reported that the victorious squadrons of the allies would soon appear in Japanese waters. The next day a Russian ship brought similar information. Harris believed that there was no time to be lost, and he at once started for Yedo. Arriving at Kanagawa on the twenty-seventh, he sent a message to Lord Hotta urging that the Treaty be signed before the fleets arrived, so that Japan might grant peacefully and with honor some of the things wrested from China after a humiliating war.

This news created a profound sensation in the castle at Yedo. A special conference of the higher officials was called, and the majority favored signing the Treaty at once. But now Lord Ii advocated delay until the Imperial approval could be obtained.[21] He recognized what grounds for criticism would be given if he acted in opposition to the Imperial will, and he also did not despair of obtaining the Mikado's sanction. Perhaps this might have been secured if the full period until September 4 had been available. But the affair seemed, to the majority of the Cabinet, to be pressing, and they reasoned against the objections of the Tairo. Lord Ii finally accepted their view, and agreed to send Iwase and Inouye, the two Commissioners of the negotiations, to Kanagawa, to prevail upon Harris, if possible, to accept a further postponement, but if unsuccessful, to sign the Treaty. The conference occurred on board the "Powhatan" early on the morning of the

[20] Commodore Tatnall did not rush off to Japan "to take advantage of the consternation certain to be created by the first news of recent events in the Peiho." As a matter of fact he delayed for eleven days at Nagasaki before proceeding to Shimoda (Griffis, *Matthew Calbraith Perry,* p. 415).

[21] Akimoto, *op. cit.,* p. 157.

twenty-ninth. Harris repeated the reasons why it would be to the interests of Japan to sign the Treaty at once, and he personally agreed to act as a friendly negotiator should trouble arise with the English and the French.[22] This promise seemed to satisfy the Commissioners, and the Treaty was signed at three o'clock that afternoon.[23]

In this decision of the Tairo, Ii Naosuke Kamon-no-Kami, we have a key to the developments of the next seven years, but one which the Foreign Ministers did not appreciate until almost the end of the period. The Treaty had been signed without the Imperial approval. In those days of increasing respect for the Throne and growing criticism of the Tokugawa Shogunate this fact involved the whole question of foreign relations in the turmoil of domestic politics. It gave to the Jo-i, or anti-foreign party, the rallying cry, "Honor the Emperor and expel the barbarians." As

---

[22] No. 20, July 31; Griffis, *Townsend Harris, First American Envoy in Japan*, p. 321; Harris sent an explanation of the Treaty in No. 27, August 7.

[23] For an unjust interpretation of the work of Townsend Harris see F. V. Dickins in Dickins and Lane-Poole, *The Life of Sir Harry Parkes*, II, 20–21: "At this juncture, before the buké and kugé could be duly consulted—and there existed no constitutional rule or precedent requiring the Shogun to consult with them generally on any subject whatever—the Yedo court was terrorized by the American envoy Townsend Harris into compliance with his demands. That astute diplomatist made, in the words of Admiral Sir James Hope, an 'adroit use of the (then recent) success of the English and French forces in China,' warning the Shogun of the dire consequences likely to result from a persistence in the policy of exclusion. The action of the American envoy was crafty but not wise. At that time the prestige of the Shogun was scarcely impaired, and the Regent Ii Kamon no Kami (for the Shogun had died during the negotiations and his successor was a minor), a man of intelligence and courage, would have known, had time been afforded him, how to smooth over difficulties at Kioto and bring the Imperial Court into harmony with his own views. It is not too much to say that to Harris's ill-advised and selfish policy were due many of the troubles that attended the emergence of Japan from her long isolation."

Aside from the errors in fact which may be noted in the quotation above, there is displayed a complete ignorance of the real work of Harris. His Treaty was signed but a few days before Count Poutiatine and Lord Elgin arrived, each supported by ships of war. Was it not better for the Japanese to negotiate with a man whom they had learned to know and to trust, unsupported by ships of war, and under no visible duress, rather than with cannon-supported envoys fresh from their diplomatic victories in China? The opinions of recent Japanese historians concerning the work of Townsend Harris could hardly be cited by Dickins in support of his charges.

the Imperial party gathered strength the Shogunate was driven to desperate devices in order to keep faith with the powerful foreigners and also to appease the hostility of the court party and its supporters. As we shall see, the Foreign Representatives had no appreciation of the difficulty in which the Shogunate was involved. Few of them had the slightest sympathy for the perplexed officials who were struggling against hitherto unfamiliar forces. It was not until the Imperial approval was finally obtained in 1865 that foreign affairs could be viewed in their own light, and from that date the unreasoned opposition to foreign intercourse rapidly waned.

In making the momentous decision to conclude the Treaty without the Imperial approval Lord Ii acted against his own wishes and out of no disrespect for the Throne. A profound student of Japanese literature and history, he held in loftiest reverence the Imperial house, even though he was Tairo of the Shogun's court. In his student days he wrote: "The first and most important feature of the Yamato spirit is reverence and loyalty to the throne,"[24] and in this great crisis he hoped, in spite of the failure of Hayashi and Lord Hotta, to be able to convince the court and win the Imperial approval. But with the unexpected reopening of the question on July 27 and with the general belief among the Cabinet that a decision must at once be made, he was resolute enough to take the responsibility of action, even though he realized fully the attacks which would be hurled against him. It was well for Japan that such a man held dictatorial powers in such a crisis. It the decision had lain with more conservative or more ignorant leaders, Japan might have entered upon the course which China had taken, a course which led to war, defeat, and humiliation.

In recent years the work of Lord Ii has been studied anew in Japan, and his fame has been rescued from the opprobrium which had been heaped upon it.[25] His biographers point out that in sign-

---

[24] Akimoto, *op. cit.*, p. 115.

[25] Satoh, *Agitated Japan,* based on Shimada's *Kaikoku Shimatsu;* Akimoto, *Lord Ii Naosuke and New Japan,* based on Nakamura's *Ii Tairo To*

ing the Treaty Lord Ii did not act in defiance of the Imperial will, in that he "was only compelled to omit the formality of reporting the matter to the throne before he carried it into practice."[26] In other words, "the Cabinet of Kioto never expressly gave orders that the country should be closed to foreign nations. All the instruction given went no farther than to require further conference among the Princes, Officers, and Barons of the land," and Mr. Shimada points out that "failure to carry out an instruction and wilful disobedience are two things that must never be confounded."[27] These conclusions are premised on the belief that the Imperial court was not really hostile to foreign intercourse, and that Lord Ii had to act in an emergency unknown to the court when its instructions, which meant delay, were given. But whether Lord Ii's conduct be deemed willful disobedience or not, the fact remains that it was so considered by the opposition at the time, and it proved to be the most vulnerable point of attack in the foreign policy of the Shogunate until the Imperial approval was finally gained.

The storm soon broke. On July 31, Lord Nariaki addressed the Tairo, as if he did not know that the Treaty had already been signed, warning him of the irreverence of disregarding the Imperial orders, and urging that a delegate be dispatched to Kyoto to learn His Majesty's will.[28] His letter, however, gave indication that even he realized that freer intercourse was bound to come. The next day a messenger was dispatched to Kyoto to advise the court of what had been done and to assure it of the Shogunate's intention to do its utmost to protect the coasts and defend the Empire.[29] On that day, in Yedo, the officials and the daimyos were summoned to the castle and advised of the whole Treaty proceedings, and once more their opinions were requested.[30] Then,

---

Kaiko. Many of the dates in *Agitated Japan* were wrongly translated from the Japanese to the Gregorian calendar.

[26] Akimoto, *op. cit.,* p. 154.   [27] Satoh, *Agitated Japan,* p. 89.

[28] Akimoto, *op. cit.,* p. 163; Satoh, *Agitated Japan,* p. 73.

[29] Satoh, *Agitated Japan,* p. 75.

[30] Text in *Japan. No. 1 (1865),* p. 39.

in order to consolidate his position against his opponents—not only those who opposed his foreign policy but those who criticized his conduct in the matter of the Shogun's heir—Lord Ii dismissed Lord Hotta and Lord Matsudaira (Iga-no-Kami) because they favored the appointment of Lord Hitotsubashi.[31] This action brings out clearly the involved state of Yedo politics at this time. Lord Hotta was one of the leaders of the pro-foreign party. His course had been a consistent one, and it was due to his enlightenment that Harris had been able to negotiate his great treaty. In favoring foreign intercourse Lord Hotta had been a doughty adversary of Lord Nariaki ever since the appearance of Perry. In the matter of the heirship, however, Hotta favored the Mito claimant, because he desired to see a man of some experience and education succeed as Shogun. In dismissing him from office, Lord Ii lost a champion of his foreign policy in order to weaken the party opposed to his policy regarding the heirship. It is interesting to note that the Foreign Representatives who visited Japan soon after this Cabinet change believed that Hotta was dismissed because of his enlightened foreign policy, and that members of the "Tory party" were in control.[32]

On the same day the Imperial approval of the appointment of the Prince of Kii was received, and August 4 was designated as the date for the formal announcement.[33] This fact inspired the opposition to a last and desperate effort to set aside the choice. Lord Nariaki, accompanied by the lords of Mito, Owari, and Echizen, appeared at the Shogun's court, and a famous interview took place between the three former, members of two of the Three Families of the Tokugawa, and the Tairo.[34] The first point of attack was the signing of the Treaty without the Imperial sanc-

---

[31] August 2. Satoh, *Lord Hotta*, p. 105.

[32] Oliphant, *Narrative of the Earl of Elgin's Mission to China and Japan*, p. 378; Alcock, July 28, 1859, in *Correspondence with Her Majesty's Envoy Extraordinary and Minister Plenipotentiary in Japan* [cited as *1860 (2648)*], p. 27.

[33] Satoh, *Agitated Japan*, p. 76.

[34] August 3. Akimoto, *op. cit.*, pp. 166–70; Satoh, *Agitated Japan*, pp. 79–86.

tion, and in defence Lord Ii argued that what he did was in accord with the Emperor's will and in view of the immediate crisis. Then the claims of Hitotsubashi to the heirship were advanced, and Lord Ii maintained that this decision rested with the Shogun alone. Lord Nariaki then demanded that the choice of an heir should be postponed until the Imperial sanction had been obtained for the Treaty. Ii replied that he fully believed the sanction would be granted when all the facts were known, and announced that Lord Manabe, of the Cabinet, would soon go to Kyoto. The interview, which was a protracted one, resulted in the victory of Lord Ii and his supporters. Yet the situation was a most embarrassing one, for against Ii were arrayed three of the great lords of the Tokugawa houses.[35]

Notwithstanding this powerful opposition the appointment of the youthful Iyemochi was proclaimed on August 4, and on the tenth the daimyos presented their formal congratulations to the Shogun and his heir.[36] On that night the Shogun was suddenly taken ill, but on the twelfth he had recovered sufficiently to call the Tairo and the Cabinet into his presence and take measures against the hostile lords. It was decided to confine Lord Nariaki to his house, to require the lords of Owari and Echizen to turn over their fiefs to their heirs, and to deny the Lord of Mito and Lord Hitotsubashi the privilege of appearing at the Shogun's court. These penalties were announced the next day, and they brought down upon Lord Ii the denunciation of the retainers of these powerful houses. On the sixteenth the Shogun died.[37]

[35] Brinkley states that "the three feudatories offered to compromise; in other words, they declared their willingness to subscribe the commercial convention provided that Keiki was appointed shogun; the important fact being thus established that domestic politics had taken precedence of foreign" (*History of the Japanese People*, p. 668).

[36] Satoh, *Agitated Japan*, p. 92.

[37] Harris' No. 31, September 20, states the Shogun died on the sixteenth, but it was later announced as of September 12. Satoh, *Agitated Japan*, p. 94, states the death as occurring on August 14. The sudden death of the Shogun gave rise to many theories at the time. Some believed he had been poisoned by Mito adherents in order that Lord Hitotsubashi might seize the Throne. The Dutch reported that he had committed suicide because of the difficulties due to the foreign situation. Townsend Harris described him as "a wretchedly-delicate-

In the midst of these momentous events, which in the eyes of nobles and officials loomed larger than did the foreign problem, came the not unexpected demands of other Powers for treaty rights similar to those which Harris had obtained. Mr. Donker Curtius hurried back from Nagasaki. The three Ambassadors who had won treaties at Tientsin now turned their attention toward Japan. Admiral Count Poutiatine was the first to arrive. Then came the Earl of Elgin and Kincardine, convoying the yacht which the Queen had sent out as a present to the Shogun, and a month later, Baron Gros. None of them brought a large force, the English and French squadrons comprising only three ships each. The first to arrive were amazed to find that the lonely American Consul General had won, unsupported, all that they well could ask.

The negotiations of three of the treaties were in progress at the same time. The American Treaty was used as a basis, and few changes were introduced. The Dutch Treaty was signed on August 18, the Russian on the nineteenth, the British on the twenty-sixth, and the French on October 7.

Two changes were introduced by Lord Elgin, one fixing the date on which the treaty would go into effect as July 1, instead of July 4, 1859, and the other removing cotton and woolen manufactured goods from the class which paid twenty per cent duty to the five per cent class. As Baron Gros later told the Japanese Commissioners, Lord Elgin did not wish to mention a date "which would recall a painful epoch for England."[38] He, in turn, selected August 15, the festival of Napoleon III. As Lord

looking man, and a victim of apoplexy" (Oliphant, *op. cit.*, p. 460). The death of the Shogun was not publicly announced until September 14. Lord Elgin was told that the Shogun was unable to see him but that an audience with his "son" might be arranged, which he did not deem it expedient to accept (*ibid.*, p. 418). Oliphant states that the British did not know of the death of the Shogun until after the French mission returned to Shanghai at the end of October (*ibid.*, p. 459). But Chassiron asserts that Baron Gros learned of the event from Lord Elgin in China (*Notes sur Le Japon, La Chine et L'Inde*, p. 59). See also *Correspondence relating to Earl of Elgin's Special Mission to China and Japan, 1857–1859*.

[38] Chassiron, *op. cit.*, p. 157. For these negotiations see Harris' No. 28, September 1; No. 30, September 11; No. 32, September 20; No. 41, December 6.

Elgin had secured a valuable concession in the reduction of the
duty on cotton and woolen goods, so he endeavored to have
French wines removed from the thirty-five per cent to the twenty
per cent class. He argued that the other envoys had failed to
mention wines because their states did not produce any, and that
Harris, who had proposed the duty, was "probably a member of
some temperance society."[39] But in this respect the Japanese refused to yield, assuring Baron Gros that if the Japanese perceived the need of wine they could change the tariff at the revision
of the schedule five years later. Lord Elgin, therefore, had made
the first breach in the reasonable tariff which Harris had drawn
up. Under the "most-favored-nation" clause all the Treaty Powers
enjoyed this tariff reduction, but Britain most of all because of
her pre-eminence in cotton and woolen manufacturing.

The negotiation of these later treaties, important as they
seemed to the European diplomats, was but a troublesome detail
to the harassed officials of the Shogunate. Of far more importance was the curbing of the increasing hostility to the administration which was evident both at Yedo and at Kyoto. Lord Ii
had already announced that it was the intention of the Government to send Lord Manabe, of the Cabinet, to explain matters to
the Imperial court, but the illness of the Shogun and the arrival
of the Russian and British envoys had compelled him to remain
in Yedo. On the day the Shogun died, however, an Imperial
order was received, requiring that either the Tairo or one of the
Princes of the Three Houses present himself at the court with an
explanation of the foreign situation.[40] To this demand Lord Ii
replied that he was too much occupied with affairs of state, while
two of the Sanke, Mito and Owari, were undergoing domiciliary
confinement, and the third was but a boy.[41] Instead, he forwarded another written explanation of the course pursued by the
Shogun's government, which differed little from the earlier statements except for its suggestion that the policy might be tried for

[39] Chassiron, *op. cit.*, p. 163.
[40] Satoh, *Agitated Japan*, p. 93.
[41] *Ibid.*, p. 103; Gubbins, *The Progress of Japan, 1853–1871*, p. 112.

ten or fifteen years and then the question finally decided as to whether the country be closed or opened to foreign trade and residence.[42] In the main it favored an open-door policy, and presented arguments in support of the opening of Hiogo, which was especially objectionable to the court.

At Kyoto a bitter feud was now in progress between the two factions of the court. One, led by Prince Kujo, the Kwambaku or Prime Minister, supported the policies of the Shogunate. The other, led by the nobles Takatsukasa, Konoye, and Sanjo, stood with the Mito party, and were stout exclusionists. But as long as Prince Kujo was Kwambaku the Shogunate was assured of Imperial favor, for no legal document could be transmitted from the Throne without his approval. The exclusionists now sought to remove from his influential office a prince who opposed them. On September 15, during the absence of Prince Kujo, six of the hostile kuge (court nobles) signed an Imperial decree which censured the Shogunate for its presumption in signing the Treaty in defiance of the Imperial will and for the failure to obey the summons to send one of the princes or the Tairo to Kyoto, and once more called for an expression of opinion from the daimyos.[43] This instruction was accompanied by a document asserting that no controversy existed between the two courts.[44] A copy of the former document, with a covering letter instructing the Prince of Mito to make the contents known to the other daimyos, was sent to the prince as senior feudatory. These documents reached him on September 23, a day before the copies reached the castle at Yedo. He replied to the court that he would act for the best, and then informed the Shogunate that he had been honored with direct instructions from the Throne.[45]

This act was another shock to the Yedo officials. It was contrary to all law and precedent for an Imperial communication to be directed to any but the Shogun. In this crisis the act also served both to humiliate the Shogunate and to support the hostile influence of Mito. To the Tairo, the thing to be done was plain.

[42] Satoh, *Agitated Japan,* pp. 96–98.   [43] Gubbins, *op. cit.,* p. 113.
[44] Satoh, *Agitated Japan,* p. 106.   [45] *Ibid.,* p. 105.

He must strike at the roots of the conspiracy in Kyoto which was undermining the prestige of the Tokugawa administration. The foreign question could bide its time.

On October 9 Lord Manabe, of the Cabinet, set out for Kyoto to act in this emergency. While he was on the way—for he did not arrive in Kyoto until the sixteenth[46]—the exclusionist party was able to persuade Prince Kujo to resign from office, and he so notified the Throne. Lord Ii, when news of this *coup d'état* reached him, sent word that the resignation could not be recognized without the Shogun's approval, and on his arrival Lord Manabe was able to persuade Prince Kujo to withdraw his application. Then the Shogun's emissary proceeded to ferret out and arrest the two-sword men who were implicated in the dispatch of the letter from the Emperor to Mito. These, principally retainers of the hostile kuge (although it is said that even peasants and townspeople were arrested), were sent to Yedo, in sedan chairs covered with nets and in bamboo cages, to be imprisoned with those who had been arrested there.[47]

With the atmosphere cleared in this manner, Manabe took up the question of foreign affairs, and on November 29 made his explanations at the Imperial court.[48] The way in which this controversy had been crowded to one side by the greater issues arising from the internal commotion is evident from the position taken by the Shogun's representative. Instead of seeking the Imperial approval because of the absolute wisdom and necessity of breaking down the exclusion laws, Lord Manabe took the position that the treaties were temporary evils which could not be avoided, that the Shogunate did not desire to cultivate friendly relations with the foreign Powers, and that as soon as adequate armaments were prepared the barbarians would be expelled.[49] In fact the author of the *Bakumatsu Gwaikodan* (*The Story of Foreign Relations in the last days of the Shogunate*) believed that

[46] Satoh, *Agitated Japan,* p. 112. Satow, "Japan," in *Cambridge Modern History,* XI, 838, gives this date as the twenty-third.

[47] Baba, *op. cit.,* pp. 31–32.

[48] Satoh, *Agitated Japan,* p. 114.   [49] *Cambridge Modern History,* XI, 838.

"the Shogunate's agents were directed to make no difficulties in regard to wording, but to accept any decree which clearly established the fact that an understanding between the Court and the Shogunate had been effected."[50] This was not easy to obtain. Shimada states that the "highest order of eloquence and wisdom" was engaged, for more than three months, until, on February 2, 1859, the Imperial answer was delivered to Lord Manabe.[51] This, in brief, approved the resolution of the Shogun, the Tairo, and the Council of State to keep the barbarians at a distance and eventually restore the old policy of exclusion, and authorized the Shogun to take temporary measures to this end.[52]

This impractical edict was considered a great victory for the Shogunate party. Lord Manabe returned to Yedo in April. There the conspirators had been tried by a special court; some were beheaded, including retainers of Mito, Echizen, and Choshiu, and others were banished to the penal colonies. At Kyoto some of the kuge of highest rank were compelled to enter monasteries and others were punished with domiciliary confinement, and the leaders of the anti-foreign party were compelled to resign their offices at the court.[53] Although these rigorous penalties curbed the opposing faction for the time, they also served to embitter the partisans who believed that their friends had been executed, exiled, and dishonored because of loyalty to the Throne.

Lord Ii recognized that only a temporary reconciliation between the two courts had been effected, and he bent his great energies toward gaining an unequivocal endorsement of the Shogunate's foreign policy.[54] He endeavored, therefore, to arrange a marriage between the Shogun and a younger sister of the Mikado, and he succeeded in securing an order from the Throne requiring Mito to return the Imperial instruction of the preceding year. Before either event was consummated, however, the Tairo had paid with his life for his courageous loyalty to his master.

This brief survey of the involved political developments of

[50] Gubbins, *op. cit.*, p. 114.   [51] Satoh, *Agitated Japan*, p. 116.
[52] *Ibid.*, p. 115; Gubbins, *op. cit.*, p. 115.
[53] Baba, *op. cit.*, pp. 33–34.   [54] Satoh, *Agitated Japan*, p. 119.

the period is absolutely essential to any study of the foreign relations of Japan. It is evident that the great question as to whether Japan should abandon her old policy of seclusion and exclusion could not be decided on its merits alone. The Foreign Representatives were unable to fathom the mysteries of the political situation and could not, for several years, understand the hidden forces which were working so powerfully against the maintenance of the new treaties. From their point of view, and according to established law, the treaties had been negotiated and concluded by the proper authorities. Harris, who knew more about Japanese politics than any other foreigner at the time, perceived the rising influence of the Mikado at Kyoto, but he did not fully realize how important his power had suddenly become. The hostile edicts from Kyoto were not made known to the envoys, nor was the latest, temporizing one published. It was not until 1863 that the American Minister, Mr. Pruyn, was able to point out the absolute necessity of securing the Mikado's approval of the Treaties, which indicates how far at sea the Representatives were in the intervening years. Even when, in 1864, some of the documents of 1858 came to light, they were taken to confirm the power of the Shogun to act on his own responsibility in foreign affairs.[55]

From the point of view of the Shogunate the period was one of tremendous embarrassment. It had signed the Treaties. Without doubt Lord Hotta and Lord Ii and most of the members of the Cabinet and the higher officials had considered that it was not only necessary but eminently proper for Japan gradually to emerge from her seclusion and take her part in the affairs of the world. Fear of the foreigners, though a powerful factor, was not the only reason for their forward-looking decision. Through the stress of many hostile forces, however, they had been compelled to act without the Imperial approval. That act placed them on the defensive at once, and involved the whole foreign question in the turmoil of internal politics. It became the weapon near at

---

[55] *Japan. No. 1 (1865)*, pp. 37–41.

hand for all the critics and opponents of the Yedo administration. All loyal Japanese, at a time when loyalty to the Mikado was being preached by students of Japanese history, denounced this irreverent act. Daimyos and their retainers, court nobles and their followers, all who were opposed to foreign intercourse, or angered at the high-handed conduct of Lord Ii, or embittered because of the decision regarding the succession to the Shogunate, or hostile to the Tokugawas, or even opposed to the Shogunate itself, all these opposition forces could unite on a common basis of denunciation of, as they deemed it, Ii's impious and cowardly act in signing the Treaties in opposition to the Imperial will and because of fear of the "foreign barbarians."

Then when the Shogunate, in order to heal the breach with the court and gain support in its campaign against its enemies, receded from its former sound position regarding foreign intercourse, and practically promised eventually to close the doors against the Western peoples, it made for itself a Procrustean bed. Its temporizing policy was bound to be assailed, and demands were sure to be made that the period of intercourse be brought to an end. Lord Ii hoped that he would be able to secure complete recognition of his foreign policy, but he was struck down too soon, and his successors were unable to carry out his plans. On the one hand they faced the foreigners, who insisted that the Treaties be lived up to in spirit and in letter, and on the other they faced the rising power of the court, which demanded that the old law of exclusion be enforced.

The careful student of the events of the next six years will be impressed, not with the infrequent attacks upon foreign nationals and the occasional violation of treaty provisions, but with the way in which the Shogunate struggled to keep its plighted faith in the presence of a bitter and general anti-foreign feeling.[56]

---

[56] It must be recognized that much of this feeling was directed not so much against foreigners as against the Shogunate and its foreign policy.

CHAPTER V

MUTUAL RECRIMINATIONS
1859–60

ALTHOUGH the new Treaties would not go into effect until the following July, one clause in the American Treaty called for immediate attention. It was the fourteenth, which provided for the exchange of ratifications at Washington, on or before July 4, 1859, although the Treaty would go into effect even if the ratifications were not exchanged by that time. This clause had been proposed by the Japanese[1] and gladly welcomed by Harris in order that the United States, the first of the Treaty Powers, might welcome the first Japanese embassy.[2] In September the Japanese Government formally applied for the use of an American steamer to convey the mission to Washington, by way of San Francisco and Panama, and it was suggested that December 7, 1858, be the date of departure.[3] Owing to the slow and uncertain means of communication at this period (a letter from Commodore Tatnall to Harris, dated Nagasaki, October 27, 1858, did not arrive until February 14, 1859), no American vessel appeared at the appointed time. During these months the effort to secure Imperial approval of the Treaties was in process at Kyoto, and the Yedo authorities were loath to pour oil upon the flames. In January 1859 Harris' old friend, Shinano-no-Kami, proposed that the mission be postponed for not more than a year, on the ground that some of the hostile daimyos were demanding the enforcement of the ancient

---

[1] Suggested by Ii to Hotta (Akimoto, *Lord Ii Naosuke and New Japan,* p. 180).

[2] Cosenza, *The Complete Journal of Townsend Harris,* p. 531.

[3] Harris' No. 29, September 6; in *36th Cong., 1st Sess., S. Ex. Doc. No. 25 (Serial Number 1031),* p. 3; also No. 41, December 6.

death penalty upon any Japanese who might leave the country.[4]
He suggested that a convention be executed agreeing to the postponement and fixing a new date, and to this Harris agreed.
Nothing, however, was done until February 27 when the U.S.S.
"Mississippi" arrived at Shimoda, prepared to receive the embassy. Harris proceeded in it to Kanagawa and tendered it to the
Government. On the next day, March 3, four commissioners
appeared at Kanagawa to negotiate a convention for the postponement of the embassy. This could easily have been done, but
Harris took this opportunity to secure, if possible, a new and
important treaty concession. It was none other than a clause
securing full religious toleration among the Japanese themselves.[5]
The Japanese Commissioners, however, refused to accept this new
article, although the negotiations were protracted for fifteen days.
On March 19 the Convention was signed. It provided that a
ratified copy of the Treaty should be placed in the hands of
Harris pending the exchange of ratifications in Washington; that
no embassy should leave Japan for any foreign nation until the
mission bearing the Japanese ratification had arrived in Washington;[6] that the article of the Treaty relating to freedom of trade
between Americans and Japanese should be published in all parts
of the Empire on July 1; and that the embassy would be ready to
leave Yedo on February 22, 1860.[7]

After this satisfactory agreement had been reached Harris
returned to Shimoda until early in May, when, under a sick certif-

[4] No. 6, January 29, 1859, in *Serial Number 1031,* p. 5. Harris reported
that the British Government was endeavoring to have an embassy sent there.
No. 8, February 22.

[5] No. 13, March 23, in *Serial Number 1031,* p. 8. Articles securing toleration for the practice of the Christian religion had been inserted in the several
Tientsin treaties of June 1858. The right of the Chinese to practice this foreign faith was thus based on treaty provisions, and any interference with
Chinese Christians became a treaty violation. The Japanese never accepted
such an article, and toleration came a few years later as an act of their own
government.

[6] This provision was introduced because Harris believed that the English
would renew the efforts made by Lord Elgin to have a Japanese mission visit
their land.

[7] *Serial Number 1031,* pp. 9–10.

icate, he took his first and only leave from his post. For a month he remained in Shanghai, enjoying the society of this growing seaport after his long years of isolation. At home his achievement had been everywhere acclaimed, and on January 7 the Senate unanimously confirmed his nomination as Minister-Resident of the United States in Japan.[8]

On June 15 Harris sailed from Shanghai on the "Mississippi" to take up his duties in Japan under the new Treaties and with his new rank. At Nagasaki he found H.M.S. "Sampson," bearing the new British Consul General, Mr. Rutherford Alcock. After remaining a few days at Shimoda he arrived at Kanagawa on the thirtieth, the day before that port was to be opened under the British Treaty.

The Japanese, on their part, had made serious preparations for the inauguration of the new commercial relations. The first question was that of the location of the new port at Kanagawa. This matter had been taken up by the Japanese Commissioners with Harris, and he had insisted upon the town of Kanagawa, which was named in his Treaty. Lord Ii, however, favored the little fishing village of Yokohama, three miles distant, where Perry's Treaty had been signed. The Tairo's reasons were of the best, for Yokohama not only possessed an excellent harbor but was also removed from the great highway, the Tokaido, along which passed the daimyo processions and where unsuspecting foreigners might come to grief at the hands of hostile two-sword men. But Harris saw in this squalid fishermen's hamlet on the swampy shores of the bay, accessible to Kanagawa only by a raised causeway, a second Deshima, where the foreigners would be isolated and trade with them strictly controlled. He protested so strongly against the selection of Yokohama—in fact, pointing out two sites on the Kanagawa side—that the Commissioners recommended that his views be accepted. The Cabinet also indorsed this opinion, but the Tairo refused to consent.[9] He determined to

    [8] Griffis, *Townsend Harris, First American Envoy in Japan*, p. 322.
    [9] Akimoto, *op. cit.*, p. 180; Harris' No. 14, March 24.

make ready a port at Yokohama in the belief that the merchants would recognize the desirability of the site. So when the Foreign Representatives arrived in June they found a new port ready for trade, with residences for the Consuls and merchants, shops, a custom house, a governor's office, and two "really imposing and beautifully constructed landing-places, with flights of well-laid granite steps of great extent."[10]

In another respect the Japanese had made ready, to the amazement of the newcomers. The Treaties provided for the circulation of foreign coins in Japan, weight for weight, and the exchange of these coins for Japanese coins during the first year. Hitherto three silver ichibus were equal intrinsically to a Mexican dollar, but now the government issued a new coin, the half-ichibu, which was equal in weight and value to a half-dollar. Although larger than the old ichibu, the new coin had a token value of only half the old one. It is easy to realize the effect upon trade of this innovation.

When Harris reached Kanagawa on the thirtieth he found that Alcock had arrived four days before and had proceeded to Yedo to arrange for the exchange of the ratified British Treaty. Alcock returned that day in order to take part in the formal opening of Kanagawa on July 1. Harris, in turn, raised the American flag over the consulate, at the temple of Hongakuji, on July 4. On the sixth Alcock took up his residence at the temple of Tozenji, in Yedo, and the next day Harris established the American Legation there at the temple of Zempukuji.[11] The first two Foreign Representatives had taken up their residence in "the capital of the Tycoon."

As Mr. Alcock aptly remarked, it was one thing for the Ambassadors to secure their treaties in 1858 from the alarmed Japanese, and quite another for their successors to make the treaties "practical, every-day realities" in the presence of the aroused hostility of the country.[12] He failed to mention that Mr. Harris,

---

[10] *1860 (2648)*, p. 9.

[11] Griffis, *Townsend Harris, First American Envoy in Japan,* p. 322; Harris' No. 31, July 4.   [12] Alcock, *The Capital of the Tycoon,* I, xvi–xvii.

who had negotiated the master Treaty of 1858, was the only one of the envoys to remain and endeavor to make the treaties work. Rutherford Alcock was appointed British Consul General in Japan after a service of fourteen years as Consul at the Chinese treaty ports. This service was not the best sort of training for a responsible post in Japan, although Alcock never carried the masterful ways of the Chinese service to the extreme reached by his successor, Sir Harry Parkes. In addition to the many laudable qualities portrayed by his biographer,[13] Alcock had two failings which affected his usefulness in Japan. He possessed too ready a pen, which led him into the writing of dispatches and minutes which were wordy in the extreme, and in which the meaning was at times almost obscured by the veil of verbiage. As the ideal of Japanese official correspondence is brevity, and as the difficulties of translating were very great at this time, it may be doubted if the perplexed Japanese Ministers for Foreign Affairs were always able to fathom the voluminous dispatches which were poured in upon them. With this readiness to write came a tendency to hasty judgments which frequently had to be soon revised, although at times they persisted in all their pristine inaccuracy.

Townsend Harris, on the other hand, entered upon his ministerial duties with a very different training and temperament. He had lived in Japan for three years, and his admiration for the people and his sympathetic understanding of the problems before the Government were pronounced. He was slow to come to a conclusion, but once decided he rarely altered his position. In his correspondence he was a man of few words, but of absolute clarity of phrase. No wonder one of the Japanese officials who had to deal with him could say: "I admired him because he did not change his views frequently, for he always spoke deliberately."[14] These differences between the representatives of the English-speaking peoples must be pointed out if we are to understand the strained relations which later developed.

The inauguration of the new treaties was apparently marked

[13] Michie, *The Englishman in China.*
[14] Griffis, *Townsend Harris, First American Envoy in Japan,* p. 307 n.

by two violations on the part of the Japanese because of the way in which they had tried to make ready for the foreigners. Against the choice of Yokohama as the open port both Harris and Alcock protested. But the question was really decided by the merchants, who promptly recognized the commercial advantages of Yokohama no matter what the political disadvantages might be. It was a great disappointment for Mr. Alcock when the representative of the great British firm of Jardine, Matheson and Company established himself at Yokohama, despite Alcock's protest,[15] and when some Dutch merchants did likewise. It was finally settled that the foreigners could reside at Kanagawa, but as a matter of fact only the Consuls and a few missionaries did so.[16] The merchants preferred the site which Lord Ii had chosen, and to him, and not to the Foreign Representatives, should be given the credit for the choice of this excellent port. In a few years the Consuls also moved over to Yokohama, although the foreign Consuls were still designated as at Kanagawa.[17]

The currency question proved more difficult of solution than that of the location of the open port. That the Japanese had the sovereign right to alter their currency could hardly be doubted, and they did not consider that they had parted with this prerogative when they signed the Harris Treaty,[18] but the circulation of a special form of currency designed apparently for the foreign trade alone might be considered a clear infraction of the Treaty, and Harris and Alcock both presented formal protests to the Ministers for Foreign Affairs. The result was that the Japanese withdrew the new coinage, and, as provided by treaty, agreed to the free circulation of dollars, and to the exchange of dollars for ichibus to the capacity of their mint, or 16,000 a day.[19] The evils from which they suffered, however, which were far greater than those of the foreign merchants, persisted. Because of the abnormal ratio of silver to gold in Japan, which was only five to one instead of fifteen to one as in the world at large, it was tremen-

---

[15] Heco, *The Narrative of a Japanese,* I, 217; *1860* (*2648*), p. 25.

[16] *1860* (*2648*), p. 54.   [17] Adams, *The History of Japan,* I, 118.

[18] Alcock, *op. cit.,* II, 415.   [19] *1860* (*2648*), pp. 48, 53.

dously profitable for the foreign merchants to import dollars, secure ichibus, exchange them for gold kobangs, and export the latter. Neither the Japanese nor Harris had any idea that this business would follow from the Treaty which they negotiated, but if it continued it would perhaps drain Japan of all her gold coins. To alter the ratio of gold and silver would have disturbed all financial transactions in Japan, and it seemed easier to introduce a new currency which would take up the impact of the new commercial relations. When this was denied to the Japanese they resorted to other means to protect their supply of gold, and in doing so legitimate trade was bound to suffer. It must always be borne in mind, however, that the Japanese were real sufferers under these new relations, and that the export of gold was the first of many grievances.[20]

That a hostile element existed among the Japanese had long been known. Mr. Harris had noted threatening incidents at Shimoda, and during his visit to Yedo, in 1857, he had several times been warned of possible danger. He, in turn, had done his part by taking every precaution against possible assaults.[21] When Lord Elgin and Baron Gros visited Yedo only rare evidences of ill will were met with. With the arrival of the foreign Ministers and Consuls, merchants, and sailors, trouble developed. In August 1859 complaints were made that members of the two missions were pelted with stones and threatened by two-sword men,[22] and on the twenty-fifth of that month the first assassination occurred.

Early in the month Count Muraviev-Amursky, Governor-General of Eastern Siberia, appeared in Yokohama with a squadron of seven vessels carrying one hundred and five guns.[23] A few days

[20] Harris' No. 34, July 22. A gold kobang was worth by assay from 17s. 6d. to 18s. 6d., but was exchangeable for four silver ichibus, equivalent to a dollar and a third Mexican [*1860* (*2648*), p. 15]. The Government forbade the sale of kobangs, but they could be had for 6½–7½ ichibus ($2.17–2.73 Mex.) and sold in China for $3.50–3.85 (Heco, *op. cit.*, I, 234). See Tilley, *Japan, the Amoor, and the Pacific*, pp. 131–35; Black, *Young Japan*, I, 41–42.

[21] Griffis, *Townsend Harris, First American Envoy in Japan*, p. 291.

[22] Harris' No. 43, September 1; *1860* (*2648*), p. 32.

[23] Tilley, *op. cit.*, p. 144.

later two more ships joined him. He had, the year before, negotiated a treaty with China which won for Russia the left bank
of the Amur River (whence his title) and gave her equal rights
to the Manchurian seacoast. His present mission was to secure
the cession of Sakhalin by Japan. Before he took up his residence
in Yedo some of his men, wandering through the city, had been
jostled and stoned by a mob. They were protected by some native
officers and escorted back to their residence.[24] On Count Muraviev's complaint the Japanese officer in charge of the district and
his lieutenant were dismissed. Muraviev landed in state on the
twenty-second and proceeded three days later to open his negotiations. On that day, however, at Yokohama, a lieutenant and
two seamen from the Russian fleet were cut down by two-sword
men. One of the seamen was instantly killed, and the lieutenant
expired during the night.[25]

This crime filled the foreign community with horror and
alarm, and many persons promptly armed themselves against a
general attack. Speculation was rife as to the cause of the assault,
the best explanation being that the attack had grown out of the
punishment of the Yedo officials, but whether made by them or by
their friends could never be learned.[26] That it was a deliberate
attempt on the part of hostile daimyos to provoke hostilities seems
less evident. Then came the question of reprisals.

Each had his own plan of what ought to be done: some were for
burning the town down, others for attacking Yedo; one or two sensible
ones proposed that the authorities should forbid their officials to wear
their swords within the districts opened to foreigners. All expected that
some severe act of retribution would, of course, be inflicted on the murderers if caught, but if not, on the Government, by the large Russian
squadron in the neighborhood, as a warning and a lesson that it would
be called to account for the life of every foreigner by all European governments combined.[27]

None of these reprisals occurred. The Japanese expressed their
sorrow and regret and promised to do all they could to arrest and

[24] *Ibid.*, p. 153.
[25] *Ibid.*, pp. 162–66.
[26] *Ibid.*, p. 173; *1860* (*2648*), p. 44.   [27] Tilley, *op. cit.*, p. 169.

punish the murderers, and one of the Governors of Kanagawa attended the funeral of the victims—much against his wishes, for it was contrary to custom and would necessitate observances for purification. Count Muraviev and Commodore Popov were satisfied with the efforts made by the Japanese, and they sailed away, leaving Captain Ounkovsky and the "Askold" to settle the matter and protect the foreign community. On September 26 the Japanese accepted Ounkovsky's proposals, which called for an expression of regret by a deputation of the highest dignitaries on the frigate, the dismissal of the Governors of Yokohama, and the apprehension of the murderers and their execution in the presence of Russian officers on the spot where the murders occurred.[28] In addition, the Japanese agreed to guard the mortuary chapel in perpetuity. No indemnity was demanded, for, as Count Muraviev proudly said, "Russia did not sell the blood of her subjects."[29]

This solution of the affair was a great disappointment to those who favored a strong policy. A feeling of the greatest insecurity prevailed; and not only did all the residents of Yokohama, with the exception of the Americans, go about armed, but the English and Dutch Consuls wore their weapons when holding interviews with the Japanese officials.[30] Before the excitement could pass away, a Chinese servant in the employ of the French consular agent was struck down on November 5.[31] As the victim had come from Hong Kong, the British Consul at Kanagawa believed that he was called upon to move in this matter; and so distraught was he that he not only determined to turn the murderers, if caught, over to Alcock for punishment, which would have been a violation of the Treaty, but he issued a notification to all British subjects to go about armed as much as possible, and gave them free permission to use a revolver or other deadly weapon, on any reasonable provocation, on any Japanese official or non-official.[32]

---

[28] *1860 (2648)*, p. 77.   [29] Alcock, *op. cit.*, I, 342.

[30] Tilley, *op. cit.*, p. 175.

[31] *1860 (2648)*, p. 81. A Japanese was executed for this murder on September 30, 1865 [*1866 (3615)*, p. 61].

[32] *1860 (2648)*, p. 82.

Mr. Alcock, in Yedo, was able to preserve a sense of proportion, and he ordered the immediate withdrawal of the notification. For this murder the best explanation seems to be that as the Chinese wore European dress he was killed by a native who had been insulted by a European,[33] or, as seems even more probable, some Japanese could not tolerate Chinese, whom they despised, aping the lordly foreigners and finding shelter under their flag.

On the day that this murder occurred in Yokohama, Townsend Harris had his second audience of the Shogun, in order to present his new credentials as Minister-Resident.[34] The growing bitterness occasioned by the ill effects of the new commerce manifested itself in a reception which was far less cordial and honorable than that in 1857. Against this Harris protested for months, and successfully, until a third and satisfactory audience was held. This episode, and the restrictions upon trade, caused Harris to despair. On November 15 he wrote: "Our affairs here are in an unsatisfactory state. The Japanese evade the faithful observance of the most important of the treaty stipulations or meet them with a passive resistance."[35] He tried in every way to convince them of the danger which such a course involved. About the same time Alcock sent a gloomy dispatch to Lord Russell: "I may begin by stating, that at this hour all Treaties recently concluded with Japan are virtually annulled."[36] The annulment, however, consisted mainly in certain interferences with trade, which

[33] Adams, *op. cit.,* I, 124.

[34] Harris' No. 51, November 7. He did not have the formal letter of credence, which was not sent to him until June 28, 1860.

[35] *Serial Number 1031,* p. 12; also Harris' No. 5, February 1, 1860.

[36] December 6, 1859. *1860 (2648),* p. 89. In reply to this dispatch Lord John Russell approved Alcock's general conduct, but said: "It were to be wished that you had not threatened war. . . . . If war is made to enforce the observance of a Commercial Treaty, we run the risk of engaging in protracted hostilities, and of earning a reputation for quarrelling with every nation in the East. Time and patience may remove many of the difficulties of which you complain. The Japanese, on their side, may well be jealous of Europeans, who insult their usages and carry away their gold. You should endeavour rather to soothe differences than to make and insist upon peremptory demands. Our intercourse is but merely begun: it should not be inaugurated by war" (February 28, 1860, *ibid.,* p. 98).

could not have been very serious, for a few months later Alcock was able to report that the progress of trade at Kanagawa and Nagasaki during these six months, "in spite of every obstacle, whether in currency, monopolies, or official interference . . . . must be a matter of surprise as well as congratulation."[37]

On the same day Alcock addressed a "strong letter" to the Ministers for Foreign Affairs requesting a conference and emphasizing the importance of this interview, for on it the question of peace or war between the two countries would depend.[38] The interview took place on December 7. Alcock found the Ministers "quite unconscious of any disregard of Treaties," and in a four-hour conference he proceeded to enlighten them. Harris and Duchesne de Bellecourt, the French Minister, supported Alcock in his complaints, and when Harris had an interview with the Ministers on the thirteenth he tried a new argument, assuring them that if because of treaty violations war should result, "the Representatives of the foreign Powers would only negotiate with the Representatives of the Mikado, and that this would overthrow the governing power then exercised by the Daimios, with the Tycoon as their Representative."[39] For the second time Harris had put his finger upon the weakest point in the Shogunate régime, but it may be doubted if he fully realized the growing influence of the formerly almost mythical Mikado.

The new year brought no relief to the nerve-racked foreign residents.[40] Despite government regulation and restriction a profitable trade was rapidly developing, and the merchant colony at Yokohama grew with it. But the menace of sudden death at the hands of some two-sword fanatic was never absent. On January 30, 1860, the Japanese interpreter of the British Legation, Dankirche (Denkichi), was struck down in broad daylight close to the gate of the Legation.[41] Dan, as he was generally called, had

---

[37] March 6, 1860. *1860 (2694)*, p. 8.   [38] *1860 (2648)*, p. 91.

[39] Harris' No. 4, January 16, 1860; *1861, Lords 18*, p. 56.

[40] A Chinese coolie was murdered in Yokohama about this time (Heco, *op. cit.*, I, 236).

[41] *1860 (2694)*, pp. 1–4.

had a remarkable career. He had been a sailor on a junk which had been blown to sea early in December 1850. One of his companions was the well-known Joseph Heco.[42] On January 22, when all hope of ever reaching Japan had waned, they were picked up by an American bark and carried into San Francisco. A year later they were sent to Hong Kong to be returned to Japan by Perry's expedition, but Heco returned to the United States before Perry arrived. Dan joined the expedition, where he was known as Dan Ketch; but he was afraid to land in Japan lest he be beheaded under the law forbidding Japanese to leave the country.[43] He was taken back to America and lived there under the Commodore's protection until his return to Japan in 1858, as linguist for Mr. Alcock. His residence in America had ill prepared him for life in his native land, especially in those parlous times. Mr. Alcock described him as "ill-tempered, proud and violent."[44] He was accustomed to wear European clothes, and, counting upon the protection of the British flag and the Colt revolver which he wore at his belt, "to swagger and to defy his countrymen."[45] The reaction of such conduct upon the Japanese samurai and ronins[46] may easily be imagined. So hated had he become that the Governors of Foreign Affairs urged Alcock to send Dan to the consulate at Kanagawa for safety, but the British Minister announced that he would see to it that his servant was protected.[47] Again the Ministers expressed their regret and promised to make every effort to secure the assassins, but these were never apprehended. Alcock then demanded that two of the Governors of Foreign Affairs attend the funeral. They agreed, but later refused as contrary to Japanese custom. Alcock insisted and

[42] Author of *The Narrative of a Japanese.*

[43] Hawks, *Narrative of the Expedition of an American Squadron to the China Seas and Japan,* I, 486.

[44] Alcock, *op. cit.,* I, 332.

[45] De Fonblanque, *Niphon and Pe-che-li,* p. 77.

[46] Samurai, a warrior who could wear two swords, and generally received a pension from his daimyo; ronin, a free lance, a samurai who had left his clan.

[47] Heco, *op. cit.,* I, 237. While these officials were spoken of as governors, a better translation would be commissioners.

they complied, "to the astonishment and dismay of the assembled thousands who lined the streets of Yedo."[48]

Within a month came a more brutal and less accountable onslaught. Two Dutch merchant captains were "literally hacked to pieces" on the evening of February 26, in Yokohama. No reason could be assigned for this deed, for the captains were known to be "remarkably quiet, inoffensive men." The feeling prevailed that this was but another attempt of the anti-foreign party, perhaps led by Mito,[49] to precipitate a general collision, for this time there were both a British and a Russian ship of war in the harbor. Captain Vyse, the British Acting Consul, however, in his warning to the British community suggested that the unruly conduct of drunken sailors may have brought about the assassination of the captains.[50]

Once more some Japanese officials were compelled to attend the funeral services, at which marines and blue-jackets from the two warships served as escorts. A collective protest was made to the Japanese Ministers for Foreign Affairs on the part of the three Foreign Ministers, and the demand of the Dutch Consul for an indemnity was supported. Alcock believed that if every life should cost the Government from twenty to fifty thousand dollars it would take better precautions to protect the foreigners. Yet the foreigners were loath to accept the protection which the Japanese offered, believing that it was designed rather to isolate than to protect them. But of the good faith of the Government and of its eagerness to do all it could to protect the foreigners there can be little doubt.

These sporadic assassinations, six in seven months, loomed large in the thoughts of the little group of foreigners at Yedo and Yokohama, but they little realized the number of Japanese who were losing their lives during these troubled days. The

---

[48] De Fonblanque, *op. cit.,* p. 79.

[49] Harris' No. 10, March 10. Mito was believed by the foreigners to be the evil spirit of the times. He was accused of having poisoned the Shogun in 1858 and of having set fire to the palace at Yedo on November 12, 1859 [Alcock, *op. cit.,* I, 357; Heco, *op. cit.,* I, 246; and *1860 (2694)*, p. 6].

[50] *1860 (2694)*, p. 9.

seriousness of the political situation was, however, brought home to them when on March 24 the Tairo himself, Lord Ii Kamon-no-Kami, was assassinated and his head taken, at the very entrance to the Shogun's castle.[51] Lord Ii was on his way to the palace to pay his respects on that festival day. Seated in his palanquin surrounded by his retainers—who unhappily, because of a belated snowstorm, wore their clumsy raincoats and had their swords wrapped in cloths—he had almost reached the Sakurada Gate when a band of eighteen ronins sprang into the procession. A shot was fired, the Tairo was stabbed to death through the sides of his palanquin, then dragged out and beheaded, and the survivors fled with their prize.

Of the assassins, seventeen were Mito samurai and one was from Satsuma; but before embarking on this bloody enterprise they had dissolved their clan connection and become ronins. Eight were killed or mortally wounded in the encounter, and eight more surrendered later. As was the custom, the Mito men had, before the attack, drawn up a statement of their reasons for this deed, and their indictment against the Tairo signaled out his foreign policy.

While fully aware of the necessity for some change in policy since the coming of the Americans to Uraga, it is entirely against the interest of the country and a shame to the sacred dignity of the land to open commercial relations, to admit foreigners into the castle, to conclude a treaty, to abolish the established custom of trampling on the picture of Christ, to permit foreigners to build places of worship of their evil religion, Christianity, and to allow the three Ministers to reside in the land. Under the excuse of keeping the peace, too much compromise has been made at the sacrifice of national honor. Too much fear has been shown in regard to the foreigners' threatenings. Not only has the national custom been set aside, and national dignity injured, but the policy followed by the Shogunate has no Imperial sanction. For all these acts the Tairo Baron Ii Kamon-no-Kami is responsible.[52]

Then followed a protest against Ii's conduct in confining some of the loyal princes and barons, and even in interfering with the Shogunal succession:

[51] Harris' No. 11, March 31; Akimoto, *op. cit.*, p. 185; Satoh, *Agitated Japan*, pp. 129–42.   [52] Satoh, *Agitated Japan*, pp. 137–40.

Therefore we have consecrated ourselves to be the instruments of Heaven to punish this wicked man, and we have assumed on ourselves the duty of putting an end to a serious evil by killing this atrocious autocrat. Our conduct, however, does not indicate the slightest enmity to the Shogunate. We swear before Heaven and earth, gods and men, that our action is entirely built on our hope of seeing the policy of the Shogunate resume its proper form and abide by the holy and wise will of His Majesty, the Emperor. We hope to see our national glory manifested in the expulsion of foreigners from the land. Thus will the whole nation be established on a basis as firm and unmovable as Mount Fuji itself.[53]

Although in the minds of his assailants Lord Ii's foreign policy was a great offense, yet it must not be forgotten that loyal samurai of Mito had grievances nearer their hearts than that. The feud between the ex-lord of Mito and Lord Ii had continued for seven years, and Ii had gained the upper hand. Not only had he confined the ex-lord to his mansion and humbled the present lord and Lord Hitotsubashi, but he had secured an Imperial order for the return of the Mikado's letter to Mito. This had occasioned a brief civil war between clansmen who would obey the order and those who would have refused to deliver up the Mikado's letter. It was seventeen of the latter who made their way to Yedo to destroy the man whom they considered a swaggering despot and the enemy alike of the Emperor, the daimyos, and the good old customs of Japan.[54]

The Foreign Ministers in Yedo now realized that if the Tairo himself could not secure his own protection, they stood little chance if a determined assault were made. However, the authorities doubled their protective measures. The Legation guards were increased, cannon were installed, and every precaution known to the Japanese was taken.

From these scenes of bloodshed it is a relief to turn to a brighter episode. On February 13 the Japanese Embassy to the

[53] This feeling of personal responsibility for the punishment of public servants whose policy did not prove acceptable was very troublesome, and resulted in the destruction of several of the most valued leaders of new Japan.

[54] Brinkley, *History of the Japanese People,* p. 671; E. W. Clement, "The Mito Civil War," in *Transactions of the Asiatic Society of Japan,* Vol. 19, Part II.

United States sailed from Yokohama on board the "Powhatan," accompanied by the Japanese war steamer "Kanrin Maru."[55] The Ambassadors consisted of the two hatamoto, Shimmei Buzen-no-Kami and Muragaki Awaji-no-Kami, and the censor Oguri Bungo-no-Kami, while fifteen officers and fifty-three servants completed the party.[56] In command of the "Kanrin Maru" was Captain Katsu, better known as Count Katsu Awa, the organizer and historian of the modern Japanese navy, while in the envoys' suite was Fukuzawa Yukichi, who became one of the most influential leaders of new Japan as founder of the *Jiji Shimpo* newspaper and the Keiogijuku University. The journey was made by way of San Francisco and Panama; at the latter place the U.S.S. "Roanoke" was waiting to convey the party to Hampton Roads. There, on May 12, the party were officially received and transferred to the "Philadelphia," on which they were carried to Washington. On the seventeenth the Ambassadors were presented to President Buchanan and the ratifications were exchanged. After three weeks in the capital there followed a brief tour of the Eastern cities, in which, in every case, the mission was received with lavish hospitality and widespread interest. At Philadelphia the Ambassadors were especially interested in the working of the mint, for they sought light on the currency problem which so embarrassed their government. As they traveled they received as presents or purchased all manner of American tools, instruments, and articles new or strange to them, and their artists were continually engaged in sketching scenes of interest and their secretaries in taking notes. On June 30 they sailed from New York in

[55] For the Japanese Embassy see *The First Japanese Embassy to the United States of America,* which contains a translation of the diary of Muragaki Awaji-no-Kami, and reprints of contemporary and later American accounts. At the request of the State Department, translations of the correspondence exchanged between the Ambassadors and the Department were supplied by the Ministry for Foreign Affairs and transmitted in Bingham's No. 926, July 31, 1879. See also Harris' No. 6, February 8, 1860; No. 21, July 5; No. 33, August 29; and No. 42, November 19; also Moore, *Digest of International Law,* V, 742–44.

[56] The censor, Oguri, was not named in the Shogun's letter to the President. The hatamoto were direct vassals of the Shogun, ranking below the daimyo.

the "Niagara," largest of our warships, arriving at Yokohama on November 9.

The first Japanese mission to the Treaty Powers had, therefore, sailed to the United States. It is impossible to estimate the effect of this visit upon some of the keen-eyed Japanese,[57] and the welcome the members received strengthened the good impression of America which Harris had labored so hard to create.

Within a year after the opening of Kanagawa it was evident to Townsend Harris that he had been too optimistic regarding the readiness of Japan for general foreign intercourse. Instead of the anti-foreign feeling dying down, it had apparently gained strength, and showed itself in the assassinations of foreigners and of the Tairo. Although he had confidence in the desire of the Shogunate to protect foreigners, he also recognized the difficulty of the task, especially in Yedo, where the streets were filled with two-sword retainers of the resident daimyos, arrogant, aggressive, and many of them bitterly anti-foreign. Therefore, on August 1, 1860, he advised his Government that the opening of Yedo to foreign residence on January 1, 1862, might lead to conflict between some of the merchants and the Japanese retainers, and thus jeopardize the promising trade which had already been established.[58] On this matter the British and French Ministers were in agreement, and each wrote to his Government requesting discretionary power to postpone the opening for one year and to renew it from time to time if it seemed necessary. In this respect they anticipated the broader request of the Shogunate a few months later.

At this point it may be well to point out some of the then more recent aspects of the anti-foreign feeling. With the general Japanese opposition, based on the violation of the ancient traditions of the land and the disobedience of the Imperial will, we are quite

[57] Heco, *op. cit.*, I, 261. Gifts from the President to the Shogun were delivered in December (No. 48, December 7).

[58] *F.R., 1862*, pp. 793–94. He had given notice in October 1859 that Niigata would not be opened on January 1, 1860, and that a more satisfactory harbor on the west coast would be agreed upon (No. 50, October 28, 1859). Belgium and Switzerland had been refused treaties early in 1860, but Portugal secured one on August 3, which reduced the duty on linens to five per cent (No. 16, May 15, 1860; No. 28, August 4).

familiar. But with the opening of unregulated trade at Kanagawa and the other ports certain immediate evils had been impressed upon the Japanese. In the first place, such was the demand for export articles that their prices rose from one hundred to three hundred per cent, and this rise in turn affected other articles.[59] The temporary introduction of a new coinage also demoralized prices. This rise in prices was especially felt by persons on fixed salaries, such as officials and retainers, and it was most evident near the treaty ports.

Then, it must be confessed, the conduct of many of the foreigners was not such as to cause the Japanese to welcome more intimate relations with them. On this point much suggestive material may be found in the state papers and the contemporary narratives. Many of the merchants had come over from China, where since the Opium War they had conducted themselves much as they pleased, with little respect for the feelings or the rights of the Chinese.[60] This was hardly a good preparation for life in Japan.

The so-called pioneers of civilization are, like other pioneers, more noted for physical energy than for gentler or more refined qualities. It is not the skilled or scientific farmer, but the strong-armed labourer, who cuts down the forest; nor is it the liberal, enlightened, prudent, and educated merchant, but the daring, money-seeking adventurer, who clears the way for commerce. What have the Japanese to learn from such men? Do they set them a profitable example in morality, in decency, in religion, in probity, in intelligence, in industry, or even in the outward forms of social intercourse? . . . . We say the Japanese are false; but did we teach them truthfulness or honesty when we bought their gold weight for weight with silver, and drained their treasury of native currency by false representations? We call them a semi-barbarous race; but contrast the courteous, dignified bearing, and the invariable equanimity of temper of the lowest official or smallest tradesman, with the insolent arrogance and swagger, the still more insolent familiarity, or the besotted violence, of many an European resident or visitor![61]

[59] *F.R., 1862,* p. 795. See No. 22, July 11, 1860, in *Commercial Relations, 1860,* pp. 403–4.

[60] In November 1859 there were only twenty resident foreign merchants at Yokohama [*1860 (2617)*, p. 2].

[61] De Fonblanque, *op. cit.,* pp. 69–70; Hodgson, *A Residence at Nagasaki,* xxix–xxxii.

Mr. Alcock made frequent severe strictures on the conduct of the foreigners,[62] and Mr. Harris reported that

unfortunately, a portion of them are neither prudent nor discreet, and they are numerous enough to imperil the safety of the orderly and well-disposed, and seriously endanger the amicable relations that have been established with so much difficulty and labor with this government.[63]

Before 1859 only a few ships touched at Japanese ports, but in that year ships were continually passing in and out of Yokohama. Heretofore the crews had been kept in fairly good control; but now drunken sailors, assaulting Japanese and entering their shops and houses, frequently gave offense.[64] Perhaps it was some outrage of this nature which brought down vengeance on quite innocent foreigners like the Russian sailors and the Dutch captains.

When it is remembered also that of all the consular representatives only the British were *de carrière,* while those of the United States, France, and Holland were merchants, unsalaried, and "mixed up with the practices objected to in others," it is easy to understand why their influence on their nationals was small.[65] Thus, in violation of law, foreigners engaged in the sale of fire-

[62] *1860 (2648),* pp. 67, 78, 83, 88; *1860 (2617),* pp. 1, 3–7.

[63] Harris' No. 26, August 1, 1860, in *F.R., 1862,* pp. 793–94. Harris had been instructed to co-operate with the British Minister in suppressing disorders committed by foreigners, and in maintaining good order and good government among them (No. 8, April 2, 1860).

[64] "The foreigners, subjects of the various Treaty Powers, at Kanagawa, have done their best to justify the policy and confirm the fears of the Japanese authorities, as to the course foreign trade would take, and its results. Nothing could well have been worse than the conduct of the body generally; and the acts of many individuals are altogether disgraceful" [Alcock to Lord Russell, November 23, 1859, in *1860 (2617),* p. 1]. "There have been, unfortunately, very many instances where Japanese have been grossly maltreated by foreigners, and no indemnity asked or paid. Indeed, it admits of some question whether it would be safe, in view of the character of the floating population of the treaty powers, at the open ports, to establish the principle of the liability of a government for the act of its individual citizens or subjects" (Pruyn to Seward, February 29, 1864, in *F.R., 1864, Part III,* p. 485).

[65] *1860 (2617),* p. 2; Tilley, *op. cit.,* p. 120. The United States did not provide salaried consuls at Kanagawa and Nagasaki until July 1, 1861. No provision was made for carrying into effect extraterritorial jurisdiction until the Act of Congress of June 22, 1860.

arms to Japanese, and in hunting within the proscribed limits.[66] This led to the *cause célèbre* in which an Englishman, Moss, shot down a Japanese officer who attempted to arrest his servant.[67] In the Consular Court Moss was found guilty and sentenced to a fine of $1,000 and deportation. Alcock, on reviewing the case, added imprisonment for three months, and ordered the fine to be paid to the wounded man as an indemnity. The Supreme Court at Hong Kong, however, released the prisoner and awarded him $2,000 damages for false imprisonment, on the ground that Alcock could only fine and deport or imprison. The Japanese could hardly understand such technicalities. If one would know the pressure which might be exerted by the foreign community to prevent justice being done in cases where a white man was the defendant, let him read Alcock's comments on consular jurisdiction in the East.[68]

The exportation of gold coin has already been mentioned. Much was shipped without manifest or declaration at the custom-house in violation of the Treaties. In September 1859 after the forced withdrawal of the new silver currency, the Government ordered that the sale of gold coins to foreigners should cease.[69] Such was the profit on both sides, however, that illicit trade continued. In order to buy these coins, and, in fact, to carry on any trade, it was necessary to secure ichibus in exchange for dollars. The mint was able to coin only 16,000 daily, which proved too few for the demand. By notification British subjects were permitted to request exchange for not more than $5,000 nor less than $1,000, and when the total demanded exceeded the supply the Japanese tried to prorate the allotments.[70] This attempt caused some of the merchants to send in false requisitions for enormous amounts in the hope of receiving a liberal issue. Even Mr. Keswick, of Jardine, Matheson and Company, applied for $4,000,000 (notwithstanding the limit of $5,000), and a Mr. Telge, who had

---

[66] Alcock, *op. cit.*, I, 330; Heco, *op. cit.*, I, 262–64.

[67] Alcock, *op. cit.*, II, 14–17; Jones, *Extraterritoriality in Japan*, pp. 54–57.

[68] Alcock, *op. cit.*, II, 25–29.

[69] Heco, *op. cit.*, I, 234.   [70] *1860 (2648)*, p. 53.

complained to the British Consul concerning the insulting conduct of a Japanese customhouse officer, asked for the exchange of $250,000,000. Other instances are noted in the special Blue-book dealing with this episode.[71] The climax was reached by Thomas Tatham, who asked exchange for "$1,200,666,777,888,999,-222,321." In November the Japanese found in the burning of the Shogun's palace an excuse for closing the mint, stopping the sale of copper, and restricting the sale of all produce desired by the foreigners; but it was certainly the difficulties at Yokohama which drove them to this measure.

With these outstanding occasions for friction, in addition to the prevailing hostility to foreign intercourse, it would have been too much to expect the new year to open upon greatly improved relations, while the problem before the Shogunate officials of maintaining the Treaties in the face of growing opposition was bound to be increasingly perplexing.[72]

[71] *1860 (2617).* Lord John Russell forwarded Alcock's dispatches regarding the conduct of British merchants to the East India and China Association with the hope that its members would use their influence on their correspondents in China and Japan to induce them to put a stop to such proceedings. American naval officers were accused of trading in gold, and even Harris himself; this he denied—see his No. 7, February 14, and No. 46, November 22, 1860.

[72] The instructions to Harris in 1858 were numbered 8 and 9; in 1859, Nos. 1 to 6 and extracts of Nos. 3 and 5 were printed in *Serial Number 1031;* and in 1860, 8 to 14 *bis* (no No. 7 was sent). Harris' dispatches for 1858 were numbered 1 to 50, and No. 29 was printed in *ibid.;* for 1859, 1 to 54, and Nos. 6, 7, 13, and 52 were printed in *ibid.;* and for 1860, 1 to 53; No. 26 was printed in *F.R., 1862,* and No. 22 in *Commercial Relations, 1860.*

CHAPTER VI

HARRIS STANDS ALONE
1860–62

THE NEW year did indeed dawn ominously on both sides of the Pacific. In the United States the secession movement had commenced, which was soon to plunge the States into the horrors of civil war—a war which, among its other effects, served to hurry the decline of American influence and commerce in the Far East. Townsend Harris was a "far-seeing War Democrat," and yet, despite his belief in the success of his cause, he must have known many hours of bitter anxiety in those days of long-delayed communication.[1]

In Japan the foreign community was threatened as never before. The first warning was given by the Government to Mr. Harris, who in turn warned Alcock, De Witt, the Dutch Consul General, and de Bellecourt. It was to the effect that some six hundred ronins from Mito were on their way to burn the foreign settlement at Yokohama and to attack the Legations at Yedo. The Japanese authorities proposed that the foreign Consuls move over from Kanagawa to Yokohama, where they could be better protected, and that the Ministers move for a time within the castle moats at Yedo. Again there was some question as to the good faith of the Government, the Consuls, for instance, refusing to move, lest they seem to abandon their right to reside at Kanagawa.[2] The Ministers also remained in their Legations, while

---

[1] The instructions for 1861 are numbered 15–25 to Harris, and 1–4 to Pruyn; of these fifteen, one was printed in *F.R., 1861,* and eight in *F.R., 1862,* as well as an unnumbered one to Pruyn. Harris' dispatches are numbered 1–64; of these, one was printed in *F.R., 1861* and ten in *F.R., 1862.* During his term as Secretary of State, Mr. Seward favored the publication of a very wide selection of the diplomatic correspondence.

[2] *1861, Lords 18,* pp. 1–6; Heco, *The Narrative of a Japanese,* I, 266.

Alcock suggested that the British admiral leave at least two ships in the bay after his departure. For a few days the alarm was great, but on January 8 Alcock believed that the crisis had passed, and expressed the opinion that the Japanese were taking all the precautions they deemed necessary. Large patrols of armed men were guarding the whole road from Yedo to Yokohama, and a daimyo with two hundred of his men and two fieldpieces was in charge of the British Legation.

On the evening of the fourteenth the swords of the ronins flashed again, and this time one of the most popular and useful of the foreign officials was brought down. The deed struck close to Mr. Harris, for it was his interpreter, Mr. Heusken, who fell. He had accompanied Harris to Japan in 1856, as interpreter, because of his knowledge of Dutch. In the intervening years he had mastered Japanese so well that he was said to know more of Japan and the Japanese and to speak their language with more fluency than any other living European.[3] He had acted not only at all of Mr. Harris' conferences with the Japanese but had also assisted Lord Elgin in 1858, and was then aiding Count Eulenburg to negotiate a treaty for Prussia. It was on his return from the Prussian Legation, on a dark and rainy night, that the blow was struck. The assassins were able to escape in the darkness. Much as Harris mourned the loss of his faithful attaché, he did not hesitate to point out that Heusken had lost his life through failure to heed the repeated warnings which had been given.[4] To go abroad at night, in these troubled times, was a dangerous proceeding for any man. Harris endeavored, by running no needless risks, not merely to save his own life but to co-operate with the Shogunate officials in their endeavors to protect him.

In this case the Japanese did all that could be expected of them

[3] De Fonblanque, *Niphon and Pe-che-li,* p. 89.

[4] No. 3, January 22; No. 21, June 7, *F.R., 1862,* pp. 797–98; No. 49, November 23, *ibid.,* pp. 804–6. See Adams, *The History of Japan,* I, 130, for the story that this murder was due to the enmity of Hori Oribe-no-Kami. The chief of this band of ronins was said to have been murdered on May 30, 1863. He had taken part also in the murder of Lord Ii, the first attack on the British Legation, and the attack on Lord Ando (*F.R., 1863,* II, 1101).

in order to arrest the guilty and punish the yakunins who had been remiss in their duty. The funeral was attended by the three Ambassadors who had recently returned from the United States —an unusual token of respect. When the Diplomatic and Consular Corps gathered to follow the body to the grave, a warning was received that they might be attacked on the way. They did not flinch, and happily no attack was made.[5]

This was the seventh assassination[6] in the foreign community since Yokohama had been opened, eighteen months before; and coming as it did after the recent alarms, it seemed to possess a most ominous import. On the day after the funeral all the Foreign Ministers met at the British Legation to consider what position and course they should take.[7] A difference of opinion promptly developed. Mr. Alcock, after summarizing the events of the past year and a half, stated his conviction that the murder of Heusken was not a "mere fortuitous rencontre with a band of bravos," but rather an incident in the recent course of terrorism and intimidation inaugurated with the alarm of the threatened ronin attack. He furthermore believed that "measures were being taken which had for their object the removal of foreigners out of the Empire, either by intimidation or by murder"; but there were no facts to show whether the officials were parties to it or only reluctant witnesses. He felt that the Representatives of the Treaty Powers should take "some action so decided and significant" that it would arouse the Ministers to a sense of danger, and also their colleagues and possibly the daimyos who had hired the assassins to kill Mr. Heusken. Such an action he believed would be the withdrawal of the Foreign Representatives to Yokohama, under the protection of the fleet, where, free from menace, they could call upon the Government to reconsider its policy and to give satisfaction for past breaches and guaranties for the future, especially as to security of life and property.

The French, Dutch, and Prussian Representatives agreed with

[5] *1861, Lords 18,* p. 6.

[6] Two of the victims were Orientals in the employ of Westerners.

[7] *1861, Lords 18,* pp. 12–25; also No. 8, February 13.

Alcock in his plan of withdrawing from Yedo. Mr. Harris was
unable to concur.

He was the oldest foreign resident in Japan; he had enjoyed long and
intimate relations with the Japanese authorities and Government, and he
still retained his faith in their good-will and desire to carry out honestly
the Treaties they had entered into. But they had many difficulties to con-
tend with, and the foreign Representatives could not desire them to do
impossibilities. They had shown no backwardness in taking measures of
precaution for the protection of all; but it was out of their power to prevent such murders as that of Mr. Heusken, who had exposed himself by
going out at night, contrary to the repeated counsels and remonstrances
received both from the Government and himself. He, for his part, felt
perfectly safe, so long as he complied with the conditions which circumstances imposed, and could not agree in the policy of leaving Yeddo. On
the contrary he thought such a step fraught with danger, that if they once
left it they would never return, and that an attempt to occupy any portion
of Yokohama with foreign troops would create such an alarm and outburst of national feeling that conflict and war would be inevitable. He
recommended that they should unite in urging upon the Government more
vigorous measures, and trust to their good faith to give effect to these.

This statement showed that the American Minister had a far
better understanding of the difficulties which confronted the Shogun's Government than any of his colleagues possessed, and in
urging a sympathetic and conciliatory policy he was again trying
to serve the best interest, not only of his own land but of Japan.
The conference of the nineteenth was followed by a second on the
twenty-first which Harris failed to attend, and concerning which
a sharp exchange of letters took place between him and Alcock.
Harris took a position which was sound at the time and which was
indorsed by later events, and which, if recognized, would have
averted much bloodshed and ill will:

It strikes me that all the arguments at the Conferences referred to, are
based upon the assumption that the Japanese Government represented a
civilization on a par with that of the Western world; that is a grave
error. The Japanese are not a civilized, but a semi-civilized people, and
the condition of affairs in this country is quite analogous to that of Europe during the middle ages. To demand, therefore, of the Japanese Government the same observances, the same prompt administration of justice,
as is found in civilized lands, is simply to demand an impossibility; and to

hold that Government responsible for the isolated acts of private individuals, I believe to be wholly unsustained by any international law.[8]

After arguing against the withdrawal to Yokohama, which Harris believed would not produce any beneficial effect, and would be an important step toward a war with Japan, he added:

I had hoped that the page of future history might record the great fact that in one spot in the Eastern world the advent of Christian civilization did not bring with it its usual attendants of rapine and bloodshed; this fond hope, I fear, is to be disappointed.

I would sooner see all the Treaties with this country torn up, and Japan return to its old state of isolation, than witness the horrors of war inflicted on this peaceful people and happy land.[9]

On January 26 the Representatives of Great Britain, France, and the Netherlands retired to Yokohama, and the Prussian Envoy followed soon after his treaty was signed.[10] On the day of the withdrawal Alcock addressed a long and querulous letter to the Ministers of Foreign Affairs protesting against the many murders, the failure to arrest and punish the assassins, and the general insecurity of life. He announced his withdrawal, and stated that he was ready to return to Yedo "whenever I can see such material guarantee for redress in respect to past grievances, and security for the future as may warrant the step."[11] It is of interest to note that when the news of this decision reached England, Lord Russell again warned Alcock not to break off relations with the Japanese, and added, "Except in a case where immediate action is required to preserve the lives and properties of British subjects, or of the subjects of foreign Powers in amity with Her Majesty, it is the desire of Her Majesty's Government that the employment, or even the menace of force should not be resorted to."[12]

[8] *1861, Lords 18*, p. 43. Alcock finally adopted this view in 1864. Harris transmitted this correspondence in No. 10, February 25, 1861.

[9] *1861, Lords 18*, p. 44.

[10] The signing of the Prussian Treaty, January 24, 1861, was, of course, in violation of the orders from the Mikado which permitted only temporary relations with the foreigners and looked to their ultimate expulsion. This Treaty omitted any reference to the opening of other ports than Kanagawa, Nagasaki, and Hakodate (Rein, *Japan: Travels and Researches*, p. 347; also No. 6, January 26).

[11] *1861, Lords 18*, pp. 7–10.   [12] *Ibid.*, p. 11.

Certain inconsistencies in this policy are at once evident. If, as Alcock had asserted, the Japanese authorities desired to force the Ministers out of Yedo, was not this retirement playing right into their hands? And why should the Japanese, who were already under heavy expense for guarding the Legations, offer any further guaranties in order to induce the Ministers to return, especially if they considered their presence a source of trouble? Harris pointed out the difficulty he had met with in securing the article providing for the residence of a Minister in Yedo, and he, at least, would not endanger the exercise of that right. So he held his post, amid the many dangers, confident that he would be safe if he observed reasonable measures of precaution.

For more than a month Harris remained in Yedo, alone and undisturbed. At Yokohama his colleagues must have been surprised at the failure of the Japanese immediately to meet their demands. A week passed before even an informal inquiry was made, and it was not until February 8 that the Ministers for Foreign Affairs formally acknowledged the dispatch of January 26, stating that repeated deliberations were necessary in order to take proper measures.[13] In the meantime Alcock instructed the British Consul at Kanagawa to gather all possible information concerning official interference with trade at Yokohama. A public meeting, attended by sixteen persons, was held on the seventh, and a committee which was appointed to gather the desired information reported two days later.[14] From that report it is evident that the one real difficulty was the currency. The merchants desired the free circulation of dollars throughout the Empire. Of the non-enforcement of contracts, however, only one case was found; of official interference with trade, only two instances; as to want of system at the customhouse and inadequate wharfage accommodation, there was no specific complaint, nor was there any as to the occupation of land at Yokohama. As to security of life and property, the committee agreed that the Government was apparently anxious to protect the foreign community.

[13] *1861, Lords 18*, p. 70.   [14] *Ibid.*, p. 58.

From this report, drawn up by a representative committee of merchants, it is evident that the sweeping charges of treaty violation could not be substantiated at this time. In fact, Alcock reported to Lord Russell, on March 3, that the trade of Yokohama more than realized the most sanguine anticipations.[15]

In order to hasten the deliberations of the Ministers, Alcock advised them on February 13 that he proposed to travel through the country and visit all the open ports.[16] Knowing how loath the Government was to have the Foreign Representatives travel in the interior, he believed that this suggestion would have some effect, and the event convinced him that he had "made no miscalculation as to the effectiveness of the new weapon brought to bear."[17] A week later Sakai Wookionoske (Ukionosuki), a member of the Second Council, arrived in Yokohama as an envoy of the Tycoon to consult with Alcock and de Bellecourt. Conferences were held on February 21, 22, and 27, to the complete satisfaction of the Foreign Representatives, and on March 2 they returned to Yedo.[18]

An analysis of the agreement made at this time, which was confirmed by the Ministers for Foreign Affairs, does not convince one that the drastic measure of striking the flags and withdrawing from the capital was by any means necessary. The most important clause was as follows: "The Tycoon, by and with his Council of State, formally engages to provide effectively for their security, together with that of the members of their respective Legations, and their exemption alike from menace and violence; and under this assurance invites them to return."[19] To be sure, there had been no "formal engagement" to this effect in the past, but the Shogun's Government had done everything in its power to protect the Legations; and, as we shall see, even this formal engagement could not prevent the onslaughts of desperate anti-foreign fanatics. Then followed certain details as to the measures for defense, notably the substitution of mounted guards, from the Ty-

---

[15] *Ibid.*, p. 82.   [16] *Ibid.*, p. 70.
[17] Alcock, *The Capital of the Tycoon*, II, 61.
[18] *1861, Lords 18,* pp. 71–82; also No. 11, March 6.
[19] *1861, Lords 18,* p. 73.

coon's troops, for the yakunins who had proved so unsatisfactory. Vigorous measures were pledged for the arrest and punishment of murderers, and, after much difficulty, the Japanese agreed to fire a royal salute of twenty-one guns for each flag as it was raised in Yedo, the salute to be returned from the foreign warships.[20]

At the same time certain complaints regarding affairs at Yokohama were brought forward and a promise was made that they would be remedied. One of these provisions called for the removal of the Consulates from Kanagawa to Yokohama. Thus the proposal of Lord Ii, of two years before, was finally accepted. It was stipulated by Alcock and de Bellecourt that the Consuls should not reside within the foreign settlement, but on the "Bluff," as "an effective innovation on the stereotyped 'Decima' policy of this Government."[21] As a matter of fact they eventually were located in the heart of the foreign settlement, where they should have been from the very beginning had not the unreasoning suspicion of the Foreign Ministers outweighed the necessities of the case.

While twenty-one cannon roared out a "royal salute," the flags of the two Treaty Powers were unfurled in Yedo, and, as Alcock affirmed, "thus ended the grave crisis—ostensibly to the satisfaction of all parties."[22] But there can be little doubt today that in remaining in Yedo and placing confidence in the good faith of the Japanese Government, in recognizing the difficulties under which it labored, and in endeavoring to co-operate with it, Townsend Harris more adequately met the needs of the hour. And his courage and confidence was not wasted upon the Japanese. One young samurai volunteered as a bodyguard for this undaunted foreigner, ready to lay down his life if some fanatic should attack his master.

---

[20] "After Mr. Heusken's murder all the Ministers but Mr. Harris left Yedo. One of the conditions of their return was that a national salute should be fired when they returned. They accordingly went up. On that day all the forts at Yedo commenced firing early in the morning at sunrise and fired all morning. When the ministers arrived they stopped for a few minutes and then the fort at Shinagawa fired the salute and then in a few minutes all the forts fired away again till sunset. The consequence was no one in Yedo but those in the secret knew that any salute had been fired" (Pruyn Papers, November 20, 1862).

[21] *1861, Lords 18,* p. 73.   [22] Alcock, *op. cit.,* II, 62.

He was Ebara Soroku, who became a leader in modern Japanese education and later a member of the House of Peers. Viscount Shibusawa, the financial genius of new Japan, then an officer of the Shogunate, has testified: "This incident won for America the good will of Japan."[23] And on April 2 Harris was received by the Shogun with "every mark of honor" when he presented his new letter of credence.

While Harris, on the ground, had adopted so conciliatory an attitude, his Government, unknown to him, stood forth as the advocate of a strong policy. On learning of the murder of Heusken, Mr. Seward, Secretary of State, on May 14 addressed a circular note[24] to the Ministers of Prussia, Great Britain, France, Russia, and Holland, proposing a joint naval demonstration in Japanese waters. Instead of postponing the opening of Yedo, as Harris had suggested, the President believed that no concession should be made, and he proposed

that those powers should announce to the government of Japan their willingness and their purpose to make common cause and co-operate with this government in exacting satisfaction, if the Japanese government should not at once put forth all possible effort to secure the punishment of the assassins of Mr. Heusken, and also in making requisitions with signal vigor if any insult or injury should be committed against any foreigner residing in Yedo, after the opening of the city in January next, according to the treaty.

With these suggestions was submitted a form of a convention for carrying them into effect: "This projected convention contemplated the despatch of a fleet of steamers adequate to impress the Japanese government with the ability and the determination of the states engaged, to secure a performance of its treaty stipulations."[25] The Ministers forwarded the proposals and the convention to their respective Governments, but before any answers were received Harris' later dispatch of May 8 cleared up the situation and the matter was happily dropped.

[23] N. Masaoka, editor, *Japan to America*, p. 19.

[24] Seward to Baron Gerolt, Prussian Minister, May 14, in *F.R., 1862*, p. 547. Moore, *A Digest of International Law*, V, 747, cites letter to Mr. Stoeckle, Russian Minister, May 20.   [25] *F.R., 1862*, pp. 814–16.

This proposition was a remarkable one, not merely in view of America's traditional policy, which was opposed to joint operations with European states, but also when the situation in the United States at the time was considered. The Civil War had begun, and the intention to blockade the Southern ports had been declared; surely the Federal Government could ill afford to spare any steamers to take part in a demonstration against Japan. The unusual nature of this suggestion inclines one to believe that it was due to foreign complications quite remote from Japan. These were weeks of great uncertainty in Washington, and of great stress in foreign affairs. Seward, especially, was at a loss how best to proceed. In his famous letter to the President of April 1 he had outlined a foreign policy of amazing vigor. Explanations of certain acts were to be demanded of Great Britain, Russia, Spain, and France, and if the two latter did not give immediate satisfaction, war was to be at once declared.[26] This proposal has been interpreted as a measure for turning the minds of the people away from threatened civil war to the excitement of a foreign contest. Yet a few weeks later Seward proposed the convention for a joint demonstration in the Orient to three of these very powers. Perhaps at this time he was anxious to strengthen the relations of the North with the European states by advocating a policy toward Japan which he felt sure they would indorse.[27] During his administration Mr. Seward consistently instructed the American Ministers in Japan and China to act in concert with their colleagues, and these instructions were carried out by Mr. Pruyn and Mr. Burlingame. But never again did the United States take the lead in proposing joint operations against Japan.

Harris' dispatch of May 8, which caused Seward to alter his

[26] F. Bancroft, *Life of William H. Seward,* II, 133.

[27] On May 21, however, Seward, irritated at Great Britain's proclamation of neutrality, drafted his dispatch No. 10 to Mr. Adams, Minister to St. James, "which, if transmitted and delivered in its original form, could hardly have failed to endanger the peaceful relations of the two countries" (Nicolay and Hay, *Abraham Lincoln,* IV, 269). President Lincoln revised the dispatch so as to remove the needlessly brusque statements. For Seward's Far Eastern policy, see Dennett, *Americans in Eastern Asia,* pp. 407–21.

policy toward Japan, covered a letter from the Tycoon to the President and one from the Ministers for Foreign Affairs to the Secretary of State.[28] The purpose of these was to request the postponement of the opening of the remaining treaty ports and cities. The Ministers pointed out that the present commerce "has led to a result generally experienced and very different from what was anticipated: no benefit has been derived, but the lower class of the nation has suffered from it already." Prices had risen, they asserted, and this fact had augmented the ancient opposition to foreign intercourse. They pleaded for delay, for seven years in fact, until "public opinion should be reassured and gradually prepared, commerce organized by degrees, prices of things find their level, and the old custom changed in such a manner that a prosperous intercourse with foreign countries may become the wish of the nation." Harris reported that this might seem to be a retrograde action, but it would not be considered such in view of the facts. Prices, he said, of all articles of export had risen in the past two years from one hundred to three hundred per cent, and complaints from officials of fixed and limited salaries were loud. He had already advised postponing the opening of Yedo, and he now perceived that the residence of foreigners in Osaka, which was located near Kyoto, might occasion hostility. Hiogo was merely the seaport of Osaka, and Niigata was of little value as a port. He requested, therefore, discretionary power to act in concert with his colleagues as might seem advisable for the interests of both countries. This request was granted by the President, and the discretion was conferred, while Seward urgently insisted that, except in the extremest necessity, no postponement be consented to unless satisfaction of some marked kind was received for the murder of Mr. Heusken.[29]

---

[28] *F.R., 1862*, pp. 794–97. The Ministers for Foreign Affairs had, on May 1, advised Harris that they could enter into no new treaties for the present, and he so informed the Foreign Offices of Austria-Hungary, Spain, Sardinia, Denmark, Norway and Sweden, and Brazil (No. 19, May 4). Yet at about this time they asked Harris to engage two mineralogists and mining engineers (No. 18, April 25); and in June they desired to purchase two merchant vessels (No. 22, June 18).   [29] No. 18, August 1, *F.R., 1862*, p. 815.

Ever since that unhappy outrage Harris had been kept informed of the efforts of the authorities to punish the assassins. He was convinced that they were acting in good faith and earnestly desired to discover and punish them. A large number of Japanese had been arrested on suspicion and some executed for other crimes.[30] Three of Heusken's mounted escort and four of the guards at the guardhouse were dismissed for neglect of duty, and, as he said, "to a Japanese official such a punishment is next to a death penalty; for it deprives him of all means of support, except beggary, as he would prefer suicide to what he would consider as the degradation of labor."[31] But the Government was never able to arrest and convict the real offenders, and before the incident was settled a far greater outrage had been perpetrated.

For the past three months the utmost quiet had prevailed in Yedo. During that time Mr. Alcock had visited China and on his return had traveled overland, in company with Mr. De Witt, the Dutch Consul General, from Nagasaki to Yedo. On July 4 he returned to the British Legation, and on the next night a "daring and murderous" attack was made.[32] A band of fourteen ronins, sworn to drive out the hated barbarians, flung themselves upon the Japanese guards at the Legation, burst into the temple residence, and wounded two of the Englishmen, Mr. Oliphant, the Secretary of the Legation, and Mr. Morrison, British Consul at Nagasaki, who was a guest. This time the guards, when they had recovered from the first shock of the attack, fought desperately, killing three of the ronins on the spot and wounding one. Of the Japanese at the Legation two were killed, and five severely and ten slightly wounded.

Such an attack upon the Representative of one of the great Powers aroused the profoundest indignation. Mr. Alcock was inclined to believe that the attack, if not instigated by the Government, was at least made with the knowledge of some or all of

[30] No. 21, June 7, *F.R., 1862*, pp. 797–98.

[31] No. 49, November 23, *ibid.*, p. 805.

[32] *1862, Com. 64*, pp. 1–25; No. 28, July 9, *F.R., 1861*, pp. 437–41; No. 30, July 12, *F.R., 1862*, pp. 799–800; Alcock, *op. cit.*, II, 151–70.

the Great Council, for "these acts of violence are all in perfect accordance with the desire they do not conceal, to extricate the country from the obligations of Treaties, and revert to the ancient policy of isolation, even at the price of a violent rupture."[33] He also placed no confidence in the Japanese guards, and secured a guard of twenty-five men from the British warship "Ringdove" the next day. In notifying his colleagues of the attack he requested their views as to what should be done.

On his part, Harris considered "the present as a crisis in the foreign affairs of Japan." If the Government was too weak to punish the guilty parties, then Great Britain might take some decided action. But he found one reason for encouragement in the stiff fight put up by the guards: "This is the first instance in which a blow has been struck in defence of a foreigner in this country, and may be considered as proof of the desire of the government to give us protection."[34]

On the eighth, Harris addressed the Ministers for Foreign Affairs, and pointed out that any failure to arrest and punish the authors of the most recent crime would result in the "most lamentable consequences."[35] For the preceding attacks no one had been arrested or punished, but this time a prisoner had been taken and a list of fourteen accomplices had been found. From these two sources enough information should be obtained to ferret out the guilty and adequately punish them. Three days later Harris had an interview with the Ministers for Foreign Affairs in which he pressed home the advice given in his letter. They told him that

[33] *1862, Com. 64*, p. 5.

[34] *F.R., 1861*, p. 437. "There is a party in this country who are opposed to the presence of any foreigners in Japan, and, in addition to this, there is a very strong dislike to the English in particular, which feeling seems to attach especially to Mr. Alcock. He was absent from this city for some three months, during which time the utmost quiet prevailed; yet within thirty-six hours after his return the attack in question was made on him." Alcock replied to this by stating that if it were true it might be more naturally accounted for by the statements made by Harris concerning the English during his negotiations of 1858 (Alcock, *op. cit.*, I, 215). An exchange of letters between Alcock and Harris at this time showed that good relations had not been restored (*F.R., 1861*, pp. 439–40; *1862*, p. 801).

[35] *F.R., 1861*, p. 439.

the attack had been delivered by fourteen men belonging to a band of desperate outlaws, "willing to make themselves the exponents of the national feelings, and who gloried in sacrificing their lives in such a cause. They attacked the British legation, hoping not only to distinguish themselves by slaying all the members of the mission, but also to bring about a war with the foreigners, and thereby a return to their old state of isolation." The Ministers furthermore said that the desperadoes were men of low degree, and were without instigators or abettors among men of high rank or station; and they hoped that as Harris "had been so long in the country, and knew its condition better than any other foreigner," he would give his testimony in support of their representations. Of the fourteen engaged in the attack seven[36] were accounted for, and every effort would be made to arrest those who had escaped; but this would be difficult, as was shown by the failure to secure all the men who had murdered Lord Ii more than a year ago. They furthermore protested that Alcock had refused to allow the Japanese guard to be posted as they had desired, and said that they were ready to afford the same protection to the Foreign Representatives that they themselves enjoyed.[37]

Alcock naturally had been carrying on an extended correspondence with the Ministers. On the seventh he described the attack, complained against the supineness and tardiness of the Japanese guard, pointed out the grievous nature of the outrage, insinuated that some daimyo must be the instigator of the deed, and asserted that "unless signal satisfaction be given, and ample security for the future, the common voice of Europe will hold the Government responsible for the acts of its subjects."[38] He followed this up on the eleventh with a letter in which he required the Ministers "without delay, to answer categorically and truly the following queries" concerning the steps taken by the Government in the matter.[39]

[36] Three were killed on the spot, one was wounded and captured, and three committed hara-kiri at Shinagawa, of whom one was taken alive.

[37] *F.R., 1862*, pp. 799–800.   [38] *1862, Com. 64*, pp. 7–8.

[39] *Ibid.*, p. 19. The Ministers frequently asked for delay in order to translate Alcock's long dispatches properly.

This dispatch, with its insinuations and demands, might well have been ignored by the Ministers. On the thirteenth they replied to his letter of the seventh, requesting that he withdraw the British guard, lest in their ignorance of the language they wound friends as well as foes, and stating that the crime had been the work of persons of low standing without any secret instigator of rank.[40]

A conference between Alcock and the Japanese Ministers took place on the twentieth. They made practically the same explanation that they had given Harris, but they frankly stated that although they would do all they could to protect the foreigners, yet in the present state of the country such attacks were inevitable; they themselves were menaced from the same hostile motives, "nor could any Government be held responsible for the isolated acts of individuals, or outrages perpetrated by bands of their lawless subjects." At this interview the Ministers presented to Alcock letters from the Tycoon and themselves asking for the postponement of the opening of the ports.[41] In the three weeks which had elapsed since the attack, Alcock found the question at issue narrowed down to this: Does the Government lack the will or the power to protect the flags and the Representatives of the Treaty Powers? His final opinion was that the Government had no "deliberate intention" to allow them to be sacrificed by assassins or by the followers of any daimyo.[42]

After his interview with the Ministers for Foreign Affairs Alcock notified his colleagues that "what line of conduct and course of general policy may eventually be best adapted to meet the exigencies of such a position, is a grave question, and full of difficulty, but one for the decision of Governments rather than Diplomatic Agents."[43] Therefore no exchange of views occurred

---

[40] *Ibid.*, p. 20.   [41] *Ibid.*, pp. 13–16.

[42] *Ibid.*, pp. 23, 28; *F.R., 1862,* p. 802. At this time Alcock had the idea, later proved to be quite erroneous, that the attack was instigated by the Prince of Tsushima in revenge for an insult offered by the Russians the preceding year (*1862, Com. 64,* p. 23; Alcock, *op. cit.,* II, 161–64).

[43] *1862, Com. 64,* p. 18. Harris declined to confer with Alcock on this subject. (See No. 32, July 31.) He later exchanged views with de Bellecourt on the state of affairs (No. 34, August 20).

among the Representatives in Japan. It should be noted that on this occasion the Dutch Consul General announced that he would not return to Yedo until further instructed by his Government, for the same reasons which had caused him to withdraw earlier in the year,[44] but Alcock and de Bellecourt remained in their Legations. It might be argued that far greater reason was given by the last attack for withdrawing from Yedo than in the case of the murder of Mr. Heusken; but this time Alcock reported that an advantage had been gained through remaining, for it held in check those who thought the Foreign Representatives could be driven from the capital by violence and intimidation.[45] Mr. Harris must have taken some comfort from his colleague's change in policy.

On the receipt of Harris' dispatch describing the attack on the British Legation, Mr. Seward assured the British Government directly "of the willingness of the United States to co-operate with it in any judicious measure it may suggest to insure safety hereafter to diplomatic and consular representatives of the western powers in Japan, with due respect to the sovereignties in whose behalf their exposure to such grave perils is incurred."[46]

When Harris finally received discretionary power to agree to a postponement of the opening of the ports it was coupled with an instruction to first secure satisfaction "of some marked kind" for the murder of Mr. Heusken. This demand caused him to review the whole incident and to determine what form the satisfaction should take. His dispatch to Mr. Seward of November 23 shows how thoughtfully he considered the whole question and

[44] No. 31, July 15, *F.R., 1862*, p. 801.

[45] *1862, Com. 64*, p. 27. Oliphant's views, as expressed to Sir Harry Parkes at Hong Kong, in September 1861 while on his way to England, were that "we must cease, for a time at least, to be the thorn in the side of the Japanese that foreigners and foreign treaties have been during the last three years; that they, the Japanese, must be allowed time to digest those treaties, which were rammed down their throats too hastily in the first instance and which are evidently disagreeing with them; that, in a word, we must slack the strain, or the string of our connection with them will snap" (Dickins and Lane-Poole, *Life of Sir Harry Parkes*, I, 450). If, as was expected at the time, Oliphant had succeeded Alcock, this slackening of the strain might have taken place.

[46] No. 23, October 21, *F.R., 1861*, p. 441.

gives further confirmation of his keen sense of fair play.[47] The satisfaction, he believed, might be accorded in one or another of three forms: "1st, by the arrest and punishment of the assassins; 2d, by a salute to our flag; or 3d, by a money payment as an indemnity." On an examination of the facts he could acquit the Japanese Government of any complicity in the murder, and he was convinced that "they have loyally and seriously endeavored to arrest and punish his assassins." A salute to the flag, under the circumstances, with no American ship to receive it, would mean nothing. A money indemnity presented two difficulties: It might be taken as a satisfaction for the murder, or as a "condition precedent" for postponing the treaty stipulation, but he had not "the least doubt that the ministers will readily agree to any demand I may make, provided it be in their power to comply with it." He knew whereof he spoke, for when he met with them in conference on the twenty-seventh they agreed to give any satisfaction in their power, assured Harris that they were making every effort to arrest and punish the murderers, and willingly agreed to pay for the support of Heusken's widowed mother the sum of $10,000, which was not to be considered payment for his blood, or an atonement for the murder, or a release from the obligation to arrest the murderers.[48]

Harris promptly notified his colleagues that he had received satisfaction for the murder of Heusken, and that he possessed discretionary power as to postponing the opening of the ports. He stated that he was convinced that it was not desirable to open Yedo at present, and he requested their opinions as to the other ports.[49] Alcock and de Bellecourt, however, were not ready to take up the question at that time. The former had recommended to Lord Russell, on August 16, that the postponement be granted, and had proposed to make a rule, under the Order in Council,

[47] Instruction No. 18, August 1, *F.R., 1862,* pp. 814–16; Dispatch No. 49, November 23, *ibid.,* pp. 804–6.

[48] No. 50, November 27, *F.R., 1862,* p. 806. Compare this sum with the £125,000 demanded for the murder of Richardson. The latter sum was exemplary rather than compensatory.

[49] November 27, *ibid.,* pp. 807–9.

suspending the opening of Yedo.[50] Oliphant, who had been wounded in the attack on July 5, had been sent home with dispatches and first-hand information for the Foreign Secretary. He arrived in London on October 28, and on November 23 Lord Russell sent out instructions covering the attack on the Legation and the postponement.[51] These, in brief, insisted upon the payment of a pecuniary indemnity for Oliphant and Morrison and the granting of a full equivalent for the postponement. Almost four months passed before Alcock attempted to follow out these instructions.

On December 6 Harris was received by the Shogun in order to deliver the President's reply to the letter of May 2. It stated, very briefly, that Mr. Harris would be instructed regarding the postponement of the opening of the ports. A similar reply had been given by Mr. Seward to the letter from the Ministers for Foreign Affairs, which added that the subject was complicated by "the yet unpunished and unatoned homicide of Mr. Heusken," but it gave assurance that "the spirit of this government is liberal and friendly towards Japan."[52]

Early in the new year two events occurred which testified to the unstable equilibrium of Japanese politics. On January 23, 1862, the second Japanese mission to the Treaty Powers steamed, in a British frigate, down the Bay of Yedo.[53] It consisted of three Ministers Plenipotentiary and a retinue of thirty-two officers and servants, under instructions to visit the Governments of Great Britain, France, Prussia, Russia, the Netherlands, and Portugal. This opening of direct relations with the European Powers was considered a hopeful sign, although the principal object of their mission was to urge the postponement of opening the additional ports.

[50] *1862, Com. 64*, p. 33.

[51] *Ibid.*, pp. 72–73. A provisional postponement was agreed to by the Foreign Representatives on December 27 (No. 59, December 30, 1861; No. 2, January 1, 1862).

[52] No. 53, December 7. President Lincoln to the Tycoon of Japan, August 1, 1861, *F.R., 1862*, p. 822; Seward to the Ministers for Foreign Affairs, August 1, *ibid.*, p. 821.   [53] Alcock, *op. cit.*, II, 377–83.

The other event was the attempt, on February 14, by a band of eight ronins,[54] to assassinate Ando Tsushima-no-Kami, one of the Ministers for Foreign Affairs. This time the escort was on the alert, and although the Minister was twice wounded his life was saved, and seven of the eight assailants were cut down on the spot. Of all the Ministers, Ando was considered the one best disposed toward foreigners, and on this account he had been singled out for destruction.[55] This event, coupled with the murder of Lord Ii, should have convinced any doubters of the difficulty which the Government was experiencing in dealing with desperadoes of this type, who considered themselves patriots.

On March 17 Alcock reported to Russell his endeavors to settle the two questions at issue—reparation for the Legation attack and postponement of opening the ports.[56] As to the first, the Japanese promptly met his demands. An indemnity of $10,000 was granted for Oliphant and Morrison, a new site for the British Legation was conceded, and the execution of two of the assailants recently captured was promised. When he demanded some equivalent for the postponement of the treaty concessions, however, the Japanese frankly confessed that they could not agree. It was their hope, if there were no further development in foreign intercourse, to allay the present national antipathy within the next six years; but if any of the new ports were opened, or any equivalent were demanded, they despaired of being able to carry out their plans. Alcock appreciated the force of these arguments, and promised on his return to London to ask his Government to send out fresh instructions and authority to make large concessions "upon the understanding always that some equivalent or corresponding advantage should be gained to compensate the loss, either in the public repeal of all hostile law and the sanction of Treaties, the improvement of our position at the open ports, or other ports in lieu." As Alcock was about to depart for England on sick leave,

---

[54] Retainers of Hori Oribe-no-Kami, who had committed hara-kiri because of a reprimand from Ando (*Cambridge Modern History*, XI, 844).

[55] Alcock, *op. cit.*, II, 395–97; *F.R., 1863*, II, 1067; Baba, *Japan, 1853–1864, or Genji Yume Monogatari*, pp. 41–42.   [56] *1863 (3709)*, pp. 15–22.

hc offered to take with him Moriyama, the interpreter, as a bearer of dispatches to the Japanese envoys there. This offer was accepted. In spite of the better relations which had been established, Alcock left on March 23 without an audience of leave of the Shogun, because he considered certain features of the proposed ceremonial derogatory to himself.

On his arrival in England the matter was taken up with the Japanese envoys, and on June 6 a memorandum was signed by Lord Russell and the Japanese.[57] This postponed until January 1, 1868, the opening of Niigata and Hiogo and the residence of British subjects in Yedo and Osaka. These concessions were made in order to enable the Japanese Ministers to overcome the existing opposition, but "they expect the Tycoon and his Ministers will in all other respects strictly execute at the ports of Nagasaki, Hakodadi, and Kanagawa, all the other stipulations of the Treaty; that they will publicly revoke the old law outlawing foreigners; and that they will specifically abolish and do away with" certain specified restrictions on commerce and social intercourse.[58] In default of the strict fulfillment of these conditions the concessions would be withdrawn and the Tycoon would be called

---

[57] *1863* (*3709*), pp. 6–8.

[58] These were: "1. All restrictions, whether as regards quantity or price, on the sale by Japanese to foreigners of all kinds of merchandise according to Article XIV of the Treaty of 26th of August, 1858. 2. All restrictions on labour, and more particularly on the hire of carpenters, boatmen, boats, and coolies, teachers, and servants of whatever denomination. 3. All restrictions whereby Daimios are prevented from sending their produce to market, and from selling the same directly by their own agents. 4. All restrictions resulting from attempts on the part of the Custom-house authorities and other officials to obtain fees. 5. All restrictions limiting the classes of persons who shall be allowed to trade with foreigners at the ports of Nagasaki, Hakodadi, and Kanagawa. 6. All restrictions imposed on free intercourse of a social kind between foreigners and the people of Japan." In addition to the question of postponement, the Japanese raised twelve other questions, most of them concerned with details, and these were properly left to be discussed and settled in Japan. But Lord Russell flatly refused to give up the escort of British cavalry which had been established at the Legation in Yedo [*1863* (*3079*), pp. 7, 13, 15, 28]. It should be noted that Russell did not act upon Alcock's suggestion that the treaties be ratified by the Mikado. The mission visited all the European Treaty Powers and secured their consent to the postponement of opening the ports on terms similar to those in the British memorandum (Alcock, *op. cit.*, II, 407).

upon to open the ports. In addition the envoys agreed to submit to the Tycoon the policy and expediency of opening Tsushima,[59] of placing glassware among the articles dutiable at five per cent, and of establishing bonded warehouses.

It has been necessary to follow this question of postponing the opening of the ports in order to note the conditions with which it was surrounded. During the next six years it was possible at almost any time to cite some violation, real or imagined, of this London Convention as a reason for demanding the immediate opening of the ports and cities.

Townsend Harris' term of service was now drawing to its close. On July 10, 1861, he had desired Mr. Seward to lay before the President his request to be recalled, on the ground of impaired health and advancing years.[60] His resignation was accepted in October by the President, with "profound regret,"[61] and Robert H. Pruyn, of New York, was appointed as his successor. He was expected to arrive early in January, as Harris had requested.

When the Shogunate Government learned that Harris was to be recalled it addressed a letter to Seward testifying to his ability, his knowledge of the country, and his friendly attitude, and begging that he be allowed to remain.[62] This letter, of course, could

[59] In 1861, from March to September, a Russian force was established on Tsushima Island, and its withdrawal was largely due to the representations of the British admiral directly, and of the British Government through its ambassador at Petrograd (Michie, *The Englishman in China*, II, 111–15). See Harris' No. 39, October 7, and No. 43, October 22, 1861. Seward advised Harris that if Japan was still alarmed he would ask the President for authority to seek an explanation from Russia. No. 6, February 5, 1862. In his instructions to Alcock of November 23, 1861, Russell had included the opening of Tsushima and the neighboring coast of Korea among the equivalents to be demanded.

[60] No. 29, *F.R., 1862,* p. 799. Mr. E. H. House, a friend of Harris' later years, states that he resigned "under a mistaken sense of his obligations" on the inauguration of the Republican administration (*Atlantic Monthly,* Vol. 47, p. 610). But the dates do not confirm this, and the statement made in his letter of resignation probably describes the case correctly. In a private note to Seward, Harris asked him to support his request.

[61] Instruction No. 24, October 21, *F.R., 1862,* p. 816.

[62] December 5, 1861, *ibid.,* p. 812. A similar letter was sent to Lord Russell concerning Alcock, on March 20, 1862, just before he left Japan on leave [*1863 (3079),* p. 10].

have no effect in view of Harris' expressed wishes and the appointment of his successor, but its expression of esteem was repeated when Harris took his leave. On April 25, 1862, Mr. Pruyn arrived at Kanagawa, and the next day Harris had his farewell audience of the Shogun and thus ended his five strenuous years as pioneer Consul and Minister in Japan.

No one can study this troubled period of Japanese affairs without gaining a high admiration for the services of Townsend Harris, but unhappily too few have scanned this, one of the most creditable pages of America's diplomatic history. Mr. John W. Foster, himself a diplomat and a Secretary of State, has paid Harris this tribute: "He reflected great honor upon his country, and justly deserved to rank among the first diplomats of the world, if such rank is measured by accomplishments."[63] Japanese encomiums are not wanting, for beyond question he is better known and appreciated in Japan than in his own land.[64] The estimate of Longford, British Consul and historian, is a noble one: "The story of how, unbacked by any display of force under his country's flag, he succeeded by his own personal efforts in overcoming the traditional hatred of centuries to even the smallest association with foreigners, is one of marvelous tact and patience, of steady determination and courage, of straightforward uprightness in every respect, that is not exceeded by any in the entire history of the international relations of the world."[65] Mr. Seward fittingly said: "It is a deserved crown of his long period of public service that the same high appreciation of his merits and usefulness is entertained by the government which sent him abroad and by the government near which he has been accredited."[66]

[63] Foster, *American Diplomacy in the Orient*, p. 186.

[64] Nitobe, *The Intercourse between the United States and Japan*, p. 115; Shibusawa, in *Japan to America*, p. 19; Hishida, *International Position of Japan as a Great Power*, pp. 111, 114, 117; Griffis, *Townsend Harris, First American Envoy in Japan*, pp. 331–33. After his return to the United States Mr. Harris lived quietly in New York City until his death on February 25, 1878. In 1909, when the Japanese Commercial Mission visited this country, its members found the grave of Harris in Greenwood Cemetery, Brooklyn, and placed a floral tribute upon it.   [65] Longford, *The Story of Old Japan*, p. 302.

[66] To the Ministers for Foreign Affairs, March 5, 1862, *F.R., 1862*, p. 822.

The opening of Japan to foreign intercourse after two hundred years of seclusion was not the work of any man or of any single agency. A combination of circumstances and a group of forward-looking Japanese and foreigners made it possible. But if one man is entitled to a full measure of praise it is Townsend Harris. His honesty and his fair-mindedness while isolated at Shimoda won the respect and the confidence of the Japanese. That victory gained, the negotiation of his great Treaty was no difficult matter, and Japan peacefully conceded almost all that China had been forced to grant after two unhappy wars. If the story of Japan's relations with the Western Powers reads so differently from that of China's bitter experience, much of the credit is due to Townsend Harris as well as to Lord Hotta and Lord Ii. After he had negotiated his revolutionary treaty Harris remained for two years to help the Japanese enter upon their new relations. He was the first to recognize the immediate difficulties created by foreign intercourse and the first to recommend that some of the concessions granted in his treaty be postponed. While the blades of the ronins were flashing he kept his poise, and his refusal to join his colleagues in their withdrawal from Yedo brought into relief the futility of their action. Above all, he tried to understand the Japanese point of view and to reconcile his country's interests and those of Japan, and in doing so he was a real statesman, for he was building for all time. The student of international relations may well consider how these problems might have been solved in Japan if all the Foreign Representatives and their home Governments could have recognized in time the fundamental wisdom of the policy of Townsend Harris.

CHAPTER VII

ROBERT H. PRUYN, MINISTER-RESIDENT
1862–63

In the selection of a successor to Townsend Harris the United States was again most fortunate in its choice of a Representative in Japan. In spite of the serious situation which had developed with the progress of the Civil War and the strained relations with England and France in the first year, Mr. Seward considered the mission to Japan one of extreme importance, and desired to have some one there whom he knew thoroughly and on whose sound judgment he could rely. Such a representative he found in Robert Hewson Pruyn, of Albany, New York. Mr. Pruyn was born in that city on February 14, 1815, of Flemish ancestry. Educated at the Albany Academy and at Rutgers College, he had been admitted to the bar in 1836, and had promptly entered upon a career of public service. First serving as attorney and corporation counsel for his native city, he later entered the State Assembly, and in 1854 was elected speaker of the House by the Whig majority. During these years he was the intimate friend of Mr. Seward and his strong political supporter. With the success of the Republican party in 1860 Mr. Pruyn was assured of an important appointment; but on the resignation of Mr. Harris, Mr. Seward, after consultation with President Lincoln, made a strong personal request that Mr. Pruyn accept the Japanese mission. He was loath to do this. At such a time, when the fate of the nation was at stake, it required a high sense of civic duty for a man to accept so dangerous, difficult, and remote a post. Mr. Pruyn did accept, however, and the event justified the confidence which Mr. Seward had placed in him. In his letter of instructions of November 15, 1861, Seward pointed out the difficulties which Pruyn would have to face, owing to the loss of national prestige during

the war and to the hostility of the Japanese to foreign intercourse:

> You will find no open questions for discussion in your mission. It is
> important to preserve friendly and intimate relations with the representa-
> tives of other western powers in Japan. You will seek no exclusive ad-
> vantages, and will consult freely with them upon all subjects, insomuch
> as it is especially necessary, at this time, that the prestige of western
> civilization be maintained in Yedo as completely as possible. In short,
> you will need to leave behind you all memories of domestic or of European
> jealousies or antipathies, and will, by an equal, just, and honorable con-
> duct of your mission, make the simple people of Japan respect, not only
> the institutions of your own country, but the institutions of christianity
> and of western civilization.[1]

On April 25, 1862, Mr. Pruyn arrived at Kanagawa, and was
conveyed to Yedo in the Shogun's steam-yacht "Emperor," the
gift of the British Government to the Tycoon.[2] His reception in
Yedo and by the Ministers for Foreign Affairs and the Council
of State was marked by the utmost cordiality. On May 17 he was
received in audience by the Shogun and presented his credentials.
Here also the evidence of good will was marked. The ceremony
was the same as that used in the case of Mr. Harris, the Japanese
refusing to make any unfavorable distinction between the Minister-Resident and his colleagues—Alcock, then absent on leave,
being an Envoy Extraordinary and Minister Plenipotentiary, and
de Bellecourt, a Minister Plenipotentiary.[3]

---

[1] No. 2, *F.R., 1862,* p. 817. The instructions for 1862 are numbered 5–29;
of these twenty-five, four were printed in *F.R., 1862,* ten in *F.R., 1863,* II, and
one in *37th Cong., 2d Sess., S. Ex. Doc. No. 33 (Serial Number 1149).* Harris'
dispatches are numbered 1–15, and Pruyn's 1, 2, 16–68; of these seventy, one was
printed in *F.R., 1862,* fourteen in *F.R., 1863,* II, one in *F.R., 1866,* II, and one
in *Serial Number 1149.*

[2] Mr. Pruyn was delayed on his way to Japan through the illness and death
of his son in San Francisco. Because of the war no national vessel was available
to convey him to Japan, as had been planned; and although the Russian Government placed the corvette "Caravala" at his disposal, he thought it unwise to sail
under a foreign flag. He, therefore, chartered the American sailing-ship
"Ringleader." No trans-Pacific steamships were then in operation.

[3] No. 20, May 17, *F.R., 1862,* p. 812. Pruyn understood that this was why
Alcock refused to take an audience of leave. Portman told Pruyn that his
audience contained unusually friendly features, such as the escort back to the
Legation. The audience is described in Pruyn Papers, May 1862.

The American Minister took up his residence in the temple Legation where Harris had held his ground during almost three eventful years. He also was for a time the only Foreign Representative in Yedo. The temple grounds were defended by a double palisade of bamboo, with frequent guardhouses. At least one hundred and sixty soldiers, later increased to two hundred and eighty-four, part being two-sword yakunins of the Shogun's forces and part troops of the daimyo in charge of protecting the Legation, were continually at their posts. No one was allowed to enter the inclosure except those whose business was known, and when any of the residents went abroad on horseback, thirty-two mounted yakunins and twenty-two fleet-footed bettoes (grooms) accompanied them. None of the Americans ever went armed, in distinction from the other foreigners, who generally wore sabers and revolvers.

In one respect Mr. Pruyn entered upon his mission under favorable circumstances. There can be little doubt that the friendliness, sympathy, and good will of Townsend Harris had caused the Japanese to feel more kindly disposed toward Americans than toward any other nationals. Mr. Pruyn felt this at once, and the Japanese in turn continued to look to him as their adviser and mediator as they had in the case of Harris. In fact the next year the French Minister confessed that the American Minister alone could secure results, and that soon "everything will have to be done through the Americans."[4]

In every other respect, however, Mr. Pruyn's position was a most difficult one. The Civil War at home caused doubts as to the very survival of the Government which he represented. It prevented the presence of an American fleet in Eastern waters to support his position, and this fact led the British and French Ministers, with ships at their call, to act together. Just as Harris won his great Treaty without the support of a squadron, so Pruyn maintained the honor and dignity of the United States practically without material backing.[5] And the three years covered by his

[4] Pruyn Papers, March 12, 1863.
[5] It must be remembered that Colonel Neale and Sir Rutherford Alcock

mission were the years which saw the culmination of the anti-foreign movement. He had to face crises far more serious than those which Harris knew. If Perry opened the gates of Japan, and Harris threw them open wide, then Robert H. Pruyn is entitled to no little credit for preventing their being closed again.

In preceding chapters the rise of the anti-foreign movement and its intricate relation with the anti-Shogunate and pro-Mikado propaganda have been pointed out. While Lord Ii lived, the Imperial court and the rebellious daimyos were cowed, the trouble-making ronins were suppressed in Yedo with a heavy hand, and, although it occasioned civil war within the clan, the Imperial order to the lord of Mito was finally turned over to the Shogunate. With the assassination of Lord Ii in 1860, however, there was no one strong enough to take his place, and the anti-foreign feeling, so long suppressed, surged forth again. "From this time the advocates of the expulsion of the 'barbarians' increased every day," says the Japanese historian.[6] Then followed the outrages already described—the murder of Heusken, the first attack on the British Legation, and the frequent alarms in Yedo and Yokohama, all well founded, for the surrounding country was infested with anti-foreign ronins.[7] On September 17, 1861, the old Prince of Mito, Nariaki, leader of the anti-foreign forces and stout antagonist of Lord Ii, died. With his death the leadership of this cause passed to daimyos of western Japan.

One of Lord Ii's measures for reconciling the court and the castle was the arrangement of a marriage between the sister of the Mikado and the boy Shogun. After the death of Lord Ii his successors were able to carry this through. In December the princess arrived in Yedo, and on March 11, 1862, the marriage took place, but, unhappily, its influence was slight. In the mean-

had the support of a powerful fleet and of troops landed in Japan. Mr. Pruyn, practically without support, except for the occasional presence of one or two ships of war, exerted a strong influence upon the leaders of the Shogunate administration.

[6] Yamaguchi Uji, *Kinse Shiriaku. A History of Japan,* translated by Satow, p. 20.

[7] *Ibid.,* p. 21.

time the ronins had struck again, this time at Lord Ando, one of
the Ministers for Foreign Affairs, because of his support of the
pro-foreign policy. "During this period the samurai deserted
from their clans in daily increasing numbers. They allied themselves with the ronins in all parts of the country to raise the cry
of 'honour the Mikado and expel the barbarian.' "[8] Not for two
hundred years had Japan known such internal commotion, and
the Shogunate seemed unable to rise to the demands of the hour.

At this time the clans of Satsuma and Choshiu (Nagato) assumed the leadership which they held throughout this troubled
period, and which they hold even to the present time. The daimyo
of Choshiu, Mori Daizen-no-Daibu, had frequently urged the
Shogunate to act in harmony with and under the orders of the
Mikado, pointing out that the treaties had been signed before the
Mikado's approval had been obtained, and that this sort of arbi-
trary government might lead to the overthrow of the Shogunate.[9]
About the same time Shimadzu Idzumi, brother of the late and
father of the then daimyo of Satsuma, while on his way to Yedo,
was addressed by a band of ronins at Himeji, on May 4, and called
upon to lead them against the Shogun's castles at Osaka and Nijo,
in Kyoto, and against the castle at Hikone of the Ii family, then
to drive the Shogunate officials out of Kyoto, to free the princes
and nobles there, and to escort the Mikado over the mountains, in
order to punish the crimes of the Shogunate.[10] Instead of proceeding to Yedo, Shimadzu turned off to Kyoto, and presented
the memorial of the ronins to the Mikado. The Emperor was delighted, and ordered Shimadzu to remain in Kyoto "to quiet the
excitement among the ronins of all parts, and give tranquillity to
the Empire."[11] A few days later the daimyo of Choshiu arrived
in Kyoto and was associated with Shimadzu in control of the
loyal ronins. These two nobles now stood forth as advocates of
the Imperial demands.

---

[8] Yamaguchi, *op. cit.,* p. 24.

[9] Baba, *Japan, 1853–1864, or Genji Yume Monogatari,* p. 49. See his letter
to the Shogun, in *1864 (3242),* p. 27.

[10] Baba, *op. cit.,* p. 45.   [11] *Ibid.,* p. 48.

Although four years had passed since the Treaties of 1858 had been negotiated, the Foreign Ministers were still uncertain as to the serious flaw in their validity—the lack of the Mikado's sanction. As we have seen, Townsend Harris had perceived the formal authority of the Mikado, and had twice threatened to carry his negotiations to Kyoto. But he believed that the Treaties had been ratified by the Mikado, except so far as they related to Osaka, and he so informed his successor.[12] Rutherford Alcock had first been impressed with the lack of validity while making his overland journey from Osaka to Yedo, in June 1861.[13] When, however, on August 14 he asked the Ministers for Foreign Affairs if the Mikado had sanctioned the British Treaty, they replied in the affirmative.[14] However, in the following March he suggested that "the sanction of Treaties" be one of the equivalents secured for postponing the opening of the ports, but Lord Russell did not accept the proposal. The French Minister, de Bellecourt, in June did not believe that they had been ratified, but the difference of opinion and information on this score caused the Ministers to determine, on June 27, 1862, "to raise no questions which would imply a doubt as to the validity of the treaties." It was left for Mr. Pruyn to point out clearly and forcefully the absolute necessity of obtaining the Mikado's approval.

It was in such a milieu of doubt and uncertainty, alarms, and sudden death that Mr. Pruyn began his mission. Happily he possessed a disposition which made for usefulness at such a time. First of all, he had the utmost consideration for the Japanese people as a whole, and especially for the harassed officers of the Shogunate. He recognized with unusual clearness, in view of the lack of accurate information, the difficult position in which they were placed, between the foreigners who demanded the fulfillment

[12] No. 35, June 30, 1862, *F.R., 1863,* II, 1035.

[13] "I think this gave me the first clear insight as to the actual relations established by the treaties entered into on the part of the Tycoon. He had made treaties, but the Mikado had never ratified or sanctioned them, and the *Daimios could not therefore be compelled to observe them*" (Alcock, *The Capital of the Tycoon,* II, 137).

[14] *1862, Com. 64,* p. 31.

of the Treaties to the letter, and the rising tide of Imperial opposition. He never doubted their anxiety to protect him and all foreigners, even when relations were most strained, and he was ever ready to distinguish between the acts of the Shogunate and those of the hostile Japanese who dealt their blows both at the foreigners and at the Yedo administration. Furthermore he preferred to think for himself and arrive at his own conclusions unswayed by the clamor of the treaty ports. In one of his early dispatches he wrote:

> I regret to say that many idle rumors are constantly agitating the foreign residents at Yokohama, many of whom are too ready to believe everything to the prejudice of the Japanese. For my part I am amazed, when I consider that two centuries of isolation have moulded the customs and opinions of this people, that there is so much freedom of intercourse and so little appearance of hostility.[15]

And again:

> I had learned to receive with distrust all the rumors and news of which Yokohama is the prolific parent, and which keep it in a state of constant alarm.[16]

Perhaps the fact that his colleagues lived almost all the time in Yokohama, in such an atmosphere, colored their thoughts and actions. As we have seen, Mr. Pruyn relied entirely upon the Japanese guards at the Legation and never asked for American forces. Although adopting such precautionary measures as the officials recommended, he considered them designed in good faith for his protection and not in order to isolate him, and while frequently making excursions through Yedo, and up and down the Tokaido to Yokohama, he never reported a hostile act or gesture.[17] In fact the cheeriness and the good will of the people were most evident.

With his colleagues Mr. Pruyn was on the best of terms except for a brief period at the time of the British ultimatum of April

[15] No. 37, July 8, *F.R., 1863,* II, 1040.

[16] No. 63, December 16, *ibid.,* p. 1056. Also Pruyn to Neale, April 30, 1863, *ibid.,* p. 1088.

[17] No. 22, May 26, *ibid.,* p. 1028; Pruyn Papers, July 7, November 20, 1862.

1863. Mr. Seward had advised the most friendly co-operation, and Pruyn's genial personality made this easy. He was fortunate in having as the British Chargé d'Affaires Lieutenant Colonel Neale, who arrived in May 1862 to take the place of Alcock, then on leave. Colonel Neale was more sympathetic than Alcock, and his views were, at first, quite in accord with Pruyn's. From the first, official meetings were occasionally held for a consideration of the general situation and in order to insure harmonious action. Soon another alarming event occurred. On the night of June 26 a single Japanese made his way through the heavy guards at the British Legation, struck down two of the British sentries, and then committed suicide. Such were the facts; what was the explanation?

Colonel Neale had taken up his residence in Yedo only as long before as the twelfth.[18] His guard consisted of five hundred and thirty-five Japanese soldiers, partly of the Tycoon's bodyguard and partly troops of Matsudaira Tamba-no-Kami, and thirty British sailors and fourteen officers and men of the British bodyguard. If the assailant was animated by unreasoning hatred of all foreigners, surely the British Legation was the last place he could have attacked with impunity. The Japanese officials told Pruyn that one of the Japanese guard "had been suddenly seized with a kind of madness." In his opinion one or all of three reasons might have led to the crime. These were: resentment at the presence of foreign soldiers and sailors as guards; some quarrel between the two kinds of guards; or an act of revenge on the part of relatives of those who had lost their lives in the preceding attack on the Legation.[19] The most reasonable explanation was the second, for Mr. Pruyn learned through his servants that one of the Japanese guards had been kicked by a British guard and had

[18] *1863 (3079)*, pp. 30–32. For an unfavorable estimate of Colonel Neale see Satow, *A Diplomat in Japan*, pp. 29–30. Satow joined the British Legation as a student interpreter on September 8, 1862. He has given us a very valuable record of the events of 1862–69.

[19] No. 31, June 30, *F.R., 1863*, II, 1034. "You know England nor France nor the United States, would allow any such thing as foreign guards to be landed in their cities" (Pruyn Papers, July 7, 1862).

been goaded on to avenge the insult. A somewhat similar story was told years later to Mr. Adams and recorded in his *History of Japan*,[20] and the author of *Kinse Shiriaku* gives about the same explanation.[21]

Mr. Pruyn at once addressed a strong letter to the Ministers for Foreign Affairs testifying to his astonishment and grief at such an outrage, regretting the want of fidelity and courage on the part of the Japanese guards, and urging the utmost promptitude and vigor in the arrest of the guilty participators, lest the repetition of such attacks degrade Japan in the opinion of the whole civilized world.[22] The French and Dutch Representatives addressed similar letters, and a lengthy exchange of notes occurred between Colonel Neale and the Japanese Ministers, in which the former sought some explanation of the attack, demanded additional measures and guaranties of protection, and complained loudly of the cowardice and inefficiency of the Japanese guards. The Ministers made such explanations as they could, and carried out every suggestion for the defense of the Legation. They also addressed a letter to Lord Russell in which they expressed the regret of the Shogun, and pointed out the measures they had taken to protect the British Representative. The question now resolved itself into one of the amount of indemnity, the Japanese, on their part, offering $3,000 for the relatives of the two murdered men;[23] but Lord Russell in his dispatch of September 22 demanded that an indemnity of £10,000 sterling, in gold, be levied upon the estate of the daimyo in charge of the Legation.[24]

As for Mr. Pruyn, he was convinced of the sincerity of the distress manifested by the Shogunate officials, and he had little fear for his own safety. Soon he was the only Foreign Minister left in Yedo, for Colonel Neale retired to Yokohama on July 15

[20] I, 170–72. [21] Yamaguchi, *op. cit.*, p. 28.

[22] *F.R., 1863,* II, 1036.

[23] *1863 (3079)*, p. 57.

[24] *Ibid.*, p. 49. In this dispatch, after stating that the admiral would take proper steps for the protection of the Legation, Russell said that it might be necessary to mount three or four small cannon on the grounds.

to await the completion of the new British Legation at Goten-yama about the end of October.[25]

For the next few weeks there was a lull in the stormy relations of the time. Mr. Pruyn endeavored to straighten out a dispute as to the proper customs duty to be levied on articles imported for use in packing tea, and hence promptly exported again,[26] and Colonel Neale instituted an inquiry among British merchants as to Japanese obstructions and restrictions on trade, but little specific information was obtained.[27] On August 21 he issued a notification that his Government had consented to defer the opening of the other treaty ports and cities for five years from January 1, 1863, and a little later Mr. Pruyn wrote that when he took up the question he would try to secure as a compensation the establishment of a bonded warehouse system and the opening of the island of Tsushima.[28]

Then, out of a clear sky, came one of the most fateful of all the anti-foreign outrages. On September 14 four British subjects, C. L. Richardson, W. Marshall, W. C. Clarke, and Mrs. Borro-daile, a sister-in-law of Mr. Marshall, were riding on the Tokaido within the treaty limits. They had gone about three miles from Kanagawa when they met the train of Shimadzu Saburo, father of the daimyo of Satsuma,[29] and, as we have seen, a leader of the Imperial faction. As to what then happened there is some dispute, but it appears that when they reached the main body of the pro-cession an order was given, a retainer drew his long sword, swung right and left, and fatally wounded Richardson, who, able to ride on for more than a mile, at length fell from his horse and was there put out of his misery. Marshall and Clarke were severely

[25] Pruyn stated that Neale withdrew because the naval captain would not leave more than twenty sailors in Yedo. There had been fifty immediately after the murders (No. 41, August 27, *F.R., 1863*, II, 1042).

[26] No. 36, July 2, *ibid.,* p. 1039. His effort to secure a relinquishment of the duty on such articles was approved (No. 23, September 25). An interesting epi-sode at this time was the return by Mr. Pruyn of a sword stolen in Baltimore, in June 1860, from one of the Japanese mission. It was recovered and trans-mitted to Mr. Pruyn by Mr. Seward.

[27] *1863 (3079)*, pp. 64–73.   [28] No. 41, August 27, *F.R., 1863,* II, 1043.

[29] Own father, but uncle by adoption.

wounded, but Mrs. Borrodaile, though attacked, escaped unharmed.[30]

Great was the excitement when the news reached Yokohama. The foreign community cried out for summary punishment and demanded that an armed force be sent at once to seize the nobleman and his escort.[31] Happily the British admiral refused to be a party to such a wild expedition, and thus immediate hostilities were prevented. Colonel Neale incurred the censure of the British community for his moderate measures, but his Government later approved his judgment and forbearance.

Mr. Pruyn received the news in Yedo late that night; he notified Mr. De Witt, the Dutch Chargé, the next morning, and they requested a joint interview with the Ministers for Foreign Affairs. After some argument the request was granted, and the two Foreign Representatives joined in a strong demand that the leader of the party (whom they understood to be the secretary of the daimyo) be arrested before he escaped to Satsuma. When the Ministers said that they could not arrest so important an officer but would have to ask the daimyo to seize him, Pruyn warned them that if he were not arrested the Tokaido might be seized. The Ministers finally authorized Pruyn and De Witt to assure their colleagues that the guilty parties would be punished whatever their position, and said that they would act promptly and vigorously. They furthermore hoped that the Foreign Ministers would use their influence to prevent the seizure of the Tokaido or any other hostile act.

This unhappy affair presented several complicating features. It was not deliberate murder, without excuse, by some irresponsible ronin. Instead, the blow had been delivered in hot blood, to avenge an insult offered, in ignorance it may be presumed, to one of the most powerful nobles in the land. According to Japanese law, when the procession of a man of high rank was passing it

[30] No. 50, September 18, *F.R., 1863,* II, 1048–51; *1863 (3079),* pp. 73–94; Black, *Young Japan,* I, 124–44; Satow, *op. cit.,* pp. 51–55.

[31] Estimated at from 200 to 1,000 followers. Baba, *op. cit.,* p. 54, says 600 well-armed retainers.

was customary for bystanders to show some mark of respect. Those who were privileged to ride would dismount, and those who stood would fall on their knees.[32] Every foreigner in Japan doubtless knew the danger involved in meeting and passing such a procession. Repeatedly the Government had warned the Legations to advise their nationals not to use the Tokaido on certain days, and in fact a request of this nature had been made for September 15 and 16, when the Imperial envoy was to pass from Yedo toward Kyoto.[33] Shimadzu Saburo was in charge of his escort and he had started two days in advance. That Clarke and Marshall recognized the danger is plain from their evidence at the inquest, and Mr. Pruyn reported that "some time before the attack was made, Mr. Marshall exclaimed 'For God's sake, Richardson, do not let us have any trouble!' To which Mr. Richardson replied, 'Let me alone; I have lived in China fourteen years, and know how to manage this people.' "[34] Although both Marshall and Clarke denied that any provocation had been given, yet the very fact that they were on horseback was an insult and gave color to the charge that they had attempted to force their way through the procession. Death alone could have wiped out such an insult from a Japanese of low class, and the retainers of this bitterly anti-foreign lord were not inclined to make an exception in the case of "barbarians." That a woman was attacked was due to sheer ignorance, for a woman was not expected to be on horseback.[35]

---

[32] Adams, *op. cit.*, I, 214; Hodgson, *A Residence at Nagasaki*, pp. 283–85; De Fonblanque, *Niphon and Pe-che-li*, pp. 95–99; Black, *op. cit.*, I, 72, 143.

[33] Even after this event some British subjects protested against being debarred from the Tokaido on days when daimyos were passing [*1863 (3079)*, p. 104].

[34] No. 2, January 14, 1863, *F.R., 1863*, II, 1064.

[35] "Shimadzu Idzumi had left Yedo on the 13th in advance of Ohara dono, and on arriving at Namamugi in Musashi, fell in with English barbarians riding on horseback. They passed through in front of Shimadzu's retinue, and behaved in a rude manner. The light infantry in front of the procession rebuked them for their rudeness, and killed three of them on the spot. After this, the military glory of the house of Shimadzu shone more and more brightly" (Baba, *op. cit.*, p. 59).

Kawakami Tajima, Minister of the Prince of Satsuma, wrote to Colonel

At this critical period of domestic politics, to have the leading Imperial supporter become involved with the most determined of the foreigners and to be compelled to punish him, was a situation which seemed to spell disaster for the Shogunate. That they could not arrest an officer of so powerful a daimyo as Satsuma they frankly confessed. At best, they could only trust that he would heed the requests of the Shogun and his Council. In the meantime they were prepared to build a new road for the use of daimyo processions, to erect more guardhouses on the old one, and to furnish guards for foreigners who desired to use it when daimyos were passing.[36] So, with sincere expressions of regret for the outrage, with eagerness to take every precaution to avoid another, but with no power to arrest and punish the actual participants in the crime then under discussion, the Shogunate officials waited for the presentation of such demands as Her Majesty's Government might deem it desirable to make. In the meantime, in order to prepare for the civil or foreign war which might grow out of the present complications, they turned to their trusted adviser, the American Minister, and asked him to arrange for the building in America

Neale, August 13, 1863 (when the British expedition was at Kagoshima) : "We have heard something about a Treaty having been negotiated in which a certain limit was assigned to foreigners to move about in; but we have not heard of any stipulation by which they are authorized to impede the passage of a road.

"Supposing this happened in your country, travelling with a large number of retainers as we do here, would you not chastise (push out of the way and beat) any one thus disregarding and breaking the existing laws of the country? If this were neglected Princes could no longer travel. We repeat that we agree with you that the taking of human life is a very grave matter. On the other hand the insufficiency of the Yeddo Government, who govern and direct everything, is shown by their neglecting to insert in the Treaty (with foreigners) the laws of the country (in respect to these matters) which have existed from ancient times. You will, therefore, be able to judge yourself whether the Yeddo Government (for not inserting these laws) or my master (for carrying them out) is to be blamed." Kawakami also stated, in this reply, that the murderers when detected should be punished by death, but said that they had escaped and were possibly being concealed by hostile daimyos [1864 (3242), p. 95].

"Passing over several years to 1863, when, owing to a wilful lady, and an after-lunch expedition on horseback—we being entirely in the wrong and the Japanese in the right—we found ourselves involved in a war with one of the chief princes" (St. John, Notes and Sketches from the Wild Coasts of Nipon, p. 204). Captain St. John later took part in the bombardment of Kagoshima.

[36] 1863 (3079), pp. 98, 102.

of three steam ships of war, which would be a match for those purchased by some of the daimyos in Holland and England.[37]

It is again necessary to turn to the developments at Kyoto during the preceding few months. From week to week the waves of opposition against the Shogunate and its foreign policy were rising higher and higher. Some of the great daimyos of western Japan were coming out in open criticism of their ancient overlord, and threats were being made that they would dissolve their allegiance to the Shogun and transact affairs of state only with the Mikado. The most outspoken of these leaders, such as Shimadzu (Satsuma) and Mori (Choshiu), as we have seen, had taken up their residence at Kyoto, and other feudal lords on one pretext or another had failed to make their regular journey to Yedo. At the court the demand was often presented that the Shogunate bring to a close the temporary foreign intercourse, as it had seemingly agreed to do, but among the leading daimyos it was understood that to break off all foreign relations would be difficult.[38] Instead, they demanded that no additional liberties be granted and the present concessions be restricted. The leaders in this open criticism were lords of the west, long resentful of the Tokugawa régime, and now glad to make use of the foreign complication to bring it to account.

The result of all this agitation at the Imperial capital, where the presence of daimyos and their retainers and the loyal ronins served to nerve the long hostile court nobles, was the sending of an Imperial envoy to Yedo to make known the Mikado's will and to secure the promise of the Shogun to respect it.[39] The kuge (court noble) Ohara Jiu-sammi was selected for this purpose. He was

[37] October 21, 1862, request by Ministers for Foreign Affairs. The cost was to be $860,000; of this, $200,000 was paid down, the balance payable on specified dates until delivery. The needs of the American Government for cannon delayed the completion of the first of these ships, and then it was detained in New York pending the outcome of the Shimonoseki affair in 1864. The "Fusiyama" finally was delivered to the Japanese at Yokohama on February 5, 1865 (*F.R., 1866,* II, 671–79; *Serial Number 1149,* pp. 1–8).

[38] For a résumé of one of the documents put forward by the anti-foreign daimyos at this time see *1864 (3242),* pp. 7–10.

[39] Baba, *op. cit.,* p. 54.

raised in rank and appointed Sayemon-no-Kami, and on June 16
he set out, escorted by Shimadzu Saburo and six hundred well-
armed retainers, arriving at the castle in Yedo on July 6. He
carried with him a letter of instruction from the Kwambaku
which summed up the evils of foreign intercourse and the discord
which it had occasioned among the people, and insisted that Osaka
and Yedo must not be opened, and that Kanagawa must be closed,
but that if the foreigners would not listen to reason, then Shimoda
might be offered in exchange.[40] The Shogun was told to permit
them to hold out a slight hope that Kanagawa might be reopened
in the future, "for the Daimios say that Japan will be able to receive foreigners without blushing in six or seven years." Finally,
"Our Envoy has received strict orders not to leave Yeddo until
you have solemnly promised to do your utmost to replace our
country in the position it occupied when the Ooranda (Dutch)
were at Nagasaki." In addition, three alternative demands were
presented: First, "The Shogun must proceed to Kioto to take
counsel with the nobles of the Court, and exert himself thoroughly; must send forth orders to the clans of the home provinces
and seven circuits, and performing within a few days the exploit
of expelling the barbarians, restore tranquillity to the empire";
or, second, five of the great maritime daimyos should be appointed
Tairo to assist in the Government; or, third, Hitotsubashi Gio-
bukio should be appointed guardian of the Shogun, and the ex-
daimyo of Echizen (Matsudaira Shungaku) be appointed Tairo
to assist the Shogunate in the conduct of domestic and foreign
affairs.[41]

The Shogun received the Imperial commands with due respect,
and on July 27 gave a formal answer that he accepted the first
and third proposals, a proceeding which indicated the helplessness
of his position quite as much as his respect for the Mikado's authority. Both of these resolutions had a serious import. Not since
the year 1634, when the third Tokugawa Shogun, Iyemitsu, en-

[40] Summarized in *1864* (*3242*), p. 8.
[41] Baba, *op. cit.,* p. 58; also Yamaguchi, *op. cit.,* p. 29; in this latter version
no choice is mentioned.

tered Kyoto, had a Shogun gone up to pay his respects to the
Mikado, and no Shogun of his house had ever done so in obedience to a command. It is not too much to say that this step marked
the beginning of the end of the Tokugawa Shogunate. Conditions
had greatly changed since the Tairo Ii had sent his minister to
overawe the court and punish the recalcitrant kuge. By the placing of Hitotsubashi and Echizen in positions of chief authority
the Yedo administration was intrusted to followers of the Mito
school.[42] The former was, of course, the son of the late lord of
Mito, and the latter was Mito's strong supporter in his struggles
with Lord Ii. Echizen, on the other hand, had from the first recognized the wisdom and the necessity of foreign intercourse.

The tide of Imperial authority was now running high. Already,
in May, a general amnesty had pardoned the court nobles and
feudal lords who had been punished by Lord Ii in 1859, and they
were released from their confinement.[43] Then, in July, the Emperor conferred posthumous honors on the late lord of Mito and
on the late kuge, Sanjo Naidaijin, both of whom had opposed
Lord Ii and had died while in domiciliary confinement.[44] Shortly
after, several of the court nobles who had supported the Shogunate policies were punished, including the retired Kwambaku,
Kujo. This act was followed by a reorganization of the Yedo
ministry and the retirement of three of the pro-foreign members.[45]
In Kyoto the ronins began their bloody work of murdering the
retainers of pro-Shogunate nobles and those who supported the
Yedo régime.

It was in the midst of these alarming conditions that the Richardson affair took place. The noble concerned was the leader of
the western anti-Tokugawa lords, and his retinue was the guard

[42] It was soon after his appointment as guardian or regent that Hitotsubashi
came to the conclusion that the power of the Shogunate should be restored to
the Emperor, and after he became Shogun in 1867 he made the surrender (Okuma, *Fifty Years of New Japan,* I, 70).

[43] Baba, *op. cit.,* p. 52.

[44] *Ibid.,* p. 55.

[45] Kuze Yamato-no-Kami and Naito Kii-no-Kami were members of the
Rojiu. Ando Tsushima-no-Kami had been removed from that office in May.

that had accompanied Ohara, the Imperial envoy, to Yedo. Such a complication at such a time was confusion worse confounded. Then another western lord, Tosa, came up to Kyoto and joined the clans of Satsuma and Choshiu, "in the repression of disorder," but really in threatening the power of the Tokugawa Shogunate. This was the beginning of the "Sat-cho-to" triumvirate.[46]

On October 17 a decision of great importance was taken by the Yedo authorities. It was no less than to relieve the daimyos and the hatamotos from the more burdensome features of the San-Kin Ko-tai system, "taking turns in official attendance at Yedo," which had been introduced in 1634 by the great Shogun Iyemitsu.[47] Under this system most of the daimyos spent alternate years in Yedo, and the others spent alternate half-years, but all were required to leave their families there, as hostages, in the power of the Shogun. The new system cut down the residence in the case of the greatest lords to one hundred days every third year, and in the case of the lesser daimyos and hatamotos to two hundred days a year, and the frequent exchange of presents between the Shogun and the feudal lords was done away.[48] The old system was troublesome and costly, but it served to keep the lords under the control of the Yedo Government, and the presence of these feudatories and their numerous retainers made the capital populous, rich, and splendid. The reason given for the change was in order that the daimyos might use for coast defenses the money saved and devote the time to administering their fiefs.[49] Coming at this moment, however, it is probable that the measure was dictated by the Kyoto party, who saw in it, and justly, a means of weakening the Shogunate. And this was the immediate effect. The daimyos, relieved from attendance at Yedo, now flocked to Kyoto; all the large temples were occupied as their

---

[46] Yamaguchi, *op. cit.,* p. 31.

[47] Baba, *op. cit.,* pp. 60–62; Gubbins, *The Progress of Japan, 1853–1871,* pp. 139–43.

[48] The daimyos, however, wished all visits to cease. See memorial of daimyos in *F.R., 1863,* II, 1109.

[49] *1864 (3242),* pp. 5–6.

headquarters, and even those of neighboring villages were in demand. "Kioto had never been so crowded since the visit of Iyĕmitsu, third Shogun, in 1634."[50] When one of the western daimyos, on his way to take up his duties at Yedo, passed by Kyoto, as had always been the custom, the action was now taken as "a slight offered to the Court and therefore a crime." Orders were given, and some of the patriotic samurai overtook him and demanded an explanation. He obeyed the orders of the court, returned to Kyoto, and took up his residence there. This incident, as well as any, indicates the temper of the times. So while Kyoto was acquiring a new splendor, the Shogun's capital fell upon evil days.

As the Shogun had not kept his promise to appear at Kyoto, a second Imperial mission was sent to Yedo, this time consisting of two court nobles, escorted by the lord of Tosa. Leaving Kyoto on December 3, they reached Yedo safely, and on January 22 delivered the Imperial message, to the effect that in the following spring the Shogun must go up to Kyoto, "and assuming the command and leadership of all the clans, wield in his hands the military prestige of the Empire, and accomplish the feat of driving out the barbarians without loss of time."[51] Shortly after this, two of the western daimyos, those of Inshiu and Chikuzen, were sent by the court on a similar mission.[52] That the Shogunate was facing a crisis was evident, even if no serious complication with Great Britain arose out of the two latest attacks on her nationals.

In order to allay, in some measure, the rising hostility of the

---

[50] Baba, *op. cit.*, p. 67.

[51] *Ibid.*, p. 68.

[52] These anti-foreign edicts got into the hands of the Ministers at Yedo in various ways. On February 16, 1863, Mr. Pruyn forwarded to Mr. Seward a translation of an edict from the Mikado to the Tycoon calling for the speedy expulsion of the barbarians. This may have been the message presented on January 22 (*F.R., 1863*, II, 1070). On June 20 he inclosed a similar Imperial message, dated the twelfth month, January 20–February 18, 1863, calling either for the expulsion of the foreigners or their removal to Nagasaki or Hakodate. This may have been delivered by the daimyos of Inshiu and Chikuzen (*ibid.*, p. 1112).

court, the Shogunate turned against its own faithful servants and punished, with heavy hand, all who had taken any prominent part in the foreign relations of the past five years. The estate of Lord Ii was reduced from 350,000 to 240,000 *koku*. Among the others who were punished either by loss of revenue, forced retirement from the headship of their clan, or domiciliary imprisonment were the former ministers and high officials, Naito Kii-no-Kami, Manabe Shimosa-no-Kami, Sakai Wakasa-no-Kami, Hotta Bitchiu-no-Kami, Kuze Yamato-no-Kami, Ando Tsushima-no-Kami, Matsudaira Hoki-no-Kami, and Matsudaira Idzumi-no-Kami, while a number of lesser officials were dismissed from office.[53] Hotta Bitchiu-no-Kami, who had actually negotiated the Harris Treaty, was pursued into his retirement, for after Lord Ii became Tairo he had resigned the headship of his clan. The Shogun also offered to descend one step in rank for his short-comings, but the Mikado graciously would not permit this, and the Shogun promised to do better and "to obey faithfully his Majesty's will in all things."

These punishments met with the approval of the court party, and shortly afterward eleven of the leading daimyos sent up a memorial which, after joining in approval of these acts, and stating that in relieving the daimyos from most of their visits to Yedo the Shogunate had not gone far enough, insisted that foreign affairs should be placed on the old basis, that the foreigners should be allowed to trade as a favor and not to enjoy the privilege as a right, and that the Shogun should go up to Kyoto as he had promised, there to consult with the Mikado.[54]

In February the Regent, Hitotsubashi, went up to Kyoto, arriving there on March 1, accompanied by Ogasawara Dzusho-no-Kami, one of the Rojiu, and followed by Echizen-no-Kami, the Tairo.[55] The ronins there were eagerly demanding that a date for the expulsion of foreigners be fixed, and in their unrest frequent murders of pro-foreign samurai occurred. In fact a few days

[53] Baba, *op. cit.,* pp. 69–71.
[54] Text in *F.R., 1863,* II, 1109–12; *1864 (3242),* pp. 49–50.
[55] Baba, *op. cit.,* p. 72.

after Hitotsubashi arrived the head of a murdered man was left at his temple residence, with a note to the effect that the Regent's views on the expulsion of the barbarians were known to be of a temporizing nature.[56] In this respect the ronins were right, for Hitotsubashi, representative of the Mito clan, and apparently advocate of the anti-foreign views of old Lord Nariaki, had learned enough during his regency in Yedo to know that any attempt to carry out the demands of the court would mean a foreign war, and to know also what would be the effects upon Japan of such a war at that time. At first a critic of the Shogunate policy, it was now his duty to follow it himself, endeavoring to prevent any clash between the ignorant courtiers and the masterful foreigners, until more knowledge and better understanding might remove the grounds for friction, or until Japan should have acquired strength enough to hold her own against any foreign foe. To temporize—that was the policy of the Yedo Government from the start.

In considering this period of unrest and agitation it must be borne in mind that the Foreign Representatives possessed only a very hazy idea of what was in progress. The Tycoon's Government naturally failed to inform the Ministers of the strength of the anti-foreign movement. It is doubtful if any *de facto* Government would have done so. It did, repeatedly, describe the general situation, the popular opposition to foreign intercourse, the hostility of the court and that of some of the great lords, but it always expressed its confidence that in the course of time the opposition would pass away. Occasionally news reached the Ministers or some of their nationals who were on friendly terms with the Japanese, and copies of the more important state papers generally came to light after some time.[57] On receiving one of these unofficial communications Mr. Pruyn and the other Ministers would endeavor to have some Japanese official, either a Minister or one of the Governors for Foreign Affairs, vouch for its correctness. This they would frequently do, although unwilling to

[56] *Ibid.*, p. 73.
[57] For examples of these rumors see Alcock, *op. cit.*, II, 167–70.

furnish an official copy directly. At an interview with the Ministers on August 12, 1862, Colonel Neale complained of this unwillingness to furnish information. "Important political changes," he said, "such as the appointment of the Gotiro, the proposed visit of the Tycoon to the Mikado, the assembly of large bodies of armed men at Miako, or any other matters of general political interest, are not communicated."[58] To which the Ministers replied that they did not consider these subjects were of interest to the Foreign Representatives, but promised to inform him in the future, and added: "We thought that the Governors of Foreign Affairs, whom we send to the foreign Ministers on matters of business, would have answered any questions which you put to them." But Colonel Neale pointed out that no information would be given by them, and "the Gorogio here smiled in acquiescence." In keeping their promise they notified the Foreign Representatives on November 2 that the Tycoon was about to proceed to Kyoto in March of the following year.[59] No reason for the unusual expedition was given, and the Ministers had to conjecture what it could all be about.

One incident in these troubled times should be cited as a forecast of better days. On the night of November 22 the American bark "Cheralie," en route from Hakodate to Shanghai, struck a sand bank and became a total loss off the coast of Hitachi Province, about a hundred miles north of Yokohama. "The officers and crew were not only saved," wrote Mr. Pruyn, "but treated with humanity and kindness by the officers and people of the province. Nothing which could be done was left undone to display good will; even a flagstaff was erected by the Japanese at the temple appropriated for the use of the crew, from which to display our national flag."[60] Now this was the province of the Mito clan, supposedly bitterly hostile to foreigners. In Yokohama the usual rumors were current as to the hostility of the Japanese, and the French Minister very kindly offered to send the French warship

---

[58] *1863 (3079),* p. 55.

[59] *1864 (3242),* p. 3.

[60] No. 63, December 16, *F.R., 1863,* II, 1055.

"Dupleix," in the absence of any American vessel, to the place to inquire into the state of affairs and offer such protection as the Americans might need. But the Japanese Government also offered the services of their warship, the "Choyo-Maru," and Mr. Pruyn very wisely decided to accept its offer. Colonel Fisher, American Consul at Kanagawa, went to the scene of the wreck in the Japanese vessel, and found that the Americans had been treated with "true kindness" by the Japanese people and officials. This incident made a deep impression upon him, and he reported:

I cannot but regard this act, as it most assuredly is, an unparalleled demonstration of the rapid advance this remarkable people and government are making towards a full emancipation from exclusiveness which is to place them speedily in the front rank of nations, if not to make it and them a Christian country and people—a nation soon to be counted as among the first and most enlightened of the earth.[61]

Surely times had changed since shipwrecked mariners had been placed in confinement and shipped in cages to Nagasaki for deportation in Dutch or Chinese ships.

The Japanese Government appreciated Mr. Pruyn's confidence in them in accepting their ship and not that of France. The United States Government, on receipt of the news of this gratifying exhibition of humanity, forwarded appropriate presents for the principal officers of the "Choyo-Maru" and those of the province.[62]

It was at just this time that the first of the British demands for reparation was presented. This dealt with the murder of the two guardsmen at the British Legation on the night of June 26. The Japanese authorities had conducted their examination into the crime, and in August had inflicted severe punishments on the Japanese guards who might in any way be considered guilty of dereliction or cowardice. The daimyo whose troops were on guard, Matsudaira Tamba-no-Kami, was reprimanded and placed under arrest. Two of the Tycoon's bodyguard were sentenced to fifty days' and five to thirty days' confinement; one was reprimanded and two left to be punished by the daimyo, while two had

[61] *Ibid.*, p. 1059.   [62] *Ibid.*, p. 1128.

died before punishment could be inflicted.[63] In other words, the Japanese considered that they had made ample reparation for the deed of a single assassin, although Colonel Neale, in order not to forestall the demands of his Government, refused to express any opinion on this point.

Before he had learned of these measures, Lord Russell had forwarded to Colonel Neale his demand for reparation.[64] It was based on the assumption that the Government was aware of the projected attack, that the daimyo had favored it, and that its purpose was to induce the British to abandon Yedo and "allow the ancient custom of non-intercourse and prohibition of trade to be reestablished." Neale was instructed to "show in every possible way that Her Majesty's Government will not be deterred from their course by these shameful murders. It would be better that the Tycoon's palace should be destroyed than that our rightful position by Treaty should be weakened or impaired." If the daimyo had betrayed his trust or had connived in the attack on the Legation, he should be openly degraded and most severely punished. A compensation, in the sum of £10,000 gold, was to be demanded for the families of the marines, and this sum should be levied on the estate of the daimyo in charge of the guard.

It goes without saying that these demands were based on erroneous premises. No well-informed man on the ground believed that either the Government or the daimyo was in any way responsible for this crime, even though the guard might have been wanting in vigilance or courage. If cable communication had existed and Colonel Neale could have kept Lord Russell promptly informed of developments, it is doubtful if such demands would have been formulated. As it was, Colonel Neale could do nothing but present them, which he did at an interview with the Japanese Ministers on December 4.[65] At this time the Ministers, without discussing the amount of the indemnity, protested against the implication that their Government was concerned in the attack on the

---

[63] *1863 (3079)*, pp. 58–60.
[64] *Ibid.*, pp. 49–51.
[65] *1864 (3242)*, pp. 12–14; Satow, *op. cit.*, pp. 61–70.

Legation, and when they asked Neale if he himself thought so he replied: "You have afforded me no substantial grounds for forming an opinion upon that subject." For the first time Colonel Neale described the punishments inflicted in August as "insufficient and unsatisfactory."

In an unusually long dispatch the Ministers, on December 20, replied to the British demands, taking up the incident with great detail, endeavoring to remove any suspicion from the Government and from the daimyo, explaining that the punishments inflicted were burdensome, especially in the case of Tamba-no-Kami, and finally stating that "the law of our land does not allow us to grant the indemnity, and we therefore decline [to pay] it." They were willing to pay $3,000 in silver to the relatives of the murdered men "for their maintenance."[66] Here the matter rested, despite considerable correspondence, for several months.

The New Year dawned with another alarm of a ronin attack. The Government warned the foreign settlement and did all it could to prevent a surprise, with complete success. Mr. Pruyn, who was in Yokohama at the time, returned to Yedo, as the Japanese advised, and thus again showed his willingness to co-operate with them for his own protection. The French and British Ministers protested to the Government against these alarms (can it be that they preferred to be surprised by the desperadoes?), but Mr. Pruyn considered them unworthy of any formal notice.[67]

The foreign community was now much alarmed by rumors, either that the Japanese were about to assume hostilities or that the British were preparing to demand redress. It was said that British troops were on their way to Japan, and a large fleet was expected.[68] On January 16 one of the Japanese guards at the unfinished and unoccupied British Legation in Yedo was killed by four ronins who sought to force an entrance.[69]

When news of the attack on the British Legation on June 26 reached Washington, the conduct of Mr. Pruyn was scrutinized

---

[66] *Ibid.*, pp. 14–16.
[67] No. 1, January 10, 1863, *F.R., 1863*, II, 1062.
[68] No. 2, January 14, *ibid.*, p. 1063.   [69] *1864 (3242)*, p. 20.

carefully to note whether or not he had failed in any way to co-operate with and sustain the British Representative. His conduct was approved, and he was instructed to persevere in the same course in the future. Moreover, he was to

especially inform the ministers for foreign affairs that, while the United States will hereafter, as heretofore, prove themselves a generous friend, yet that the safety of all representatives, citizens and subjects, of all the treaty powers, must and will be insisted upon, as an indispensable condition of the continuance of the relations between this country and Japan, which have been so happily established.[70]

On receipt of a later dispatch from Mr. Pruyn, Seward replied that the President earnestly hoped that the Government of the Tycoon might

practice such diligence, in bringing all persons connected with the transaction to condign punishment, as will give assurance to the British government, and to the other treaty powers, that the rights and safety of foreigners in Japan will hereafter be inviolably protected.[71]

On receiving these dispatches Mr. Pruyn, on January 27, 1863, addressed the Ministers for Foreign Affairs and conveyed to them their more important passages. In addition he wrote:

It has afforded me sincere pleasure to be able to inform the President that the Japanese government is sincerely desirous of extending this protection, and of securing to the citizens and subjects of the treaty powers all the rights conferred upon them by treaty.

Coming at a time when another of the Treaty Powers had charged them with complicity in the murderous attack on the British Legation, this kindly letter must have been well received. The closing advice of the American Minister may well be quoted:

The cultivation of this feeling of good will, and the faithful observance of their reciprocal obligations by Japan and all the powers with which treaties have been made, not in a narrow spirit, constantly asking how much can be withheld, but in an enlarged spirit of liberality, which shall ever ask how much can with propriety be done, will result in great advantage to Japan and the world. And I indulge the hope that the friendship which now animates all these governments will be greatly increased and be perpetual.[72]

[70] No. 24, September 25, 1862; *F.R., 1863,* II, 1053.
[71] No. 25, September 29; *ibid.,* p. 1054.   [72] *F.R., 1863,* II, 1065.

When Mr. Pruyn reported the punishment inflicted by the Government upon the daimyo and the guards at the British Legation, Mr. Seward replied on January 31 that the President hoped "that the proceedings of the Japanese government, in this painful transaction, may be satisfactory to the British government."[73] In reply to a later dispatch of Mr. Pruyn he sent this word of deserved approval:

> The President does not fail to observe that some of the agents of some others of the treaty powers pursue, in their intercourse with the Japanese, a course more energetic, if not more vigorous, than that which you have followed under the instructions of this department. He, nevertheless, approves your decision to persevere in your past course, which, so far at least, has attained all desired objects, while it seems to have inspired the Japanese authorities with sentiments of respect and friendship towards the United States.[74]

Before this dispatch reached Yedo, however, Mr. Pruyn had, on his own motion, refused to follow his colleagues in their high-handed course, and this note must have comforted him in his isolation.[75]

On the very day that these moderate dispatches were being framed in Washington, the American Minister in Yedo again demonstrated his reasonable attitude. Two Governors for Foreign Affairs waited upon him, as they had already done in the case of his colleagues, in Yokohama, and frankly said that the difficulties between the Shogun and the Mikado might lead to civil war, not between the two principals, but between the Shogunate and the great daimyos of Satsuma and of Choshiu, who had hitherto influenced the Mikado. The Tycoon had appointed his guardian, Hitotsubashi, as an ambassador to the Mikado, and the Tycoon himself would go up in March. Between them they would remove these prejudices from the mind of the Mikado and defeat the machinations of the hostile daimyos. Much as they desired peace, yet civil war might take place, and in this event they asked "what would be the feeling and action of the United States."[76]

---

[73] No. 35, *ibid.*, p. 1066.   [74] No. 33, January 31, 1863, *F.R., 1863,* II, 1065.
[75] See chapter viii.   [76] No. 10, February 16, *F.R., 1863,* II, 1066–69.

To this Pruyn replied

that the government of the United States would, of course, be deeply interested in such a struggle, and that all the moral support it could render, and all material support which would be justified by international law, would doubtless be given; and that it was my opinion that, if called on by the government of the Tycoon for aid, all the treaty-powers would be justified in giving it, in self-defence, and would give it if, as was said, the object of the hostile daimios was to drive out foreigners.

The Governors replied that "they supposed the United States and Russia would have this disposition, but feared England and France might act contrary."

The next matter to be discussed was the new site of the Legations. After the first attack on the British Legation, on July 5, 1861, Alcock had asked for and received a new site "on a commanding table-land, having a tolerably direct communication with the water."[77] This was at Goten-yama, an attractive piece of land to the west of the scattered temporary temple Legations, part of which had been used by the people as a pleasure resort. On this site the Legations of all five of the Treaty Powers were to be erected. The grant of this site to the foreigners aroused no little opposition among the people, who would lose their park, and among the hostile daimyos, who pointed out that the elevated site commanded the five forts in the bay and the main road into the city.[78] One of the reasons given for the assault on Lord Ando in 1862, and of his punishment the next year, was because he had granted this concession, and it was realized by the beginning of 1863 that the establishment of the Legations there would result in difficulties. It was said to be a common remark among the people: "The British have our plum-garden, but the blossoms will be red."[79]

Under these circumstances the Japanese asked Pruyn if he and the other Ministers would accept another site.[80] The French Min-

---

[77] Alcock, *op. cit.*, II, 179.   [78] *F.R., 1863,* II, 1067.

[79] Note the murder of a Japanese guard there on January 16.

[80] The Japanese offered to build the Legation and charge ten per cent of the cost as rent. Seward wrote that he would recommend the offer to Congress (No. 37, March 20, 1863).

ister was said to be willing, but the British Chargé could not act until the return of the Minister, Sir Rutherford Alcock. Pruyn at once consented to accept "any location equally convenient and pleasant," and addressed a letter to that effect to the Ministers for Foreign Affairs, in which, after commenting on the popular opposition, he added: "I do not wish that the American flag shall ever be regarded as an emblem of hostility, either by the people or government of Japan, but only as an emblem of friendship and good will." The correctness of the Government's views on this matter was demonstrated that very night, for at 2:00 A.M. (February 1) the unfinished British Legation was destroyed by an incendiary fire.

In reporting this latest incident to Lord Russell, Colonel Neale said:

The inference would seem to be that the Japanese Government has connived at the accomplishment of this act as the only effectual solution of the pressure brought to bear by the Mikado and his party upon the Tycoon. It is equally possible that the retainers and partizans of the hostile Daimios, intent on carrying out the desires of their Chiefs, may have accomplished a portion of the work allotted to them by the destruction of the residence at Goteng-yama, despite all the efforts of the Government to restrain them.[81]

The Government, however, affirmed that the disaster was due to no dereliction of its guards;[82] and years afterward it was learned that among the incendiaries were two men who became two of the greatest of Japanese statesmen, Ito and Inouye, then young samurai of the bitterly hostile Choshiu clan.[83]

At the interview with the Japanese Governors it was suggested that Mr. Pruyn would find it more pleasant to live in Yokohama and only occasionally visit Yedo on business, in which case the Japanese Government would assume all the additional expenses. This proposal he declined, however, saying:

I had not come to Japan for my pleasure; that I had refused to leave Yedo when the other ministers did, because I had supposed I would serve

---

[81] *1864 (3242)*, p. 21.					[82] *F.R., 1863*, II, 1070.
[83] Michie, *The Englishman in China*, II, 62 n.; Yamaguchi, *op. cit.*, p. 33 n.; Rein, *Japan: Travels and Researches*, p. 349 n.

my own country, and Japan also, by remaining; that when I could render such service better by departing than by remaining, I was willing to converse on the subject; but that such time had not arrived, and, in my judgment, was not likely to arrive.

His assumption was doubtless correct, that the Japanese desired to be able to report to the Mikado, at the great meeting in Kyoto, that no foreigners resided in Yedo.

It was now evident to the Foreign Ministers that a crisis was impending. It was felt that the rule of the Shogun was being threatened by the Mikado, supported by some of the most powerful and wealthy daimyos of the Empire. The French Minister and many other foreigners and Japanese believed that when the Tycoon went up to Kyoto he would be deposed. Mr. Pruyn believed that the Tycoon had "sufficient power to maintain his position, even against the Mikado."[84] Colonel Neale felt that although the Tycoon's Government did not seek to break off relations with the Treaty Powers, it was showing signs of yielding to the pressure exerted by the opposition forces.[85] If it should be overthrown, a desperate effort might be made "by their less well-informed or reckless successors to accomplish the Mikado's imputed desire to expel or extirpate foreigners, especially from this settlement, so unpalatably contiguous to the capital." He therefore addressed Rear-Admiral Kuper, at Hong Kong, and pointed out the advisability of a considerable naval demonstration in Japanese waters, not merely to insure the maintenance of treaty rights, but at the same time to "afford a powerful moral support to the Tycoon's Government in its well-disposed but wavering and timid policy in regard to foreign intercourse."[86]

On the receipt of this strong representation the Admiral prepared to proceed to Japan with all the available strength of the British navy. But before his squadron sailed into the bay of Yedo a new situation, bristling with difficulties, had developed.

[84] No. 10, February 16, 1863, *F.R., 1863,* II, 1068.
[85] To Russell, February 10, 1863, *1864 (3242),* pp. 24–25.
[86] February 2, 1863, *ibid.,* p. 22.

CHAPTER VIII

EXCLUSION AGAIN DECREED
1863 [1]

THE EVENT which so profoundly affected not only the foreign relations but the domestic affairs of Japan was the presentation of the British ultimatum demanding reparation for the attack on Mr. Richardson and his companions on September 14, 1862. Earl Russell's dispatch was dated December 24, and was received by Colonel Neale about March 14, 1863. Earl Russell stated:

> In fixing the reparation to be required, Her Majesty's Government have had to consider the anomalous state of political rule in Japan. They find two parties who are responsible to the British Government: first, the Government of Yeddo, who, when British subjects are attacked and murdered on the highroad in full daylight, by persons who are known, nevertheless allow those persons to remain unpunished; secondly, the Daimio Prince of Satsuma, whose relation, Simadzoo Saboolo, permitted, if he did not actually order, his retainers to commit this horrible crime, and who do not punish it.

This was an extraordinary decision, as far as the canons of international law were concerned. The British Government had treaty relations only with the Government of Yedo, and from it alone should redress have been demanded. But Colonel Neale was instructed to demand reparation from both parties. From the Japanese Government he was to ask for:

> 1. An ample and formal apology for the offence of permitting a murderous attack on British subjects on a road open by Treaty to them.
> 2. The payment of £100,000 as a penalty on Japan for this offence.

From the daimyo of Satsuma he was to demand:

---

[1] The instructions for 1863 are numbered 30–55; of these twenty-six, fourteen and one telegram were printed in *F.R., 1863*, II, four in *F.R., 1864*, III, and two in *F.R., 1866*, II. The dispatches are numbered 1–85; of these, thirty-one were printed in *F.R., 1863*, II, and twelve in *F.R., 1864*, III.

1. The immediate trial and capital execution, in the presence of one or more of Her Majesty's naval officers, of the chief perpetrators of the murder of Mr. Richardson, and of the murderous assault upon the lady and gentlemen who accompanied him.

2. The payment of £25,000 to be distributed to the relations of the murdered man, and to those who escaped with their lives the swords of the assassins on that occasion.

The measures to be taken by Neale were also prescribed:

If the Japanese Government should refuse the redress you are thus instructed to demand, you will inform thereof the Admiral or Senior Naval Officer on the station, and you will call upon him to adopt such measures of reprisal or blockade, or of both, as he may judge best calculated to attain the end proposed.

You will at the same time communicate the substance of your instructions to the Envoys and Naval Commanders in Japan of other European Powers; and you will concert with the British Admiral, and the naval officers of those Powers, arrangements for the safety of foreigners during coercive operations.

If the Daimio Satsuma should not immediately agree to and carry into effect the terms demanded of him,

the Admiral should either go himself or send a force to the territory of the prince sufficient to blockade the port or to shell the residence of the prince there. Certain steamships which the prince had bought in Europe might be seized or held till redress was obtained.

During these operations, whether against the Government of Japan or the Prince of Satsuma, care must be taken by the Admiral to protect the ports where British persons and property may be in jeopardy.

The distinction between the Government and the Daimios is one that must be kept in view.

The Prince of Satsuma is said by one of the Japanese Ministers to be a powerful Daimio, who could not easily be coerced by the Japanese Government. He must not, nor must the other Daimios, escape on that account, the penalty of their misdeeds.[2]

---

[2] *1864* (*3242*), pp. 1–2. These demands were criticized in debates in the House of Lords, July 10, and House of Commons, July 21, 1863 (*Hansard's Parliamentary Debates,* 3d Series, Vol. 172, pp. 502–36, 1186–98). Lord Stanley said in the House of Commons, February 9, 1864: "If the murder of a British subject took place under anything like similar circumstances in a European country, you would insist on the punishment of the offender and demand compensation; but you would not demand a sum amounting altogether to about L. 150,000 and proceed in satisfaction to seize property of much greater value" (*ibid.,* Vol. 173, p. 361).

Such was the reparation demanded by a great nation, than which, as Colonel Neale admonished Mr. Pruyn, none "more frankly, loyally, and assiduously watches over, and administers to, the interests of its subjects abroad and at home."[3] But once more the demands of Downing Street were drafted without consideration of what might happen to be the situation in the Far East.[4] We have seen that all the Representatives were convinced that a crisis was threatening in the early part of 1863; that the Shogun was about to go up to Kyoto to fight for his place and power; and that Colonel Neale had requested naval support, not merely to defend treaty rights but also to afford a strong moral support to the Shogun's Government. Nothing could arouse more bitter anti-foreign feeling than the presentation of such humiliating demands; nothing could weaken the prestige of the Shogunate more than to accept them humbly; and nothing could rally more effectually the hostile daimyos of the west to the standard of hostility to the foreigners than the punitive measures directed against their fellow daimyo of Satsuma.

It is of interest to note Colonel Neale's views as to what would be adequate reparation, expressed in his dispatch of March 2, forwarded before he had received the above-mentioned instructions.[5] The result of various communications with the Japanese Ministers concerning the outrage, he wrote,

has led to the conviction that the Tycoon's Government is powerless to afford reparation, inasmuch as that reparation necessitates the arrest of the malefactors within the domain of the Prince of Satsuma, an attempt to effect which would, in all probability, hasten to a climax the gathering elements of civil war in this country. The urgent necessity for active measures on the part of the Tycoon's Government to constrain the Prince to deliver up the criminals is not as yet sufficiently apparent to the Mikado and nobles hostile to foreign intercourse. Extraneous pressure,

---

[3] *F.R., 1863,* II, 1082.

[4] As Sir Rutherford Alcock was in England at this time it is very probable that his advice was sought by Lord Russell in framing these demands. As early as March 6, 1860, he had suggested an indemnity of from $20,000 to $50,000 for every foreigner slain [*1860 (2694),* p. 8]. Compare this demand with Mouraviev's action in 1859 and with Harris' in 1861.

[5] *1864 (3242),* pp. 34–35.

coming from a powerful nation, would not only afford a ready reason to this Government for the adoption of such stringent measures as are possibly within its reach; but there are strong reasons to entertain the belief that the Tycoon and his Government would view with passive satisfaction Satsuma, Nagato, and Tosa (the three powerful Daimios who are hostile alike to the Tycoon's Dynasty and to foreign intercourse), made aware of the contingency of Her Majesty's Government exacting redress, if needs be, at the ports of their own seaboard possessions.

With these views, Colonel Neale must have been surprised, to say the least, when he received Earl Russell's dispatch with its heavy demands upon the Shogun's Government.

The ominous instructions were in Neale's hands by March 14, but he refrained from presenting them until Rear-Admiral Kuper and his squadron arrived.[6] On the twenty-second the Admiral entered the bay in the "Euryalus," flagship, accompanied by the "Rattler" and the "Racehorse." The "Centaur" and the "Kestrel" were already in port, and the "Argus" soon arrived, while the "Pearl," "Encounter," "Coquette," "Ringdove," "Cormorant," and all other available vessels on the China station were to follow. An imposing squadron was to give weight to the British demands.

While waiting for this force to gather, Neale advised Earl Russell of the steps he proposed to take in carrying out his instructions. These were to direct the hardest blows against Satsuma, rather than the Tycoon, so that

the scene of hostilities would thus also be removed to a distance from the Tycoon's Court and capital, while the news which would percolate throughout the Empire that Satsuma had been humbled in his independent career, would afford, I have reason to believe, actual satisfaction to the Yeddo Government.

He proposed, moreover, to do all that he could to secure redress in both cases without recourse to coercion, and he would point out to the Japanese

the essential difference between measures of reprisal should they be forced upon us for the purpose of awakening in them a knowledge of the serious necessity of affording redress, and a declaration of war, as declared between nations, founded upon great political differences.

[6] *1864 (3242)*, p. 35.

He would also point out that the penalty now imposed in thousands would expand into millions should Japan drift into open hostilities with Great Britain. Finally—and this might lead one to believe that the Chargé d'Affaires was not whole-heartedly in sympathy with what he was about to do—he wrote:

Impressed with the fact that the difference which we have at issue with the Japanese Government is restricted to a demand for reparation arising out of the occurrence of two isolated outrages which we have no proof were perpetrated with the knowledge or acquiescence of the Tycoon's Government; impressed, moreover, with the humble conviction that, apart from these lamentable occurrences and the first attack on the Legation, no hostile or defiant conduct has been exhibited towards us by the Japanese Government during the course of our relations with this country,—although, indeed, want of confidence and distrust has ever been perceptible, —I shall devote my best endeavours to avert a serious interruption of our commercial relations, which may fairly be said to be prosperous; keeping at the same time steadily in view the paramount duty with which I am charged, of carrying into effect, in letter and in spirit, the instructions with which I am furnished by your Lordship.

While Neale was waiting for the gathering of the squadron he was advised by the Ministers for Foreign Affairs, on March 30, that the Tycoon had resolved to start for Kyoto on the next day.[7] To this Neale replied that he was about to present, in two or three days, certain demands for reparation, the peremptory and explicit nature of which would require "the most serious deliberation and prompt attention of the Tycoon's Government within a restricted period of time." The Ministers, however, naturally refused to delay the departure of the Shogun. From their point of view, no doubt, it would have been to the last degree unwise for the Tycoon to put off his long-promised visit to Kyoto, made in obedience to the Imperial commands, in order to receive some new demand of one of the foreign Powers. They did not say as much, but they did naïvely remark that they could not promise a speedy answer to Neale's demands, as they did not know how important the matters might be.[8]

It was indeed unfortunate that the Shogun and two of the

[7] *1864 (3242)*, p. 38.   [8] *Ibid.*, p. 39.

Rojiu[9] were about to leave the capital, but it should not be forgotten that the great event of the moment was the approaching conference between the Shogun and the Mikado at Kyoto. It was even more unfortunate that the most threatening of all foreign complications should come just at this critical time. It should also be noted that Colonel Neale delayed presenting the ultimatum for at least twenty-three days, in order to have the support of a powerful fleet.

It was on April 6 that Mr. Eusden, of the British Legation, delivered the ultimatum to one of the Japanese Governors for Foreign Affairs in Yedo. It was a long document, but phrased in the clearest English.[10] In addition to the reparation demanded for the Richardson murder, which would not be "deviated from, modified or discussed," the indemnity of £10,000 for the two marines was now "peremptorily demanded." Twenty days were allowed for a categorical reply on the part of the Japanese Government, and at the end of that time, if the answer were anything but a positive acceptance, the Admiral would, within twenty-four hours, "proceed to enter upon such measures as may be necessary to secure the reparation demanded." It was suggested, and the point was repeated in a second letter, that a high officer accompany the British to Satsuma to advise that daimyo to comply with the demands.

The first reaction of this astounding ultimatum upon the two Japanese Ministers for Foreign Affairs who were left in Yedo was anxiety to prevent the British from resorting to direct action against the lord of Satsuma. "It is to be feared," they wrote, "whether the said undertaking may not originate an unexpected calamity, increase confusion tenfold and create discord amongst us; and it causes us great sorrow (to think) that this undertaking might injure (put aside) the law of our Empire and cause many irregularities. Therefore it is desirable that the said mission of men-of-war to (the domains of the Prince of) Satsuma should be given up." They requested that the settlement of this point be

---

[9] One was already in Kyoto with Hitotsubashi; two would remain in Yedo.
[10] *1864* (*3242*), pp. 40–44.

left in their hands, and said, therefore, that they could not send an officer of high rank with the British man-of-war to Kagoshima.[11]

Colonel Neale had some appreciation of "the disturbed political condition" of the country, and was not reluctant to defer the proposed expedition; in fact he wrote to Earl Russell that "circumstances may render its forced delivery inexpedient; as, for example, the prompt offer of the Tycoon's Government to satisfy the redress and reparation made upon its quasi independent vassal."[12] In other words the British Chargé was ready to modify the strict letter of his instructions, which called for reparation from Satsuma as well as from the Tycoon. In this way the matter rested, the Ministers assuring Neale that the Tycoon could not receive their message until the twelfth or thirteenth, and he, in turn, leaving them in doubt as to his intentions concerning Satsuma.[13]

The attitude of the Representatives of the other leading Treaty Powers toward these demands should now be noted. The French Minister, M. de Bellecourt, and Captain Massot, of the corvette "Dupleix," had received their instructions to act in perfect accord with the policy pursued by the British Government, and de Bellecourt so informed the Rojiu on April 21.[14] Colonel Neale counted upon this "moral, if not material, cooperation"; and when Admiral Jaurès arrived on the twenty-sixth, he unreservedly expressed the "entire sympathy" entertained by France with the justice of the British demands.[15]

The American Minister, on the contrary, had received no instructions, and therefore had to act on his own responsibility and in the light of existing conditions. He had to bear in mind the friendly relations between his Government and Japan, as well as his instructions to maintain harmonious relations with the Treaty Powers, and Seward's proposal, early in 1861, for a joint naval demonstration. His position was bound to be a difficult one. Officially neutral, his views concerning the justice of the British de-

[11] April 8, *1864* (*3242*), p. 45.   [12] April 14, *ibid.*, p. 40.
[13] *Ibid.*, p. 45.   [14] *F.R., 1863*, II, 1090.   [15] *1864* (*3242*), p. 52.

mands were very different from those of his colleague of France. In reporting the ultimatum to Mr. Seward he wrote:

It is to be regretted that this demand should have reached here at this particular juncture. It is well known that the Tycoon has been summoned to Kioto by the Mikado; that all the great daimios will shortly assemble there, and that the Mikado has been influenced to regard the treaties with displeasure. At this meeting, and within a few days, the foreign policy of this government will probably be determined, and I fear that this demand of the British at this time will weaken the influence of the Tycoon and his supporters, and inflame the passions, and increase the influence, and add to the number of daimios opposed to foreign trade.[16]

Three weeks later he added:

I have felt from the outset that the course of the British government has been a most extraordinary one. No one can deny that the occurrence of September, however unfortunate, was purely accidental. It is conceded that under the same circumstances a Japanese would have been killed. It is likewise conceded that the nationality of none of the parties attacked was known. Indeed, the governor of Kanagawa despatched a messenger that evening to our consul, under the impression that one of the wounded men was an American. And yet I have strongly urged a compliance with the demand, though I view it with feelings I shall not permit myself to express.[17]

In urging compliance, therefore, Mr. Pruyn was not moved by the justice of the cause, but, frankly, by a desire to save the Japanese from having to pay a far larger demand later, based upon the expenses of the British fleet and the business losses of British merchants. If, however, the Japanese would not agree, he advised Mr. Seward that he would recommend to them to propose submitting the whole case for settlement to the President of the United States or the Emperor of Russia, or both, or even to the British Government. He also informed him of the deplorable results which might follow should the British Chargé insist that the demands be complied with

without modification or even discussion. . . . . No country is so susceptible of defence as this. There are no roads for artillery. The whole country is intersected by ditches and canals and covered by rice fields. The people, or rather the two-sworded men, are as reckless of life as any people that

[16] No. 15, April 10, *F.R., 1863,* II, 1071.   [17] No. 22, May 3, *ibid.,* p. 1079.

ever existed, and no hostile force can hold any considerable portion of this empire without the sacrifice of thousands of lives and millions of money.

Mr. Pruyn promptly notified Colonel Fisher, the American Consul at Kanagawa, of the serious aspect of affairs, and of the possibility that the Japanese might not be able to comply with the demands within twenty days because of the absence of the Tycoon and most of the Ministers for Foreign Affairs, and recommended that citizens of the United States

pursue their business as usual, avoiding excitement, sacrifice of property, and all exposure to danger. Their position, until other wise determined by the action of the government of the United States, or by hostile acts of the Japanese government or people, which are not apprehended, must be that of entire neutrality.

He also recommended that they form an organization so that they might act in concert. This step was not to indicate any separation of interests from those of the other Treaty Powers, but, as he pointed out, "thus far nothing has disturbed the peaceful relations between the government of the United States and that of Japan, and it is to be hoped that nothing will change those relations."[18]

From the Japanese point of view it was of the utmost importance that the British demands be not discussed until after the close of the Tycoon's conference with the Mikado at Kyoto. But the Tycoon reached the capital only on the twenty-first, and the ultimatum would expire on the twenty-sixth. In this crisis the two Ministers for Foreign Affairs in Yedo turned to the American Minister for help.[19] They requested him to mediate for the grant of an extension of the time limit, and they said, "From the treaty such great friendship may be expected; and also, because we experienced your friendly feeling on more than one occasion." This, of course, referred to the second article of the Treaty of 1858.

Mr. Pruyn advised the Ministers to place the matter frankly before the British Chargé, pointing out to him the necessity for

[18] April 9, *F.R., 1863,* II, 1073. [19] April 19, *ibid.,* p. 1077.

having such an important matter settled by the Tycoon and his full Council, and also to ask the friendly interposition of the French Minister. He then proceeded to Yokohama to consult with the British and French Representatives. Colonel Neale was unwilling to grant the extension asked; but on receipt of the letter from the Ministers in which it was stated that the Tycoon would be back in Yedo within thirty days (by May 20), he agreed, on the twenty-fifth, to an extension of fifteen days from April 27, that is, until May 11.[20] This extension did not allow for the return of the Tycoon from Kyoto, nor was it Neale's intention to do so. It merely granted time for a new exchange of dispatches between the Ministers in Yedo and the Tycoon and his counsellors in Kyoto. It is interesting to note, in passing, that the Ministers thanked Mr. Pruyn for his friendly interposition, and informed him that they attributed the successful result of their application entirely to his mediation;[21] but Colonel Neale took pains to inform them that the days of grace were granted in consequence of their appeal in writing to him, and indirectly to his colleague, the Minister of France.[22] This statement would indicate that all was not well between the representatives of the English-speaking peoples. Such was the case.

On April 16 a conference took place at the British Legation in Yokohama which was attended by the British Admiral, Chargé, and military officer, the French naval captain, and the commander of the Netherlands naval force, for the purpose of considering the protection of that port.[23] It was their decision that "there was not a sufficient force at present in Japan to guarantee perfect security to the foreign community at Yokohama in the event of an attack in force by the Japanese," and the residents there were advised to adopt such measures as might be in their power for their security before the ultimatum expired on the twenty-sixth. Mr.

---

[20] *F.R., 1863,* II, 1078. Note Neale's explanation to Russell, and his reply to the Japanese Ministers, in *1864 (3242),* pp. 52–53, 53–54. See the Sanke Owari's statement on the twenty-sixth (*ibid.,* p. 79).

[21] No. 21, May 3, *F.R., 1863,* II, 1077.

[22] *1864 (3242),* p. 54.   [23] *F.R., 1863,* II, 1080.

Pruyn, who was, of course, in Yedo, was informed of this decision by Colonel Neale; and in reply, after expressing his regret that he was not notified of the meeting so that he could have explained his views more fully, he ventured to advocate a policy of moderation.[24] At the time of the delivery of the ultimatum he had received from Colonel Neale the impression that the British fleet was sufficient to protect the treaty ports; now it seemed that the combined forces of Britain, France, and Holland would not suffice. If the problem were one of unprovoked attack by the Japanese, he would have no observation to offer, for he did not consider that such an attack was at all likely to be made; but if it were concerned with the hostilities which might ensue from the measures resorted to by the British to enforce their present demands, he felt it his duty to point out the disastrous effects of allowing the Japanese to gain a temporary advantage which would arouse the whole country and possibly destroy all the advantages which the Treaty Powers had gained. "It appears to me," he said, "the dictate of wisdom, that no coercive measures be resorted to by any power, unless ample means be at hand for the defence and protection of life and property at the settlement." It would be unwise, he considered, to establish such a precedent, for some one of the Treaty Powers, with a force wholly inadequate to protect the foreign residents, might hereafter attempt to do what Great Britain, with its powerful fleet, now proposed. The Japanese, he maintained, would not be able to discriminate between the various nations in case of hostilities, and therefore the United States and Great Britain, having the largest commerce and the largest interests at stake, were most concerned in the preservation of peaceful relations.[25]

This candid statement brought forth from Colonel Neale a spirited defense of the British policy, in which he stated that the views of Mr. Pruyn, "though doubtless applicable and just when

[24] *Ibid.*, p. 1081.

[25] Mr. Pruyn believed that the Japanese would have fought the British if they would not have been involved with other Powers (Pruyn Papers, April 26, May 4, 1863).

regarded in the sole light in which you have presented them, namely, that of commercial interests . . . . are wholly inapplicable when weighed in the balance against the offended dignity of a great nation." He then proceeded to accuse American citizens of supplying arms and munitions to the Japanese at this critical juncture, and asserted, on the basis of current reports, that they were aiding the Japanese in making preparations for resistance, a report which, if it could be proved, he said, would ill accord with Mr. Seward's policy of joint action and a joint demonstration as proposed in 1861.[26]

To this Mr. Pruyn replied in a letter of unusual length, conciliatory in tone, but also perfectly frank.[27] He had not attributed to Neale a desire to act with undue haste, because he understood perfectly that he was acting under explicit instructions, nor did he presume to express an unfavorable opinion as to the action of the British Cabinet. He was interested, however, not in commerce, but in the safety of American citizens, and on this account he was ready to renew the suggestion, made in his former letter, that no measures of retaliation be taken before the Powers were better prepared for defense. As to his own attitude, he had from the very day after the murder made every effort to arouse the Japanese Government to the necessity of prompt and vigorous action and ample reparation. He had repeatedly advised that the present demands be met. His interpretation of Mr. Seward's proposal in 1861 was, however, different from that of his colleague.

If I rightly understand Mr. Seward's proposition, he desired to establish the principle that the treaty powers, recognizing their identity of interest and their exposure to a common danger, should abstain from separate action and make common cause in maintaining common rights, and securing the common safety of their citizens and subjects. It was a wise suggestion, because it insured unity of action and moderation and equity of demand; it was humane likewise, because necessarily attended with peaceful results.

He brought out the difference between Seward's policy and the British program by citing the case of Mr. Heusken's murder,

---

[26] April 20, *F.R., 1863,* II, 1082.   [27] April 30, *ibid.,* pp. 1085–88.

when "for the sake of a salutary precedent, a specific demand for redress was waived" and the sum of $10,000 was accepted for the support of the widowed mother. Finally, the charge that American citizens were supplying the Japanese with arms was refuted, for such few sales as had been made were made openly and in time of peace.

It was at this juncture that Mr. Seward's dispatch of December 13, 1862, dealing with the Richardson affair, arrived, and Pruyn read it to the Governors for Foreign Affairs on May 1.[28] It expressed the hope that the Japanese authorities would bring the offenders to punishment and make reparation without delay, and added: "You cannot too strongly advise the government of Japan that it can only have friendship, or even peace with the United States, by protecting citizens and subjects of foreign powers from domestic violence."

The next development in this interesting situation could hardly have been anticipated. The time limit of the British ultimatum would expire on May 11, and if the demands were not complied with the British fleet would commence operations. The members of the Rojiu in Yedo had, on April 30, begged that the full extension of thirty days be granted. This request was the occasion of a conference between the British and French diplomatic and naval officers. On May 3 two of the Governors for Foreign Affairs came down to Yokohama seeking an interview with the allies, which was granted on the fourth and fifth. On the night of the third the Japanese residents of Yokohama, alarmed at the approaching hostilities, began to leave the city and supplies ceased to come in. This alarm and panic continued for several days, and on the sixth several foreigners, including three Americans, were badly handled by certain Japanese, who demanded sums of money due, or believed to be due, on contracts. Under these circumstances the Representatives of England and France announced

[28] Instruction No. 29, *F.R., 1863,* II, 1054; Dispatch No. 17, May 1, 1863, *ibid.,* p. 1076.

[29] Pruyn sent this information on the twelfth, by telegraph from San Francisco.

that they had offered their naval forces to the Tycoon for service against the hostile daimyos!

The reasons for this offer were summed up by Colonel Neale as follows:

1st, the avowal of the Tycoon's government itself of the opposition it encounters in its relations with foreigners, on the part of certain powerful daimios specifically named; 2d, upon the knowledge which has been conveyed to us of peremptory and arrogant written appeals addressed to the Tycoon and his counsel, by eleven of the most influential of those daimios, against all intercourse with foreigners, and the authenticity of which is not denied by the government envoy; and, finally, upon a correspondence between the Mikado and the Tycoon; wherein the former enjoins the immediate expulsion of foreigners.[30]

In order that this proffer of assistance might be placed before the Tycoon, an additional term was granted to the ultimatum, which would now expire on the twenty-third, but this extension was granted on the distinct condition that the authorities would stop the evacuation of Yokohama by the Japanese and would assure, further, the provisioning of the town.[31] If these conditions were not carried out, it would be considered an initiation of hostilities on the part of the Shogunate. It was implied that if the Tycoon refused this offer the allied fleet would resort to measures of coercion.

This decision was taken by the British and French Representatives on May 5. De Bellecourt promptly advised Mr. Pruyn, and Colonel Neale wrote a letter on the sixth.[32] In reply to the former, Mr. Pruyn stated that the propriety of giving support to the Tycoon by all the Treaty Powers had been recognized for almost a year, and would be quite in accord with Seward's proposal of 1861.[33] Moreover, he had told the Japanese in February last that in the case of civil war the United States and all the Powers would doubtless support the Tycoon if asked to do so. But should mean-

---

[30] *F.R., 1863,* II, 1092–93. In 1864 the four Treaty Powers came to the support of the Shogunate in the Shimonoseki operations.

[31] *1864 (3242),* p. 55. Mr. Pruyn was informed by Neale that the ultimatum would expire on the twenty-first (*F.R., 1863,* II, 1093).

[32] *Ibid.,* pp. 1088–90, 1092–94.   [33] *Ibid.,* pp. 1091–92.

while the Tycoon accept the assistance of the fleets of Great
Britain and France, he had no observation to offer, for he had not
been invited to the allies' conferences nor had his opinion been
asked in respect to the results of their deliberations. This offer
to support the Tycoon, coming while the demand for an enormous
indemnity was still pressing, might well have astounded the
harassed Japanese officials.

Left in ignorance by his colleagues of what had taken place,
Mr. Pruyn learned from the Japanese officials of the proceedings
at the Yokohama conferences. He reported to Mr. Seward that

they had several times declined the offer of assistance to the Tycoon,
fearing that the knowledge even that such a proposition had been made
might disturb the peace of the empire; but that finally, as the ministers
and admirals were not satisfied with their answer, the government has
reluctantly agreed to despatch an officer in whom they had entire confidence to the Tycoon

to make known this offer and return with his reply.[34] This Governor left Yedo on the eighth and was expected back from Kyoto
on the twenty-third. It was Mr. Pruyn's opinion that

unless a collision shall have taken place at Kioto, or the civil war, which
I wrote you on the 16th of February last was feared, shall break out or
appear imminent, I do not anticipate the offer will be accepted. I believe
that if the alternative be distinctly presented, a foreign war will be accepted, if thereby a civil war may be averted, calamitous as it may prove.[35]

In this respect he was right, for when the term expired on the
twenty-third the Ministers declined the offer of assistance, and
offered to pay the demand of £110,000 at some future day, "after
the Tycoon has succeeded in quieting the troubles which prevail."
To have made the payment at this time would have precipitated
civil war.[36]

At this juncture, when war between Japan and England and
France seemed imminent, Mr. Pruyn and the American colony
were relieved to have the U.S.S. "Wyoming" enter the bay on
May 11. On the morning of the twenty-fourth, however, the

[34] No. 25, May 8, *ibid.,* pp. 1094–95.   [35] See Pruyn Papers, May 11, 1863.
[36] No. 30, May 26, *F.R., 1863,* p. 1098.

American Minister suffered a disaster which is all too common in Japan. This was the destruction of the Legation in Yedo by fire —not an unusual incident in a land where houses are built of light wood and paper, but smacking of incendiarism at this time of internal commotion. Mr. Pruyn was ready to "suspend judgment," reporting to Mr. Seward:

I desire to believe, for the sake of this government, as well as our own, that this fire was purely accidental. Still, for weeks, and even for months past, repeated attempts have been made to induce me to leave Yedo.[37]

Despite certain suspicious circumstances, the authorities who investigated the event always maintained that the fire was accidental, and the yakunins on guard, more than five hundred that night, did all that they could to save property and protect the residents.[38]

The next day Mr. Pruyn took up his abode in temporary quarters and remained there until the 31st. He had planned to go to Yokohama on June 1, but that afternoon he was informed by one of the Governors for Foreign Affairs that the Government had learned of a conspiracy to attack the Legation that very night, and although it would do all it could to arrest the conspirators, yet some might escape and trouble be made. It would relieve the Government greatly if Mr. Pruyn would retire temporarily to Yokohama, and this he agreed to do.[39] Although he hoped to return early in July, it was actually two years before the American Legation was again permanently established in Yedo.

It is now necessary to turn to Kyoto and follow the developments there during the great conference between the Mikado and the Tycoon. In the last chapter it was stated that the Regent, Hitotsubashi, had preceded the Shogun, arriving in Kyoto on March 1, and finding there a state of great agitation and insistent demands in many quarters that the Mikado's decrees for the expulsion of the foreigners be carried out at a definite date. On

---

[37] No. 29, May 26, *F.R., 1863,* pp. 1097–98.

[38] No. 38, June 22, *ibid.,* p. 1115.

[39] No. 31, June 12, *ibid.,* p. 1100.

April 8 a council was held at the palace attended by the Regent and the Tairo, princes of the blood, kuge of high rank, and the leading daimyos in Kyoto, at which a new mandate for the expulsion of the foreigners was read. In this the Mikado expressed his belief that the date should be fixed, and that all who had ideas on the subject, "even low-class two-sworded men and people of the baser class," might present their opinions to the Gakushiu-in.[40] On this day and the next some of the leading kuge and greater daimyos appealed to the Regent to fix the date, while Mori, of Choshiu, took the matter up with the Kwambaku. Hitotsubashi replied to all these demands that nothing should be done until the Tycoon arrived, when the date would certainly be fixed.

But the agitation could not be quelled. On the ninth all Kyoto was talking of an astounding act of sacrilege. Some of the hostile samurai entered the temple of Tojiu-in, where wooden images of the Ashikaga Shoguns were preserved, cut off the heads of three of them, and pilloried them in the bed of the river in the heart of the city. This act was designed to call attention to the usurpation of the Mikado's power by the Shoguns. The Shogun's military governor in Kyoto, the lord of Aidzu, caused his retainers to ferret out the perpetrators of this sacrilege, and some were killed and others thrown into prison. This caused Mori, of Choshiu, to come forward in defense of the ronins—and at the same time of the Mikado—but Aidzu would not relent. One result was that Mori became the idol of the ronins, and his influence among them and at the court was unbounded.

Word had now reached Kyoto of the British demands, and on April 15 the Shogun's representative at Kyoto (the Shoshidai) issued a notice to the thirty-six principal daimyos concerning the situation, and stating that

three demands have been preferred in satisfaction; but as none of them can be accorded, we intend to reject them entirely. As this refusal will probably cause immediate war, we request you to assemble around your

---

[40] Baba, *Japan, 1853–1864, or Genji Yume Monogatari,* pp. 80–81. The Gakushiu-in was the school for nobles in Kyoto.

sovereign [the Mikado] like a wall, and to make the necessary preparations for war.[41]

This notice must have rejoiced the hearts of the anti-foreign party, into whose hands the British were, in ignorance, apparently playing.

On April 21 the Shogun, accompanied by a noble retinue of counsellors, daimyos, hatamotos, eight or nine hundred soldiers, and two thousand servants, entered Kyoto. More than two hundred years had passed since the Imperial capital had seen such a spectacle. On the twenty-fourth he paid a visit of ceremony to the palace to inquire after His Majesty's health and to present his gifts to the Mikado and the court, and, according to the precedent created by Iyemitsu, he distributed a large sum of money among the townspeople. His advisers had hoped that he could hurriedly transact the business in hand and return to Yedo by May 1, but this did not fit in with the plans of the court party, who desired to keep him in Kyoto until the plans for the expulsion of the foreigners had been formulated to their satisfaction. So on the twenty-eighth the Mikado and the Tycoon proceeded, in magnificent state, to visit the shrines at Upper and Lower Kamo, "as a preliminary."[42]

The result of the first conference between the Mikado and the Shogun was the acceptance by the latter, on May 6, of the Imperial commands to expel the barbarians. This was to be done by peaceful negotiation if possible, but if not, then they were to be swept away, and it was suggested that, depending upon circumstances, the Mikado himself might conquer the foreigners.[43]

The news of this decision was promptly transmitted throughout the Empire, for on May 14 the Governor of Hakodate, in distant Hokkaido, issued a proclamation to the inhabitants that

the treaty between European countries and Japan is finished. Henceforth Hakodadi and Nagasaki will be the only ports opened to foreigners. If the foreigners, however, persist in their claims, a war will break out.

[41] *F.R., 1863,* II, 1107.   [42] Baba, *op. cit.,* p. 84.

[43] May 6, notification to the o-metsukes, to be transmitted to the feudal lords and retainers; May 8, notification made to the daimyos in the presence of the Gorogio (Rojiu) in Nijo Castle, Kyoto (*F.R., 1863,* II, 1113–14).

He also assured his people that there was not the least chance of war breaking out in Hakodate.[44]

The first decision, however, failed to fix a specific date for the expulsion, and thus, of course, could not satisfy the extremists. The Tycoon and his advisers, on their part, perceived what was meant by the presence of the British and French fleets at Yokohama at this time and what would follow if relations with all the seven Treaty Powers were abruptly terminated. Again they struggled to find some loophole. The opportunity to negotiate with the Powers would enable them to temporize, and in time all might be well. With the situation in Kyoto in mind it is easy to understand why the Tycoon refused to accept the offer of British and French aid. It would have meant a wide-waged civil war.

In order to nerve the Shogun to carry out the expulsion plan, it was arranged that on May 28 the Mikado and the Shogun, with their suites, would visit the shrine of Hachiman, god of war, at Otokoyama, where "the Mikado was to present to the Shogun in the presence of the God a sword of justice for the expulsion of the barbarians."[45] But the Shogun suddenly fell ill, and was unable to attend. Then the Mikado ordered that the Regent Hitotsubashi should receive the sword, but at the last minute he "suddenly fell sick" and went down from the shrine before the presentation.

In consequence of this the honest patriots were greatly incensed, and declared that the Bakufu officials did not sincerely intend to drive out the barbarians; that all of them, including Hitotsubashi, were deceiving the Imperial Court, and that the villany they thus displayed, and in constantly urging the Shogun to return to Yedo, was beyond the power of words to stigmatize. And they clamoured loudly that since this was so, the Mikado himself should proceed to conquer the barbarians in person, without waiting for the Bakufu.[46]

The patriots were right. The Shogunate officials did not sincerely intend to drive out the barbarians, and yet in the threatening environment of Kyoto they felt the presence of a *force majeure*. A few days later, on June 5, another audience was held, and on

[44] *1864 (3242)*, p. 64.   [45] Baba, *op. cit.*, p. 88.   [46] *Ibid.*, p. 90.

that fateful day the date for the expulsion of the barbarians was fixed. June 25 was the day appointed by the Mikado, and the daimyos were notified to that effect and instructed to defend their coasts and, when invaders came, sweep them away.[47] Satsuma and many of the maritime daimyos had returned to their fiefs after the decision to expel the barbarians had been reached but before the date was fixed, and the news was swiftly forwarded to them.

Although forced to accept this alarming decision, the Shogunate officials recognized the hopelessness of their position. The Tairo, Echizen-no-Kami, who had stoutly advocated foreign intercourse, begged leave to resign his office, and when the Mikado refused his request, he departed for his fief without Imperial permission.[48] The Shogun again begged leave to return to Yedo, but this was refused, for the lord of Mito had been appointed by the Mikado to proceed there in his stead and "expel totally the foreigners, and sweep them away as it were with a broom." His commission from the Tycoon was far more moderate. He was told "to do what is right and proper, in order that the good name of Japan may not be lost."[49] The Shogun was permitted to visit his castle at Osaka and he was there when the day of expulsion arrived. Hitotsubashi had, in the meantime, returned to Yedo. And there the scene shifts. How was the expulsion edict to be carried out?

The situation at Yedo and at Yokohama was much as follows: The ultimatum covering the British demands and the Anglo-French offer of assistance expired on May 23. The officials in Yedo, knowing of the decision taken at Kyoto on the sixth to expel the foreigners, and doubtless under explicit instructions, refused the offer of assistance, and proposed to pay the indemnity at some later date. This refusal was the subject of several inter-

[47] Baba, *op. cit.,* p. 87. Tycoon to Rojiu, June 6 (*F.R., 1863,* II, 1124). Notice to daimyos (*ibid.*). Notice by Governor of Yedo, June 9, *1864 (3242),* p. 68.

[48] June 6. Baba, *op. cit.,* p. 87. He notified his agent in Yokohama that the Mikado was under the influence of Satsuma and the anti-foreign daimyos (*F.R., 1863,* II, 1108).

[49] *F.R., 1863,* II, 1106. He reached Yedo about the end of May.

views between the British Chargé and the Japanese Governors. In the meantime the news of the decreed expulsion aroused the ronins to greater activity, and the Shogunate to increased efforts to protect the foreigners. It was a curious situation: an allied fleet menacing Yedo, and the Yedo authorities straining every nerve to prevent hostile operations on the part of impetuous Japanese. On May 31 the Governor of Kanagawa summoned the Consular Corps to a conference, in which he stated the danger of attacks from ronin bands, and urged that the foreigners at Kanagawa move over to Yokohama for safety. This request applied only to the American Consul and to missionaries. He then stated that the Yedo authorities would reinforce the daimyos' troops on guard at Yokohama by some of their own troops, commanded by officers of the rank of hatamoto, "gentlemen of birth and breeding, much superior to the daimios' officers," and that "any unnecessary threatening display of firearms would be felt by them as a special indignity."[50] It is interesting to note that this scrupulous endeavor to protect the foreigners, at this exciting period, was received with suspicion, the British Consul writing:

Undoubtedly the Japanese Government is quite capable of creating a fictitious alarm, and under its cover compassing their darling object of controlling the movements or (it may be) getting rid of this community.

The protracted discussion concerning the payment of the indemnity was brought to a close with the pronouncement of a new ultimatum fixing ten days as the limit for compliance. The Japanese wished to extend the payment over a long term, from ten months to ten years, but Colonel Neale insisted that six weeks was the maximum time allowance. This declaration was accepted by the Governors for Foreign Affairs on June 8 and approved by the three members of the Rojiu on the eleventh, and the formal agreement was signed on the fourteenth, calling for a first payment of $140,000 (Mexican) on June 18 and $50,000 weekly thereafter, the last payment being due on July 30.[51] It should be noted that this agreement was signed after word of the decision to expel foreigners on the twenty-fourth must have reached Yedo, and with the approval of the lord of Mito, who had been sent up to "expel totally the foreigners, and sweep them away as it were with a broom."[52]

The news which had come up from Kyoto as to the decision to expel foreigners and the appointment of Mito for that purpose caused Mr. Pruyn, for the first time, to feel the necessity for an American naval force in Japanese waters. His opinions on this question had undergone a great change. Just as the presence of Perry's formidable fleet had opened Japan, so, he felt, "it is both natural and undeniable that the same means must be relied on, for some time at least, to preserve to the world what was thus gained."[53] It was in his opinion the presence of ships of the United States, France, and Holland, as well as of Great Britain, which doubtless caused the Japanese to abandon or at least to suspend the expulsion decrees, and he recommended to Mr. Seward that the Treaty Powers combine to maintain a permanent fleet in Japan for some time. The promise to pay the indemnity seemed to mark a change in the policy of Mito, hitherto so hostile to foreigners, and if his change in policy were approved by the Mikado and the hostile party, all would be well; but if the latter re-established their influence over the Mikado or insisted that a more vigorous agent be appointed to carry out the "exterminating war," or if the fleet should be withdrawn, the foreigners might be overwhelmed.

When they agreed to pay the indemnities the Yedo officials took up the question of Satsuma and after explaining anew the difficulties of the situation offered to pay the £25,000 demanded of that daimyo at once and to postpone the arrest and punishment of the murderers.[54] This offer Colonel Neale refused to consider, and while the negotiations proceeded he was amazed to receive on

[52] On June 9 the governor of Yedo had warned the inhabitants that negotiations regarding the closing of the ports would soon be opened and war might result. He urged the preservation of order [*1864 (3242)*, p. 68].

[53] No. 34, June 16, *F.R., 1863*, II, 1104–6.

[54] *1864 (3242)*, p. 70.

the seventeenth, the day before the first payment of the indemnity was due, a statement to the effect that the money would not be paid the next day. An explanation was offered, on the twentieth, to the effect that an order had been received from the Mikado not to pay the indemnity and that this must be obeyed

in the first place, because it emanated from the Mikado, and secondly, because they feared an outburst of public indignation if not complied with; also, if not carried out, the Tycoon might have to pay for it with his life.[55]

Colonel Neale had now no alternative but to place the matter in the Admiral's hands on the twentieth and to request him to adopt "prompt coercive measures of reprisal."[56] But on that day the French Minister learned the real situation—that the Yedo authorities had received orders from the Tycoon for the expulsion of the foreigners. Mr. Pruyn at once sent for the Governors for Foreign Affairs, and when one appeared the next day he asked why he had not been informed of this important decision. The answer was that although the orders had been received, the Yedo authorities had proposed to disregard them.

They were not disposed to reflect the wishes and views of the Tycoon; that the Mikado had been prejudiced against the foreigners by bad men at Kioto, that he had given such orders; that the Tycoon was obliged to obey them, or he would lose his office and life; but that the ministers at Yedo knew that the orders could not be executed; they had neither ships-of-war nor arms to accomplish this; besides, the Tycoon had made the treaties and wished to observe them.

Near midnight on the twenty-second, Mr. Pruyn was informed by the Governor of Kanagawa that the British indemnity would

[55] *Ibid.*, p. 71. At an interview between the Governor of Kanagawa and the Consular Corps the former stated that the Tycoon had been willing to pay the indemnity and that he had so ordered before he left Yedo, but that he would lose his life if he paid now. The Governor also twice affirmed that the Tycoon did not leave Yedo until after April 6, when the demand was presented. This was hardly possible. The Foreign Ministers were told that the Tycoon would leave on March 31. He arrived in Kyoto on April 21, which would hardly have given time enough for a state progress if he left after the sixth. The apparent contradiction was due either to faulty interpretation, which might always cause difficulty, or to the Governor's speaking from memory. There was no apparent reason for deceiving the Consuls on this point.

[56] *Ibid.*, p. 73; *F.R., 1863,* II, 1117.

be paid on the twenty-fourth, that Ogasawara Dzushu-no-Kami, the Minister for Foreign Affairs, who had been at Kyoto during the first days of the great conference, would go up there again for the purpose of changing the hostile views of the Mikado, and that before leaving he desired to see all the Foreign Representatives at Yokohama.[57] The next day the Governor informed the French Minister, who in turn advised his colleagues, that the purpose of the interview was to notify them that orders had been received for their expulsion and to request them to leave. He replied that a communication of such importance should be reduced to writing, and in fact suggested a form, which was modified, however, by the Japanese. The French Minister was given to understand that nothing would be done pending negotiations, which would have to cover a considerable period in order that the Ministers might receive instructions from their Governments. In other words the Shogunate was going to consider the fixed date, June 25, to refer to the beginning of negotiations for the closing of the ports, rather than to the actual expulsion.

By five o'clock on the morning of the twenty-fourth the total indemnity of £110,000, or $440,000 (Mexican), was paid to the British Chargé and hurriedly transferred to the warships in the harbor.[58] Later in the day the Minister, Ogasawara, arrived on the Shogun's steam-yacht "Emperor," and shortly afterward the Foreign Ministers received a communication much as follows:

I have the honor to inform your excellency that I have received full powers to act on the subject herein stated.

I have received orders from his Majesty the Tycoon, now residing at Kioto, and who received orders from the Mikado to cause the opened ports to be closed and the foreigners (subjects) of the treaty powers to be removed, as our people will have no intercourse with them; hence negotiations on this subject will afterwards take place with your excellency.[59]

[57] *F.R., 1863,* II, 1118.

[58] A satisfactory written apology as demanded by the ultimatum was sent by the Rojiu on July 3 [*1864 (3242)*, p. 80].

[59] *F.R., 1863,* II, 1120. Three other translations are given in *1864 (3242)*, p. 74. Mito reported to the Mikado that the Richardson affair and the closing of the ports should not be confused, that the indemnity had been paid and then negotiations on the other point commenced; see Baba, *op. cit.,* p. 92.

The three Ministers sent immediate replies, for no time was available for a conference. Although they had been told that there was no intention of enforcing the orders, yet they felt that their replies should deal with the written notice and not with the verbal explanations. In each case, therefore, a strong reply, refusing to abandon the Treaties, was returned. Mr. Pruyn stated:

> A solemn treaty has been made by the government of Japan with the United States granting to its citizens the liberty to reside and trade at these ports. The right thus acquired will not be surrendered, and cannot be withdrawn. Even to propose such a measure is an insult to my country, and equivalent to a declaration of war.

He warned the Government of the folly of attempting to carry out such a course, announced that life and property of American citizens would be defended to the last extremity, and declared that the Government would be held responsible for any consequences and liable for any losses which might result.[60]

The French Minister asserted that the proposal was without precedent in the history of civilized nations and might bring some chastisement upon those who conceived it; in the meantime he intrusted the safety of his nationals to the French Admiral, who would take all necessary measures by land or by sea against any one violating the spirit of the Treaty.[61] Colonel Neale also considered the indiscreet communication "unparalleled in the history of all nations, civilized or uncivilized," and, in fact, "a declaration of war by Japan against the whole of the treaty powers, and the consequences of which, if not at once arrested, it will have speedily to expiate by the severest and most merited chastisement."[62]

The Foreign Ministers, therefore, would not even discuss the right of the Japanese to denounce the Treaties. As a practical proposition their attitude was eminently sound. It would have been unfortunate for Japan, and for the world, if the Treaty Powers had consented to withdraw from Japan and permit that country to retire into her old seclusion, even though for only a few

[60] *F.R., 1863,* II, 1121.   [61] *Ibid.,* p. 1123.   [62] *Ibid.,* p. 1124.

years. In spite of temporary disadvantages, some of which persisted for more than thirty years, it was well for Japan to solve the problem of how to take her place in the great family of nations. It would have been far more unfortunate if expulsion by force had been attempted, with its resulting war and its legacy of debt and sorrow and hate.

But as a matter of equity, the right was not all on the side of the Treaty Powers. If the choice lay between denunciation of the Treaties and civil war, who would deny the right of the Japanese to rid themselves of such calamitous engagements? Also, if the Treaties had been ratified by the *de facto* but not the *de jure* power, could their sanctity be unqualifiedly asserted? These are moot points, and there is much to be said on both sides. Finally, it must be remembered that when Perry opened the doors of Japan, the message which he bore contained this suggestion, which made a deep impression at the time:

> If your imperial majesty is not satisfied that it would be safe to abrogate the ancient laws which forbid foreign trade, they might be suspended for five or ten years, so as to try the experiment. If it does not prove as beneficial as was hoped, the ancient laws can be restored. The United States often limit their treaties with foreign States to a few years, and then renew them or not, as they please.[63]

If ever a nation is justified in denouncing its treaty obligations, surely the Japanese were justified in doing so in June of 1863.

Happily the question was not going to be pressed at the time. Ogasawara was on his way to Kyoto to convince the Mikado of the futility of his commands. Hitotsubashi, the Regent, reported from Yedo that the Imperial mandate could not be enforced, and, realizing his guilt in not carrying out the duty of expelling the barbarians, he humbly awaited his punishment and begged to be allowed to resign his present office.[64] The Imperial court seethed

---

[63] Hawks, *Narrative of the Expedition of an American Squadron to the China Seas and Japan*, I, 257. This provision was not incorporated in any treaty. The Japanese referred to it in an interview with Colonel Neale as late as January 4, 1864 [*Japan. No. 1 (1865)*, p. 5].

[64] Baba, *op. cit.*, p. 93. He reached Yedo on June 24 (Heco, *The Narrative of a Japanese*, I, 326).

with indignation at the "cowardly and temporizing action" of the Yedo officials, but it refused to allow the Shogun to return to Yedo in spite of the pleas of his advisers that only through his presence could the result be achieved.

In the midst of this period of uncertainty and confusion the American Minister made the one positive contribution toward a happy solution of the problems at hand. On June 27 Mr. Pruyn forwarded to Mr. Seward a dispatch of weightiest import.[65] His proposal was none other than to advocate a joint naval demonstration, as suggested by Mr. Seward in 1861, designed not for the protection of the treaty ports, but for securing the ratification of the Treaties by the Mikado. Until that was obtained, he said, the public mind of the country will not be quieted, "the position of foreigners must continue precarious, and their presence occasion intrigues, and perhaps civil war, because not sanctioned by the rightful sovereign, which the Mikado doubtless is, theoretically and practically, should the daimios gather around him." He pointed out how this was to be accomplished, by making a naval demonstration at Osaka, twenty miles from Kyoto, backed, if necessary, by a land force to move on Kyoto. This was a statesmanlike proposition, if the Powers intended to insist upon the maintenance of the existing Treaties, and, to the best of our knowledge, Mr. Pruyn was the first diplomat adequately to realize the importance of such a step. He not only pointed out what should be done, but he showed exactly how it might be, and later was, accomplished.

To arrange such a demonstration would require reference to the home Governments, and, even if they approved, the plan could not be carried out for many months. Before the proposal was framed, however, an event occurred in far western Japan which was to have wide-reaching effects.

[65] No. 45, *F.R., 1863,* II, 1125.

CHAPTER IX

CHOSHIU TAKES THE OFFENSIVE
1863–64

THE ALARMING news which reached Yokohama on July 11 was none other than that one of the great daimyos, Choshiu, the leader of the anti-Shogun and hence anti-foreign faction, had taken literally the Mikado's order for the expulsion of the foreigners, which had set the date for June 25, and had fired on the first foreign vessel which tried to pass through the Straits of Shimonoseki.[1] This vessel was the little American steamer "Pembroke," which was en route from Yokohama to Shanghai, and the attack was delivered by two armed vessels at 1:00 A.M., June 26, while she lay at anchor near the entrance to the straits. Happily no lives were lost and little damage was done, but the American flag had been fired upon by a foe which carried the national flag of Japan.[2]

Mr. Pruyn learned of this attack on the evening of the eleventh, first from a Governor for Foreign Affairs, dispatched from Yedo, and a little later from a letter written by the owners at Shanghai, covering an affidavit and a request for $10,000 damages.[3] Early the next day he sent for the Governor and learned that the vessels belonged, not to the Shogun, but to the lord of Choshiu, and that they carried the Government flag in disobedience to orders. Mr. Pruyn pointed out the serious nature of the insult to the American flag, assured the Governor that ample satisfaction would be de-

[1] No. 48, July 24, *F.R., 1863,* II, 1129–37. A telegram was also sent this day, *ibid.,* p. 1141.

[2] One of the vessels carried the Government flag, the red sun on a white field, whereas when the "Medusa" was attacked later the Choshiu flag of blue and white was used.

[3] The damages were for loss of time, loss of freight and passengers through not being able to visit Nagasaki, and recompense for the deadly peril to which the crew were subjected.

manded, and said that he would expect to receive some statement from the Japanese Government concerning this serious offense. The Governor was unwilling to approve an American punitive expedition, and begged that Mr. Pruyn do nothing until the Yedo authorities should act.[4]

At this time there happened to be in the harbor of Yokohama the American steam war vessel, "Wyoming." Commander Mc-Dougal had been present at the interview between Mr. Pruyn and the Governor, and he had decided that the proper course was to proceed to Shimonoseki and seize or destroy the two offending vessels. In this decision he had the cordial support of the American Minister, for the following reasons: If the outrage were not promptly punished the inaction would be attributed either to fear or to weakness, and great encouragement would be given to the hostile daimyos; on the other hand, the Shogun's Government would no doubt welcome any punishment meted out to the leader of the anti-Tycoon and anti-foreign forces, which would, in effect, aid it in its attempt to curb the opposing faction; and, finally, it was especially important, in view of the Civil War at home, that the United States should be ready to protect its nationals, lest it be deemed too weak to do so. It was felt that Choshiu was carrying out, in good faith, the expulsion edicts, and was using the national flag to cover his proceedings. "His acts, if justified by the government, constituted war; if disavowed, were acts of piracy."[5]

With Minister and Commander in such accord and ready to assume the responsibility, there was immediate action. The "Wyoming" sailed the next day, the thirteenth, for the purpose of capturing the two vessels and delivering them to the Shogunate,[6] but without the slightest idea that Choshiu would fire upon an American ship of war.[7] But that aggressive daimyo evidently meant business, as the news which reached Yokohama indicated.

[4] Heco, *The Narrative of a Japanese,* I, 335.

[5] No. 48, July 24, *F.R., 1863,* II, 1131.   [6] *Ibid.,* p. 1139.

[7] Heco, *op. cit.,* I, 338. Heco accompanied Commander McDougal as interpreter.

On July 8 the little French steam gunboat "Kienchang" was fired upon by the ships and by the batteries on shore, and on the eleventh the Netherlands steam sloop "Medusa" was attacked and replied vigorously. News of these attacks reached Yokohama on the fifteenth and sixteenth. In the meantime the "Wyoming" had reached the straits on the sixteenth and had been fired on by six of the shore batteries. By good seamanship the vessel was kept close in to the batteries, and most of their shells passed over her deck. Commander McDougal steered between the bark and the brig on the one side and the steamer on the other, receiving from and delivering broadsides into each ship, and succeeded in sinking the steamer and the brig.[8] This punishment effected, he returned to Yokohama, having lost four seamen killed and seven wounded (one of whom died later). The first blow in defense of treaty rights had been struck by the United States.

When the news of the attack on the "Kienchang" reached Yokohama, Admiral Jaurès sailed on the sixteenth, with two vessels, for Shimonoseki. Arriving there on the twentieth, he landed a small force and destroyed one of the batteries, burned a small village and caused other destruction.[9] Six of the seven batteries

[8] The steamer "Lancefield," renamed "Koshin Maru," had been purchased from the British firm of Jardine, Matheson and Company for $115,000; the brig "Lanrick," formerly in the opium trade, from the same firm for $20,000; and the bark had been built in Japan (*F.R., 1863*, II, 1133). These values are stated differently; see *1864* (*3242*), p. 87, and *41st Cong., 2d Sess., S. Rept. No. 250* (*Serial Number 1409*). The "Lancefield" was later repaired and was sold to an American firm in 1865 (*Serial Number 1319*). The officers and men of the "Wyoming" were allowed prize money for the destruction of "hostile vessels in the Straits of Shimonoseki." See Appendix in Vol. II.

[9] Mr. Pruyn wrote to Commander McDougal on the fifteenth, begging him to co-operate with Admiral Jaurès in the destruction of the batteries (*Serial Number 1409*). This letter, apparently sent down with the French expedition, did not reach McDougal. Its purpose was to inform him that batteries as well as the two ships had fired on the "Kienchang," and that even if the ships had escaped he should not return "without vindicating our flag and taking full satisfaction for the outrages upon it." On the twentieth, Admiral Kuper sent a vessel to communicate with Admiral Jaurès and co-operate with him if needed [*1864* (*3242*), p. 84]. It was expected that she would be fired upon and thus all four of the leading Treaty Powers would be involved. But she was informed that she would not be fired upon unless she fired first—a hopeful sign (Pruyn Papers, August 3, 1863).

were left intact. Happily the Kokura clan, on the south side of the straits, took no part in these engagements, or the foreign ships would have suffered greater loss; but for this neutrality the clan was sharply censured by the Mikado. Notwithstanding these acts of reprisal by the American and French ships of war, the Straits of Shimonoseki remained closed, nor were they forced open for more than a year.

The position of Choshiu was therefore clear. Acting upon its own interpretation of the Imperial order it had struck the first blows against the foreigners, blows which, in its opinion, were bound to involve the hated Shogunate in difficulties. But what would be the attitude of the Yedo authorities, and what further steps would the aggrieved Powers take? These were questions of immediate interest.

From the point of view of the Shogunate this blow, aimed more at it than at the foreigners, came at a most unfortunate period. The anti-foreign party was in the saddle at Kyoto, and the Shogun was still detained there, almost as a hostage for the carrying out of the expulsion edicts. The British indemnity crisis had just been passed and the indemnity paid, while the Satsuma phase of that complication still loomed threateningly. And the Treaty Powers had flatly refused even to negotiate regarding the closing of the open ports. At such a time the opening of hostilities by Choshiu upon the flags of the United States, France, and Holland might easily incite the other hostile daimyos and precipitate the general war which the Shogunate had so long tried to avoid. The Governors for Foreign Affairs had promptly disavowed the actions of Choshiu, and had promised that the Government would investigate the circumstances; but on July 23 Sakai Hida-no-Kami, a vice-minister, while repeating these statements, also said that if it were found that Choshiu acted under orders of the Mikado, "the Tycoon would be compelled 'exteriorly' to approve his conduct, but that 'interiorly,' of course, he would disapprove, and continue the friend of the foreigners."[10] In other words, although no known edict could justify the conduct of Choshiu, yet

[10] *F.R., 1863,* II, 1134.

the Yedo authorities did not know what secret orders might have issued from the hostile court of Kyoto, and, just as in the matter of closing the ports, the Shogun might have to indorse openly a course which he really disapproved.

On July 25 the representatives of France, the United States, Great Britain, and the Netherlands signed a memorandum to the effect that it was necessary, for the maintenance of treaty rights, to proceed immediately to the reopening of the Inland Sea, and therefore expedient to request the naval officers to take all necessary measures.[11] It was agreed also to establish a combined action of the naval and military forces available, and to notify the Tycoon's Government of this decision, in order that it might take the requisite measures with its own means, and thus render it unnecessary for the agents of the Treaty Powers to proceed with the operations. This memorandum, marking the commencement of joint action instead of Anglo-French co-operation, was forwarded by each of the Representatives to the Japanese Ministers for Foreign Affairs, with a covering letter calling for the immediate chastisement of Choshiu.[12] Mr. Pruyn even intimated that the Treaty Powers might have to pass by the Government of the Tycoon and address themselves directly to the Mikado, and "by such arguments and means as they have in their power, cause him to give indemnity for the past and security for the future."[13] Immediate action, either by the Shogunate or by the Powers, was not, however, forthcoming.

The events at Shimonoseki had served to delay, but not to prevent, the presentation of the British demands upon Satsuma for the murder of Richardson. On July 15 Colonel Neale had requested Admiral Kuper to order a portion of the squadron to proceed to Kagoshima.[14] So quiet were affairs at Yokohama, despite the open warfare at Shimonoseki, that the Admiral proposed to take almost all his squadron to Satsuma, leaving only three vessels behind. On August 3 Neale notified the Rojiu that within three days he would leave for Kagoshima, and suggested that a high

[11] *F.R., 1863,* II, 1144.		[12] *1864* *(3242),* p. 89.
[13] *F.R., 1863,* II, 1146.			[14] *1864* *(3242),* p. 82.

official be sent with the squadron. The Rojiu at once replied begging that the expedition be delayed; but the next day a vice-minister informed Neale that an official would be sent in one of the Tycoon's steamers. The vessel failed, however, to arrive in time.[15]

The British squadron, consisting of seven vessels, left Yokohama on August 6, and entered the Bay of Kagoshima on the evening of the eleventh.[16] The next day Colonel Neale delivered his letter for the daimyo, which had been written on April 9.[17] This called for the immediate acceptance of the demands:

First. The immediate trial and execution, in the presence of one or more of Her Majesty's naval officers, of the chief perpetrators of the murder of Mr. Richardson, and of the murderous assault upon the lady and gentlemen who accompanied him. Second. The payment of £25,000 sterling, to be distributed to the relations of the murdered man, and to those who escaped with their lives the swords of the assassins on that occasion.

At no time would Colonel Neale or the Admiral land in order to discuss the demands, and the invitation of the Japanese that they do so was looked upon as treachery. Finally, on the thirteenth, a written reply was delivered on board the flagship.[18] This letter, signed by the minister of the lord, while deprecating the murder and asserting that the assassins had escaped, promised that if the accused were taken and found guilty they would be executed and British officers would be invited to be present. But the fault lay with the Shogunate, it insisted, in failing to insert in the treaties the ancient laws of the land.[19] This question should be decided between the Shogunate and Satsuma, and then the money indemnity could be arranged. The letter closed with the affirmation that "our government acts in everything according to the orders of the Yeddo Government."

[15] An officer was sent in the Tycoon's steamer "Emperor," but was delayed and arrived after the attack [*Japan. No. 1 (1865)*, p. 68].

[16] *1864 (3242)*, pp. 90–92.

[17] Satsuma had been notified of the demands long since by the Yedo authorities.

[18] *1864 (3242)*, p. 95.   [19] See chapter vii, note 35.

This reply was considered to be utterly unsatisfactory, and the Admiral was called upon to resort to such preliminary measures of coercion as might bring the daimyo to terms. He at once followed out the suggestion in Earl Russell's dispatch of December 24, 1862, and seized three small steamers belonging to the daimyo, which had been purchased for $300,000 (Mexican), with the intention of holding them until Satsuma complied with the demands. The immediate effect was what might have been expected. Scarcely had the three steamers been lashed alongside three of the British ships when the batteries opened fire upon the squadron, "an act which," Admiral Kuper reported, "it became necessary immediately to resent, in vindication of the honour of the flag, and as a punishment for the outrage."[20] The squadron then engaged the batteries, having first set fire to the captured ships. A storm was brewing, which rose to a typhoon during the night, so that the fires started by the shells swept over the town and destroyed half of it, as well as an arsenal, a gun foundry, and five large Loochoo junks. The next day the action was renewed, a temple, mistaken for the palace of the daimyo,[21] was shelled, and the entire town was believed to be in ruins. As "every act of retribution and punishment within the scope of operations of a small naval force" had been accomplished, the squadron returned to Yokohama, having lost fifty-six officers and men killed or wounded.[22]

It is interesting to note that Colonel Neale considered that he had now carried out "in letter and in spirit" the onerous instruc-

[20] *1864 (3242)*, p. 97.

[21] Adams, *The History of Japan*, I, 327; Satow, *A Diplomat in Japan*, pp. 84–89. The engagement occurred on August 15 and 16.

[22] The Japanese historian (Baba, *Japan, 1853–1864, or Genji Yume Monogatari*, p. 105), after describing this action, states: "The land and sea strove together like a couple of bulls, until the robber vessels, unable to endure it any longer, were entirely defeated, and fled in disorder to the ocean. When these affairs were reported to the Imperial Court, letters of approval were sent to the clans of Satsuma and Choshiu." Captain St. John, who was present at the action, wrote: "The result of our attack on Kagoshima was to induce the Prince of Satsuma to grant our demands. He evidently was not aware how he had really driven us off" (*ibid.*, p. 206).

tions of last September concerning the Richardson affair.[23] The damage wrought at Kagoshima, in his opinion, covered the demands made upon Satsuma. On his return to Yokohama, however, he advised the Ministers for Foreign Affairs that Satsuma had stated that it could do nothing toward complying with the demands until it had received orders from the Tycoon's Government, and he requested them to take the necessary steps lest he be compelled

to engage the Admiral again to proceed with his fleet to the territory of Satsuma, and continue, much against our desire, the hostilities which have momentarily been suspended in order that the Tycoon's Government should again have the opportunity of satisfactorily terminated [*sic*] this matter.[24]

Here the dispute rested for more than two months, with occasional queries from Colonel Neale. Early in November two envoys arrived in Yokohama from Satsuma. After three days of discussion they agreed on the sixteenth to pay the indemnity of £25,000 and to give a written engagement to continue the search for the assassins and to punish them when discovered.[25] After some delay the money, $100,000 (Mexican), was duly paid on December 11, the written promise was delivered, and Colonel Neale agreed to use his good offices toward the purchase by Satsuma of a ship of war in England.[26]

The "Kagoshima affair" is considered by all historians to be the cause of the sudden change of front of Satsuma, from leadership in the anti-foreign faction to an appreciation of the strength of the foreigners and the futility of trying to expel them. There can be no doubt that the men at Kagoshima learned a remarkable lesson, and it is to their credit that they did not need to have it repeated. But Satsuma had not been rabidly anti-foreign. The presence of steamships, shipyards, foundries, and modern fortifications are proof of that. Although at this time, for other reasons, there was a brief conciliation between Satsuma and the Shogunate, it soon came to an end, and this haughty western clan realized

[23] *1864 (3242)*, p. 92.   [24] September 24, *ibid.*, p. 110.
[25] *Ibid.*, p. 116.   [26] *Japan. No. 2 (1864)*, pp. 1–7.

that it could oppose the Shogunate with other and better weapons than unreasoned hostility to foreigners.[27]

In order to follow through the Kagoshima affair, events as late as December 1863 have been discussed. It will now be of service to turn back and endeavor to follow the developments at Kyoto, which was, when last under consideration, the center of a determined anti-foreign agitation. The date for the expulsion had been fixed for June 25, and the Shogun was detained in Kyoto practically as a hostage. At about the same time came the news, from Yedo, that the British indemnity had been paid, and from Choshiu that the first shots had been fired at the foreigners. The former was received with indignation, and the latter with loud acclaim.

Just about this time, July 4, a high court noble was murdered in Kyoto by three Satsuma samurai. This deed moderated the admiration of the court for that clan, and it was removed from its honorable post of guardian of the Inui gate of the palace.[28]

At Yedo there was much alarm because of the enforced residence of the Shogun at Kyoto. It was commonly reported that he would be deposed, and perhaps put to death. He had gone up to the court in April, intending to stay for ten days at the most; now, almost three months had passed. It was determined to rescue him by force, if necessary, and an attempt was made to secure the loan of some of the foreign warships at Yokohama as transports.[29] When the Representatives of the United States, France, and Eng-

---

[27] The action at Kagoshima was the subject of an extended debate in the House of Commons on February 9, 1864, resulting in the defeat of a resolution expressing regret for the burning of the town contrary to the usages of war among civilized nations (*Hansard's Parliamentary Debates,* 3d Series, Vol. 173, pp. 335–422). Regret was expressed in the Royal Speech at the opening of Parliament, on February 4, 1864 (*ibid.,* p. 4). It is interesting to note that after these criticisms Colonel Neale, who had reported the damage as amounting to £1,000,000 and 1,500 casualties (November 17, 1863), later reported (January 16, 1864) that the inhabitants had retired from the town before the attack, and that the damage, caused by the typhoon rather than by the squadron, was slight. The assassin of Richardson was never punished, although in later years he was well known (Michie, *The Englishman in China,* II, 56). Colonel Neale was rewarded by a Companionship of Bath.

[28] Baba, *op. cit.,* p. 96.   [29] *F.R., 1863,* II, 1131.

land refused to allow their national vessels to sail under the Japanese flag (although Mr. Pruyn offered the services of the "Wyoming" to bring the Shogun back by sea), several British merchant vessels were chartered. Loaded with troops, and commanded by Ogasawara Dzusho-no-Kami, the most active member of the Rojiu, they proceeded to Osaka.[30] This resolute proceeding was successful, without the use of arms, and the Shogun was able to leave Osaka by sea on July 24. But Ogasawara suffered for his loyalty, and for having paid the British indemnity, and at the demand of the court he was punished by the Shogun, being deprived of his title and honors and confined in the castle of Osaka.[31]

So far, to the disgust of the court, the Yedo authorities had done nothing toward expelling the foreigners except to give notice of future negotiations. At Kyoto another Imperial edict urging action and citing the example of Choshiu was issued.[32] A court noble, escorted by troops from western clans, proceeded to Choshiu as an Imperial visitor. Another noble was sent to Yedo to warn the Shogun that his delay in expelling the barbarians was most improper, while in September others were sent to visit some of the coast daimyos.[33] The court was in earnest in its anti-foreign campaign, even if the Shogunate was not.

In order to strengthen its weakened prestige, the Bakufu determined to send envoys of its own to some of the western clans, and also to investigate the attacks on foreign vessels at Shimonoseki. On September 8 the Shogun's ship, "Choyo Maru," was fired on by the Choshiu forts, and two of the envoys, who were compelled to land, were assassinated by ronins. And yet, in spite of this direct insult, the Shogunate felt itself too weak to strike at its open foe.[34]

[30] Left Yokohama on July 11 and 13. Other troops left on the twenty-third.

[31] Baba, *op. cit.*, p. 100. For an entirely erroneous survey of these events, but the best information then available to the Foreign Representatives, see Pruyn to Seward, No. 60, September 28, 1863, in *F.R., 1864*, III, 447–79, in which it is stated that a conspiracy existed to depose and assassinate the Shogun and place Hitotsubashi in his stead. Ogasawara was said to have been at the head of this conspiracy and to have been punished on its discovery. It was believed that the prince of Mito was at the bottom of it.

[32] Baba, *op. cit.*, p. 100.   [33] *Ibid.*, p. 101.   [34] *Ibid.*, pp. 102–3.

Meanwhile the prestige of the court steadily increased. The daimyos continued to flock into Kyoto, and many of them, great and small—more than a hundred, it is said—built residences there or enlarged their old sites, so that the town was full of troops. Never had it been so prosperous.[35] The victories reported by Choshiu and Satsuma over the foreigners were welcomed by the court, and letters of approval were sent to the clans. But the Yedo authorities at the same time sent out a warning to the daimyos not to proceed to hostilities until all efforts at negotiation had failed.[36]

With the announcement of this temperate advice, the hotheads were more than ever convinced that nothing could be expected of the weakling Yedo administration, and the cry arose that the Mikado should take the field in person in the Phoenix Car. In Kyoto the ronins struck down "traitorous" officials and tradesmen with impunity. The court, now completely under the influence of the Choshiu party, approved of the proposal that the Mikado take the field; a military review was held in his presence on August 18; a week later it was announced that he would visit the shrines in Yamato and at Ise before undertaking the expulsion campaign in person; and on the twenty-seventh a prince of the blood, Arisugawa, was appointed generalissimo.[37] At this time a band of ronins, led by a former court noble, took the offensive in Yamato, attacking a Shogunate revenue office there, and proclaiming themselves the vanguard of the Emperor's army. Evidently the antiforeign forces had gathered overwhelming strength.

It was, indeed, the high watermark of the exclusionist agitation. Never again was it so near achievement. When its prospects seemed most fair, suddenly they were blighted. On September 30 a *coup d'état* was executed in Kyoto which destroyed for several years the influence of Choshiu and weakened the anti-foreign party. The enemies of the clan—and there were many among the Tokugawa officials and court nobles—charged it with planning to seize the person of the Mikado when he visited the shrines of Yamato, and thus become dictator of the Empire.[38] The palace

[35] Baba, *op. cit.*, p. 104.   [36] *Ibid.*, p. 106.   [37] *Ibid.*, p. 107.
[38] *Ibid.*, pp. 110–18; Yamaguchi, *A History of Japan*, pp. 45–46.

revolution was successfully carried through. The Choshiu forces were expelled from the city, and seven court nobles of high rank, who were accused of furthering the designs of the clan, retired with them. Satsuma troops were restored to their guardianship of one of the palace gates, the act marking a breach between the two powerful anti-foreign clans. This *coup d'état,* however, was based upon internal rather than foreign affairs. The Mikado announced during the confusion that his personal campaign was only postponed, and on October 1 the clans were instructed to expel the barbarians at once, without further orders from the Shogunate.[39]

But without the aggressive leadership of Choshiu the anti-foreign campaign lacked vigor. The Shogunate officials in Kyoto, regaining their courage, now began to punish the hitherto swaggering ronins, and many of the latter fled to Choshiu or joined marauding bands in the provinces. As the Japanese historian says: "From this time the scheme of expelling the barbarians fell to pieces like ice during a thaw, and the prestige which had accrued to the Imperial Court seemed to be lessened again by its own acts."[40] In the meantime Choshiu made repeated efforts to win pardon for itself and for the seven kuge, but the Mikado was obdurate. The rising influence of the Shogunate was evident in a new Imperial edict, very different from those which had gone before, to the effect that as the Shogunate was engaged in negotiations for the closing of the ports its directions were to be followed in all things, and no rash or violent actions should be committed.[41] This development at Kyoto explains what otherwise seemed inexplicable at Yokohama.

In spite of all the expulsion edicts which were known to the foreigners—and the many others of which they had no inkling—the community at Yokohama did not consider the situation by any means desperate. To be sure, Mr. Pruyn, in a dispatch of July 24 describing the Shimonoseki operations, very correctly stated: "The current is now setting strongly against us,"[42] be-

[39] Baba, *op. cit.,* p. 118.   [40] *Ibid.,* p. 121.
[41] *Ibid.,* p. 128.   [42] *F.R., 1863,* II, 1134.

cause he feared the Ministers at Yedo might be overawed by the hostile daimyos. In spite of all that had happened, he never failed to express his great sympathy with the Government in its troubles; and although entire harmony existed among the four Foreign Representatives he would act with them only if they would not go too far.[43] Within a few days this alarm subsided, as was evident from the departure of almost the entire British fleet to press the demands against Satsuma. A private letter of Mr. Pruyn's at this time gives a good idea of the situation at Yokohama:

I received yesterday a letter which Mr. Brown is translating said to be a summons from the Tycoon to some of the most powerful Daimios to meet him at Yedo to arrange for the expulsion of foreigners. He is now free from actual restraint, whether this movement is serious or not we cannot even anticipate. The rulers of Japan are performing a play on a grand stage, which is farce, comedy and tragedy intermingled. We cannot tell until the curtain falls and the actors walk the streets of everyday life, which will predominate. All we can now do is to watch the motions and guess which is the prevailing tone. The faces are masked and no feature or emotion betrays the real feeling. We have all kinds of rumours to which I have learned to pay no attention and all kinds of speculation to which I never attribute any value. Meanwhile everything goes on merry as a marriage bell and the disinterested observer, neither blinded by interest or led away by feeling would be inclined to laugh at the idea of danger. We have business and pleasure flowing freely in their accustomed and almost well-worn channels—everything seen almost in palpable open conflict with what is heard. We have no marrying and giving in marriage because there is no raw material, but with that exception we are as unconcerned as the antediluvians and yet a storm may come here as suddenly and out of as clear a sky.[44]

So, although the closing of the ports was mandatory, commerce prospered, and a boom in land values at Yokohama occurred just about the time of the Kagoshima affair.[45] Mr. Pruyn then believed the Shimonoseki difficulty would be settled by the Shogunate, though perhaps not speedily enough, and early in September he believed it would be quite safe for him to take up his residence again at Yedo and purposed to do so as soon as his quarters were ready. In the meantime the Representatives awaited instructions

[43] *F.R., 1863*, II, 1135; Pruyn Papers, July 22. [44] Pruyn Papers, August 3. [45] *1864 (3242)*, p. 101; Heco, *op. cit.*, II, 11.

from their Governments as to the course to pursue toward Choshiu.

This calm merely preceded another storm, one not so violent, however, as those which had gone before. On October 14 occurred another unprovoked murder of a European near Kanagawa. This time it was a French officer, Lieutenant Camus, of the Third Battalion of the Chasseurs d'Afrique, who, while riding alone, was cut down by three two-sword men.[46] Great was the indignation; but it was now realized that little could be done except to demand of the Tycoon's Government that it run down and punish the offenders. The drastic demands based on the Richardson affair were not repeated, nor was it now considered wise or proper to hold the Shogun's Government responsible for the murderous acts of private fanatics. Another phase of the renewed ronin activity was the pressure which these outlaws exerted to stop the commerce of Yokohama, this time striking at the source by intimidating the merchants of the interior who were shipping goods to the seaport. Under these circumstances the Rojiu begged Mr. Pruyn not to return to Yedo.

A few days later Mr. Pruyn and Mr. van Polsbroek, the Netherlands Consul General, proceeded to Yedo in response to an urgent invitation of the Ministers for Foreign Affairs. The interview was held on October 26, and its purpose was to request the Foreign Representatives to ask their Governments to consent to the closing of Yokohama and to have the trade transferred to Nagasaki and Hakodate, while the notification of Ogasawara that the foreigners would be entirely expelled would be withdrawn.[47] The reasons for this request were stated as follows:

The unsettled state of things in our realm is increasing. We are apparently approaching a revolution; there may be a general uprising among the people who hate foreigners, and to our shame we must confess that we have no power to suppress this insurrectionary movement.

It is principally owing to the opening to trade of Yokohama that this deplorable state of things exists.

[46] *F.R., 1864,* III, 450; *1864 (3242),* p. 110.
[47] No. 70, *F.R., 1864,* III, 450–56.

If a continuance of trade at Yokohama be persisted in, the state of affairs will grow worse. Trade will suffer, and no doubt disappear in consequence, and then the friendship will be destroyed. It was to establish friendly relations that the treaties were made, as may be seen in the heading of each of them. Friendship is the corner-stone; trade is subordinate to friendship. We have always considered that the framers of the treaty intended it as an experiment, to last as long as it would not prove injurious to Japan. In order to perpetuate this friendship, it is of the highest mutual interest that the port of Yokohama be closed to trade, and, in our opinion, this is the only way to allay the prevailing excitement.

There was, of course, a great measure of truth in this exposition; and yet, as events proved, there were other ways of quieting the agitation than by closing Yokohama. The request itself, so much less drastic than that presented four months before, marked a lessening of the anti-foreign pressure at Kyoto; and it must be remembered also that the anti-Choshiu *coup d'état* had occurred on September 30. This new proposal was presented to the American and Netherlands Representatives first because the first treaties had been made with them, but also, no doubt, because it was felt that they would be more apt to accept it than their colleagues of Great Britain and France. But on this point there was no illusion. Mr. Pruyn and Mr. van Polsbroek both assured the Ministers that they were convinced that the Treaty Powers would never consent to the closing of Yokohama to trade, nor could they themselves enter into any negotiations. They further said "that the treaties were never meant to be experiments, but that it is explicitly stated that they were made to perpetuate friendship and commerce between our respective governments and their citizens and subjects," and they refused to withhold the proposal from their colleagues.

When, the next day, a similar invitation was extended to all the Ministers to visit Yedo, they refused either to go there or to receive at Yokohama any envoys charged with such a communication. The most they would agree to do was to forward the proposal to their respective Governments. Colonel Neale, in addition, warned the Rojiu that any hostile acts by the Government or by any daimyo would be resented by corresponding acts of retribution,[48] while Mr. Pruyn took the opportunity to repeat his friendly advice:

> Let it be at once proclaimed that his Majesty the Tycoon will faithfully observe the existing treaties and require his subjects to do the same. Peace in Japan will be secured by such an exhibition of good faith and vigor. A contrary course invites to a resistance of the authority of the Tycoon. It holds out expectations which will never be realized, while it encourages a defiance of his authority which may subject him to the twofold danger of a civil war and of serious difficulties with all the treaty powers.

This advice called for too strong a policy for the weak and temporizing Yedo officials to adopt at this juncture. One valued suggestion of the American Minister was accepted. He had twice urged the Rojiu to withdraw the expulsion letter presented by Ogasawara on June 24, on the ground that it might be considered by the Treaty Powers as the equivalent of a declaration of war and hence render Japan liable for all the expenses incurred by them in protecting their interests, and also on the ground that it announced the settled policy of the Government to close the ports, and thus left no opportunity for negotiation with the Powers.[49] He went over this ground again with three Governors for Foreign Affairs on November 9, with such conviction that the Rojiu, on the eleventh, notified all the Foreign Representatives that the former opinion of the Government had been changed and that it was desirable that the letter of Ogasawara be returned.[50] This change in policy was received with much satisfaction by all the Foreign Representatives, the British Chargé very naturally believing that the pressure exerted by the British fleet had contributed very largely to the happy result.[51]

The Rojiu, however, had not abandoned their proposal to close Yokohama, and they doubtless reasoned that as the mission in 1862 to the Treaty Powers had been so successful another mission might succeed in this difficult emergency. On November

---

[48] *1864 (3242)*, p. 114.   [49] *F.R., 1864*, III, 456.   [50] *Ibid.*, p. 457.

[51] *1864 (3242)*, p. 115. On November 6 Admiral Kuper notified the Governor of Kanagawa that he would not permit the Japanese to erect certain projected batteries for the defense of Yokohama, and they were in consequence given up (*ibid.*, p. 114).

30, therefore, they turned first to the American Minister and asked his advice as to how such a mission would be received in Europe and the United States. Mr. Pruyn could not speak for the European states, but he could say that in the United States their proposals would be listened to patiently and would be carefully considered, though he could hold out no hope of success.[52] Also, at their request, he agreed to transmit any communication they desired to the Government of Russia, which at that time had no Minister in Japan. The most likely explanation of this move, to Mr. Pruyn, was that the Government sought to gain time, as it had failed in its endeavors to commence negotiations with the Foreign Representatives at Yokohama.

Although they had received little encouragement from the most kindly of all the Representatives, the Japanese still pondered over the new mission. Finally, an opportunity was presented during the discussion growing out of the murder of Lieutenant Camus. The French Minister, M. de Bellecourt, favored a mission of apology and regret, and Admiral Jaurès believed that an autograph letter from the Tycoon to the Emperor Louis Napoleon would go far toward settling the affair.[53] So it was determined that a mission should leave in February, nominally designed "to deprecate the anger of France," but actually commissioned to visit the European Treaty Powers and secure, if possible, their assent to the closing of Yokohama. This meant that for at least six months no active measures were likely to be taken at Yokohama, and, as we have seen, the Shogunate had warned the daimyos against any overt acts, and the Mikado had issued orders to the clans to follow the Shogun's instructions.

At this point something should be said as to the attitude of the American Government toward the amazing developments in Japan during this critical year. Several things should be borne in mind in this connection. The United States was involved in the great Civil War, and the summer of 1863 marked the high tide of the Confederacy. Although the relations with the European Powers

---

[52] No. 80, December 1, *F.R., 1864,* III, 463–64.
[53] No. 3, January 4, 1864, *ibid.,* p. 472.

had improved, yet there was still every reason to preserve a good understanding with them. For this reason, if for no other, Mr. Seward continually counseled the American Minister to sustain and to co-operate in good faith with the Legations of the Treaty Powers. He was also told to deserve and win the confidence of the Japanese Government, if possible.

It may be not altogether easy to apply these two principles in the conduct of details. You will however make the best effort to do so, and will be permitted to judge which of them must give way in any case of irreconcilable conflict.[54]

So when Mr. Seward learned of the British demands, which had impressed Mr. Pruyn so unfavorably, he warned him to lend them his moral support as long as the British sought no conquest or exclusive advantage; but the naval forces were only to protect American lives, and were not to unite in hostilities against the Japanese.[55] Mr. Pruyn, furthermore, was to use his moral influence to procure or to preserve peace between the other Powers and Japan, but force would be used to protect the Legation and American citizens.[56] As it took at least four months for dispatches to be exchanged between Yokohama and Washington, although occasionally brief messages were telegraphed from San Francisco after the overland wire was opened on October 24, 1861, Mr. Seward wisely left to Mr. Pruyn a large discretion, and when the assaults on Americans early in May were reported, Mr. Pruyn was allowed to judge whether a pecuniary indemnity, in addition to the punishment of the offenders, should be insisted upon, or whether the claim should be put over until after the British demands had been adjusted.[57]

When, however, Mr. Pruyn reported, on June 9, that the Legation in Yedo had been burned and that he had been compelled to take refuge in Yokohama, then, on September 1, Mr. Seward penned an instruction[58] which called for specific reparation. It

---

[54] No. 45, July 10, 1863, *F.R., 1863*, II, 1129.

[55] No. 42, June 29, *ibid.*, p. 1126.

[56] No. 43, July 7, *ibid.*, p. 1126.   [57] No. 45, *ibid.*, p. 1129.

[58] No. 46, in reply to fourteen dispatches from Mr. Pruyn, May 26–June 24 (*ibid.*, pp. 1148–50).

was based upon certain conclusions derived from Mr. Pruyn's reports:

First, the facts submitted by you raise a strong presumption that the act of firing the residence of the legation was committed by incendiaries, with a purpose at once political and hostile to the United States, and that the government of Japan could probably have foreseen and prevented it, and that they have, at least, given to it tacit assent and acquiescence.

Secondly, The President is satisfied that your removal of the legation from Yedo to Yokohama was prudent and wise, in view of the circumstances then existing in Japan, and the proceeding is approved. But it is equally clear that the government of Japan ought to have so controlled those circumstances as to have rendered the removal unnecessary; and that it is bound to provide for your safe return to Yedo, and for the secure and permanent re-establishment of the legation in that capital. . . . .

Fourthly. It is with much regret that the President has arrived at the conclusion that the government of Japan has failed to keep its faith, solemnly pledged by treaty, with the United States. . . . . The friendship of this country cannot be secured by the government and people of Japan, nor would it be of any avail, if the United States should fail to maintain their own dignity and self-respect in their intercourse with Japan with the same firmness which they practice in regard to all other nations.

Then followed the five demands: (1) indemnification for all the losses suffered through the burning of the Legation; (2) diligent search to discover and punish the incendiaries; (3) proper and adequate guaranties for Mr. Pruyn's safe return to Yedo, and the permanent re-establishment of the Legation there without delay; (4) the full observance of the treaties between the United States and Japan; (5) a reasonable indemnity, to be fixed by Mr. Pruyn, for the injuries sustained by American citizens at the hands of Japanese, and the bringing of the transgressors to justice. The Tycoon's Government was to be informed that the United States would, "as they shall find occasion," send additional forces to insist upon these demands.

It should be noted that although certain categorical demands were to be preferred, yet they were in the nature of indemnities or guaranties, and carried no punitive measures. In this way they differed widely from the heavy British indemnities.

This dispatch, for some reason, was long delayed in transmission. On December 14 Mr. Pruyn wrote that he had received no letters since those dated July 10 but had received copies of the instruction of September 1 through the courtesy of the French and the British Minister, for Mr. Seward had forwarded copies to their respective Governments.[59] His dispatch to the Rojiu of December 21 was based on the copies, before the original instruction had reached him. In presenting the American demands Mr. Pruyn reviewed all the circumstances connected with the burning of the Legation and the assaults upon Americans in Yokohama, and he assessed the damages at $10,000 in the first instance and $20,000 in the second, and in addition $2,000 for an American citizen, George Horton, who had been deported by the Japanese from the Bonin Islands. If the sum of $32,000 was not paid within thirty days, he reserved the right to make such additional demands as might be required by further instructions or the course of events.[60]

Before the presentation of these demands, Mr. Pruyn had already secured the consent of the Rojiu to the payment of $10,000 damages for the "Pembroke," although the amount had not been received. He had expressed his willingness to settle the attack upon the "Wyoming" and the insult to the flag without any money indemnity, provided a sum was paid to provide annuities for the families of the dead and for the wounded.[61] Furthermore a correspondence regarding the return of the American Legation to Yedo had been in progress for several months.[62] Now, without any ship of war to support him (for the "Jamestown" had gone on December 28 in search of the Confederate cruiser "Alabama"), Mr. Pruyn was called upon to secure redress by argument alone.

In their reply of January 18, 1864, the Rojiu refused to pay any damages for the burning of the Legation lest it be taken as a confession that the fire was caused "by secret instigation of criminals," which would be "an extraordinary indignity for our government." This question they proposed to have their new embassy take up with the Washington authorities. As to the other

[59] No. 81, *F.R., 1864*, III, 465.   [60] *Ibid.*, pp. 466–72.
[61] No. 76, November 28, *ibid.*, p. 458.   [62] *Ibid.*, pp. 460–63.

indemnities, they would investigate and confer with Mr. Pruyn later.[63]

To this the American Minister replied that the payment of the claim would not "necessarily involve the idea . . . . of the complicity of the government in these lamentable occurrences," and he warned them that the President's decision would not be modified or abandoned, and that it would be useless to send envoys to Washington while affairs in Yokohama were in so unsatisfactory a position. Their refusal, he asserted, was additional proof that no justice could be expected unless a minister was supported by a permanent and strong naval force, and it would be his duty to summon the force now in Chinese waters and make use of it if necessary for the maintenance of the national dignity and the rights of American citizens. In closing he reminded them that the United States had not yet agreed to the postponement of the opening of Osaka, Hiogo, and Niigata, and it would be justified in withholding such consent altogether and notifying the Treaty Powers that it regarded such ports as now open under its treaty with Japan.[64]

This statement introduced a new subject for discussion, which had been overlooked by the Japanese, and it came just when they were anxious to have their affairs in order before the new mission to negotiate for the closing of Yokohama should sail. Mr. Pruyn was approached on the matter of granting the assent of the United States to the postponing of the opening of the ports, and the result of the conferences was a convention lowering to five per cent the duty on several kinds of imports and placing articles used in the preparation and packing of tea on the free list.[65] On the same day, January 28, Mr. Pruyn consented to the extension of the time for opening Yedo, Osaka, Hiogo, and Niigata, to five years from

[63] *F.R., 1864,* III, 476–77.

[64] January 20, *ibid.,* pp. 477–78. England had given her consent in the London Protocol of June 6, 1862.

[65] These terms were practically agreed upon in January, 1863, and Pruyn had been instructed to sign such a "Treaty" (No. 43, July 7, 1863), but the signature was delayed for a full year [*F.R., 1864,* III, 482–84; *Japan. No. 1 (1865),* p. 9].

January 1, 1863. A few days later the Ministers, by proclamation, reduced the duties on certain other imports to six per cent.[66] These tariff reductions, as well as the signature of the Swiss Treaty and the long-delayed exchange of ratifications of the Prussian Treaty, were all considered due to the desire of the Government to propitiate the Treaty powers before the arrival of their envoys. This was the third modification of the reasonable tariff drawn up by Townsend Harris in 1858; but as the whole tariff would be subject to revision after July 1 following (according to the Treaties of 1858), the Japanese doubtless thought the concession a small one. It was the Treaty of June 25, 1866, which bound Japan by a disadvantageous conventional tariff until 1899.

In spite of this friendly interlude, the American claims remained unsettled; yet so encouraged was Mr. Pruyn at the turn in the reactionary tide that he counseled moderation in pressing them. He wrote to Mr. Seward:

> The dictates of an enlightened humanity have justified the friendly and patient forbearance which has heretofore characterized our relations with this government; and it is pleasant to believe that such forbearance is still compatible with our true interests as being best calculated to overcome the obstacles arising from the laws and institutions of the government and the prejudices of the ruling class.[67]

Similar moderate views were entertained at this time by Colonel Neale, the British Chargé. On March 1 he wrote to Earl Russell that trade was flourishing, and the general results at the close of the last year were "satisfactory beyond all expectation"; that no aggressive or seriously obstructive acts might be expected from either the Tycoon or any of the daimyos, at least while the envoys were in Europe; that although Choshiu still closed the Straits of Shimonoseki, yet, "unless for the purpose of vindicating our right

---

[66] Articles to be admitted at five per cent duty: machines and machinery; drugs and medicines; iron, in pigs or bars; sheet iron and iron ware; tin plates; white sugar, in loaves or crushed; glass and glassware; clocks, watches, and watch chains; wines, malted and spirituous liquors. Mr. Pruyn inserted the provision for spirituous liquors in order not to appear unfriendly to France. The Japanese themselves reduced the duty on jewelry, perfumery and soap, books, paper, mirrors, arms, cutlery, and drawings.

[67] No. 20, February 29, 1864, *F.R., 1864*, III, 484.

of passage, I am not aware of any detriment sustained to our commerce or navigation in this country by this temporary obstruction"; that "the real designs of the rulers of this country in regard to foreigners in the future, whether they tend towards peace and amity, or to stoppage of trade, aggressive acts and war, are not . . . . matured or determined even by the Tycoon's Government itself, or by the principal feudal chiefs"; and, finally, "an expectant and defensive policy, with a strong naval force in these waters, and a moderate military contingent available in China, if meanwhile our commercial relations are continuedly prosperous, would seem, I humbly conceive, to be the best adapted to meet the actual and present position."[68] Fifty years later such a policy would have been summed up in the two words, "watchful waiting."

Such were the views of the Representatives of the two leading Treaty Powers in Japan about March 1, views which counseled "friendly and patient forbearance" and an "expectant and defensive policy." But in a short time all this was changed and a strong policy, to secure peace by making war, was substituted. For that change two things were responsible—the lack of telegraphic communication with Japan, and the return to his post of Rutherford Alcock, the British Minister.

Sir Rutherford—for he had recently been created a Knight Commander of the Bath—had left Yedo in March 1862. He had been present in London when the first Japanese envoys had agreed to the Convention of June 6 of that year, and his views had doubtless influenced Earl Russell when he drafted his crushing demands for indemnities in the Richardson affair, in December. A year later, in December 1863, he left England for Japan, and arrived at Yokohama on March 2, 1864. When about to leave, Earl Russell had given him certain very general instructions, in view of the uncertainty concerning affairs in Japan which then prevailed.[69] These instructions called, however, for a defensive policy. He was to require from the Tycoon and the daimyos the execution of the

---

[68] *Japan. No. 1 (1865)*, p. 12.   [69] December 17, *ibid.*, p. 1.

engagements of the Treaty; he was to consult with the Admiral and any military officer in Japan as to the means of strengthening and holding Yokohama; but the abandonment of Nagasaki in case of attack was suggested. The Admiral, if Alcock agreed, was authorized to destroy the batteries which had been erected to interrupt the passage of British merchantmen, "and which shall have evinced their hostile purposes by some hostile act," but their hostile purpose must be clearly proved. The Admiral was to take care "that no unarmed and peaceable towns should be bombarded, but when fired upon the ships of war must return the fire with vigor and rapidity." In other words, the Government was unwilling to authorize the destruction of another town like Kagoshima—and it must be remembered that to the date of these instructions no British ship had been fired upon at Shimonoseki. Further instructions warned Alcock that the modifications in the Treaty agreed upon at London in 1862 were to be considered binding unless expressly revoked,[70] and also that although he might call upon the naval and military forces for assistance, yet when operations had been decided upon their execution was to be solely in the hands of the naval and military commanders.[71] He was to have "no authority to direct either of them to undertake any operation, or to interfere with their directions as to the manner in which any operation should be conducted," nor could they undertake any military or naval operations without his concurrence, unless some sudden emergency should call for immediate action. Further evidence of the moderate opinions which prevailed at Downing Street is found in the passing of an additional Order in Council on January 7, 1864, which authorized the British Consul General in Japan, whenever it should appear that the unrestricted entrance or passage of British ships or vessels into any straits or other waters of Japan "may lead to acts of disturbance or acts of violence, or may otherwise endanger the maintenance of peaceful relations and intercourse" between British subjects and those of Japan, to make and enforce any rule or

[70] December 19, *ibid.*, p. 1.   [71] December 24, *ibid.*, p. 2.

regulation for the purpose of prohibiting or regulating such entrance or passage. British ships of war were authorized to use force to carry out such regulations, and if need be to seize the offending ship and take her to some port in Japan so that the navigators might be brought to trial.[72] This Order in Council certainly was designed to avoid trouble in the Straits of Shimonoseki.

The development of Sir Rutherford's views after his return to Japan can be traced with some accuracy through the voluminous dispatches which he forwarded to Earl Russell or to his colleagues in Yokohama. As dean of the Diplomatic Corps, with experience going back to 1859 in Japan, and earlier still in China, his views were worthy of careful consideration and, when supported by his forceful character, soon prevailed upon all his colleagues. Under Alcock's leadership they revised their own opinions and set aside the instructions of their Governments. Nothing but the apparent success of his policies saved him and his colleagues from severest censure, and today it is possible to think of that success as more apparent than real.

It will be remembered that, some years before, Sir Rutherford and Townsend Harris were not on the best of terms. Their different attitudes toward Japan precluded any common understanding. But the events of the past two years had seemingly given some support to Alcock's earlier views, so that after his first conference with Mr. Pruyn, on March 16, the latter was able to write: "We find ourselves in very fair accord and I think we will walk well together. There need be no conflict as the interests of our respective governments harmonize, and yet he and Mr. Harris quarrelled like old women."[73] Already the policy of co-operation had been set forth in the joint memorandum of July 25, 1863, and it was incumbent upon Alcock to maintain this joint action, but if possible under his own direction.

At the end of the month Alcock sent to Earl Russell a long

[72] *Japan. No. 1 (1865)*, pp. 3–4. The right of foreign ships to enter the Straits of Shimonoseki was not questioned at the time, although this narrow strait was wholly within the jurisdiction of Japan.

[73] Pruyn Papers, March 16, 1864.

dispatch, summing up the developments of the past two years and stating his conviction that the end of conciliation and forbearance by the Treaty Powers had been reached.[74] This conclusion, however, was based upon premises both false and erroneous. After describing the concessions made when the first envoys visited Europe, he wrote:

> The avowed object of the second Mission is to declare that all the hopes held out by the Tycoon of the probable results of the first concessions have been illusory. He is not stronger but weaker than he was. His Government is not more but less able to hold its own and protect foreigners from the hostility of the opposing Daimios; and now what he has to propose is no longer concession or even alliance offensive and defensive, but absolute withdrawal from the country as the sole condition of peace.

As to the first statement, we have already seen the weakening of the anti-foreign agitation at Kyoto, the expulsion of Choshiu, the pro-foreign views of Satsuma, and the Mikado's edict to follow the directions of the Shogun in regard to foreign affairs. As to the second, the very mission of the envoys was proof of the improvement in foreign relations. In June 1863 the Foreign Ministers were served with notice that the Mikado had given orders that all the ports be closed; but this letter had been withdrawn, and in February 1864 the envoys were dispatched to negotiate regarding the closing of Yokohama only. The idea of "absolute withdrawal" had not been mentioned for several months until Alcock himself revived it. In this dispatch there were inclosures describing the conferences then in progress at Kyoto in which several of the staunch pro-foreign daimyos were taking a prominent part, as well as telling of the attack by Choshiu upon a steamer of Satsuma,[75] thus indicating the open breach between the former leaders of the anti-foreign faction. It would have been easy to find in recent developments a vindication of the policy of "friendly and patient forbearance."

---

[74] March 21, *Japan. No. 1 (1865)*, pp. 13–16.

[75] On January 26. The steamer belonged to the Tycoon and had been loaned to Satsuma. It was burned, and twenty-six Satsuma men were lost. Choshiu explained that it was mistaken for a foreign vessel (*ibid.*, p. 17).

Two weeks later Alcock wrote[76] that although

there is the strongest ground for believing that there will be no material improvement until measures of hostile and coercive character are resorted to—measures sufficiently decisive and uncompromising to carry conviction into the minds of all who are responsible, and the ruling classes generally, that there are some Treaty Powers at least who possess both the will and the ability to maintain in their integrity all the rights conferred by Treaties, and secure their full observance with the strong hand,

yet the time was not ripe. In the first place, the Americans had no ships, the French but one, and the Dutch but two, in those seas; and, secondly, it might be well to wait until more was learned of the decision taken at Kyoto concerning foreign affairs. For coercive measures Alcock found ample justification in the acts of Choshiu in firing upon foreign flags and in sinking native junks laden with produce for the foreign trade. Other grievances requiring redress were the virtual exclusion of the Foreign Representatives from Yedo, and "the suspension of all the functions of Government there, so far as foreigners are concerned, by the prolonged absence of the Tycoon and his Ministers"; the isolated attacks upon foreigners at the treaty ports; and even the murder of Japanese merchants at Osaka and elsewhere, avowedly for trading with foreigners. One may search in vain through these dispatches of the British Minister for any appreciation of the difficult position in which the Tycoon's Government was placed, or any sympathy with it in its endeavors to keep faith with the foreigners and preserve order within the land. But to consider the absence of the Tycoon and some of his Ministers from Yedo, in order to take part in a conference of the most vital significance at Kyoto, as a grievance "requiring redress," seems to reach the summit of arrogance.

In the meantime Alcock and Mr. Pruyn had engaged in several conferences on the state of affairs, and their views were presented in an exchange of letters.[77] Alcock's letter of April 22 surveyed at great length the situation as he understood it, and arrived at certain conclusions: first, "that there is a settled pur-

---

[76] April 14, *Japan. No. 1 (1865)*, pp. 18–20.   [77] *F.R., 1864*, III, 495–502.

pose to get rid of foreigners, and either to expel them from the Japanese territories altogether, or, failing this, to lock them up within the fortified barriers of Nagasaki, where entrance and escape are alike difficult, if not impossible, without the consent of those who hold the keys"; secondly, that the Treaty Powers must decide between the active and the passive policy; thirdly, that the conduct of Choshiu amply justified any action on the part of the Powers; and, finally, that an attack upon Choshiu by all the Powers with or without the Tycoon's consent might either prevent an attack upon the foreign communities or else precipitate a war now, when the Japanese would have to act at a disadvantage before their preparations were completed. These views were based on the premise that hostilities were bound to occur sooner or later, and that the offensive would really be the best defensive.

Mr. Pruyn's reply, dated May 13, while accepting much of Alcock's reasoning, arrived at a very different conclusion:

> In view of these facts, what is the duty of the treaty powers? Manifestly to insist on the observance of the treaties, and neither to surrender nor postpone any rights now acquired. At the same time, they should, in my opinion, exercise great moderation and forbearance in their treatment of the government, and give it credit for sincerity, as far and as long as possible; sympathize with and aid it in its difficulties, and strengthen it as far as may be safe, to enable it to resist any probable combination of the Daimios, of whom the Tycoon is not the sovereign, and who are in a great measure independent.

But the wisdom of punishing Choshiu evidently appealed to him, and he was ready to meet with his colleagues and concert such measures as seemed essential to the preservation of treaty rights.

On May 1, Sir Rutherford forwarded another long dispatch to Downing Street, to the effect that advices from Kyoto were convincing proof that the Government was determined to expel the foreigners as soon as it had made the necessary preparations, and that a decision would soon have to be made whether the Powers would calmly await "the full-maturing of all their schemes of treachery and violence to effect their avowed object, the destruction of trade, and the expulsion of foreigners, in violation of all existing Treaties, or anticipate such hostile action by taking at once some effective steps to place our relations on a more secure and less derogatory footing?"[78] On May 6, for the first time, he developed his plans for an attack upon Choshiu, "the most violent and rash of his class," which would tend to paralyze the whole body of daimyos.[79] He also summoned more troops from Hong Kong to guard Yokohama while the projected operations were in progress.[80]

These dispatches, increasingly strong in tone, caused consternation in the Foreign Office at London. The Kagoshima operations had recently been severely criticized in Parliament. The Government was not disposed to blunder into another war in the Far East, and Alcock was promptly advised to that effect.[81] On July 26 Earl Russell replied to Alcock's dispatches of May 1, 6, and 14, and after rejecting his proposal "to make war for the sake of forestalling war," continued:

> There is another course of policy which appears preferable, either to precipitating hostilities, or to the abandonment of the rights we have acquired by our Treaties. This course of policy appears in conformity with the views so moderately and carefully expressed by the minister of the United States.[82]
> This policy consists in—
> 1. Giving every encouragement and support to such of the Tycoon's Ministers, and to such of the Daimios as are favorable to foreign trade, and thus lead to the ultimate weakening of the feudal system and of the protectionist theory of Japan.
> 2. To make arrangements with the Japanese Government for the protection of the foreign settlement at Yokohama.
> 3. To keep for the present a strong squadron in the Japanese seas.
> 4. To endeavour to establish an understanding with the Governments of France, the Netherlands, and the United States, with a view to our common interests in Japan.

[78] *Japan. No. 1* (*1865*), pp. 27–29.

[79] *Ibid.*, pp. 32–36. In this dispatch Alcock commented at length on the memorial of the eleven daimyos early in 1863. The anti-foreign views of several of them had, however, altered considerably in the year that had passed.

[80] *Ibid.*, p. 43.   [81] *Ibid.*, p. 44. Two wars had been fought with China.

[82] This refers to Pruyn's letter of May 13. The sentence "This . . . . States" is omitted from the dispatch as printed in *Japan. No. 1* (*1865*), p. 44, but Alcock gave Pruyn a copy of the dispatch as he received it, which is published in *F.R., 1864,* III, 556, and Lord Lyons showed a copy to Mr. Seward (*ibid.,* p. 594), both of which contained the sentence.

In another dispatch of the same day Earl Russell wrote:

> Her Majesty's Government positively enjoin you not to undertake any military operations whatever in the interior of Japan; and they would indeed regret the adoption of any measures of hostility against the Japanese Government or Princes, even though limited to naval operations, unless absolutely required by self-defence. The action of the naval and military forces of Her Majesty in Japan should be limited to the defence and protection of Her Majesty's subjects resident in Japan, and of their property, and to the maintenance of our Treaty rights.
>
> It may be hoped that the power vested in you by Her Majesty's Order in Council of the 7th of January last, to prohibit, or regulate, or restrict, the entrance or passage of British ships into straits or waters of Japan, when such entrance or passage may lead to acts of disturbance or acts of violence, or may otherwise endanger the maintenance of peaceful relations or intercourse between Her Majesty's subjects and the subjects of the Tycoon of Japan, will enable you to prevent the occurrence of the necessity for any such measures of hostility to obtain redress for injuries done to British vessels.[83]

The British Government had, therefore, refused to support its aggressive representative in Japan, and instead it had adopted as its own the policy of moderation and forbearance laid down by the American Minister. More than that, it sent copies of Russell's instruction to the other Treaty Powers, and expressed the hope that a concert might be established. The acquiescence of the United States and France was promptly given; the Netherlands alone favored action against Choshiu, but it preferred if possible to have it come through the Tycoon's Government.[84] In an instruction of August 20 Mr. Seward informed Mr. Pruyn of the President's approval of the four points laid down by Earl Russell, and emphasized it by a statement that it would probably be inconvenient to keep a naval force continually in the Japanese seas, but that the United States would endeavor to have a vessel appear there sufficiently often to make a suitable impression upon the Japanese Government.[85] But before these pacific instructions could reach Japan the offensive had already been assumed.[86] If there had been telegraphic communication, the only joint naval operations of the Treaty Powers would never have occurred.

[83] *Japan. No. 1 (1865)*, p. 45.   [84] *Ibid.*, pp. 54–55.
[85] No. 71, *F.R., 1864*, III, 594.
[86] Alcock received the instructions before September 30.

CHAPTER X

THE JOINT EXPEDITION AGAINST CHOSHIU
1864 [1]

THE PROPOSAL "to make war for the sake of forestalling war" had been put forward by Sir Rutherford Alcock on the strength of his understanding of the probable attitude of the Mikado, the Tycoon, and the leading daimyos toward foreigners.[2] It is unfortunate that the Shogunate did not deem it advisable to keep the Foreign Ministers well informed of the political situation within the country; and yet its course was intelligible. To have told the foreigners of the full force of the opposition might have encouraged them to do what had occasionally been threatened—pass over the Shogun and deal directly with the Mikado at Kyoto. Nor could the Yedo authorities speak freely of movements concerning which they were not themselves fully informed, or tell the Ministers that the anti-foreign policy which they had been forced to accept was but a blind, and that they hoped to temporize long enough to overcome the opposition of the hostile nobles and the court.[3] There was, to be sure, abundant written evidence of the

[1] The instructions for 1864 are numbered 56–86; of these thirty-one, nineteen were printed in *F.R., 1864*, III, one in *F.R., 1865*, III, and one in *F.R., 1866*, II. The dispatches are numbered 1–77; of these, forty-three were printed in *F.R., 1864*, III, and three in *F.R., 1865*, III.

[2] "It is possible that Sir Rutherford Alcock's fears were well founded, but to the writer, himself a resident in Japan at the time, it has never appeared probable that the policy of expulsion was seriously entertained by any party in, or likely to be in, power" (Dickins and Lane-Poole, *The Life of Sir Harry Parkes*, II, 33–34).

[3] A slightly similar situation prevailed during these years of civil war in the United States. Mr. Seward, Secretary of State, was very frank in his conversations with the Foreign Ministers, especially Lord Lyons, but he gave expression to his own point of view, which at times did not agree with the facts. Not infrequently his dispatches to the American Representatives abroad were designed rather for consumption in America than for effect in Europe. So the Tycoon framed letters and orders which might quiet the restless daimyos but which he had no desire to act upon in dealing with the foreigners.

hostile disposition of both the Kyoto and the Yedo administration, but there was also reason to believe that the crest of the anti-foreign wave had been reached and passed. As Mr. Pruyn had said of this baffling period, "Everything seen [is] in palpable open conflict with what is heard." With such ignorance of the real situation misunderstandings were bound to occur. The amazing thing is, not that there were so many, but that there were so few.

After the expulsion of Choshiu from Kyoto on September 30, 1863, there had been a weakening of the anti-foreign agitation at the capital accompanied by an increase in the prestige of the Shogunate, until, as we have seen, the Mikado gave orders that "the directions of the Bakufu were to be followed in all things, and that no rash or violent actions must be committed." This declaration had encouraged the Yedo officials to revise their demands upon the foreigners, and instead of seeking their entire expulsion to ask only that Yokohama be abandoned. On November 13 Shimadzu Saburo, of Satsuma, visited Kyoto for the third time in order to advocate a second great conference there for the purpose of aiding the Shogun in "performing his duty against the barbarians, and in giving peace to the empire."[4] This proposal was adopted by the court, and the Shogun was requested to make a second visit to Kyoto.

Once more he was preceded by Hitotsubashi, his guardian, who reached Kyoto on January 5, and a month later the Shogun left Yedo, arriving in Kyoto on February 22. Instead of being severely reprimanded by the Mikado for so continually putting off the date of expulsion of the foreigners, as many expected, he was received with honor and promptly promoted to the rank of third minister at the Imperial court (Udaijin). On February 28 the Shogun and his suite had audience of the Emperor, at which an Imperial speech was read by one of the nobles.[5] In this the Emperor ascribed his own want of virtue as the cause of their present unhappiness:

---

[4] Baba, *Japan, 1853–1864, or Genji Yume Monogatari*, p. 129.
[5] *Ibid.*, pp. 132–33.

At home the laws put aside, the bonds of society loosened and the people groaning under a weight of misery; on all sides there is evidence of dissolution and ruin. Abroad, we are exposed to the insults of five great continents of haughty barbarians, and the calamity of being swallowed up by them threatens us at every moment.

He then stated:

The subjugation of the ugly barbarians is a fundamental law of our policy, and we must set an army on foot in order to strike awe into them and chastise them. But We like not in truth a reckless attack upon the barbarians. Do you therefore ponder an efficient scheme and submit it to Us. We will then discuss its merits with care, and come to a firm and irrevocable determination.

The Mikado also named five of the great daimyos who might be depended upon in this emergency, and the Shogun was instructed to work with them. This speech, while still calling for the expulsion of the foreigners, was much more restrained than the edicts of the preceding year had been.

On March 5 an Imperial letter[6] was presented to the Shogun, which lamented the weakness of the land:

After a peace of more than two hundred years, Our military power is insufficient to put down our foreign enemies, and We therefore fear lest to revive recklessly the law of punishment and warning would be to plunge the state into unfathomable disasters,

but found comfort in the reforms introduced by the Bakufu. In regard to foreign affairs there was this surprising statement:

But contrary to all anticipation, Fujiwara Sanetomi and others, believing the violent words of low and vulgar fellows, and disregarding the condition of the Empire and the safety of the state, have falsified our command, and issued orders to soldiers of low rank to expel the barbarians, and madly to raise up war to destroy the Shogun.

The violent servants of the Saisho of Nagato have made a tool and a plaything of their master, have without provocation fired upon barbarian ships, have murdered the messengers of the Bakufu, and have for their own purposes seduced away Sanetomi and others to their province. Such mad and violent people must certainly be punished. Nevertheless, as all this arises from Our want of virtue, we sincerely feel unspeakable re-

---

[6] Baba, *op. cit.*, pp. 134–36; *Japan. No. 1 (1865)*, p. 30; *F.R., 1864*, III, 502–3. Three different versions.

pentance and shame. Moreover, We are of opinion that if our war vessels are compared with those of foreigners, it will be seen that they are as yet insufficient either to destroy the fierceness of the proud barbarians, or to manifest the dignity of our country abroad; but on the contrary we receive constant insults at their hands. You must therefore, as you have frequently asked permission to do, fortify the important harbours of the Inland Sea, with the whole resources of the empire, subjugate the ugly barbarians, and carry out the Law of Punishment and Warning made by the former Emperors.

The letter, therefore, approved the cautious policy of the Shogunate, and decreed punishment for Choshiu and the fugitive court nobles. It was received by the Tycoon and the daimyos present in Kyoto, and was forwarded to those who were absent.

The Shogun's reply was presented on the twenty-first.[7] In it he expressed regret for all his shortcomings, especially in failing to close the port of Yokohama, and he promised to carry out all the instructions then received:

The protection of the seaboard is a matter of course, and he will carry to the highest degree of perfection the military defences of every province; he will put an end to the contemptuous treatment we receive from the barbarians, and will prepare vessels of war; in the end he will revive the great law of Punishment and Warning, and cause the dignity of our country to be known beyond the seas. To all these things will he give his most diligent attention.

He would, however,

strictly observe the Imperial wish that Punishment and Warning should not be recklessly entered upon, and he hopes to be able to devise such a plan as shall ensure certain victory. As he has already sent envoys to foreign countries to speak about the matter of closing the port of Yokohama, he hopes, at all events, to be able to accomplish that; but as the dispositions of the barbarians are hard to fathom, he will continue to be most diligent and energetic in the fortification of the seaboard.

Copies of these letters came into the possession of Sir Rutherford Alcock in April, and became the evidence on which he based his conclusions that the Japanese were about either to expel the foreigners or to lock them up at Nagasaki. At the time both

[7] Baba, *op. cit.*, pp. 137–39; *Japan. No. 1 (1865)*, p. 31; *F.R., 1864*, III, 504–5. Different versions.

documents were considered weak and temporizing by the exclusionists. "By speaking thus, after having previously proclaimed the 'expulsion of the barbarians,' the Court brought upon itself the reproach of inconsistency," wrote a contemporary historian.[8] The Emperor also wondered if the Shogun had really understood his commands, which elicited another statement from the latter that "the barbarians must not be expelled without deliberation."[9]

During the rest of his stay in Kyoto the Shogun steadily gained in favor and influence.[10] This fact is evident in the stern repression of the anti-foreign ronins in Kyoto, in the distribution of high court honors by the Mikado among the leading retainers of the Shogunate, in the refusal of the Mikado to pardon Choshiu and the seven fugitive court nobles, and finally in the conferring on June 3 of full powers on the Bakufu, in all matters, including the closing of Yokohama and the punishment of Choshiu and the seven nobles. The Shogun, in turn, issued a new law which greatly increased the prestige of the court, providing among other things that the Shogun and the daimyos should go up to Kyoto in the future to receive investiture on succeeding to their offices or fiefs. From every point of view this visit to Kyoto was more encouraging than that in 1863, and when the Shogun returned to Yedo on June 23 there was great joy among all the officials, great and small, "who were glad to think that, by the aid of the Shimadzu family, the Tokugawa family had been reinstated, and their happiness was shared by the town, down to the very lowest classes."[11] But this satisfaction was not shared by Choshiu, or by the anti-foreign ronins who had gathered there. The restored influence of the Shogunate at Kyoto was to be maintained by the presence there of Hitotsubashi, who had been appointed protector of the Imperial palace, the daimyo of Aidzu, staunchly loyal to the Tokugawas, who was military governor of the city, and the ex-daimyo of Echizen, the most outspoken of all the pro-foreign lords.

As we have seen, the deliberations at Kyoto were considered menacing by the Foreign Representatives, and it was generally

[8] Yamaguchi, *A History of Japan,* p. 53.   [9] *Japan. No. 1* (*1865*), p. 32.
[10] Baba, *op. cit.,* pp. 141–44.   [11] *Ibid.,* p. 144.

believed that a determined effort was about to be made to close Yokohama. Frequent conferences were held by the four representatives of the United States, Great Britain, France, and the Netherlands, and on May 18 Mr. Pruyn, for the first time, expressed the hope "that the position of affairs at home will permit the President to despatch a strong re-enforcement to the squadron in the China seas." In his opinion the withdrawal of the ships then in the harbor would be the signal for an instantaneous outbreak, and the United States "should participate in protecting our common rights and interests."[12]

About this time the Rojiu sent a high official to communicate to the British Minister certain information concerning the proceedings at Kyoto, "and the satisfactory result attained, after innumerable difficulties," and also to urge the Powers not to proceed against Choshiu, as the Tycoon proposed to initiate punitive measures against that daimyo himself.[13] This announcement was received with suspicion, and its purpose was believed to be solely to gain time until the Rojiu were ready to turn against the foreigners.[14] In reporting this to Earl Russell, Alcock asserted that the Treaty Powers were reduced to three alternatives: to be shut up in Nagasaki or Hakodate, to withdraw from Japan altogether, or to maintain treaty rights in their integrity with effective force.

[12] No. 36, *F.R., 1864,* III, 493.

[13] *Japan. No. 1 (1865),* pp. 45–49. Typical of the uncertainty of the times, and of Alcock's attitude of mind, is the fact that he preferred to accept as correct, instead of the information presented by the Shogunate official, which really was accurate, certain information "previously received from other and at least as reliable sources." This budget of news contained such false information as that Choshiu had appeared before the Council at Kyoto (whereas the Mikado resolutely refused to pardon him); that Aidzu had committed hara-kiri, and later that he had been murdered by a Satsuma ronin; that Echizen had been denounced as a traitor and had left the Council, for his own safety; and that "the final triumph of the more violent members of the Council hostile to foreigners" had been attained.

[14] It was at this time that Alcock demanded that the Japanese provide accommodations for the British marines and the Twentieth Regiment, on the ground that the perpetual menace of danger and the efforts for the expulsion of the foreigners directed by the Tycoon's Government made their presence necessary. The Japanese granted the desired quarters. This would seem to indicate that the Shogun, at least, had no immediate intention of attacking Yokohama.

Pending the receipt of specific instructions, he felt that the Representatives on the spot would have to decide between one of two courses:

They must either consent to wait passively the course of events, until acts of violence or treachery for the expulsion of foreigners from Yokohama are in full operation, or anticipate attack, and, if possible, avert it, by striking a blow at Choshiu's batteries, closing the Inland Sea to commerce, which may cause the hostile Daimios, as a body, to pause and recoil before the immediate consequences to themselves of a conflict with one or more of the Treaty Powers.

Alcock had determined upon a course of proceedings—a joint attack upon Choshiu—as early as the beginning of May, but he was not prepared to carry it immediately into effect or to urge it too forcefully upon his colleagues. As the result of repeated conferences of the four Representatives a Protocol was agreed to on May 25 and formally signed on the thirtieth.[15] It is interesting to note that in forwarding the unsigned draft to Earl Russell, on May 25, Alcock now pointed out that the enemy which the Treaty Powers had to face was the body of six hundred daimyos, which controlled both Executive and people, and that as the former could not be conciliated "we must either accept the gage he throws down or retire from the conflict."[16]

The preamble of the Protocol[17] stated that the Representatives of Great Britain, France, the United States, and the Netherlands, "being fully convinced of the increasing gravity of the existing state of affairs in Japan, have thought it right to unite in order to consider, in concert with each other, the nature of the situation, and to organize by mutual understanding the means for prevent-

[15] In sending a first rough draft of this Protocol to Mr. Pruyn on May 18, Alcock pointed out that "the object I believe we should all desire to have in view is to affect [affirm] our right of action in any direction without binding ourselves down to the time or the mode—and if possible to deter the government from proceeding to extremities until we ourselves were better prepared or our governments had time to give specific instructions and means to carry them out" (Pruyn Papers).

[16] *Japan. No. 1 (1865)*, pp. 49–50.

[17] French and English texts, *ibid.*, pp. 50–53. The Protocol was signed on May 30.

ing its aggravation." Three points were then considered: the silence of the Government regarding the joint declaration of the previous July dealing with the hostile acts of Choshiu; the communications made by the Rojiu with regard to closing the port of Yokohama; and the joint measures necessary to be adopted "to preserve the rights guaranteed by Treaties, to secure the safety of their countrymen, and to stay the Governor [*sic*] of the Tycoon in the course of open reaction upon which they have entered." As to the first point, it was resolved to recall to the attention of the Government the collective declaration of July, and to make a fresh effort to cause it to remove the obstacles which obstructed the navigation of the Inland Sea; as to the second, the Protocol simply recorded the four statements of the Rojiu that Yokohama should be closed, and especially similar statements recently made to the British and French Ministers; and as to the third, it was held to be the duty of the Representatives to summon the Government of the Tycoon formally to withdraw the declaration of its determination to close the port of Yokohama, and, in default of a satisfactory reply and pending the final decision of their respective Governments, to reserve to themselves

in the first place the right of declaring collectively to the Tycoon's Government that they consider them responsible for the least injury which may be caused to the persons or properties of their countrymen, and of afterwards taking in concert such measures as they may judge necessary for assuring, each according to the means of action which he has in his power to dispose of, the safety of the foreign communities at Yokohama, as well as the maintenance of the rights guaranteed by Treaties.

A copy of this Protocol was at once forwarded to the Rojiu by each of the Ministers, under an identical covering note.[18]

On receipt of Alcock's dispatches of May 21 and 25 and the draft Protocol, Earl Russell at once recalled the forceful British Minister, and again criticized his views on Japanese affairs.[19] On August 18 he repeated his belief that the navigation of the Inland Sea was not necessary to foreign commerce as long as Kyoto

[18] *Ibid.,* p. 53; *F.R., 1864,* III, 506.
[19] August 8, *Japan. No. 1 (1865),* p. 54.

and Osaka were closed, and instructed Alcock not to call upon Admiral Kuper to attack Choshiu but to turn all their attention to the defense of Yokohama.[20] There is today much reason to believe that in this paragraph Earl Russell expressed a sound judgment concerning the situation in Japan: "If the Tycoon and the Mikado see that the British position is strong, and that the British naval and military forces are effective, they will, by degrees, if not at once, drop all thoughts of violating the existing Treaties, and of expelling foreigners from Japan." It must be considered a great pity that the lack of prompt communication prevented a trial of this reasonable course of action.

The reply of the Rojiu to the Protocol was not presented until June 30, and was, from the point of view of the Foreign Representatives, entirely unsatisfactory.[21] In regard to opening the Inland Sea, the Ministers stated that they were considering this action, but that time would be required to carry out their arrangements, and they requested that for the present this matter be left to them to manage. As to the closing of Yokohama, they had explained fully the reasons for this through their envoys sent abroad. At this point the interpreters of the American and British Legations failed to agree. The American version gave the impression that the Japanese were still deliberating on this matter and hoped to tranquilize the public feeling, while the British translator considered the closing of the port to be the only plan calculated to calm the national feeling and restore good relations.

On receipt of this long-delayed reply, the Foreign Representatives again considered the situation, and on July 5 came to the decision to open the Inland Sea if the Government failed to do so within twenty days.[22] For this purpose there were available one American, fifteen British, four Dutch, and three French ships of war.

This decision was followed by the drafting and signing, on July 22, of a very comprehensive memorandum which restated

[20] *Japan. No. 1 (1865)*, p. 56.
[21] *Ibid.*, p. 67; *F.R., 1864*, III, p. 528.   [22] *F.R., 1864*, III, p. 517.

the views already expounded by the British Ministers.[23] After agreeing that the punishment of Choshiu was the action best qualified to meet the exigencies of the hour, the Representatives agreed to five principles which would serve as a basis for future co-operation: (1) the neutralization of Japan; (2) the maintenance of treaty rights; (3) the protection of the open ports against any attack, considered by them improbable, in consequence of any operations in the Inland Sea; (4) the determination not to ask for or to accept any concession of territory or any exclusive advantage, in the open ports or elsewhere in Japan; (5) the abstaining from all interference in the jurisdiction of the Japanese authorities over their people, as well as from all intervention between the contending parties in the country.

They furthermore agreed that as soon as the naval commanders should report that they were ready to act, the Representatives would each send an identical note to the Rojiu, covering certain specific points, among them that if within twenty days there was no change in the Choshiu situation the naval and military authorities would proceed to action without further notice; that they would not even discuss the closing of Yokohama; and that the non-fulfillment of the London Convention of 1862 would cause the Powers to insist upon the immediate opening of Yedo, Osaka, Hiogo, and Niigata.

The framing of this extended statement had been the work of many days, during which the American Minister was in Yedo, and before it was actually signed there seemed to be a chance that hostile operations might be avoided. It had been reported, by way of Nagasaki, that the daimyo of Choshiu was willing enough to come to terms if the Powers would approach him peacefully and consider his justification for his deeds.[24] Just at this time two young Choshiu samurai returned from England (where they had been sent by their daimyo to be educated), alarmed at the news which had reached them there of the threatened attack, and eager to convince their lord of the folly of opposing Great Britain

---

[23] *Ibid.*, pp. 528–33; *Japan. No. 1 (1865)*, pp. 62–66.
[24] Pruyn Papers, July 19.

alone, to say nothing of the combined fleet of the Powers. Sir Rutherford and his colleagues believed that it would be wise to co-operate with these young men and to use them as dispatch-bearers to the obstinate feudal chief. Admiral Kuper agreed, and two British ships of war left Yokohama on July 1, to carry Ito Shunsuke and Inouye Bunda (later Prince Ito and Marquis Inouye) to Choshiu. Each of the four Representatives sent letters of advice and warning to the daimyo.[25]

The youthful envoys landed at Totomi on July 26, and the two vessels cruised about, making surveys, and gathering information concerning the batteries, until August 6, when the Japanese returned with an oral answer from their lord.[26] It was to the effect

that the hostile attitude of their lord was the result of orders received from the Mikado and the Tycoon, and that acting under these circumstances, he was unable to change his policy. Being, however, perfectly aware of the strength of the European Powers, and that it would be useless to endeavour to thwart their designs or refuse compliance with their demands, he requested a delay of three months, during which time he would communicate with the Mikado, and endeavour to obtain the recision of the present orders.[27]

In private conversation the envoys stated

that their Daimio had been originally favourable to foreigners, but had gone too far now to retract, and that they did not believe the matter could be settled without war. They also suggested it as a good measure that the foreign Representatives should throw the Tycoon overboard, and going to Osaka, demand an interview with the Mikado's Ministers, and conclude a Treaty with him. They spoke with great bitterness of the Tycoon's Dynasty; that they kept all trade, not only foreign, but native also, to themselves by seizing all places where trade was likely to develop itself, as Nagasaki and Neegata; and they [said] that these feelings were shared by most of the people of the country.[28]

On the arrival of the ships at Yokohama, on August 10, after this unsuccessful mission, it was felt that the time for action had come.

---

[25] *F.R., 1864*, III, 534; *Japan. No. 1* (*1865*), pp. 72–73. Satow accompanied this party (*A Diplomat in Japan*, 96–100).   [26] *Ibid.*, p. 74.

[27] The ships would not wait until a written statement to this effect from the daimyo could be procured.   [28] *Japan. No. 1* (*1865*), p. 75.

It was at this time, while the joint expedition against Choshiu was pending, that the American Minister was able to settle satisfactorily the claims which had been subject to dispute for many months. It will be remembered that the Japanese had rejected the claim for damages due for the burning of the American Legation, on the ground that such a payment would be considered an acknowledgment that the Government was responsible for the action of the incendiaries. Mr. Pruyn had taken pains to show that the responsibility consisted solely in the failure of the Japanese guards to take proper precautions, rather than in any complicity of the Government.[29] The Rojiu at first refused to accept this proposition,[30] a step which led Mr. Pruyn to assume that the claim had been finally rejected, and caused him to reply that the United States would demand the payment of all the expenses caused in enforcing these proper demands.[31] On the other hand, a compromise was effected concerning another claim, and $1,000 (Mexican) was paid as an indemnity in the case of George Horton.[32]

With the various claims unsettled, Mr. Pruyn decided that the only thing to do was to proceed to Yedo and deal directly with the Rojiu. In addition he proposed to strengthen his position by taking, for the first time, a guard of American sailors and marines with him into Yedo. This was done, not because of any fears for his personal safety, as he felt as secure in Yedo as ever, but because he felt the presence of the foreign guards would serve to expedite his negotiations.[33] He had heretofore consistently been opposed to the landing of troops while his country was at peace with Japan, but the Rojiu had refused to guarantee his safety in Yedo and he felt that their disclaimer gave him the opportunity he needed to bring this pressure.[34] So on July 14, with the "Jamestown" lying off the shore, and with a guard of sixty-five marines and sailors, he again took up his residence in Yedo. During a pleasant stay of three weeks, marred by no threatening incidents,

[29] May 24, *F.R., 1864*, III, 518. [30] June 10, *ibid.*, p. 519.

[31] June 11, *ibid.*, p. 519. [32] *Ibid.*, p. 516.

[33] Pruyn Papers, July 12. [34] *Ibid.*, August 2.

"not an unpleasant word, or even an unfriendly look," and in which he entertained numerous guests, he brought all the outstanding questions to a satisfactory conclusion.[35] He received $10,000 in payment of the public and private losses at the burning of the Legation; an agreement to pay by September 5, $11,200 as principal and interest on the "Pembroke" claim; an agreement that if the claims for damages to American citizens at Yokohama were not settled within thirty days, they would be submitted to the arbitration of the Emperor of Russia; and, finally, an agreement to rebuild the American Legation and have it ready for occupancy at the close of the year.[36] Mr. Pruyn took especial satisfaction in the provision for the arbitration of the sole unadjudicated claim, and well he might. It marked the introduction of that principle in Japan, and by accepting it he felt that the Government acknowledged the sanctions of international law.[37] But what an apparent contradiction existed—at Yedo the Rojiu accepting this advanced principle of international comity, and at Yokohama the Foreign Representatives formulating plans for maintaining, by the use of force, the treaty rights of the Powers!

[35] *F.R., 1864,* III, 541.

[36] No. 52, August 10, *ibid.,* pp. 535–37. Eleven thousand two hundred dollars is wrongly printed as $1,200. See Pruyn Papers, August 11, September 10. While Mr. Pruyn was in Yedo word was received that some batteries in Choshiu had on July 11 fired upon the little American steamer "Monitor," which had put into a harbor there presumably to obtain wood or coal, water, and fresh provisions. He took up the matter with the Japanese Governors for Foreign Affairs, but was willing to wait for further consideration until they had received reports from the Governor of Nagasaki. Mr. Pruyn was not disposed to make any claim in favor of the owners, as no damage had been done, because this ship had entered a closed port in Satsuma in 1863, "and it would be unwise to encourage owners of vessels brought to this country for sale, to enter the ports of hostile Daimios, or any ports not open to trade" (No. 49, August 8, 1864, *F.R., 1865,* III, 517). The affidavit of the master of the "Monitor" is printed in *Japan. No. 1 (1865)*, pp. 69–70. When news of this attack reached Washington the President suspended the departure of the steam gunboat "Fusiyama," built at New York for the Japanese Government (*F.R., 1864,* III, 596). Satow erroneously states that "this afforded fresh justification of the action adopted by the foreign representatives" (*op. cit.,* p. 102).

[37] The claim was settled without the necessity of arbitration. But in 1875 the Emperor of Russia arbitrated the case of the "Maria Luz" between Japan and Peru.

As we have seen, no action would be taken under the memorandum of July 22 until the naval officers should have agreed to the feasibility of the proposed expedition. So on the return of the two British ships from Choshiu, on August 10, this preliminary step was taken. In requesting Captain Cicero Price, of the U.S.S. "Jamestown," to attend a conference of the commanding officers, Mr. Pruyn stressed the importance of co-operation on the part of the United States (even though its force was insufficient) "either in the display of our flag in the inland sea, or in the defence of Yokohama."[38] The conference took place on August 12 on board the British flagship, and was attended by Vice-Admiral Kuper, Rear-Admiral Jaurès, Captain Price, and Captain de Marr, of the Dutch navy. They decided that they were prepared to act in conformity with the policy set forth in the memorandum, but that, as they would have to take the greater portion of the naval force and some of the troops, they would not leave Yokohama "until they shall have been relieved entirely by their respective ministers from all responsibility with regard to the defence and security of the settlement."[39]

The Ministers considered this proposal, and on the fifteenth gave the desired assurance.[40] They furthermore requested them to proceed with all convenient speed to open the straits and to destroy and disarm the batteries, and informed them "that the political situation renders it desirable that there should be no considerable delay in the commencement of operations." Even if Choshiu were intimidated and failed to fire on the fleet, the batteries were to be destroyed and such measures taken as would secure a material guaranty against any further hostilities on his part. The officers were also requested to enter into no negotiations with the prince, reserving all questions for the action of the Tycoon's Government and the Foreign Representatives, and they were asked to avoid any demonstration in force in the vicinity of Osaka, lest it give rise to some new complication, "and in order not to change the character of this expedition, which ought to be regarded no other-

[38] July 24, *F.R., 1864,* III, 546.   [39] *Ibid.,* p. 547.   [40] *Ibid.*

wise than as a chastisement to be inflicted on an outlaw or a pirate."[41]

Two features of this new memorandum should be noted. In the first place, the proposal in the memorandum of July 22 that a *note identique* be sent to the Rojiu giving it twenty days in which to settle the Choshiu difficulty was now dropped, and the operations were to be promptly commenced. More important than this decision is the statement that the expedition was nothing more than a punitive one directed against an outlaw or pirate. In the past few weeks the situation had greatly improved at Yokohama. Probably no well-informed foreigner believed for a moment that the Shogunate would lead any hostile campaign against the Treaty Powers. The expedition against Choshiu was now considered advisable in order to strengthen the hands of the Tycoon; it was carried through with the secret approval of his Government; and its results were welcomed. As such it was primarily an interference in the domestic politics of Japan, and in addition it was expected greatly to improve the relations between the Shogunate and the Treaty Powers.[42]

[41] On the twelfth, Sir Rutherford Alcock delivered a memorandum to Takemoto Kai-no-Kami, a confidential official of the Shogunate, pointing out the futility of the anti-foreign policy of the Government, and urging, instead, a policy of freer intercourse and unrestricted trade. It proposed, in order to meet certain causes of complaint, that ports be opened in the territories of daimyos who desired it, that all restrictions on the movement of goods into the open ports be withdrawn, that monopolies of trade and burdensome restrictions be removed, that a royalty or share of the customs receipts be paid to the Mikado, and that the ancient law against foreigners be removed. In return for these more cordial relations the Treaty Powers, or at least those now acting in concert, would guarantee the neutrality of Japan [August 12, *Japan. No. 1 (1865)*, pp. 75–79].

[42] At an interview with Takemoto Kai-no-Kami and two other Japanese officials on August 13, Pruyn informed them "that this expedition was not an act of hostility to his [the Tycoon's] government, but for its maintenance, and in the interests of peace, which I and my colleagues were satisfied could thus be more effectually secured" (No. 54, August 13, *F.R., 1864*, III, 542). "I believe he [the Tycoon] would have been hurled from power if we had not crushed the hostile party" (Pruyn Papers, September 30, 1864. see also August 12, August 25). About this time Alcock received a letter from an unknown Japanese which gave a very accurate summary of the internal situation and urged that Choshiu be punished. It was written before the Kyoto *coup* of August 20.

For the usual interpretation of this section see Moore, *Digest of International Law*, V, 750. "The proceedings of the treaty powers in this instance were

It was arranged, therefore, that the allied expedition should leave Yokohama on August 20. The only American ship of war in Japan was the sailing ship "Jamestown," which would have had to be towed to Shimonoseki and which would have been useless during the operations there. In order that the American flag might be represented in the fleet, Mr. Pruyn and Captain Price chartered the little American steamer "Ta-Kiang" (600 tons), placed a 30-pound Parrott gun and eighteen men from the "Jamestown" on board, and hurriedly prepared her for the voyage.[43] Although the Shogun's Government had given its assent to the expedition in its eagerness to have Choshiu, the most recalcitrant of the daimyos, punished, it arranged that a deputation from the Rojiu should wait upon the Foreign Representatives on the nineteenth and request that the operations be abandoned, to whom the Ministers were to reply that no further delay was possible.[44] Early that morning the European mail-steamer entered the port with the Japanese flag at the fore, and all were amazed to learn that the envoys, who had left for Europe in February, had unexpectedly returned, having signed a Convention in Paris, but without visiting any other capitals.

Before the envoys had reached Europe the Treaty Powers had agreed, at the instance of Great Britain, that they would not even consider closing the port of Yokohama.[45] The envoys were in-

---

not intended nor considered as an act of interference in the political affairs of Japan. Their object was the enforcement of treaty rights, with the approval of the government that granted them; and the effect which the expedition may have had on the fortunes of parties in Japan was purely incidental." It has been shown that the passage of the straits was a doubtful treaty right, and that Great Britain had no desire to enforce it. There is every reason to believe that the straits could have been opened in the fall of 1864 without striking a blow. For the wrong done by Choshiu in firing on the foreign ships the clan had been punished by the "Wyoming" and the French force. A careful study of all the steps leading to the expedition has convinced the author that the real object was that cited in the text—to strengthen the Tycoon through the punishment of the most active of the hostile daimyos, and as such it was a logical development of the Anglo-French offer of 1863.

[43] She was referred to in Congress later as a "Chinese junk."

[44] No. 54, August 13, *F.R., 1864,* III, 542. Minutes of this conference in *Japan. No. 1 (1865),* pp. 81–82.

[45] *Ibid.,* pp. 7, 11, 12, 17. Russell's note to the British ministers abroad is dated April 20.

formed of this in Paris and decided that it would be useless to
proceed further; so after several conferences with M. Drouyn de
Lhuys, the French Minister of Foreign Affairs, they signed a Convention on June 18, and promptly departed for Japan. This Convention[46] bound the Tycoon (still spoken of as "His Majesty the
Emperor of Japan") to pay, within three months after the return
of the envoys, an indemnity of 140,000 Mexican piasters for the
attack upon the "Kienchang," of which 100,000 would be paid by
the Tycoon's Government and 40,000 by the authorities of Choshiu; secondly, to open the Straits of Shimonoseki within the
same period and to maintain them free at all times, "having recourse, if necessary, to force, and, in case of need, acting in concert with the Commander of the French naval division"; finally,
to reduce the tariff on certain articles—these being, however,
covered by the reductions made in January and already mentioned.
At the same time the envoys paid an indemnity of $35,000 for the
family of Lieutenant Camus, and promised that the Government
would take all measures necessary to arrest and punish his murderers.

The news of this Convention was most disappointing to both
the Shogunate and foreigners. It bound the Japanese to do something which they could not do, and it withdrew the French from
the concert of the Treaty Powers. The Government frankly
wished that their envoys had been drowned, and in fact promptly
punished them, and the Foreign Ministers had to countermand the
sailing orders of the fleet, pending the ratification of the Convention by the Tycoon.[47] They at once addressed letters to the Rojiu
asking whether or not the Tycoon would ratify the Convention
and was prepared to open the Inland Sea.[48] To this the Rojiu replied with unusual promptness by a messenger on August 24 and
by letter on the evening of the twenty-fifth,[49] that the Tycoon had
resolved to annul the Convention. The Foreign Representatives
therefore met in conference on the afternoon of the twenty-fifth

---

[46] *Japan. No. 1 (1865)*, pp. 25–27.

[47] *F.R., 1864*, III, 548.

[48] August 19, *ibid.*   [49] *Ibid.*, p. 549.

and drafted a new memorandum.[50] This called upon the naval commanders to proceed, with as little delay as possible, to open the straits. But it went further than that, and requested them to seize some important position in or commanding the Straits of Shimonoseki and to hold it as a guaranty that an indemnity should be paid by Choshiu to cover the expenses of the expedition, "and until possession can be given to the Tycoon, or authorities deputed by him, of the whole line of territory coasting the straits now appertaining to the Prince of Nagato." As there was a possibility of securing an open port in or near the straits, the naval officers were requested to furnish such information as they could gather concerning Shimonoseki and the other ports. The indemnity mentioned above was to cover the costs of the joint action, and was not to prejudice the right of each Power to prosecute claims arising out of separate grievances.

With these instructions, the commanders soon had their forces in order, and on August 28 and 29 the expedition of seventeen ships put out from Yokohama. On the latter day the Foreign Representatives sent in their long-delayed identical notes to the Rojiu, which pointed out that as the Tycoon was unable to punish Choshiu the Treaty Powers would have to do so; that they refused to entertain any proposition looking toward the closing of Yokohama; and that the Tycoon would be held responsible for any disturbances there during the absence of the fleet and the responsibility would be enforced by reprisals not merely at Yedo but at Osaka and Kyoto.[51] This note must be considered as designed for general consumption, for a perfect understanding existed between the foreign and Japanese officials. One of the latter had informed the Representatives that in order to keep the daimyos quiet while the expedition was away the Government would send another embassy, which would, however, go only as far as Shanghai.[52] On September 1, after the fleet had departed, some members of the Foreign Office called upon the Ministers to go through the farce of asking that the vessels should not sail.[53] Mr. Pruyn wrote at

[50] *Ibid.*   [51] *Ibid.*, p. 550.
[52] Pruyn Papers, August 25.   [53] Pruyn Papers, September 2.

the time: "Everything remains quiet here. . . . . No stranger would suppose that war was actually in progress in any part of the country."

Before the fleet had sailed, news had reached Yokohama concerning remarkable developments at Kyoto just at this time.[54] Late in July certain ronins and anti-foreign samurai had gathered in Choshiu and organized themselves into bands of irregular troops (*Kiheitai*). They determined to proceed to Kyoto, drive away the hostile officials, and force the court to pardon Choshiu and the exiled court nobles.[55] By the end of July these bands had reached the environs of Kyoto, and had been reinforced by clansmen who had fled from the city. The irregulars now sent up petitions to the court, praying for the pardon of Choshiu, his son, and the nobles, and for a renewal of the campaign against the foreigners. In Kyoto opinions differed as to what should be done, but the Tokugawa officials were resolute in advocating the severe punishment of these threatening bands. The Mikado, under their influence, refused to answer the petitions. On July 30 some of the troops moved nearer to Kyoto, a proceeding which caused much excitement in the city, the closing of the Nine Gates of the palace, and the rushing to their posts of the Tokugawa retainers. In the meantime the daimyo of Choshiu had sent up two of his karo (officials) with bodies of troops, presumably to keep the irregulars in order, but their arrival enraged the anti-Choshiu faction at the capital. Although many of the court nobles opposed the decision, yet the Shogunate officials, supported by some of the high court officers, secured an edict from the Mikado, on August 19, that the clansmen who had come up to Kyoto, and the Choshiu provinces from which they came, should be severely chastised for their attempt to intimidate the Imperial court. This edict made civil war inevitable. The next morning the various bodies of Choshiu clansmen hurled themselves upon several of the palace gates, presumably to punish and destroy the daimyo of Aidzu,

---

[54] News reached Yokohama on August 26 [Heco, *The Narrative of a Japanese,* II, 59; *Japan. No. 1 (1865),* pp. 89–92].

[55] Baba, *op. cit.,* pp. 147–239.

military governor of the city and leader of the Shogunate partisans there, and hostile to Choshiu, but actually to secure control of
the Mikado. The fighting lasted all day, clansmen of Aidzu, Kuwana, Echizen, and Satsuma being in opposition to those of Choshiu. The latter were defeated and driven out of the city, while a
fire, started during the fighting, destroyed the greater part of the
Imperial capital. This ill-timed and unsuccessful *coup* caused Choshiu to be outlawed, made possible a strong demonstration of
Tokugawa retainers as a punitive expedition, and seemed to mark
the speedy destruction of that aggressive anti-Shogunate house.
It should be noted that the defeat came just before the visit of
the joint expedition to Shimonoseki. It is not unreasonable to
believe that its far-reaching effects might have rendered the foreign demonstration quite unnecessary. In fact the Imperial court
promptly deprived the Mori family and its branches of all its
titles, and issued orders that the clan be punished. Some twenty of
the clans were ordered to put troops in the field, and the Lord of
Owari was appointed commander-in-chief.[56] As the clansmen were
unwilling to co-operate with the foreign fleet against Choshiu, the
Yedo authorities begged that the fleet be recalled.[57] But while the
discussion was going on at Yokohama, the fleet was carrying out
its orders at Shimonoseki.

The joint expedition which sailed from Yokohama on August
28 and 29 consisted of nine British, four Dutch, and three French
ships and one (chartered) United States steamer.[58] The whole
squadron assembled at the appointed rendezvous in the Inland
Sea and proceeded to the Straits of Shimonoseki. No attempt was
made to negotiate with Choshiu, and the attack upon the batteries
was commenced by the British flagship on the afternoon of September 5, when five batteries were silenced, and a landing party
spiked most of the guns in one of them. The next morning the
action was resumed, and a party of British, French, and Dutch

---

[56] Yamaguchi, *op. cit.,* p. 61.   [57] Pruyn Papers, September 10.

[58] Vice-Admiral Kuper's report, September 15, in *Japan. No. 1 (1865),*
pp. 99–103. Pruyn's reports are No. 61, October 1, *F.R., 1864,* III, 553, and No.
62, October 12, *ibid.,* pp. 553–57. See Satow, *op. cit.,* pp. 102–32, for his remi-
niscences.

sailors and marines assaulted and took possession of the eight principal batteries and, after spiking the cannon and destroying the magazines, returned to the ships. On the seventh, landing parties brought off the guns captured the day before, and on the eighth, the two remaining batteries were silenced and their guns taken off, sixty-two pieces of ordnance being eventually taken away. While this was being done, an envoy of the daimyo appeared, under a flag of truce, and sought to negotiate for a termination of hostilities.[59] He brought a letter from his lord stating that henceforth the straits would be unobstructed, and he offered copies of letters to show that in firing upon the foreign ships the daimyo had acted under the direct orders of the Mikado and the Tycoon.[60] The admirals determined that before any discussion could take place they must receive a written request from the daimyo, and two days were allowed for this to be secured, during which an armistice was declared. On the tenth the chief councillor of the daimyo came on board and presented identical dispatches for each of the four commanders.[61] In this letter the daimyo stated that, when he had learned of the foreigners' demands, through the letters brought by Ito and Inouye in July, he had sent his son to Kyoto to learn the Emperor's will, but that the conflict of August 20 had caused his son to turn back before his mission was accomplished. He then sent two of his retainers (one of them was the late Prince Ito) to the rendezvous of the fleet to notify the admirals that he would not offer any opposition to the passage of the straits, but unhappily the fleet had already departed.[62] He then said: "I felt no enmity towards you, nor did I wish to bring disaster upon my own people. My sole desire is that you will grant peace." And the karo who brought this message stated: "My Prince's feelings are exactly the same as your own.

[59] *Japan. No. 1 (1865)*, p. 113; *F.R., 1864*, III, 578.

[60] These letters were printed in *Japan. No. 1 (1865)*, p. 113, but the date decreed for ceasing communications with the barbarians (tenth day of the fifth month) was wrongly translated as June 20, instead of 25, 1863, thus occasioning much confusion in later documents and secondary accounts.

[61] *Japan. No. 1 (1865)*, p. 114; *F.R., 1864*, III, 558.

[62] If this letter had been delivered, there might have been no hostilities.

He not only wishes a cessation of hostilities, but is also desirous to have intimate relations with you."[63]

Although the admirals desired to negotiate directly with the daimyo and his son, the former wrote that in view of the affair that had recently taken place in Kyoto they had gone into retirement.[64] Two of the chief councillors met with the two admirals on the fourteenth and drew up the following agreement: (1) All ships of all countries passing through the straits would be treated in a friendly manner; they could purchase supplies; and in stress of weather their people could land at Shimonoseki; (2) no new forts would be built, nor the old ones repaired; (3) a ransom would be paid for the town of Shimonoseki, which "might justly have been burnt," and the whole expenses of the expedition would be defrayed by the prince.[65] This agreement was ratified by the daimyo and his son.

Admiral Kuper was convinced of the inexpediency of holding a position in or near the straits, as desired by the Ministers, and therefore returned to Yokohama, leaving three vessels at Shimonoseki for a few weeks, as a guaranty against any immediate infraction of the terms of the agreement.

The joint naval demonstration at Shimonoseki had been a great success. The batteries had been destroyed, their cannon carried away in triumph, the straits opened, and the daimyo humbled, and all this had been accomplished with the loss of only twelve killed, fifty-six wounded, and one missing, in the allied squadron.[66] It must be remembered, however, that the position of the lord punished in 1864 was very different from what it had been when he gave the offense in 1863. Then he was high in influence at the Imperial court, and leader of the western daimyos in their opposition to the Shogunate and, nominally, to foreigners. Now, after

[63] *Japan. No. 1 (1865)*, pp. 114–16.   [64] *Ibid.*, p. 117.   [65] *Ibid.*, p. 119.
[66] *Ibid.*, p. 111. Satow wrote later: "Having beaten the Choshiu people, we had come to like and respect them, while a feeling of dislike began to arise in our minds for the Tycoon's people on account of their weakness and double-dealing, and from this time onwards I sympathized more and more with the *daimio* party, from whom the Tycoon's government had always tried to keep us apart" (Satow, *op. cit.*, p. 129).

the events of September 30, 1863, and August 20, 1864, he was
a discredited outlaw, with every man's hand against him, crushed
by an Imperial edict which deprived him of his titles and called
upon the Shogun and his vassals to punish him. Naturally the
Yedo authorities were much gratified at what had been done, although somewhat mortified "that so little valor and capability of
resistance had been displayed."[67] With the batteries demolished
and stripped of their cannon, the punitive expedition of the twenty-one daimyos could now hardly fail.

This was the second and the last time an American ship of war
took part in hostilities in Japanese waters, the next participation
of American forces in joint operations in the Far East coming
thirty-six years later, during the Boxer Rising in China. The little
chartered steamer "Ta-Kiang," proudly floating the American
flag, was by no means an idle spectator of the stirring events at
the straits. The big Parrott gun did good service; the light draft
of the vessel enabled it to be used to tow boats with landing parties
in to the shore; and all the wounded were taken on board the ship
and conveyed to Yokohama.[68]

The gratification of the four Representatives at Yokohama was
tinged with misgivings because of the instructions which reached
Sir Rutherford Alcock while the fleet was still at Shimonoseki.
Among them was Earl Russell's of July 26, which laid down a
policy of moderation, based on Mr. Pruyn's ideas, and which
stated that he advocated a concert of the Powers in favor of this
plan. Accordingly on September 28 Alcock framed two dispatches,
one which told of the remarkable success achieved at Shimonoseki,
and the other which would serve as a vindication of the course
he had pursued.[69] Sir Rutherford took up every point in Russell's
instruction and maintained that he had anticipated each one "in a
great degree, if not in every particular." Thus, whereas Russell
had held "that while a prosperous trade is carried on it would

[67] No. 62, October 12, *F.R., 1864,* III, 553.

[68] The men from the "Jamestown" who served on the "Ta-Kiang" received
prize money. See Appendix in Vol. II.

[69] *Japan. No. 1. (1865),* pp. 111, 119–22.

be unwise to snap asunder the chain of friendly relations, and to make war for the sake of forestalling war," Alcock replied that the trade in silk at Yokohama had been stopped for some two months before it was finally resolved to send the expedition to the Inland Sea. It should be observed that there is no specific reference to this interference with the silk trade in the long memorandum of July 22, nor did Alcock mention it in any dispatch to Earl Russell until that of September 7, where the statement is based upon the complaint of a dealer in Yokohama of September 6.[70] The trade in cotton and tea had not at that time been affected. But Earl Russell's full approbation of Alcock's conduct, expressed on December 2, was primarily on the ground of the interference with the silk trade. On this point the dispatch should be quoted:

Your despatch of the 28th of September is a successful vindication of the policy you have pursued.

My despatches of the 26th of July were written with a view to discourage the interruption of a progressive trade by acts of hostility, and to forbid recourse to force while the Treaty was generally observed. Those despatches you will understand remain in full force.

But the documents you have sent me, which arrived by the last mail, show that the silk trade was almost wholly interrupted by the Tycoon, who seemed to be preparing to abet or to abandon the project of driving out foreigners according to the boldness or the timidity of our demeanor.

In this position there could be no better course than to punish and disarm the Daimio Prince of Nagato.[71]

With the arguments used by Alcock in his vindication we are familiar: that the operations were conducted with the Tycoon's assent; that it was necessary to punish Choshiu, the outlaw and common enemy of civilized nations, and to strike a blow at the leader of the anti-foreign daimyos; that this was the best way of encouraging and supporting the Tycoon and the daimyos favorable to foreign trade—witness the prompt removal of the restrictions on silk—and that it was the only effective way to protect Yokohama from hostile operations.

Mr. Pruyn also prepared a dispatch justifying his conduct, in which he stated: "It is my belief that the result of the expedition

[70] *Ibid.*, pp. 89, 92.   [71] *Ibid.*, pp. 127–28.

to the straits of Shimonoseki has greatly contributed to, if it has not secured, altogether, our safety in Japan."[72] Nothing was said in this dispatch about the silk trade; instead it was pointed out that the operations were really designed to sustain the Tycoon's Government,

which, if prostrated, would leave us without a friend, and liable to be involved in the struggle which would ensue.[73] The best place to defend the open ports was, therefore, manifestly at the Straits of Shimonoseki, where the strength of the hostile party might be broken before it was ready to be precipitated on these ports.

In this dispatch Mr. Pruyn brought out very clearly the real situation:

Though the treaties are to some extent the cause of trouble in Japan, they are, to a much greater extent, the pretext eagerly embraced by intriguing and ambitious Daimios, some of whom are known to aspire to the Tycoonship, each hoping that, with the fall of the Tycoon, and the favor of the Mikado secured, that high position would not be beyond his reach.

On the receipt of this dispatch Mr. Seward on December 14, expressed the President's full approval.[74]

With the return of the victorious squadron the Representatives proceeded to consolidate the good results of the demonstration. On September 18, the day after the first news had reached Yokohama, the four Ministers held a conference with three of the Yedo officials, led by Takemoto Kai-no-Kami, the principal Governor of Foreign Affairs and confidential agent of the Tycoon, who had acted as the chief Japanese negotiator in all these meetings.[75] This conference brought out the fact that the defeat of Choshiu had tremendously strengthened the Tycoon, and that he would no longer have to temporize and equivocate in his dealings with the Treaty Powers. The French Minister advised that the Tycoon now secure the sanction of the Mikado to the Treaties, and even

---

[72] No. 62, October 12, *F.R., 1864,* III, 553–58.

[73] An evidence of the temporary restoration of the Tycoon's power was the order of September 30, canceling the one of 1862 which relieved the daimyos from residence in Yedo (*ibid.,* p. 577).

[74] No. 86, *F.R., 1865,* III, 229.   [75] *Ibid.,* pp. 561–65.

asked if the Mikado might not receive the Foreign Representatives at Kyoto. His British colleague pointed out that the time had come for the Tycoon to give up once and for all his temporizing policy, and that either the authority of the Mikado and the Tycoon must be reconciled, or the Powers would have to find some other means of securing their rights than through the Tycoon. Mr. Pruyn in turn suggested that the Straits of Shimonoseki be placed under the Tycoon, and that possibly some port there be opened.

On September 23 Takemoto Kai-no-Kami returned with a message from the Rojiu to the effect that they had finally resolved to abandon their double-faced policy and henceforth to make not even a pretense of closing Yokohama, and that they would send one of their number to Kyoto to inform the Mikado of this decision and to "obtain his sanction to the public renunciation of such a policy, and, if possible, his acceptance and ratification of the treaties."[76] In the meantime they begged that the foreign ships be withdrawn from the straits, as they interfered with the Tycoon's operations against Choshiu. It was suggested that this might be done if the Tycoon would enter into negotiations either to pay the indemnities promised by Choshiu, or to open Shimonoseki or some more convenient port in the vicinity, at the option of the Treaty Powers.

It was peculiarly gratifying to the American Minister to find his colleagues at last adopting a policy which he had urged, even to the details, on June 27, 1863.[77] Mr. Seward had promptly taken up with the Treaty Powers the desirability of securing the Mikado's ratification of the Treaties, but the plan had been rejected by Great Britain on November 10, on the ground that the power and the right to make treaties resided in the Tycoon, as stated by Satsuma's envoy to Colonel Neale at Kagoshima.[78] Now the wis-

---

[76] *F.R., 1864,* III, 565–67.   [77] Pruyn Papers, October 10, 1864.

[78] *Japan. No. 1 (1865),* p. 19; *F.R., 1863,* I, 420, lviii–lix, cxxv. Lord Palmerston stated in the House of Commons on February 9, 1864, that there was no doubt "as to the binding nature of the treaty as having been made only by the Tycoon" (*Hansard's Parliamentary Debates,* 3d Series, Vol. 173, p. 416).

dom of this step was self-evident. Before the Ministers went up
to Yedo for their conferences with the Rojiu, letters to the Tycoon were drafted by Pruyn, Alcock, and Roches, urging him to
secure the Mikado's ratification of the treaties.[79]

At the first conference in Yedo, on October 6, the Rojiu agreed
unconditionally to pay the indemnities promised by Choshiu, but
they could give no promise as to the opening of a port there, pending the outcome of the mission of one of their number to Kyoto.
They agreed to make every effort to secure the Mikado's ratification. The next day a conference of a more confidential nature
took place, attended by only the British and American Ministers,
as representatives of their colleagues.[80] At this meeting the Rojiu
agreed to the appointment within eight days of plenipotentiaries
to arrange the details of the promised indemnities. Alcock then
developed his plan for conciliating the Mikado and the daimyos
by permitting them to share the profits of the foreign trade, and
pointed out that if the Treaties were not ratified the Powers would
insist upon their full execution, including the opening of the cities
and ports. On their ratification, moreover, he would send away
the British troops at Yokohama, no longer necessary to meet the
hostility created by the Mikado and the daimyos. He suggested,
as Mr. Pruyn had done a year before, that while these negotiations were going on at Kyoto, the Foreign Representatives should
proceed to Osaka with a portion of the squadron, but the Rojiu
objected to this as liable to be construed by the Mikado and the
daimyos as an attempt to coerce the Mikado with foreign aid.
Alcock further suggested that thirty days be set in which to obtain an answer from Kyoto, and the Rojiu hoped that this period
would suffice. Other subjects of discussion were met in the same
conciliatory manner, and the Rojiu promised to remove all interference with the silk trade, to take up certain matters concerning
the improvement of Yokohama, to permit the export of silkworm
eggs, and to consider granting the Legations another site in Yedo,
in lieu of Goten-yama.

[79] October 4, 5, *F.R., 1864,* III, 559–61.   [80] *Ibid.,* pp. 569–75.

Shortly after the Representatives had returned to Yokohama, the ships left at Shimonoseki returned, and on the British vessel were four Choshiu officials, sent to explain the hostile deeds of their lord and to urge indulgence in the matter of the promised indemnities.[81] On August 10 the chief envoy had an interview with Alcock and Pruyn, and stated his case.[82] It was a strong defense of Choshiu, for it stressed the unsuccessful attempt of the daimyo to secure the withdrawal of the Mikado's edict, "and thus the prince's good intentions in respect to foreigners had been frustrated." In regard to the indemnity, the envoy was told that the Tycoon's Government had agreed to assume the responsibility and to pay it. As in the case of Satsuma, only one lesson was necessary to teach Choshiu the futility of opposing the Treaty Powers.

The plenipotentiary promised by the Rojiu came to Yokohama before the appointed time, and a Convention was agreed upon on the twelfth, which was signed by the four Foreign Representatives and Sakai Hida-no-Kami on October 22.[83] The preamble, which was of especial significance, was framed by the American Minister.[84] It stated that

the representatives of the United States of America, Great Britain, France, and the Netherlands, in view of the hostile acts of Mori Daizen, Prince of Nagato and Suwo, which were assuming such formidable proportions as to make it difficult for the Tycoon faithfully to observe the treaties, having been obliged to send their combined forces to the Straits of Simonoseki in order to destroy the batteries erected by that Daimio for the destruction of foreign vessels and the stoppage of trade, and the government of the Tycoon, on whom devolved the duty of chastising this

[81] Typical of Mr. Pruyn's generous attitude and of his sound judgment in his reference to this humbled daimyo: "I must confess this prince has my sympathy; an open foe is much preferred to a deceitful and doubtful friend. He has acted with consistency, vigor, and boldness. He now desires peace, and his past history will probably prove a guarantee for his future sincerity. If, as I think is highly probable, he shall escape the destruction now threatened [by the Tycoon's punitive expedition], perhaps, on payment of a large fine, little damage need be apprehended from his open hostility, and probably as little from his secret opposition" (No. 62, October 12, *F.R., 1864,* III, 557).

[82] *Ibid.,* pp. 575–77.   [83] *Ibid.,* p. 583.

[84] Pruyn Papers, October 31.

rebellious prince, being held responsible for any damage resulting to the interests of treaty powers, as well as the expenses occasioned by the expedition. . . . .

It fixed the amount payable at $3,000,000, to include all claims for indemnities, ransom, or expenses, payable in six quarterly instalments of $500,000 each, beginning from the date when the Representatives should advise the Tycoon's Government of the ratification of the Convention and of their instructions. Finally, "inasmuch as the receipt of money has never been the object of the said powers, but the establishment of better relations with Japan, and the desire to place these on a more satisfactory and mutually advantageous footing is still the leading object in view," therefore if the Tycoon preferred to offer in place of the indemnity the opening of Shimonoseki or some other eligible port in the Inland Sea, the Powers would have the option to accept the port or insist upon the money payment.[85]

It will be observed that this Convention said nothing about the proposed ratification of the Treaties by the Mikado. That matter was considered to be well understood after the friendly conferences at Yedo. The determination of the amount of the indemnity was interesting. Mr. Pruyn had already received $11,200 in payment of the claim of the "Pembroke." The Japanese envoys had promised, in Paris, to pay $140,000 for the attack on the "Kienchang," but that Convention had been annulled by the Tycoon. It was felt that this amount should serve as a standard for appraising the indemnities for firing upon the national ships of the United States and the Netherlands. Beyond that, Alcock and Pruyn thought that the balance of any indemnity should be divided in proportion to the force sent to the straits by each of the Powers.[86] So they advocated a lump sum of $2,000,000, to be divided as follows: Great Britain $1,000,000; France $440,000; Holland $290,000; and the United States $270,000.[87] The French Minister,

[85] The ministers believed that the port might be accepted in either full or part payment of the indemnity (*F.R., 1864*, III, 582).   [86] *Ibid.*

[87] Pruyn Papers, October 31. Pruyn's first estimate for the United States was $150,000 for indemnities and $20,000 for expenses (Pruyn Papers, October 10).

on the other hand, won approval of his suggestion that the sum be fixed at $3,000,000, and that its division be left to the home governments, in case an indemnity was paid instead of a port being opened.[88] A memorandum to this effect was drawn up by Mr. Pruyn, which provided also that at least $140,000 be paid to the United States, France, and the Netherlands before the other distribution was made, and this agreement was signed by the four Representatives on the twenty-second. The French Minister thought that the moral support given should also be taken into account; and as the United States had given more moral than material support, Mr. Pruyn agreed with him, but this principle was not incorporated in the memorandum. It was believed at the time that the distribution would be on the basis of the ships and men on duty in Japan.

With the signing of this Convention[89] it was felt that all the

---

[88] Pruyn approved the larger sum because he thought the demand for it would be more likely to induce the Tycoon to open a port instead of paying it. Satow believed: "The fixing of an indemnity was intended only to provide a means of pressure upon the Tycoon's government in order to procure the Mikado's ratification of the treaties, and the consequent extension of commercial relations" (*op. cit.*, p. 132).

[89] Alcock received his letter of recall on October 10, just before the Convention negotiations began. He wrote Mr. Pruyn that he would turn his steps homeward "very joyfully," for "I have done the work I came out determined to undertake, and I never could retire at a happier moment" (Pruyn Papers, October 10). Mr. Pruyn believed that the British Government was "afraid of the Peace party as a general election is approaching and so he will be home ready for the meeting of Parliament and to be offered as a sacrifice if needful." He also felt sure that "a great triumph awaits him. There is nothing so successful as success and the Ministry will be obliged by public sentiment to make ample atonement to one who has aided so much in gratifying the national pride and also in the improvement of business" (Pruyn Papers, October 12). The Japanese Minister for Foreign Affairs on October 27 addressed Earl Russell asking that Alcock be sent back to Japan, and spoke of the deep regret with which he had learned of his approaching departure. Alcock's reply to his letter of recall is dated November 19, 1864, and is a lengthy consideration of his proceedings and defense of his conduct [*Japan. No. 1 (1865)*, pp. 148–54]. To this Earl Russell replied on January 31, 1865, stating that "the energetic course you pursued in concert with the Representatives of the other Treaty Powers in these altered circumstances has been entirely approved by Her Majesty's Government." Russell also wrote that he would wish Alcock to return to Yokohama after he had reported on the present state of affairs in Japan (*ibid.*, p. 155). Instead, he was promoted to the post at Peking. Sir Harry Parkes, who met Alcock at Hong Kong, on his way home, wrote as follows: "He is full

perplexing questions arising out of the Shimonoseki affair had been settled, but in the sequel the Shimonoseki Convention, as it was called, was to occasion no little controversy.

of talk and feels very jolly, because satisfied that he is in the right and the Government is in the wrong, in which I entirely agree, and they will have to indemnify him in some way for his recall. He left home with full sanction of the Government to employ force to bring the recalcitrant daimios to book whenever he could get a chance and force. A battalion of marines and a regiment of infantry, in addition to the whole navy of the station, were furnished him for this express purpose. But when the Manchester party raised an outcry against the first symptom of force being employed, the Government would not declare that they had authorized the course, but as a sop to Bright and Cobden recalled their Minister. It is . . . . unlike Lord Palmerston, who has always backed his men; but he is not in the Foreign Office and has to give way to his colleagues occasionally, I fancy" (Dickins, *op. cit.,* I, 478). Satow states that an invitation for a diplomatic officer to return home is equivalent to removal (Satow, *op. cit.,* p. 134).

CHAPTER XI

THE MIKADO RATIFIES THE TREATIES
1865 [1]

As A military operation the opening of the Straits of Shimonoseki had been an unqualified success. As far as could be seen at the time, it had been a great political success as well. The Tycoon had certainly been strengthened in his position, and most of the difficulties in the way of improved foreign relations had apparently been removed. But was the success real? In little more than three years the Shogunate was to pass away, and in the new government Choshiu was to play a prominent rôle, which the clan plays even to this day. The operations, therefore, did not save the Shogunate, nor did they destroy Choshiu. Their effect was, for a time, to stem the current which was flowing strongly in favor of the Imperial restoration; but bombardments and memoranda, protocols and conventions, could not for long save the doomed Shogunate.

The first fruit of the improved relations was the report that the Mikado was now in full accord with the foreign policy of the Tycoon. A vague statement to this effect was sent to each of the Ministers on November 22 by Abe Bungo-no-Kami, the member of the Rojiu who had just returned from Kyoto.[2] On being returned by them as not explicit enough, it was again transmitted, with a confidential note to the effect that as soon as Choshiu and the hostile parties were punished, the Mikado would be informed, and a definite arrangement would be made.[3] Although the Min-

---

[1] The instructions for 1865 are numbered 87–94 (to Pruyn), and 1–8 (to Portman); of these sixteen, five were printed in *F.R., 1865,* III. The dispatches are numbered 1–22 (Pruyn), and 23–75 (Portman); of these, twenty-three were printed in *F.R., 1865,* III, and nine in *F.R., 1866,* II.

[2] *F.R., 1865,* III, 231.   [3] *Ibid.,* p. 232.

isters had hoped for the formal ratification of the Treaties by the Mikado at this time, yet they felt that much of practical value had already been gained.[4]

This good understanding between the Yedo authorities and the Foreign Representatives was suddenly jeopardized by another atrocious murder on the part of irreconcilable ronins. Two British officers, Major George Walter Baldwin and Lieutenant Robert Nicholas Bird, of the Twentieth Regiment, stationed at Yokohama, were cut down by two ronins on November 21, 1865, near the Daibutsu image at Kamakura.[5] One was evidently instantly killed, and the other lingered until evening. The assassins made good their escape. Such were the facts. Great was the indignation at Yokohama, and genuine was the horror and regret of the Rojiu. But a better appreciation of the difficulties in which the Shogunate was involved now prevailed, and no attempt was made to hold the Government responsible for the acts of these fanatics. The crime was a more brutal and less explicable one than the murder of Richardson, but the day of enormous indemnities and sporadic bombardments had passed. Sir Rutherford Alcock, in dealing with this tragedy, followed the principles laid down by Townsend Harris in 1861, and it must have given the American ex-minister some pleasure to read Alcock's dispatch to Earl Russell of December 23. After pointing out the difficulty of arresting such criminals, especially in a feudal state like Japan, he added:

These are perplexing and difficult conditions to deal with; and as nothing can ever be gained by insisting upon impossibilities, even if such a course could be defended as just or right, I am disposed, while pressing our demands for full justice to be done and urging the utmost diligence and energy in the pursuit of the murderers, to accept what has been al-

---

[4] "The explanation given is perfectly Japanese. The Mikado was never seriously opposed to foreigners and did not contemplate their exclusion and thought the Tycoon would understand his decree was only issued for effect at home and not to be acted on. And the Tycoon unfortunately not comprehending this, and believing the Mikado in earnest felt himself obliged to carry out those orders though fully sensible that he would fail in his efforts. What can you do with such a government?" (Pruyn Papers, November 19, 1864).

[5] *Japan. No. 2 (1865)*; *Japan. No. 3 (1865)*; Satow, *A Diplomat in Japan*, pp. 135–40.

ready done as a satisfactory instalment. I believe it may be all that, with the best good will, they have hitherto been able to effect.

On its part the Shogun's Government, strengthened by the good accord with the Mikado and by the foreigners' punishment of Choshiu, made strenuous efforts to arrest and punish the offenders. The Governor of Kanagawa, on the advice of the British Minister, was dismissed because of his delay in reporting the crime. On December 16 two ronins were publicly executed in Yokohama as accomplices of the assassins, although the charge against them was that they compelled certain farmers to contribute funds for the purpose of exterminating the foreigners and expelling them from Yokohama. At the same time the Government posted proclamations ordering the arrest or destruction of assassins of Europeans in the future, and holding the communities responsible for any failure to report traces of fugitives.[6]

A few days later one of the actual assassins was arrested and was beheaded on December 28, in the presence of a large body of Japanese and almost the whole foreign community. Two battalions, of the Twentieth Regiment and the Royal Marines, and half a battery of Royal Artillery were drawn up in a square around the execution ground. The Foreign Representatives were invited to be present, but the Americans, British, and French officials refused to attend, as it would be regarded by the Japanese as a degradation and might give the impression of vindictiveness. The Dutch Consul-General, who had not learned of this decision, was present. This was the first time that a two-sword man had been publicly executed for an attack upon a foreigner. It was indeed a sign of bettered relations; but more blood was to flow before the misguided patriots could be brought to sheathe their blades.[7]

[6] Both Alcock and Pruyn took credit for this proclamation [*Japan, No. 3 (1865)*, p. 3; Pruyn Papers, December 17, 1864].

[7] In reporting these murders to Earl Russell, Alcock spoke of "the long series of barbarous murders in which foreigners have been the victims," and references to "the long and dismal list" were frequent at the time. In fairness it must be said that in more than five years since Kanagawa had been opened eleven Europeans had been murdered. In view of the bitter hostility to the

At about this time two internal disturbances which had threatened the authority of the Shogunate and taxed its resources were brought to what seemed to be a successful termination. One was the Mito civil war, which arose out of clan politics of some years before and which culminated in the fall of 1864 in a little civil war in the fief, in which one side rallied to its support those who favored the anti-foreign views of the late ex-lord of Mito.[8] The Shogunate sent troops to the support of the party in power, then advocating liberal foreign policies. It was this campaign which prevented the Tycoon from moving against Choshiu as promptly as he would have liked. The strife came to an end in January 1866 with the surrender to the daimyo of Kaga of the "Righteous" (anti-foreign) party, and with the execution of seven hundred and twenty-nine of the prisoners early in March.[9]

The punitive expedition against Choshiu achieved an easy but a temporary success. Under the command of the ex-lord of Owari the forces of twenty-one daimyos moved to the frontier of Choshiu and "demanded an explanation." Within the clan a *coup d'état* had been effected, and the faction opposed to the former policies was now in control.[10] It therefore caused the three karo who had taken part in the Kyoto emeute to commit hara-kiri and sent their heads to the commander-in-chief, who transmitted them to the Mikado. The daimyo and his son were confined in a temple, and certain other officials were placed in domiciliary confinement. Five of the seven kuge who had fled to Choshiu in 1863 were surrendered and were placed in the custody of Satsuma, Chikuzen, and Higo. After these manifestations of repentance, the punitive expedition retired to Osaka, in February, and it was felt that final sentence would be pronounced after a consultation between the Mikado and the Shogun. That the western daimyos

Europeans and to the Shogun's foreign policy, this number must be considered amazingly small.

[8] Clement, "The Mito Civil War," in *Transactions of the Asiatic Society of Japan*, Vol. 19, Part II.

[9] *Japan. No. 1 (1866)*, p. 12.

[10] Yamaguchi, *Kinse Shiriaku. A History of Japan*, pp. 69–70.

would not approve of the destruction of the house of Mori was generally believed.

It was this difficulty in carrying out the proposal to confiscate some or all of the provinces belonging to the daimyo of Choshiu which caused the Shogunate to come to the conclusion that it would be better to pay the heavy indemnity of $3,000,000 rather than open a port in the Inland Sea. This notice was given by the Rojiu on April 5, with the statement that the first payment would be made in the sixth month (August), the second a year later, and the others as provided by the Convention.[11]

This decision was received with regret by both the American Minister and the British Chargé, Charles A. Winchester. Mr. Pruyn and Sir Rutherford Alcock had, from the first, preferred a new port to a heavy indemnity; Mr. Pruyn had very soundly pointed out that indemnities of this kind were really paid by the foreign merchants in enhanced burdens on commerce, and he had expressed the opinion that the great Richardson indemnity had been met in exactly that way.[12] In this view he was supported by Mr. Winchester.[13] But as long as the Japanese preferred to pay the indemnity rather than open the port, the powers could not insist otherwise. There was one chance for further discussion, and that lay in the request of the Japanese that the second payment, instead of being made within three months, be postponed to one year after the first. Mr. Winchester first saw the possibilities in this postponement, and in reporting the Japanese request he suggested that the Treaty Powers take advantage of the long period between the first and second instalments "to effect some arrangement which, by securing general advantages, such as the opening of Hiogo, or a revision of the tariff, will be compatible with a reduction of the total amount of the indemnity."[14]

The four Representatives considered in conference the proposal of the Rojiu and decided to accept the first payment, under reservation, but to refer to their home governments the question

---

[11] *F.R., 1865,* III, 247.   [12] No. 65, October 29, 1864, *F.R., 1864,* III, 582.
[13] April 12, 1865, *Japan. No. 1 (1866),* p. 15.   [14] *Ibid.,* p. 15.

of altering the date of subsequent payments.[15] Ten days after
this conference, on April 25, Winchester made a suggestion to
Earl Russell which shaped the course of the later negotiations.
It was

whether the deviation proposed by the Japanese might not fairly be made
the basis of a joint counter-proposition on the part of the foreign co-
signatories to take, as equivalent to the moiety, or two-thirds of the indemnity, some such concessions as the opening of Hiogo on the 1st of
January, 1866; the written adhesion of the Mikado to the Treaties; and
the reduction of import duties, now levied at 5, 6, and 20 per cent. on
different classes of goods, to a uniform rate of 5 per cent., a change which
would be a great convenience to foreign commerce, and, by stimulating
consumption, would probably be attended with no material diminution of
profit to the Japanese revenue.[16]

This proposal of the British Chargé was in keeping with the
Anglo-American policy of commercial development. The only
new feature was the reduction in the tariff, for the Mikado's
ratification had been promised, and Hiogo would be open anyway
after January 1, 1868. If the opening of Shimonoseki or a similar
port were considered equivalent to the entire indemnity, then these
concessions were surely worth half or two-thirds of it. The Dutch
and French governments, however, favored the payment of the
full amount. It was now a question as to whose views should
prevail.

At this time it was becoming more and more evident that many
of the daimyos were eager to have commercial relations with the
foreigners, and that one cause of their hostility to the Shogun was
the restrictions placed upon their trade at the open ports, all of
which were within the Tycoon's domain. It was for this reason
that Mr. Pruyn advocated the opening of Osaka, where the
daimyos had long enjoyed privileges of trade.[17] Mr. Winchester
believed that if the Tycoon would not agree to open some ports in

---

[15] *Japan. No. 1 (1866)*, p. 18. It should be remembered that no payment was
due until after the Convention had been ratified by the Powers. It was not ratified by the United States until April 9, 1866.

[16] *Ibid.*, p. 19. Winchester felt that the payment of so large an indemnity
would seriously tax the impoverished resources of the Tycoon.

[17] *F.R., 1865*, III, 249.

western Japan the daimyos would open them themselves, and the conduct of Choshiu in purchasing supplies from Shanghai was cited as a case in point.[18] On several occasions he pointed out to officials from Yedo the folly of trying to bar the daimyos from foreign trade, and even stated that Great Britain had the right to deal directly with the feudatories, but had no intention of adopting such a policy prematurely.[19] Of course the object of these suggestions was to induce the Shogunate to open the desired port in the Inland Sea.

Early in May the American Minister, Mr. Pruyn, left Japan to enjoy a well-earned vacation at home. When he sailed out of the Bay of Yedo it was with every intention of returning at the expiration of his leave of absence. After his return to Albany a combination of personal reasons caused him to proffer his resignation on October 25, and he retired from the diplomatic service.

The career of Mr. Pruyn has been sketched in the preceding pages, but in this place a few words of summary may well be added. He may be considered an excellent representative of the American diplomat of his day—untrained in diplomacy, but well supplied with sound judgment, high principles, and sympathetic insight.[20] His colleague, Sir Rutherford Alcock, was an excellent British representative, ever jealous of British rights and interests, and quick to support or maintain them. But Robert H. Pruyn, like Townsend Harris, was more than an American diplomat. He could see more than American rights and interests; his vision was broad enough to permit him to see the interests of Japan as well. Hence of all the diplomats in Japan in his day he possessed the best understanding of the embarrassing problems created by foreign affairs, and he also retained to the end the greatest sympathy

[18] *Japan. No. 1 (1866)*, p. 24; Satow, *op. cit.*, p. 147. It was this exclusive policy of the Shogunate which turned the British Legation against it.

[19] *Japan. No. 1 (1866)*, pp. 27-28.

[20] Charles Sumner, chairman of the Senate Committee on Foreign Relations, is reported to have said that Mr. Pruyn's correspondence was unsurpassed in ability by any other American envoy, with possibly the single exception of Hon. Charles Francis Adams (*National Cyclopedia of American Biography*, XIII, 439).

for the Shogunate in its difficulties. His policy was a simple one. He would maintain the treaty rights intact, but he would not commit a wrong to preserve a right. "Moderation and forbearance" were the principles which he believed would serve best in such unsettled days. Perhaps, as an American, he could not approve of the threatening attitude of Britain and France in 1863 because he realized what would have been the effect in his own land if during the early days of the Civil War a similar interference had been carried through.[21] When he finally joined Alcock in the expedition against Shimonoseki, it was because he was convinced that it would serve to strengthen the lawful authority of the Shogunate.

These principles were manifest in his dealings with the Japanese. In settling claims he kept in mind the real situation in Japan and never sought to impose exemplary damages, but was content merely to secure modest sums to cover reasonable losses. For the murder of Mr. Richardson, Great Britain demanded and received £125,000, and destroyed the town of Kagoshima; but for firing on the American ship of war "Wyoming" all that Mr. Pruyn asked was a provision of annuities for the families of the slain and for the wounded. The exaction of the enormous indemnity did not save the lives of Major Baldwin and Lieutenant Bird a year later, nor did the modest demand of Mr. Pruyn encourage the Japanese to attack Americans with impunity. In assenting to the heavy Shimonoseki indemnity, Mr. Pruyn did so in the hope that it would result in the opening of a port rather than in the payment of money.

To Mr. Pruyn was due the recognition by the Japanese of the principle of international arbitration, as well as the first definite proposal that the Treaty Powers should unite in securing the Mikado's ratification of the Treaties. It was a great pity that he could not have remained in Japan a few months longer to see his proposal carried out. The credit for securing the ratification has

---

[21] Japan was happily spared a foreign war at this time. But in 1857, while China was in the throes of the terrible Taiping Rebellion, demands for increased treaty rights were made which resulted in the war with Great Britain and France.

gone to the man who executed rather than to him who devised the plan.

In Mr. Pruyn's absence the Legation was intrusted to Mr. A. L. C. Portman as Chargé d'Affaires. A Hollander by birth, he had first visited Japan as Dutch interpreter with Commodore Perry and had returned with the Japanese embassy in 1860. Early in June he was able to move the Legation once more to Yedo.

Soon after Mr. Pruyn left Japan the Choshiu problem, which had been dormant for several months, again became acute.[22] The revival was due to another clan revolution which this time put the old controlling element back in power. But although they were members of the former anti-Shogun and anti-foreign party, they had dropped all their hostility toward foreigners, and instead had doubled their hatred of the Shogunate. At this time, also, a reconciliation was effected between Satsuma and Choshiu, at the instigation of Saigo Kichinosuke, the Satsuma samurai who later became commander-in-chief of the Imperial forces. Henceforth these clans agreed to work side by side for the restoration of the Mikado and the abolition of the dual government. When news of this *coup* reached Yedo—although the agreement between Satsuma and Choshiu was not known at the time—the Shogun again proclaimed his intention of punishing Choshiu, and called upon the vassal daimyos for aid. This time there was a difference of opinion among the retainers as to the wisdom of renewing punitive measures, and the ex-lord of Owari, who had commanded the first expedition, now urged caution before proceeding on a second. The Shogunate stood firm, however, and on June 9 the Shogun left Yedo for Osaka to direct the operations in person.

The renewal of hostilities caused the Foreign Representatives to consider the obligations of neutrality and also their relations with Choshiu under the Shimonoseki arrangements. On January 21 the Rojiu complained that Choshiu was carrying on illicit trade with foreign ships in the straits, and the Ministers then issued warnings against their nationals' carrying on trade at other than

[22] Yamaguchi, *op. cit.,* pp. 70–76; Murdock, *A History of Japan,* III, 750–55.

treaty ports or selling munitions of war to others than the Japanese Government.[23] In May it was reported that foreign adventurers were flocking to the support of Choshiu, and the notorious General Burgevine, fresh from his exploits during the Taiping Rebellion, was said to be among them.[24] The Foreign Representatives met and signed a memorandum, on June 21, which was addressed to the commanders of their national naval forces.[25] This stated that although the commanders ought to oppose the rearmament of the batteries of Choshiu, and even proceed to disarm them if they should have been rearmed, yet, as this act might bring about conflicts and complications, they were requested to make such remonstrances as they deemed appropriate and to inform their respective Representatives. They were also to keep the straits open for legitimate traffic, and to lend their aid in the repressing of contraband trade; they were to prevent the Tycoon's ships from going too far in the prevention of unlawful commercial operations; and when hostilities should have commenced they were either to warn merchant ships or even to prevent them from entering the straits if there was actual danger. The Representatives expressed their desire that "the strictest neutrality should be observed in all that concerns the military operations between the Tycoon and the Prince of Nagato." At the same time Mr. Winchester issued an official notification, based upon the provisions of the Treaty and on the Order in Council of January 23, 1860, warning British subjects of the penalties attached to illicit commerce, especially in arms and munitions of war.[26]

On July 18 the successor of Sir Rutherford Alcock landed at Yokohama. In Sir Harry Smith Parkes the British had a forceful and courageous representative who was able to dominate the diplomatic body during his eighteen years of service in Yedo and Tokyo.[27] With twenty-four years of eventful experience in China

[23] *Japan. No. 1 (1866)*, p. 7.   [24] *Ibid.*, pp. 23, 24, 27.

[25] *F.R., 1865*, III, 252.   [26] June 22, *Japan. No. 1 (1866)*, p. 43.

[27] For an uncritical biography see Dickins and Lane-Poole, *Life of Sir Harry Parkes;* for a very different estimate see House, "The Martyrdom of an Empire," in *Atlantic Monthly,* Vol. 47, pp. 610–23.

to draw upon, he was prepared to take the leadership among his colleagues, and this post he never relinquished. Thus the newcomer was able to reap the harvest which his predecessors had so laboriously tended.

It now becomes necessary to follow the negotiations among the Treaty Powers concerning the wisdom of accepting the Shimonoseki indemnity. In reporting the naval success at Shimonoseki and the terms agreed to there, Alcock had, on September 28, 1864, asked for instructions as to Russell's willingness to accept the opening of Shimonoseki or a similar port in lieu of the ransom and the indemnity.[28] Russell had promptly replied, on December 3, that the Government would renounce any money payment "if greater or equal advantages can be secured by stipulations to be obtained from the Tycoon or the Mikado." Russell then tried to secure the consent of the other Powers, and was informed by France and the United States that their Representatives were intrusted with discretion to act as seemed wise.[29]

After the terms of the Convention reached Europe, France took the lead and announced early in January that she would prefer the payment of the indemnity to the opening of a port, and the Netherlands agreed.[30] But now Great Britain preferred to wait until Alcock had returned and made his report. On March 30 Russell instructed Sir F. Bruce to ask Mr. Seward what was the opinion of the United States in this matter, advising him at the same time of the disagreement between England and the two continental Treaty Powers.

Before any agreement could be reached on this question the Japanese apparently removed it from the realm of discussion by announcing that they would pay the indemnity rather than open a

[28] *Japan. No. 1 (1865)*, p. 126.   [29] *Ibid.*, pp. 136, 147.

[30] *Japan. No. 1 (1866)*, p. 1. These reasons were advanced by M. Drouyn de Lhuys, the French Minister for Foreign Affairs: "In the first place that Shimonosaki was no port at all, but an open roadstead, not always safe; secondly, that the port of Osaca, not a great way off, must, according to Treaty, soon be opened; and, thirdly, that money was a substantial penalty which once received could not be recalled, whereas permission to trade at Shimonosaki might be rescinded at any moment." See also *F.R., 1865,* II, 353.

port. However, in requesting a modification of the terms of payment they at once opened the door for further discussion. Earl Russell, on June 21, instructed the three British Ministers to notify the Treaty Powers to which they were accredited that the British Government believed the whole amount of the indemnity ought to be paid in 1866.[31] Support of this view was received from France and the Netherlands.

On July 6, however, Earl Russell received Mr. Winchester's dispatch of April 25, which suggested the waiving of half or two-thirds of the indemnity in return for the opening of Hiogo, the written adhesion of the Mikado to the Treaties, and the reduction of the import duties. He at once instructed the Ministers abroad to take up this proposal with the respective governments.[32] If the Shogun would not accept these terms, then the indemnity was to be promptly paid, the final instalment being due on October 1, 1866. If he would accept neither of these conditions, the concessions made in 1862 should be withdrawn, and the opening of Osaka and Hiogo from January 1, 1866, should be insisted upon. If the Powers agreed, the British Minister in Japan would be instructed to act in concert with his colleagues.

The Netherlands, preferring the payment of the indemnity, at first accepted Lord Russell's scheme only on condition that the other Powers would agree, but later sent instructions to their agent in Japan to act as Russell had suggested.[33] The United States, unable to act until the Treaty was ratified by the Senate, was still disposed to concur nominally and co-operate in the plans proposed by Great Britain.[34] The French Government continued to prefer the indemnity; in fact it held that the Powers had no choice in the matter as long as Japan offered to pay.[35] As to the proposed delay, it thought the Ministers on the ground could determine best whether or not the delay should be accorded.[36] M. Drouyn de

---

[31] *Japan. No. 1 (1866)*, p. 17.　　　　[32] July 12, *ibid.*, pp. 20, 21.

[33] *Ibid.*, pp. 29, 32.　　　[34] August 15, *ibid.*, p. 48.　　　[35] *Ibid.*, p. 30.

[36] Note the erroneous interpretation of the French position by Sir Harry Parkes later. Russell sent a summary of M. Drouyn de Lhuys' dispatch to Parkes in his dispatch of July 26. There is no record of any American sugges-

Lhuys also took up the question of the distribution of the indemnity. He believed that the "moral influence" pointed out by the
Americans should be considered, and his proposed division called
for $2,000,000 to be distributed on the basis of the forces em-
ployed, $420,000 to France, the United States, and the Nether-
lands, for attacks on their flags, and the balance, $580,000, to be
divided equally. This refusal of France to join with the other
Powers in revising the demands prevented the new joint action
which Earl Russell had endeavored to organize. But what the
Foreign Minister was unable to bring about by dispatches, Sir
Harry Parkes was quite able to accomplish through his forceful
personality.

The instructions which Earl Russell forwarded to Parkes on
his appointment to Japan were of a very general nature.[37] He was,
in brief, to maintain all the advantages gained by the Shimonoseki
operations and to cultivate the most cordial relations with his
colleagues. Among the advantages thus gained were:

Either the confirmation of the Treaties by the Mikado, or the formal ad-
mission that the Tycoon having, as the Prince of Satsuma said, the treaty-
making power, required no sanction from the Mikado for the conclusion
and execution of the Treaties with European Powers and the United
States of America.

At this late date the British Foreign Minister was unable or
unwilling to appreciate the absolute necessity of securing the
Mikado's assent to the Treaties.

After the French reply had brought to a close the proposed
concert for the revision of the Shimonoseki Convention, Earl
Russell sent an instruction on August 23 which actually directed
Parkes only "to ascertain the real state of affairs" in conjunction
with his three colleagues and in communication with the Rojiu.[38]
The dispatch pointed out the contradictory assertions of the Japa-
nese as to the validity of the Treaties, but maintained that the
British Government had properly assumed that the Tycoon had the

tion that "moral influence" be considered. See chapter x for discussion at the
time the Convention was negotiated.

[37] April 8, 1865, *Japan. No. 1 (1866)*, p. 8.   [38] *Ibid.*, p. 36.

power to conclude them; it then developed the view that the Tycoon's Government had deccived the Treaty Powers in stating that the attacks on foreigners were due to the opposition of the Japanese people and the ill will of some of the most powerful daimyos, whereas both Satsuma and Choshiu had said that their hostile deeds were committed under orders from the Tycoon; and it recalled that the Powers had accepted the representations of the Tycoon's Government and had agreed to postpone the opening of some of the treaty ports but now it was said that the people and the daimyos would welcome the inauguration of trade at those places and that the principal daimyos were ready to open their own ports. If these assertions were true, then the British Government was unwilling to exclude its subjects from the treaty ports upon insufficient grounds. Parkes was also advised that his Government would prefer "a large and healthy extension of commerce" to the payment of money indemnities; but if Japan insisted upon the payments, then they must be made at the stipulated times.

This instruction, which was received on October 23, really called for an investigation and a report,[39] and a man of less initiative and assurance would doubtless have followed the letter of his instructions. Sir Harry Parkes knew, however, what his Government desired, and he proceeded to accomplish it. Basing his action upon a misinterpretation of Russell's dispatch of July 26, he at once summoned the French and Dutch Representatives to a conference and easily convinced them of the wisdom of his proposals.[40]

[39] Lord Clarendon, Russell's successor, was waiting for Parkes's "report" as late as November 22 [*Japan. No. 1 (1866)*, p. 59].

[40] In his reply to Russell's dispatches of July 24 and 26 and August 23, Parkes wrote, on October 30, that he understood Lord Russell had arranged with M. Drouyn de Lhuys that the question of securing other compensations in return for the remission of two-thirds of the indemnity should be submitted to the four Representatives in Japan "in order that they might decide on the course to be adopted or to report to their Governments in the event of disagreement." This was not the case. M. Drouyn de Lhuys had only suggested that the Representatives in Japan should decide whether or not to permit the Shogun to delay the payments of the indemnity. France at this time stood out squarely for the payment, and her position was reaffirmed as late as November 16 (*ibid.*, p. 59).

The Japanese, true to their promise of April, had offered to pay the first instalment within the sixth month, which ended on August 20. Although this sum was not due until after the Representatives had announced to the Shogunate the ratification of the Convention and the receipt of their respective instructions, yet on consultation they determined to accept the first payment.[41] The receipt, which was given on September 4, expressly stated that the acceptance of this sum should not affect in any degree the right of the Powers to demand, if they saw fit, the punctual payment of the whole indemnity in quarterly payments as stipulated in the Convention.[42] At this time Mr. Portman suggested to Mr. Seward that if he deemed too large the full amount of $3,000,000—"so much larger than originally intended"—a portion of it, say $500,000, might be employed in the improvement of the foreign and Japanese settlements at the open ports, in drainage, street cleaning, and so on. "In no manner that I am aware of," he added, "could any portion of such indemnity be employed to greater advantage and be of more lasting benefit to both our political and commercial relations with this country."[43]

In other words, early in September it looked as if the payment of the indemnity would proceed, with or without the grace desired by the Shogunate. However, on the receipt of Russell's instructions Sir Harry Parkes, as we have seen, entered into a conference with the two Representatives in Yokohama, on October 26. He stated the British views concerning the remission of the indemnity and the three concessions to be secured in lieu thereof,[44] and he wrote, "I had the satisfaction of finding that these views were concurred in by M. Roches." With the French Minister won over in spite of his instructions, the way was clear. M. Roches explained that he had changed his views because he

---

[41] *F.R., 1865,* III, 256.

[42] *Ibid.,* p. 259. Delivery of the $500,000 commenced on August 22, but as it was not possible to examine more than $50,000 a day, it was continued until September 1. The money was at first deposited in two of the foreign banks in Yokohama and later transferred to the British commissariat chest there, and drafts for the amount were made available for distribution among the Powers in London.   [43] *Ibid.,* p. 257.   [44] *Japan. No. 1 (1866),* p. 64.

had not felt that the opening of a single port, as mentioned in the Convention, was a fair compensation for the surrender of all of the indemnity, while the three concessions now outlined would be quite equivalent to two-thirds of it. It was understood that the Tycoon would still have the option of paying the indemnity or accepting the new proposals, but in the former case the payments would have to be punctually made.[45]

With this understanding effected, it became necessary to consider how the new negotiations might best be carried out. Parkes then suggested that as the Tycoon and four of the five members of the Rojiu were at that time at Osaka, and as their return might be long delayed on account of the Choshiu operations, it would be expedient for the Representatives to proceed there and discuss with them the questions at issue.[46] "And it also occurred to me," he wrote,

that whatever result might attend our negotiations, the appearance of a fleet off Osaca could not fail to exercise a beneficial effect both on the Daimios who surround the Court of Kioto, and have had little opportunity of satisfying themselves of our power, and also on the people generally of that vicinity, whom it is well to begin to accustom to the sight of foreign visitors.[47]

His colleagues agreed with this proposal, M. Roches believing that their appearance at Osaka might give the Tycoon an excuse for postponing hostilities against Choshiu and might thus afford another opportunity of avoiding the outburst of civil war. A memorandum to this effect was promptly drafted, and was signed on October 30, on the arrival of Mr. Portman from Yedo.[48] The meat of this document was the statement that the four Representa-

[45] As late as November 16 the French Government felt that the extension of time asked for by the Shogunate should be granted; *Japan. No. 1 (1866)*, p. 59.

[46] Pruyn had advised this on June 27, 1863, and Alcock on October 6, 1864. See chapters viii, x.

[47] He also explained to Russell "that Osaca at this time would present more favourable opportunities than Yeddo for acquiring the information which your lordship instructs me in your despatch of the 23d of August to procure on the disputed question of whether the opening of Hiogo to foreign trade involves danger to the Tycoon's Government."

[48] *F.R., 1865*, III, 266–67. French text in *Japan. No. 1 (1866)*, pp. 65–67.

tives had agreed to transfer their negotiations to Osaka and to invite the naval commanders to proceed there and to remain during the negotiations. A long preamble was designed to reconcile the divergent instructions of the Representatives and to establish the wisdom of acting upon the proposals put forward by Great Britain.[49]

On that day notes, similar in expression, were addressed to the Rojiu by the four Representatives to the effect that they were about to proceed to Osaka to negotiate with the Ministers at present with the Tycoon for the solution of all that related to the convention of October 22, 1864.[50] When the news of the proposed expedition reached Yedo the sole remaining Minister of the Rojiu, Midzuno Idzumi-no-Kami, and a Vice-Minister hurried to Yokohama on the twenty-ninth and called upon Parkes and Roches, "for the professed purpose of dissuading us from the proposed movement."[51] Parkes explained that "the objects of the expedition were strictly of a friendly nature," and the Japanese officials, in turn, promised to keep order in Yokohama during their absence. The seriousness of the situation was evident, however, from the fact that this was the first time a member of the Rojiu had called upon a Foreign Minister at his own residence.

It was arranged that the joint expedition should sail from Yokohama on November 1.[52] The British furnished five ships, the French three, the Dutch one; but, as had so frequently happened, there was no American ship of war available, and so the American Chargé d'Affaires proceeded to Osaka in the British frigate "Pelorus." The squadron arrived off Hiogo on the fourth, and the next day letters were sent ashore to the Japanese Ministers at Osaka. These letters announced the arrival of the four Representatives in the Bay of Osaka for the purpose of determining with the Japanese Ministers "certain questions of grave importance arising out of the Convention of October 22, 1864." Sir

[49] It was again asserted that France had favored the settlement of this question by the representatives in Japan. See note 40. Mr. Portman had received no instructions on this subject.

[50] *F.R., 1865*, III, 267; *Japan. No. 1 (1866)*, p. 68.

[51] *Japan. No. 1 (1866)*, p. 65.   [52] *Ibid.*, p. 65.

Harry Parkes, while stating that the visit was undertaken in the most friendly spirit, spoke of the long delay that had occurred since the signing of the Convention, and announced that he and his colleagues would demand "a prompt and satisfactory settlement of the questions referred to." He added:

It will give the Undersigned the most sincere satisfaction to learn that the adjustment of these questions may be greatly facilitated by their Excellencies being provided with the formal approval of the Treaties by His Majesty the Mikado, which their Excellencies in October last admitted to be essential to the maintenance of a good understanding between European nations and Japan, and which they then promised to obtain.

In closing he took occasion to say that he was accompanied by Admiral King, commander-in-chief of all the naval forces of Her Britannic Majesty in China and Japan, and that his letter was dated from the Admiral's flagship.[53]

In order to avoid confusion it should be remembered that there really were no "questions of grave importance" arising out of the Convention of 1864. The Japanese had done everything they had agreed to do. They had even paid the first instalment of the indemnity almost a year before it was due. They had, to be sure, asked for a delay of some months in making the second payment, but until they failed to make that payment their attitude was absolutely correct. It must also be remembered that the Convention said nothing about the ratification of the treaties by the Mikado. The Yedo officials had agreed that this was desirable, but they had carefully refrained from doing more than promise that they would do their best to secure the ratification. The Foreign Representatives, backed by a powerful fleet, at a time when civil war was threatening, were going to demand "a prompt and satisfactory settlement" of new questions, instead of any that had arisen from the late Convention.

The Japanese did not question the right of the Foreign Ministers to request a conference with the Rojiu at Osaka, and it was arranged that Abe Bungo-no-Kami would meet them on shipboard on the ninth. He was unable to keep the first appointment,

[53] *Japan. No. 1 (1866)*, p. 78.

but did appear on the eleventh. At that time he conferred with the British Minister and the American and Dutch Representatives on board the British flagship,[54] and later with the French Minister on his vessel. At the former conference considerable discussion centered upon the London Protocol of 1862. It was pointed out that the postponement of the opening of Hiogo and Osaka was granted on certain conditions. These had not been lived up to, and therefore Great Britain could insist upon the immediate opening of those places.[55] At the same time the Shogun had asked for a postponement of the date of paying the Shimonoseki indemnity. The Powers would not permit "these repeated delays and evasions," and would insist upon punctual payment of the indemnity. Therefore the Powers offered as an alternative the proposals

to remit to the Tycoon two-thirds of the money stipulated in the Convention of October 22, 1864, in return for the immediate opening of Hiogo and Osacca to trade, the formal consent of the Mikado to the treaties and the regularization of the tariff on a basis of five per cent.[56]

It was pointed out in support of these requests that

in virtue of the London Convention of 1862, the opening of Hiogo and Osacca might be demanded at any moment, and a revision of the tariff can be claimed under the treaty itself.[57] A formal announcement by the Mikado of his approval of the treaties is, therefore, the only additional measure that is now asked, and this is simply a mark of friendship, which ought to be granted without hesitation, and which the Japanese ministers promised to obtain upwards of a year ago.

Lord Abe pointed out the difficulties of the Shogun's position

---

[54] Minutes of conference in *F.R., 1865*, III, 268–72.

[55] On December 19, 1863, Russell had instructed Alcock that the modifications set forth in the London Convention "are binding on Her Majesty's Government until they are expressly revoked" [*Japan. No. 1 (1865)*, p. 1]. No revocation had since been made. On July 12, 1865, Russell informed the other Powers that if Japan would not grant the new concessions or would not pay the indemnity promptly, then the modifications granted in 1862 should be withdrawn. But no action was taken on this proposal. In raising the question at Osaka the Representatives went beyond any instructions they possessed.

[56] It was stated that the Representatives had received instructions to insist upon either payment or acceptance of the alternative, a statement which was not correct.

[57] The tariff was subject to revision "if the Japanese Government desires it," after July 1, 1864, but at the desire of foreign governments only after July 1, 1872.

which had caused his Government to be unable to fulfill the conditions of the London Convention, and he craved the indulgence of the Treaty Powers. He also maintained that the opening of Hiogo and Osaka was out of the question at the present time. To this the Ministers replied that if the Shogun would not open them, the Powers might insist upon this point under the original Treaties, and then the Shogun would have to open the ports and lose $2,000,000 as well. The suggestion was made that there was nothing in the Treaties to prevent the Powers from opening trade with the daimyos at their own ports if the Shogun failed to reciprocate their friendship and consideration.[58]

These demands naturally made a deep impression upon the Japanese Minister, and he asked that the conference be adjourned to the next day for their consideration. At that time a messenger reported that in order that the whole question might be discussed by the Tycoon and the Rojiu the Minister would have to postpone the conference until the fourteenth. On the latter day a Vice-Minister and the principal ometsuke of the Tycoon came in the place of Lord Abe, and announced that although the Tycoon agreed to the justice of the Representatives' demands, it would take time for him to convince the Mikado.[59] They repeatedly assured the Ministers that the Tycoon was now resolved to settle once and for all the ratification of the Treaties. But an audience with the Mikado would be necessary, and so they asked that a delay of fifteen days be granted for this purpose. To this the Representatives replied that at most they would wait for eight or ten days, and in order to induce the Shogun to come to a prompt decision they added, "In the interval we may find it convenient to visit Shimonoseki or other places in the Inland Sea."

Here matters rested for a few days. In Kyoto there was great excitement.[60] The leading Shogunate officials urged the court to

[58] The Treaties designated certain ports and cities which were to be opened for trade and residence. How the Representatives could propose to trade at other places and still consider the Treaties in force is a mystery.

[59] Minutes of conference in *F.R., 1865*, III, 272–74.

[60] *Japan. No. 1 (1866)*, pp. 82–85; *F.R., 1866*, II, 189–91.

ratify the Treaties, lest war between Japan and the allied Powers ensue.[61] The conservative party, however, was not easily dislodged. On the nineteenth, Abe Bungo-no-Kami and Matsumae Idsu-no-Kami, two of the Rojiu, were dismissed by order of the Mikado, and stripped of their titles. The news was confirmed by messengers sent from the Rojiu on the twenty-first. Believing that it meant a reactionary movement in Kyoto, the four Representatives promptly addressed identic notes to the Tycoon, which were delivered in Kyoto on the twenty-third. These notes insisted that unless a categorical reply to the proposals was made, in writing, within the allotted ten days(which would expire on the twenty-fourth), they would consider "that its absence denotes a formal refusal of our conditions on your Majesty's part, and we shall, in that case, be free to act as we may judge convenient."

This letter, with its scarcely veiled threat, produced an immediate effect. On the afternoon of the twenty-fourth a member of the Rojiu and other officials came aboard the flagship to announce that the Mikado had ratified the Treaties and that the Tycoon had agreed to the downward revision of the tariff, but that instead of opening Hiogo and Osaka, the Tycoon would rather pay the full indemnity at the times stated in the Convention.[62]

Thus the Foreign Representatives, acting either without or in defiance of instructions, but under the masterful leadership of Sir Harry Parkes, gained two of their three demands without having

[61] Yamaguchi, *op. cit.*, pp. 77–78. For address of Shogun to Mikado praying for ratification of Treaties, see Adams, *The History of Japan*, II, 24–27.

[62] *Japan. No. 1 (1866)*, p. 86. The text of the Mikado's assent as communicated by the Rojiu to the Foreign Representatives was a follows: "The Imperial consent is given to the Treaties, and you will therefore undertake the necessary arrangements in connection therewith" (*ibid.*, p. 86). Yamaguchi states that at the time the consent was given the Bakufu was ordered to revise the hitherto existing treaties, and the opening of the port of Hiogo was prohibited (*op. cit.*, p. 78). This led Sir Ernest Mason Satow, the translator, to state in a note (p. 77 n.): "With characteristic duplicity they omitted from this copy the postscript in which the opening of Hiogo was forbidden and a revision of the Treaties commanded. As there is no article in the Japanese language the omission of these two conditions made it apparent that the Mikado had given his consent to the Treaties as they then stood, which was not his intention." These orders were annulled by an imperial decree on June 26, 1867, and Hiogo was opened at the stipulated time. See Murdock, *op. cit.*, I, 759; Satow, *op. cit.*, p. 155.

to relinquish a penny of the Shimonoseki indemnity. Naturally the report of their success was received with great satisfaction, and their proceedings met with the approval of their governments.[63] However, a careful study of the whole episode serves to discount the achievement, and leaves but little credit to be divided among the participants. Once more the Powers had imposed their will upon Japan.[64] Is it to be wondered at if she remembered some of these bitterly learned lessons? Nothing more was said about the opening of Hiogo and Osaka under the terms of the London Convention, and those ports were opened in due course on January 1, 1868. The tariff was revised in 1866 and remained in force until the long-delayed revision of 1899. Of greatest immediate value was the ratification of the existing Treaties by the Mikado; but how unfortunate it was that this essential Imperial recognition should have been linked with a demand for a downward revision of the tariff! The indemnity was eventually paid in full, and the United States, be it said to its credit, later returned every penny of its share.[65]

As long as the Treaties remained unratified the foreign relations of Japan were bound to be unsettled. Foreign affairs could not be determined on their merits, but became the football of domestic politics. Even after many of the daimyos were convinced of the wisdom of widening their relations with the West, they still found political capital in the Tycoon's unauthorized dealings with the foreigners. Although when Perry arrived few Japanese would have questioned the right of the Shogun to deal with foreign affairs as he pleased, yet with the weakening of the Shogunate

[63] *Japan. No. 1 (1866)*, p. 87; *F.R., 1866*, II, 199.

[64] Parkes to Earl Russell, November 25, 1865: "Speaking after the event, I can assert with confidence that had it not been for the presence of the allied fleet on this occasion, the Tycoon would not have been persuaded to make to the Mikado those energetic remonstrances and representations without which union between these rulers on the subject of the Treaties, and the foreign policy they render necessary, would not have been effected" [*Japan. No. 1 (1866)*, p. 81]. At a dinner that night Parkes said to Vice-Admiral King, "but after all it was you who did it, Admiral, for without you and your magnificent ship, we should not have made the slightest impression" (Satow, *op. cit.*, p. 154).

[65] See Appendix in Vol. II.

and the rise of the Imperial power, there were as few in 1865 who did not recognize the Mikado's supremacy in such fundamental matters as these. The members of the Rojiu frankly admitted this. After the Mikado's sanction was won, the Treaty Powers were freed from their dangerous dependence upon the Shogunate. There were still some Japanese who yearned for the old ways, and hated the foreigners who desecrated the sacred land of the Kamis, but there was no powerful party in the state whose motto was "Honor the Mikado and expel the barbarians." Thus when the restoration of the Emperor came in 1868, it was a very easy matter for direct relations to be established between the Treaty Powers and the new Government.[66]

The most interesting period of Japanese foreign relations is that between 1858 and 1865, when the Shogunate tried to keep faith with the foreign Powers, in spite of a hostile court and powerful feudatories; when Japan learned her first lessons in modern diplomacy and international intercourse; and when the Foreign Ministers groped their way through the haze of Japanese politics until they found in the Mikado the ultimate source of power in the state. In mastering this situation American diplomats played a leading part. Townsend Harris was ready to negotiate at Kyoto if the Yedo authorities were unable to grant his requests; and it was Robert H. Pruyn who first pointed out the absolute necessity of having the Treaties ratified by the Mikado. And the latter would have made a joint naval demonstration at Osaka, much as Parkes finally arranged; but it may be doubted if he would have linked a request of such fundamental importance with demands for additional commercial concessions.

The policy of the United States during this period was easy enough to define but difficult indeed to carry out in the presence of the uncertainty which prevailed in Japan. The American Government insisted that treaty rights be maintained, sought no selfish advantage, and urged the constant co-operation of the Treaty Powers. Because of the unity of interest of all foreigners in China

[66] Treat, "The Mikado's Ratification of the Foreign Treaties," *American Historical Review,* April 1918, Vol. 23, pp. 531–49.

and Japan, the United States abandoned its traditional isolation and worked in concert with the Treaty Powers in both countries. When, however, treaty concessions were prematurely granted, America was willing to postpone their enjoyment. So Harris was the first diplomat to advocate deferring the opening of the additional ports and cities and the first to receive discretionary power to grant the Japanese request. There were also times when the American Representatives could not support their colleagues, as when Harris stood alone in Yedo and when Pruyn sought to temper the British ultimatum in 1863. If the Americans, after the treaty-making of Perry and Harris, were forced out of their position of leadership by the British Ministers, Alcock and Parkes, it does not follow that their influence was lost. Both Harris and Pruyn stood consistently for a policy of moderation and forbearance in dealing with the Japanese during those troubled years, and there could be no co-operation among the Foreign Ministers unless their views were recognized. If Harris, in 1860, or Pruyn, in 1863, had joined their colleagues of England and France, war between the Treaty Powers and Japan might have occurred. Yet, when American interests were openly attacked and the guilt was plain, the American Minister was not afraid to strike with the limited means at hand. It was an American ship which fired the first shot in defense of treaty rights; but there was a world of difference between the work of the "Wyoming" at Shimonoseki and that of the British squadron at Kagoshima a month later.

Americans, therefore, can read the story of these days with pardonable pride. In Perry, Harris, and Pruyn they find three worthy representatives of their nation, in whose record there is scarcely a line which, after half a century, one would erase. These men laid the foundation of what has been termed the "traditional friendship" of America and Japan. Others builded upon it. Though some have tried to undermine the edifice so honorably reared, yet may it endure "till the little stone grows into a mighty rock, thick velveted with ancient moss." It will endure if the principles of respect for treaty obligations, mutual understanding, and unselfish good will prevail on both sides of the broad Pacific.

CHAPTER XII

AFTER the successful negotiations at Osaka, Mr. Portman returned to Yedo, but Sir Harry Parkes proceeded to Shanghai and at Shimonoseki met some of the officers of Choshiu. This was the first of several contacts with the feudal clans which were to have much to do with the development of Sir Harry's policy in the next two years. He reported to Lord Clarendon that the Choshiu men accepted the Mikado's decree as authentic and admitted "that it would be generally respected by the Daimios."[2]

Mr. Portman, in his dispatch of December 5, 1865, stressed the importance of the Mikado's ratification, which was, in truth, of far greater value than even the reduction in the tariff, and, he added:

> The Tycoon is under lasting obligations to the four powers for the action taken by them so opportunely for his interests and the true interests of Japan, and by sanctioning the treaties, the Tycoon is recognized as the *de facto* chief of the government of this country.[3]

On December 1, all daimyos and others were notified that the Mikado had ratified the Treaties.

On all sides the improvement in the position of the Shogunate was recognized. Portman believed that the Choshiu rebellion could now be settled without coercion, especially as the Mikado's action had deprived the clan of any cover of legality and destroyed its hope of receiving foreign aid or sympathy.[4] At the

---

[1] The instructions are numbered 9–26, with two duplicate numbers (to Portman), and 1–7 (to Van Valkenburgh); of these twenty-seven, six were printed in *F.R., 1866*, II. Portman's dispatches are numbered 1–34, with one duplicate, and Van Valkenburgh's, 35–67; of these sixty-eight, nineteen were printed in *F.R., 1866*, II, and five in *F.R., 1867*, II.

[2] *Japan. No. 1 (1866)*, p. 86.

[3] *F.R., 1866*, II, 191.   [4] February 15, 1866, *F.R., 1866*, II, 199.

same time, some of the coastal daimyos resented the monopoly of foreign trade at the Shogun's ports. Portman believed, in December, that the restrictions on trade at the open ports would be removed, so that the daimyo agents could trade directly and not through the customhouses,[5] and such a notification was issued in April 1866, with the proviso that arms, munitions, and ships of war could be purchased only by permission.[6] But Choshiu, and doubtless some of the other clans, were carrying on a clandestine trade, and foreign adventurers were frequenting their ports.[7] A further evidence of the security which the Shogunate felt was seen in the proclamation of May 23 permitting Japanese to travel abroad under passports issued by their Government,[8] although it was not until November 6 that a form of such passport was submitted to the American Minister.[9] Thus the seclusion system, which had been decreed in 1636, came to an end, and the process of setting aside both seclusion and exclusion, which began in 1854, may be said to have been completed. This could not have been attempted had not the Shogunate felt strong enough to defy conservative criticism.

The first matter of business confronting the foreign diplomats was the negotiation of the new tariff convention. Soon after his return from Osaka Mr. Portman had asked the Ministers for Foreign Affairs to appoint commissioners for this purpose, and they assured him that the matter would be taken up as soon as they had received official communications from Osaka.[10] They should have added that nothing could be done before Sir Harry Parkes returned from his visit to Shanghai, for he was to play the major rôle in the negotiations. These began early in January, and although the negotiations at Yedo were conducted with unusual facility the frequent references to Osaka delayed the final signature until June.[11]

[5] *F.R., 1866,* II, 191.

[6] *Ibid.,* p. 205.   [7] *Ibid.,* p. 199.   [8] *Ibid.,* p. 209.   [9] *Ibid.,* p. 227.

[10] Portman to Midzuno, November 30, 1865, *ibid.,* p. 194.

[11] Satow, *A Diplomat in Japan,* p. 157.

In the meantime the Shogunate was embarrassed by the Cho-shiu war and the resulting lack of funds. A peaceful solution had not been arrived at, and in January 1866 the feudal levies were again ordered to take the field. The Shogun, Iyemochi, was be-lieved to be personally hostile to the Mori family, and the latter reciprocated his animosity in addition to their hatred of the Sho-gunate. Three additional penalties were proclaimed upon Choshiu, including a heavy forfeiture of revenue, the retirement and con-finement of the Daimyo and his son, leaving the succession to a grandson, and the extinction of the families of the three karo who had taken part in the Kyoto emeute of 1864.[12] As no reply was received within the stipulated thirty days, the Mikado, on July 18, ordered the resumption of hostilities. Fourteen crimes were spec-ified in the indictment which was then published, the second in the list stating that the attack upon the foreign ships in 1863 was due to a wicked scheme to annoy the Tycoon's Government rather than to carry out the Imperial will.[13] The war was carried on vigor-ously from July until the death of the Shogun gave an excuse for suspending operations in October. In these engagements the Cho-shiu men gave an excellent account of themselves, while some of the leading clans refused to take part in the punitive measures.[14] A French man-of-war was reported to have attempted to intervene on the Imperial side, but Sir Harry Parkes visited Shimonoseki in August and, as in December 1865, made known the neutrality of his country in this civil strife.[15]

The Choshiu operations, which have been only touched upon here, must be kept in mind when the relations between the Powers and the Shogunate are being considered. They placed the latter in the position of needing some help from the Powers, and thus gave them an advantage when they sought something from the Shogunate. The Shogun's officials were placed in the weak posi-tion of seeking help in the first instance and, as had happened in

[12] Yamaguchi, *Kinse Shiriaku. A History of Japan,* p. 80.
[13] *F.R., 1866,* II, 211.
[14] Yamaguchi, *op. cit.,* p. 85.   [15] *F.R., 1866,* II, 213.

1865 and was to happen many times in the future, it was the Shimonoseki indemnity which forced their hands. In the conventional accounts of the career of Sir Harry Parkes frequent reference is made to the invaluable advice which he gave the Shogunate and Imperial officials. It must have been a mere oversight that not only did he fail to advise them that the indemnity payments were not due in the first instance until all the Powers had ratified the Convention of 1864 (and the United States did not do so until April 9, 1866) but he never failed to join his colleagues in taking advantage of their ignorance. His greatest diplomatic achievement, the Osaka negotiations of 1865, had its origin in the request of the Shogunate for a postponement of payments which had actually commenced long before they were due. So when, in February 1866, the Shogun's minister asked for a postponement of the third instalment, which really was not due until January 1867, the Foreign Representatives graciously agreed to accept a promissory note for the amount, payable in three months. In reporting his action to Mr. Seward, Mr. Portman recognized that he had no authority to accept this money, in view of the failure of the Senate to approve the Treaty, but he did not feel like dissenting from the opinion of his colleagues, and he hoped his action would be approved.[16]

But on April 13 the Rojiu addressed to the four Ministers a request that the three remaining instalments be postponed, giving as their reason the third article of the Convention, which stated that the object of the Powers was not the receipt of money but the establishment of better relations with Japan.[17] The Imperial ratification of the Treaties and the tariff negotiations which were in progress were certainly evidences of the latter. Mr. Portman, however, did not feel that a fair equivalent for the concession had been offered,[18] and while Mr. Seward agreed with him, his eagerness for co-operation led him to say that concurrence with the other Powers was doubtless more important than even the correct-

[16] February 15, 1866, *F.R., 1866*, II, 199.
[17] *Ibid.*, p. 204.   [18] April 22, *ibid.*, p. 204.

ness of the decision which might be adopted.[19] Sir Harry Parkes, however, advised his Government that the Representatives had determined to await the result of the tariff negotiations before submitting the application for postponement to their respective governments. This, as we have just seen, Mr. Portman did not do. Sir Harry further advised Lord Stanley "that he had intimated to the Gorogio that his recommendation of their proposal must greatly depend upon the spirit in which they should meet the representatives in these negotiations."[20] His recommendation had not been received in London by August 23. In other words, the postponement of the undue indemnity payments was tied in with the tariff negotiations.

It should be added that in 1866, after some little correspondence, the Powers accepted the generous proposal of the British Government that the indemnity be divided, when and as received, in equal parts, after $140,000 each had been set aside for damages and expenses incurred by the United States, France, and the Netherlands at Shimonoseki before the joint expedition, thus awarding the three Powers $785,000 each, and Great Britain, which had borne the major expense of the joint expedition, only $645,000.[21]

On June 25 the Tariff Convention was signed by Midzuno Idzumi-no-Kami, a member of the Rojiu and a Minister of Foreign Affairs, and by Mr. A. L. C. Portman, Sir Harry Parkes, M. Leon Roches, and M. Dirk de Graeff van Polsbroek, the Representatives of the United States, Great Britain, France, and the Netherlands. Rarely has the negotiation of so important an agreement received so little contemporary attention. This was due to the fact that both parties failed to appreciate the significance of their work. In form, and according to the understanding of the signatories, the Convention simply established modifications in the tariff of import and export duties annexed to the Treaties of

[19] July 18, *ibid.,* p. 210.
[20] Lord Stanley to C. F. Adams, August 23, *ibid.,* p. 176.
[21] See Appendix in Vol. II.

1858. And the same provision which was found in those Treaties applied to these amendments, that they would be subject to revision on July 1, 1872. Thus the Shogun's Government was ready to meet the desires of the four Powers, as set forth at Osaka in November 1865, in the firm assurance that the reduced tariff would be in operation for only a few years; and the foreign negotiators, and their governments, also looked upon the Convention as a temporary measure. As a matter of fact the tariff there agreed upon was to remain in operation until August 1899 and was to be the occasion of continual protest by the Japanese Government for some twenty-two years.

Although the preamble stated that the four Representatives had received from their respective governments "identical instructions for the modification of the Tariff [of 1858]," in the case of the American Representative the only instruction he had received was a brief approval of his conduct at Osaka. The report of Sir Harry Parkes, after the Convention was signed, does not refer to any previous instructions, and it is at least doubtful if any specific ones were forwarded to him. It was not deemed necessary to supply the four Representatives with the customary "full powers" to negotiate, for the Convention was considered merely a modification of the 1858 tariff, yet the Japanese negotiator had received such. Contemporary writers, some of them in a position to know what was going on, such as Adams, and Satow, and Black, the journalist who has given us so detailed a record of the period, mention the negotiations in the briefest terms. After the signature, Sir Harry sent two long dispatches to Lord Clarendon,[22] explaining the purpose of the several articles, and Mr. Portman also reported in briefer terms.[23]

It is not easy, with the available materials, to reconstruct the negotiations. Sir Harry Parkes took the lead in working out the new provisions.[24] M. Roches tried to have the Japanese declare

---

[22] Both were dated July 16. Only an extract of the second was printed, which omitted Parkes's remarks on the new tariff [*Japan. No. 1 (1867)*, pp. 7–11]. [23] Portman to Seward, No. 34, July 14, 1866.

[24] Dickins, *The Life of Sir Harry Parkes*, II, 64.

Yokohama a free port, and stated that M. Drouyn de Lhuys, the French Foreign Minister, had tried to secure this concession from the Japanese envoys in 1864 but found them unable to act.[25] Mr. Portman supported the French proposal, having in mind the desirability of placing Yokohama on an equality with Hong Kong, but the proposal was not accepted by Sir Harry.[26] The delay in completing the negotiations was due in large part to the frequent references by the Japanese officials to the Shogun and his principal Ministers at Osaka.[27] In fact it is probable that pressure was brought to bear upon the Japanese to secure their signature before July 1, for they finally agreed to act without securing the last advices from Osaka respecting Articles IX and XI.[28] Mr. Portman had hoped that the new American Minister, General Van Valkenburgh, would arrive in time to sign the Convention, but he affixed his own signature in order to allow time for drafting the bonded warehouse regulations before July 1.[29]

As might have been expected, this revision of the tariff of 1858 covered far more than a reduction in import and export duties.[30] All the stipulations of the former Treaties remained in force, except the tariff articles, but additional facilities for foreign commerce were added. The new tariff, which was to go into effect on July 1, 1866, was substituted for the Harris tariff of 1858 as modified by Lord Elgin a few months later and at other times as already mentioned. It reduced the rate of duty to five per cent *al valorem,* but fixed specific duties (based on the average of prices for the past five years) on eighty-nine enumerated articles.[31] A few duty-free goods were listed, and opium was prohibited. A similar export tariff was drawn up, with specific duties on fifty-three articles (arrived at in the same way), with gold and silver coins and gold, silver, and copper free, and with certain goods prohibited, such as rice, paddy, wheat, and barley, flour made from the foregoing, and saltpeter. Aside from the articles on which

[25] *Ibid.,* p. 68.   [26] Portman's No. 34.   [27] Dickins, *op. cit.,* II, 69.
[28] *Japan. No. 1 (1867),* p. 16.   [29] Portman's No. 34.
[30] Note the "revision" of the treaties with China in 1858.
[31] *Japan. No. 1 (1867),* p. 7.

specific duties were laid, and these covered almost every conceivable article of commerce, goods would be taxed at the rate of five per cent ad valorem.

It was perfectly true that the levying of the *ad valorem* duty was fraught with difficulties, inconveniences, and often hardship for the foreign merchant. Goods were unfairly declared and either a haggling with the officials took place, or bribes were used. If the valuation placed by the customhouse was rejected by the merchant, the Government could take over the goods at its valuation, and these goods were then sold, a practice which, in fact, ran counter to the Treaty provision that the Government would not engage in trade. The fixing of specific duties would facilitate the operations of the customhouse and the transactions of the merchants. It would probably improve the receipts from duties, but, it should be added, these duties were to be revised from time to time, so that, with rising prices, the five per cent *ad valorem,* which was the basis of the tax, would actually be received. With revision delayed until 1899, the five per cent, low as it was, was reduced to an average of three per cent, which was a gross violation of the plain intent of the agreement at Osaka and of the Convention of 1866.

Sir Harry, and the British merchants, understood this chance of profit or loss under the specific duties. On the one hand, he saw to the reaffirmation, in Article II, of the right to claim revision of the tariff in 1872 (which would be insisted upon if prices fell) ; and, on the other, he incorporated a provision that the export duties on tea and silk might be revised after two years, on six months' notice, on the basis of the average value of those articles during the preceding three years. This was inserted because the merchants felt that prices had been high in 1864 and 1865 but would be lower in 1866 and 1867, and that the specific duties should be based on the lower prices. For a similar reason it was provided that after six months the duty on lumber might be changed to a specific one, for the information then at hand as to prices prevailing at Hakodate, from which port lumber was exported, was too incomplete to risk a specific rate.

The third article abolished the permit fee of $1.50 whenever goods were landed or shipped. These fees were the perquisites of the interpreters, and the more permits a merchant took out at the customhouse the more friendly were the officials, while it was possible to create delays in order to issue several permits on a single shipment.

The establishment of a system of bonded warehouses, in Article IV, caused the most difficulty. As we have seen, M. Roches and Mr. Portman favored a free port. Sir Harry favored the warehouse system. Some arrangement was necessary, for no provision was found in the 1858 Treaties for the reshipping of goods without the payment of duty. Lord Russell had urged a warehouse system upon the Japanese envoys in 1862 and they had promised to recommend it to the Government on their return, but nothing had been done. Parkes now pressed for this arrangement, and he found unexpected support from Mr. Portman, who claimed the right of free re-export under the seventh article of Perry's Treaty of March 30, 1854. But Portman preferred the use of a system of drawbacks for a time, perhaps two years, until the Japanese could prepare for the warehouse system. The Japanese, however, objected strongly to a drawback system, because of the frauds which might be attempted. When they found that they must yield they accepted the broadest of the proposals and promised to open a bonded warehouse at Yokohama at once and at Nagasaki and Hakodate within three months.[32]

Article V extended to goods moving to the ports for export the same freedom from transit duties or other taxes (except such road or navigation tolls as were levied upon all native traffic) as was enjoyed by foreign imports moving into the interior, under the 1858 Treaties.

The sixth article stated that a free mint would be established, and the Japanese Government would propose to the Powers that the existing currency provisions in the Treaties be modified. Under the Treaties foreign money should pass current in Japan for its corresponding weight in Japanese coin. At the custom-

[32] *Japan. No. 1 (1867)*, p. 7; Portman's No. 34.

house 100 Mexican dollars were accepted as 311 bus (or ichibus). In exchanging dollars for ichibus, for the use of the official establishments of the Powers, the rate of 298 ichibus per 100 dollars had been adopted, the difference (13 ichibus) being allowed to cover the cost of recoinage. As the merchants could exchange only a limited amount of dollars for ichibus at the official rate, the result was that dollars were discounted, sometimes as much as fifteen to thirty per cent. In such times, the foreign officials enjoyed a handsome profit on their exchange.[33] In 1866, however, the heavy importation of foreign goods had strengthened the demand for dollars, so that their value had reached around 300 ichibus a hundred. With the establishment of the mint, foreign coins could be exchanged for Japanese coins, allowing a discount to recover the cost of recoinage.[34]

The seventh article called for the drafting of regulations by the Governor of each open port and the foreign Consuls to put an end to certain abuses and inconveniences connected with trade, such as delays and confusion in the customhouse, landing and shipping of cargoes, and hiring of boats, coolies, and servants. And at each port one or more covered landing-places should be erected to protect cargoes.

The eighth article made a treaty right of the permission already accorded Japanese subjects to purchase sailing or steam vessels, but not ships of war. The duty was fixed at three ichibus per ton for steamers, or one ichibu for sailing ships, which Parkes thought considerably less than one per cent of the value of the vessels.

The ninth and tenth articles Parkes considered "to embrace

[33] Satow, *op. cit.*, p. 26. In September 1862 the current exchange was 214 ichibus for 100 dollars, while the foreign officials received 298 ichibus.

[34] It is interesting to compare the reports of Parkes and Portman on the existing exchange operations. Portman admitted that "profits occasionally accrued to [foreign] officials," while Parkes stated that "the foreign officer was enabled to obtain the value of his money in native coin," and it was entirely the fault of the Japanese Government that the foreign merchants had to circulate dollars at a discount of fifteen to thirty per cent. But Satow, *op. cit.*, p. 26, points out that a Minister whose salary was £3,000 a year made a fine profit, and he was ashamed as he looked back at his own conduct, as a junior officer in the British Legation, in those days.

the most important stipulations of the Convention." Portman referred any discussion of them to General Van Valkenburgh, because of their political importance. In brief, the ninth article placed upon record as a treaty stipulation the permission accorded by the proclamation of April previous to all Japanese merchants to trade directly with foreign merchants not only at the open ports but, should they be authorized to travel abroad, in all foreign countries. And this right was specifically extended to daimyos and their agents. The tenth article confirmed the right of all Japanese subjects to ship goods to or from any of the open ports of Japan, or of any foreign Power, either in vessels owned by Japanese or in those of any Treaty Power. It also gave a treaty sanction to the passport regulations, proclaimed on May 23, and furthermore permitted Japanese to accept employment in any capacity on board the vessels of any Treaty Power.

Parkes pointed out:

In giving the Japanese credit for these timely concessions to the progressive spirit of their countrymen, I am not insensible, my Lord, to the proneness of this Government, in common with other Oriental States, to avoid, when they can do so, the execution of engagements which conflict with a traditional policy. It is to be expected, therefore, that close watchfulness combined with patient persuasion will be needed on the part of the foreign Representatives to ensure full effect being given to all the important provision of these two Articles. We may find that the passport system is not conducted with the liberality we could desire; or that the rigid system of espionage and control, upon which all government in this country is based, is not readily relinquished in the management of foreign relations; but the distinct recognition in this Convention of the principle that foreign trade or intercourse with foreigners, either at home or abroad, is open to all Japanese subjects, must in itself give an impetus to advancement, and may be relied on to work out in the end, its own fulfilment.[35]

As conditions were at the time, Sir Harry was right. The abandonment of the seclusion policy was now made a treaty engagement. Any deviation from the liberal policy evinced by the Shogun's Government could become the subject of represen-

[35] *Japan. No. 1 (1867)*, p. 9.

tations, perhaps even sanctions, on the part of the four Treaty Powers. "Close watchfulness combined with patient persuasion" would be the policy of the Foreign Representatives. Happily for Japan, neither the then Government nor the one which was soon to replace it took a backward step.

"Another instance of liberality on the part of the Tycoon's Government," in Parkes's opinion, was found in the eleventh article, which promised that Japan would light and buoy the approaches to all the ports. In fact he hoped these safeguards would be extended to dangerous parts of the coast. For his active interest in encouraging the Japanese to build up a lighthouse service, with British personnel and materials, Sir Harry deserved well of all mariners.

The final (twelfth) article shows the informal nature of this very important Convention. It was to go into effect on July 1, 1866, before it could be ratified by the foreign governments. And in place of a formal exchange of ratifications each party would notify the others when the approval of his Government had been obtained. While Lord Stanley and Mr. Seward promptly approved the action of their Ministers, the United States Senate did not advise ratification of the Convention until June 17, 1868, and the Convention was never proclaimed by the United States.[36]

Speedy work was necessary in order to complete the details of the warehouse system. Rules and regulations were drawn up and approved by both sides on June 29. In view of the inexperience of the Japanese, some foreign help would be needed, and on the suggestion of Parkes and at the request of the Rojiu each Representative recommended a suitable person. The Rojiu selected Mr. Benjamin Seare, an Englishman, as General Instructor, for two years at $600 a month, and Mr. Hogg, an American, as Assistant, for one year at $300, and these appointments were understood to be of a temporary nature, and quite unlike the appointments in the Chinese customs service. At Nagasaki and Hakodate the Japanese hoped to rely upon native officials trained

[36] Instruction No. 86, May 20, 1871. For a text of the Convention, see Malloy, *Treaties and Conventions,* I, 1012–21.

by Mr. Seare. It should be noted that the Bonded Warehouse Regulations and Tariff of Storage Charges were approved by the Foreign Representatives on June 29, and no portion of them could be changed without their consent.

In view of the recognition by the foreign diplomats of the supremacy of the Emperor, as shown by the demand for his ratification of the early Treaties, at Osaka in 1865, it is surprising that no effort was made to secure his approval of the Tariff Convention. As we have pointed out, the Convention was signed before final reference to even the Shogun could take place, and it went into operation almost immediately. Neither Parkes nor Portman considered, in their dispatches, the necessity of securing the Emperor's approval. In the English text the use of the term "Government of Japan" avoided any reference to either Emperor or Shogun. It is a perfectly reasonable inference that the Foreign Representatives considered the new concessions so desirable that they would accept any kind of a Convention, trusting to their ability to secure Imperial sanction later if necessary.[37]

Immediately after the tedious negotiations were ended Sir Harry set out for a visit to the daimyos of Satsuma and Uwajima, and on his return touched at Nagasaki and Shimonoseki. The cordial reception extended him served to wipe out the sting of the Kagoshima bombardment of 1863, and Satsuma clansmen now became on good terms with the British Legation.[38] At the very end of the year, E. M. Satow, a student interpreter, made a similar visit to secure information.[39] In this way, Sir Harry became the best-informed diplomat at Yedo, and his contacts were mainly with anti-Shogun clansmen. The active participation of Satow in anti-Shogun politics was a feature of this period.

On August 12, the new American Minister arrived at Yokohama. General Robert B. Van Valkenburgh was, like his two

---

[37] Lord Stanley promptly advised Parkes of the approval of Her Majesty's Government of the new Convention. August 31, *Japan. No. 1 (1867)*, p. 7. Mr. Seward, on September 10, merely acknowledged the receipt of the Convention and stated that it would be submitted to the Senate at the ensuing session.

[38] Dickins, *op. cit.*, II, 66–67; Black, *Young Japan*, II, 2–7.

[39] Satow, *op. cit.*, pp. 167–69.

predecessors, a New Yorker.[40] A lawyer by profession, he had
served three terms in his state legislature. In the early days of
the Civil War he had been active in raising regiments for the
Federal service, and had entered Congress in 1861. While still
a member, he had taken the field as Colonel of the Hundred and
Seventh New York Volunteers, and had been in action at Antie-
tam. Re-elected to the Thirty-eighth Congress, he had served
until 1865, when for a time he had acted as Commissioner of
Indian Affairs. In December he was appointed Minister-Resident
to Japan. He was a typical American diplomat of the period,
devoid of technical experience but somewhat acquainted with
public affairs. Fortunately he could rely upon Mr. Portman, who
had been attached to the Legation since 1860 and had previously
visited Japan as an interpreter with Perry. Portman's usefulness,
as a Dutch interpreter, was diminishing as the student interpreters in the British Legation improved in knowledge of Japanese.
For much of his information concerning internal affairs General
Van Valkenburgh had to rely on such translations as Parkes
would furnish him. Had it not been for two able American
linguists, Dr. J. C. Hepburn and the Reverend S. R. Brown, near
at hand, the American Legation would have been forced to rely
almost entirely upon British sources for access to Japanese materials.

Van Valkenburgh's arrival almost coincided with a renewal
of activity in the Choshiu campaign, for the Emperor, on July 18,
had ordered the Tycoon to commence hostilities. The Shogun's
officials now desired to stop the illegal trade which was supplying
Choshiu with arms and munitions. On July 24 Mr. Mangum,
the American Consul at Nagasaki, had received a request from
the Governor that he advise American ships not to anchor in the
ports of Suwo and Nagato (Choshiu). He referred the request
to Mr. Portman, who at about the same time had received a

[40] President Johnson had appointed Chauncey M. Depew, of New York, to
this post November 11, 1865, and he had been confirmed by the Senate (Seward
to Depew, November 23, 1865), but Depew declined the post to accept
the attorneyship of the New York and Harlem Railroad. He rose to prominence
in the Vanderbilt railway interests and in the Republican party, serving for a
time as Senator from New York.

similar request from the Rojiu, which included a request for the prohibition of American ships passing through the Straits of Shimonoseki. Portman, on August 4, had instructed Mangum to warn American citizens as desired, and Mr. van Polsbroek issued a similar warning. Choshiu, on its part, asked that American ships should not approach the coast by night, and always show their colors, lest they be taken for enemies. On August 28 Van Valkenburgh had a long interview with Sir Harry Parkes, and they arrived at an understanding. Parkes, on September 1, issued a notification, based on the Order in Council of March 9, 1865, warning British ships to avoid the war zone and a second one regulating British traffic through the straits. The latter was amplified by a notification of September 5. Van Valkenburgh, on the eleventh, issued a notification in strong terms, based on the Act of June 22, 1860, warning American ships not to visit any but the three open ports, and citing the capital penalty prescribed for taking part in a rebellion against the governments of either China or Japan.[41] Parkes had withdrawn from his earlier position of neutrality in this civil war.

On September 27 Van Valkenburgh reported to Mr. Seward that it was believed the Tycoon had died in the latter part of August.[42] An official statement, forwarded to him on the sixteenth, advised him that the Tycoon had been unwell for some time, and that in case of his death Hitotsubashi would succeed. The latter had, in fact, been ordered to assume command of the army and navy as the Tycoon's representative. But this was only an example of the custom of Old Japan of withholding notice of the death of a sovereign, or high dignitary, until all necessary arrangements could be made. Iyemochi had, in fact, died at the castle in Osaka on August 28. Dr. Bauduin, of the Medical College at Nagasaki, had been sent for, but he arrived a day late. He was able to report that death had been caused by heart disease, aggravated by dropsy, although the rumor was current that the young Tycoon, for he was only twenty-one, had been poisoned.[43]

---

[41] For the documents cited above see *F.R., 1866*, II, 214–19.
[42] *Ibid.*, p. 220.   [43] Black, *op. cit.*, II, 28.

It was generally felt that the senseless Choshiu war would now be ended, for Hitotsubashi was known to be personally friendly to the Mori family.[44]

Yoshinobu (better known by his Chinese name, Keiki) was son of the old prince of Mito, but, having been adopted by the Hitotsubashi family, he was eligible to the Shogunate. Son of a leader of the anti-foreign nobles, and the unsuccessful claimant to the Shogunate in 1858, he had, however, realized the necessity of maintaining the Treaties and foreign relations during his regency for the boy who had been chosen instead of himself. At this crisis in the Shogunate, with no heir to the office, Hitotsubashi tried to refuse the appointment offered by the Emperor. As a price for acceptance, he asked for full confidence, not only in domestic but in foreign affairs.[45] This the Emperor promised, and he further agreed to a peace with Choshiu, which was proclaimed on October 3, giving the death of the late Shogun as an excuse.[46] Hitotsubashi then summoned some of the most influential feudatories to Osaka, and pleaded for their co-operation, but not until January did he finally accept the appointment as Shogun. Much was expected of this enlightened prince.[47]

In August the Italian frigate "Magenta" visited Yokohama, and about September 1 Van Valkenburgh heard rumors that a treaty had been concluded.[48] He promptly reminded the Rojiu that some five years before the Japanese Government had requested the American Minister to notify Austria, Brazil, Denmark, Italy, Spain, and Sweden that treaties could not then be made. If Japan had now made a treaty with Italy, it would be well for the United States to advise the other Powers of the readiness of Japan to negotiate. He was told that Denmark had applied through the Netherlands' Consul General, and Hawaii through Mr. E. M. Van Reed, an American citizen who acted as

---

[44] *F.R., 1866,* II, 220. Van Valkenburgh was officially informed, on October 5, that the Tycoon had died at 6:00 A.M. on September 20, and that Hitotsubashi had succeeded to the Throne on that day (*ibid.,* p. 222). He did not accept this statement as authentic (*ibid.,* p. 223).

[45] Black, *op. cit.,* II, 30.　　　　　　　　[46] Yamaguchi, *op. cit.,* p. 89.

[47] *Ibid.,* p. 91.　　　　　　　　[48] *F.R., 1866,* II, 220.

Hawaiian Consul General. Japan was now ready to treat with the other Powers as soon as duly accredited Ministers should arrive, but preferably not until peace was restored in the Empire. The Italian Treaty had been granted because during the war between Italy and Austria Italy would have no place of refuge for her men-of-war in Eastern seas. This was similar to the reason, it might be added, which gained Admiral Stirling's Treaty in 1854.

At about the same time General Van Valkenburgh was approached by one of the Governors of Foreign Affairs and told that the Government desired to purchase some eight of the warships used by the United States in its Civil War for use against Choshiu, and later the number was raised to ten. The most he could do was to forward their request.[49] Rear-Admiral Bell, whom he consulted, recommended that a "messenger" be sent by Japan to complete the transaction, and this resulted in the naval mission of the next year.[50] It will be recalled that Mr. Pruyn had been asked to have three small steam warships built in 1862. After many delays and difficulties, due in part to the American Civil War and to the Shimonoseki hostilities, only one ship, the "Fusiyama," arrived at Yokohama, on January 23, 1866. Mr. Portman reported, "the Japanese authorities informed me that she arrived in excellent condition, and that they are very much pleased with her." One of the duties of the naval mission was to settle the outstanding account with Mr. Pruyn.[51]

The close of 1866 was marked by the great fire in Yokohama on November 26, and an even greater one in Yedo on December 14. The relations between the Powers and Japan were on a

[49] No. 43, September 29, 1866. A description of the ten steam vessels desired was transmitted in No. 45, October 4.

[50] *F.R., 1867,* II, 17.

[51] *F.R., 1866,* II, 671–79. For an entirely inaccurate account of this transaction see Dickins, *op. cit.,* II, 63, which states that the price was $600,000 for one ship—instead of $860,000 for three steamships—and that the Yedo Government refused to accept the one that was delivered. In compensation, the American Government offered the ram "Stonewall Jackson" [*sic*]. Dickins had evidently relied upon Black (*op. cit.,* II, 199), and added a few embellishments of his own.

more satisfactory basis than they had ever been. The new Shogun was enlightened, capable, and experienced. The reactionary court had given no recent signs of active opposition to foreign intercourse. The Convention of 1866 had placed foreign commerce on a firmer and more profitable basis, and all trace of the exclusion system had been wiped out. Only the deep and persistent animosity of the western clans for the Tokugawa family and its paramount power threatened the new peace which had dawned.

By the end of the year the Japanese Government had, of its own motion, modified one of the provisions of the new tariff. The Choshiu war and a bad harvest had caused high prices for rice. In Yedo, rice riots had broken out. Van Valkenburgh and Parkes urged the Government to permit the importation of foreign rice, mainly from China, which could be sold at half the cost of Japanese rice, the price of which had risen from one cent a pound to about five and a half.[52] On November 12 the former addressed the Rojiu in these terms, and on the seventeenth he received a copy of the proclamation which had been issued. Rice might now be purchased in foreign countries, and Japanese could freely purchase the same from foreign merchants. And Van Valkenburgh also advised Mr. Seward that the Government was importing rice for the poorer people.[53]

[52] No. 54, November 5, 1866, *F.R., 1866,* II, 226.

[53] No. 57, November 20, 1866, *F.R., 1867,* II, 16–17. In 1865, a dispute between the American and British Consuls at Yokohama arose out of the action of Mr. Fisher in arresting a British subject for contempt and sending him to the British Consul for trial. The documents may be found in Portman's dispatches of March 5 and April 16, 1866. Mr. Seward, who was a staunch advocate of co-operation in the Far East, promptly recalled Mr. Fisher, and advised General Van Valkenburgh: "You will need to instruct the United States Consuls in Japan to refrain from Consular meetings and combinations which may be designed, or calculated to divide and alienate the commercial representatives residing in that empire" (No. 18, May 9, 1866).

CHAPTER XIII

THE LAST DAYS OF THE SHOGUNATE
1867 [1]

THE NEW year opened auspiciously. General Van Valkenburgh, on January 12, transmitted certain translations which he had received from Sir Harry Parkes, which seemed to show the growth of an enlightened spirit even in the Imperial court.[2] On October 8, 1866, twenty-two kuge had presented the following advice to the Emperor, in person: That a council of daimyos be assembled, that the Choshiu war be ended, that a definite policy be followed, and that pardon should be granted to kuge then undergoing punishment. The immediate result was an order of the Mikado that the kuge who had committed this breach of reverence be confined to their residences, and the daimyos of Aidzu and Kuwana, respectively the protector of the Emperor's person and the Shogun's representative at Kyoto, were instructed to furnish the required guards. But this was soon followed by an order to some of the leading daimyos to come up to Kyoto immediately for counsel, and their decisions would be presented to the Emperor by the Chinnagon (which was the title of the Shogun designate, before his formal investiture). Hitotsubashi, as we have seen, had urged the assembling of such a council, and he had received strong advice from the daimyo of Echizen, who had urged that he decline the office of Shogun until the daimyos had approved his appointment.

It was not until January 10 that Hitotsubashi was invested with the title of Shogun. And on February 3 the Emperor Komei

---

[1] The instructions are numbered 8–40 (one number repeated, and one not used); of these thirty-three, eleven were printed in *F.R., 1867,* II. The dispatches are numbered 1–80; of these thirty-six were printed in *F.R., 1867,* II, and two in *F.R., 1868,* I.

[2] *F.R., 1867,* II, 21–22.

died in his palace at Kyoto.[3] Within a few days an enlightened and experienced man had assumed the administrative headship of the state, and an old Emperor, who had been the very soul of the anti-foreign policy, had been succeeded by a boy (Mutsuhito, born November 3, 1852), who would follow the advice of his counsellors. But more than that, Hitotsubashi, as a member of the Mito house, had been taught to respect the one fundamental House law: "If the Shogunate should be so unfortunate as to take up arms against the Emperor, our descendents must observe the motto, 'Loyalty knows no blood relationship.' "[4] This was to determine his conduct in the troubled days which were to come.

Even before he had assumed the formal title of Shogun, Hitotsubashi had invited the Foreign Representatives to an audience at Osaka, where he was detained by affairs at the Court.[5] But the death of the Emperor caused the reception to be postponed until the fifty days of mourning were over.

Indicative of the improved relations was the signing of a treaty with Denmark, on January 12, in which the Netherlands Consul General, van Polsbroek, acted for Denmark.[6] But the Shimonoseki indemnity again raised its head, and, as the Representatives held that the three final payments were all past due, they insisted that the instalments be paid on May 15, August 15, and September 15.[7] When the first-named day arrived, the Rojiu again asked for a postponement, for two years, although they hoped to be able to complete payment within one. This time Van Valkenburgh approved, and commended the favor to his Government on the ground that the Japanese had carried out their engagements for the opening of the two ports and two cities in so liberal a manner as to satisfy himself and his colleagues for the present

---

[3] *F.R., 1867,* II, 27. Satow says the death occurred on January 30 but was officially announced as of February 3 (*A Diplomat in Japan,* p. 189).

[4] Okuma, *Fifty Years of New Japan,* I, 63.

[5] *F.R., 1867,* II, 27. This invitation was precipitated by the request of the French Minister for an audience to present a letter to the Shogun (Satow, *op. cit.,* p. 174).

[6] *F.R., 1867,* II, 24.

[7] The Japanese Ministers were advised on March 7, *ibid.,* pp. 29–30.

and to inspire him with confidence for the future. Moreover, he added, the object of the Treaty Powers was not the receipt of money, but the establishment of better relations with Japan.[8] Mr. Seward made no comment on the first dispatch, but in reply to the second he stated, on July 12, that the Department had no authority to grant a postponement of the indemnity, that the Senate must consent to any change in the Convention, and that the best procedure would be to conclude an additional article which would be submitted to the Senate, provided, of course, all the other parties also consented.[9] We shall see that this strict interpretation was not to be followed.

The official mourning for the Emperor had passed, and no word came from the Rojiu about the proposed audience at Osaka. The Foreign Ministers had long felt the necessity of making arrangements for the promised opening of Osaka and Hiogo on January 1, 1868. In fact there was some doubt as to whether the Shogun could accomplish it, for the opposition in the Court and among some of the powerful daimyos was well known. On December 24, 1866, Van Valkenburgh had asked for authority to act in concert with his colleagues, but no instruction was forthcoming.[10] In April following, the four Ministers, after consultation, announced to the Rojiu that they intended to visit Hiogo and Osaka and, at the latter place, discuss the necessary regulations with the Shogun's Government.[11] To this the Rojiu replied, on the twelfth, that the audience would positively take place early the next month. On the twenty-third Van Valkenburgh informed the Rojiu that he proposed to leave for Osaka about the twenty-sixth, with the ships of war "Shenandoah" and "Wyoming."[12] The British and Dutch Ministers left Yedo on the fifteenth, and the French on the twenty-third, but Van Valkenburgh delayed until the twenty-ninth, waiting for instructions from Seward, which never arrived, and for assurances that the ports would be opened according to the Treaty.[13]

The reception of the four Ministers by the Shogun was grati-

---

[8] May 18, *ibid.*, p. 37.   [9] *F.R., 1867*, II, 45.   [10] *Ibid.*, p. 21.
[11] *Ibid.*, p. 31.   [12] *Ibid.*, p. 32.   [13] *Ibid.*, p. 32.

fying in the extreme, and an augury of better days. On May 2
the first three were informally received by the Shogun, and Van
Valkenburgh on the third. The official audience of all four took
place on the fourth, the first audience which had been granted in
some five years.[14]

Van Valkenburgh wrote:

His Majesty the Tycoon is 31 years of age and of extremely pre-
possessing appearance. There is that about him which stamps him as a
gentleman; such simple dignity and such an air of perfect breeding, only
equalled by his intelligence, which is as superior as it is unassuming. Our
conversation ran principally on our army and navy matters, and the manner in which it was conducted on his part showed that he was well con-
versant with the subject.

The friendly nature of the audience, during which Van Valkenburgh sat at the Shogun's right hand, furnished

a fair indication of the wonderful progress that has been made in our intercourse with this people; but even this it strikes me cannot be compared,
viewed in the light of progress, with the extremely handsome entertain-
ment that followed.

It is earnestly to be hoped that the friendship of the Japanese Government, and their desire as exhibited on this occasion to increase the cordiality of their relations with the United States, may prove to have been
a well-sustained effort, and that no reaction to the admirable feeling displayed be in store for us.

Even more reassuring were the negotiations which followed,
and by which the regulations for the trade and settlement at
Hiogo and Osaka were drawn up. In both instances the Japanese
had adopted a most generous attitude. The negotiations went on
with unaccustomed smoothness and celerity.

No more angry discussions and heated arguments (in which the heat
and anger of our chief [Sir Harry Parkes] were opposed to the stolid
calm of the imperturbable Japanese Ministers) such as had characterized
our official interviews at Yedo. At the word of the new Shogun an entirely new line had been adopted, and a serious endeavour was made to
convert the treaty of friendship into a reality.[15]

[14] For Van Valkenburgh's account of the audiences, and the text of the
addresses of Parkes on May 2 and Van Valkenburgh on May 4 and the Shogun's replies, see *F.R., 1867,* II, 32–36; also see Satow, *op. cit.,* pp. 199–200, and
Lord Redesdale, *Memories,* I, 389–96, for British accounts, and Black, *Young
Japan,* II, 40–42, for an account by van Polsbroek.   [15] Satow, *op. cit.,* p. 198.

Thus wrote Satow, who was present at the discussions, but the triumph of the Shogun over his opponents did not please this friend of the anti-Shogunate clansmen, and, he wrote, "I hinted to Saigo [of Satsuma] that the chance of a revolution was not to be lost. If Hiogo were once opened, then good-bye to the chances of the *daimios*."[16] So while the Ministers were delighted at the friendly attitude of the Shogun and his officials, a young foreign diplomat was busily engaged in fomenting a revolution.

While most of the responsibility for drawing up the land regulations at Hiogo and Osaka fell upon Sir Harry Parkes,[17] the Japanese officials evinced "the greatest promptness and liberality" throughout the conferences, and the sites selected were "unsurpassed for convenience in every respect."[18] The land regulations contained an improvement over those at Yokohama, for the annual rent would cover not only the ordinary land-tax but a sum sufficient to maintain the roads and drains, sanitary conditions, and good order. On May 18, Van Valkenburgh was able to report to Mr. Seward that the arrangements for Osaka and Hiogo had been agreed upon and an understanding arrived at for the opening of Yedo and Niigata.[19]

While the negotiations were in progress a circular was issued by the Government which described the reception accorded the four Foreign Representatives at Osaka, and laid down certain instructions for social intercourse between Japanese and foreign Ministers, a notable feature of which was an injunction to deal straightforwardly in the future.[20]

While General Van Valkenburgh was at Osaka he received a most interesting letter from the Rojiu, dated May 10.[21] It was to the effect that they had learned that France had engaged in war with Korea, and that an American merchant vessel, the "General Sherman," had been treated with great cruelty. The Shogun proposed

to tender friendly advice to Corea and to endeavor to induce that country, with due regard to the friendship which should govern the intercourse between neighbors, to mend its course in future.

[16] *Ibid.*, p. 200.   [17] *Ibid.*, p. 198.   [18] *F.R., 1867*, II, 38.
[19] *Ibid.*   [20] *Ibid.*, pp. 43–44.   [21] *Ibid.*, pp. 36–37.

A letter would be sent, by two emissaries,

and if, on reflection of the wrong that has been committed and through our influence, he should sue for peace, we hope that the flag of the United States will return; that retaliation will be abandoned and the means for friendly intercourse be found.

While it was, of course, uncertain whether or not the Koreans could be persuaded from persisting in their course, yet it was the wish of the Shogun

that no effort be left untried, with the object of promoting peace in this part of the world, and we further request your excellency to use your best endeavor in the same direction.

The Shogun's Government, which had embarked upon a policy of the fullest foreign intercourse, was now ready to urge a similar policy upon its hermit neighbor. Mr. Seward expressed his thanks for this friendly gesture, but added that

the government of the United States will feel obliged, should no satisfactory explanation or apology be furnished by Corea, to consider how proper reparation can be obtained and honor maintained.[22]

And he tentatively proposed to France a joint punitive expedition.[23]

The Shogun's Government acted in good faith. Hingama Desho-no-Kami, a member of the second council, was appointed in May as envoy to Korea. He at once sent a messenger to the daimyo of Tsushima, who controlled the Japanese trade at the port of Fusan, asking him to secure permission for him to visit Korea as a duly recognized envoy. The Korean Government replied that the proposition was a new and strange one and would have to be considered, and the decision would be later communicated. When no further word was received, messengers were again sent to Tsushima, urging the importance of the mission and of its reception by the Korean Government. Van Valkenburgh believed that the envoy would not be received, and in this he was correct.[24]

[22] *F.R., 1867*, II, 46.
[23] Dennett, *Americans in Eastern Asia*, pp. 418–21.
[24] November 20, *F.R., 1867*, II, 75.

During the negotiations at Osaka the basis on which settlements would be laid out at Yedo and at Niigata (or another port on the west coast) was agreed upon. Sir Harry, in May, proceeded to inspect the port of Tsuruga, while Van Valkenburgh proposed to visit the west coast after his return to Yedo.[25] On May 22 he reached the capital, inspired "with perfect confidence for the future," but it was not until the end of June that he could start on his visit of inspection. On this voyage he visited Hakodate, Niigata, Nanao, Mikuni, Tsuruga, Miyazu, and Nagasaki, returning to Yedo a month later.[26] It took little examination to convince him that Niigata was inferior to Nanao, Tsuruga, and Miyazu, and he awaited the return of Sir Harry Parkes before coming to a decision with all his colleagues.[27]

After his return he advised the Department that on June 14 an American sailor, George Bunker, had been murdered at Nagasaki, and that while he had been at that port two British sailors had also been fatally slashed as they lay asleep in the street. Van Valkenburgh was correct in his assumption that these crimes had been committed by the retainers of daimyos residing in other provinces.[28] The American incident was quickly closed, but Sir Harry Parkes took up the murder of the British sailors with vigor. The fact that they lay in a drunken stupor, in a bad part of the town, did not lessen his indignation.[29] Being at the time at Osaka, he was able to deal directly with the Shogun's Minister, using "extremely warm language," and he had an interview with the Shogun himself.[30] He then went directly to Tosa, for Tosa men were suspected of being the assassins, and there received a very straight reprimand for his rough language from Goto Shojiro, leading Minister of the daimyo.[31] The most the daimyo would do was to promise to investigate the affair and punish any Tosa man who was implicated. At Nagasaki further investiga-

---

[25] *Ibid.*, p. 40; Satow, *op. cit.*, p. 202.   [26] *F.R., 1867*, II, 47–50.

[27] Sir Harry visited the west coast again in August. Mitford and Satow, at this time, crossed overland from Niigata to Osaka (Satow, *op. cit.*, pp. 231–51).

[28] *F.R., 1867*, II, 51.   [29] Satow, *op. cit.*, p. 251.

[30] *Ibid.*, p. 252.   [31] *Ibid.*, p. 267.

tion was held, but without result.[32] Parkes held the matter open to be used to exert pressure on the Shogunate at some suitable time. A year later it was learned that the assassins were nine Chikuzen men, "which was rather an unfortunate conclusion for Parkes,"[33] and due punishment was meted out by the Imperial Government in February 1869.[34]

In August 1867 the diplomatic corps had been augmented by the arrival of Count de la Tour of Italy, Kint de Rosenbeck of Belgium, and Herr von Brandt of Prussia. The Yedo authorities were proceeding with plans for the opening of the city on January 1; a desirable site had been selected for the foreign settlement; and a Western hotel was being constructed under the supervision of an American architect. Van Valkenburgh was disposed to limit the entrance of Americans to those engaged in legitimate trade.[35]

It was at this time that the treatment of Japanese Christians first became a subject of diplomatic intervention. When Van Valkenburgh was at Nagasaki, in July, he learned that many native Christians had been arrested, tortured, and imprisoned under an old law of Japan. He at once wrote to Bishop Petit-Jean, the Roman Catholic prelate, and was advised that some 20,000 native Christians were estimated to be in Japan, mostly in the island of Kyushiu, and near to Nagasaki. French priests (in violation of the Treaties, it should be said) visited them, preaching and administering the sacraments. No notice was taken by the officials until the Buddhists protested too strongly, and then, about the middle of July, some sixty-three men, women, and children had been arrested and imprisoned at Urakami, about four miles from Nagasaki. It was not known whether or not they had been tortured or what their punishment would be.

Van Valkenburgh at once asked for an interview with the two Governors of Nagasaki, and on July 29 he expressed to them his regret at the occurrence, and endeavored to induce them to release the prisoners. This they were unable to do, although they

[32] Satow, *op. cit.,* p. 273.   [33] *Ibid.,* pp. 266, 393.
[34] Dickins, *The Life of Sir Harry Parkes,* II, 76–77.
[35] *F.R., 1867,* II, 55.

promised that the prisoners would be well treated and that no more arrests would be made until instructions were received from the Rojiu. Hearing that two more arrests had been made, he again discussed the subject with the Governors on August 8, but they replied that the later arrests were not because the persons were Christians. On his return to Yedo, August 20, he addressed the Rojiu on the subject, assuring them that he would in no manner interfere with the internal regulations of Japan but pointing out the regret with which the President would learn of the action at Nagasaki, and stressing the effect produced on the Western Powers by such an exhibition of intolerance. He ventured to assume that his remonstrances at Nagasaki had resulted in instructions for the release of the native Christians, and he requested an official statement that they had been released, that their property be restored, and that "an absolute forgetfulness of the past may be considered as a guarantee against similar ill-advised acts for the future."[36]

Before any reply was made by the Rojiu, Van Valkenburgh had received an instruction from Mr. Seward on the very matter.[37] It seems that on November 13, 1866, Bishop Horatio Potter and the members of the Foreign Committee of the Protestant Episcopal Church of the United States had memorialized the President asking that instructions be sent to the American Minister to endeavor to secure full toleration of the Christian religion and protection for all missionaries. They stated that Secretary Marcy had given such an instruction to Townsend Harris and that the latter had made strenuous efforts to insert a clause granting religious toleration into his Treaty. They believed that simi-

---

[36] *F.R., 1867,* II, 56–58. Sir Harry Parkes learned of the arrest of the Urakami Christians when he visited Nagasaki in September. Satow was told that the Omura officials wanted to execute all the Christians, according to law, and were indignant because the Shogun's officials at Nagasaki would pardon all who would recant. They planned to induce all the daimyos in Kyushiu to unite in demanding punishment of the Shogun. This would, in effect, be a manifesto against the Government, and Satow, while pleading for tolerance, saw no objection if the demand were made to annoy the Shogun's administration (Satow, *op. cit.,* pp. 275–76).

[37] September 9, *F.R., 1867,* II, 59.

lar efforts were being made to induce the British Government to obtain such modification in the Japanese laws, and they felt that the present moment was an auspicious one for the United States to renew its efforts. Mr. Seward, to whom the memorial was referred, replied that Mr. Marcy had given no such instructions,[38] that he himself feared that any attempt to induce the Japanese to change their policy would be premature, but that he would instruct Mr. Van Valkenburgh to make inquiries and, if he should find the prospect at all favorable, to co-operate with the British Minister, should the latter also have been instructed to endeavor to have the disabilities against Christians removed.[39] Mr. Seward, however, failed to forward the promised instruction, and a year later the Evangelical Alliance of the United States, through a committee, inquired what progress had been made under the instruction. This resulted in the long-delayed instruction of September 9, 1867, in terms similar to the promise made a year earlier to Bishop Potter.

Seward's instruction of September 9 crossed Van Valkenburgh's dispatch of August 23, and on receipt of the latter Seward promptly, on October 7, approved the conduct of the Minister and instructed him to prosecute those measures, if necessary, to secure the release of the prisoners and to prevent any renewal of religious persecution at Nagasaki. He added that the incident seemed to be a suitable occasion for an appeal by the Representatives of all the Treaty Powers to the Japanese Government to repeal and abrogate the law which prohibited Christianity, and therefore he instructed Van Valkenburgh to confer diligently with his colleagues, and, "while treating the Japanese Government and authorities with perfect respect and conciliation," with the concurrence of his colleagues to press the application, if possible, to a successful conclusion. A copy of this instruction was communicated to each of the Treaty Powers.[40]

To this Van Valkenburgh replied on November 12, forwarding additional details regarding the arrests, but giving his opinion

---

[38] Harris had tried later, in 1860, to secure a toleration article.
[39] *F.R., 1867,* II, 60.   [40] *F.R., 1867,* II, 63.

that the present moment would be ill-chosen for urging the matter in the earnest and energetic manner it demanded. Sir Harry Parkes, he reported, had not received any instruction on the subject.[41]

As France was the recognized protector of the Roman Catholic church in heathen lands, M. Roches was more actively concerned with the arrest of the Urakami Christians than any of his colleagues. His discussions with the Shogunate officials convinced him of their liberal views, and gave him an insight into the difficulties which they faced. Some of the daimyos had protested against the spread of Christianity and the alleged tacit approval of the Tycoon. They had vowed that they would enforce the fundamental laws against the faith and would not hesitate to behead any European priest or Japanese Christian who entered their territories. The Tycoon recognized that in time toleration would replace the barbarous law then in force but that a premature and unsuitable measure would jeopardize the future. M. Roches appreciated this situation and was ready to co-operate with the Government. He even promised to warn Monseigneur Petit-Jean, Apostolic Prefect of Japan, to avoid any act which might be calculated to uphold any Japanese Christians in resistance to the authorities. On this understanding the officials promised to release the prisoners. He also instructed the French Consular Agent at Nagasaki to prevent any priest from going to Urakami or elsewhere for missionary purposes,

for, during the great state of excitement which now prevails in the south of Japan, the presence of a Catholic missionary in the midst of the Japanese population would be sure to cause incalculable evils, where a sound policy and the true interest of our religion admonish us to make every effort to avoid such a result.[42]

The desire of the Shogun's Government to purchase warships in the United States had resulted in the appointment, in February, of two Commissioners, with a suitable suite, to proceed to the

[41] *Ibid.*, pp. 68–72.

[42] These documents were transmitted to the American Government by the British Foreign Secretary in 1870, when the matter was again under discussion (*F.R., 1870,* pp. 485–86).

United States for this purpose, as well as to inspect navy yards, arsenals, foundries, and machine shops, and to settle the accounts with Mr. Pruyn.[43] The business was speedily consummated, and on July 6 Mr. Seward could advise the American Minister that the iron-clad ram "Stonewall" had been purchased for $500,000, of which $100,000 was to be paid to Van Valkenburgh in Japan.[44] The Commissioners had made a very agreeable impression on all who had had the pleasure of meeting them, and on their return the Rojiu, on September 28, transmitted to Mr. Van Valkenburgh a formal letter of thanks for the kind treatment of the Commissioners, who had succeeded in their mission and had satisfactorily settled the outstanding account.[45]

Other items of interest which were reported by the American Minister were the signature of a Convention at St. Petersburg, on March 18, Russian Calendar (March 30), for the joint occupation of Sakhalin;[46] the attempt, in June, to negotiate a treaty for the Kingdom of Hawaii, whose Commissioner was Eugene M. Van Reed, an American citizen;[47] the arrangements for the foreign settlement at Yedo, in October;[48] the new arrangement, a month later, for the establishment of a Japanese municipal office, with a foreign director, at Yokohama;[49] and the appointment of the first Consul to represent Japan abroad, in this case Mr. Charles Walcott Brooks, at San Francisco, who was selected from several persons recommended by Van Valkenburgh. For the past nine years he had served as Commercial Agent at that port without pay.[50]

---

[43] F.R., 1867, II, 24.   [44] Ibid., p. 45.

[45] Ibid., p. 64. The ram "Stonewall" (not "Stonewall Jackson," as sometimes given) was a Confederate iron-clad which has been built at Bordeaux for the Danish navy. Rejected by that Government, she had been bought by the Confederates, and had been surrendered to Federal naval officers at Havana, on May 19, 1865 (F.R., 1865, II [Spain, passim]; also F.R., 1872, Part 2, Vol. IV, p. 358).   [46] F.R., 1867, II, 61.

[47] Ibid., p. 42. The Japanese Government later refused to deal with Van Reed because he was engaged in trade at Yokohama (No. 61, November 4).

[48] F.R., 1867, II, 66, 79–81. The opening of Yedo was postponed by a proclamation of November 27.   [49] Ibid., p. 73.

[50] Ibid., pp. 73–74. He was relieved in 1873 and personally thanked by the Emperor (No. 343, January 23; No. 8, October 21 in F.R., 1874, I, 652–54).

But the most important events, in respect to both the internal affairs of Japan and the foreign relations of the country, were to happen late in the year. On November 7 Van Valkenburgh forwarded a copy of the proclamation which announced the assumption by Hitotsubashi of the title of Shogun, on October 18, which he was "inclined to accept as a favorable omen for the continued improvement of our political and commercial relations with Japan."[51] But nine days later he was visited by one of the Governors for Foreign Affairs, who placed in his hands an official statement that "the Tycoon has hereafter no authority to confer or make arrangements with reference to any of the internal affairs of Japan."[52] This was followed by an interview the next day in which an explanation was given of this surprising information. It was not until December 2 that a dispatch could be sent off to Washington, and by that time Van Valkenburgh had obtained copies of the more important documents—the Shogun's notice to his vassals of his resignation, the Emperor's acceptance, his proclamation to the daimyos and officials, the Shogun's recommendation that a council of daimyos and clansmen be held, and the Emperor's reply that, pending the assemblage of the lords, the Shogun should continue to arrange for foreign affairs in consultation with two or three of the clans acquainted with such matters.[53]

Hitotsubashi, while ascribing the unsettled affairs in the country to his own "want of virtue," pointed out that

our intercourse with foreign powers becomes daily more extensive, and our foreign policy cannot be pursued unless directed by the whole power of the country. If, therefore, the old régime be changed and the governmental authority be restored to the imperial court; if the counsels of the whole empire be collected, and the wise decisions received, and if we unite with all our heart, and with all our strength, to protect and maintain the empire, it will be able to range itself with the nations of the earth. This comprises our whole duty towards our country.[54]

[51] *F.R., 1867,* II, 67.   [52] *Ibid.,* p. 76.   [53] *Ibid.,* pp. 77–78.

[54] Van Valkenburgh described this document as a memorial from the Tycoon to the Mikado announcing his resignation. It was, as stated above, an announcement to the Tokugawa vassals, and its concluding paragraph stated: "However, if you have any particular ideas on the subject, you may state them without the slightest reserve." He was told that it was issued on November 3.

The Shogun's resignation of his inherited powers was thus due primarily to the pressure of foreign affairs and the necessity for Japan to conduct these relations as a united power. It will be seen, from time to time, that all the great political innovations of the next few years were due to the necessity of reform in order that Japan might "be able to range itself with the nations of the earth." By failing to understand this, many of the foreigners, including most of the Foreign Representatives, were to make many errors in interpreting the march of events in the first years of New Japan.

Few indeed were the foreigners who were prepared for such a startling announcement as was made in Yedo on November 16. The explanation which the local officials gave was that six of the powerful daimyos had shown such opposition to the Shogun because of his liberality toward foreigners, had so taken advantage of every opportunity to prejudice the Emperor against him, and had made it so disagreeable for him, that he had surrendered his powers to the Emperor. But he would still carry out the foreign Treaties until some further arrangements were made by a council of the great daimyos.

In this study we cannot examine in detail the secret intrigues which brought about a loose alliance of western clansmen to overthrow the Shogun and the Tokugawa family. We need only recall that in the west were most of the great Tozama lords, who were by tradition hostile to the Tokugawas. Taking advantage of the bitter controversy over the Treaties, they had worked for the humiliation of the Shogun. Even after the Emperor had approved the 1858 Treaties, in 1865, they continued their hostility, but their agents were forced to work under cover, for the legiti-

Satow, *op. cit.*, p. 283, accepts November 8 as the date of the Shogun's resignation, following Gubbins, *The Progress of Japan, 1853–1871*, p. 305. Yamaguchi, *Kinse Shiriaku. A History of Japan*, p. 97, gives the date as November 19, but many errors are found in translating Japanese dates into the Western calendar in the English version of this valuable work. Murdoch, *History of Japan*, III, 769, states that it was presented November 9, and accepted on November 10. It should be noted that the official announcement was made to Van Valkenburgh and Parkes in Yedo on November 16. Other translations of these documents may be found in McLaren, "Japanese Government Documents," in *Transactions of the Asiatic Society of Japan*, Vol. 42, Part I, pp. 1–2; Okuma, *op. cit.*, I, 138–39.

mate basis of opposition had been removed. The work of certain
able young clansmen, of Satsuma, Tosa, Choshiu, and a few other
fiefs, brought about a general understanding, and it was true that
the Shogun, who longed for peace, was so harassed that only two
courses were open, a bitterly fought civil war or the relinquishment of his great powers. It is at least probable that if the issue
had been clearly drawn in 1867, the faithful Tokugawa vassals
and their sympathizers could have crushed the loose league of hostile westerners; but the war would have been hard fought and it
would have left Japan helpless in the face of foreign exploita-
tion or aggression. Hitotsubashi, a real patriot, chose the course
which meant great sacrifice for himself but, he hoped, peace and
unity for Japan.

We should, however, note here any foreign participation in the
development of this anti-Shogun movement. In general, the foreigners in Japan, with few exceptions, supported the Shogun and
looked upon him as the defender of their treaty rights. This was
due to many reasons. In the first place, the Shogun's Government
had negotiated the Treaties and had maintained them against the
opposition of the Emperor, his court, and the western clansmen.
The new Shogun, Hitotsubashi, was considered to be a liberal
man, and he had given many signs of his desire to improve the
relations between Japan and foreign countries.[55] Although by
1865 it was generally recognized that the Emperor was the supreme authority in the state and his approval of the 1858 Treaties
was considered an absolute necessity (and for this sound interpretation Sir Harry Parkes is entitled to full credit), few indeed
of the foreigners would have welcomed a transfer of foreign
affairs to the Imperial court, with its long record of unreasoning
hostility. Furthermore, few foreigners were able to come into
contact with members of the so-called "Daimyos' party." The
four open ports were in the Shogun's territory, and the officials
there were all his retainers. At Yedo, the members of the Legations, who alone could reside there, occasionally came in contact
with the representatives of the daimyos at their *yashikis*. At

---

[55] This was the basis of Sir Rutherford Alcock's pro-Shogun policy in 1864.

Nagasaki, most of the western lords had resident agents, and some intercourse took place between them and the Consular and foreign-merchant bodies. But at Yokohama and Hakodate, the agents were, with few exceptions, representatives of loyal clans.

Of the Foreign Representatives, Sir Harry Parkes had made the greatest effort to establish friendly relations with the western daimyos. He visited Shimonoseki, in Choshiu, in December 1865, Satsuma and Choshiu in July and August 1866, Awa and Tosa in September 1867, and, in addition, the west coast in May and August 1867, and was at Osaka in April, May, and August 1867. On each of his visits to western Japan he touched at Nagasaki. There is no available evidence that Sir Harry took part in the political intrigues which were rife among the western daimyos, and he gave repeated expression of his confidence in the new Shogun.[56] If there was any doubt in his mind about the existing régime, it was probably due to the friendliness which the Shogun's Government had shown to France and French nationals, who had been engaged to form a military mission and who had been given contracts for a dock yard at Yokosuka and for military supplies.[57]

But some of the junior members of Sir Harry's staff had boldly plunged into the troubled waters of Japanese politics. Ernest Mason Satow, then a student interpreter, but later Sir Ernest and Ambassador to Japan, has frankly told us of his activities and those of his associate, Algernon Freeman-Mitford, later Lord Redesdale. Satow, it seems, first began to sympathize with the daimyo party when he saw much of Ito, Inouye, and other Choshiu clansmen at the time of the Shimonoseki expedition in 1864. During his first years in Japan, from September 1862 on, the devious and vacillating conduct of the Shogun's Ministers, due to political conditions of which the foreigners were but slightly aware, turned this high-spirited young Englishman against the Yedo régime. His contacts with the hostile clansmen convinced

---

[56] Satow, *op. cit.,* p. 299, states that Parkes had contributed "as far as lay in his power" to the downfall of the Shogun.

[57] Anglo-French rivalry was a feature of the diplomatic scene in Yedo (Satow, *op. cit.,* pp. 173, 174, 254, 255, 277; Dickins, *op. cit.,* II, p. 74).

him that the Shogunate was deliberately impeding the fullest intercourse between the foreigners and the Japanese, in order to confine all commerce, and the resulting revenues, to the Shogun's ports. He came to believe that notwithstanding the apparently anti-foreign attitude of the Shogun's opponents the foreign relations of Japan would be in friendlier hands if the western clansmen could at least participate in the administration, and from this position he soon advanced to one which advocated the overthrow of the Shogunate and a "reformation of the Constitution" which would substitute the Emperor and a Council of Daimyos for the Shogun's administration. In March 1866 he began to write articles for the *Japan Times* which occasionally touched upon political conditions. Some of these, especially those which advocated the changes mentioned above, were translated into Japanese and widely circulated.[58] Satow thus became popular with the daimyos' party, and his Legation won favor. In addition to accompanying Sir Harry on his visits to Osaka, Tosa, and the west coast, he made a special visit to Kagoshima and Uwajima in December 1866, traveled overland from Osaka to Yedo in May 1867, and overland from Nanao to Osaka in August 1867. On all these travels Satow was in constant communication with the samurai leaders of the anti-Shogun league. He was even more pronounced in his opposition to the Shogun than many of his Japanese visitors.[59]

Many instances of Satow's advice may be found in *A Diplomat in Japan,* which was based on his diary of this period. As this is a chronological narrative, with few generalizations, it is not easy to fathom Satow's policy or purpose. But antipathy to the Shogun's administration, a poor opinion of Hitotsubashi himself, confidence in the western clansmen, eagerness to halt the rising influence of the French and to supplant them by the British

[58] Satow, *op. cit.,* pp. 159–60.

[59] Saigo, of Satsuma, wrote Okubo of a talk with Satow in Osaka, August 1867, in which the latter advocated action before the Shogun, with French help, would be able to crush his foes, and suggested an understanding with England so that the French would not intervene. "Satow's language about the Bakufu," he wrote, "is very insulting" (*ibid.,* p. 255; and Redesdale, *op. cit.,* II, 397–412).

as the first and best friends of the league, and the hope that the British constitution would be accepted as a model for the new government are all clearly evident.

If it is agreed that the diplomatic representatives of a foreign country (and by this we mean all the members of a Legation or Embassy) should refrain from interference in the domestic affairs of a country in which they reside, then the conduct of Satow, Mitford, and perhaps other members of the British Legation was censurable in the extreme. While the British Orders in Council of March 9, 1865, proclaimed heavy penalties for British subjects participating in war, rebellion, or insurrection against the Tycoon, certain members of its own Legation were vigorously advocating these very breaches of the peace. As Satow hinted to Saigo at Osaka in May 1867, "the chance of a revolution was not to be lost. If Hiogo were once opened, then good-bye to the chances of the *daimios*."[60] On the other hand, the activities of Satow made it easy for the new government to enter upon friendly relations with the British Legation in 1868, and for the next four years Sir Harry Parkes was the principal adviser of the Imperial officials, while the early attempts at political reorganization were strongly influenced by British practices. It is useless to speculate as to the real effect of Satow's intrigues, just as it is useless to consider whether or not Japan could not have worked out a reorganization of the government under an enlightened Shogun, without the miseries of a civil war. The fact remains that in these troubled years, the British Legation, informally to be sure, threw its influence on the side of the revolutionists, while the French Legation supported the Shogun. Von Brandt, of Prussia, and the Count de la Tour, of Italy, could be counted upon to support M. Roches. Van Polsbroek, of the Netherlands, would support Parkes.[61] Van Valkenburgh was neutral, but his sympathies were clearly with the Shogun.

When Satow was at Nagasaki in September 1867, he was shown a document by Hikozo (better known as Joseph Heco, a naturalized American citizen), which was said to have been

[60] Satow, *op. cit.*, p. 200.   [61] *Ibid.*, p. 173.

signed by the daimyos of Satsuma, Tosa, Geishiu, Bizen, and Awa and presented to the Shogun, advising him to resign his office and allow the government to be reconstituted.[62] This was the famous memorial drafted by Goto and presented, in the name of the daimyo of Tosa to the Imperial court at Kyoto on October 27.[63] And as we have seen, Hitotsubashi promptly followed the course so strongly outlined. On December 4, Ogasawara Iki-no-Kami, one of the Ministers for Foreign Affairs, advised Sir Harry Parkes that the Shogun's resignation had been presented on November 19 (*sic*). And two days later he presented to Van Valkenburgh and his colleagues a long statement explaining the action. This was an unusually frank and accurate résume of the political situation, of the problems created by foreign intercourse, and of the necessity for a strong and united government, and it pleaded for the friendship and sympathy of the foreign governments, with an assurance that no fears should be held for future relations.[64]

The Foreign Representatives continued to conduct affairs with the Shogun's Ministers in Yedo, and on November 26 concluded arrangements for the opening of Niigata and the harbor of Ebisuminato on Sado Island.[65] These ports, and the city of Yedo, were to be opened on April 1 next. And as final arrangements would have to be completed for the opening of Osaka and Hiogo on January 1, the six Ministers agreed to proceed to Osaka, late in December, to superintend the opening of those important places personally.[66]

[62] *Ibid.*, p. 272. Heco (*The Narrative of a Japanese,* II, 97), states that this was given him by Kido. It was signed by representatives of three daimyos, and was forwarded to the Kyoto Government.

[63] Murdoch, *op. cit.,* III, 768–69. For original form of this letter, cf. Satow, *op. cit.,* p. 379.

[64] Van Valkenburgh transmitted these documents in his dispatch of December 13 (*F.R., 1868,* I, 606–9). A similar document was handed to General John A. Dix, in Paris, by the Japanese Chargé, and may be found in a different translation (*ibid.,* pp. 446–48). See also Gubbins, *op. cit.,* pp. 306–12.

[65] *F.R., 1868,* I, 605.

[66] *Ibid.,* p. 606. Before leaving for Osaka, Van Valkenburgh, after protracted negotiations, accepted $10,000 (Mexican) in settlement of the claims of Messrs. Robertson, Schoyer, and Stearns for outrages at Yokohama in May 1863 (No. 34, April 3, 1868).

CHAPTER XIV

CIVIL WAR AND NEUTRALITY
1868 [1]

G ENERAL VAN VALKENBURGH left Yokohama for Hiogo and Osaka on December 21, 1867, in the U.S.S. "Shenandoah," arriving at the former port on the twenty-third. Seven English war vessels and three American had assembled there, and by the twenty-eighth their number had been increased to eight and six, with at least two French warships. At Hiogo, the American Minister found the Japanese busily preparing the foreign settlement, but the work was not yet completed. On the twenty-eighth he sailed over to Osaka, where he found the British Minister had arrived on the twenty-fourth.[2] Sir Harry Parkes had wisely sent three of his staff, Satow, Mitford,[3] and Noel, to Osaka early in December to make arrangements for the British Legation, and his foresight gained for the British the most comfortable and convenient quarters in the city. Satow used the time at his disposal to counsel with clansmen of Satsuma, Tosa, and Choshiu, all hostile to the former Shogun. The French, Italian, and Prussian Representatives[4] arrived by the thirty-first, but van Polsbroek was delayed at Hiogo. Negotiations with the Shogun's officials proceeded satisfactorily; on the thirty-first the regulations for the opening of Hiogo were agreed upon, and on January 1, the port of Hiogo and the city of Osaka were opened as the Shogun had promised. The discussion, in which Parkes and Van Valkenburgh took the lead, then turned to the regulation for Osaka, and

---

[1] The instructions are numbered 41–100; of these sixty, twenty-two were printed in *F.R., 1868,* I. The dispatches are numbered 1–145; of these, seventy-four were printed *ibid.,* as well as six unnumbered reports from Mr. Portman.

[2] Satow, *A Diplomat in Japan,* p. 292, gives the date as the twenty-fourth, Van Valkenburgh as the twenty-third.   [3] Later Freeman-Mitford.

[4] Von Brandt was Chargé of the Prussian Legation.

the terms on which land would be sold in the two settlements.[5] In private interviews Sir Harry had brought pressure on the Japanese negotiators by insisting on reparation for the Nagasaki murders of 1867. He also threatened to send for a couple of regiments if the Tycoon did not send all Japanese troops away from Osaka, where they might come into collision with foreigners. As these were mostly daimyos' troops, even Satow

could not help feeling that it was unfair of him to meddle in this way in Japanese domestic affairs and thus add to the Tycoon's embarrassment, for as the *daimios'* forces had taken Ozaka merely as a stage towards advancing on Kioto, where else could they go except to the capital?[6]

Choshiu troops had been sent to Osaka, but since they did not wish to go there, as a clansman told Satow, "they thought it a great piece of luck that the English Minister had proposed to the Tycoon's people what they most desired."[7]

On January 4, 1868, news reached Osaka of momentous events at Kyoto. A palace revolution had occurred on the third, the troops of Aidzu, a loyal Tokugawa vassal, had been replaced at the palace gates by those of Satsuma, Geishiu, and Tosa, and decrees hostile to the Tycoon had been issued in the boy Emperor's name. On the seventh Hitotsubashi returned to Osaka, for although he had been deprived of the office of Shogun he had refused to fight his foes "so near the palace of the Mikado."[8]

Sir Harry at once sent a letter requesting an interview with "His Highness the Tycoon" the next day. The reply, which was a refusal, referred to Hitotsubashi as "Uyesama," the title borne by the head of the Tokugawa family.[9] Impatient, the British Minister planned to send Locock and Satow to the castle on the eighth to insist upon an interview, when he learned that the former Shogun would that very afternoon receive M. Roches, the French Minister, and would receive Parkes the next day. On hearing that the French Minister had gained the first audience, Sir Harry's "wrath was unbounded"; he claimed priority on the ground of superior diplomatic rank, and, in a pouring rain he set

[5] *F.R., 1868,* I, 610–12.   [6] Satow, *op. cit.,* p. 293.   [7] *Ibid.*
[8] *F.R., 1868,* I, 620.   [9] Satow, *op. cit.,* p. 300.

out for the castle, with his armed escort. In the very audience chamber he exchanged words with Roches, who properly condemned this breach of courtesy, and then the ex-Shogun gave them both an explanation of what had occurred in Kyoto.[10] At his request, the six Ministers called upon him in a body on the tenth, when M. Roches (who had been designated doyen by his colleagues in spite of Sir Harry's protests) made the address, to which the Uyesama replied.[11] While the ex-Shogun condemned the conduct of the daimyos who had seized the reins of power, abolished the office of Shogun, and demanded the surrender of almost all his lands, he refused to follow the advice of his loyal retainers and precipitate a civil war.

But, as my original object in laying down the governing power was to insure unity among all classes of the people, such excess of zeal was contrary to the course I had resolved on. However much I might be in the right, I certainly would not be the cause of a national convulsion. In order to avoid such an unfortunate disturbance I came down to Osaka.

That he denied the validity of the Imperial decrees, issued at the instance of his foes, was evident from his announced intention to observe the Treaties and conduct foreign relations until the form of government should be settled by "a general discussion by the whole country," by which was meant a general council of daimyos.

No word, however, came to the Foreign Representatives from the newly constituted Imperial Government at Kyoto. Satow learned from Terashima that the Emperor's proclamation to the Foreign Powers on his assumption of the government had been delayed until the surrender of 2,000,000 *koku* of the Shogun's lands had been arranged. This would form the nucleus of the Imperial revenues, and it was even suggested that all the daimyos contribute part of their lands for this common purpose. Satow and Mitford pointed out that if a general council of daimyos were

---

[10] Satow, *op. cit.,* pp. 300–302. For a memorandum of this audience, cf. *F.R., 1868,* I, 620–21.

[11] *F.R., 1868,* I, 621–22, for the texts. For a different translation of the Uyesama's reply, see Redesdale, *Memories,* II, 422–24, from von Brandt, *Drei und dreissig Jahre in Ost-Asien,* II, 170–72.

promptly held, the Tokugawa vassals would control a majority of the votes and reinstate the Tycoon in his former position. They counseled delay.[12] The Foreign Representatives, therefore, continued to discuss their affairs with the Tycoon's officers, and daily conferences were held, up to and including January 27, at which the land regulations for Osaka and Hiogo were considered in great detail.[13] On the fifteenth, Sir Harry Parkes had a private audience with the Uyesama, and Van Valkenburgh was received on the twenty-third.[14] The civil war, which had seemed so imminent on the seventh, now seemed remote. That Hitotsubashi had no desire to oppose force to force seemed clear.

On the twenty-sixth, the ex-Shogun had sent forward an advance guard toward Kyoto, and he planned to follow. The next day his men were attacked by the troops of Satsuma, and other hostile clans, at Fushimi. Immediately, on the twenty-seventh, the Rojiu sent a circular to all the Ministers advising them that the Tycoon's forces were engaged in putting down a rebellion of Satsuma, and asking them to issue orders to their countrymen to abide by the Treaty provisions as to the sale of contraband, the entering of non-open ports, and the prohibition of the sale of arms and ships of war to any but the Japanese Government. Having been assured that Satsuma was the only rebel at that moment, that if others were drawn in, the Government had every confidence of its ability to crush them, and that it would take every precaution to protect the Treaty nations, Van Valkenburgh issued the desired warning to the United States Vice-Consul at Nagasaki on the twenty-ninth.[15] The battle raged on the twenty-seventh, twenty-eighth, twenty-ninth, and thirtieth, the Tokugawa troops, weakened by treachery, retiring before a resolute foe. About midnight on the thirtieth the several Legations were warned that the Tycoon could no longer protect the foreigners in Osaka,[16] and the American Minister was asked to permit the Tycoon to take refuge on the "Iroquois" until one of his own

---

[12] Satow, *op. cit.*, p. 306.   [13] *F.R., 1868,* I, 635.

[14] Satow, *op. cit.*, p. 306; *F.R., 1868,* I, 635.   [15] *F.R., 1868,* I, 640.

[16] A similar warning to withdraw to their ships was given the foreigners at Hiogo on February 1 (*F.R., 1868,* I, 640).

ships should arrive. This was granted, and about 2 : 00 A.M. on the thirty-first the Tycoon went aboard the American warship, remaining about two hours, after which he transshipped to the "Kaiyo Maru" and steamed toward Yedo.[17]

Early on the morning of the thirty-first the five Ministers, except Parkes, made their way in a body and on foot to the fort at the mouth of the river, and late the next afternoon the Italian, Prussian, Netherlands, and American Ministers embarked on the "Iroquois." M. Roches boarded the "Laplace," and Sir Harry Parkes, who had first moved to the British vice-consulate in the settlement, went aboard the "Rattler" on February 2. Some feeling had arisen between Parkes and his colleagues, the former at first insisting on remaining at Osaka until all the Legation property had been removed, and finally leaving only in order to preserve a semblance of harmony. The mob promptly pillaged the French Legation, but spared the British until a later day, which led Satow to believe that they could distinguish between the pro-Shogunate French and the pro-Imperial British.[18] Temporary Legations were now established at Hiogo, and there the Ministers remained during the exciting weeks which followed.

With the events of the civil war which broke out at Fushimi, on January 27, 1868, and was to last until the surrender of Hakodate in June 1869 we are not concerned. The military operations, and the political intrigues afford a fascinating subject for investigation, which has never been adequately presented in any Western history.[19] For our purposes we must confine our attention to the diplomatic questions and incidents which arose from

---

[17] *F.R., 1868,* I, 636. Dickins, *The Life of Sir Harry Parkes,* II, 82, erroneously intimates that he boarded a French ship and hinted at French help.

[18] Satow, *op. cit.,* pp. 312–14.

[19] Valuable source material may be found in *F.R., 1868,* I, 605–845. Almost all of these documents were placed before the Senate in three earlier documents, indicative of the interest in the subject—*40th Cong., 2d Sess., S. Ex. Doc. No. 65* (June 18, 1868), *No. 65,* Part 2 (July 10), and *No. 80* (July 20)—these may be found in *Serial Number 1317.* A Japanese factual narrative is Yamaguchi, *Kinse Shiriaku. A History of Japan.* A contemporary British account is found in Satow. A journalist's account is given by Black, in his *Young Japan.* One of the best secondary accounts is found in Murdoch, *A History of Japan,* Vol. III.

the political revolution and the civil war. The first involved the
attitude of the Foreign Ministers toward the new Government
and, conversely, the attitude of the latter toward foreigners and
the existing Treaties. This led to the question of neutrality during the ensuing civil war. It is safe to say that when the Shogun
was driven from Osaka he had the sympathy of almost all the
foreigners in Japan, and of the Foreign Representatives except
Sir Harry Parkes. M. Roches, the French Minister, had been the
most intimate adviser of the Shogun, and he was suspected of
having offered aid to his cause, an offer which, with rare patriot-
ism, Hitotsubashi had refused to accept.[20] General Van Valkenburgh, while in every act staunchly neutral, never failed to show
his sympathy for the Shogun and his supporters, and until the
very end he hoped against hope that the western clansmen would
be punished as he felt they deserved. And the Englishman,
John R. Black, editor of the *Japan Gazette,* at Yokohama, was
strongly of the opinion that the Shogun had been badly treated
and that every constitutional reform could have been carried out,
under this enlightened administrator, without the evils and passions of civil war.[21] It was natural for all the Foreign Representatives, except Sir Harry, to suspect the conduct of Kyoto
officials, who had been so stoutly anti-foreign in the past, and
every act which seemed to confirm this suspicion was seized upon.
But the British Minister, thanks to his brilliant young staff, knew
that the anti-foreignism of the western daimyos was only a mask
with which to conceal their hatred of the Shogun. Fortunately,
the Osaka negotiations of 1865 had brought about the recognition of the Mikado as the head of the state, and his approval of
the Treaties had been secured. To support the Shogun, or his
followers, against the Imperial forces would be to support rebellion, and foreign aid on one side would as surely have been
countered by foreign aid on the other. A firm neutrality was
necessary, but where partiality was so pronounced an impartial
neutrality would not be easy.

[20] *Serial Number 1317,* p. 25. A paragraph omitted in *F.R., 1868,* I, 665.
[21] *Young Japan,* II, 42–44, 109, 242.

Events now marched with startling significance. Most of the Foreign Ministers reached Hiogo on February 1, where the Shogun's representatives were hastily preparing to leave for Yedo. Sir Harry Parkes followed on the second. On the third the local officials withdrew, and the protection of the city was in the hands of the Ministers and their forces.[22] Great was the uncertainty as to what would happen when Imperial troops marched in, and the worst possible impression was created the very next day when a small force of Bizen men entered the settlement and wounded with lances two French soldiers who tried to cross before their advance. The karo in command then gave orders to fire on all foreigners in sight, and the Ministers of the United States, Great Britain, Prussia, and Italy were endangered. The fire was promptly returned by the American marines, French sailors, and British infantrymen on shore, and reinforcements were promptly landed. The offending clansmen were put to flight, and the settlement was strongly guarded.[23]

Only prompt action on the Imperial side saved a very ugly situation, in view of the fact that most of the Foreign Representatives were decidedly pro-Shogun. The Ministers at once agreed to instruct the naval commanders to seize all the Japanese steamers in port in order to prevent hostile measures on their part, and to invite them to take charge of the defense of the settlement. Four notices were posted for the information of the townspeople, describing the attack, explaining why the Japanese ships were seized, advising the people to go about their business without excitement, and forbidding armed men to pass through the settlement.[24] The situation was tense. Parkes, who was in touch with members of the Imperial party, urged them to hurry an envoy to Kobe (as the foreign settlement at Hiogo will hence-

---

[22] *F.R., 1868*, I, 637.

[23] *Ibid.*, pp. 641–46, 649–55. Satow (*op. cit.*, p. 319) states that the incident was created when an American sailor was shot as he crossed in front of them, an insult which, according to Japanese ideas, deserved mortal chastisement. Another version may be found in Redesdale, *op. cit.*, II, 428–33. He quotes von Brandt, who also was present.

[24] *F.R., 1868*, I, 646.

forth be called) as soon as possible,[25] and on the eighth Higashi-Kuze, a court noble, met the six Ministers and presented a copy of the Emperor's proclamation, dated the third, which announced to all foreign nations and their subjects that permission had been granted the Shogun, Tokugawa Yoshinobu, to return the governing power in accordance with his own request, that henceforth the Emperor would exercise supreme authority in both internal and external affairs, and that officers would be appointed to conduct foreign affairs.[26] Higashi-Kuze was well chosen for this delicate mission. Van Valkenburgh wrote:

We found him a very intelligent and quick man, evidently desirous of cultivating friendly relations with foreign powers, and continuing on the part of the Mikado the same terms heretofore existing between those powers and the Tycoon.

The interview lasted for two hours, and the envoy assured the Ministers that the Emperor would disapprove of the Bizen onslaught, while he promised to forward to Kyoto any demands which they would put in writing. He further offered to assume entire protection for the foreigners at Kobe and guaranteed there would be no recurrence of similar outrages. Officials would soon be installed at Hiogo and Kobe, and the Ministers would then be able to return to Osaka. "Our conference was pleasant; the bearing of the envoy was all we could desire; his replies to inquiries prompt and to the point, and we were all very favorably impressed with him," wrote Van Valkenburgh. That very afternoon the foreign sailors and marines were re-embarked, and troops of Satsuma and Choshiu assumed protection of the settlement.[27]

The next day the demands were agreed upon and given to the envoy. They called for a full and ample apology by the Mikado's Government to each Representative, with a solemn assurance for protection in the future and the capital punishment of the officer who had given the order to fire, in the presence of officers from

---

[25] Satow, *op. cit.*, p. 321.   [26] *F.R., 1868*, I, 659.

[27] Roches was not so favorably impressed (Satow, *op. cit.*, p. 325). He presented a long argument in favor of the Shogun on the sixth and left for Yokohama on the ninth. Von Brandt's argument for neutrality was informally approved by his colleagues (*F.R., 1868*, I, 666–69).

the different Legations.[28] Goto was at once sent to Kyoto with the demands, which were promptly acceded to, and the Ministers were so informed on the fourteenth.

On the tenth a second interview was held with Higashi-Kuze, "which passed off as pleasantly as the former one," and at which renewed assurances were given of the Emperor's desire to protect foreigners and faithfully execute the Treaties. At his request, a committee, consisting of Parkes and von Brandt, was appointed to furnish him with copies of all Treaties, Conventions, and Agreements made by the foreign Powers with Japan. This was done at a conference on the eleventh, at which it was pointed out that the only way in which the Ministers could prevent their nationals from carrying troops for the Shogun between the open ports would be for the Mikado to issue a formal declaration of war against the Tycoon, notify it officially to the Foreign Representatives, and demand that no foreign merchant vessels carry troops for either belligerent. Such a declaration would be considered by the Ministers, who would preserve a strict neutrality, as they had *de facto* relations with both parties. Higashi-Kuze also gave a very informing account of the *coup d'état,* from the Imperial point of view.[29] The same day the appointment of four very able men as superintendents of the Kobe customhouse was announced, including Ito and Terajima. On the thirteenth the appointment of Prince Yoshiakira as Chief Administrator of Foreign Affairs, to be assisted by Sanjo, Higashi-Kuze, and Date, was announced; and on the fourteenth, Parkes and von Brandt held their second interview, at which the Bizen reparations were discussed, and a formal ratification of all outstanding Treaties was presented, as well as a declaration of war against Tokugawa Yoshinobu.[30]

The result of these assurances was the agreement of the Ministers to issue neutrality proclamations, which was done on the eighteenth.[31] But a troublesome question was presented by the foreign-built war vessels which had been bought abroad and were

---

[28] *F.R., 1868,* I, 660.
[30] *Ibid.,* pp. 663–64.

[29] Memorandum in *F.R., 1868,* I, 661–63.
[31] *Ibid.,* pp. 672–76.

then on their way to Japan. Of these the most powerful was the ram "Stonewall," purchased by the Shogun in the United States, while two ironclads were expected from France, and several had been bought in England by western daimyos.[32] After some discussion the Ministers agreed on the eighteenth (but the memorandum was not signed until the twenty-eighth) that the delivery of war vessels to either party would be a breach of neutrality, and that they would use their utmost endeavors to prevent such until they received instructions from their governments or peace was restored.[33] Van Valkenburgh, on the nineteenth, instructed Portman, at Yedo, to retain the "Stonewall" under the American flag at Yokohama or to send her to Hong Kong, and on the twenty-fourth he asked Seward for instructions.[34] The "Stonewall" arrived at Yokohama on April 24, and her disposition became the major problem of neutrality in the following months.[35]

Taking advantage of the good relations which had been established at Kobe, Satow and Dr. Willis, of the British Legation, visited Kyoto, which they entered on the eighteenth, traveling by house boat and palanquins from Osaka. Both were received cordially by their Japanese friends, and Dr. Willis rendered helpful service to the wounded. The visit gave a good opportunity to ascertain the political situation at the capital, but Satow was recalled by Parkes on the twenty-third, because of the unsatisfactory turn which the Bizen affair had taken.[36] The execution of

[32] Satow, on the thirteenth, had urged the prompt issuance of the declaration of war in order to prevent the delivery of the ships to the Shogun. He did not mention the British ships consigned to the daimyos (Satow, *op. cit.*, p. 330).

[33] *F.R., 1868,* I, 677–78.   [34] *Ibid.,* p. 676.

[35] While the new régime was winning the confidence of the Foreign Representatives at Kobe, an incident was precipitated at Nagasaki by the French Consul, who refused to recognize the *de facto* officials. It seems that the Governor had left the port on the eighth, and an armed guard of American and British sailors had landed to protect the customhouse. The retiring Governor had intrusted the port to the daimyos of Hizen and Chikuzen, but the agents of the western daimyos had taken control and been recognized by all the other Consuls. This situation was corrected when an Imperial representative arrived. It confirmed the pro-Shogunate sympathies of the French officials (*ibid.,* pp. 680, 683).

[36] Satow, *op. cit.,* pp. 332–41.

the condemned officer had not been carried out, and the suspicion had arisen that the Emperor might be as little able to punish a clansman as the Shogun had been in the past.[37] M. Roches returned from Yedo on the twenty-seventh with four men-of-war, convinced at last of the hopelessness of the Shogun's cause. During his absence, says Satow:

> Sir Harry was now in high spirits and in very good temper. We had no more of the interviews with Japanese officials at which he used strong language, and interpreting for him, which used to be a painful duty, was changed into a labour of love. Success makes a man kind, and certainly Sir Harry had been successful.[38]

The same day Higashi-Kuze informed the Ministers that the Bizen retainer had returned to his native province, but that he would be at once sent to Hiogo for punishment.[39] This was followed by a conference on March 1, between the Ministers and Date, of the Imperial Foreign Office, at which Date reported that the execution would take place the next day and the Mikado's apology would then be given. This assurance brought the Ministers to agree that on the fifth they would return to Osaka and reestablish their temporary Legations there.[40]

But on the morning of the second, Godai and Ito called unofficially on the Ministers and asked if the man's life could not be spared. Van Valkenburgh believed that this was a mere formality, which was followed in every case of the death sentence. For almost four hours the six Foreign Representatives debated the proposal, and all but Parkes and van Polsbroek opposed it. The officer, Taki Zenzaburo, was permitted to commit hara-kiri late that evening, in the presence of representatives of the Legations.[41] The formal apology in the name of the Emperor was presented the next day.

On the fifth, the Ministers returned to Osaka, where they found the temporary British Legation burned and the other

---

[37] *F.R., 1868*, I, 678.   [38] Satow, *op. cit.*, p. 332.

[39] *F.R., 1868*, I, 679.   [40] *Ibid.*

[41] *Ibid.*, pp. 688–96. Mitford and Satow also were opposed to clemency (Satow, *op. cit.*, p. 343). For a famous description of this impressive event, cf. Mitford, *Tales of Old Japan*, pp. 355–63. Another officer was sentenced to imprisonment.

Legations pillaged.[42] There had been some talk of an audience with the Mikado on his first visit to Osaka, and this had again shown the division which prevailed among the Ministers. M. Roches firmly opposed accepting an audience, and Parkes as firmly favored it; Van Valkenburgh, von Brandt, and de la Tour were unwilling to commit themselves too deeply with the Imperial party, and pleaded a prompt return to Yokohama as a reason for not accepting; and van Polsbroek seemed indifferent.[43] But the verbal invitation for them to be received at Kyoto was not given until midnight of the eighth, and then the bearer linked it with news of an alarming nature.[44]

That afternoon a clash had occurred between a surveying party of French sailors from the "Dupleix" and Japanese guards at Sakai, on the bay, seven miles from Osaka, and eleven men were killed and five wounded by Tosa clansmen.[45] The first word was brought by Japanese officers, and promptly, at 1 : 30 A.M. on the ninth, the Ministers assembled at the French Legation to discuss the startling situation. Apparently the punishment inflicted for the Bizen affair had created no real guaranties for the safety of foreigners. All the old suspicion of the Imperial party and their samurai supporters surged up anew. The Ministers themselves were not sure of their own safety, and all night they considered the measures which should be taken. But in the morning the alarm was quieted by the prompt appearance of officials, who expressed the keen regret of the Government and promised prompt satisfaction. That afternoon most of the Ministers returned to Kobe, and Sir Harry followed the next day. On the twelfth, Van Valkenburgh, de la Tour, and von Brandt departed for Yokohama, leaving to M. Roches the settlement of the Sakai affair, with Parkes as intermediator.[46]

The immediate effect of the outrage was the postponement of

---

[42] Satow was told the Osaka people had wrecked the various legations because they thought the Court was hostile to foreigners (Satow, *op. cit.*, p. 344).

[43] Satow, *op. cit.*, p. 349.   [44] *F.R., 1868*, I, 698.

[45] *Ibid.*, pp. 697–700. Note the several attacks on surveying parties in Korea later.

[46] *F.R., 1868*, I, 704.

the opening of Yedo and Niigata, for, as Van Valkenburgh reported, no Japanese Government was strong enough to protect the foreigners from the "general and savage hatred" against them which then existed.[47] But once more the Imperial officials acted with such celerity and good judgment as to avert the direst effects of the most grievous wrong the foreigners had suffered since the first Treaties. Parkes had advised them to accept the demands promptly, if they were moderate, but if they exceeded the demands of justice then to appeal to the French Government and the Treaty Powers.[48] He approved the execution of a large number of Tosa men, but no pecuniary indemnities—certainly a reversal of British policy as shown in the Richardson affair. The French demands, in the light of existing precedents were moderate enough. They called for (1) the execution of all who had participated in the attack; (2) an indemnity of $150,000 for the families of the murdered men; (3) an apology by the principal Minister for Foreign Affairs on board the French flagship; (4) an apology by the daimyo of Tosa, also on board the "Venus"; (5) and the exclusion of all Tosa armed men from the treaty ports.[49] These demands were presented on the twelfth, and the next day Parkes and van Polsbroek advised the Japanese to accede to them, while at the same time they accepted the invitation to an audience at Kyoto. Very promptly, on the fourteenth, came word that the demands had been accepted, and that two officers and eighteen men of Tosa would commit hara-kiri the very next day.[50] But when the expiation occurred only eleven lives were sacrificed, for the French naval witness begged that the remaining men be spared.[51]

[47] *F.R., 1868,* I, 706.   [48] Satow, *op. cit.,* p. 352.
[49] *F.R., 1868,* I, 711.   [50] Satow, *op. cit.,* p. 354.

[51] He stated that, as the hour was late, he felt that he should return to his ship (*F.R., 1868,* I, 713). The Japanese believed that eleven were sacrificed on the principle of a life for a life (Satow, *op. cit.,* p. 354, and note). Redesdale states that Captain du Petit Thouars could not stand any more executions and prayed that the others be spared (*op. cit.,* II, 446). The report that these Tosa men had been canonized was transmitted by Van Valkenburgh on May 26 (*F.R., 1868,* I, 743), and November 4 (*ibid.,* p. 833). Seward brought the latter dispatch to the attention of the Representatives of the Treaty Powers in Washington, No. 108, January 11, 1869.

During all these exciting weeks, Van Valkenburgh had been without instructions from Washington. By the use of the mail steamer from Yokohama, and the overland telegraph, a message could reach Washington in about twenty-two days, but the Minister and the Department rarely made use of the telegraph.[52] Mr. Seward's first instruction was forwarded on March 24, in reply to Van Valkenburgh's No. 3, of January 16, and it advised the practice of a wise discretion, adhering to the existing Government while it still maintained its power, and taking a position neither adverse to, nor prematurely in favor of, any political power which might arise during these convulsions.[53] Mr. Van Valkenburgh had, in fact, followed out the very course which was here outlined.

After the prompt satisfaction for the Sakai murders, M. Roches changed his mind and decided to accept the invitation to Kyoto. On March 23, Roches, van Polsbroek, and Parkes were to be received by the Emperor, the first audience which had ever been granted to Europeans. The two former were received, after Parkes had failed to arrive at the stipulated time, for the latter had been attacked by two Japanese as he set forth for the palace surrounded by guards of Japanese and British soldiers. One of the assailants was promptly dispatched, and the other, severely wounded, was degraded and decapitated. Parkes was then received by the Emperor on the twenty-sixth, who testified to his horror at the detestable crime.[54]

The scene now changed to Yokohama, with the return there of Parkes, Roches, and van Polsbroek. In the meantime the advance guard of the Imperial forces had entered the city, the former Shogun had retired as head of the Tokugawa family, a youthful prince had succeeded him, and many of the former vassals had withdrawn from the city most indignant at the high-handed proceedings of the western lords and their clansmen, who now had complete control of the new régime. The non-resisting

[52] *F.R., 1868*, I, 633.   [53] *Ibid.*, p. 705.

[54] Satow, *op. cit.*, pp. 358–63; Redesdale, *op. cit.*, II, 449–61; *F.R., 1868*, I, 718. Imperial proclamation announcing penalties for attacks on foreigners, March 28.

attitude of the former Shogun furnished no guaranty that a war to the finish would not be fought between his loyal retainers and the daimyos who supported the Imperial Government. This uncertainty led to the decision to land forces to protect Yokohama, in co-operation with the present Shogunal troops there,[55] and later to take steps to prevent the landing of armed Japanese at the port.[56] The Ministers also asked the new Government to send administrators to Yokohama to relieve the Tokugawa officials.[57]

At about this time the Ministers received copies of the Kyoto *Government Gazette,* of March, which contained a memorial of six of the great western daimyos advocating the most enlightened foreign policy and the reception of the Ministers at the Court, a memorial dated February 29, and a reply of the Daijokwan (Government) which indorsed these views.[58] Okubo, of Satsuma, had even memorialized that the capital be removed from Kyoto to Osaka.[59] They did not know that on April 6, in Kyoto, the young Emperor had proclaimed the famous oath, the five articles of which were to be the charter of his wise and enlightened reign. Soon after the resignation of the Shogun, in the previous November, Sir Harry Parkes had applied to his Government for letters of credence addressed to the Emperor. These had arrived late in March, but it was not until the middle of May that he felt that he could leave Yokohama. On the twenty-second of that month, in the Nishi Hongwanji temple at Osaka, Parkes presented to the Emperor his new credentials, the first addressed to him by any foreign state. And during this visit he learned of the new measures which had been taken to proscribe the Christian faith.[60]

On April 26 the two envoys of the Emperor entered the Shogun's castle at Yedo, and presented the Imperial demands to the Shogun's representatives. They were accepted in their entirety, and on May 6 the late Tycoon summoned his army, navy, and treasury to surrender.[61] These orders were not obeyed; many of

---

[55] April 2, *F.R., 1868,* I, 707.   [56] April 17, *ibid.,* p. 721.
[57] April 4, *ibid.,* p. 722.   [58] *F.R., 1868,* I, 725–27.   [59] *Ibid.,* p. 728.
[60] Satow, *op. cit.,* pp. 368–70.   [61] *F.R., 1868,* I, 735–43.

the troops left the city, the warships for the most part retired from off Yedo to an anchorage at Yokohama, and the treasury was largely depleted. It was evident that in spite of all that Hitotsubashi could do, the Imperial authority could not be established in eastern Japan without a struggle.

This gave point to the situation created by the arrival of the "Stonewall" at Yokohama on April 24. Van Valkenburgh, acting in accordance with the agreement of the Ministers of February 18, placed her under the charge of the senior American naval officer, raised the American flag in place of the Tycoon's and drew a draft on London for £4,416, 13s., 4d., to cover expenses to July 1.[62] Simultaneously, in Washington, Mr. Seward was formulating an instruction based on Van Valkenburgh's dispatches of March 1. It contained an unhesitating approval of all the latter's proceedings except his proposal to keep the "Stonewall" under the American flag. This was deemed impracticable. The vessel had been delivered to the Japanese Government in American waters, it was under the Japanese flag, her officers and crew were employees of the Japanese Government. "No diplomatic, consular, naval or military agent of this government has a lawful right to reduce her into possession or to interfere with her movements." But this strong statement was modified by an intimation that his course must be determined by events, and that so long as he continued to exercise a wise discretion, "and at the same time co-operate in prudent measures with the representatives of the treaty powers in Japan," his conduct would be approved.[63] If a Pacific cable had been in operation, it is possible that this powerful ship would have been released to join the Shogun's navy. When Mr. Seward learned that Van Valkenburgh had acted contrary to these instructions (which had not yet

[62] Telegram to Seward, April 28, 1868 (*ibid.*, p. 733; see also Black, *op. cit.*, II, 199). On May 9, two Imperial Commissioners for Foreign Affairs took over the administration of Kanagawa (Yokohama), and at their request the Ministers agreed, on the eleventh, to withdraw the foreign guards the next day (*F.R., 1868*, I, 743). They were landed again in July (*ibid.*, p. 780).

[63] April 30, *F.R., 1868*, I, 733–34. This was the first instruction addressed to Van Valkenburgh, dealing with the political situation, since March 24, and the next was not forwarded until May 20.

reached him), he wrote on May 20 that the proceedings in the case of the "Stonewall" were "entirely irregular," but, under the circumstances, the President had decided to honor his draft, and he must bring the situation to an end as soon as possible. The United States would expect a full reimbursement from Japan.[64] Van Valkenburgh telegraphed on June 5, that he had paid off the crew of the "Stonewall," and had drawn a second draft for some £7,100.[65] This reached the Department on the twenty-eighth. But on the eighth, Mr. Seward had forwarded an instruction dealing with recognition.

You will, without special instructions, recognize the authorities which shall seem to be accepted, and approved by the Japanese people, proceeding, however, in this respect, as on all other occasions, upon due consultation and in harmony with the representatives of the other western powers.

When recognition was made, or ready to be made, Van Valkenburgh was to ask payment for all arrears due on the "Stonewall" and then turn her over to the authorities. But he was instructed that it would be expedient, and perhaps necessary, to secure at the same time a recognition, if not an immediate liquidation, of the indemnity debt.[66] Thus, again, the Shimonoseki indemnity was to be used as a *quid pro quo*. We must now turn to another problem which had given rise to co-operative action.

When Sir Harry Parkes went down to Osaka in May, to present his new credentials to the Emperor, he learned that the new Government had revived the old proclamations against the Christian and other "evil" (or "pernicious") sects. He had at once protested against this intolerance, and Satow, who was with him, tried to have the specific term "Christian" deleted. But they were

[64] *F.R., 1868,* I, 734–35. This was confirmed by a telegram of May 26, approving his conduct and omitting any reference to its irregularity.

[65] *Serial Number 1317,* Part 2, p. 1.

[66] *F.R., 1868,* I, 756. On July 27, the Department advised Van Valkenburgh that the balance on hand, left by the Japanese Commissioners, amounted to $30,732.71, not quite enough to meet his first draft, which equaled $30,982.66, although falling rates might permit it to be sold for a sufficient sum. He was, on delivery, to demand the final payment with interest, and a sum equal to meet the second draft for £7,128/16/4, as well as any other expenses incurred in detaining the "Stonewall" (Instruction No. 58).

told that the popular hostility to Christianity was still intense and that to have refrained from denouncing it would have been tantamount to approval. The active proselyting of the French Roman Catholic missionaries at Nagasaki was a special reason for action. Parkes had received an instruction from Lord Stanley in the matter, and he left a copy with the Japanese Ministers.[67]

At about the same time, and independently, Van Valkenburgh had learned of the new proclamation, at Yokohama. It seems that when the two Commissioners for Foreign Affairs had taken over the administration of Yokohama, on May 11, they had given him copies of the *Official Gazette* published at Kyoto, ending with number nine. But number six was missing, and on securing a copy he found it contained the following proclamation, issued in April:

> Proclamation Board No. 3.
> The Christian and other evil religions are strictly prohibited. Any person suspected of violating this commandment must be reported to the proper officers, and the reporter will be rewarded.

He at once informed M. Roches, and invited his co-operation, and on the twenty-sixth he addressed the two Commissioners, disclaiming any intention of interfering in the internal affairs of Japan but pointing out how such an edict would affect the friendly relations between their respective governments and urging a reconsideration and repeal. Parkes returned on the twenty-ninth, and reported on his conversations at Osaka. But nothing could be effected at Yokohama.[68]

The Consuls at Nagasaki, on their part, had sent in a remonstrance to the local officials on May 12, to which the latter replied, on the thirty-first, after reference to Kyoto, that they must strictly enforce the law. On June 8, the Imperial Government issued a stringent decree, distributing some 4,010 Christians among thirty-three western daimyos, who were to send their agents to Nagasaki to receive them, in groups of from thirty to two hundred fifty each, and it stated:

[67] Satow, *op. cit.*, pp. 368–69; *F.R., 1868,* I, 750–51.
[68] May 30, *F.R., 1868,* I, 749–51.

The Christian religion being strictly prohibited by the law of the empire, the violation of this law is considered a serious matter; therefore after the people shall have been placed in charge of the Daimios, care should be taken to induce them to renounce their evil ways, and if there be any who refuse to repent severe punishment must be inflicted.

These people shall be rigidly excluded from social intercourse until it shall have been proved that their hearts are purified.

They shall be employed as laborers on ground requiring improvement, such as mines, coal mines, etc.

They shall live in forests. For a period of three years one ration for each person per day shall be allowed to the Daimios.

Van Valkenburgh, who reported these events on July 8, expressed some sympathy with the Government, for, he wrote:

There appears to be no doubt that, under pretense of professing Christianity, those people, who belong to the humblest and most ignorant classes, neglected their avocations, held so-called religious meetings at night, when often gross licentiousness prevailed; and hard labor in isolated places is the means adopted to cure them from immoral practices.

And he and his colleagues were convinced that no measures calling for the interference of the Christian Powers would be carried out by the Mikado's Government.[69]

In this connection we have another example of the difficulties occasioned by slow communications. Van Valkenburgh's dispatch of May 30 had been interpreted by Mr. Seward as signifying a prohibition of the practice of Christianity by foreigners, as well as native subjects, which would have been a violation of the eighth article of the Treaty of 1858. His instruction of July 14 stated that the United States could not acquiesce in or submit to the Mikado's proclamation. This was to be notified to the Foreign Representatives, and Van Valkenburgh, in concert with them, was to proceed with firmness.

If it shall be necessary, you will distinctly inform the Japanese authorities that this government will regard it to be an imperative duty to protect the lives and property of citizens of the United States against any persecution which may be instituted under the Mikado's proclamation.[70]

[69] *F.R., 1868,* I, 766–67.

[70] *Ibid.,* p. 757. A copy of this instruction was transmitted to Mr. Thornton, the British Minister, and to Baron de Stoeckl, the Russian Minister, in Washington, by Mr. Seward (*ibid.,* pp. 431, 486).

But when the dispatch of July 8 was received, a more moderate
instruction followed on September 5. The protest of the Consuls
at Nagasaki was approved.

> Humanity, indeed, demands and expects a continually extending sway
> for the Christian religion. Nevertheless it can wait the slow but steady
> and secure progress of conversion which is always effected sooner or later
> by a diffusion of knowledge and calm persevering appeals to the reason
> and consciences of men.
>
> You may forbear from making a formal representation to the gov-
> ernment of the Mikado on the subject of the late decree, until it shall be
> more clearly seen that the measure of persecution thereby commenced is
> likely to take effect. In that event you will protest earnestly and firmly,
> but not without moderation and kindness, against the recent severe meas-
> ure which the Mikado's government has adopted, and will warn him of
> the grave political consequences which may be expected to follow so great
> an error.[71]

In June the Foreign Ministers had to face several questions
involving neutrality. Van Valkenburgh reported, on the fourteenth, that southern troops were being conveyed to the north in
British steamers, and although he had called this to the attention
of Parkes, at a conference of all the Ministers, no action had been
taken.[72] On his part, he had instructed the American naval
commander to seize an American steamer, the "Kaga no Kami,"
which had been chartered to transport Imperial troops, which
was done on the twelfth. He had refused to turn the "Stonewall"
over to the Imperial authorities, and he was dubious of the formal
statement of the Minister for Foreign Affairs, received on the
thirteenth, that the war was over.[73]

Again, on July 2, a request was made that the "Stonewall"
be sent to Osaka, where the Emperor would receive her in person,
to which Van Valkenburgh replied that only when peace was
restored or he had received specific instructions would he surrender her. The rumor that the delivery would take place brought
Enomoto, Commander of the Tokugawa navy, to Yokohama, to

---

[71] *Ibid.,* p. 811.

[72] Seward forwarded this statement to the American Minister in London
and instructed him to bring it to the attention of Her Majesty's Government
(September 3, *F.R., 1868,* I, 349).

[73] *Ibid.,* pp. 758–59.

protest, the point he made being that it would be unfair to deliver the "Stonewall," which had been paid for by the Tycoon, to the Emperor, while some of the western daimyos retained foreign-built ships in their own control.[74]

That peace had not been restored was very evident when, on the fourth, the first serious fighting took place in Yedo. This was the attempt of the Imperial troops to seize the Miyasama, who was defended by Tokugawa volunteers in the Uyeno temple and shrines. The volunteers were defeated, but the Miyasama escaped to the north, to lend a color of legitimacy to the cause of the northern daimyos as supporters of a rival Mikado, as had happened before in Japanese history.[75]

This news was the more disconcerting because on the preceding day, at Yokohama, Higashi-Kuze had stated that, as perfect tranquillity existed at Yedo, the Foreign Representatives and merchants might with perfect safety return there and from that day the Mikado's Government would be responsible for the safety of the Legations and the merchants, provided the latter remained in their houses. This meant that the opening of Yedo was near at hand. But some of the foreigners were even more interested in the opening of Niigata, where silkworm eggs might be obtained; yet the Imperial authorities were reluctant to comply, because the war was still raging on the west coast. On this question the Representatives were divided, those of Italy and Prussia insisting that the port be opened on July 15, and despite the protests of their colleagues they advised their nationals on June 24 that they could trade at that port on the fifteenth. Van Valkenburgh reported that even before that date foreigners of several nationalities had gone there, no Americans among them.[76] But he and

[74] July 3, F.R., 1868, I, 763.

[75] F.R., 1868, I, 772-75. The Miyasama, Rinoji-no-Miya, was a prince of the blood, and according to custom, was Lord Abbot of the Uyeno monastery. He was under the influence of the chief priest, a stout supporter of the Tokugawas (Black, op. cit., II, 208).

[76] July 13, F.R., 1868, I, 776-78; July 22, ibid., pp. 781-82. The Italian Government protested against Van Valkenburgh's refusal to co-operate in this démarche. Long after the port was opened, he was instructed to join in the request (No. 3, August 24, 1869).

Parkes renewed their warnings to their nationals, for the presence of foreigners in that disturbed region might lead to new complications. As an earnest of its good intentions, Higashi-Kuze stated that the new Government would open Osaka as a port of entry, and not merely as a place for residence, and the date was set for September 1. The long-delayed arrangements for the sale of land-leases at Osaka and Kobe were also agreed upon.[77]

Late in July an English steamer arrived at Yokohama bringing sixty or seventy Choshiu officers and men with the object of seizing the "Stonewall" and carrying her to the Inland Sea. Van Valkenburgh was convinced that Choshiu was the last clan to whom the ship could be intrusted, because of its old hostility to foreigners, and he reported new expressions of anti-foreignism from that quarter.[78] At this time foreign adventurers were assisting both parties, and he feared that a union of the opposing forces might be made on a common basis of hostility to foreigners.

New advices from Nagasaki now reported that instead of 4,010 Christians having been banished, only some 120 had been punished. Sixteen of these who, according to law, had been condemned to death, had been reprieved on the representation of the Consuls. But there was no reason to believe that the faith would be tolerated, and under the present circumstances it was not prudent to do more than had already been done.[79] To this dispatch Mr. Seward replied on October 5, approving Van Valkenburgh's conduct, but still apprehensive of trouble between foreign Christians in Japan and the officials of an infuriated people, through the sympathy shown by the former for native Christians.

When one foreign Christian shall have suffered martyrdom in Japan for his faith, Christendom will be shocked to its centre, and it may demand that the policy of forbearance and encouragement which the treaty powers have hitherto practiced in Japan shall be reversed.

He therefore hoped that the Foreign Representatives might not only urge the Japanese Government, in a firm and friendly man-

[77] *F.R., 1868,* I, 785, 786.   [78] *Ibid.,* pp. 788–91.
[79] August 15, *ibid.,* pp. 796–803.

ner, to adopt a more humane policy, but also seek and obtain the freedom of the native Christians now suffering under the existing persecution.[80]

This instruction was based not only on Van Valkenburgh's dispatch of August 15 but also on a statement of British policy as communicated by Mr. Thornton to Mr. Seward on September 24.[81] Lord Stanley's decision was based on the reports of Sir Harry Parkes and the documents which had been given by the latter to Van Valkenburgh and sent to the Department on May 30. Sir Harry had been warned of the necessity of proceeding with caution.

A rupture with Japan would paralyze a trade which promises to be of great value, while its immediate effect would scarcely be other than to increase, for a time at least, the pressure for persecution which the governing powers in Japan, however well disposed, might be unable to withstand.

A common action on the part of the Christian Powers "to repress or revenge a policy of systematic religious persecution" would, in the opinion of Lord Stanley, expose the Japanese Government to serious danger. Sir Harry, therefore, was instructed to act, as far as possible, in concert with his colleagues in behalf of native Christians, but to go no further than friendly representations and remonstrance,

unless, indeed, the persecution of native Christians should lead to a similar persecution of foreign Christians, and among them British subjects, in which case her Majesty's minister would be justified in applying to the commander of her Majesty's naval forces in the waters of Japan for his co-operation in protecting their persons and property, at the same time holding the Japanese government responsible for any wrongs done to them.

Mr. Seward, on October 12, furnished the British Legation with a copy of his instruction to Mr. Van Valkenburgh of the fifth.[82]

---

[80] *F.R., 1868*, I, 828.　　　　　　[81] *Ibid.*, p. 432.

[82] *Ibid.*, p. 433. In August, Herr von Brandt was insulted when two retainers of Higashi-Kuze, Minister for Foreign Affairs, dragged his Japanese coachman from his box. The explanation was the well-known one, that a commoner must kneel when a lord passed by. The incident was settled by a public apology, for Higashi-Kuze assumed the full blame and could not punish his retainers (*F.R., 1868,* I, 815–17).

The new Government, hard pressed for funds, had issued non-convertible paper money, which caused much dissatisfaction among native and foreign merchants.[83] It also proposed to revise the export duties on tea and silk, which, according to the Convention of 1866, could be done in 1868, on six months' notice. At the time this provision was inserted the foreign merchants thought prices would fall and the specific duty could be reduced, but, as it turned out, a readjustment would probably result in an advance. The export duty on tea in 1868 amounted to about one cent a pound.[84]

Van Valkenburgh's dispatches of June–July were acknowledged in sixteen instructions of September 3–8, which approved his conduct throughout, and, in respect to the "Stonewall," took the position that the United States had dealt with the Tycoon as the head of a government and not as head of a clan, and that it was necessary to wait for the people of Japan to decide who was the head of their Government.[85]

On September 18, Higashi-Kuze again requested the delivery of the "Stonewall," and when he found that this could not be done in the face of the neutrality proclamations he asked that they be withdrawn.[86] Van Valkenburgh was willing to act in concert with his colleagues, but at this time, the prospect of trouble loomed at Niigata. The last postponement had fixed the opening for April 1, and no extension had been granted. The Italian and Prussian Representatives had authorized their nationals to visit the port on and after July 15, and Satow had advised the Japanese to enforce neutrality themselves by setting up a blockade there.[87] This advice was taken.[88] Two questions were presented here: one was the opening of the port, which was in the hands of Tokugawa supporters; and the other was the supply of munitions to the foes of the Government.[89] That foreign vessels were engaged in a contraband trade was unquestioned, and so was

---

[83] *Ibid.,* p. 795.   [84] August 19, *ibid.,* p. 804.

[85] September 4, *F.R., 1868,* I, 811. Seven of these instructions were printed (*ibid.,* pp. 810–14).

[86] *Ibid.,* p. 821.   [87] Satow, *op. cit.,* p. 380.

[88] About September 1 (*F.R., 1868,* I, 823).   [89] Black, *op. cit.,* II, 230–31.

the right of the Government to blockade the port and seize blockade runners.

During these months a bitter conflict was raging in the northeast, where a league of daimyos supported the Tokugawa cause. In order to strengthen the Imperial régime in the eastern provinces, it was decided to have the Emperor visit Yedo. Van Valkenburgh reported this on September 17, with a statement that the name of Yedo would be changed to East Kyoto (Tokyo).[90] But execution of the plan was delayed by an unexpected turn in the military situation. On October 5, the Tokugawa fleet, of some eight vessels, sailed from Yokohama to the north, to throw in their lot with the hard-pressed northerners. In a long statement they announced their purpose "to repress the arrogance of the southerners and to aid the distressed people of the north in the maintenance of their just rights."[91] Even as late as November 7, Van Valkenburgh did not believe that the south (west) would subjugate the north (east) nor, if so, could hold it in submission long.[92] But on the previous day the castle of Wakamatsu, stronghold of the Aidzu clan, surrendered. This was reported to all the Foreign Representatives on the sixteenth, and, wrote Satow:

> It was a pleasure to us to see how the countenances of some of those who had to listen to the story fell, for they had counted on a desperate resistance on the part of Aidzu to defeat the imperialist party and frustrate the policy of the British Legation.[93]

But the American Minister, in reporting this interview, on November 20, stated that he had been advised later that Aidzu had not surrendered, that the southerners were surrendering to him, and that steps were being taken to prepare Yedo against a northern attack![94] On November 26 the Emperor entered Yedo. The war was practically over, except for the operations of the Tokugawa fleet in Hokkaido.

With the restoration of peace on the main island, the Japanese Commissioners at Yokohama again announced that peace had been

---

[90] *F.R., 1868,* I, 820.   [91] *Ibid.,* pp. 829–32.   [92] *Ibid.,* p. 837.
[93] Satow, *op. cit.,* p. 388.   [94] *F.R., 1868,* I, 839–41.

restored, but that very day Van Valkenburgh had learned from the Consul at Hakodate in Hokkaido (Yezo), that the Tokugawa fleet had arrived off that port. After consultation, on December 11, the Ministers decided to send the French frigate "Venus" and the British corvette "Satellite," later joined by the "Argus," to Hakodate to protect all foreigners there and to enforce neutrality so far as their own nationals were concerned—for French officers were serving on the rebel ships.[95] On the fourteenth, a Japanese official again applied for the surrender of the "Stonewall," for use in the Hokkaido campaign, and Van Valkenburgh repeated his inability to comply.[96] When, next day, he learned that an American merchant steamer, "Mars," had been chartered to convey Imperial troops to Hakodate, he warned the agent and succeeded in having the charter canceled, although he was prepared to seize the steamer if necessary.[97]

At this juncture, Sir Harry Parkes took the position that the Tokugawa naval forces were pirates, and refused to enforce his former prohibition against British vessels engaging in the transportation of men and munitions.[98] This was a breach in the existing co-operation among the Foreign Representatives.

When the Ministers met in conference, on the twenty-first, Van Valkenburgh was too ill to attend. Von Brandt reported to him that Parkes had stated that he could not prevent British vessels from leaving port with troops or articles contraband of war, but, as he would not recognize the belligerent rights of the Tokugawa naval forces at Hakodate, the British war vessels there would prevent British ships from entering that port with such cargoes. While von Brandt considered these views wrong, and not in harmony with the proclaimed neutrality, he was unwilling to have German merchants debarred from the profits of this carrying trade, and he was returning the papers of German vessels at Yokohama, leaving the merchants to act as they pleased, with

---

[95] No. 130, December 14, 1868.   [96] No. 131, December 16.

[97] No. 134, December 18. Southern troops were being transported in chartered [British] steamers (*ibid.*).

[98] Based upon the Special Order in Council of May 14, 1868 (*ibid.*).

the express understanding that in no case could they claim the protection of their Government while engaged in such a trade. American merchants were also clamoring for a share in this carrying trade, which Van Valkenburgh was not prepared to permit, and he again instructed the several American Consuls to remind their nationals that neutrality must be strictly observed. In fact he intimated that views might well be exchanged by the Department with the British and North German Governments so that the cordiality of the co-operative policy might remain unimpaired.[99]

During the year two incidents furnished opportunities for the American Minister to state emphatically the attitude of his Government toward the nefarious coolie traffic. It will be recalled that the Kingdom of Hawaii had endeavored to secure a Treaty through Mr. Van Reed, an American citizen who had been informally received as Hawaiian Consul General at Yokohama. But when the Japanese authorities found that he was a merchant consul they refused to negotiate with him. The Hawaiian Government then requested Mr. Van Valkenburgh to act for them, and furnished him with a commission to conclude a Treaty.[100] Before any action could be taken the Japanese authorities formally complained about the high-handed conduct of Van Reed in shipping Japanese coolies to Hawaii without proper passports. It seems that he had contracted to supply 350 coolies, and the Tokugawa officials had granted passports for 180 of these, before they had withdrawn from Yokohama. The Imperial Commissioners, however, refused to furnish the remainder on the ground that no Treaty existed with Hawaii. They did offer to do so if one of the accredited Ministers would sanction the transaction, and Van Reed agreed to consider this alternative. But on May 25, the "Scioto" sailed, without a proper clearance, and in spite of notice that the Imperial authorities did not recognize the passports alleged to have been given by the late Government.

---

[99] No. 138, December 24. Mr. Seward approved Van Valkenburgh's conduct, and made the desired representation to the British and North German Governments. He expressed surprise at Sir Harry's position, and hoped he should have the power necessary and would wield it in the interest of the co-operative policy (No. 118, February 17, 1869).   [100] No. 42, April 24, 1868.

Mr. Van Valkenburgh had previously been advised of Van Reed's operations, and as the "Scioto" was a British vessel he had informally called Sir Harry's attention to the proceedings, but no action was taken before the latter left for Osaka. In reply to the Japanese protest he could only point out that he was powerless to interfere with a British ship, much as he regretted the occurrence. But he felt he had one recourse, and that was to issue a regulation applying the Act of Congress of February 19, 1862, which prohibited the Chinese coolie trade, to Japan, and, until otherwise instructed, he would apply its provisions to Americans shipping coolies in foreign as well as American vessels.[101] Mr. Seward, however, found this regulation "without sufficient foundation in law," and therefore invalid and ineffectual. Van Valkenburgh would have to rescind it, but application would be made to Congress to amend the Act of 1862 so that it could be applied. The spirit of the regulation was approved, and in response to the Minister's request, copies of the Senate Resolution of January 16, 1867, and a State Department Circular of January 17, both of which denounced the traffic, were inclosed.[102]

In September the Japanese asked for the return of the laborers and the punishment of Van Reed, which could not be brought about under the existing American law. By that time, Van Valkenburgh had learned that the "Scioto" coolies had been landed at Honolulu on June 19, and disposed of at $70 a head, under a contract to labor for three years at a fixed rate of wages.[103]

The other instance was the ill-omened bark "Cayalte." On August 19 this American-built ship arrived at Hakodate with forty-two Chinese coolies on board. Stains of blood in the cabin supported the suspicion that the master and crew had met with

---

[101] "This government entirely disapproves of the shipment of their people in any other capacity than as voluntary emigrants; they will be able, no doubt, to prevent similar shipments in future, and there is every reason to hope, therefore, I am happy to say, that I shall have no infringement to report of the resolution issued, of which I trust you will be pleased to approve" (May 29, *F.R., 1868*, I, 746–48).

[102] July 15, *ibid.*, p. 778.

[103] No. 96, September 18, 1868; No. 51, May 17, 1870.

foul play. The coolies could give no information as to the nationality of the ship. Investigation by the American Consul, and later by an American naval officer, seemed to show that the ship was owned in Chile, that she had been engaged in the South Pacific coasting trade under the American flag, and that, when last heard of, she had sailed from Callao for one of the northern ports of Peru, for a banker of Lima to whom the coolies were under contract to labor. A "sea letter, crew list, clearance and other papers, signed and sealed by the U. S. Consul at Callao" were found on board. The crew, it appeared, had been murdered by the coolies, who had spared the master on condition that he navigate the ship back to China. He had escaped on some island where he had landed to obtain provisions. As the ship was deemed unseaworthy she was left for the winter at Hakodate, in charge of the Japanese authorities. Some time later, Van Valkenburgh received a visit from the Peruvian Consul at Macao, the seat of the coolie trade, who claimed the ship, and asserted that the coolies were worth $20,000. Van Valkenburgh refused to take any action until it could be proved that he had a perfect right to do so.[104]

The immediate reaction of the State Department was that, as it was doubtful if any American citizens were interested in the vessel, the American Government could certainly take no part in reducing the coolies to servitude. Van Valkenburgh's conduct in abstaining from interference was approved, and Mr. Seward would be disappointed "if the authorities of Japan do not sympathize with those of this country and of China in detestation of the Coolie Trade."[105] When the later dispatches showed that the ship was owned by a Portuguese captain and a Peruvian banker, that it had carried a Peruvian crew, and that the American flag had been assumed to protect the ship during the war between Spain and Peru, the Department again refused to give effect to the use of the American flag which was "a fraud and abuse." The suggestion of Admiral Rowan that the coolies were guilty

---

[104] No. 121, November 23; No. 129, December 5; No. 132, December 18, 1868.

[105] No. 111, January 12.

of piracy under the law of nations was answered by the statement that their real motive was not robbery or plunder or general hostility but to effect their return to their native land. And the language of the Supreme Court in the "Amistad" case was quoted:

We may lament the dreadful acts by which they asserted their liberty and took possession of the "Amistad," and endeavored to regain their native country, but they cannot be deemed pirates or robbers in the sense of the law of nations (15 Peters R. 594).[106]

[106] No. 119, February 19, 1869. Although the "Cayalte" was the subject of further correspondence (Van Valkenburgh's No. 41, June 3; De Long's No. 83, November 20, 1869; Davis to De Long, No. 4, August 27, 1869), the status of the ship was unchanged. In the last instruction the Department held that even if the vessel were American and American-owned, it was clear that she was engaged in the coolie trade, in violation of the Act of February 19, 1862. But as no one came forward to claim the ship, it was sold by Consul Hawes, in 1873, for 500 *rio*. Minister Bingham reported that it was then generally believed that the ship was American (No. 25, December 5; No. 34, December 20, 1873).

CHAPTER XV

THE NEW RÉGIME
1869 [1]

THROUGHOUT the struggle in 1868, the American Minister, while careful to observe all the duties of a neutral, was avowedly sympathetic with the Tokugawa cause. His dispatches stressed every favorable report from the northern battlefields, as well as those which indicated dissension among the Imperial supporters. The Satsuma clansmen, as the prime movers in the anti-Tokugawa confederacy, were especial objects of suspicion. When, in December, many of the Satsuma and Tosa clansmen returned to their homes, for the campaign in Honshiu was practically over, Van Valkenburgh believed their influence and control of the Emperor had completely disappeared, and that their disgrace would soon be proclaimed.[2] And a few days later he wrote:

The struggle is stripped of much of its interest, when considering, that after all there is no political principal at stake, all pretence to the contrary notwithstanding. The movement to unite the whole of Japan under the sceptre of the Mikado is not a bona fide one, and there is not the remotest prospect of the people being benefited by the results.[3]

Like most foreigners, and many Japanese, Van Valkenburgh saw in the struggle only an attempt on the part of the western clansmen to seize the power which had so long been denied them. Like

---

[1] With the close of 1868, the period of very full publication of diplomatic correspondence, which had marked the tenure of William H. Seward as Secretary of State, came to a close. No volume of *Foreign Relations* was issued for 1869–70. The instructions for 1869 are numbered 101–26 (to Van Valkenburgh), and 1–8 (to De Long); of these thirty-four, one was printed in *41st Cong., 2d Sess., S. Ex. Doc. No. 58, Serial Number 1406.* The dispatches are numbered 1–94; of these, one was printed in *F.R., 1870,* two in *Serial Number 1406, Doc. No. 52,* and two in *Serial Number 1406, Doc. No. 58.* Fortunately, for 1869 some valuable material may be found in *Japan. No. 3 (1870).*

[2] No. 131, December 16, 1868.   [3] No. 135, December 19, 1868.

them, he feared that Satsuma would try to set up a new Shogunate under its daimyo, and he believed that only when all elements in Japan were brought into the new Government could the country become consolidated. In this he was correct, and the wise statesmen of the new régime understood this quite as well as did he. Revenge would have to give way to moderation.

But the withdrawal of the British Minister and the North German Chargé from the co-operative policy in respect to neutrality, complicated the international situation. Sir Harry Parkes had taken the position that Admiral Enomoto and his associates, who had seized the island of Hokkaido, were pirates and unworthy of belligerent rights. But Van Valkenburgh knew some of them as able and distinguished officers of the late Shogunate and quite as responsible as the northern daimyos who had hitherto been treated as belligerents. He therefore instructed the Consul at Hakodate to enter into relations with the *de facto* government there, the officers of which had been elected by the samurai and which was looked upon as an experiment in republican institutions.[4] But the march of events was to resolve this problem. On January 1, Niigata and Tokyo were opened to foreign residence, after a delay of a year, and on the fourth the Representatives of Italy, France, and the Netherlands were received in audience by the Emperor, and those of the United States, the North German Confederation, and Great Britain the next day. This friendly reception caused Van Valkenburgh to report:

If the Sovereignty of the Mikado be only nominal at present, it is to be hoped, that it may become a reality at an early day, as it seems impossible that this Country can ever be reunited and strong under any other chief than the one, whose recent reception of the Foreign Representatives has given such satisfaction to all.[5]

In the following days the Imperial Representatives continued to press for the withdrawal of the declarations of neutrality, on the ground that the war was over and peace had been restored. By this time Parkes was supported by Outrey (the new French

---

[4] No. 134, December 18, 1868; Black, *Young Japan,* II, 240.

[5] No. 3, January 7, 1869.

Minister) and van Polsbroek, and he set out to bring the other three Ministers to his point of view.[6] On January 15, Iwakura, the Minister for Foreign Affairs, discussed the matter with the Ministers in Yedo, and they agreed, on the twenty-third, after several meetings, to acknowledge that the war was over and asked for a short delay in which to arrange for the simultaneous withdrawal of their notifications.[7] On the twenty-seventh they agreed to postpone the withdrawal until February 10, and Van Valkenburgh believed the report from Hakodate would show the opposition there to be stronger than was generally believed.[8] But he finally recognized that peace had been restored, and on February 8 he joined in a memorandum signed by all the Foreign Representatives to this effect. The notifications of neutrality would be withdrawn, and the "Stonewall" would be turned over to the Imperial forces.[9] The Hokkaido campaign, however, had by no means ceased, and the "Stonewall" was used by the Imperialists in the final operations which ended with the surrender of Hakodate on June 26.[10]

In view of Van Valkenburgh's consistent attitude in opposition to the withdrawal of neutrality when it had previously been requested by the Imperial authorities, some explanation is necessary for his approval of the memorandum of February 8, in which the Foreign Representatives declared:

---

[6] Satow, *A Diplomat in Japan*, p. 402.   [7] *Ibid.*, p. 406.

[8] No. 9, January 28.

[9] No. 12, February 9. This final payment was $116,160.41 (Mexican). No. 19, March 8.

[10] No. 51, July 15. The final discussions of neutrality were complicated by the action of the British and French Ministers in presenting to Iwakura a memorial from the Tokugawa commanders at Hakodate, asking that the island of Hokkaido be conferred upon the head of the Tokugawa clan, to be colonized by his retainers, who could not subsist on the 700,000 *koku* allowed by the Court. This reached Tokyo on January 22. Iwakura finally agreed to receive it, but would not forward it to the Emperor, who had returned to Kyoto. The Representatives of the United States, Italy, and Prussia feared that the British and French naval commanders at Hakodate had entered into arrangements of a special nature with either belligerent, and warned the Imperial authorities that they would not sanction any departure from the co-operative policy (No. 9, January 28). Parkes joined in presenting the memorial, lest Outrey gain prestige by acting alone (Satow, *op. cit.*, p. 408).

The undersigned having been officially informed of the cessation of the state of war formerly existing in Japan, and having satisfied themselves of the non-existence of belligerents in this country have agreed upon withdrawing their respective notifications of neutrality and to discontinue the enforcement of the measures agreed to by their memorandum of the 28th of February, 1868.

His dispatch of February 9 was devoted mainly to a report of the punishment meted out to the northern daimyos, who, "partly by force and partly by friendly mediation . . . . were induced to proceed to Yedo to arrange matters with the Mikado's authorities in person." Then, after reporting that the punishments were not in accord with the assurances held out when they agreed to surrender, and expressing the opinion that fresh outbreaks might be expected, he came to the surprising conclusion:

Whatever means have been employed, the result has been unquestionably a cessation of hostilities and peace has been restored as far as known in all parts of Japan. There was no ground therefore any longer to decline rescinding the declarations of neutrality issued in February 1868, and in compliance with the application of the Mikado's Authorities it was unanimously resolved by the Foreign Representatives that the proper time had arrived for that measure.[11]

Yet in subsequent dispatches he reported the strong position of the Tokugawa retainers in Hokkaido, and the measures taken to subdue them. In other words, Van Valkenburgh knew perfectly well that hostilities had not ceased. He had, however, been led to accept Sir Harry Parkes' contention that the rebels in Hokkaido were not "belligerents," and the latter took all the credit for bringing his reluctant colleagues to his point of view.[12] But Sir Harry's success was due not to arguments but to deeds. When he refused to forbid British vessels entering the service of the Imperial Government, in which he was reluctantly followed by the North German Chargé, he admitted his nationals to the most profitable carrying trade in Japanese waters. As he would no longer co-operate with his colleagues, they must adopt his policy or subject their shipowners and traders to the loss of a desirable commerce. This, without doubt, accounts for the change in

---

[11] No. 12.   [12] Satow, *op. cit.*, pp. 401–8.

policy of four of the Representatives, for only van Polsbroek originally supported Parkes's position. Other foreign ships were at once chartered, and the "Hermann," a steamer of the Pacific Mail Company (American) was wrecked off the east coast on February 13, with about four hundred Imperial troops on board.[13]

This explanation is necessary because it sheds some light on the relations between the several Legations in Yedo and the Imperial authorities throughout 1869. Sir Harry Parkes was first in influence, because of his consistent partisanship for the Imperial cause, which had culminated in his victory over his colleagues in the neutrality dispute. And he was also the most sympathetic of the Ministers in dealing with the new régime. In those days of readjustment there were many incidents which showed signs of the old anti-foreignism and reaction. As he wrote to Lady Parkes, he was battling with the reactionary spirit,[14] and again, "I stick by this nascent Government and try to keep them in the right groove."[15] Fortunately, the real leaders of the new Government were neither anti-foreign nor conservative, and they justified all the trust which Sir Harry reposed in them.[16]

The French Legation was under suspicion, not only because of its intimate relations with the Shogunal Government but espe-

[13] No. 15, February 23. One result of the withdrawal of neutrality was to cause long-drawn-out discussions between the American Representatives and the Imperial officials. On July 21, Van Valkenburgh reported that the American steamer "Peiho" had been seized by Imperial officers at Aomori opposite Hakodate (No. 56). After considerable delay she was finally released in September. Thus arose the famous "Peiho" claim, which the Japanese resisted on the ground that the vessel was engaged in an illegal traffic (No. 69, October 10). This claim was not settled until 1883. Van Valkenburgh had an additional reason for modifying his previous course in the attitude of the Department toward the retention of the "Stonewall." Just as the discussion among the Representatives at Yokohama had reached a climax, he received an instruction of January 11, 1869, which stated: "The detention of the Stonewall is becoming inconvenient and of some concern. I sincerely hope that before long she may be transferred on just terms to a proper Government in Japan" (No. 107).

[14] June 7, 1869, Dickins, *The Life of Sir Harry Parkes,* II, 119.

[15] June 12, *ibid.*

[16] His dispatches, printed in *Japan. No. 3 (1870),* contain a great deal of material on political conditions in Japan in 1869, especially in the translations of documents inclosed, and testify to his optimistic view of developments.

cially because French officers (members of the military mission and deserters from French ships) had fought with the Hokkaido rebels.[17] French nationals were assaulted at Yokohama, although British nationals were also threatened, and an attempt was made to burn the French Legation on the night of May 5. These hostile acts led to the reoccupation of guardhouses in the native city by the British and French troops.[18]

And General Van Valkenburgh, during the remainder of his mission, was as critical of the new régime as Sir Harry was optimistic. The reorganization of the Government, in which an Assembly of feudal retainers was a prominent feature; the voluntary surrender of their lands and powers by the daimyos; the financial difficulties, which led to a flood of inconvertible paper and even debased coins, all were reported in dubious or even hostile terms. And as a discordant note repeated suspicions arose of the daimyo of Satsuma and his conservative clansmen. The continued punishment of the Japanese Christians furnished support for his unfavorable views.

In his rôle of adviser to the new Government, Parkes had tried to bring them to tolerate Christianity, for no measure would win greater support among the Treaty Powers. On December 21, 1868, during a conference at Yokohama in which this subject was brought up, Satow reported that Parkes "unfortunately lost his temper over the arguments used by Kido, and made use of very violent language such as I do not care to repeat."[19] The

---

[17] Parkes wrote to Lady Parkes, June 25: "All the Frenchmen have left Enomoto at Hakodate, and have given themselves up. They have been forwarded on to Saigon by M. Outrey—to be dealt with as the French Government may direct. They deserted Enomoto on the evening of a severe defeat, which does not say much for their prowess. After instigating the Japanese to revolt, and countenancing them so long as they could do so without risk, they leave them on the first appearance of danger. This has added to the discredit they had already acquired, and will not improve the French reputation in Japan" (Dickins, *op. cit.*, 120–21).

[18] No. 36, May 20.

[19] Satow told Parkes that he had hurt Kido's feelings and that while "that sort of thing may have a good effect in a particular case, it makes the Japanese dread interviews with you" (*op. cit.*, p. 399). On another occasion, when they were discussing the Sermon on the Mount, Yoshida, referring to Parkes's vio-

Japanese officials, however, promised to write notes to the Foreign Representatives announcing the Mikado's intention to show clemency to native Christians.[20] These were not sent until several weeks had passed and rumors of renewed persecutions had led to persistent representations by the Foreign Ministers.[21] On January 27 the Prime Minister assured them that officers would be sent to the Goto Islands to stop the persecutions there. After a conference, the Ministers addressed similar notes to Higashi-Kuze, on February 9, asking for prompt news of the repression of such measures, and Van Valkenburgh added that he had received instructions informing him of the deep impression produced on his Government by the report of the deportation of the Urakami Christians in the previous July. He ventured to suggest that those Christians be restored to their homes, for his Government

will not fail to see in such a measure a further proof of the regard of the Mikado's Government for the feelings of those Foreign Powers, with whom they seek to cultivate friendly intercourse.[22]

Within a few weeks Van Valkenburgh was informed by Outrey that the Goto Christians had been released and returned to their homes.[23] Yet, as conflicting reports continued to be received from Nagasaki,[24] he directed Mr. Portman to visit that city and investigate the situation. Portman left Yokohama on April 10 and returned on the twenty-sixth. While he was unable to visit Omura and the Goto Islands he learned from natives of those places that perfect tranquillity prevailed there. He did visit Urakami, and found no signs of official interference or control, and he reported

that he is inclined, from all he has seen and heard on that occasion, to concur in the opinion expressed to him by intelligent and well informed foreign residents of Nagasaki, that the reports of persecutions of native Converts to Christianity in Kiusiu have greatly been exaggerated, and that in many instances they probably have had no foundation whatever.[25]

lence in conference, said to Satow: "Now in his case, when he gets in a rage, so far from offering him the other cheek, I feel inclined to kick him out of the room" (*ibid.*, p. 403).   [20] Satow, *op. cit.*, pp. 398–99.

[21] No. 8, January 27.   [22] No. 13, February 10.   [23] No. 18, March 2.

[24] No. 24, March 30.   [25] No. 30, April 27.

The next month, however, M. Outrey laid before his colleagues a very circumstantial report of the persecutions in the Goto Islands, prepared by the Roman Catholic Bishop. It stated that some four hundred Christians had been arrested in the villages there and seventeen had died from starvation, cold, and torture. While Van Valkenburgh was still inclined to the opinion that such reports were often exaggerated, if not entirely unfounded, he joined with his colleagues in an identical letter to the Ministers for Foreign Affairs, of May 18. This compared the previous statements of the Japanese officials, that no persecutions had occurred there, with the detailed report which they transmitted, and pointed out that the inquiries should be prosecuted until the truth should be ascertained.[26]

While the Government itself would have preferred toleration, it could not march too far in advance of the popular wishes in the matter. Van Valkenburgh reported, in July, that in the Assembly an almost unanimous opinion had been expressed in favor of the repression of Christianity but of lenient measures to that end, while a few members insisted that foreigners coming to the country should be compelled to trample on the Cross, as of old. From the Consul at Nagasaki he learned that the imprisoned Christians had been released so that they might work in the fields, and he hoped that they would not again be confined.[27]

This was the last reference to the Japanese Christians in the correspondence of 1869, but the problem was by no means settled, and it was to disturb the relations between Japan and the Western Powers for the next three years. While the Foreign Representatives had no color of right to interfere in this domestic situation, for the practice of Christianity by native Japanese was not a treaty right, they went as far as they possibly could by advice and warning to bring the Government to tolerate the faith which they all professed. And the best friends of Japan sought

---

[26] *F.R., 1870,* pp. 453–54.

[27] No. 59, July 28. Parkes to Clarendon, June 26, 1869, refers to the anti-Christian feeling then prevailing and advised discretion on the part of missionary bodies and foreign governments [*Japan. No. 3 (1870)*, p. 23].

to remove the occasion for the most effective criticism of the enlightenment of the new régime. The question which was presented by these and other incidents was as to whether the Tokyo administration shared these views or was strong enough to repress them. Van Valkenburgh was able to report, in October, that nothing further had been heard of the persecutions of Christians, while the anti-foreign movement, which at one time had appeared quite threatening, was in abeyance.[28]

Although the Emperor had given his assent to all the existing Treaties,[29] there was a very general feeling in Government circles that the Treaties negotiated by the Shogunate should be speedily modified in certain particulars. As soon as neutrality had been withdrawn, Higashi-Kuze proposed to the Foreign Representatives that the Treaties of 1858 be revised before the stipulated time (1872), in order to bring them "in harmony with the new state of things."[30] This may be considered the first attempt of the Japanese to secure a revision of the Treaties, which was not to be gained until 1894 (1899). The Ministers could only reply that they would await his views as to the alterations desired.[31]

But even before this, the Imperial Government had assumed a freedom of action in matters of diplomacy which was viewed with some alarm by the Powers. During the negotiations of the Treaty with Sweden, which was signed on November 11, 1868, the Japanese Ministers had tried to insist that only *consules missi,* and not *consules electi,* should be received from Sweden, and it further announced that it would cancel all existing Treaties unless the Powers accepted the same provision. The antipathy of the Japanese to merchant-consuls has already been pointed out. The Italian Government asked the other Treaty Powers for their views on this question. Mr. Seward, while sympathetic with the desires of the Japanese Government, referred the matter to Van

---

[28] No. 72, October 15.   [29] *Supra,* chap. xiv.   [30] No. 14, February 16.

[31] When Van Valkenburgh reported the conclusion of the Treaty with Austria-Hungary he stated that it conferred no privileges not already enjoyed by the United States. However, this example of the old Treaties was so well framed that it became the maximum statement of foreign rights down to 1894.

Valkenburgh for an expression of his opinion.[32] As the Treaty did not eventually contain the disputed clause the matter was dropped, but the attitude of the Japanese Foreign Ministers was typical of the new spirit.

In addition to the unfavorable impression created by the enforcement of the anti-Christian edicts, there was some ground for suspicion of the new Government because of the renewal of assaults upon foreigners. Under ordinary circumstances these incidents would have been the subject of individual representation on the part of the Minister of the nationals involved. But it must always be remembered that the Imperial party had a reputation (not well founded, it should be said) for anti-foreignism, and most of the Foreign Representatives were continually on the alert lest the reactionary samurai get out of hand. The insults to British subjects, and assaults on French nationals, which have been mentioned, led to simultaneous protests on the part of the five Representatives, in which those of the United States, Italy, and North Germany supported the action of their colleagues of Great Britain and France. They also led to the reoccupation of the guardhouses in the native city by British and French troops.[33] The assassination of Yokoi Heishiro, an Imperial official, at Kyoto on February 16, because he advocated a liberal foreign policy and the toleration of Christianity, was not understood until the British Legation, in May, secured a copy of the manifesto, which was posted by one of the sympathizers of the assassins near the scene of the crime.[34] A few days later Van Valkenburgh reported that many of the samurai who had joined the western clans in overthrowing the Shogunate had done so on the understanding that the foreigners and their religion would be immediately driven out. They were incensed at the failure of the Government to carry out this promise, and the attempt to stop the second visit of the Mikado to Yedo, in April, was ascribed to some of them.[35]

[32] No. 114, February 2.
[33] No. 36, May 20. The troops were withdrawn in July (No. 52, July 17).
[34] No. 38, May 25.　　　[35] No. 40, May 29. Black, *op. cit.*, II, 254.

In the Assembly,[36] which convened on April 18, frequent references were made to foreign affairs, and no little hostility was manifest, despite the efforts of the Government to curb this antiforeign feeling. This led the Foreign Representatives to address identical notes to the Minister for Foreign Affairs, on July 17, asking for information as to the competence of the Assembly, and pointing out that no vote or proceeding on its part could modify the Treaties already concluded with the foreign Powers, except with the full consent of those governments. They were informed that questions affecting Treaties could be discussed in the Assembly, but that no measures could be carried out except after due negotiations. To matters proposed by individual members and on petitions from private individuals the Government paid no attention, while even the measures approved by the Assembly had to be submitted to the Emperor for his sanction.[37]

Another matter which involved only four of the six Powers, was the readjustment of the duties on tea and silk. While a mere detail in the comprehensive tariff of 1866 it became linked with the old bogy, the Shimonoseki indemnity, and thus assumed an especial importance. The six months' notice had been given by the Japanese in August 1868.[38] After some little delay beyond the six months, the four Representatives agreed to discuss the matter with the Japanese Ministers on May 1.[39] The conference was friendly, for the claim of the Japanese was well founded. But before the revised rates could be agreed upon, the balance of the Shimonoseki indemnity ($1,500,000, Mexican) came due on May 15.[40] While the Imperial authorities recognized this indebtedness, they were unable to liquidate it. It was then agreed that the Representatives would submit to their governments a proposal to postpone the indemnity payment in return for a continuance of

[36] The Kogisho was composed of samurai representing the feudal fiefs.

[37] No. 54, July 18; *Japan. No. 3 (1870)*, pp. 36–38.

[38] *Supra,* chap. xiv.

[39] No. 28, April 14.

[40] The delay was due to the refusal of the Representatives to discuss the tariff in view of the recent attacks on French nationals in Yokohama, and until satisfaction had been granted (No. 36, May 20).

the existing low export duty on tea and silk. The loss in revenue to the Japanese would more than balance the interest waived by the four Powers. The arrangement took the form of an agreement (which was signed on June 1) to revise the tariff, on a five per cent basis, to take effect on January 1, 1870, and a formal statement by the Japanese that they would postpone the collection of this increased duty until 1872 (when they thought the whole tariff would be revised) in return for the postponement of the indemnity payment, without interest, until May 15, 1872. Mr. De Long, the new American Minister, was instructed on September 10, to sign such a convention if the other Representatives were similarly authorized.[41]

It was to be expected that during the civil war and the days of reconstruction in Japan some of the Powers might be suspected of trying to fish in troubled waters. That Japan was able to pass through this crisis with so little foreign intervention was due, on the one hand, to the success of the co-operative policy and, on the other, to the unusually competent leaders who took up the reins of government. To be sure, unfounded suspicions arose concerning the conduct of Britain and France, the stoutest advocates of the opposing parties, but the other Treaty Powers held the scales in favor of strict neutrality. When some British ships appeared off Hakodate to protect their nationals, late in 1868, a rumor spread that Britain was about to acquire the large and undeveloped island of Hokkaido.[42] A few months later, however, the conduct of Russia gave real occasion for alarm. Van Valkenburgh reported, on September 22, 1869, that the Russians had expelled the Japanese officials from Sakhalin (Karafuto), and

---

[41] *Serial Number 1406, Doc. No. 58,* pp. 10–13. This instruction was delayed in transmission. Mr. De Long wrote, on December 13, that the higher duties would be collected on January 1 following, if the agreement to postpone the indemnity was not approved. In the absence of his instructions his colleagues had agreed to each give verbal notice to the Japanese that the date should be postponed to February 1 (No. 85, December 13). This dispatch was received on February 5, 1870, and a telegram was at once sent off (*ibid.,* p. 14). The formal approval of the June 1 agreement was not announced to the Japanese until March 7, 1870 (No. 28, March 9, in *Serial Number 1526, Doc. No. 151*).

[42] Adams, *The History of Japan,* II, 165 n.

were engaged in fortifying the tip of the island commanding the straits of La Perouse.[43] The joint occupation of this island had been agreed upon by the Convention of March 18 (30), 1867, and in some quarters it was anticipated that Russia would change this into complete possession.[44] The Tokyo officials, occupied with all the pressing problems of internal reorganization, proposed to colonize the island with farmers.[45]

From the point of view of the foreign merchants the principal difficulty created by the civil war and reconstruction was the stagnation of trade produced by the fluctuations in the currency. As late as October 1868 the exchange value of Japanese ichibu in Mexican dollars was high, but early in that month the native coin began to depreciate, owing to well-founded rumors that certain daimyos were issuing debased and spurious coins.[46] The Foreign Representatives, in concert, protested against these counterfeits, and the authorities promised to stop further issue.[47] Foreigners had speculated in these debased coins and tried to have their Representatives demand their redemption, a measure which would have bankrupted the Government. Sir Harry Parkes, as usual in this period, took the lead in urging moderation, while he sharply warned the Government of the consequence of such issues. The effect on trade was immediate, for the Japanese merchant, buying foreign goods in dollars, now had to exchange four ichibu for a dollar, instead of three.[48] The Government now began to issue paper money in Tokyo and compelled the people to accept it. The first issues had been made at Kyoto and Osaka, and sums had been remitted to various daimyos for circulation in their fiefs, on the understanding that they would be redeemed in tenths annually

[43] No. 66.

[44] *F.R., 1867,* II, 61. A different translation is found in *British and Foreign State Papers,* 1870–71 (Vol. LXI, 1877), pp. 558–59. It gives a wrong Japanese date—25th day of the 7th month of the 3rd year of Keio, instead of 2nd month; the signatures are garbled; and the Russian's (Strezmonkow) is omitted. A third version is found in No. 85, September 20, 1870.

[45] No. 71, October 12.

[46] No. 24, March 30. Ichibu pieces were issued of copper silver-gilt, instead of silver, and two bu coins of lead and tin, instead of gold.

[47] No. 32, April 29.   [48] Dickins, *op. cit.,* II, 115, 117.

over a period of from ten to thirteen years. But now larger sums were emitted and it was rumored that the circulation of gold and silver would be forbidden.[49] This led to a second joint protest of the Representatives in July.[50]

The stagnation of native trade which followed the issue of large sums of paper money extended to foreign commerce. Repeated conferences were held between the Representatives and the Japanese officials, and it was finally agreed that until the debased coin should be redeemed it would be received in payment of duties at the open ports. This was considered satisfactory to foreign interests as well as honorable to the Government.[51] In Yedo the paper money was freely used, but all metallic currency had passed out of circulation excepting cash, and these were mostly of iron.[52] With the report that the Government had purchased the Hong Kong Mint, which would be set up at Osaka under British supervision, and that the paper would be eventually redeemed at par, business revived, and no further representations were necessary.[53]

The inauguration of President U. S. Grant, on March 4, 1869, brought about the customary changes in the American foreign service. Hamilton Fish, of New York, succeeded William H. Seward, who had served as Secretary of State for the quite ex-

[49] No. 43, June 23.

[50] No. 53, July 17. In his dispatch of July 20, Van Valkenburgh inclosed a bulletin of information from the Department for Foreign Affairs for the Japanese students at the United States Naval Academy, Annapolis. It summarized the political changes which had taken place, described the Assembly then in session, reported the surrender of the Hakodate rebels, and told of the increasing numbers of foreigners residing at the open ports and cities. In regard to the currency it stated: "Since spring the minting of coins has been stopped and paper money issued. This circulated at some discount for a while—but since the 5th month the rate of exchange between metallic and paper currency has been abolished; and it has been ordered that paper must pass at par. Paper was to circulate during thirteen years but as new coins will be issued an arrangement for the exchange of paper for new coin has also been made, and the term of thirteen years has been shortened to four years (that is up to the year Saru). In consequence of the issue of paper the price of all articles has advanced, but this will soon come down, as soon as the people discover the convenience of paper money" (No. 55).

[51] No. 60, August 26.   [52] No. 61, August 28.   [53] No. 66, September 22.

ceptional term of eight years and who had earned a place as one of the ablest of all the Secretaries. A successor for General Van Valkenburgh was found in the Honorable Charles E. De Long, of Virginia City, Nevada, and he was commissioned on April 21.[54] Not until October 30 did he arrive at Yokohama, and on November 11 the two Ministers were received by the Emperor, when Van Valkenburgh presented his letter of recall, and De Long his letter of credence. So prompt an audience was welcomed as another sign of the enlightenment of the Imperial court.[55]

While, as we shall see, the appointment of De Long was by no means a happy one, a change in the American Representative was most desirable. General Van Valkenburgh had served through three difficult years in Japan. Arriving, in 1866, when the new Shogun had given convincing signs of his wisdom and liberality, he had thrown his sympathies to the Tokugawa cause during the civil war. His conduct had been irreproachable, and he had faithfully lived up to the co-operative policy, which was the very corner stone of Seward's diplomacy in the Far East, but he was in no position to evaluate fairly the efforts of the new leaders, who were trying to create a New Japan in the face of appalling difficulties. His dispatches dealing with internal political affairs, which cannot be discussed in this study, contain many opinions and predictions which were not justified by the actual march of events.

Perhaps a typical example should be cited, that of the surrender by the feudal lords of their lands and powers. The offer of the daimyos of Satsuma, Choshi, Hizen, and Tosa was reported on March 30, 1869, without comment or details.[56] A month later (April 29) the report was confirmed but its significance minimized

[54] Van Valkenburgh was informed of De Long's appointment in Instruction No. 125, June 28. A letter of recall from the President to be presented to the Emperor was inclosed. No word of appreciation or thanks for his services was tendered. After his retirement from Japan he served as Associate Justice of the Supreme Court of Florida from May 20, 1874, until his death, August 1, 1888.

[55] A new letter of credence, addressed to the Emperor, had been forwarded to Van Valkenburgh on March 3, 1869, No. 120, but had not been presented.

[56] No. 24.

because of the belief that the four daimyos designed to secure a monopoly of offices and a cash annuity in exchange for their revenues.[57] On May 29 he reported that all the provinces of western and southern Japan were divided between two parties, one favoring and the other opposed to the surrender of the fiefs.[58] On June 23, he believed that the matter had been dropped altogether,[59] but on August 28, he reported that a considerable number of the daimyos had been received by the Emperor on the second and notified of his acceptance of their sovereign rights.[60] Yet even at this date he did not understand the terms of the surrender, for he reported that either the daimyos retained ten per cent of their revenues for their own use or that the Emperor received ten per cent for the general government. And he ventured this opinion:

The movement I am further inclined to believe, will prove not to have been a bona fide one, but to have been chiefly intended by the Daimios represented as a demonstration less of loyalty to the Mikado than of apprehension of Prince Satsuma,—a suspicion of whose designs has lately ripened into overt declarations of resistance to his well known ambitious pretensions.

Yet Satsuma was one of the leaders of the movement to return the fiefs to the Emperor!

And in one of his last dispatches (October 15) he wrote:

The liabilities of the Mikado's Government are in excess of the assets. Arms, munitions, money and ships of war have been surrendered only nominally by some Daimios, and by the others not even so; a distinct refusal to comply with the Imperial wishes in this respect has in some cases been met with. Commissioners or tax collectors, sent into the Provinces, have sometimes failed to report their return; and it cannot always be ascertioned, whether they absconded with the money, or were assassinated. And, yet, while the Yedo Government is daily growing more unpopular in that city, and within the limited extent of territory, where their authority is not nominal, but real, they actually issued an order abolishing Daimios, reducing them in rank, and appointing them governors of their provinces or territories, though removable, it is understood, at the Mikado's pleasure.[61]

[57] No. 32.   [58] No. 40.   [59] No. 43.   [60] No. 61.   [61] No. 72.

At the same time Sir Harry Parkes was supplying the British Foreign Office with translations of many of the important documents of this period, so that the Blue-book, *Japan. No. 3 (1870)*, has been a veritable source book. Lord Clarendon was far better informed of the real situation in Japan than was Mr. Seward. A few years later this criticism of Van Valkenburgh would apply with equal force to Sir Harry Parkes, for he also proved himself as unadjustable to new conditions as his American colleague had been. Each in his turn could confess

> The time is out of joint: O cursed spite,
> That ever I was born to set it right.

CHAPTER XVI

SHIRT-SLEEVES DIPLOMACY
1870 [1]

CHARLES E. DE LONG, the fourth American Minister-Resident in Japan, was a native of New York. As a young man he had joined the gold rush to California, where he had toiled as a miner and in other humble capacities. Gifted with personal qualities which made for political leadership in those rough days, he had risen to become a member of the California Assembly and then the Senate. When new mining areas were opened in the infant state of Nevada, he migrated there, in 1863, and entered the political life of the smaller community.[2] Twice he had been defeated for the United States Senate, and in 1869 the political situation had made it desirable to the faction in control to remove De Long from the scene, and for this reason his appointment as Minister to Japan was urged upon President Grant. Possessed of the most meager formal education, inexperienced in affairs except in the turbulent politics of the two mining states, self-educated as a lawyer, De Long was as ill-prepared for a diplomatic appointment to a court as formal as that of Tokyo as could be imagined. That he achieved a moderate success may be ascribed to his native intelligence, but that he should fail to measure up to the requirements of the post was inevitable.

In one of his first dispatches he reported that the political situation "probably was never during our intercourse with this

---

[1] The dispatches are numbered 1–131; of these, seven were printed in *F.R., 1870*, two in *41st Cong., 3d Sess., S. Ex. Doc. No. 25 (Serial Number 1440)*, and two in *42d Cong. 2d Sess., H. Mis. Doc. No. 151 (Serial Number 1526)*. The instructions are numbered 9–49; of these forty-one, two were printed in *F.R., 1870* and three in *Serial Number 1440, Doc. No. 25*.

[2] *Representative and Leading Men of the Pacific,* edited by Oscar T. Shuck, pp. 219–24.

country more complicated than at the present moment." While the Legation was officially established at Yedo, all the Foreign Representatives maintained temporary quarters at Yokohama, where the archives of the American Legation had been deposited since 1863. This was "extremely expensive and embarrassing," and if the Emperor should be forced to return to Osaka or Kyoto, a third residence would have to be established near his person. At Yokohama a post office, jail, and hospital were very much needed, and there was a rent allowance only for the jail. Several claims had been placed in his hands for settlement, growing out of the disturbed conditions in 1868–69, and these he was investigating, with the assurance that "in no case shall I make any demand upon the Japanese Government unless expressly authorized to do so."[3]

A month later he described his unenviable situation with the frankness of an inexperienced diplomat. Holding the title of Minister-Resident he was outranked by the Ministers Plenipotentiary and Envoys Extraordinary of Great Britain, France, Italy, and Holland. The Legation staff had not been increased since its establishment, although the interests of the United States had greatly expanded.[4] The high cost of living, the unfavorable exchange, the inadequate quarters provided in Yedo, all depleted his modest salary. In comparison with his humble station he described the imposing establishments of the British and French Ministers, with their adequate salaries, their residences at Yokohama and Tokyo provided, their well-trained staffs, their mounted guards supported by garrisons at Yokohama and men-of-war at their disposal. He recommended the erection and furnishing of a permanent Legation in Tokyo, the establishment of a mounted guard of twenty-five or thirty men, with at least one warship at his service,[5] and the increase of his pay and rank. He again urged

[3] No. 81, November 17, 1869.

[4] De Long brought with him a friend, and former miner, F. C. Farrington, who was to act as his secretary in return for his expenses and no salary. This was promptly disapproved (No. 24, February 22, 1870; No. 299, October 26, 1872).

[5] De Long relied for protection on his revolver and such mounted native policemen as might be detailed as an escort.

the need of a post office, jail, and hospital at Yokohama, and pointed out that whereas heretofore American prisoners had been boarded in the British jail, the increase in their own prisoners had made this inconvenient.[6] There was much truth in this indictment of the inadequate provision which the American Government made for its diplomatic and consular service in Japan— as in all other lands—but it was to be many years before Congress could be moved to improve the situation.[7] In order to improve his diplomatic status he was commissioned Envoy Extraordinary and Minister Plenipotentiary on July 14.

De Long's first co-operative action with his colleagues was in connection with the postponement of the Shimonoseki indemnity.[8] Then came the proposal of the Japanese Foreign Office to remove the difficulty involved in the free export of coal for steaming purposes by permitting all shipments in steamers to be free of duty, while collecting the export duty on shipments in sailing vessels. This was accepted unanimously by the Foreign Representatives.[9] The Government also announced that it would prosecute foreigners trading at unopened ports, and requested the Ministers to instruct their Consuls to punish such offenders. Such a notification was duly issued.[10]

Early in 1870 the treatment of Japanese Christians again brought about co-operative action. On January 1 the Japanese Foreign Ministers replied to the identical letters of the Representatives of May 18, 1869. They stated that, on further investigation, they had learned that on Goto Island there were some one thousand native Christians. Of these, 335 had been reconverted to their national religion, "after having been gradually advised and disciplined"; 593 had been imprisoned; and 140 had escaped

---

[6] No. 88, December 27, 1869, *Serial Number 1406, Doc. No. 52,* pp. 3–10.

[7] On October 20, 1870, De Long asked for a steam launch to expedite his movements to and from Tokyo (No. 99).

[8] See *supra,* chap. xv.

[9] No. 86, December 14, 1869, *Serial Number 1406, Doc. No. 52,* p. 2. At this time coal could not be shipped economically by steamers. Later a controversy arose when the practice developed (Dickins, *The Life of Sir Harry Parkes,* II, 261).

[10] No. 87, December 21, 1869, *Serial Number 1406, Doc. No. 52,* pp. 2–3.

from confinement. It was reported that some of the latter had conspired to rise against the authorities, and they were again arrested and those who would not confess "were coerced in the usual way." They were not struck by iron rods, nor was fire put in their mouths as alleged, and their treatment was much better than that of ordinary criminals. But as rumors of ill-treatment had again been heard, they had sent other officers to investigate. This was followed by a letter of the seventh, which stated that the sentences of deportation would be carried out in the case of those Christians at Urakami who had escaped exile in 1869, for the reason that only in this way could difficulties between the Christians and the unfriendly country people be avoided.

On the tenth, when the latter communication was delivered, De Long received from the Consul at Nagasaki the copy of a protest addressed by all the Consuls to the Governor there, on January 2, against this deportation of some seven hundred Christians at Urakami. Sir Harry Parkes happened to arrive at Nagasaki on the third, and he had promptly investigated and urged delay, which the local officials could not grant. Proceeding to Kobe, he had sent in a full account of his proceedings to the Japanese Ministers, on the seventh, and warned them of the ill effect of such measures upon the good opinion of all Western States.

De Long immediately, on January 10, added his protest, and M. Outrey wrote a similar letter the next day. On the seventeenth, the four Representatives at Yokohama joined in a request for a conference and requested that the deportations be immediately suspended until the Government could consider the joint representations which the Ministers proposed to make. That day De Long received a reply to his protest of the tenth which may be cited as a satisfactory presentation of the Japanese point of view:

As you are aware, the profession of Christianity has been prohibited in our country from ancient times; but in consequence of the promise we made last year, that those Christians should be treated leniently, they have been left undisturbed at their homes. Every possible advice to change their Christian belief was given them. In return they insulted the deities, thrones, and temples, quarreled with the other inhabitants, and committed various lawless acts.

Should these acts be left unrestrained, the local administration would be embarrassed; and our government, having no other means, sent those people to various other places to be educated. Orders were therefore issued to Nagasaki to simply remove them and to inflict no punishment whatever; and after careful consideration it was deemed by our government that this is the most lenient measure that could be adopted.[11]

The conference at Tokyo, on the nineteenth, was an impressive occasion, and its immediate results were reassuring. Sanjo, Iwakura, and Terashima, accompanied by eight members of the State Council, met with Parkes, Outrey, De Long, and von Brandt. A memorandum of the discussion, in which all the principals took part, contains much information. In general, the Japanese insisted that the Christians were trouble-makers and that the measures of correction had been enforced with kindness. Missionaries, in violation of the Treaties, had visited the villages, but instead of protesting to the Foreign Representatives the Government had thought it easier to deal with their own subjects. Iwakura insisted that Japan desired friendly relations with all the Powers, "but we must be allowed to govern our own people," and he now asked the Ministers to control their missionaries. Such a promise was given by Outrey and De Long. In his opening remarks Sanjo stated that the Government, on its own part and without any foreign pressure, had decided to suspend the deportations, and the next day two officers would leave with appropriate orders.[12]

All now seemed to be well, but on the twentieth came word from the Netherlands' Consul at Nagasaki that some 3,170 men, women, and children had actually been sent away from Nagasaki, on native and foreign vessels, some of them steamers. This news produced surprise and chagrin among the Representatives, although the action had taken place before the new orders could arrive, and led to a highly colored dispatch from De Long to the Department on the twenty-second. Fears were entertained for

[11] In No. 10, January 17, *F.R., 1870,* pp. 455–59.
[12] In No. 13, January 22, *ibid.,* pp. 462–68.

the safety of the missionaries at Nagasaki, and the French Minister had sent the gunboat "Flamme" there. The officials who had spoken so fairly on the nineteenth were accused of dissimulation, in order to gain time. The sole offense of the Japanese Christians, in De Long's opinion, was their faith, which threatened the Shinto religion and the divine claims of the Mikado. The Government, he wrote,

fear the advance of Christianity more than they do the consequences of wounding the sensibilities of the Christian powers, and, entrenching themselves behind the legal shield of an abstract right on their part to manage their own internal affairs without foreign interposition, they intend by such practices as these to maintain this faith and the government based upon it until forced to abandon them.

He then stated as a fact what is of prime significance in this whole controversy—that the Tycoon's Government had been overthrown because of its liberal foreign policy and the Mikado's party had succeeded by an appeal to the anti-foreign sentiments of the daimyos and others.

Hence, we have in this government one impliedly and expressly pledged to hostility to foreigners and the Christian faith; and from such a government, so intended and so committed, I can see no hopes of effecting aught for important or general good relative to this subject by simple remonstrances. Thus, then, the issue stands framed; and thus simplified, the Christian powers may now know the exact spirit and disposition of this government relative to this question.

So far he had acted according to instructions given his predecessor. These had now been exhausted, and he solicited additional ones,

so full and complete that I may know the full extent to which I may proceed should exigencies of a very grave nature arise, which is not improbable, as I fear that these authorities will become much emboldened by the success of this movement, if they find that, for any considerable length of time it is allowed to pass unmet by aught else than remonstrances and vague warnings.

For the present he would follow the course already pursued, in concert with his colleagues, although conscious of its perfect inefficiency.[13]

[13] No. 13, January 22, *F.R., 1870,* pp. 460–62.

This dispatch indicates that De Long, at the very beginning of his service, had adopted the old opinion that the Imperial régime was anti-foreign because it was anti-Christian. There was no recognition of the difficulties confronting the Japanese officials, who were trying by mild measures to bridge over the gap between the old relentless persecution and the new toleration which would in time come. And there was a slightly veiled request for instructions which would permit more drastic measures than "remonstrances and vague warnings." His reference to an "abstract" right to manage their own internal affairs without foreign interposition struck a false note in a dispatch from an American Representative.

A second dispatch of the same day, which dealt with the political situation, ascribed the persecution to a desire to conciliate the Shinto priesthood, the bigoted country squires, and the daimyo retainers, while the show of independence of foreign feeling flattered the anti-foreign party.[14] This was followed, on the twenty-third, by the transmission of two reports, received from Sanjo and Terashima, and prepared by the Governor of Nagasaki, which related exactly how some 2,810 Christians had been deported and stating that 185 were awaiting transportation. While the treatment as described was kindly in the extreme, De Long saw no reason to modify his previous views.[15]

On the twenty-eighth the Japanese Ministers visited Yokohama to hold a second conference, which, however, could not be assembled, and in its place they left a long memorandum which they asked to be transmitted to the Treaty Powers. This was an argument in support of the loyal way in which the Government had lived up to its engagements to permit foreigners to worship according to their own religion and to build churches, in proof of which it pointed out that missionaries had even been engaged as teachers in Government schools and that anyone could translate and sell all sorts of books, even such as related to religion, but that the conduct of the foreign missionaries gave great dissatisfaction, and the actions of the native Christians were such "as

[14] No. 14, *ibid.*, pp. 468–71.   [15] No. 16, *ibid.*, pp. 471–72.

would undoubtedly be punished in all other countries." If the missionaries would apply themselves to their own people, according to the Treaties, it stated that the Government would not have to cut them off from those Japanese who sought information on religious matters, and would have no objection to restore the exiles to their homes. In conclusion it stated:

The Japanese government are desirous that their people be instructed in arts and sciences, in which your country is superior, instead of being instructed in religion, and they are, above all, desirous that the existing friendship between our countries may increase more and more.[16]

The postponed conference was held on February 9, and it resulted in the following memorandum signed by Parkes, Outrey, De Long, and von Brandt:

The Japanese government having declared that the action of some foreign missionaries in preaching outside of the limits of the foreign settlement has caused serious disturbances, and is one of the reasons for which the government thinks the removal of the native Christians from the neighborhood of Nagasaki is a political necessity, the foreign representatives do not hesitate to declare that they, on their part, will do everything in their power to restrain the foreign missionaries from such acts, and will punish them therefor if such acts be persisted in; provided, that the native Christians who have already been deported from Urakami are all brought back.[17]

Thus the matter was restored to the footing it had had in 1867, when a similar promise was made by M. Roches. The last clause is significant—the Foreign Representatives would enforce their treaty obligations only on condition that Japan would refrain from doing something which it had every legal right to do.

Further details of the humane measures adopted at Urakami were reported by De Long on April 12. The employment of Protestant missionaries in public schools at large salaries he ascribed to an attempt to stop their proselytism, a view which overlooked the unique opportunities which such employment offered.[18]

The discussion was now removed to the foreign chancelleries.

[16] In No. 20, February 10, *F.R., 1870,* pp. 472–74.
[17] *Ibid.,* pp. 474–75.   [18] No. 41, *ibid.,* pp. 475–78.

Mr. Fish replied to De Long's dispatches of January and February in an instruction of April 18. He approved the individual and co-operative efforts of De Long to prevent the persecution of the native Christians. But he took the position that:

These deplorable acts of the Japanese Government, however cruel or uncalled for, do not seem to have been done in violation of any treaty or agreement between Japan and the United States. They rather appear to have been done in the exercise of the internal authority which that government claims to possess over its subjects.

Until the views of the Treaty Powers could be ascertained, the Department could give no other instructions than to continue to act in the same spirit. The American Ministers at London, Paris, and Berlin would be asked to ascertain whether or not those governments contemplated sending any further instructions to their diplomatic or consular officers.[19]

The same day such instructions were forwarded to the European Legations. They were based on De Long's dispatches and manifested apprehension for the safety of foreigners in Japan. Before sending instructions to the diplomatic and consular officers in Japan, and to the officers of the Asiatic squadron, the President desired to ascertain what the European Powers proposed to do,

in order that should there be an apparent unity of purpose in Europe, the policy of the United States may be made to conform to it so far as our interests will allow.

Inquiries were to be made if the facts concerning the deportations had been reported to the respective governments; if so, whether any new instructions were proposed; and whether or not any new instructions or new steps were being considered to safeguard foreigners and their interests and "the maintenance of the policy inaugurated by the government of the Tycoon."[20]

John Lothrop Motley, the American Minister in London, addressed Lord Clarendon, as instructed, on May 22. His Lordship's reply showed a sound understanding of conditions in Japan. While desiring to use its influence in favor of the native Chris-

[19] No. 16, *ibid.*, p. 478.   [20] *Ibid.*, pp. 479–80.

tians, Her Majesty's Government did not think it advisable to put such pressure upon the Mikado as might imperil his position with his subjects in general. It would be unwise to add to his difficulties by urging him to set at defiance the religious principles of his people. The Government, therefore, did not contemplate giving any new instructions or taking any new steps for the safety of foreigners, while reposing full confidence in the judgment and discretion of Sir Harry Parkes, in the assurance that he would neglect no means for securing those ends. A copy of Clarendon's instruction to Parkes, of April 20, was given to Motley, which approved the former's conduct, and suggested ways in which the Representatives could further the interests of the converts, especially by impressing upon them that they should show their rulers that the Christian religion was not incompatible with their duties as good subjects. This instruction was also forwarded to Lord Lyons, in Paris, for the information of the Minister for Foreign Affairs, with the suggestion that France might send out an instruction to the same effect to its Representative in Japan. Attention was called to a statement made to Parkes by one of the Japanese Ministers,

that the distribution of the converts in nineteen different localities is more calculated to facilitate the propagation of Christianity throughout Japan than their unmolested residence in the locality in which they have heretofore been permitted to reside.

A few days later the French Embassy discussed the situation with the British Foreign Office. Mr. Hammond, who received the French First Secretary in the illness of Lord Clarendon, developed the British position, which was based on Sir Harry's reports. At this time the Foreign Office had not received a copy of the Yokohama memorandum of February 9. Lord Clarendon approved what Hammond had said, in an instruction to Lord Lyons of April 30. When, some weeks later, the French Government again took up the matter, in connection with the inquiry of the United States, Lord Clarendon had before him a dispatch from Parkes which told of the promise, made by M. Roches in 1867, to restrain the Catholic missionaries. He concurred in the prudence of the instructions issued by M. Roches to the French Consul at Nagasaki, and felt that the Japanese Government had a fair claim to ask that they should be acted upon, and in reporting this discussion to Lord Lyons, on May 23, he added,

if the French government adopt M. Roches's views and instructions there is every reason to believe that the differences which have arisen out of the late proceedings of Roman Catholic missionaries in Japan will be brought to a close.[21]

The British Government had, therefore, resolved this problem into the only element which concerned the Treaty Powers, and that was the conduct of the missionaries. With the treatment of Japanese subjects the Powers had no right to interfere, and time and forbearance could be counted upon to handle this phase of the matter. Mr. Fish, therefore, closed the matter for the present, by transmitting all the correspondence to De Long, on June 18, with the comment that further instructions would be unnecessary.[22]

While the treatment of native Christians was the subject of joint representations, the threatened conflict between Japan and Russia for the possession of Sakhalin was also a matter of concern to the Foreign Representatives individually. De Long reported, on January 3, that no hostilities were intended by Japan, although steps had been taken to colonize the disputed island, but, on the eleventh, he revised this judgment and anticipated trouble in the coming spring or summer, perhaps for the purpose of consolidating the opposing factions in the country. He had asked the Japanese Ministers for a statement of their northern boundary claim, and had been told that it ran between the Kurile (Chishima) Islands of Etorop and Urup.[23]

Some weeks later, in the course of a conference on other matters, the Ministers brought up this controversy with Russia and

[21] All the documents above were transmitted by Motley to Fish (No. 345, June 2, *F.R., 1870,* pp. 480–86).

[22] No. 22, *ibid.,* p. 486. It is perhaps probable that the Department's lack of confidence in De Long's judgment dates from this incident.

[23] No. 3, January 3. This was based on the Russo-Japanese Convention of February 7, 1855. Sakhalin was to remain in joint possession.

requested the mediation of the President of the United States. They did this because neither Japan nor Russia had accredited envoys at the court of the other, because of the well-known friendly relations between Russia and the United States, because of the proximity of the American coast to the region in dispute and the probability that the American Government would feel an interest in the question arising from the activity of American fishermen in those seas, and because of the second article of the Treaty of 1858.[24]

De Long, in reply, gave assurance of the perfect willingness of his Government to carry out the provisions of the existing Treaties, but reminded them that they must exhibit a similar disposition. He pointed out several instances where his predecessors and himself had had reason to complain of their non-fulfillment of treaty obligations, and warned them that as long as they continued to deny full commercial intercourse and continued their illiberal measures in relation to freedom of religious belief and worship

they could not reasonably expect the sympathy of the Christian Powers in controversies of this nature between themselves and another Power which in all its possessions allowed perfect freedom of commercial intercourse and religious belief.

But before he could lay the matter before the Department he requested a statement of the controversy, a full list of all proofs in support of their claims, and a complete history of all transactions between the two governments in the matter.[25]

In compliance with this request, the Japanese Ministers, on March 15, presented two memoranda: one a formal request for mediation; and the other a statement of the points to be proposed to Russia. In the latter, the division of Sakhalin along the fiftieth parallel was proposed, Aniwa Bay would be opened as an "open

[24] "The President of the United States, at the request of the Japanese Government, will act as a friendly mediator in such matters of difference as may arise between the Government of Japan and any European Power."

[25] No. 85, September 20. In this dispatch De Long narrated the discussions which had been proceeding for several months. The statement in the text is based upon it and the documents inclosed.

port," and provision would be made to respect lands cultivated by the nationals of either party beyond the new line on paying ground rent to the proper authorities.

De Long did not consider these documents as full or as formal as the gravity of the occasion required, and on March 18 he asked for a more explicit statement and a complete history of the controversy. The Japanese then asked to withdraw their first statements and submit others, which was done on the twenty-third. But there was little change in the new memoranda. The request for the President's mediation was withdrawn, but the American Government was asked to transmit the Japanese proposals to Russia, "and kindly negotiate the matter with the Russian Government." And in the terms proposed, one word only was changed: Aniwa Bay would be opened as were the "other ports" in Japan.

Again De Long insisted upon substantial proof of the Japanese claims, and to satisfy him the Foreign Office sent members of their staff to go over all their records with Mr. Portman. They also gave him a copy of the Convention of 1867.[26] After this interview, Portman, in August, drew up a list of eighteen questions for the Japanese to answer in writing, and asked for maps, original letters, documents, or other written or printed proof. The replies, submitted on the twenty-eighth, furnish a valuable summary of this long-standing controversy. The questions were not taken up in the order Portman had arranged them, and only ten were answered; but this was due in part to the confusion in the records consequent on the change in Government at Tokyo. Some questions which could have been answered were, why the Japanese had asked De Long to aid them instead of Parkes or von Brandt, and what forces could be used to protect Aniwa Bay if opened to foreigners, or to support the Japanese claim to Sakhalin.

From this Japanese statement it appears that Count Poutiatine

---

[26] This was described as "Copy of Proposal to Japan by Russia, St. Petersburgh, March 18 [30], 1867, signed by Weletsky, Chief of Asiatic Department, Counsellor of College."

(in 1853–55) had been instructed to negotiate a boundary line, with specific reference to the southern coast of Sakhalin, and Count Muraviev had had similar instructions in 1859; and that after the Convention of 1862, the Russians had proposed a delimitation of the boundary *in situ*. This had resulted instead in the mission to St. Petersburg which had agreed upon the joint occupation Convention of 1867, an arrangement subsequently approved by the Shogun's Government. The Russian Consul at Hakodate had come to Japan to exchange the ratifications of the Treaty of 1858, and he had called himself the Consul for Japan and had been so accepted. The Japanese claimed that their contacts with Sakhalin had begun in 650 A.D., and referred to a history of the island published in 1716–35. The Shogun's Government sent an official to investigate conditions there in 1786, and a trading-post was erected by the daimyo of Matsumai in 1790. In 1792 and again in 1801 officials had been sent there, and colonization encouraged. The first visit of the Russians was reported in 1806. When they had settled at Aniwa Bay, about 1806, the Japanese had protested to Count Poutiatine, who had ordered their removal. Concerning the recent reports that the Russians had fortified the southern coast the Japanese knew nothing definitely.[27]

The Japanese now urged De Long to submit the matter to his Government at the earliest possible moment, fearing the effects of longer delay, and he was on the point of compliance when, on September 14, some officials came to inquire as to the truth of reports printed in the *Japan Herald* that the Russians were preparing to establish a penal settlement on Sakhalin and that the United States would not intervene or mediate in the matter. De Long knew no basis for such reports, but he reminded the Japanese that he had received no formal letter stating that all the facts, so far as they knew them, were in his hands, nor had they supplied him with the requested map. The letter and map were promptly forthcoming, and on the twentieth De Long forwarded

[27] See also Takekoshi, *The Economic Aspects of the History of the Civilization of Japan*, III, 164–69, 177–92, 288–324.

all the documents and the map to Mr. Fish with an indorsement of the Japanese claims and the hope for immediate and favorable action, feeling convinced "that successful action in the premises upon your part will go very far to advance American influence and promote American interests here."[28]

On receipt of this request for mediation, Mr. Fish addressed an appropriate instruction to Mr. Curtin, at St. Petersburg,[29] to which the Russian Government replied unfavorably, on the ground that it would create a precedent for intervention in some other matters by European states.[30] The Russian Government then instructed its Chargé to inform Mr. Fish that it would not be disposed to receive favorably an offer of mediation from the United States, but that if the good offices of the latter could secure the assent of the Japanese to the claims of Russia, it would give the Japanese material interests (*intérêts réels*) and a satisfactory guaranty that the aggressions which the Japanese Government apparently apprehended might follow such a recognition would not take place. De Long was instructed to inquire whether or not the Government would settle the disputed question on such a basis; and should such be the case, he could say that it would afford the President great pleasure to render all the aid in his power in bringing about such an adjustment.[31]

Mr. De Long was annoyed at the Russian position. He

[28] During the controversy between De Long and Portman, which came to a head late in the year, the latter reported to the Department that the first clash had come over the drafting of the above-mentioned dispatch of September 20. Portman had advised De Long against submitting it to the Department, on the ground that the matter had been imperfectly stated and partly misrepresented by the Japanese authorities. The Minister had threatened to suspend him if the dispatch was not promptly prepared according to his manuscript draft (Portman to the Department of State, Yedo, December 20, 1870). In this connection it should be remembered that Portman was personally hostile to De Long, and perhaps resented any kudos which might derive from successful mediation; he was also on bad terms with the Foreign Office because of his previous support of the Shogun and the refusal of the new authorities to confirm his railway concession.

[29] November 11.

[30] Curtin to Fish, December 9. Both inclosed in Instruction No. 51, to De Long, January 17, 1871.

[31] No. 51, January 17, 1871.

thought a perfect reply would be to point out that the American Treaty with Japan differed from those of Europe in this very provision for mediation. But in compliance with his instructions he reported, vaguely, to Terashima, that the Russians had raised some objection to accepting mediation. Pressed for particulars, and unable to refer to the Russian correspondence, he offered the good offices of the President to secure a compromise, and intimated that material advantages, perhaps an indemnity, might be obtained. And when he was asked why the Russians had refused to accept the mediation already offered, he volunteered an explanation that the grounds were purely technical, because Japan had never attempted to deal directly with Russia. The inexperienced diplomat was handling the business very clumsily.

To his surprise—and gratification—he was advised that in January the Japanese had asked the Russian Government to send a Plenipotentiary to meet their Commissioners to adjust and settle the question. This offered a way out of the *impasse*.

From any other than Japanese Authorities this might be considered offensive, but it is so exactly like them that I am not surprised nor offended, but rather gratified, as I think their action furnishes an excellent reason for our Government to decline absolutely in the future to have anything to do with this business, should it be deemed desirable to pursue such a course.[32]

In reply to this dispatch Mr. Fish simply stated that it did not seem necessary to give further instructions. And then he proceeded to give the first of many lessons in diplomacy to the American Representative. In the matter of mediation the President could not act unless both parties to the controversy accepted him as mediator. And in regard to "material interests," the Russians had given no intimation as to what they meant. Mr. Terashima might have inferred, "from your suggestive statement," that a pecuniary indemnity was intended. If an opportunity was presented, De Long was to explain to Terashima that his statement was derived from other sources than the instructions from his Government.[33]

[32] No. 168, March 14, 1871.   [33] No. 78, April 28, 1871.

This attempt of the Japanese to obtain the President's mediation has many significant features. It was the first resort to the mediation clause in the 1858 Treaty made by the Imperial authorities.[34] It furnished an opportunity for the American Minister and his Government to show their good will for Japan, and it indicated a growing expertness on the part of the Japanese Foreign Office. Under ordinary circumstances they would have turned to Sir Harry Parkes for help, but they recognized that mediation on the part of Great Britain would have been unfavorably received by Russia. The United States was the most impartial friend of both parties, and the Treaty of 1858 furnished a sound basis for the appeal. On the other hand, the interpretation by Mr. Fish of the mediation clause was to be helpful in later controversies.

While the Christian deportations and the Sakhalin boundary dispute involved the United States in discussions with certain of the European Powers, they were not matters of importance in the relations between that country and Japan. In fact, the year 1870 was free from any incidents of more than trifling importance. These can be briefly summarized, taking them up in order: (1) matters under discussion between the United States and Japan; (2) matters involving other Powers; (3) claims and concessions; (4) matters of general interest.

The first incident in which the American Minister acted on his own responsibility involved the right of access to the island of Amakusa, near the entrance to Nagasaki harbor. The Treaties of 1858 provided that foreigners might go to any part of the Imperial [Shogun's] domain in the vicinity of the port. Up to December 1869 foreigners had visited Amakusa freely, but then the Governor prohibited all foreigners from going there. De Long's inference was that the English, who were working coal mines on Takashima, a more remote island, had influenced the Japanese to close Amakusa in order to prevent Americans and others from opening competing mines. He considered this an

---

[34] The Shogun's Government had applied in 1863 for Mr. Pruyn's mediation with Great Britain.

abrogation of an undoubted treaty right, and complained to the Japanese Ministers, who first acknowledged that the island was Imperial territory and then stated that they had authorized the order in question and intended to enforce it. He then applied for instructions, believing that a firm but respectful insistence upon this and all other treaty rights might induce the authorities to rescind this objectionable order.[35]

Mr. Fish, in reply, pointed out that it was necessary to ascertain if the island was "imperial domain" and if it was fairly in the vicinity of Nagasaki.

In determining this the Department relies upon your well known firmness in maintaining the just rights of your countrymen on the one hand, and on your sense of justice on the other hand, which will not permit you to claim for this Government more than it is fairly entitled to.

Should the facts be determined in the affirmative he was "firmly but respectfully and without resorting to threats" to demand that the order which excluded Americans from the island be rescinded. And in conclusion he wrote:

The Department is at a loss to understand your request for instructions to insist not only upon this, but upon all other Treaty Rights.

No information has been received here of a violation of other Treaty Rights by orders of the Japanese government. I have no hesitation, however, in saying that if it shall come to your knowledge that such violations take place, you will without waiting instructions from the department take official action to prevent further violation and to secure redress for what may have been done.[36]

On receipt of this instruction De Long wrote the Consul at Nagasaki for more information, and inquired of his colleagues as to their interpretation of the Treaty. Satisfied of the correctness of his position he addressed the Foreign Office on November 27, demanding that the order of exclusion be rescinded, and that orders be sent to the authorities and people at Amakusa not to interfere with or injure American citizens visiting that island. In reply, on December 21, the Japanese Ministers gave a complete refusal. This led De Long to announce, on the twenty-seventh,

[35] No. 62, July 2.   [36] No. 33, September 15.

that he would instruct the Consul at Nagasaki to notify American citizens that they were at liberty to visit Amakusa and that in doing so they would receive the protection of their Government, while he warned the Japanese Government that any attempt to enforce the order of exclusion would bring it into direct and inevitable collision with the authorities of the United States. Such instructions were sent to Nagasaki on January 8, 1871.[37]

On January 22, 1871, De Long reported that he had brought the matter up at a conference of the Foreign Representatives, called for another purpose, and that all but Sir Harry Parkes had approved his action. The latter reserved an opinion until he had heard further from the Japanese authorities. The others had agreed to support De Long at a conference with the Japanese on the twenty-fourth, and von Brandt had assured him that he intended instructing his Consul at Nagasaki in similar terms. De Long had also asked Admiral Rodgers to touch at Nagasaki on his return to China and confer with Mr. Mangum, the Consul, while he had privately advised the latter not to publish the notification to Americans until the Admiral had arrived or he had heard again from De Long, in the event that he should fear the least trouble. Rodgers had suggested that De Long confer with him at Kobe, but smallpox on the "Benicia" had prevented the voyage. De Long further reported that his colleagues believed that many of the Urakami Christians were held as "prisoners in slavery" at Amakusa, and that was the reason why foreigners were forbidden to visit the island.[38]

---

[37] No. 134, January 10, 1871.

[38] No. 139, January 2 (22), 1871. This dispatch, No. 139, is dated January 2, 1871, and is so filed. Its number and contents indicate that it was written after No. 134, of January 10. The correct date is unquestionably January 22. A further complication arises from the dual numbering of these dispatches. De Long continued the numbering of Van Valkenburgh's dispatches in 1869 instead of starting a new series. Thus his first seventeen dispatches were numbered 77, 79–94, while No. 1 was dated January 2, 1870. The Department instructed him to correct this error, and on December 31, 1870, he changed No. 126 to No. 144 (to take up the discrepancy of the seventeen numbered dispatches and one unnumbered sent before sailing from San Francisco). The Department later decided it would be less confusing to retain De Long's numbers for 1869 and 1870, and therefore renumbered those after 126 (144). Hence De Long in

De Long's dispatch of January 10 brought down upon him a sharp reprimand from Mr. Fish. On three counts his conduct was disapproved: he had gone beyond the limitations of his instructions; he had threatened the Japanese Government; and he had issued unauthorized instructions to the Consul at Nagasaki. The latter would receive direct instructions from the Department to notify American citizens to pay respect, for the present, to the order of the Japanese Government excluding them from the Island of Amakusa.[39]

In blissful ignorance of the attitude which the Department would take, De Long plunged into his first battle with the Japanese. On January 29 the Foreign Ministers informed him that permission would be granted foreigners employed by Japanese to visit Amakusa to work coal mines, but De Long would not listen to such a compromise. The same day he received a letter from Admiral Rodgers in which the latter supported the Japanese contention on the ground that the island lay outside a 22.5-mile radius of Nagasaki, which the Admiral considered the equivalent of 10 Japanese *ri*. De Long found, on inquiry, that 24.5 miles was more nearly correct, and he so advised the Admiral in no uncertain terms. On February 2 the matter was discussed, with others, at a conference of the Japanese and Foreign Ministers. The Japanese conceded that the island was Imperial territory when the Treaty was made, but claimed that as the Treaty did not specify islands only the mainland was included. To this De Long replied that as the Treaty did not exclude islands, hence by a fair construction they were included, and his colleagues were unanimous in demanding that the ten-*ri* radius should be allowed in all directions around Nagasaki.[40] This forced the Japanese to

his (renumbered) 139 refers to his No. 52, which, renumbered, was filed as No. 134. The Department was trying to number correctly De Long's early dispatches as late as June 14, 1872 (Instruction No. 130).

[39] No. 62, March 2, 1871. As Mr. Portman was under suspension, De Long had to draft and prepare these dispatches. His unconventional spelling and grammatical construction must account, in part, for Mr. Fish's increasing asperity.

[40] Ten *ri* was the distance within which foreigners could travel around the other open ports. It had not been so specified at Nagasaki.

recede to De Long's contention, that only the islands in the vicinity of Nagasaki be accessible, and they made such an offer. De Long then asked them to withdraw their order, and, in refusing, they asked him to suspend his orders to the American Consul.

I then informed them that this I could not honorably do nor should not, that I had requested the Admiral of the American fleet to repair there to sustain the consul, and that he had gone there; that if one American was arrested by their authorities for visiting Amakusa that I should request Admiral Rogers [*sic*] to at once arrest every Japanese official in Nagasakie [*sic*] and put them in irons on board of his ship.

To his support came his colleagues, and the Japanese finally yielded and agreed to send orders to suspend the prohibition pending negotiations. De Long then, in turn, agreed to request Americans not to visit Amakusa for the time being. Admiral Rodgers, after conference with Consul Mangum at Nagasaki, revised his former opinion, and the breach with De Long was healed. The Minister closed this long dispatch on a note of self-congratulation for having met this test and won.

In that letter [to the Admiral] I told him what I now beg leave to assure you which is that the policy I have adopted in dealing with this people is never to demand anything not clearly right; to follow such demand with all of the explanations and proofs a man would ordinarily use to convince a child; but when after all of this is done my demand is met with sullen and unreasoning refusal as was the case in this instance to have my rights or fight for them if but a pin's worth of consideration is involved.[41]

The only comment of the Department on this achievement was a curt instruction to act upon the instructions of March 2, and in so far as native Christians were concerned to be guided by that of April 18, 1870.[42] This tempest in a teapot suggests the marked difference between the methods of the American Minister and those of the Department of State. It also brings out the readiness of the Foreign Representatives to make use of De Long's

[41] No. 155, February 20, 1871.

[42] No. 69, April 14. De Long referred to this matter in his dispatches of March 16, No. 171, and May 19, No. 193. In the former he reported that although Terashima had stated that orders had been sent to Nagasaki rescinding the prohibition, Mangum had advised him that the Governor had denied receiving such; and in the latter he transmitted a copy of the orders sent.

bellicose demands to insist upon a concession even greater than he had demanded.

It was at this time that the United States, as the only American Power having treaty relations with Japan, became involved in events which were to occasion some little annoyance in later years. Both Hawaii and Peru desired the good offices of the American Representative in Japan, and in both cases the interests at stake were incompatible with American policy. The Kingdom of Hawaii was primarily interested in securing Japanese labor, and if it could have its way that labor would be coolie (indentured) labor. The Republic of Peru, so recently involved in the "Cayalte" case, sought safeguards against any further interference with its Chinese coolie trade. We have seen that the Shogun's Government, in 1867, had refused to negotiate with Van Reed, an American citizen representing Hawaii, because he was a "Merchant Consul," and his conduct in shipping the "Scioto" coolies in violation of Japanese regulations had made him obnoxious to the Imperial Foreign Office.[43] General Van Valkenburgh, early in 1868, had received a commission from the Hawaiian Government to negotiate a treaty, but in the absence of instructions from Washington he had taken no action. In October 1869 the Japanese had sent agents to Hawaii to inquire into the treatment of the Japanese laborers taken there on the "Scioto" in 1868,[44] which showed a commendable interest on the part of the new Government in the welfare of its subjects in foreign lands and met with the approval of the American Government.[45] They returned in March 1870, and although Terashima informed De Long that the Government was well satisfied with their report a very condemnatory statement of conditions in Hawaii was issued in the press of Yokohama. Some 105 Japanese laborers remained under contract, and De Long offered this suggestion to the Department:

The impression exists in the Japanese mind, that the Sandwich Islands are in fact an American Colony; and I now beg respectfully to submit,

---

[43] Hawaii was, however, generously granted most-favored-nation treatment pending treaty negotiations.

[44] No. 75, October 24, 1869.   [45] Instruction No. 8, December 20, 1869.

that if the Hawaiian Government could be induced to free those laborers, and send them back to their homes, while it would avert any difficulty, that may grow out of the bitter feeling above referred to, which unquestionably exists,—such action would be simply just, consistent with our abhorrence of bondage, even in a mild form—and of undoubted benefit to our relations with this country.[46]

A month later he reported additional developments. It seems that when Van Valkenburgh had advised the Japanese to proceed against Van Reed in the American Consular Court they had been on the point of doing so, which led the latter to appear before the American Consul in order to relinquish his American citizenship and declare himself henceforth a Hawaiian subject. It was now reported that the Government had asked Sir Harry Parkes to use his good offices in concluding a Treaty with Hawaii. De Long then took it upon himself to address the Japanese Ministers, insisting upon delay and urging that no action in the matter be taken until the opinion of Mr. Fish was procured. His motive, he assured the Department, was to secure such safeguards that the judicial authority of the American officials in Japan should not be weakened.[47]

No comment was forthcoming on De Long's first dispatch, but the second elicited a very suggestive statement:

In reply, I have to state that I am not aware of the reason which may have actuated my predecessor in omitting to instruct Gen. Van Valkenburg [*sic*] upon the subject of the proposed treaty between Hawaii and Japan. No objection is now perceived to the conclusion of such an instrument, either under the auspices of the British Minister or those of the Minister of the United States. You will, however, give the Japanese Government distinctly to understand that although our citizens in the Sandwich Islands are numerous and some of them hold high office there, this government is not on that account responsible for the policy or for the acts of the government of Hawaii which is as independent of us as the government of Japan itself.

If citizens of the United States who may have been residents of the Sandwich Islands visit Japan and there violate the law, they must not be allowed to do this with impunity merely because of their domicil in those islands. On the contrary it is believed that this government has no option to claim jurisdiction over them, unless they can show that they have been duly naturalized pursuant to the laws of Hawaii.[48]

---

[46] No. 43, April 16, 1870.   [47] No. 51, May 17.   [48] No. 24, June 23.

Peru, on the other hand, followed the correct course of first approaching the State Department. On March 15 its Minister in Washington asked the United States to permit its Ministers in Japan and China to act as Ministers of Peru. Mr. Fish could not grant this request, but he did instruct De Long to attend to any matters which might be intrusted to him by Peru, "so far as this can be done compatibly with other instructions from this Department."[49] The proviso certainly referred to matters arising from the coolie trade. Mr. De Long advised the Japanese Foreign Office in these terms in June.[50]

In this year the Japanese, who had learned much about neutrality in 1868–69, were first called upon to proclaim and enforce it on their part. They were to find that in this, as in many other respects, their hands were not as free as those of the Treaty Powers. The situation was produced by the war between Prussia and France, and it led to acrimonious discussions between the Representatives of these countries, in which all the foreign agents were involved, as well as the inexperienced but well-meaning Japanese Foreign Office. On September 23 a proclamation of neutrality was published in the *Japan Mail,* at Yokohama, but no copy was furnished to the Foreign Representatives. On October 4, a "revised copy" was transmitted, and duly published.[51] On the eleventh, von Brandt met the Representatives of the neutral Powers—Great Britain, the United States, the Netherlands, and Spain—and protested against the conduct of the French corvette "Sinois" in pursuing the North German merchant steamer "Rhine" out of the harbor of Yokohama, for the latter had escaped capture only by returning to her anchorage. The French ship had also fired a gun across the bow of a British bark at the entrance to the bay and forced her to show her colors. Von Brandt also laid before his colleagues certain amendments which he wished to propose to the proclamation of neutrality, such as that merchant ships should be allowed twenty-four hours after leaving a Japanese port before they could be followed by a bel-

[49] No. 15, April 13.   [50] No. 56, June 20.
[51] No. 92, October 10, *F.R., 1870,* p. 188.

ligerent ship, and that the Japanese Government should prohibit the use of its ports by either belligerent as a base of operations. To these principles his colleagues assented, and von Brandt announced that he would at once lay these demands before the Foreign Office in Tokyo. He further stated that if these demands were refused, he would require the immediate removal of the French forces and stores at Yokohama, and the abandonment of their hospital and barracks.[52]

The neutral Representatives believed that M. Outrey should be informed of this proceeding; so they met him in conference on the thirteenth. To their surprise they learned that the first proclamation of neutrality had been objected to by Outrey, that it had been revised in the light of amendments proposed by both Outrey and von Brandt, and that the second proclamation "partook of the nature of an international convention, and was not subject to alteration or change by the Japanese Government without consent of the representatives of the belligerent powers."

This statement led the colleagues to agree that it would be inappropriate for the Japanese Government to alter the proclamation at the dictation of one of the Representatives concerned without the knowledge or consent of the other. They decided to accept the proclamation, with a proviso that it was issued under exceptional circumstances and was not a precedent for the future.[53]

Von Brandt returned that afternoon from Tokyo, and reported that he had secured the desired amendments. He announced that he would insist upon their enforcement and that any deviation or hostile actions by the French would be construed as an insult to his flag and would occasion an immediate attack upon the French ships of war. He now explained that he had left out of the second draft the provisions now inserted because of an agreement between M. Outrey and himself, which, it should be said, was promptly denied by the former. On being informed of von

---

[52] A French garrison had been established at Yokohama since 1864.

[53] De Long had in mind that the British and French both had garrisons and depots at Yokohama and he did not want the terms of the proclamation to form a precedent in case the United States should become involved in war.

Brandt's proceedings, M. Outrey at once notified the Foreign Office that he would not accept the amendments, and protested against their right to amend or alter the proclamation without consulting him. But very late that evening came the letters advising the Representatives that the proclamation had been amended, as von Brandt had desired.

The neutral Ministers again convened on the fourteenth, and tried to persuade von Brandt to make some concession, which he would do only in respect to merchant ships if M. Outrey would accept the second amendment. That night Terashima arrived in Yokohama, filled with regret at the occurrence and eager to do anything to adjust the matter. Parkes and De Long advised him to meet with all the neutral Representatives the next morning, while they would previously confer with M. Outrey and try to secure his acceptance of von Brandt's offer. M. Outrey, however, in view of the way in which von Brandt had obtained the amendments, refused to make the slightest concession. The neutral colleagues could then only advise Terashima to call upon Outrey and von Brandt individually, learn what each demanded, and, if possible, meet their requests. He did so, but he could only report that Outrey was adamant while von Brandt was willing to have the amendments withdrawn if he could obtain a guaranty that the French would not use the ports as a base of supplies. Terashima thought that von Brandt would expect this guaranty from the neutral Representatives.

Such a guaranty the Representatives could not give, and they so informed Terashima, that evening. De Long then withdrew from further discussion of the matter, as he felt the Government could not act or refuse to act without offending one or the other of the belligerents, and he feared that he might be suspected of influencing the action of the Japanese, thus involving his Government in what seemed to be an inevitable misunderstanding.[54]

This incident deserves a place in our narrative because the

[54] No. 102, October 22, 1870. De Long reported on February 16, 1871 (No. 149), that the German bark "Persia" had been pursued from her anchorage at Yokohama by the French corvette "Dupleix." For any loss sustained Germany would hold Japan responsible.

Japanese had to learn the conduct of diplomacy in the school of experience. The precedents which were created in these early days were filed away for use later. And it explains why the Japanese were to make vigorous efforts to procure the evacuation of the British and French garrisons and depots at Yokohama, which were bound to involve them in difficulties should either of these restless Powers become involved in war.[55]

Until the Japanese had promulgated a civil code and set up courts with adequate jurisdiction, the settlement of claims of American citizens against the Japanese Government and its nationals would at times call for diplomatic intervention. And, on the other hand, the Japanese Government had just claims against the United States which were the subject of repeated representations on its part. De Long reported, on July 7, that the claim of Dr. A. M. Vedder, for $3,125 (Mexican), had been paid in full,[56] and on the twelfth that $20,885 (Mexican) had been paid to Walsh, Hall & Company for rice delivered.[57] But the claim of the latter for the redemption of debased *nubus* received in trade caused lengthy complications.[58] The trouble arose from the fact that these coins were not remitted from the firm's agents at Niigata and Hakodate in time to be stamped within the time limit set at Yokohama. A long-drawn-out correspondence ensued, in which the Japanese demanded confirmatory details from the ports and finally denied the force of the evidence submitted. De Long's recommendation to the Department was that an assistant be allowed him who would investigate all such claims and whose decision would guide him in demands upon the Japanese. He also asked for another assistant who would combine the duties of secretary and interpreter to the Legation.[59] An alternative solution would be to have the Consul at Yedo act as Examiner and

---

[55] For the British garrison, cf. *Correspondence with Her Majesty's Minister in Japan respecting British Troops in that Country, 1867 (3831)*.

[56] No. 65.   [57] No. 66.

[58] A third claim of this firm for over $18,000 was pending (No. 106, November 5).

[59] At this time his only assistant held the office of Dutch Interpreter.

Judge of Claims.[60] That the Department paid no attention to this request was perhaps due to his earlier report, in April, that outside of Yokohama there were almost no Americans resident in Japan. At Nagasaki there was an agency of the Pacific Mail Steamship Company and two firms; at Niigata, only the Consular Agent; at Hakodate, the Consul and his two sons; at Kobe, four residents; and at Yedo, four missionaries and three temporary visitors.[61]

Mr. Fish, however, took this opportunity to instruct the American Minister on the policy and practice of his Government in the matter of claims. The Walsh, Hall & Company claim for the redemption of debased coin was deemed "ungracious," although De Long had pressed it. To Mr. Fish it was inconceivable that there were no courts in Japan, as De Long had reported, for the Treaty of 1858 referred to them, and American creditors of Japanese subjects were to find relief there, waiting for diplomatic intervention until the denial of justice was established. "If the Minister will instruct his countrymen on this subject he will be relieved of the duties of an attorney in private controversies."

Claims founded on contract express or implied between the Japanese Government and American citizens had not been regarded as subjects of public intervention. But they had, when the merits of the claim appeared clear, been commended to the attention of diplomatic representatives for the unofficial exertion of their friendly influence to procure an examination and equitable adjustment by the Government concerned.

It was not deemed advisable to ask Congress to provide for an Examiner of Claims in Japan.

The Minister should not be deprived of his full responsibility about urging claims, but it would be well for our Ministers everywhere to refrain from anything like a peremptory presentation of a claim until after it has been examined in this Department, except in cases of urgent emergency. The Government has frequently found itself at quite an advanced stage of the discussion of a doubtful claim, before this Department had any information, or, if any, inadequate information for a judgment upon the case.[62]

60 No. 106, November 5.   61 No. 40, April 10.
62 No. 56, January 21, 1871. An extract is printed in *F.R., 1871,* pp. 584–85.

Against the United States there lay the claim of the British owners of the steamship "Aroostook" for services connected with the search for the survivors of the warship "Oneida." And the Japanese Government was pressing for land rents due for the Legation at Tokyo, the Consulate lot at Hakodate, and the Consulate and hospital lots at Yokohama. De Long reported:

A few days since His Exellency [*sic*] the Chief Minister for Forign [*sic*] Affairs remarked to me: Why is it that you are so prompt in compelling the Japanese Government to pay claims of all kinds to your government and its citizens and yet you will never pay any claims that are present against your government? This remark although made with seeming good nature carried with it a shameful truth that put the blush upon me. . . . . To this I could make no reply except to admit that this was so; to attribute it to negligence and to promise again to submit to my government their request for payment of these rents. In conformity with my promise, and in renewal of my unanswered despatch upon this subject of the 27th of last December, No. 88: I respectfully repeat, that rents are due these people for these premises. That common justice and fair dealing requires us to surrender the various pieces of property held by the Government of the United States back to the Japanese; or to pay them their demands for rent.

And he urged that Congress be asked to appropriate the necessary sums.[63]

It is generally believed that the first attempt of the Japanese to introduce railways dates from the unsuccessful efforts of Horatio Nelson Lay, an Englishman, who secured a concession for a line from Tokyo to Osaka, with a branch to Yokohama, in 1870. This carried with it a loan of £1,000,000, which was needed to liquidate the pressing debts of the new Government. Lay's unauthorized proceedings in London brought about the repudiation of the agreement.[64] But as a matter of fact a concession for a line from Tokyo (Yedo) to Yokohama was granted to Mr. Portman in the last days of the Shogunate (1867). The fact that the Shogunate had given valuable contracts to French engineers, and had employed a French military and an English naval mission, as well as employed Englishmen in the new lighthouse department, was the basis for the American official's

[63] No. 119, December 14, 1870.   [64] Black, *Young Japan*, II, 279–82.

request. The Imperial Government refused to confirm the concession, and admitted that the concession in question had since been awarded to Lay and the capitalists he purported to represent. Portman tried to secure a confirmation by direct appeals to the new Foreign Ministers, in 1869, but Van Valkenburgh left the dispute for De Long's attention. The latter engaged in a lengthy correspondence with the Japanese Ministers in 1870, without result. Finally, in August, he transmitted the entire correspondence to the Department.[65] One detail is of interest. The Japanese Ministers distinctly assured him that Lay was introduced and recommended to them by Sir Harry Parkes, and De Long was of the opinion that Parkes's standing with the new régime was so influential that the Japanese felt constrained to cancel the prior concession to Portman in order to meet Parkes's wishes. Sir Harry, in a public statement, denied that he had used his influence to further Lay's schemes.[66]

A second concession which De Long supported was for a submarine cable between Yokohama and San Francisco.[67] While no comment was made by the Department concerning Portman's railway concession, it did warn De Long, in regard to the cable, that while his efforts to establish such communication were approved, "the policy of this Government is opposed to the grant of exclusive rights or of monopoly privileges to any line,"[68] and it forwarded a copy of the proposed concession to Mr. Cyrus W. Field, of Atlantic-cable fame, for his examination.[69]

From year to year a considerable portion of the dispatches from Tokyo had to deal with matters arising under the extra-territorial jurisdiction of the United States. Even to enumerate

[65] No. 73, August 8.

[66] Parkes reported the Lay concession in his dispatch of April 21, 1870. He stated that toward the close of 1869 he had been informed by the Japanese Government that it proposed to construct a railway between Yedo and Kyoto. The proposal had received much discussion in the Council. He did not intimate that he had supported Lay [*Japan. No. 3 (1870)*, p. 95].

[67] No. 63, July 2; No. 110, November 20.

[68] No. 34, September 21.

[69] No. 54, January 20, 1871.

these cases, and the issues involved, would require a volume.[70] Occasionally, however, questions were raised which brought out the difficulties involved in such a treaty right, and these will be briefly referred to from time to time. The first case that perplexed De Long was a decision of the Consular Court at Nagasaki to deport Elias Tolman to China.[71] The Department, while approving this action, on the facts as reported, added:

A doubt, however, may reasonably exist as to the propriety of sending him to China, whither it appears he was sent, and where his presence is likely to be as obnoxious as it was in Japan.[72]

In reply, De Long inquired how a sentence of exile or deportation was to be carried out, for no foreign country would receive the offenders, and it was doubtful if the Department would approve sending them to California. He asked for explicit instructions.[73] These he received, but hardly in the terms anticipated, for the Department replied that the United States did not approve the banishment of American convicts from Japan to the United States or to China.[74] The inference, which it would not have been safe to act upon, was that it approved banishment to some other land. De Long then suggested that if deportation was illegal, the provision for its exercise should be eliminated from the rules and regulations for the Consular Courts recently issued by him.[75]

---

[70] For a general discussion, see Scidmore, *Outline Lecture on the History, Organization, Jurisdiction, and Practice, of the Ministerial and Consular Courts of the United States of America in Japan.* Extraterritorial cases which were the subject of diplomatic correspondence in 1870 were Hoeflich *vs.* Myers, No. 29, March 14; Einstein *vs.* Lemuel Lyon (U.S. Consul) and H. W. Denison (Marshal) at Yokohama, No. 30, March 21, No. 52, May 20; and No. 67, July 16; G. W. Lake *vs.* W. P. Mangum (Consul) and D. L. Moore (former Consul) at Nagasaki, No. 80, August 21.

Arising from the extraterritorial jurisdiction was the question of registering American firms at the Consulates. The registration of a German firm was canceled after protest from the German Chargé (No. 70, August 2). De Long's action was approved, and the Department held that the registry of firms or commercial houses at the Consulates was inadmissible (No. 36, October 20). New regulations, applying only to individuals, were issued in November (No. 113, November 26).

[71] No. 4, January 4.   [72] No. 12, March 22.   [73] No. 58, June 21.
[74] No. 31, September 10, *Serial Number 1440, Doc. No. 25,* p. 39.
[75] No. 108, November 20.

However, he issued the necessary instructions to all the American Consuls.[76]

We have referred above to De Long's attempt to draft and put into operation a code of regulations for the United States Courts in Japan. On his arrival at his post he found that no regulations had ever been framed and that those in force in China had generally been followed without formal adoption. He set about remedying this defect, but before submitting his draft he asked for instructions as to how he should harmonize the Act of June 22, 1860, under which these courts were constituted, with the Constitution of the United States, for he had grave doubts of the constitutionality of the regulations previously issued in China. He had special reference to the failure of the Act of 1860 to provide grand and petit juries, which were guaranteed under the Constitution in criminal cases and in civil cases involving more than twenty dollars.[77] In reply Mr. Fish gave this cryptic advice: "it is not deemed wise to listen to doubts upon questions which long usage has settled."[78]

Undeterred by this lack of encouragement, De Long went forward, and, on the basis of the Civil Code of California, drafted an elaborate Code of Regulations, of which some 267 clauses dealt with civil cases, and twenty-five with criminal. This was to be followed by a Code of Criminal Procedure and codes for the settlement of estates and for bankruptcy; but he postponed drafting these until Mr. Fish had passed upon his first effort. As the approval of all the American Consuls in Japan was obtained, this body of regulations came into effect, subject to revision by Congress.[79]

Mr. Fish replied that he would lay the Regulations before Congress, but he ventured to point out six objectionable articles

[76] No. 113, November 26.   [77] No. 46, April 20.   [78] No. 20, June 10.

[79] No. 87, September 20. The manuscript copy, transmitted with No. 87, fills Vol. XV of Dispatches from Japan. The printed copy, transmitted in No. 96, October 19, was laid before Congress, and may be found in *Serial Number 1440, Doc. No. 25*, pp. 2–39. De Long reported (No. 141, January 28, 1871) that he drew these regulations "in some haste, with no books, no assistance, and whilst somewhat otherwise engaged with diffusing duties."

in the draft, among others their references to a federal divorce law and to the common law.[80] In due time Mr. Fish submitted the draft to the President, for revision by Congress, and suggested for the consideration of the legislature the propriety of limiting the powers of Ministers to make decrees and regulations, in the sense that it was limited in the Consular Regulations of the Department, "to acts necessary to organize and give efficiency to the courts created by the acts."[81]

In a later instruction, Mr. Fish pointed out that the confirmation by Congress was desirable to resolve any question as to the validity of certain of De Long's regulations.[82]

Another instance of De Long's lack of training and experience was brought out when Sir Harry Parkes discussed with him a complaint which had come from the British Consul at Hakodate against Mr. E. E. Rice, the American Consul at that port. It seems that the latter had failed to render aid to the former to recover an alleged deserter from the British ship "Southland," at Yokohama, who was then on the American steamer "Augusta." De Long agreed with Sir Harry, and wrote a letter of reproof to Rice.[83] The Department took occasion to inform him:

that there is no law or treaty authorizing the surrender of sailors in such a case, and Mr. Rice is not therefore in error in refusing but if the British authorities as a matter of comity are willing in such cases to surrender American seamen there is no objection to the surrender by Consuls of the United States of British seamen in return.[84]

[80] No. 48, December 20, *Serial Number 1440, Doc. No. 25,* pp. 40–42.

[81] President Grant to the Senate and House of Representatives, January 27, 1871, *ibid.,* p. 1.

[82] No. 83, May 20, 1871.   [83] No. 86, September 20.

[84] No. 39, November 5. De Long was occasionally involved in difficulties with the Department because of his ignorance of the regulations. Thus he appointed General Paul Frank as Vice-Consul at Hiogo and Osaka (No. 95, October 19), and he was instructed that such appointments were made on the nomination of the Consul, with the Minister's approval in advance (No. 42, December 6). Japan at first refused to accept General Frank but finally recognized him (No. 143, February 12, 1871). When Mr. Rice, Consul at Hakodate, appointed the British Consul at Niigata to act as Commercial Agent for the United States there, De Long refused to approve (No. 115, December 12). The Department approved his decision but again pointed out that the Consul had the right to nominate, while the Minister approves (No. 57, January 30, 1871).

And on an earlier occasion the Minister, in an excess of zeal, had brought upon himself loud complaints from the British community. The U.S.S. "Oneida" was sunk in a collision with the Peninsular and Oriental steamer "Bombay," at the entrance to the bay of Tokyo, on January 24, 1870. The failure of the "Bombay" to stand by and rescue the survivors, while explained by the Captain as due to his belief that so slight a collision could not have been serious, caused no little recrimination. De Long personally took part in the proceedings of the Naval Court of Inquiry which was held at the British Consulate, and his vigorous interposition aroused much unfavorable comment.[85] Dickins alleges that the charge was deliberately made that the English steamer had purposely run down the American vessel.[86] Captain Eyre was acquitted of blame for the collision, but his certificate was suspended for six months for failing to stand by. De Long, who had chartered the "Aroostook" to search for survivors, was commended for his promptness and energy, and his presence at the inquiry was approved.[87] The Russian corvette "Veadnuck" also rendered De Long valuable assistance.

Finally, the acrimonious dispute between De Long and his only staff assistant, Portman, must be alluded to. The charges and counter charges, which fill the correspondence, need not be evaluated at this late day. Perhaps there was much to be said on both sides, but some little weight must be attached to the fact that Portman had served acceptably under Harris, Pruyn, and Van Valkenburgh, while De Long managed to quarrel with almost every American official in Japan. The quarrel, between men of such different temperaments, came to a head in September over the drafting of a dispatch on the Sakhalin mediation. De Long then demanded the removal of the archives from Portman's residence to the Legation at Yokohama and, when compliance was not immediate, sent Denison, the Marshal of the Consulate, to

[85] No. 17, February 1; No. 23, February 22; No. 25, February 23; Black, *op. cit.*, II, 284–86.

[86] Dickins, *op. cit.*, II, 159.

[87] No. 14, April 9.

remove them forcibly.[88] The archives, he reported, were in a state of confusion, and the filing was long in arrears. De Long also learned for the first time that Portman's commission was not as secretary but as Dutch interpreter, and he commented upon the latter's inability to help him in conferences with the Japanese.[89] He therefore asked for his dismissal. While the Department regretted this controversy, it instructed De Long to recommend another interpreter if he so desired.[90]

In the meantime the dispute had taken a new form, involving the title to a lot in Yokohama which had been set aside for the Legation and which Portman alleged had been released to him by Van Valkenburgh. In the course of this dispute, De Long recommended the suspension of Portman as interpreter, and that his pay be withheld from September 16.[91] As Portman would not surrender the title deed to De Long, the latter sent the Marshal with a writ of suspension (December 3), and issued an order of arrest.[92]

Mr. Portman's long letter to the Department, of December 20, ascribed De Long's proceedings to his "reckless craving after sensation." But it was not a pretty situation, this dispute between the American Minister and his only staff officer.[93]

A very promising development during the year was the increasing number of Japanese students, travelers, and officials who visited the United States. On August 21 De Long transmitted

[88] H. W. Denison later served as Adviser to the Japanese Foreign Office, 1880–1914.

[89] No. 103, October 22. Portman's commission as interpreter to the Legation was dated June 27, 1861.

[90] No. 45, December 13. On October 12 (No. 94), De Long had asked for the appointment of James Russell Hiltz as a student interpreter. No such appointment was provided for by law (Instruction No. 44, December 12).

[91] No. 111, November 22. [92] No. 122, December 22.

[93] The suspension of Portman was approved in Instruction No. 55, January 20, 1871. In response to Portman's complaint, of December 20, 1870, Mr. Fish replied that the latter's statement did not differ materially from De Long's; that the suspension had been approved; and that if De Long now failed in his political or ministerial duties to Portman, as a private citizen, the latter could appeal to the Department; and if he failed in his judicial duties, the law gave Portman remedies (March 4, 1871).

the thanks of the Japanese students at Annapolis for their kind treatment, thanks which had come to him through the proper channels.[94] The next month he sent on a letter of introduction for Asuma Takahiso Katsu-no-Miya, a member of the Imperial House who with a suite of eight young noblemen was proceeding to the United States for education.[95] In December he reported that Ito Hirobumi, Second Assistant Minister of Finance, was about to visit America to study the financial system,[96] and a little later the Government requested permission for Katsu Koroku to enter Annapolis.[97]

[94] No. 81.   [95] No. 84, September 20; unofficial, September 22, 23.
[96] No. 114, December 9.

[97] No. 120, December 17. De Long had not been at his post six months before he applied for a brief leave of absence (No. 49, May 7). But he also took the precaution of seeking the good offices of his friend, Senator Stewart, of Nevada, and it was on his request that the leave was granted (notation on De Long's No. 55, June 20). A sixty days' leave to commence on or before September 15 was allowed him (Instruction No. 25, July 11). De Long did not take the leave within the time set, and he renewed the request on September 22 (No. 90). This was followed by a statement that he would not avail himself of it, if granted, at the present time, because "affairs are wearing a very threatening aspect" (No. 93, October 11). The Department, on October 25, granted him sixty days leave exclusive of passage to and fro (No. 37, October 25). But this second permission was not availed of (No. 124, December 22).

CHAPTER XVII

JAPAN SEEKS REVISION OF THE TREATIES
1871 [1]

THE SHADOW of the "Amakusa" incident lay over the American Representative as the new year dawned. This may in part explain the pessimistic tone of De Long's dispatch of January 19, one of the longest of his efforts and one which portrays clearly his convictions at the time. As it has never been printed it deserves a rather full treatment. He began:

I have the honor to report that universal peace, universal discontent and increasing poverty is a correct summary of the internal condition of the Japanese Empire at present.

The desire for foreign luxuries had led the people to yield up the accumulated wealth of centuries, without thought for its replacement.

Ambitious and childlike they have ventured into every field; especially into the one of making their nation a great naval, military and commercial power.

They had purchased "at the most ruinous prices" ironclad and wooden warships, merchant steamers, the most modern arms and munitions. They had constructed a mint at Osaka, which

forms a most striking illustration of the mistaken and hasty efforts these people have been advised into and are making to reach national greatness.

To meet the immense outlay of money for such purposes they had been driven to the adoption of various expedients. They first debased their coins, then issued a flood of paper money, then

---

[1] The dispatches are numbered 132–264 (De Long), and 1–11 (Chargé Shepard); of these 144, ten were printed in *F.R., 1871*. The instructions are numbered 50–127, but No. 75 was not transmitted; of these 77, two were printed in *F.R., 1871*.

borrowed five million dollars abroad; and now the Government actually engaged in trade. The latter took the form of farming privileges, which led

into constant violations of the treaty rights of foreign powers; generally trifling in each individual case but extremely annoying and amounting in the aggregate to gross violations.

Among these violations of freedom of trade, which caused the foreigners to besiege their Representatives with complaints of every nature, were the duty collected on goods brought into the treaty ports for sale, the tax levied on Japanese employed by foreigners, the passport tax on Japanese traveling on foreign steamers, the system of special inspection and duty on freight shipped on such steamers, and the privilege granted to certain Japanese to deal in silk, silkworm eggs, and tea and to attend auction sales by foreigners. However, "the difficulty of correcting these grievances lies mainly in the difficulty of proving them," for the Japanese would not testify against their rulers.

The remedy for this state of affairs, which De Long proposed, was to insist, when the revision of the Treaties took place in 1872, that the whole Empire be unreservedly thrown open to foreign intercourse and trade.

Until then the boundaries of treaty ports and the ignorant guards at their gates will continue as they do now to paralyze trade, more deeply enslave their own people, prevent the spread of Christianity and make men martyrs for their faith. That time is near. Action should be taken and success is sure, for the Japanese have already learned that they cannot resist what the great powers unite in demanding neither will they do so. I am satisfied that this movement would be aided by all of the support that the people and many of the Daimios could safely give to it.

De Long then reported how he had pointed out to a daimyo the way in which he might bring prosperity to his people by opening all his ports to foreign trade and by putting his soldiers to work, at least for part of their time, raising stock and working mines.

For the present not much could be accomplished, because the Foreign Representatives could not agree as to what was best. De Long, for his part, was under instructions not to ask for the appointment of any of his nationals by Japan, and his country could not compete with European nations in the sale of manufactured goods there.

I have a very simple line of duty to follow and that is to see that my countrymen enjoy all of the rights guaranteed to them by the treaties; with no reason to fear a loss of favor with the Japanese authorities if I am exacting upon this subject.

But those of his colleagues who were seeking the patronage of the Government, trying to make loans, to procure employment for their countrymen, and to secure all possible trade for their own people, naturally would prefer to tolerate a small wrong rather than risk a greater advantage.

Complete co-operation being impossible when such a diversity of views and interests exists as does here amongst foreign representatives, I would suggest the propriety of a slight relaxation of that rule so earnestly enjoined upon my predecessors by Mr. Seward and which the instructions that I received when entering upon the discharge of my duties entails upon me. If I could read my instructions so as to co-operate when co-operation could be obtained but to none the less insist upon a right that was plain even when no co-operation could be obtained I believe that I could serve my country's interests better in the future than I have done in the past.

De Long then developed at some length his sympathy for the former Shogun and his distrust of the new régime, and he stressed the fact that the anti-foreign, anti-Christian party was in the saddle. Without mentioning Sir Harry Parkes, he charged that the influence which encouraged, advised, and made successful that "direful revolution" now palliated and excused its shortcomings in order to control its patronage.

With the overthrow of the Tycoon, America's prestige in Japan went down, for with him into exile went all of those rulers whose minds first imbibed impressions of foreign power and wisdom from the shadows of Perry's fleet and the wise counsels of our first Minister, Mr. Harris. Since then no exhibition of our power or greatness has ever been made in these seas whilst other nations have carefully made displays of theirs. Therefore it is not to be wondered at if America holds but a low rank in Japanese estimation; but this I consider as but an immaterial consideration by the side of the greater ones that I have mentioned. The cabinets of the great powers can open Japan in 1872 to civilization by concerted action.

Without such action it must be considered as indefinitely postponed, and millions of people, naturally brave, charitable, and kind, who pant for freedom, must remain enslaved in a thraldom of physical and mental servitude of the most revolting nature. A servitude rendered worse by such foreign relations as Japan now has than if it had none at all for as I have shown the wants and consequently the exactions of the titled classes have been increased which has produced a corresponding degree of severity in the slavery and serfdom of the masses.

I submit that no line should be allowed to be drawn upon this land beyond which the light of Christianity and civilization may not be shed, when simple unity of demand will at once strike such a barrier down.

And in conclusion, De Long reported that rebellion was in the air, and he believed it would occur the next spring. The daimyos, it seemed, resented the ascendancy of the kuge (court nobles), "a landless, portionless, powerless lot of drones in the political hive," who filled all the headships of the various Departments of State and, as members of the Council of State, formed an impassable circle between the daimyos and the Throne. The success of such a rebellion depended upon whether or not the discontented could agree upon the distribution of positions following a return of the old order.[2]

While De Long was incorrectly informed in some particulars, extravagant in some statements, and inaccurate as a forecaster of events, it is important for us to know the kind of information he was sending to the Department of State. By this time, however, Mr. Fish and his assistants had learned to discount De Long's opinions. In a brief reply Mr. Fish stated that he would take the dispatch into consideration, but

meanwhile you will observe the existing instructions on the subject of co-operation of the American Representative with those of other Powers in Japan.[3]

There was to be no withdrawal from the co-operative policy of Seward. Happily the enlightened conduct of the new régime (in the year which saw the abolishment of feudalism) caused De Long to modify his views as the months passed.

---

[2] No. 136, January 19, 1871. De Long stated: "The question of making public certain portions of this dispatch I submit entirely to your discretion." The quotations above and in the following pages have been edited to correct De Long's unconventional spelling and punctuation.

[3] No. 63, March 2.

If the later practice of confining a dispatch to a single topic had been followed by De Long, he would have divided his No. 136 into at least three dispatches, which could have been indexed as "political," "Treaty revision," and "the co-operative policy."[4] Of the three subjects, Treaty revision was now to come forward on the eve of the year when the existing Treaties might be revised. The first proposal for revision, as we have seen, came from the Japanese in 1869.[5] In January 1871, De Long thought of revision only as a means of opening the entire Empire to foreign intercourse and trade. That the Japanese might have other notions did not occur to him.

On May 16 he discussed the matter again. At this time both Sir Harry Parkes and Baron von Brandt were about to go home on short leave, and each would travel across America. They would doubtless call upon Mr. Fish and, if he desired it, discuss the subject of revision. For the Secretary's information De Long had gathered all the views he could from the Japanese Ministers and his colleagues, and he inclosed a memorandum drawn up by von Brandt and one given by Mr. Terashima, one of the Ministers for Foreign Affairs, to Sir Harry Parkes. The latter, De Long surmised, had been prepared by Sir Harry in the first instance. He was also very happy to report that, in an unofficial interview, Lord Iwakura had agreed with De Long that Japan should be opened freely to trade and settlement like the other nations with which Japan had treaties. Iwakura he considered "a man of vastly superior ability and power to the Ministers for Foreign Affairs." He also surmised that Sir Harry would try to persuade his Government, with the support of France, Holland, and America, to postpone again the Shimonoseki indemnity payment.[6] This would strengthen not only Sir Harry's influence in Japan but also the Imperial credit and would aid the British loan and railway undertaking. De Long was by no means in favor of

---

[4] This suggests the difficulty of using the "Diplomatic Register" (an index to the dispatches) in the Department of State, where an attempt is made to summarize each dispatch in a line or two.

[5] *Supra,* chap. xv.   [6] This was based on articles in the *Japan Mail.*

such a concession unless some American advantage would accrue. Without waiting for instruction he had given notice to Japan that the United States would ask for a revision of the Treaty on July 4, 1872, for the notice had to be given one year in advance.[7]

The two memoranda transmitted by De Long are of significance as indicating the views of certain of the interested parties on the eve of the struggle for Treaty revision. Von Brandt's memorandum, which must have been hastily drafted or copied, for the twelfth point is omitted, dealt with the extension of treaty rights.[8] It may be summarized as follows:

1. Revision of the tariff, on the basis of five per cent, or "the most advantageous course," the maintenance of the existing duties.

2. Substitution of a tonnage due for the present entrance fee.

3. Lighthouse and harbor dues to be based on tonnage. Provided the management of the funds and the supervision of lights and harbors be left entirely in the hands of the Japanese, or of an international commission to be paid by the Japanese and composed of an American, English, French and German member. Harbor Masters to be appointed by this commission.[9]

4. Right of travel and trade in the interior. Consular passports to be introduced (to be refused to missionaries if the Japanese Government insists).

5. Foreign ships to be allowed to transport Japanese goods between opened and unopened ports, on payment of a license fee to meet the expenses of Japanese Custom House officers sent with them.

6. The Mexican dollar to be legal tender if the new monetary system should not prove beneficial or efficient.

7. The ten-*ri* treaty port limit at Nagasaki to be demanded.[10]

8. Permission to foreigners to acquire real property, within two or three *ri* of the open ports, and perhaps in some of the silk-growing provinces.

[7] No. 191, May 16. The notice was given verbally on May 5. On June 30 a formal notice was presented by the Japanese Ministers (No. 211, July 4, *F.R., 1871*, p. 595). The Japanese notes were presented to the Treaty Powers on June 30 because, under the most-favored-nation clause, revision might be demanded on July 1, 1872, under the British Treaty.

[8] Of von Brandt, De Long wrote: "He is a gentleman with many of whose views I fully coincide, and who can and will willingly explain most matters with which I have been connected here that you may not fully understand from my despatches" (No. 191, May 16).

[9] This was designed to curb the influence of the British in lighthouse and harbor administration. Cf. Black, *Young Japan*, II, 287.

[10] See *supra,* chap. xvi.

9. The right of the Foreign Ministers, either singly or jointly with the Japanese authorities, to impose taxes upon their countrymen for municipal purposes, and of the foreigners to superintend the expenditure of these monies, as well as to regulate jointly with the Japanese authorities the internal affairs of the foreign settlements.

10. Drawbacks to be introduced, within twelve months as in China.

11. The lower duty (*bansha*) enjoyed by the Chinese at Nagasaki to be introduced at all the ports, or this privilege to be abolished there.[11]

12. [Omitted.]

13. Rivers to be opened to foreign steamers for a certain distance.

14. Interior custom houses between the foreign and Japanese settlements to be abolished, as well as all other taxes imposed to favor trading monopolies.

15. The Christian question to be left entirely alone.

16. Establishment of a mixed court.

In this list of *desiderata,* which would have enlarged considerably the treaty rights of the foreigners, the only points which would have pleased the Japanese were those affecting Christianity and the missionaries, and these were negative—a willingness to refrain from pressing for privileges not already accorded.

Terashima's memorandum, which was presented by Sir Harry Parkes at a conference of the Foreign Representatives on May 13, if it really originated with him and not with Sir Harry as De Long intimated, represented merely a starting-point, from which the Japanese had already advanced when negotiations began in Washington the next year:

1. The standardization of all treaty texts, preferably according to the recent Austrian Treaty [1869].

2. Tonnage dues in place of clearance and entrance fees. Lighthouse dues to be provided for.

3. Indemnification of the Government for expenses incurred in relieving shipwrecked crews and saving property.

4. Revision of the article in the Treaty of 1866 which allowed daimyos' retainers to trade freely with foreigners.

5. Revision of the article prohibiting the importation of opium.

6. Standardization of the terms used for the titles of sovereigns, and elimination of the term Tycoon Denka.

7. Trade regulations to be made more definite.

8. The Treaties to be made reciprocal. At present they applied only to

[11] Paske-Smith, *Western Barbarians in Japan and Formosa in Tokugawa Days, 1603–1868,* pp. 197–99.

foreigners coming to Japan, and in return only granted the right to establish a Japanese diplomatic agent at the foreign capitals.

9. Reservation of the coasting trade to Japan.

10. Revision of the tariff.

11. Regulation of the municipalities at the open ports.

That the Department was not satisfied with this memorandum
is evident from the instruction of September 19, which directed
De Long to ascertain, if possible, the changes desired by the Japanese Government, and to submit his own views as to what might
be advantageous to the United States.[12] This he was able to do
in person, for on December 23 he sailed from Yokohama in
company with Lord Iwakura and his mission to the Treaty
Powers.

The first enlargement in the terms outlined in the Terashima
memorandum came in August, when Japan proposed the negotiation of an extradition Treaty with the United States.[13] The
Department paid no attention to this request, expecting, no doubt,
to have it considered at the time of Treaty revision.

Aside from the question of revision, two other incidents during the year involved the co-operative policy. The first arose from
the attempted assassination of two British subjects, Dallas and
Ring, teachers in the Government College, in Tokyo, on January
14.[14] The Ministers for Foreign Affairs promptly notified De
Long, and in his reply, on the fifteenth, after stating that he was
convinced "of the utter insecurity of foreigners, even within the
treaty limits of the open ports of your Empire," he suggested the
only way to prevent such crimes, which was the prohibition of
the carrying of arms within the treaty limits, except by officials,
soldiers, and officers on duty. At a conference of the Foreign
Representatives, on the seventeenth, it was agreed to recommend
disarming throughout the Empire, and De Long forwarded such
a proposal on the twentieth.[15]

[12] No. 107.   [13] No. 232, August 21.

[14] Black, *op. cit.*, II, 324, states that the attack occurred on the twelfth, but
Adams, *The History of Japan*, II, 235, gives the evening of the thirteenth. In
the United States documents the name Ring is repeatedly given as King, owing
to difficulty in deciphering the dispatches and inclosures.

[15] No. 137, January 20, *F.R., 1871*, pp. 582–84.

The Japanese Ministers, in reply, pointed out the social significance of the sword, but said that they would investigate the right of every man in Tokyo to wear this weapon, and that samurai committing offenses would be arrested. The cogency of this letter caused De Long to report "they have recently made very rapid progress, or otherwise have foreign advisers and excusers."[16] The Department must have viewed De Long's precipitate action with misgivings, for he was informed

that the interference of an American Minister in such a case should be confined to co-operative action with his colleagues, which it is assumed was the case in this instance.[17]

The second case was of far more importance, for it involved the whole fabric of extraterritorialty. Early in January the Japanese Ministers had requested the Foreign Representatives to put in force a "game law" at the treaty ports. At the request of his colleagues, De Long drew up such a law, only to find that what was desired was a law to prohibit hunting by foreigners in temple-groves, castle-moats, and on game preserves, and to prohibit the use of firearms in cities and near dwellings. The Representatives then asked for an exact statement of what was desired, and the Ministers outlined the regulations they proposed, which called for the payment for damage to crops, and for the arrest of offenders by Japanese policemen, who would conduct them to the proper Consul.

De Long suggested that the Japanese promulgate a law of this nature, with a penal clause in it, and that then the Foreign Representatives should notify their people and instruct their consular officers to enforce it. But to this Sir Harry Parkes replied "that British subjects could only be tried and punished in Japan for

[16] No. 152, February 16, *ibid.,* p. 585.

[17] No. 64, March 2. De Long reported, on May 20 (No. 194), that two Japanese soldiers had been tried and executed for this assault. Echizen and Tosa petitioned that officials might lay aside the two swords, and it was granted, except with ceremonial dress (Black, *op. cit.,* II, 320). In 1873 the samurai might lay aside their swords, and in 1876 it was made compulsory. The action was a part of the general program for the abolition of feudalism, and cannot be attributed to foreign suggestions.

violation of British law," and he called De Long's attention to the fact that such was the rule with all other foreigners. In this light De Long interpreted the fourth article of the Treaty of June 17, 1857. Parkes then proposed to issue regulations of his own, and De Long, following his lead, submitted a draft for the approval of Mr. Fish. De Long wrote to Fish:

This matter again brings squarely before us the necessity for Congress to legislate generally for our people here, or vest the power with the representatives to make regulations, and give them the force of law until passed upon by Congress.

You are aware that we have but little Federal legislation regulating mere municipal matters, defining crimes, or providing punishments for many offenses. We have no common law on the subject; but have left each State to regulate these matters for itself. I therefore find myself unable to help these authorities, to prevent these mean wrongs that foreigners here occasionally engage in; such as shooting birds and hares in temple-groves, burial-grounds, &c., and shooting ducks and geese in castle-moats, and in a hundred other ways outraging Japanese ideas of civility and decency, besides imperilling themselves and the peace of each community. This is but a fair illustration of the necessities that almost daily arise for some legislation for the government of our people in Japan.[18]

The regulations which Sir Harry proposed to issue were based upon Sections 85 and 96 of the Orders in Council of March 9, 1865, and, as such, would have to be approved by one of Her Majesty's Principal Secretaries of State.[19] They defined, as offenses, the practices complained of by the Japanese, and on conviction before a British Consul or other court the penalty would be imprisonment up to one month, or a fine not to exceed $100, or both. Although the penalties might be considered slight, and no provision was made for damage to crops, Sir Harry no doubt felt that he had co-operated generously with the Japanese. But the difficulty, which here arose for the first time, was as to the method followed. A study of the early Treaties, on which the right of extraterritoriality was founded, affords convincing evidence that the Japanese surrendered only the right to try and punish foreign offenders. There is no evidence that either in the

[18] No. 162, March 8, *F.R., 1871*, pp. 586–88.
[19] *British and Foreign State Papers, 1864–65*, pp. 136–75.

minds of the Japanese or the foreign negotiators there was an intent to set aside the laws of Japan. But Sir Harry, and the other foreign diplomats, exercised these extraterritorial powers according to laws or rules laid down by their own governments. Thus Sir Harry found his powers defined by the Orders in Council of 1865, rather than by the Treaties. These Orders (in turn based on the statutes of 6–7 Victoria, cap. 80, and cap. 94) defined crimes as those which would be so considered under British law, or which might be so defined by regulations issued by the Minister under these Orders. Hence the violation of Japanese law was no crime, unless it involved the violation of a British law or a regulation duly issued by the British Minister. So, through the years, the Japanese Government, supported by the American Government and its Ministers, appealed to the Treaties in support of their contention that Japanese laws must be respected in Japan; but the British (and later the German) Minister could not go beyond the Orders or Decrees which defined their powers.

As this was the first time such a question had come before him, Mr. Fish made it the subject of a carefully reasoned instruction, which was to serve as a precedent in the Department for many years:

In reply I have to say that the mode of action originally proposed by you, viz; that the Japanese Government should promulgate the law and that the foreign representatives should notify it to their people and instruct their Consular officers to enforce it, seems to me preferable to that recommended by the Minister of Great Britain. The following is a precedent for the course proposed by you.

On the 1st of June, 1868, Mr. Williams, then Chargé d'Affaires in China, decreed as a regulation which should have the force of law in the Consular Courts, a prohibition by the Chinese Government of the use of a certain channel of the Yangtsze river by steamboats. The British Minister adopted the same line of conduct. My predecessor Mr. Seward, referring to the regulation promulgated by Mr. Williams, in an instruction to Mr. Browne, February 9, 1869, remarked, "that this regulation, as a notification to citizens of the United States of the consequences of an order of the Chinese Government made in the exercise of the police of its internal waters is reasonable and necessary for the security of navigation and is approved. . . . . It is certainly judicious to avoid, as I understand Mr. Williams has avoided, the assertion of a power in the Minister to make that unlawful which was not forbidden by the laws of the United States or of China."

The reference of the British Minister to the 4th Article of our treaty of 1854 [1857], to show that Americans can be punished in Japan only for violation of American law is not conclusive. The article provides that Americans committing offences in Japan—it is not in terms declared whether the offence is one against Japanese law or American law—shall be tried by our Consuls and *punished according to American laws*. This is capable of a construction which refers to American laws only for the measure and mode of punishment. There is undoubtedly some difficulty in referring to American law for punishment when that law not having defined the offence has prescribed no punishment for it. But difficulties are inseparable from the system of mixed jurisdiction, and we must feel our way through them as best we can by the aid of analogy. Thus while neither our statutes nor the common law make any provision for securing decent respect for Pagan temples, groves or other enclosure having in the estimation of their frequenters a sacred character, while the common law gave such protection to Christian churches and cemetaries, the ground upon which the desecration of such places is to be regarded in this country as punishable at common law must probably be its tendency to disturb public order and provoke breaches of the peace. The wanton outraging of the veneration paid by the Japanese to their groves and temples has the same tendency, and ought therefore to fall within the analogy of the common law, and to be punishable in some way. Many offences of this character fall within the range of police regulation which has necessarily a local character.

I am unwilling to say that Americans in Japan are wholly exempt from regulations reasonable in themselves but which we are incompetent to frame from want of familiarity with Japanese peculiarities national and religious. Foreigners in Japan as in any other country are subject to its jurisdiction except so far as it is limited by express or tacit convention. All that has been sought by the Christian powers is to withdraw their subjects from the operation of such laws as conflict with our ideas of civilization and humanity, and to keep the power of trying and punishing in the hands of their own representatives. It is proper therefore for the latter, when they find a Japanese regulation, not found, in our case, in the statutes or the common law to acquaint their countrymen with the fact of such recognition and that it will be enforced according to our methods and in our tribunals. This combining the sanction of the two Governments avoids on the one hand the assertion of the absolute immunity of our citizens from any Japanese regulation however reasonable and necessary, and on the other hand of an unqualified legislative power in our diplomatic and consular representatives—a position which it seems judicious to maintain until Congress shall act on the subject.[20]

[20] No. 87, May 21, 1871.

In this instruction Mr. Fish developed the legal interpretation
and the sensible operation of extraterritoriality in Japan. The
limitation upon Japanese jurisdiction was confined to the power
of trying and punishing foreign nationals, but otherwise Japanese
law was to be respected. The position taken by Sir Harry Parkes,
on the authority of the Orders in Council, "that British subjects
could only be tried and punished in Japan for violation of British
law," met with no favor in the mind of an eminent lawyer like
Mr. Fish. And there was no practical disadvantage in the procedure outlined by Mr. Fish. As long as the power to try and
punish remained in the Consular Courts there was no danger in
recognizing all Japanese law, and especially those which the Government might especially design for the control of foreigners. An
objectionable Japanese law would not be enforceable in a Consular
Court. If the British Government had appreciated the validity
and wisdom of the American interpretation, which was repeatedly
brought to their attention, a great deal of the entirely unnecessary
bitterness which was to grow up between Japanese and British
officials would have been removed. The resentment was based not
so much on what the British diplomats did as on the way in
which they did it.

The implications of the extraterritorial system were involved
in the consideration of De Long's Consular Court Regulations.
While these had been proclaimed in 1870, subject to the revision
of Congress, Mr. Fish had questioned the authority of De Long
in the premises and had sought the action of Congress to resolve
any doubts as to their legality.[21] De Long replied with a defense
of those rules which Mr. Fish had specifically questioned, and
with an argument for the validity of the whole code. What is of
especial interest was De Long's frank acceptance of the method
by which extraterritorial rights had expanded beyond their treaty
implications.

With regard to the general question of jurisdiction which you so
happily express the two different views about; I beg leave to submit this
suggestion: Inasmuch as this country and others has by treaty conceded

---

[21] See *supra,* chap. xvi.

this right of extraterritoriality to our citizens; a doctrine so very essential to their personal and pecuniary security in such countries which have no written laws and no courts; and inasmuch as these governments do not question the most liberal view taken by any of the foreign powers as to the extent of this right; is it not very unwise that the first suggestion of such doubts should come from ourselves. In other words would it not be the best course to claim all of the privileges necessary to insure the security of our people who are here, at least until that claim is questioned by these governments.

And inasmuch as the establishment of some *certain* rules of law for our peoples' government here is what is required, and as now the question as to what the rights of citizens here are and what rules they are governed by is one of great doubt and much dispute; would it not be the wisest course for Congress to assume that this doctrine carries with it the right and privilege of Congress to legislate for the government of American citizens here as it does for their government in territories.[22]

Before he had received Instructions No. 83 and No. 87, De Long repeated his arguments for Congressional sanction of the law-making power of the Minister. He pointed out that under the Act of June 22, 1860, the American judicial tribunals in Japan must act in conformity with the laws of the United States or the common law, including equity and admiralty. And if no remedy could be found, the Minister should, by decrees and regulations, "supply such defects and deficiencies." But there were few Acts of Congress which were applicable, and the "common law" was impossible of strict definition. He recommended the repeal of the Act of July 1, 1870, the latest statute dealing with extraterritoriality, and he suggested that he report in person on this matter, as well as the approaching Treaty revision, the Shimonoseki indemnity, and the treatment of native Christians.[23]

[22] No. 141, January 28. Mr. Fish replied that in calling the attention of Congress to certain points in the Regulations he was not expressing his personal judgment. But he repeated that Congressional action was necessary (No. 83, May 20, 1871).

[23] No. 203, June 17, *F.R., 1871*, pp. 590–94. This was followed by a personal letter to Mr. Fish urging the necessity of a visit to Washington. In reply, Acting Secretary J. C. B. Davis informed him that there was no necessity for such a visit but the Secretary would be glad to see him if his own affairs brought him there (August 23). But again De Long turned to a higher power, and on November 7 he was advised that the President had directed that a leave be granted, as his presence was desired for a month or so (No. 121).

Although the year was free from diplomatic incidents of a major nature, De Long was much occupied with the pressing of claims on behalf of American citizens against Japan. The instruction of January 21[24] had not reached him, and he plunged into the battle with the Japanese Ministers. Two new cases had come up, one arising during the Japanese civil war,[25] and another involving an American who was *persona non grata* with the Japanese. E. M. Van Reed, whom De Long described as "one of our most respectable citizens," was a Californian who had been in the employ of the American firm of Augustine Heard & Company.[26] He had incurred the resentment of the Imperial officials by his friendship with the old régime and especially because of his conduct in the "Scioto" coolie affair. Late in 1870 he had opened an exchange or auction room in Tokyo. Then when Van Reed returned to the United States on a business trip the authorities forbade the Japanese to transact business at this exchange. To the remonstrances of Consul Shepard and Minister De Long, the Ministers replied that the exchange was considered a species of gambling. De Long would not accept this explanation, for he alleged that other nationals were doing the same thing in Tokyo and that Japanese were conducting exchanges there and in Yokohama. He concluded, therefore, that this action was intended as a personal punishment of Van Reed, or as an unjust discrimination against Americans.

> I could not admit as a principle that the Japanese Government should prohibit Americans at the ports opened by treaty to trade from conducting a business that was lawful by American laws and the laws of all other civilized states.

He thereupon demanded the withdrawal of the restriction, which was refused, and he informed the Ministers that should Van Reed, on his return, present a claim for damages he would feel compelled to recognize and present it.

---

[24] See *supra,* chap. xvi.

[25] Walsh, Hall & Company at Niigata, see *infra,* footnote 35.

[26] Townsend Harris had had some trouble with him in 1860 (No. 3, January 12, 1860). He had claimed Hawaiian citizenship in 1868.

Van Reed, on his arrival, offered to forego all claims if he were allowed to continue his business. This refused, he placed in De Long's hands a claim for heavy damages, based on the profits at the time of closing. The latter considered this "an unanswerable claim for a large sum of money." But, as De Long queried the Department, what should he do? "What extremes would I be justified in resorting to in any case when these authorities bluntly and firmly refuse to settle a demand that I know to be just and proper?" Only two courses seemed open to him: to abandon the claim, or to direct American citizens to pay all dues (customs, land rents, etc.) to the Consul, from which such claims could be deducted and the balance paid over to the Japanese Government.

> This latter method is a harsh one I admit, one almost bordering upon war; but what else is to be done? Such a course has been pursued by some of the other Ministers in some cases and in one or two instances I have threatened to do it before I obtained a settlement of demands; but it has always been my intention to take your advice before actually resorting to any such an extreme expedient. . . . . One good lesson firmly lived up to I am satisfied will do a great deal of good.

The Secretary's views he solicited, "without delay," as to the validity of the claim and the measures which should be used to enforce it.[27]

Mr. Fish, after a considerable delay, asked for more information about the claim (for De Long had transmitted none of the evidence), and instructed him that he was not to withhold acknowledged dues in order to enforce payment of a claim.[28] De Long apparently sensed that the delay in sending the instruction he desired was due to the faulty way in which he had presented the case, for on May 10 (the day before Fish's instruction was forwarded) he sent on the complete record. The final instruction, signed by William Hunter, Acting Secretary, was to the effect that Japan had the right to prevent its subjects from assembling to bet upon the price of staples: "I am not able to see any infraction of our treaties with Japan in the treatment of Mr. Van

[27] No. 146, February 14.   [28] No. 79, May 11.

Reed's customers."[29] The divergence of views between the Minister and the Department in this and in so many other cases was marked, and the necessity for curbing the impulses of the impetuous diplomat was very evident.

De Long did not take kindly the instruction sent him on January 21, and he replied in a long dispatch on March 1. First he defended his support of the *nubu* claim of Walsh, Hall & Company, and then he took up the advice that American claimants be referred to the Japanese courts. There were, he insisted, no written laws and courts. Moreover, the Japanese authorities had urged the Representatives to give notice that all contracts must be approved by the Japanese Government in order to be enforceable. But this, it appeared from his dispatch, applied only to contracts made by or on behalf of the former daimyos. The daimiates had been abolished in 1869 and the estates returned to the Crown; thenceforth no clan officer could make contracts without the approval of the Government, and De Long was so advised on March 27, 1870. This led to a conference between the Representatives and the Japanese Ministers in which some of the difficulties incident to the abolition of feudalism were brought out. The Government could not forbid clan officers from making contracts with foreigners, because that would violate the Convention of 1866. Nor could it assume all the debts due foreigners by the daimyos, when their property was surrendered, because the amount was not known and some of the daimyos had not yielded up their estates. Claiming that the wishes of the Ministers were not clearly known, a written statement was requested, and this, in turn, was not considered satisfactory. The Representatives therefore made no reply and refrained from issuing the notices requested. But early in the next year, the Ministers announced that the daimyos were prohibited from pledging any of the revenues of their districts for the purchase of ships, machinery, or other articles from foreigners for their own private use; that all purchases and contracts must first obtain the authorization of the Japanese

[29] No. 93, July 1.

Government, through the indorsement of the contracts by both the
Foreign and Finance Departments; and that the Government
would undertake to make the daimyos pay their debts and, should
they fail to meet their engagements, would assume their legal liabilities.[30] Again the Foreign Representatives discussed the matter
with the Japanese Ministers and the former unanimously agreed
to issue no notices and to take no action.

De Long based his position upon clauses of the Treaty of 1858
and the Convention of 1866, but he was influenced even more by
his belief that the announced policy was a subterfuge designed to
cripple the trade of foreigners, for, in his opinion, the daimyos
possessed all the wealth and power that they ever did. Thus, he
argued, if foreigners must make contracts with the Foreign and
Financial Departments they must also settle them there, and without the intervention of their diplomatic Representatives they
would be helpless. "The American commercial community doing
business here would stand aghast with dismay," if De Long followed his instructions and did nothing about enforcing these
contracts.

The present practice, in disputed claims, was for the Consul
and the Governor to discuss the matter and agree, if possible, and,
if not, then for the Minister to bring it before the Japanese Ministers. Otherwise steps must be taken to compel them to establish
courts. Henceforth, however, De Long would refer all claims to
the Department before pressing them in Tokyo.[31]

To this Mr. Fish replied that as the *nubu* case had been settled,
further discussion was unnecessary, and he admitted that De
Long's last dispatch had pointed out certain equities not previously brought forward. But in respect to the prohibition of
trade on behalf of the ex-daimyos he supported the contention of
the Japanese Government. In these regulations he saw no violation of the Treaties between the two countries, and he took it for
granted "that the several notifications which were given to you

[30] Ministers for Foreign Affairs to De Long, January 11, 1871.

[31] No. 161, March 1, 1871. The several letters from the Japanese Ministers
were inclosed.

were communicated to the American merchants in Japan." And as for the intervention of the American Minister, he stated:

It was not the purpose of the framers of the Treaty, and it is not desirable that the diplomatic representative of the United States should become an attorney for the collection of debts against Japanese subjects through the channels of the Japanese Department of Foreign Affairs. It is the duty of the Japanese Government to furnish a proper tribunal for that purpose.

But before giving further instructions De Long was directed to ascertain from his colleagues, if possible in writing, how the private debts of English, French, German, and Dutch traders were enforced against the Japanese.[32]

To this "interesting despatch" De Long replied that the notices had not been published although their publication had been requested by the Japanese authorities. In refraining from doing so, he and his colleagues had felt that the Japanese were trying to violate treaty provisions. But, "as I now learn that my views and your own do not coincide, I will, if you think proper publish them"—which meant a further delay of about four months. At this time he transmitted statements from his British, Dutch (also in charge of German interests), and French colleagues as to the way they handled private claims, which supported De Long's previous assertion, and he also submitted a reply from the Ministers for Foreign Affairs on the same subject. The latter he interpreted to mean that the Japanese had no courts, but thought of having some; that if a case could not be settled by the Consul and Governor, then it would be considered by the Foreign Representative and the Ministers, the latter employing a tribunal to hear evidence.

De Long again adverted to the difficulties which prevailed in a land without courts, published laws, rules of evidence, or precedents, and he apprehended that even should the Government engage a foreign jurist to act as a judge he would find his position one of great anxiety and difficulty. He had urged upon the Ministers the idea of establishing a mixed court, composed of foreign and native judges, and the adoption of some code of laws.

[32] No. 84, May 20.

They had agreed as to the necessity of such a step, but had done nothing about it. In the meantime, while he had not notified his countrymen that he would no longer attend to their claims, he had privately made known the Department's views to those who had sought his intervention. For the present he would only present claims and attempt to secure their allowance, "if possible, without any contention," but, if they were rejected, would submit the proofs and the reply of the Ministers to the Department for instructions. And, in conclusion, he described several pending claims and again asked for some assistance in handling them.[33]

While De Long's stubbornness might have brought down upon him a sharp reprimand, Mr. Fish handled the matter with becoming moderation. He pointed out that the Dutch Minister had observed that the practices in vogue do not " 'seem to be consistent with the spirit of most of our treaties' "; that courts did exist in Japan, to which foreign subjects had the right to appeal directly; and that there was no separation between judicial and administrative functions. Mr. Van der Hoeven also looked to the approaching revision of the Treaties "for the only practical remedy for the present unsatisfactory condition of affairs." Mr. Fish continued:

I am inclined to concur in his view of the subject and as the United States were the first Power to conclude a treaty to be careful that it shall be the last that can be accused of a violation of provisions which the other Western Powers have borrowed from our model.

In respect to claims upon contract between citizens of the United States and the Government of Japan, I am quite sensible of the large private interests which press for your aid in their adjustment without the delay of a reference to this Department. But the citizens who are concerned entered into such contracts without the privity of this Government, for purposes of private gains having no reference to the large political considerations which must control its action, putting their own estimates upon the equity, the promptitude and the pecuniary solvency of the party with whom they contracted, and as we are warranted from experience of commercial habits to believe, charging what they deemed an adequate premium for the hazards they incurred. I do not deem this, especially in view of the avoiding of all embarrassing discussions, so far as practicable until the revision of the treaties, an opportune time for modifying my previous instruction.

[33] No. 222, July 17.

Mr. Fish also hoped that the employment of Mr. Peshine Smith in the Japanese Foreign Office would facilitate De Long's intercourse with the Ministers and permit a temporary adjournment of every question not requiring immediate solution.[34]

De Long's final reference to the matter was incorporated in a long dispatch in which he discussed the abolition of feudalism and the appointment of Iwakura as Minister for Foreign Affairs. It seems that in August he had appealed to the Dainagons (Cabinet) to establish courts. The occasion was a protest against the conclusions of the Ministers for Foreign Affairs on one of the claims. In his letter he compared, in detail, the administration of justice in Japan and that in the West, and he stressed the importance of making justice sure and prompt, of providing for the cross-examination of witnesses, and of setting up rules of procedure. His proposal, Lord Iwakura advised him on September 3, was being seriously considered.[35]

[34] No. 113, October 14.

[35] No. 238, September 4, *F.R., 1871,* pp. 597–604. The claims which De Long handled in 1871, as reported by him, were: Walsh, Hall & Company, *nubu;* settled by the Government (No. 161, March 1). Walsh, Hall & Company, exchange of coins; submitted to the Department (No. 163, March 10), rejected by De Long (No. 220, July 16), action approved by the Department (Instruction No. 103, August 30). Walsh, Hall & Company, for loss of property at Niigata in 1868; De Long doubted its validity but submitted the papers to the Department (No. 173, March 17); his conduct was approved, and the Department stated: "It is a general and accepted rule that parties resident at a place which becomes the theatre of war, foreign or domestic, stand upon the same footing with the subjects of either of the contending parties. They must abide the chances of the country in which they choose to reside and take their share of the calamities incident to war without the hope of compensation" (Instruction No. 80, May 11). Walsh, Hall & Company, claim against the Uji clan for $23,-220; the note was alleged to have been signed by a former officer of the clan with a stolen seal (No. 222, July 17). F. C. Farrington against the prince (daimyo) of Awa on a contract as a miner; Farrington was dismissed after nine months, and claimed fifteen months' pay under contract (No. 222); the Department referred De Long to its Instruction No. 113. Schultze, Reiss & Company against the daimyo of Nambu for $100,000 loaned, payable in copper, silk, or money; De Long considered this a good claim and "addressed most urgent appeals to the Foreign Office for despatch in investigating and settling this matter"; Schultze was an American citizen, and Reiss was Consul for the North German Confederation and used his influence to further the matter (No. 222); settlement was made by the Japanese Government, paying $110,000 (Mexican) on the note, and interest, a total of $145,000 (No. 259, December 21). Walsh, Hall & Company for loans to Tosa, Numata, Mito, and Taisher (Taishu, the

On four occasions, during the year, the American Minister became involved in matters under discussion between Japan and other Powers. These can be briefly mentioned. First came the request from the Hawaiian Consul that he arrange a treaty for his country with Japan. The Japanese Ministers set up a condition precedent that Van Reed (an American citizen) be dismissed from his office as Consul for Hawaii. With this De Long complied, and he asked for the Department's approval of his conduct and for instructions.[36] On this occasion his course was approved.[37] · The Hawaiian Government then furnished De Long with a letter from the King to the Emperor, and with a commission as Envoy Extraordinary and Minister Plenipotentiary. The negotiations were speedily completed (between August 15 and 19) and the ratifications were at once exchanged, putting the Treaty into immediate effect. He now asked for advice as to continuing to act as envoy for Hawaii.[38] On this point he was informed that he could not accept such an appointment except with the consent of Congress, although there was no objection to the use of his good offices.[39]

The Sakhalin mediation, which had been discussed in 1870, was finally dropped as narrated in the previous chapter.

For a second time Japan became interested in American activities in Korea. In 1871 Mr. Low, the American Minister to China, proceeded to Korea, with an escort of warships, to investigate the loss of the "General Sherman" in 1867, and, if possible, to negotiate a commercial treaty.[40] In May, Lord Date, Minister of

Chinese name for Tsushima) ; some $800,000 was involved; De Long did not forward these claims to the Department because a judicial department for examining claims had been organized; $600,000 was paid, and $200,000 was pending (No. 259, December 21).

On the other hand, certain claims were presented against the United States: De Long again recommended the payment to the owners of the "Aroostook" (*supra*, chap. xvi) (No. 156, February 21). The Japanese Government pressed for the rent of consular lots (No. 138, January 21), and De Long recommended payment (No. 204, June 19). It also presented a claim against E. E. Rice, Consul at Hakodate, for supplies furnished (No. 264, December 22).

36 No. 151, February 16.   37 No. 68, April 7.
38 No. 231, August 21.   39 No. 127, December 21.
40 *F.R., 1871 (China)* ; Dennett, *Americans in Eastern Asia,* p. 453.

Finance, and Sawa Nobuyoshi, Chief Minister for Foreign Affairs, inquired particularly about the object of the United States in sending a fleet to Korea, and as to whether or not hostilities might ensue.

They then mentioned to me that in the past Corea had acknowledged Japanese sovereignty by the payment of yearly tribute, which however that Government had ceased for some years past to pay; that the Japanese authorities had been too completely occupied in the administration of the internal affairs of their own Empire to do more than to send some Commissioners to Corea empowered to adjust the relations of the two countries.[41]

At this time, three Commissioners were at Fusan, the port in Korea open to Japanese trade and residence, and the Government feared for their safety. De Long was requested to use his good offices with Mr. Low and Admiral Rodgers to secure protection for them, should it be necessary and should they seek it. Mr. De Long was happy to show the friendliness of the United States, and he sent, by a Japanese messenger, letters as requested.[42] The Department, uncertain of the outcome of the expedition, suspended decision on the subject.[43]

Finally, Mr. De Long intervened, in a well-intentioned way, in the treaty negotiations between Japan and China. Early in the year he heard rumors that Japan was about to send an embassy to China to form an offensive and defensive treaty. Believing that China was in a somewhat critical condition and that Japan should not become openly committed to Chinese theories or involved in their disputes, he tried to prevent the attempt.[44]

Having no right to demand any information about this matter and not being asked for advice it was somewhat indelicate to undertake to obtain the necessary information.

[41] It is doubtful if De Long correctly reported the remarks about a yearly tribute. The "tribute" really consisted of presents offered by a mission of respect on the accession of a Shogun (Treat, *The Far East,* p. 284).

[42] No. 188, May 15.

[43] No. 92, June 22. The Americans became involved in hostilities at the mouth of the Han River, remote from Fusan.

[44] De Long had previously furnished letters of introduction to American officials in China for the Japanese Commissioners who went there in 1870 (No. 100, October 20, 1870).

But he pressed his inquiries and counsel until he obtained a promise that no treaty would be asked for or accepted unless similar to the one between Japan and the United States, and he would be kept informed of all the proceedings of the embassy. On June 20 he was advised of the appointment of the mission, with Lord Date, daimyo of Uwajima, as Envoy Extraordinary and Minister Plenipotentiary, and Date asked him for aid in obtaining the assistance of American officials in China. Not only did De Long promise this, but he was able to present to Date the American Consul General at Shanghai, Mr. George F. Seward, who happened to be in Japan at the time. On the twenty-sixth an official assurance as to the terms which would be incorporated in the treaty was given him. Comparing the two nations, De Long held that Japan was

a power to be welcomed as an ally and dreaded as a foe by all civilized states should trouble occur with China or our troubles with Corea enlarge and increase.

To allow Japan from inattention to drift into an alliance with China at this critical period I regarded as calamitous, therefore I have earnestly sought to prevent it, and I hope I have been somewhat instrumental in doing so although I do not know that any such action was contemplated by this government.

And he also feared that the mission would return empty-handed, for the Chinese, "underrating the power of this nation," would expect Japan to concur in their theories regarding the encroachments of the Western Powers. The Japanese were somewhat perturbed, but as they had promised, a year previously, to send the mission, they determined to proceed.[45]

To his gratification, Mr. Fish deemed De Long's action "statesmanlike," and it received the full approval and commendation of the Department. "It is the wish of this Government," he wrote, "to cherish at all times the most friendly relations with Japan."[46]

On November 18 De Long reported that Lord Date had returned, having concluded and exchanged ratifications of the

[45] No. 213, July 6.   [46] No. 101, August 24.

Treaty.[47] Pending the translation of the document he was unable to report its contents, and it was evident that he had not been
kept informed of the progress of negotiations.[48] The next year,
however, the terms of this Treaty became the subject of diplomatic consideration.

It was at this time that Japan began to seek American citizens
as advisers in the civil departments of the Government. First
came the request for two assistants, one for the Customs and the
other for the Internal Revenue Department. In transmitting
this request, De Long pointed out how much they could do to
strengthen the Legation and increase the rapidly growing good
will for the United States. But, he added,

> I would like that persons should be selected who would (in all matters
> wherein they might properly do so) support this legation in its efforts to
> extend and promote American influence and who to some extent at least
> would accept advice from it.

Mr. Ito, Vice-Minister of Finance, later Prince Ito, who was then
in Washington, would make all necessary arrangements.[49]

The Department was glad to be of such assistance as it could,
but Ito had already left Washington.[50] Again the Japanese made

---

[47] He was in error as to the ratifications. For the text of the Treaty as
signed by Lord Date and Li Hung-Chang at Tientsin, September 13, 1871, see
Statistical Department of the Inspectorate General of Customs, *Treaties, Conventions, etc., between China and Foreign States,* II, 507–83.

[48] No. 249, November 18. Mr. Low wrote De Long, from Peking, October
7, that he had met Date at Chefoo, on the latter's way from Shanghai to
Tientsin, and had impressed upon him the importance of negotiating a treaty
on the basis of equality. After the Treaty was signed, Date visited Peking, and
he told Low that the Treaty did not differ materially from that between the
United States and China. Until it had been submitted to his Government he
could furnish no copies, but he had based his Treaty on the German and
Austrian ones with China, the latest to be concluded. From unofficial sources
Low learned that the only substantial difference was a modification of the
extraterritorial clause, the new Treaty conceding this right mutually at all the
open ports in China and Japan and nowhere else. In the interior, the nationals
would be subject to the territorial law. (This provision was a vast improvement
on the clauses in the other treaties negotiated with China and Japan.) As the
Treaty did not contemplate the sending of Ministers by either country, Low
tendered his good offices to Date in case Japan ever needed them, and he intended to make the same offer to the Chinese on behalf of De Long (Inclosure
in No. 249).

[49] No. 195, May 21.   [50] No. 91, June 22.

the request,[51] and the Department was ready to act whenever Mr. Mori, recently appointed Chargé, should make application.[52] Finally Mori asked for an adviser in internal revenue and taxation, and George W. Williams was recommended and appointed. He was indorsed by the Secretary of the Interior, by Senator O. P. Morton, of the Committee on Foreign Relations, and by the Commissioner of Internal Revenue.[53]

Next came a request for a competent legal adviser. De Long hoped that a gentleman of unquestionable honor and ability both as a lawyer and as a diplomat would be chosen. He dissented from the thought that it would be advantageous to deny Japan such assistance.

I believe that all advantages foreign powers might gain over them through their ignorance of international law, would be far less in importance, besides being more unworthily gained, than what will result from having them represented by an able advocate, who, while he would prevent unworthy advantages from being taken of this government, would also counsel them against insisting upon unjust and unreasonable things, likely to produce mischief and trouble.[54]

The Department recommended to Mr. Mori, Mr. E. Peshine Smith, at the time Examiner of Claims.[55] But De Long had picked up rumors that George F. Seward, then Consul General at Shanghai, was to assist Japan in the Treaty revision negotiation, while a Mr. Saville was to be Commissioner of Customs. He could not conceal his annoyance at this development.[56] He was reassured by the information that neither of the gentlemen had ever been officially recommended for any post.[57]

The famous Agricultural Mission of General Horace Capron and his associates was apparently engaged without the intervention of the American Minister. In order to colonize and hold the Hokkaido against the Russians, a Colonization Department

[51] No. 228, August 3.   [52] No. 111, September 22.

[53] No. 122, November 21.   [54] No. 219, July 15, *F.R., 1871*, pp. 595–97.

[55] No. 109, September 21. Mr. Smith had prepared memoranda on several of De Long's dispatches dealing with claims, consular jurisdiction, etc. De Long failed to advise the Foreign Office of this recommendation, and Chargé Shepard corrected the oversight in July 1872 (No. 54, July 20, 1872).

[56] No. 250, November 20.   [57] No. 128, January 11, 1872.

was established in 1871. General Capron, then Commissioner of Agriculture in Washington, was engaged to organize its activities at a reputed salary of $20,000.[58] With his associates he arrived early in September, to be most cordially received, Lord Iwakura expressing pride and pleasure that the United States had spared them to help Japan, and De Long rejoicing in their arrival. Japan, he reported, was a great nation, well deserving of assistance.[59] His views had changed greatly from the pessimism which had marked the early days of the year. On the same steamer came a party of army and navy officers seeking employment in Japan—Lieutenants Wasson, Dunwoodie, Jones, Hoag, and Poillon. As they brought letters from Mr. Fish and others, De Long felt that he could set aside his instructions which forbade him to recommend any citizen to the Japanese. On this occasion his conduct was approved.[60]

Japanese students came to America in increasing numbers. Adams reported that forty to fifty sailed in one steamer that summer,[61] and the next year Lanman stated that to that time some five hundred had visited the United States and some two hundred were then in residence.[62] The former was impressed with the ill effect of such travel and hasty learning upon many of these young men (a criticism which was later to be made of Chinese students). But that many of the Japanese were unusually serious in the pursuit of their studies was testified by their later careers of service. The introduction of the new educational system, which brought Western learning to the schools of Japan, met the needs of many later students.

In order to give a picture of the practical difficulties which the

[58] Black, *op. cit.*, II, 328–29. General Capron was engaged directly by Governor Kuroda, in charge of the Kaitakushi (Colonization Department). He had visited the United States early in 1871, on his way home from England. After his new appointment he returned and, in conference with Chargé Mori, made arrangements with Capron (Lanman, *The Japanese in America*, p. 45). For the accomplishments of Capron and his associates see *Reports and Official Letters to the Kaitakushi by Horace Capron, Commissioner and Adviser, and His Foreign Assistants.*

[59] No. 239, September 4, *F.R., 1871*, pp. 604–5. Cf. Adams, *op. cit.*, II, 290–92.					[60] No. 114, October 17, *F.R., 1871*, p. 605.

[61] Adams, *op. cit.*, II, 251.					[62] Lanman, *op. cit.*, p. 55.

American Minister faced at this time, some reference should be made to conditions under which he worked. Late in 1870, Mr. Fish inquired why the Legation could not return to Yedo (Tokyo), as tranquillity had apparently been restored there.[63] To this De Long replied that the diplomatic corps actually resided at Yokohama. There could be found the British, French, Italian, Belgian, and American Ministers, and the Dutch, Spanish, North German, and Austrian Chargés. Only the British, French, and Americans retained Legations in Tokyo, and these were used only when occasion necessitated. The American Legation was "made of paper," undefended, unfurnished except for such private property as De Long had purchased from Van Valkenburgh, and situated a mile from the British Legation and over three miles from the Foreign Office and the foreign concession. A person living there would be banished from all foreign society and at the mercy of any assassin or mob, to which the attack on Messrs. Ring and Dallas and a prior assault on Consul Shepard in his room at the foreign hotel in Tokyo gave point. He then developed the idea that formerly the Foreign Ministers had insisted upon living in Yedo because the Government was anxious to have them withdraw. The right to live there having been established, there was no necessity to insist longer upon it even though the Japanese were eager to have foreigners reside there. In order to secure unity of action among the Foreign Representatives it was necessary to have frequent conferences, and these usually took place in Yokohama rather than in Tokyo. At both places he needed a residence, and at Yokohama he had bought and furnished a dwelling, while at Tokyo he had at his own expense furnished the old Legation. The journey to Tokyo, which he had to make frequently and at all seasons, was a difficult and dangerous one, for De Long had no guards or attachés, as had Parkes, and he again asked for a steam launch so that he could complete the round trip in a single day.[64]

Since the dismissal of Portman, De Long had been without an interpreter or translator or even a secretary. His dispatches in

[63] No. 41, December 5, 1870.   [64] No. 142, January 30.

these months were written in his own hand. In February he recommended that Reverend J. C. Hepburn, a missionary and one of the ablest students of the Japanese language, be appointed interpreter.[65] The appointment was made, and Dr. Hepburn was commissioned as interpreter to the Legation, at a salary of $2,500.[66] Hepburn served only from February 18 to June 15.[67] In addition to Dr. Hepburn, De Long tried to obtain permission to retain a native clerk and translator whom he had privately employed. This was Hayashi Tozaburo (later Count Hayashi Tadasu), a young samurai who had visited Europe and America. De Long reported that he was a brother of the former physician to the Shogun, but he really was a son. From him he had obtained much valuable information, and he transmitted two memoranda prepared by Hayashi, one explaining the meaning of the reign name Meiji, and the other a survey of Christianity in Japan.[68] As Hayashi was a staunch vassal of the former Shogun, it is probable that De Long's doubts about the stability and purpose of the new régime received some support in this quarter. The appointment could not be made, because no appropriation existed; but even when De Long was allowed an additional $500 for his contingent fund he was directed to dismiss his native clerk.[69]

De Long was at his wit's end, without a secretary or an interpreter. In October, when he visited Hakodate, he engaged Nathan E. Rice as interpreter and brought him to Tokyo.[70] This appointment was confirmed as of October 16, and Rice later accompanied De Long on his visit to the United States.[71]

[65] No. 153, February 18.

[66] Fish to Hepburn, April 20. Commission dated April 6.

[67] Hepburn to Fish, June 15; No. 202, June 16; Instruction No. 105, September 12.

[68] No. 167, March 14, *F.R., 1871,* pp. 589–90. See Pooley, editor, *The Secret Memoirs of Count Tadasu Hayashi,* pp. 3–7.

[69] No. 82, May 20; No. 85, May 20.

[70] No. 241, October 8, *F.R., 1871,* p. 606. The Department did not approve compensation for Hepburn until September 12 (No. 105).

[71] Fish to Rice, March 20, 1872; Hale to Rice, April 5, 1872. In his annual message to Congress, December 4, 1871, President Grant recommended that provision be made for student interpreters in Japan and China. He renewed this request December 2, 1872.

Although De Long had been commissioned Envoy Extraordinary and Minister Plenipotentiary on July 14, 1870, no new letters of credence had been issued. De Long had called attention to this in February 1871, and the proper credentials were dispatched on April 19.[72] These were presented at an audience on June 9.[73]

Although $6,000 had been appropriated in 1866 for the erection of a jail at Yokohama, nothing had been accomplished because of the inadequacy of the amount.[74] Van Valkenburgh, in 1869, had appealed for a new appropriation, and this request was to be brought to the attention of Congress.[75] De Long, soon after his arrival, had stressed the need for such a building, for American prisoners had been boarded in the British jail. Rent for a jail had then been provided, but no adequate quarters could be found. The Act of July 1, 1870, provided $750 for the actual rent of a prison at Yokohama (Kanagawa), and up to $2,500 for the wages of keepers and the care of offenders; at the other open ports a maximum of $2,500 each was allowed. But even the next year Consul Shepard was asking for authority to hire a jail, pay a jailer, and board the prisoners. This request was referred back to De Long *for decision*. The Department apparently held De Long responsible for the failure to provide a rented jail when an appropriation for a new building was lacking.[76]

On several occasions De Long and Shepard, the Chargé, incurred reproof for their failure to observe the regulations of the service. Colonel Charles O. Shepard, of New York, had been appointed Consul at Yedo in 1869. Two years later the Department decided to abandon the Consulate there, apparently as part of the move to force De Long to reside in Yedo, and Shepard was appointed Consul at Kanagawa (Yokohama), on the death of Lemuel E. Lyon, of Oregon. On March 22, De Long reported

[72] No. 144, February 13; Instruction No. 71.

[73] No. 200, June 12. Inclosures give the speeches exchanged.

[74] Instruction No. 9, January 28, 1867.

[75] No. 11, February 2, 1869; Instruction No. 2, August 24, 1869.

[76] No. 96, August 12, 1871.

that he was inclosing Shepard's oath and bond, duly signed, but he must have overlooked the inclosure, for on April 17 he telegraphed (one of the few occasions when he made use of this means of communication)[77] that the documents were going forward by the next mail, and he requested that Shepard's commission be sent immediately. The Department's reply, on April 22 (an unusually quick response), was that the commission would not be issued until the papers were received. In fact it was not until November 1 that Shepard's commission was dispatched.

Neither De Long nor Shepard had any intention of closing the Yedo Consulate. On December 20, De Long was advised that the Department did not intend to continue this post.[78] But when Shepard acted as Chargé he appointed three Acting Vice-Consuls at Yedo in succession. He was sharply reminded that the power to nominate a Vice-Consul belonged to the Consul, and, if approved by the Minister or Consul General, the Department would appoint, and without its sanction there could be no appointment. As this was the third time he had appointed one "it is desirable that it may be the last of the kind."[79]

Colonel Shepard first served as Chargé when De Long made his visit to Hakodate.[80] This was due to a dispute which had arisen between Elisha E. Rice, former Consul, and Ambrose C. Dunn, then Consul, and it involved Dunn's actions in the case of the claim of Japan for certain lands which Rice alleged belonged to him. The dispute had been reported by De Long on Decem-

[77] The message traveled by way of Nagasaki, Hong Kong, and Colombo to England and New York.

[78] No. 126.

[79] No. 5, March 21, 1872. Cf. No. 21, February 24; No. 23, March 15; No. 38, May 16; Instructions No. 9, April 19, and No. 14, July 2, 1872.

[80] When De Long was planning to avail himself of the leave of absence granted to him in 1870, he queried as to whom he should leave in charge—the Consul at Yedo, Shepard, or the interpreter, Hepburn (No. 154, February 18, 1871). The Department instructed him to designate Shepard (No. 77, April 28). But De Long, who had the misfortune to quarrel with many of his subordinates, replied that he would prefer to turn to Mr. Mangum, Consul at Nagasaki. (This statement is omitted from No. 203, June 17, as it appears in *F.R., 1871*, pp. 590–94.) As the Department ignored this proposal, De Long had to appoint Shepard.

ber 13, 1870,[81] and Rice laid his charges directly before the Department. De Long was instructed to suspend Dunn, pending an investigation of the charges and counter charges, and to report on the validity of Rice's land claims.[82] The Department seemed to have prejudged this dispute when it appointed E. E. Rice Consul at Hakodate for the second time.[83] De Long promptly suspended Dunn, and when E. E. Rice returned home, he placed Nathan E. Rice, his son, in charge of the Consulate.[84] It was not until September 6 that he was able to leave Yokohama to conduct the investigation. He was away from his post until November 8, taking advantage of the opportunity to explore the Hokkaido and to return overland across Honshiu. His dispatches contained a full account of his travels, and included some pertinent observations, such as that Japan was not overcrowded and that there was no danger of a coolie exodus to the United States.[85] He could not pass upon the merits of the dispute until he had obtained further proofs in Yokohama, but, as N. E. Rice had entered his employ as an interpreter, he appointed his brother, George E. Rice, as Acting Vice-Consul, and recommended that he be given the full appointment.[86] The Department, however, gave the appointment to John Hart Hawes.[87]

The extraterritorial cases which came up to the Minister (for, of course, most of these were handled by the Consuls in the first instance) were of a very perplexing nature. George Wilkins Lake, who had been a thorn in the flesh of the American officials at Nagasaki, was now suing, in the Ministerial Court, Consul Mangum and the former Marshal, L. M. Dent, for abuse of power and false imprisonment.[88] But while the case was pending the Gov-

---

[81] No. 117.   [82] No. 59, February 17, 1871.

[83] No. 67, March 22.   [84] No. 177, April 18; No. 206, June 19.

[85] No. 243, October 8; No. 246, November 12.   [86] No. 242, October 8.

[87] No. 125, December 19. Before leaving Yokohama, De Long reported that he had appointed C. A. Longfellow as secretary and left Shepard as Chargé (No. 240, September 4). He was reminded that the technical appointment of a Chargé rested with the Department, while Mr. Longfellow could not receive any diplomatic position (No. 115, October 17).

[88] No. 197, June 6; Instruction No. 97, August 17; No. 260, December 21.

ernor of Nagasaki demanded Lake's deportation because of his
previous conviction in the Ministerial Court as well as the non-
payment of his debts to certain Japanese.[89] At the same time an
action lay against Lake in Mangum's Court on behalf of a native
woman for the support of herself and her illegitimate child. While
the Department considered it unfortunate that Mangum should
be the judge, in view of Lake's suits against him, it did not see
how De Long could have designated any other Consul to act.[90]
Mangum, it seems, had acted on the Governor's request, and had
ordered Lake to leave Japan by October 1, but when Colonel
Shepard was Chargé he issued an order staying Mangum's decree.[91] His action was approved in an instruction which stated
that Lake should be allowed one year from his dismissal from
jail in which to arrange his affairs.[92] The process of deportation,
it seems, was not going to be a reliable method of ridding the
ports of undesirables.[93]

[89] No. 223, July 17.   [90] No. 104, August 30.
[91] No. 6, October 21.   [92] No. 124, December 19.

[93] De Long was not satisfied with the instruction he had received forbidding
the registration of firms (see *supra,* chap. xvi). He returned to the subject
on July 7, and sought additional instructions, pointing out that the practice
prevailing among his colleagues was for a firm composed of members of different nationalities to be allowed to choose the protection it desired, and when
no choice was made to consider it under the protection of the country of the
senior member; and he made special reference to the firm of Schultze, Reiss
& Company, doing business at Yokohama and Kobe, whose senior member was
an American, while Mr. Reiss was the North German Consul at Yokohama. He
had directed the consular officials to keep this firm on the registry, thus giving
Fish's instructions a future rather than a retroactive effect (No. 214). Mr.
Fish saw no reason for modifying his instruction, basing his decision on instructions sent to Consuls in the Barbary States in 1853 and 1864. He suggested
that perhaps Mr. Reiss sought the protection of the United States for his firm
because, as Consul of the German Empire, he forfeited the protection of his
state in commercial affairs. And he found this an opportunity to indicate his
attitude in general toward extraterritoriality: "I am aware that there are certain embarrassments to the creditors of mixed firms in pursuing their remedies
against the partners before the Consular Courts of their different nationalities.
These embarrassments have been found so great in Egypt as to induce some of
the principal European powers to consent to abrogate the judicial powers of
their Consuls in favor of Mixed Tribunals to be established by the Egyptian
government. But be the embarrassments what they may, it is to be borne in
mind that so far as they affect our own citizens, the latter voluntarily encounter them by preferring on the whole a residence in Japan to remaining at

During the year, De Long's controversy with his former interpreter, Portman, increased in intensity. The issue was now joined as to the title to Portman's lot in Yokohama, and when he refused to surrender the title deed he was arrested and confined, from June 27 to June 30, for contempt of court.[94] Portman poured forth his grievances to the Department and begged its intervention. Among other things he charged that De Long

had received and encouraged under his roof some Japanese who conspired against their government—whether those people were bona fide conspirators, or whether they were spies of some Daimio, I am unable to say.[95]

The Department instructed De Long that the United States had no interest in the lot in question, and directed him to take steps to have its title confirmed to Portman.[96] And it replied to Portman that it could neither condemn nor approve his arrest because it did not know whether De Long's mandate was a ministerial order or a judicial writ.[97]

Bearing in mind that the American Minister had no secretarial assistance and himself prepared some 133 dispatches, with many inclosures, it is not surprising that he confined his correspondence

home." And he remarked that the Treasury Department would be interested in knowing if Schultze, Reiss & Company had paid the Internal Revenue taxes on sales, profits, etc. "The correlative rights of allegiance and protection are founded upon personal status and character. They involve also correlative burdens" (No. 108, September 19). De Long saw fit to argue the point again, on the ground that the last instruction had contained no specific directions. He averred that the firm had submitted itself to American jurisdiction, and was prepared to pay any taxes which were demanded. And he asked where a company, composed of members of different nationalities, could be sued under the extraterritorial system. The members, as individuals, were subjected to their national courts, but should the Department's position be insisted upon it would compel a reorganization of all mixed firms (No. 245, November 8).

Another question involved the fees to be charged Japanese plaintiffs in Consular Courts (No. 145, February 13). He was instructed to conform to the practice in the courts of the other Treaty Powers (No. 76, April 24). As a result, he notified the Consuls not to charge any costs against Japanese litigants (No. 210, July 4).

[94] No. 218, July 14.   [95] July 21. This passage probably refers to Hayashi.

[96] No. 110, September 21. De Long took steps as directed (No. 244, November 8).

[97] September 21.

to the many concrete matters which called for attention. Unlike Sir Harry Parkes, who kept his Government well informed on political developments in Japan, De Long rarely referred to them. It would be difficult to reconstruct the events of this amazing year from his dispatches. The abolition of the feudal system, for example, was the subject of a long but ill-informed dispatch on September 4. He had first been informed of the appointment of Iwakura as Minister for Foreign Affairs, in place of Sawa, on August 29, and two days later he was advised that the *han* (fiefs) had been replaced by *ken* (prefectures).[98] De Long confused the territory with the feudal lord, and described the *han* as princes or daimyos. At the Foreign Office, on the third, he had been told of the removal of the daimyos from office and of the order that they should henceforth reside in Tokyo, ten per cent of their former revenues being allowed for their support. His explanation was that the daimyos had been gradually supplanted in power by the local legislatures, presided over by a *karo* (clan officer), and that the lords were happy to escape all responsibility and expense and to retire to a position of ease and freedom, with more money to spend than they had been able to enjoy out of their full reve- nue.[99] Six or seven of these *karo* had been appointed Ministers of Departments, such as Okubo, Goto, and Okuma, while others had been created *sanji,* or counsellors. The attempt to do away with all hereditary rights except in the Imperial house, to dis- pense with all useless offices, and yet to leave the kuge and daimyos eligible to office, and to centralize the government by extinguishing clanship, he considered wise and desirable and, if it could be ac- complished without bloodshed, it would advance the nation in a day to a position some nations had taken years to accomplish.[100]

[98] The Imperial decree was dated August 29 (Adams, *op. cit.,* II, 277).

[99] This was also the opinion of F. O. Adams, the British Chargé (Adams, *op. cit.,* II, 278–79).

[100] No. 238, September 4, *F.R., 1871,* pp. 597–99. There were, of course, no local legislatures, and the *karo* were the hereditary advisers and officers of the daimyos. De Long's estimate of the effect upon the income of the daimyos was not justified by the event. Mr. Fish wrote that De Long's report would "excite a profound interest in this country, where every indication of progress in the Empire of Japan is viewed with satisfaction" (No. 119, October 26).

Several items foreshadowed improved commercial relations. The difficulties created by the debased coinage and irredeemable paper would soon be removed by the new coinage produced by the mint from Hong Kong erected at Osaka, and old coins would be redeemed.[101] The mint was opened on April 4, with the diplomatic corps in attendance. After the exercises, De Long, accompanied by Hepburn and Hayashi, the Ministers of Holland and Spain, and the Dutch Vice-Consul at Osaka, visited Kyoto, the first Foreign Representatives to enter the old capital since the visit of the three Ministers and the attack upon Parkes, in 1868. De Long's impressions were unfavorable, and he reported

that this Mikado's government, as at present constituted, is the anti-foreign party of Japan, inimical to foreigners, fostering and encouraging the prejudices and hatred of their sect, displaying this feeling on all proper occasions of safety to themselves, and really meditating on, or hoping for, a period when they may relapse into their former condition of seclusion.

From Kyoto the party proceeded to Lake Biwa and Nara, and back to Osaka and Kobe.[102]

De Long reported the opening of the Yokosuka dockyard and naval arsenal on March 18,[103] but he overlooked the opening of the first stage of the railway between Yokohama and Tokyo in September.[104] He also reported in May that some Japanese desired to exhibit native products at the exhibition of the Mechanics Institute in San Francisco.[105] And in August he stated that the application of the Asiatic Commercial Company (made through him) to land a cable in Japan had been granted but that he would not seek a specific grant until instructed by the Department.[106]

The visit of the American fleet, in November, gave rise to two

[101] No. 166, March 13.

[102] No. 180, April 18. This unfavorable report was typical of De Long's views early in the year. The presence of Hayashi may account in part for his interpretation of some of the events. De Long forwarded three sets of the new coins on April 21.

[103] No. 179, April 18.   [104] Black, *op. cit.*, II, 332.

[105] No. 187, May 15. The Japanese, in later years, were frequently represented at international exhibitions.

[106] No. 230, August 17.

incidents. On the one hand, De Long tried to induce the Emperor to visit the squadron, but the best he could obtain was a promise that in the future the American fleet would be the first to be visited. And on the other, he sought a ceremonial audience for Admiral Rodgers and his staff. When this was refused he pressed the invitation to visit the fleet. The Ministers then agreed to the ceremonial audience on this occasion only, but never again to any but diplomats. Admiral Rodgers wisely accepted a private audience.[107]

Toward the end of the year the Japanese were preparing to send Lord Iwakura and his mission to visit the Treaty Powers. De Long notified the Department, on November 22, that he would now take advantage of his overdue leave and accompany the mission to Washington.[108] In December he took leave of the Emperor and presented Colonel Shepard as Chargé, and on the twenty-third he left Yokohama, in company with Iwakura and his party of forty-eight officials and fifty-three students and attendants.[109]

[107] No. 248, November 17.
[108] No. 251.   [109] No. 255, December 6.

CHAPTER XVIII

THE IWAKURA MISSION
1872

WHILE the progress of the Iwakura mission from capital to capital around the world has been frequently described, the most important of its negotiations, judged by both its immediate and its later significance, has never been narrated. The discussions which took place between Mr. Fish and the Ambassadors in Washington, between March and July, 1872, and which almost resulted in a revised treaty, can now be treated in the detail they deserve.

Mr. Adams, the British Chargé, believed that the idea of a mission to the Treaty Powers had taken form in the minds of the Japanese Cabinet after the abolition of feudalism had been decreed on August 29, 1871. Its purpose was to explain to the Powers the changes which had taken place in Japan since the Restoration and to describe the actual state of the country and the future policy of the Government.

They also thought it important, on their part, to take measures for learning the institutions of other countries, and for gaining a more precise knowledge of their laws, commerce, and education, as well as of their naval and military systems.

The first plan was to send Iwakura as Ambassador, with Kido and Okubo as Councillors. But the idea developed until Iwakura was supported by four Associate Ambassadors, and a large company of officials, students, and attendants.[1] De Long did not report the appointment of the mission until November 22.[2] And

---

[1] Adams, *The History of Japan,* II, 305–7.

[2] No. 251. Official confirmation was given by Chargé Mori in a letter of January 12, 1872.

as we have seen, he accompanied it when it set sail on December 23.

The Embassy was an imposing one. The Ambassador Extraordinary was Iwakura Tomomi, a kuge, Minister for Foreign Affairs and Minister of the Left (Junior Prime Minister). As Vice-Ambassadors Extraordinary were Kido Takayoshi, member of the Council of State; Okubo Tosamichi, Minister of Finance; Ito Hirobumi, Acting Minister of Public Works; and Yamaguchi Massouka, Assistant Minister for Foreign Affairs. Twelve secretaries of different grades, one attaché, ten Commissioners who held high office in the Government, and twenty-one junior officers of various departments completed the official personnel. In addition five young women accompanied the mission to the United States to enter schools there (the first Japanese women to be sent abroad for an education), and fifty-three young gentlemen and servants, employed in various capacities.[3]

The Pacific Mail steamer "America" entered the Golden Gate on January 15, 1872, and the first of many hospitable receptions occurred. In his first public utterance, through an interpreter, Lord Iwakura described the mission as "one of investigation." On another occasion Ito read a speech in English in which he described the results already derived from his observations in the United States the year before. Minister De Long, on his part, described the progress which had been made in recent years:

Who of you all, gentlemen, can fail to see in this sight [the noble array of Japanese dignitaries] the harbinger of greater events still to follow, that shall place Japan, in a very brief future, in complete alignment with the most advanced nations of the earth? We are proud of the past, proud of the present, and confident of the future. In this spirit I am sure the whole heart of the American nation will leap up to welcome the noble Ambassadors of our sister nation.

While at San Francisco, Charles Wolcott Brooks, who had served as Consul for Japan for the previous three years, and as

---

[3] Lanman, *The Japanese in America,* pp. 7–9, for the names of all the officials. The idea of sending young women to study in America originated with Kuroda who, on his two visits, had been impressed with the education and respect which American women enjoyed. He at once recognized the importance of literate mothers in forwarding the great educational program of the Empire.

Commercial Agent for nine years earlier, was attached to the mission.

The next reception was at Sacramento, where the legislature of California and the citizens paid their respects. But the visit to Salt Lake City was prolonged to seventeen days because of a snow blockade.[4] During their stay in Chicago, late in February, the envoys took the opportunity to present to Mayor Joseph Medill $5,000 for the relief of sufferers from the Great Fire. On the twenty-ninth of the month they arrived in Washington.

Congress had already appropriated $50,000 for the entertainment of the mission, and General William Myers had been placed in charge of the arrangements. On March 4, the President of the United States, Ulysses S. Grant, received the Embassy in a formal audience. On this occasion Iwakura read an address, and presented the letter of credence. The latter, after naming the Ambassadors and their titles, continued:

We have . . . . invested them with full powers to proceed to the Government of the United States, as well as to other Governments, in order to declare our cordial friendship, and to place the peaceful relations between our respective nations on a firmer and broader basis.

The period for revising the treaties now existing between ourselves and the United States is less than one year distant. We expect and intend to reform and improve the same so as to stand upon a similar footing with the most enlightened nations, and to attain the full development of public right and interest. The civilization and institutions of Japan are so different from those of other countries, that we cannot expect to reach the desired end at once.

It is our purpose to select from the various institutions prevailing among enlightened nations such as are best suited to our present condition, and adopt them, in gradual reforms and improvements of our policy and customs, so as to be upon an equality with them.

With this object, we desire to fully disclose to the United States Government the condition of affairs in our Empire, and to consult upon the means of giving greater efficiency to our institutions, at present and in the future; and as soon as the said Embassy returns home we will consider about the revision of the treaties, and accomplish what we have expected and intended. . . . .[5]

[4] Brigham Young, the Mormon leader, requested Iwakura to call upon him. He was told that the first call must be made on the Ambassador. But Mr. Young was then under domiciliary confinement in charge of a Federal officer.

[5] Dated December 15, 1871.

According to this letter of credence, the powers of the Embassy were limited to these ends: to declare cordial friendship, to place peaceful relations on a firmer and broader basis, to disclose the condition of affairs in the Empire, and to consult upon the means of giving greater efficiency to its institutions. Only on the return of the Embassy would Treaty revision be considered.

This was understood in advance by the President, for his address, which described and accounted for the prosperity and happiness of the United States, made but one direct allusion to the purpose of the mission: "It will be a pleasure to us to enter upon that consultation upon international questions in which you say you are authorized to engage." Consultation, however, was a different matter from negotiation.[6]

After other hospitalities in Washington, including a reception by Congress on March 6, and the usual sight-seeing excursions of the time, the Embassy took up the most important of its duties, the discussion of Treaty revision with the American Secretary of State.[7]

In advance of the discussions the Department had prepared, (a) a memorandum on revision based on De Long's despatches of 1871, Nos. 191, 211, 232; (b) a copy of von Brandt's points; (c) a copy of the Japanese memorandum inclosed in De Long's No. 191; (d) a brief memorandum on "Revision of Treaty"; (e) and a draft Treaty in Hunter's handwriting but with amendments and notes in another hand. This draft, as revised, became (18).

---

[6] For the reception of the Embassy in the United States see Lanman, *op. cit.*, pp. 10–37.

[7] For these very important discussions *F.R., 1872,* furnish no information whatever. This was in part due to the presence of Mr. De Long in Washington. The archives of the State Department, fortunately, contain a volume entitled "Japanese Embassy / Minutes of Conferences / Drafts of Treaties Submitted, &c. / 1872 / Department of State." Its contents comprise twenty-four items bearing upon the negotiations. They will be cited by figures in parentheses indicating the number of the document as arranged in the volume. As an indication of the fullness of the minutes, it may be said that 114 folio pages were required to cover the eight interviews.

On Monday, March 11, the first interview took place at the Department of State. The American officials included Mr. Fish, Mr. Charles Hale, Assistant Secretary of State, and Nathan E. Rice, interpreter to the United States Legation in Japan. The five Japanese Ambassadors were accompanied by Mori Arinori, Minister of Japan, Mr. Charles W. Brooks, and one of the secretaries of the Embassy.[8]

The interview began with a statement of the progress which had marked the recent years in Japan. The first question involved the powers of the Embassy. While they could only discuss points, they were prepared to sign a protocol setting forth the result of the conferences. Mr. Fish then remarked that the Emperor's letter gave them only the power to discuss, but that they could sign a record of what transpired, which would form a basis of the revision. But they pointed out that revision would take place only after their return from Europe. In this case, said Mr. Fish, a protocol would be obligatory and would simply precede a formal treaty. To which Iwakura replied that whatever they did must be subject to the approval of their Government, a condition which Mr. Fish reserved for his Government as well. A discussion then arose as to when the final revision would take place, Mr. Fish pointing out that the terms of one-third of the United States Senators would expire on March 3 next, while Iwakura desired to have the final date extended to July 1, 1873.

In regard to the general situation Mr. Fish asked certain questions and was told that all the Treaties would be revised at the same time, that in dealing with the other Powers the Embassy could only discuss but not sign, that all the new Treaties would be alike, and that they would contain equal privileges. Although Japan had informed the other Powers of its desires, no reply had yet been received from any of them. Mr. Fish then announced that the United States would postpone the revision for one year (from July 4, 1872), if the other Powers would do so, and would expect the benefit of any advantages conceded to them but not

---

[8] The minutes of interviews were signed by Mr. Hale (6).

detrimental to any rights enjoyed under the present Treaties, to which Iwakura assented.

The Secretary then asked if Japan wished to enter upon the revision, and if they would point out the portions of the existing Treaties which they wished changed and what new points they would wish to introduce. Iwakura replied that there were a great many articles which they would wish to change in detail, but he would now mention only the most important in compliance with Mr. Fish's request for a general idea of the principal changes desired. The seven desires then set forth may be considered the *sine qua non* of the Japanese diplomats of 1872.

I. Tariff autonomy.

II. A definition of neutrality in time of war.

III. "A revision of the regulations establishing Consular Courts, the judicial power of Consuls to cease upon the establishment of a national code in Japan, based on the best laws of the United States and European countries."

IV. A revision of the provisions respecting coinage and currency.

V. Reciprocal extradition of fugitives from justice.

VI. A prohibition of the landing of organized military forces in Japan.

VII. "A stipulation that, in case of serious difficulty between the United States and Japan, there shall always be an attempt at pacific solution before a resort to reprisals or acts of war."[9]

Some conversation ensued on these matters, in which Mr. Fish pointed out the difficulty involved in an attempt to define neutrality, but thought some general principles might be stated, as in the recent Treaty between the United States and Great Britain, and did not see the application of the sixth point to the United States. Lord Iwakura agreed that the United States had never landed troops in Japan. The Japanese then proposed to present, for revision, the trade regulations, personal rights, and perhaps some other matters, and Mr. Fish promised to submit his points at the next interview.

[9] Number I referred to the Convention of 1866; II, to the difficulties which arose during the Franco-German War; III, to the Treaties of 1858; IV, to the Convention of 1866; V, to the proposal made by Japan to the United States in August 1871; VI, to the presence of British and French garrisons and depots in Yokohama. VII was a most enlightened proposal. Compare these points with the alleged Japanese memorandum of 1871.

He then reverted to the difficulty entailed by the lack of power of the Embassy to conclude a treaty, and to the changes which might take place in the American executive and legislative offices after March 3. If a treaty were not made before that day it might fail. However, he thought it well that they should discuss matters and see how near they could come to agreement, the accepted points to be put in writing but not necessarily signed in any formal or binding way. To all this Iwakura assented; in a few days he would be ready to give a definite answer as to the extension desired, and he would be glad to conclude a treaty before March next—in fact the Embassy would endeavor to arrange their movements in such a way as to make this possible.

At this first interview the readiness of the United States to proceed to a speedy revision of the Treaty was made clear. Nowhere else, on their travels, did the Ambassadors meet with such a co-operative spirit.

The second interview took place two days later, on the thirteenth.[10] Iwakura at once repeated what Mori had already told Mr. Fish, that they would, if necessary, send some of the Associate Ambassadors to Japan to obtain full powers in due and proper form. "The personal instructions of the Ambassadors themselves," he said, "are broader in their terms than the letter of credence." But in the meantime the conference might proceed, pending the receipt of full powers. To this Mr. Fish assented, on the understanding that it was a conference and not an agreement.

Without expressing an opinion on the points presented by the Ambassadors on the eleventh, Mr. Fish then placed before them eleven points to which he thought attention should be drawn. They were, in brief:

  I. Foreign ships to be permitted to visit ports not now opened to foreign trade. (Under an occasional or annual license fee.)
 II. Lighthouse and harbor dues. (Reasonable charges based on tonnage. Harbor dues to be under the joint control of the native authorities and the Foreign Representatives.)

10 Yamaguchi was not present (8).

III. Treaty limits, especially at Nagasaki, to be extended.

IV. Travel and trade in the interior. (Passports to be issued by the Consuls and viséed by the Foreign Minister.)

V. Foreigners to be allowed to lease, possess and occupy real estate within the Treaty limits, and in all towns open to foreign trade, and within a limited distance therefrom. (To acquire such property either from the Government or from natives, and to transfer the same among themselves or to natives.)

VI. Freedom to natives to enter the employ of foreigners, and to employ foreigners, within the Treaty limits and open ports.

VII. No restriction, direct or indirect or by means of license or special permits, to be placed on commercial intercourse between natives and foreigners. (No duties to be levied on articles being brought to the open ports, but this was not to interfere with any regular, uniform, and generally collected taxes.)

VIII. Uniform import and export duties, irrespective of the country concerned. (All smuggling to be prevented.)

IX. Municipal Regulations. "The establishment of some system whereby either by the separate action of the Foreign Representatives or conjointly with the Japanese authorities, a tax may be levied on the Foreign Residents for municipal purposes, to be expended for the maintenance of a sufficient police system, & for Sanitary regulations in the Treaty Ports or towns where the tax is levied."

X. Freedom of speech, the press, and of conscience, and toleration of religious opinions and observances of worship. ("No persecutions on account of religious belief—no indignities to be offered to the ceremonials or to the symbols of any religious faith or creed. If such indignities be offered by the individuals they should be punished.")

XI. The most-favored-nation clause.[11]

A comparison of the seven points presented by the envoys with the eleven submitted by Mr. Fish shows how far apart the two parties were at the beginning of the negotiations. The two principal *desiderata* of the Japanese—tariff autonomy and the speedy

[11] Pencil notations indicate that points III, V, VI, VII, and VIII were agreed to by the Japanese, which is not confirmed by the reply (9). As De Long's views on revision were presented to the Department orally we can assume that they followed in the main the memorandum of von Brandt. A comparison of the eleven points given above with von Brandt's sixteen shows the following similarities: I, (5); II, (3); III, (7); IV, (4); V, (8); VI, (none); VII, (14); VIII, (none); IX, (9); X, the Christian question to be left entirely alone (15); XI, (none—as it was already in the Treaties). The only comparisons with the Japanese memorandum of 1871 are II, (2) and IX, (11).

relinquishment of extraterritoriality—were not mentioned by the Secretary. In fact, his points dealt with the modification, for the most part in details, of the existing Treaties.

The discussion was now resumed on the points previously presented by the envoys.[12] Iwakura explained that the abolition of consular jurisdiction was not to take effect immediately, but only after a modern code, based on the best Western laws, had been established. To this Mr. Fish added, "when satisfactory courts have been established," to which Iwakura assented. This brought out the first official statement as to the attitude of the United States toward the eventual abolition of extraterritoriality:

There will be no difficulty about that. The Government of the United States will be glad to withdraw the consular jurisdiction as soon as there are satisfactory local courts to take its place. The difficulty will be to know when the courts are satisfactory.

In respect to neutrality, Iwakura said that Japan did not want to be held responsible for violations by foreigners resident in the country, to which Mr. Fish replied that he would like to have their views in writing but that all other countries were responsible for the acts of people residing in them. Okubo then explained that in regard to coinage and currency the Embassy proposed that the Japanese and Mexican dollars be considered of equal value, which Mr. Fish thought could perhaps be accepted. To the mutual extradition of criminals he had no objection, for the United States had such treaties with many Powers, and all that was necessary was to define the crimes to be made extraditable. And although he had no objection to the article forbidding the landing of troops in Japan, if the other Powers would agree to it, he felt that it might have the appearance of placing the United States under suspicion, although it had never landed troops.

On the seventh point, for the pacific solution of difficulties, Mr. Fish remarked that this was already the law of the civilized world, and inquired what was the object sought by putting it in the Treaty. Iwakura replied that it was of general application,

---

[12] At this point Mr. Fish asked if the Treaty between Japan and China had been ratified. He was told the ratifications had not been exchanged.

without special reference to the United States. Mr. Fish's comment was: "It does not appear to me to be a very good provision to be put in the treaty," but if the other Powers agreed the United States would make no objection. This led Iwakura to remark that they would reconsider this point. The next interview was arranged for the sixteenth, for some of the Associate Ambassadors were being sent back to Japan, as had been intimated, and they would have to leave about the twentieth.

On the sixteenth, Mr. Brooks read an English translation of the envoys' observations on Mr. Fish's eleven points.[13] The whole tenor of this reply was toward acceptance of the improvements in commercial and other relations proposed by Mr. Fish but provision of them by the sole act of Japan, without the intervention of treaty stipulations. A summary, therefore, is instructive as indicating how far the Japanese had advanced toward the principle of autonomy and reciprocal engagements. The articles were numbered to correspond with Mr. Fish's points.

I. The Japanese Government is willing to open new ports from time to time, but the selection of the ports and the proper time for opening them would be settled from time to time by the Japanese Government after consultation with the Foreign Powers.

II. The Japanese Government will establish harbor regulations and fix the necessary dues. It considers itself at liberty to employ foreigners in carrying out these regulations. Reasonable lighthouse dues will be collected from all foreign vessels according to tonnage.

III. The treaty limits at Nagasaki will be extended, by notification given by the Government of Japan when the ratifications of this treaty are exchanged.

IV. Travel in the interior will be permitted. Passports for each journey, limited to specific times, will be furnished on the request of any duly accredited Foreign Consul, who shall vouch for the general good character of the applicant. These privileges to take effect one year after the formal ratification of this treaty.

V. Foreigners may be allowed to lease and occupy real estate for residence within treaty limits at the open ports, provided no such leases shall hereafter be construed to conflict with the mining rights and laws of Japan.

---

[13] Yamaguchi again absent (9).

> After two years from the ratification of the treaty land within five *ris* may be leased, and after two years further these limits will be extended five *ris*.

VI. No objection.

VII. Agreed to.

VIII. Agreed to.

IX. Municipal regulations will be established by the Japanese Government, the general rules governing which will first be made public, and published by authority. Taxes necessary to support and enforce these regulations will be levied and collected by Japanese officers appointed to this duty.

X. Under consideration.

XI. Agreed to.

Commenting upon some of these points, Mr. Fish was told that all mines belonged to the Government and no licenses had hitherto been granted to foreigners; and that although no provision was made for the opening of new ports it was the policy and purpose of the Government to do so. He then asked if they desired an explanation of any of his points, and a spirited discussion ensued.

Lord Iwakura at once took up the tenth point (freedom of speech, of the press, and of conscience, and religious toleration), and asked if it was to apply to everybody in Japan, or only to the resident foreigners. Mr. Fish replied:

> We wish to apply it to all. We think it necessary to the development of a nation that every individual shall have liberty to think as he pleases; let him think as he pleases, provided he does not act against public law. Any interference with freedom of thought among the Japanese is prejudicial to the interests of everybody in Japan, the foreign residents included. Without desiring to interfere in your internal affairs, we nevertheless think it desirable in the common interest that everybody under your government, or resident in your country, should have liberty to think as he pleases.[14]

Mori then observed that as the Japanese Government was then liberal, and disposed to grant the privileges of thought and action to the people as fast as it was safe to do so, it was hardly necessary to have such a treaty provision. This led Mr. Fish to suggest that perhaps such a provision would strengthen the hands of the

---

[14] The Japanese Christians, at this time, were acting "against public law."

Government and confirm its liberal tendencies. He asked them to consider this point again.

The discussion now turned to the seven points presented by the envoys. As to tariff autonomy, Mr. Fish thought they would have more difficulty elsewhere than with the United States. But he took the rather doubtful position that until Japan threw the whole country open to foreigners he was not sure that it ought to claim all the privileges that other Governments exercise.[15]

If this was the case, then Iwakura inquired as to what sort of limitation on customs duties the United States would propose. Mr. Fish was not prepared to go into details, but thought it might be a classification of articles subject to certain duties for a specified period of years.[16] Mori again argued for autonomy on the ground that the Government favored the promotion of commerce, and of its own accord would always be anxious to fix rates to encourage it. "But," replied Mr. Fish, "this policy is of recent date—there might be a reaction." And even when Mori offered to give assurance that the present policy was fixed and permanent, Mr. Fish pointed out that nobody could tell what their policy would be in the next generation. "Then you lack confidence in our Government," charged Mori. "It is a lack of confidence in human nature," was the reply. Mori then developed reasons, from the nature and situation of Japan, for the permanence of the present policy, and Mr. Fish reassured him by saying that the United States would not be as tenacious on this point as other Powers but that Japan would probably have to agree upon some limitation of duties until it was ready to throw the whole country open to foreigners.

As for the other points—Mr. Fish still awaited the views of the Ambassadors on neutrality; the United States would be prepared to withdraw its consular jurisdiction whenever Japan established and put into operation a satisfactory code of laws and

[15] This was an early disclosure of a vicious circle. Japan would not open the country to foreign trade and residence (except under a passport) because of extraterritoriality, and because she would not do so she was denied tariff autonomy and freedom from extraterritoriality.

[16] This was the nature of the existing conventional tariff.

satisfactory courts to administer them, "but," he pointed out, "it will require some time after the establishment of the courts to prove that they are satisfactory"; and he considered there would probably be no difficulty as to extradition, although neither country would agree to surrender its own citizens. In regard to the sixth and seventh points (the landing of troops and peaceful solution of difficulties), he would probably not object to putting them into the Treaty, but he perceived no particular reason for doing so.

The fourth interview took place on the eighteenth.[17] Okubo and Ito were about to return to Japan (on the nineteenth) and they wished to take back exact information on all the points upon which an agreement had been reached. Little had been agreed upon, in the opinion of Mr. Fish, and the envoys were not prepared to say which new ports would be opened and when. One assurance he could give them:

You are desirous of having the entire control of your tariff of customs dues; very well; if we can come to a satisfactory agreement with you on other points, we will agree to your wishes in this regard.

And he repeated his offer for the withdrawal of consular jurisdiction on the conditions previously laid down.

The Japanese were now willing to incorporate the opening of ports in the Treaty, and they said:

If you allow us control of the tariff we will agree to open such ports as are necessary for the interests of foreign commerce and to provide that they shall be opened at the time of the ratification of the treaty.

Mr. Fish then asked for a draft of the proposed articles, as they could go no farther without definite propositions before them. The discussion, however, continued. Harbor regulations were taken up, and Mr. Fish supported the present regulations and the right of the Consuls to have a voice in framing regulations and appointing the administrative officers. The envoys thought the Japanese Government should make all appointments, a right which Mr. Fish did not think would be accorded by the foreign Powers,

---

[17] Iwakura was ill and absent (10).

at least before the next revision of the Treaties. He also advanced his proposal for foreign participation in municipal (treaty-port) government. He then inquired if Japan intended to abolish export duties, and was told that this would be done as soon as the new internal revenue system was fully established. On their part, the envoys desired the omission of existing treaty provisions which permitted the export of rice and wheat and copper coins. Both parties agreed that the existing trade regulations could be continued with slight modifications.

In regard to the conventional tariff, Mr. Fish suggested two rules dealing with imports: (1) no duties so high as to be prohibitory; (2) ample notice to merchants all over the world as to changes—probably twelve months' notice. And the Ambassadors added that their Government should be free to discriminate against certain imports, such as opium and wine, to which Mr. Fish had no objection.

He then explained the provision in the Constitution of the United States prohibiting the levying of export duties, and the Ambassadors present agreed to an article that the two Powers reciprocally agree not to charge export duties. This agreement was, of course, reserved for the assent of Lord Iwakura. Minor alterations in the trade regulations were then suggested, as to the deposit of ship's papers and the computation of tonnage dues.

Then there occurred an exchange of views, so interesting in the light of later events, that it deserves full quotation.

The Secretary of State. Does Japan have secret treaties with any Power,

The Ambassadors. Never, and probably never will.

The Secretary of State. Are you willing to enter into an understanding with the Treaty Powers that you will not have secret treaties?

The Ambassadors. We would wish to know why you put that question.

The Secretary of State. Because some European Powers make secret treaties. The United States have never had a secret treaty. Such treaties are always liable to involve the parties making them in trouble with Powers who have not secret treaties.

The Ambassadors. We have not considered this subject.

The Secretary of State. This provision might be made reciprocal: The United States and Japan agreeing each that it will not make a secret treaty, or, that if it should make such a treaty, it will give notice to the other party to this stipulation.

The Ambassadors. This is a new thing for us to hear, we will think of it.

A long conversation ensued on the subject of liberty of thought and conscience, in which Mr. Fish repeated the views he had already expressed and called attention to the discussions in Tokyo in 1870.[18] No agreement could be reached, and Mr. Fish suggested a separate treaty. Mori, for the Ambassadors, asked for the Secretary's views in writing, to which a formal reply could be given.

The fifth interview took place on the twenty-seventh.[19] The discussion began as to the opening of new ports. Japan would agree to open two ports within one year after the ratification of the Treaty, and three other ports as the demands of commerce required. Tsuruga, Kagoshima, Otaru, Ichinomaki (near Sendai), and Shimonoseki were named by the Ambassadors, and any two selected by Mr. Fish would be opened first. After some conversation as to when the remaining three would be opened, Iwakura proposed that one of them would be opened within one year after request, and two more within four years, so that the entire five would be open within five years after the date of ratification. To this Mr. Fish assented.

Then the subject of harbor and municipal regulations was considered. The Japanese Government desired that these matters be left entirely within its control, but Mr. Fish repeated his conviction that as long as the foreign residents were restrained within certain contracted limits the Japanese Government must allow a certain degree of extraterritoriality. He was willing to have the limitation of a temporary nature, ceasing when Japan was prepared to remove the restrictions affecting foreigners. To which Lord Iwakura replied:

> The Japanese Government is wholly in earnest in the desire to facilitate intercourse with foreign countries. We wish that the Independence and Sovereignty of Japan may be recognized and respected. That is the point we start from.

---

[18] See *supra,* chap. xvi.   [19] De Long was present (11).

Of the sincerity and good faith of the Japanese Government
Mr. Fish had no doubt; but he still felt that for the present a
certain amount of supervision over the rights of their nationals in
Japan seemed necessary for the foreign governments. He suggested that foreign participation in municipal regulations might
cease as soon as Japan conceded to foreigners the right to reside
within ten *ri* of the open ports. To this proposition Iwakura
assented. Similar views were exchanged about harbor regulations,
and Mr. Fish proposed a limitation upon general foreign participation by suggesting that the Consuls of the five nations having
the largest tonnage at each port (and with authority weighted in
proportion to the tonnage of their respective nations) act with
the Japanese officials in arranging the harbor regulations and
choosing the administrative agents. This suggestion Iwakura
would take under consideration. Mr. Fish again suggested that
the Ambassadors submit a draft in writing at the next meeting.

The meeting arranged for March 30 did not take place, because of the illness of Iwakura. A long delay now occurred, during which the Ambassadors traveled extensively in the Northern
states. On April 23, Mori transmitted to the Secretary of State
the Protocol and Supplementary Articles proposed by the Embassy. These were forwarded on the twenty-sixth to Minister
De Long, in New York City, with a request for his views, and
he replied very promptly on the twenty-eighth.[20] Within the Department the Japanese drafts were subjected to thorough consideration.[21]

The Japanese draft of the Protocol of a treaty between the

---

[20] No. 267.

[21] The draft Protocol (12) was mimeographed and circulated for the use
of the American officials. A copy (13) contains comments and additions in
blue pencil, black pencil, and red ink. A memorandum was also drawn up
listing the points upon which an agreement had been reached in the five interviews, some of which were omitted from the Protocol and others of which
appeared in a different form. The draft of the Supplementary Articles (15)
was also mimeographed, but only a few pencil comments were made on the
copy in the files (16). If the drafts had resulted in a treaty, it would have
been interesting to trace the effect of these various comments upon the later
negotiations.

Empire of Japan and the United States of America contained a preamble and fifteen articles. A very brief summary will indicate how the Japanese views had developed since the original seven points were presented by Iwakura at the first interview.

I. Preamble.
"It shall be the mutual aim [of both parties] to promote between the two countries the best relations of friendship, each party respecting under all circumstances the sovereign rights and dignity of the other."[22] Provides for the appointment of Diplomatic Agents.

II. A conditional most-favored-nation clause. "It is stipulated however, that they [the people of either country] shall submit themselves to the laws, decrees and established usages governing native subjects or citizens."[23] The coasting trade reserved to each country.

III. Most-favored-nation treatment of merchant vessels.

IV. Reciprocal privileges and most-favored-nation treatment of imports and exports. No duties on goods imported and stored for the use of the navies of either country.

V. Appointment of Consuls, etc., but if they shall be engaged in trade they shall be subjected to the laws and usages governing private individuals.

VI. Mutual aid in the arrest and imprisonment of deserters.

VII. The reciprocal right to lease land, subject to law.

VIII. Reciprocal engagement to protect the person and property [of the subjects or citizens] of the other within their respective territories. Access to courts on most-favored-nation terms. Testimony to be taken from citizens of either nationality in the courts.

IX. Prohibited imports to be subject to the laws of either country. No unreasonable restrictions upon commercial or civil intercourse between their respective citizens. The right of either to employ citizens of the other in any lawful capacity.

X. The reciprocal right of freedom of conscience, worship, and burial.

XI. Protection and assistance for shipwrecked men and goods.

XII. Reciprocal extradition for certain offences.

[22] Red-ink notation: "This clause seems unnecessary—the introduction of 'sovereign rights' is probably to exclude 'extraterritoriality.' Cannot yet be conceded."

[23] Red-ink notation: "American citizens cannot be subjected to the laws & decrees &c. of Japan until the Japanese have demonstrated a capacity of administering justice."

XIII. Negotiations to precede reprisals or war. No landing of foreign military organizations on the soil of either country.

XIV. Abrogation of all former treaties. This treaty to remain in force for ten years, and if official notice is not given one year before the expiration then it shall continue until twelve months after notice has been given.

XV. Provision for ratification and exchange.

The outstanding features of this draft are the recognition of the independence and sovereignty of Japan, the use of reciprocal engagements, of the conditional most-favored-nation clause, and of a fixed period for the life of the Treaty.

The draft of the Supplementary Articles stated that they would be engrossed in a decree of the Emperor.[24]

I. The opening of five additional ports within five years from the ratification of the treaty.

II. The extension of the limits of the foreign settlements, within six years the right to reside and lease land would extend to the travel limits—ten *ri* from each port. In the case of Nagasaki and Hiogo the travel limits would be extended to ten *ri*.

III. Travel in the interior on Japanese passports.

IV. Alteration in custom duties to be effective only six months after official notice.

V. Continuance of Consular jurisdiction until properly organized courts are established, to be notified by the Government of Japan.

VI. Custom duties to be payable in Japanese gold yen, but in case of necessity Mexican dollars would be received as an equivalent.

VII. Special licenses to be granted American vessels to engage in the coasting trade between the open ports of Japan.

On June 1 the discussion was renewed in the sixth interview.[25] After remarking that the two drafts did not correspond with the points previously agreed upon in the interviews, which Iwakura admitted and was prepared to explain, Mr. Fish inquired if the Ambassadors had received their full powers. He was answered in the negative, but they believed they would arrive in due time. The discussion, however, could continue, and Mr. Fish proposed to submit a draft.

The American drafts of a treaty and accompanying schedule

---

[24] (16).   [25] Okubo, Ito, and De Long were absent (17).

were submitted on June 8.[26] The treaty draft contained a preamble and twenty-four articles; the additional articles (beyond the
fifteen of the Japanese draft) were due to the division of certain
articles, the elaboration into four articles of the provisions respecting Consuls, and a similar amplification of the article for extradition. The Treaty contained no reference to extraterritoriality,
nor any provision for its expiration, but it did incorporate the
conditional most-favored-nation clause in respect of trade, commerce, and navigation. It waived the right to participate in drafting harbor regulations, but retained the approval of the Consul
in the case of the appointment of a foreign harbor master; it limited religious tolerance to the respective nationals; it continued
all non-conflicting provisions of the Treaties of 1854 and 1858;
and it included clauses for pacific steps before hostilities and forbidding the landing of military forces in time of peace without
proper permission.

The schedule, which was to be put into force by an Imperial
decree issued on or before the ratification of the Treaty, and which
was to form a part of the Treaty, consisted of five articles. They
defined more carefully the provisions proposed in the Japanese
Additional Articles. Passports would be issued by the Japanese
Government on the request of the Consul, but again nothing was
said about the abolition of extraterritoriality.

The Japanese took the American drafts under consideration
and on July 10 returned them with their proposed amendments.[27]
In general, they tried to restore some of the articles omitted by
Mr. Fish, including the limit on the life of the Treaty and the
eventual abolition of extraterritoriality. From this time the negotiations would have proceeded on the basis of the American
drafts with the Japanese amendments, for the texts of the latter
contain pencil notes by an American official, viz., "disagree,"
"accepted," "insist."

[26] Treaty (18); Schedule (22). No. 22 is bound out of order in the volume.
It is preceded by (20), which is the same schedule, as amended by the Japanese
and submitted to Mr. Fish on July 10, along with their amendments to the
American draft Treaty (19).
[27] (19) and (20).

On July 20 the discussion was resumed.[28] Mr. Fish began by
alluding to a letter which had in the meantime been received from
Colonel Shepard, the American Chargé.[29] It had been addressed
by Soyeshima and Terashima, Ministers for Foreign Affairs, to
De Long, on May 24. It read, in part:

It was the intention of the Japanese Government . . . . to despatch
to your Government [Iwakura and his associates] and to empower them
to consult with your Government upon the points of the Treaty proposed
to be revised and upon their return to Japan to revise said Treaty.

H.M. the Tenno has now invested the above named Ambassador
Extraordinary and Associate Ambassadors Extraordinary with full power
to negotiate and sign regarding the revision of the present Treaty, at
such place as may be convenient for that purpose, if agreeable for both
parties.

We beg leave to request that you will be kind enough to communicate
to your Government our intentions.

He then inquired if the Ambassadors were prepared to proceed
with the negotiation of a treaty to be signed in Washington.
Iwakura replied that his instructions directed him to request that
the United States send a delegate, with powers to sign a treaty,
to such other place as might be convenient. Such a request had
been submitted informally when Iwakura had visited Mr. Fish
at his residence in New York, and the latter had consulted the
President, whose directions were stated as follows:

. . . . that the proposition is inadmissible. In the first place it would not
comport with the dignity of the United States,—after having received at
the seat of Government the Embassy spontaneously sent by the Emperor
of Japan,—to follow the Ambassadors across the Atlantic for the purpose
of concluding elsewhere the treaty. In the second place, the Government
of the United States has always declined to be a party to a Congress or
Conference for the conclusion of any treaty of commerce or amity.

Iwakura then suggested that one of the Ambassadors remain in
the United States to sign the Treaty, as the two Associate Ambassadors were shortly expected back from Japan. This could
be arranged, said Mr. Fish, if they brought full powers. That
they had such powers was very certain, Iwakura replied; but their

---

[28] De Long was absent (21).   [29] No. 43, May 25, 1872.

instructions called for a conference in Europe, and no decision could be arrived at until the envoys had discussed the whole situation. Okubo and Ito were expected on the twenty-second, and the next interview was arranged for three o'clock that day.

The eighth and last interview took place at the stipulated hour on July 22. Okubo and Ito had arrived that morning, but they were too fatigued to attend the conference. The proceedings were soon concluded. Mr. Fish inquired if the returning envoys had brought full powers authorizing the Ambassadors to sign a treaty. And Iwakura replied:

I will explain the circumstances which I am today for the first time able to do with exactness. Our Government has an earnest desire to make a treaty with the United States. It has, however, accepted the proposition that the treaty shall be signed at some point in Europe, convenient to both nations, in the expectation that a conference might take place at some point which would be attended by representatives of all the nations with which Japan has treaties. In this expectation our Government has decided not to authorize us to sign a treaty in Washington. We are bound by these instructions not to make use here of the full powers which the Associate Ambassadors have brought with them. We regret very much that the government of the United States has declined to send a delegate to Europe.

Mr. Fish then announced that he would report this result to the President,

[who] will no doubt appreciate the necessity under which the Ambassadors find themselves of conforming to their instructions, but it will be a source of very great regret to him to learn that his efforts to establish, on a more enlarged and firmer basis, friendly relations between the United States and Japan have failed for the present. The Embassy which the Emperor of Japan of his own motion sent to the United States has been cordially welcomed; and the President has the strongest desire to make a treaty, here and now, on the most favorable terms. If the conclusion of a treaty be postponed until after the Ambassadors have entered into negotiations with European Powers of course the United States will be free to act without regard to what has heretofore passed or to what might now be agreed upon.

Iwakura then expressed regret at reaching no present conclusion, and Mr. Fish voiced his hope that at some future time, not remote, an arrangement might be made satisfactory to both parties. But Iwakura was less optimistic. If the United States declined to send a delegate to a conference in Europe, he feared that it was quite possible that the European nations might decline. And such was to be the case. In conclusion, Mr. Fish remarked that the several interviews had been held on the understanding that full powers to sign a treaty would be produced when Okubo and Ito returned. To this Iwakura assented. The full powers had been issued, but accompanying instructions precluded the use of them in Washington.

On July 23 the Ambassadors took leave of the President, and on the twenty-seventh they left Washington.

Thus ended, without result, the first and most likely chance which Japan had to secure revision of the early Treaties. We have seen that the United States was not only willing and anxious to sign such a treaty but that in the course of the discussions the American Secretary of State had steadily modified his first views to the advantage of Japan.[30]

It is always futile to consider what might have happened, but on this occasion an inference or two may well be offered. If the Japanese Ambassadors could have signed a treaty with the United

[30] Ariga, the distinguished Japanese professor of International Law, states that the decision to make use of a European conference, instead of individual negotiations, was due to the advice given to Iwakura by the German Minister, von Brandt, who visited Washington while the mission was there. The latter pointed out that under the most-favored-nation clause each Power would demand some additional concession which would be applicable to all (Stead, editor, *Japan by the Japanese*, pp. 155–57). In the first place, von Brandt himself does not refer to this in his memoirs. Secondly, his visit to Washington occurred while Ito and Okubo were on their way to Japan to obtain the full powers, and on their return they brought instructions to negotiate only in a European conference. A more reasonable explanation may be found in the statement made by Soyeshima to De Long that Iwakura had sent Ito and Okubo to Japan to secure power to conclude the Treaty in Washington but they took upon themselves to change the plan and proposed a European conference, giving assurances to the Cabinet that the United States and other Powers would assent. Soyeshima was pleased with the refusal of the United States as he preferred to have the negotiations take place in Tokyo (No. 286, September 30, 1872). Ariga also gives three proposals which the envoys submitted to the Cabinet: the gradual enlargement of the treaty port limits, the preparation of courts and laws to take the place of extraterritorial jurisdiction, and the grant of religious tolerance. He states that Ito and Soyeshima (one of the Ministers for Foreign Affairs) were directed to frame a draft treaty.

States, along the lines indicated by the stipulations which had been accepted up to the breaking off of negotiations, there is at least some reason to believe that the British Government, which was next approached, would have entered into the discussion in a friendly spirit. Sir Harry Parkes was then in England, on leave, and he was the outstanding friend and supporter of the new Imperial Government among the Foreign Representatives in Japan. I very much doubt if he, and the Foreign Office which would have been guided by his views, would have permitted the United States to enjoy alone the good will which a friendly revision would have entailed. Even if Britain had whittled down some of the concessions which the United States was prepared to make to Japan, even if a conventional tariff, with low schedules, had been demanded, there would still have been a treaty, and Japan, while gaining less than she desired, would still have gained something. But when it was known that the United States would not take part in a revision conference in Europe, there was no incentive to make even a gesture of friendship for Japan. And so although the Japanese Ambassadors were hospitably received and royally fêted as they traveled through Europe, they were able to do no more than to explain the desires of their Government when revision negotiations should take place.[31]

On the other hand, the patient consideration of Mr. Fish was by no means without result. The comparison between the friendliness of the United States and the self-interest of the European

[31] Important documents dealing with the discussions in London may be found in *F.R., 1873*, pp. 408–16. They were transmitted to Mr. Fish by Sir Edward Thornton, the British Minister, at the direction of Lord Granville. They are entitled: No. 1, Memorandum by the Japanese Ambassadors Respecting the Shimonoseki Indemnity; No. 2, Observations of Sir H. Parkes on the Memorandum of the Japanese Embassadors; No. 1, Memorandum of an Interview between Earl Granville and Iwakura, Chief Embassador of Japan, at the Foreign Office, November 22, 1872; No. 2, Memorandum of an Interview [between the same], November 27, 1872 (Parkes, Terashima, and Yamaguchi were present); No. 3, Memorandum of an Interview [between the same], December 6, 1872.

For a summary of the conversations in Paris, see *ibid.,* pp. 265–66. Count de Remusat reported that the Ambassadors did not possess powers to enter into negotiations, which could not be undertaken until they returned to Japan.

Powers was brought home to the observing Japanese. The return of the Ambassadors was to mark the rebirth of American influence in Japan, since its eclipse with the fall of the Shogunate; and just as American influence rose, so the star of Sir Harry Parkes passed into eclipse.[32]

The immediate results of the Embassy were to be found in the realm of domestic affairs rather than in foreign relations. The information acquired by the members of the party, each one specializing in matters affecting his own department or service, was of the greatest value in shaping the course of the reforms of the following years. Kido, Okubo, and Ito were to be the great constructive leaders of the next few years, until death and assassination removed the former and left Ito to be the father of the Constitution and the pre-eminent statesman of the Meiji era.[33]

---

[32] "But soon after the return of the Iwakura mission in September a change began to manifest itself in the relations of the Government with the Foreign Representatives in general and with Sir Harry Parkes in particular . . . . most of the subsequent diplomatic troubles in Japan can be traced to the influence of Iwakura and his colleagues after 1873, aided and furthered by incompetent foreign advisers" (Dickins, *The Life of Sir Harry Parkes,* II, 179). "But from some cause or another, since its return, more difficulty has been experienced by foreign Ministers, in dealing with the Japanese Government, than ever was known before" (Black, *Young Japan,* II, 346).

[33] In Europe the mission visited England, France, Belgium, Holland, Prussia, Russia, Denmark, Sweden, some of the German States, Italy, Austria, Hungary, and Switzerland. They arrived in Yokohama on September 13, 1873. "The diary of the mission in five illustrated volumes carefully compiled by the scholars accompanying the mission, and published by the Imperial Government, furnishes most interesting and instructive reading even to this day. It contains the history, statistics, politics, finance, and military organization of the countries passed through, and one can readily imagine how much the stories told by this mission contributed to open the eyes of the Japanese public to the things going on abroad. We can also imagine how the thoughts and ideas of the leading men of Japan composing the mission became differentiated from those of their colleagues remaining at home. Hence, though attended with little diplomatic result, the importance of this mission in the history of Japan's external relations can hardly be overestimated" (Ariga, in Stead, *op. cit.,* p. 157).

CHAPTER XIX

THE "MARIA LUZ"

1872 [1]

With the impetuous American Minister at home on leave and a young Consul in charge, and with the Iwakura mission engrossing the attention of the Department in Washington, it might have been expected that the first half of 1872 would pass without any major diplomatic discussion. As a matter of fact the year proved to be one of the most uneventful in the whole story of Japanese-American relations. With the exception of claims and counterclaims, which still afforded grounds for petty irritation, there were few questions which called for discussion between the two countries, and these were of trifling significance. On the other hand, the American Representatives were involved in many incidents which called for correspondence with and from the Department, and these will, for the most part, make up the record of the year.

Colonel Charles O. Shepard assumed charge of the Legation on December 23, 1871, when De Long sailed with the Iwakura mission.[2] His relations with the Minister had not been friendly, and these were to develop later into a bitter dispute. The small number of his dispatches (forty-five in six months) indicate the

[1] The dispatches of Chargé Shepard are numbered 12–57, and those of Minister De Long, while he was in the United States and after his return in August, 265–326; of these 108, three were printed in *F.R., 1872*, six in *F.R., 1873*, and one in *42d Cong., 3d Sess., H. Mis. Doc. No. 96 (Serial Number 1572)*. The instructions are numbered 128–164 to De Long, and 1–20 to Shepard; of these fifty-seven, four were printed in *F.R., 1873*.

[2] Colonel Shepard was appointed Consul at Yedo in May 1869, transferred to Kanagawa (Yokohama), April 1871. He served as Chargé from September 6 to November 8, 1871, and from December 23, 1871 to August 10, 1872. His compensation as Chargé was $4,500, being his salary, as Consul, of $3,000 plus 15 per cent of De Long's salary.

uneventfulness of his term, and fifteen of these dealt with domestic events. In fact he queried the Department as to what sort
of local matters he should report and received this cryptic reply:
"all that is of sufficient importance to report should be reported.
The Department cannot prescribe limits."[3]

A brief reference to the contents of these dispatches will
indicate the domestic events which Shepard thought worthy of
comment. On January 1 the Emperor visited the government
dockyards at Yokosuka,[4] and a little later the suppression of a
peasants' revolt against the telegraph in Himidzu (*sic*) province
was reported.[5] The exportation of rice was permitted for the
first time, notwithstanding the opposition of the other Foreign
Ministers based on the Convention of 1866.[6] For the first time
the Emperor received the Foreign Representatives at a New
Year's reception (February 10).[7] The pardon of the former
Shogun and of Admiral Enomoto was reported in March, the
former being made an officer of the fourth class.[8] The opening
of an exhibition in Kyoto led to a liberal granting of passports
to encourage foreign attendance.[9] An attempt of ten Buddhist
priests to lay their grievances before the Emperor resulted in a
clash with the palace guards, and the death of five of them. They
were protesting against the neglect of their faith and the tolerance which was now being shown to Christianity.[10] The Great
Fire of April 3, which destroyed 6,000 houses in Tokyo, was
reported.[11] An account was given of the new political subdivisions
(prefectures) and the manner of appointing the governors.[12] The
tea districts were visited, and a long dispatch described the growth,
culture, and preparation of this important article of commerce.[13]

---

[3] No. 35, April 20; Instruction No. 13, June 7.   [4] No. 15, January 23.
[5] No. 16, January 23.   [6] No. 17, January 23; No. 22, February 26.
[7] No. 19, February 17, *F.R., 1872*, p. 321.
[8] No. 25, March 22.   [9] No. 28, April 10.
[10] No. 29, April 11. Cf. Black, *op. cit.*, II, 357, which states that the priests
were Shinto, and that four were killed. Shepard received his information from
the Foreign Office, while Black was in Yokohama.
[11] No. 30, April 13, *F.R., 1872*, p. 322.   [12] No. 32, April 16.
[13] No. 36, April 20; No. 39, May 18; No. 49, June 20, *Serial Number 1572*.

The Department was advised of the appointment of Terashima as Minister to Great Britain and of the promotion of Mori to that rank in Washington.[14] The opening of the railway between Yokohama and Tokyo was noted.[15] And an account of the changed condition of the priesthood and the new liberties allowed them made an interesting dispatch.[16]

The first question to call for an exchange of correspondence involved the already discussed Sino-Japanese Treaty of 1871.[17] De Long, from New York, had suggested to the Department the propriety of attempting to secure a copy of the Treaty from Iwakura,[18] and at the interview on March 13 Mr. Fish had inquired as to its status and had been told that the ratifications had not been exchanged. A month later a dispatch was received from Eugene Schuyler, American Chargé at St. Petersburg, which reported that a copy of the Treaty had been received at the Foreign Office. He inclosed a translation of an article in the *Journal de St. Petersburg,* from its Peking correspondent, "who is usually very well informed, and has access to sources of intelligence not open to all the world." The correspondent dismissed the reports of an alliance between the two countries, and pointed out that the two Empires had negotiated on an almost equal footing, notwithstanding the preponderance always claimed by China.[19]

In March the *North China Herald* (Shanghai) printed what purported to be a translation of the Treaty. This led Chargé Shepard to address an inquiry to the Foreign Office as to the accuracy of the second article, which read, as reported:

China and Japan being friendly, either party shall, in case of experiencing injustice or wrong from another State, be entitled to assistance or good offices of the other.

Such a clause, he pointed out, might be construed into an offensive and defensive alliance.

---

[14] No. 44, June 10.   [15] No. 45, June 13.   [16] No. 51, June 25.
[17] See *supra,* chap. xvii.   [18] March 11.
[19] Russia, No. 166, March 25, 1872, *F.R., 1872,* pp. 484–85. The article, dated January 27, was in error as to the date of the Treaty, placing it in November instead of on September 13, 1871.

He was advised, in reply,

that Article II of the Treaty in Chinese version is similar to the clause of the Treaty made between the United States of America and China, and it is not alliance, as you say.

The Japanese Government however have duly considered your note and determined to open negotiation regarding omission of the objectionable clause in question by means of an official who will shortly be despatched to China.

In a subsequent interview Shepard suggested that the article might better be omitted, and the Ministers assured him that, as the Treaty had not yet been ratified, they would adopt his view. At their request he pointed out several desirable amendments, and they stated that an officer would soon be sent to China to amend the present text.[20] It should be pointed out at this time that the text printed in Shanghai, and copied elsewhere, was accepted by many contemporary and later writers as authentic and in force. The question was to be raised again in 1873.[21]

The next subject brought up once more the Shimonoseki indemnity. On May 8 the Japanese Ministers requested Shepard to recommend to his Government a further postponement of the $1,500,000 which was payable to the four Powers on May 15. The reason for making such a request so near the date of liquidation was because Iwakura had been instructed to handle the matter directly in Washington, but he had been able to reach no conclusion. The postponement was to run only until some arrangement had been completed by the envoys. Shepard reported his "astonishment and indignation" at the fact that the matter had not been mentioned until seven days before payment was due. While he felt that the United States had a right to demand immediate payment, he would wait for instructions, "in view of private information concerning the possible disposition of the

[20] No. 31, April 15. Inclosures: Shepard to the Ministers, March 27; their reply, April 9.

[21] Cf. Black, *Young Japan,* II, 356. The dates given in Stead, editor, *Japan by the Japanese,* p. 154, are wrong. Ariga, or his translator, had great difficulty in adjusting the dates for the first five years of Meiji with the Gregorian calendar.

whole or part of·the amount in question."[22] No instruction was forthcoming.

A month later Colonel Shepard wrote a dispatch which was to involve him in an acrimonious controversy with his superior in the following year. As it was included in *Foreign Relations* for 1872 it deserves a word of comment in order to correct the printed record. It told of a dispute between his colleagues of England, France, and Russia as to the proper ceremonial to be used in an Imperial audience. From the beginning of intercourse with Japan the Foreign Representatives had been on their guard to prevent the use of observances in any way comparable to those which prevailed at the court of China. In this instance audiences had been requested for Mr. Watson, the new British Chargé, Admiral Jenkins, U.S.N., a French Admiral, and Mr. Butzou, the new Russian Chargé. When it was intimated that the Emperor would receive these officers sitting, on the ground that it was an audience of courtesy and not official, Mr. Watson declined the audience, and his French and Russian colleagues supported him. Colonel Shepard reported that he had taken no part in this *démarche,* with the result that as a particular mark of gratitude and friendship the Emperor received Admiral Jenkins and himself standing, although it was not to be considered a precedent. Thus, he wrote, "through kind words a courtesy has been *offered* me which threats and demands were impotent to effect."[23]

So far so good. But when, next year, De Long's eyes fell upon Shepard's self-congratulatory dispatch, he searched the Legation files for confirmatory evidence. According to his report, the various letters and papers which related to this episode were missing and he had to reconstruct the events from the Japanese records and statements of the British and French Ministers. On the basis of these materials he charged that not only did Shepard

[22] No. 41, May 18. There is no record of any discussion of this nature between Mr. Fish and Lord Iwakura. The matter was discussed by the envoys in London and Paris (*supra,* chap. xviii, footnote 31), and presumably in The Hague.

[23] No. 46, June 16, *F.R., 1872,* pp. 322–33. Cf. Black, *op. cit.,* II, 390.

concur in the British Chargé's demand but wrote a note so offensive that Soyeshima permitted him to withdraw and destroy it, and more, he presented to the Emperor as secretary of the Legation, Mr. E. H. House, an American school teacher and special correspondent of the *New York Tribune*. While making due allowance for the intensity of De Long's feelings, we must admit that the documentary evidence which he furnished the Department seems to confirm his allegations.[24]

Of the usual run of incidents involving Americans in Japan the Legation was remarkably free during Shepard's incumbency. So far as his dispatches show, no claims were presented and no cases came before him in the Ministerial Court. He was able to report that a jail was actually being built in Yokohama by the Japanese for the use of the Consulate and that in time American prisoners would not have to depend upon the hospitality of the British cells.[25] He also noted a dispute between Vice-Consul Mitchell and Admiral Rodgers as to the authority of naval officers to arrest deserters in a Japanese port.[26]

And on one occasion a well-meant but gratuitous suggestion of Shepard's met with the disapproval of the Department. He had ventured to suggest to the Ministers for Foreign Affairs that they consider the advisability of the Emperor's acquiring a knowledge of the English language from a foreign teacher.[27] His note was disapproved, and Acting Secretary Hale advised him: "Neither your instructions, nor the usages of diplomatic intercourse, warrant the tendency of such advice."[28]

The best-known incident with which the name of Colonel Shepard is associated is that of the Peruvian coolie ship, "Maria Luz." His official report was simple enough:

[24] No. 445, July 7; No. 451, July 17; No. 463, August 20, 1873.

[25] No. 33, April 16. The arrangements were made by Vice-Consul Mitchell, which occasioned some solicitude in the Department (Instruction No. 138, September 20; Dispatch No. 301, November 5).

[26] No. 40, May 18. This dispatch was referred to the Secretary of the Navy (Instruction 15, July 5).

[27] No. 47, June 18.   [28] No. 18, July 25.

On the 10th inst. [July] Capt. Hereiro, of the Peruvian Bark "Maria Luz" was driven into this port, under stress of weather and applied to me, as the authorized representative of Peru, for protection and assistance. Upon enquiry I ascertained she had on board "coolies" in transit from Macao to Callao. This being the case, I felt it my duty to return the enclosed reply, which, as will be seen, declines all action or assistance whatsoever.[29]

The letter to Captain Hereiro (July 10) read:

Although always ready and anxious to render aid and assistance to vessels bearing the Peruvian flag and engaged in legitimate business, I *cannot,* under the circumstances, extend my protection.

The "Coolie Trade" is prohibited by the laws of the United States, and as your ship, by your own confession is engaged in that trade, I withhold my official name, aid and sanction, and I therefore decline to assist or protect you in any manner whatsoever.

Colonel Shepard's proceedings were promptly approved by the Department.[30]

The situation was by no means as simple as Shepard's dispatch would indicate. And it was not until De Long had returned to his post that the Department received adequate information.[31] It seems that on July 7 the "Maria Luz" put into Yokohama to repair damages. On board were 232 Chinese coolies bound from Macao to Peru. A few evenings later one of them swam off to H.M.S. "Iron Duke," whose officers delivered him to the British Consul, and the latter turned him over to the Japanese authorities.

---

[29] No. 55, July 20. The Captain's name is often written Heriero.

[30] No. 133. August 29, *F.R., 1873,* p. 524. In 1873, when De Long was under criticism for his conduct in this case, he charged that Shepard had altered the Legation records, sending to the Department a copy of his note to Captain Hereiro, which stated that he had confessed his participation in the coolie trade, and filing a copy which omitted this statement (No. 357, March 6, 1873). De Long's explanation of this discrepancy was that Shepard had been trying to supplant him and had set a trap to get De Long involved in an unpopular support of a coolie trader. In fact, De Long averred that Shepard had told him, on his return to Japan, that Hereiro had denied having any coolies on board, claiming that his cargo was sugar, some rice, and some Chinese passengers (emigrants). This was well calculated to lead De Long to disapprove of Shepard's action in refusing to render aid, and to cause him to do so (No. 418, June 3, 1873). These dispatches must be interpreted in the light of the bitter controversy which was raging between De Long and Shepard in 1873.

[31] This confirms De Long's charges that Shepard was careless in handling the Legation affairs and in communicating with the Department.

To them he told a pitiful story of conditions on the vessel, but he was returned to the ship nevertheless.[32] Mr. R. G. Watson, the British Chargé, then went off to the bark, and, on the strength of the suspicious circumstances he observed there, wrote to Soyeshima, on August 3, urging an investigation. His letter, he urged, might form the basis for the inquiry, and he pointed out that Peru had no treaty with Japan, and that no other Power would interfere.[33]

It will be observed that the Japanese had not acted when the Chinese fugitive was in their hands, that Shepard had declined to assist Captain Hereiro on July 10, and that it was probably the assurance in the last part of Watson's letter which had encouraged them to move in the matter. A year later it was brought out that Shepard had supported the request of Watson for an investigation.[34]

With these assurances the Japanese acted promptly. A preliminary investigation was held, which led to a general inquiry, in the course of which the coolies were landed as witnesses. Their eventual freedom resulted from the refusal of the Japanese to compel them to return to the ship and perform their contracts.[35]

---

[32] This did not deter a second coolie from trying to escape, but this time the British naval officers made up a purse for him and set him free (Black, *op. cit.*, II, 375).

[33] *F.R., 1873*, pp. 529–30. Shepard wrote a similar letter stating, "I earnestly second Mr. Watson's request that some steps be taken to look into the matter. The officers if found guilty should be severely punished." He did not advise the Department of this, and De Long transmitted a copy in his No. 357, March 6, 1873.

[34] *Ibid.*, p. 608.

[35] For the notice to Captain Hereiro to appear in court, dated August 6; a report of the visit of E. S. Benson (Municipal Director of Yokohama) to the "Maria Luz" on the eighth, and of Hayashi Gotenji and G. W. Hill, on the fourteenth; a report of a consular meeting in Yokohama on August 29, in which the action of the Governor in holding the first inquiry was disapproved by the German, Portuguese, Italian, and Danish Consuls, with the British approving, Shepard declining to express an opinion, and the French Consul holding the Governor strictly responsible; the reply of Governor Oye Takee (Oi Taki) to Ed Zappe, Acting Consul General for Germany, on August 30, in reply to the latter's protest, in which the Governor stated that the judgment would be delivered in accordance with the findings of the Court, see *F.R., 1873*, pp. 594–601. Black (*op. cit.*, II, 376) states that a large majority of the com-

Before proceeding with the latter developments we must note the return of Mr. De Long to his post on August 10. His sixty days' leave, with a reasonable allowance for time in transit, had actually lasted for seven and a half months.[36] The cordial welcome which the Iwakura mission had received, and in which De Long had participated much like a teacher showing off his apt pupils, had put him in an amiable frame of mind, for the time at least, as far as the Imperial Government was concerned. His salary had been raised to $12,000, and he was bringing back with him his nephew, Egbert De Long Berry, of Dutchess County, New York, who had been appointed secretary of the Legation. Nathan E. Rice, who had accompanied De Long to Washington as an acting interpreter, was soon to return as the regular incumbent. The Minister was now to have the staff he had so long needed; but its usefulness would depend upon De Long's judgment of men.

The first matter which called for his attention was that of the "Maria Luz." He promptly reversed the decision of Shepard, which had been approved by the Department, and came forward as the protector of Peruvian interests in Japan. At the request of Captain Hereiro he asked the Ministers for Foreign Affairs, on August 31, for information. He first called attention to certain correspondence between the Peruvian Captain and the Kanagawa Kencho (Prefectural Government), and pointed out that he had been requested to act for Peru and had hitherto been fully recognized and treated with by the Japanese Government. He then asked if it was true

That by and with your advice and direction the investigation at the Kencho in Yokohama was called and held?

If the Chinese summoned by your authorities and brought on shore from the Maria Luz to give testimony as witnesses are now, by your direction, held in custody?

munity thought the judges were in the wrong legally, however much everyone must sympathize with their humanitarianism.

[36] The Department took note of this, and refused to approve his salary warrant from April 29, two months after he arrived in Washington, until July 1, sixteen days before he sailed from San Francisco.

If you authorize and sustain the Kencho in refusing to return them on board the Maria Luz?

And if these things are true, by virtue of what law, custom, or precedent such action has been or is now being taken?[37]

The reply, which was promptly forthcoming, must have given the American Minister a distinct shock. In it we can observe the keen reasoning, and even the phraseology, of E. Peshine Smith, the American adviser to the Foreign Office. The signature was Soyeshima's, but the draft had been prepared by Smith. It began by refusing to admit that Japan was under any obligations to receive any communication from De Long on behalf of the Peruvian Government, and the answer it gave was for Hereiro's information and not for Peru's. The investigation had been conducted by the Kanagawa Kencho at the request of Soyeshima, who had been informed by the British Chargé that cruelties had been committed on the "Maria Luz."[38] The Chinese witnesses were not being held in custody but they remained on shore of their own free will. They were kept under surveillance in case they were summoned in any suit based on their alleged contract, and the decision of the Kencho not to return them against their free will had been fully approved. And, in conclusion,

I decline for the present to enter into any argument in justification of the action of the Kencho or of the foreign office. I content myself with saying that I know of no law, custom or precedent which requires this government, or any other government, to force any person to return to a ship against his will unless he be a fugitive, criminal, or a deserting seaman. While the comity of nations may require the restoration of a criminal, it does not require the restoration of a seaman who violated his contracts and deserts from his vessel unless there is an express treaty providing for such restoration.[39]

[37] *F.R., 1873,* pp. 527–28. The correspondence mentioned above was a request of Captain Hereiro that the Chinese "passengers" be sent back that day (August 30), as they were bound by legal contracts deposited in the Kencho, and the reply of the Kencho, the same day, that as the Chinese declined to return they could be compelled to do so only after an action before the Kencho. The latter, it said, had no right to force these persons on board ship, against their will, merely at his request.

[38] Watson's letter of August 3 was transmitted.

[39] September 2, *F.R., 1873,* pp. 528–29.

De Long reported his intervention on September 3. He informed the Department that Captain Hereiro had been found guilty as charged but had been pardoned because of his long detention. In relating his own actions he said

In my note, however, I was careful to disavow any intention or desire to influence them in their actions or conclusions, and expressed in strong terms the abhorrence of my government and of myself for the coolie trade.

But these thoughts were not expressed in his letter to the Ministers of August 31, but in a letter of September 3, after he had received Soyeshima's reply. He also reported that, in answer to their objections, he had sent them a copy of Instruction No. 15 (April 13, 1870).[40] But this only confirmed the Ministers' contention, for in it De Long had been instructed to attend to any matters which might be intrusted to his charge by the Government of Peru, "so far as this can be done compatibly with other instructions from this Department." The closing phrase certainly referred to coolie cases.

The dispatch of September 3 was mislaid, and went forward with one of September 27.[41] This covered thirteen inclosures which shed considerable light on the controversy. They included the five letters which have been referred to above and in addition De Long's letter to the Ministers of September 3, with its protest of his antagonism to the coolie trade and his inquiry as to whether or not there was any objection to his acting for Peru. To this Soyeshima replied on the twenty-first, that, following the precedent of Mexico in 1867, De Long might act privately, but not in an official capacity. While the citizens of Peru who came to Japan must submit themselves in all respects to the laws and tribunals of the Empire

they will none the less be treated with justice and humanity. It may even happen that they will be regarded more favorably than other foreigners who betray distrust by insisting upon their being under the jurisdiction of their respective consuls.

[40] See *supra*.

[41] *F.R., 1873*, pp. 524–52. The two dispatches arrived on November 1. Instruction No. 15, which he inclosed, was not printed.

De Long took exception to this statement, and Soyeshima not only explained that he meant to imply no unjust discrimination against Americans who might insist upon their extraterritorial privileges but substituted a revised note, on the twenty-seventh, which concluded "it may even happen that they will obtain favor unexpectedly."

The inclosures also showed that even before he had addressed the State Department, De Long had written to the Minister of Foreign Affairs of Peru, on August 19, explaining his efforts to protect Peruvian interests. But his note disclosed that although he had written for instructions (in the "Cayalte" affair) in 1870, he had never received any reply to his dispatches. He was at the time co-operating with the Spanish Chargé, Don Tibrucio Rodriguez y Munoz, who had gone to Hereiro's aid when Shepard had failed him. In a second dispatch (September 5) De Long had sent to Lima copies of his correspondence with the Japanese Foreign Office up to September 2.[42]

And, finally, he inclosed a newspaper report of the trial in the Japanese Court (Sabansho) of the two cases against the coolies. The Court would not decree a specific performance of the contract nor award damages to the plaintiffs.[43]

---

[42] *F.R., 1873,* pp. 532–33. De Long again reported the discussion of extraterritoriality in No. 286, September 30.

[43] *Ibid.,* pp. 533–52. The report was printed in the *Japan Gazette* (Black's paper) and not in the *Japanese Gazette* (presumably a Government publication) as stated in the dispatch. The trial took place on September 18, 19, 20, 21, and 23, and the decision was rendered on the twenty-seventh. G. W. Hill, an American legal adviser, sat on the bench with Governor Oye; Peshine Smith examined the witnesses on behalf of the Government; F. V. Dickins (an English barrister and the biographer of Sir Harry Parkes) was counsel for Captain Hereiro, and introduced a *yoshiwara* contract as evidence that such contracts were enforceable in Japan; the Portuguese Consul sat on the bench throughout the trial, and other Consuls at different times. The suit was entitled:

"Between Senor Armero, of Macao, China, a Spanish subject, by his agent, Don Ricardo Hereiro, master bark, Maria Luz, a Peruvian citizen, plaintiff, and Li Chong, a Chinaman, passenger by the said bark, defendant;

"And between Don Ricardo Hereiro, master of the Peruvian bark Maria Luz, and a Peruvian citizen, plaintiff, and Lai Taim, a Chinaman, a passenger by said bark, defendant."

The pleadings, testimony, cross-examinations, and decision are given. The

Anyone who was familiar with the consistent attitude of the American Government toward the coolie trade, in all its ramifications, would have been able to predict its reaction to De Long's proceedings. If he had made use of the cable in the first instance and requested instructions before intervening, or if he had reported promptly his reversal of Shepard's decision and then awaited confirmation, he would have been spared some of his later difficulties. But, as we have seen, his first report was not posted for more than three weeks, and the Department received the whole record two months after De Long's impetuous action. In turn, it kept the matter under consideration for over a month, and December 5 arrived before its displeasure was embodied in an instruction which was to start the new year for De Long in anything but a pleasant manner.

In the meantime, the American Minister was facing an array of complications. American newspaper correspondents in Japan, including the doughty E. H. House, had soundly criticized him for his support of the coolie trade and had asserted that his actions had displeased the Japanese Government. The latter, taking advantage of De Long's intervention, had asked him to take charge of the "Maria Luz" on behalf of the Peruvian Government, and when he assented he found that he had a crew of a dozen insubordinate and desperate characters on his hands, whom he had to pay off and ship to Hong Kong.

The dispatch conveying this information[44] crossed the Department's instruction of December 5. Mr. Fish began by quoting

latter was carefully framed, and contained citations to English and American authorities.

Pending the trial, the cost of surveillance of the coolies was charged to the Captain, $20 a day. Dickins protested this, in a letter of September 14 to the Kencho which may be found in these inclosures.

[44] No. 306, November 21, 1872, *F.R., 1873,* pp. 555–63. In this dispatch De Long defends himself from attacks in the American press, and avers that he had followed Shepard's course up to the conviction of the Captain (on August 30). The inclosures, dealing with his troubles with the crew, cover six pages. The Department approved his proceedings, but the United States assumed no responsibility to the bankers for the money they had advanced at De Long's request. Their security consisted of a lien on the vessel (No. 161, December 28, *ibid.,* p. 567).

Shepard's report and the Department's approval of his proceedings. He then pointed out the exact terms of the instruction of 1870 under which De Long was to represent Peru in any case specifically and properly intrusted to him, and he reminded him that in the case of Hawaii, also, he had been directed only to use his good offices.

It does not appear that the Peruvian government had in any way intrusted to your charge the case of the Maria Luz, or that that government had made any communication to you with regard to any occasion that might arise for the exercise of your good offices. On the contrary, it is stated in your dispatch that no answer whatever has been returned by the Peruvian minister of foreign affairs to communications which you have heretofore addressed to him.

Under these circumstances, it is regretted that you deemed it proper to take any steps which might wear the aspect of giving the support and countenance of the United States to a vessel suspected by the Japanese government, not without reason, of complicity in a nefarious traffic, of a character particularly odious to the Government and people of the United States.[45]

This, however, did not close the case of the "Maria Luz," and a further discussion of it, in connection with the Peruvian mission to Japan, ensued the next year.

Turning from this episode to the other activities of the American Minister, we note that in one of his first dispatches he was able to assure the Department that the failure to negotiate a treaty with the Iwakura mission had not harmed the interests of the United States. A contrary report was in circulation, and certain incidents seemed to confirm it, but the assurances of Soyeshima set De Long's mind at rest. The Foreign Minister, in fact, preferred to have the revision negotiations take place in Tokyo.[46]

Some weeks later, however, Soyeshima brought up a question of grave import. He asked De Long what would happen if the Commissioners appointed by Japan should disagree with all or some of those appointed by the Treaty Powers. The American Minister properly replied that the Treaty of 1858 provided a method of revision, and that there must be an agreement. To this

---

[45] No. 151, December 5, *F.R., 1873,* pp. 563–64.   [46] No. 286, September 30.

Soyeshima dissented, and Peshine Smith, who was present as his adviser, remarked:

that such a construction made the treaty as it was forever binding, as the most favored nation clause found in all the treaties would enable one dissenting Power to prevent the revision of all as the empire could not afford to have different treaties with different Powers.

This also might prove to be the case, and it brought out the difference between revision, by mutual agreement, and termination. De Long reported this discussion, with additional arguments in support of his views, and asked for instructions.[47] In this case he was supported, and he was told that should the question come up again he was to insist on the views he had presented to the Foreign Minister.[48]

No questions of importance involving American interests arose during the last four months of 1872. There was a controversy at Hiogo (Kobe) as to the right of the Japanese to erect buildings along the sea wall, in front of the native town and foreign settlements.[49] On this matter the Department reserved an opinion until it could obtain the exact terms of the land leases,[50] and when it was forthcoming[51] it took the view that the lessees had a full right to the water frontage to the water-mark. This interpretation De Long's successor was to present to the Imperial Government.[52]

The repeated warnings of the Department had curbed De Long's propensity to press the claims of his nationals; yet some cases were reported. The first was one which came to him with the support of the Department. It was that of Dr. William Hozier against the daimyo of Tosa for breach of contract. The facts came to the Department from Vice-Consul Frank, at Hiogo, and after due investigation De Long was instructed to bring the matter before the Minister for Foreign Affairs. The claim was for

[47] No. 296, October 20. In the files there is a report, by Henry O'Connor, of the Bureau of Claims, which holds that the Commissioners must *decide* and *insert* the new terms.

[48] No. 167, January 18, 1873.

[49] No. 284, September 29.   [50] No. 180, March 8, 1873.

[51] No. 407, May 26, 1873.   [52] No. 3, September 1, 1873.

$17,500 for the unexpired time of the contract (three and a half years), but the Department felt that an award of $10,000 alleged to have been made by a referee, Mr. Alt, was just and equitable to both parties. It was carefully pointed out that this was a proper case for the exercise of good offices, and a special reason was found in the fact that contracts with foreign advisers should be so promptly and fully kept as to encourage others so employed or to be employed.

The suggestion of this consideration in your presentation of the case is advised in the confidence that the Government of Japan has too much magnanimity and too much friendship for the United States not to attach to it its true significance.[53]

Shepard failed to report any action, and before De Long's report of October 6 was received the Department again brought it to the attention of the Legation. It was not, however, a claim to be easily settled.[54]

Two other claims came to the Department from Hiogo, but these were received less sympathetically. They were on behalf of Smith, Baker & Company and Schultze, Reiss & Company against the daimyo of Yodo, for goods furnished to the amount of $8,100 and $10,000, respectively. The claims had been disallowed on the ground that the agent was a fraudulent pretender. In these cases De Long was to present the subject unofficially, while assuring the Foreign Minister that his Government looked with confidence for an early liquidation. A saving clause was added to the instruction:

The claims being based upon contract it must be presumed that the claimants took into consideration the honesty as well as the pecuniary ability of those to whom the merchandise was furnished. It is not customary for this Department to authorize official interference in cases of this character.[55]

These claims also were to go over to the next year.[56]

---

[53] No. 2, March 19.

[54] De Long's No. 289; Instruction No. 147, November 21.

[55] No. 132, August 22. The copy kept in the files gives the name of the daimyo as "Yedo" and "Tedo." Yodo is correct.

[56] De Long reported (No. 314, December 4), that $645.41 had been paid Schultze, Reiss & Company on a claim for sales of silk.

Finally, De Long asked for instructions as to an old claim. Allmand & Company claimed damages to the amount of 50,000 *bus,* with interest at 12 per cent since August 10, 1865, because they had not been allowed to buy silkworm eggs to fill a contract then in hand. In this case the Department refused to intervene.[57]

De Long had been the subject of scathing criticism in House's correspondence in the *New York Tribune* for his efforts to introduce Americans into Japanese employ and for his support of doubtful claims. In defense, he explained to the Department that he looked upon American advisers as *quasi* commercial agents for Japan who would further the development of American trade and he had embraced every opportunity to secure official positions for them. And he insisted that he had never collected a claim under a *demand* for payment. Such as he had presented were, he held, proper claims, while others he had never presented and some he had withdrawn when, on investigation, he became convinced of their injustice.[58] To which the Secretary observed:

It is presumed that you do not present any claims except in pursuance of instructions from this Department, and that due note has been taken of the observations [in Instructions 84, 113, and 2 to Shepard].[59]

On the other hand, the Japanese Government continued to press its just demands for rents due. These included a claim against E. E. Rice for the rent of the consular grounds at Hakodate, and against the United States for rents at Yokohama and Yedo.[60] The Department had recommended an appropriation to

[57] No. 321, December 13; Instruction No. 181, March 8, 1873.

[58] No. 307, November 21.

[59] No. 165, January 4, 1873. A suggestive incident was the request of a jewelry firm in Chicago for the Department's assistance in collecting a bill for watches furnished Frank C. Farrington. The Department sent the letter on to De Long for his information and such action as he might deem proper (No. 136, September 20). De Long reported that although Farrington had come out with him as his secretary he had long since been dismissed on instructions (No. 299, October 26). The Department then notified the jewelers that it could not help them, as Farrington was not an official and De Long was not involved (No. 158, December 18).

[60] No. 280, September 17; No. 291, October 16; No. 313, November 30. These contain many inclosures.

cover some of these claims, and such a bill had passed in the
House of Representatives on May 20. It asked De Long for
more information, and when this was forthcoming it repudiated
the conduct of Rice, when Consul at Hakodate, in 1857–58, and
of his son, George E. Rice, Acting Vice-Consul, in leasing two
lots in 1871, but it did not pass upon the validity of the claim
advanced by Japan.[61]

Among his activities in support of American interests De
Long secured a concession for a cable from the United States to
be landed in Hakodate.[62] The concessionaires were Governor
John N. Goodwin and his associates. Mr. Fish made his views
known in no uncertain terms.

> I have now to state that in future you are expected to ask instructions
> from this Department before making application for concessions of this
> nature. The Department has never felt itself under obligation to recognize
> such concessions unless obtained under proper instructions.[63]

With his initiative curbed by instructions in the matter of
recommending American advisers, of pressing claims, and of
seeking concessions, the American Minister was forced to play
a passive rôle which ill suited him.

One other gesture he made, with the general end of furthering
the influence of his countrymen, which had quite unexpected repercussions. At the request of the respected American missionary
and scholar, Dr. John C. Hepburn, De Long arranged for the
presentation to the Emperor of a copy of the Bible and one of
Hepburn's Japanese Dictionary.[64] While the Christian community
in Japan hailed this event as a sure sign of better times and as
confirmation of the increasing tolerance of the Government, Mr.
Fish instructed De Long that the presentation would not have
been approved if he had consulted the Department.[65]

After his return from the United States there came to a head
a controversy which had arisen at Kobe between the American

---

[61] No. 140, October 18; No. 153, December 5; No. 168, January 20, 1873.
[62] No. 287, September 30.
[63] No. 186, March 19, 1873.   [64] No. 304, November 10.
[65] No. 160, December 28. As we shall see, De Long erroneously ascribed
his recall to this incident.

Consul and his colleagues. In 1871 Mr. Stewart had withdrawn from the Municipal Council.[66] De Long supported his action, and thus the United States was unrepresented. But on the eve of his departure De Long arranged with his colleagues, verbally, that if they would instruct their Consuls to spend less money on salaries and more for the public good he would request the Consul to return. Colonel Shepard gave instructions along these lines to General Frank, then Vice-Consul. But soon afterward the Council elected a Mr. Trostig as superintendent and engineer at "a large salary," which led Colonel Shepard to instruct Mr. Turner, the new Consul, not to recognize Mr. Trostig until further orders, basing his decision on the presence of unauthorized members in the Council. But one of these members had been, in fact, deputed by Mr. Turner, which led De Long to disapprove his conduct and to confirm Shepard's instruction. The issue was further complicated by the fact that since Turner had withdrawn, the American residents, on his notice, had refused to pay land rents to the Municipal Council and these, with some funds on hand, had been held until Shepard had directed their delivery. But one firm, Walsh Hall & Company, refused to pay certain back taxes.

All of which brought to the front the question of Consuls sitting on Municipal Councils. De Long himself did not approve of the existing situation, and he reported that he had tried to induce his colleagues to agree upon a system which would place the settlements under the control of the residents and the Japanese authorities. He asked for instructions as to whether he was to have anything to do with these bodies in the future or should direct the Consuls to apply directly to the Department for advice and instruction.[67]

---

[66] His reasons were: the action of the Council in making its sessions private; the appointment of a local editor as paid reporter, thus enabling him to "scoop" the proceedings; and the use of funds for official salaries rather than for sanitary and police needs. Underneath was the general British-American touchiness. The favored editor represented a British paper, whereas his rival (although an Englishman) represented an American-owned enterprise.

[67] No. 276, September 14. He made a good point when he said that the presence of Consuls in the Municipal bodies had produced bad feeling.

To the specific request of De Long the Department paid no attention. To the general problems presented by the dispatch it could give only a general answer, for it lacked the precise information necessary to guide it. It expected Consuls who were members of such Councils to act with a due sense of responsibility and to exercise their powers with such discretion and intelligence as to obviate the necessity for instructions. Even should a Consul have the right to withdraw from the meetings because of dissatisfaction, it should be exercised only in extreme cases and after very careful deliberation:

It is difficult to see that any advantage to the United States or their citizens can be gained by the withdrawal of their Consul from a Council of which he is rightfully a member.

In respect to the right of representation, Mr. Fish held that a Vice-Consul in charge certainly had all the rights of a Consul, and that a Deputy or Vice-Consul might properly be sent to represent the Consul, his powers to be determined by the rules or usages of each Council. And the power to withhold rents or taxes, if it existed, should be exercised only in a case of manifest error or of unquestioned wrong: "Advice to resist or withhold payment of a duly assessed tax, as a general rule, is disorganizing and unjustifiable."[68]

An insight into the strained situation at Kobe may be gained from the protest of the British Chargé that the American Consul there had refused to arrest and try certain nationals charged with assaulting British subjects. It seems that the *Hiogo News* had referred to Dr. Tryon, of the U.S.S. "Colorado," as "Dr. Spindleshanks." When a public apology was demanded the wording was changed, but this did not restrain Dr. Tryon and Lieutenant Emory from assailing Messrs. Johnson and Walsh. Measures

---

[68] No. 162, December 30. In preparing this instruction a memorandum of December 13 by Geo. L. Berdan, of the First Diplomatic Bureau, was used. It is appended to De Long's dispatch. "A thorough examination made of the indices and all correspondence from the United States Legation in Japan from the year 1858 to present date, fails to elicit any information upon the subject of Municipal Councils in that country." In fact, they were based upon the land regulations drawn up for the several ports, and the Hiogo regulations were printed in *F.R., 1868,* I, 786.

were finally taken and Dr. Tryon was fined five dollars in the American Consular Court.[69]

From time to time the American Minister reported on developments in Japan. On September 30 he mentioned the mutiny of the Second Regiment, composed of Tosa men, as well as two local risings of which he had learned little. The cable across the Straits of Shimonoseki had been laid, and with the completion of the overland wire Tokyo and Washington would be in direct communication.[70] The railway between Yokohama and Tokyo was opened in the Emperor's presence, on October 14.[71] Statistical information from the Japanese Blue-books for 1871 was transmitted in November.[72] And a veritable paean of progress went up in his dispatch of November 21:

> I beg leave to advise you that at no time during my residence here have I ever witnessed a more prosperous or promising state of affairs. Perfect order prevails throughout the empire and *Progress* seems to be now more than ever the watchword of this people.

The new railway, the telegraph between Osaka and Yokohama, the bountiful crops, the amazing results of General Capron's activities in the Hokkaido, the prosperous condition of Mr. Verbeck's college in Tokyo, the preparations to establish a Postal Department, a Bureau of Public Printing, and an arsenal, all aroused his admiration.[73] A report on the new army followed,[74] and the same day he reported that edicts had been issued forbidding public bathing and the appearance of naked children or people incompletely clad in the streets. A tax had been levied in Tokyo for cleaning the streets, and the daimyo residences there, the *yashiki*, were to be sold.[75] And finally he reported that the old calendar would be changed, and the third day of the coming twelfth month would be designated the first day of the first month of the two thousand five hundred and thirty-third year after Jimmu Tenno, and the sixth year of Meiji.[76]

---

[69] No. 277, September 15. [70] No. 286, September 30. [71] No. 295, October 20.
[72] No. 303, November 6. [73] No. 307, November 21. [74] No. 316, December 6.
[75] No. 317, December 6. De Long continued to speak of Tokyo as Yedo.
[76] No. 324, December 21, *F.R., 1873*, p. 565. He also forwarded two notifica-

De Long's difficulties with the Departmental Regulations have already been mentioned. Some mistakes were repeated, and new ones were made.[77]

With some of his colleagues, at least, De Long was in good favor. When Mr. Van der Hoeven was ordered home to take part in the anticipated negotiations with the Iwakura mission, he left his Legation in charge of De Long.[78] For his good offices De Long received the cross and insignia of Order of the Dutch Lion.[79] And as he had done in Van der Hoeven's case, so he gave a letter of introduction to Mr. Fish to Mr. H. Calice, the Austrian Minister-Resident.[80] In both cases De Long thought an exchange of views in Washington would further the revision negotiations.

While some of the ablest statesmen of New Japan were travel-

tions published at the request of the Government, one to the effect that Japanese could not convey any lands to foreigners or pledge the title deeds as collateral security, and the other that the Government could not guarantee the certainty or expedition of messages sent by telegraph, because of the inexperience of the operators (No. 325, December 24, *ibid.,* p. 565).

[77] When De Long granted a leave to Mr. Denison, Marshal at Kanagawa, he appointed an Acting Marshal (No. 283, September 29). He had to be reminded that no such office existed (No. 143, November 4). Also, when Consul Mangum was about to take leave he nominated Charles L. Fisher as Vice-Consul, and De Long approved; but Fisher was Marshal of the Consular Court, and a Vice-Consul must give a bond, filed with the Secretary of State, before he could qualify (No. 152, December 5). Mangum had also nominated an Acting Marshal, with De Long's approval, but this was disapproved as in the case at Kanagawa (No. 154, December 5). De Long was instructed that Fisher was to continue as Marshal, and that he could appoint a temporary Vice-Consul (No. 159, December 21).

Indicative of the parsimony which prevailed in the foreign service in these years were De Long's difficulties with his contingent funds. His charge for $125 for coal, wood, and oil was disallowed (No. 142, October 18; No. 169, January 20, 1873). And he was reprimanded for charging $258.60 for the repair of the flagstaffs at Yokohama and Yedo, as the United States had only one Legation in Japan (No. 150, November 25). His explanation was deemed satisfactory, but he was told, in the future, to accompany all extraordinary expenses with a full explanation (No. 185, March 10, 1873).

An aftermath of his dispute with Portman was disclosed when he reported that he had issued a passport to him and the Department observed that he had charged a fee of $6 instead of the legal $5 (Instruction No. 145, November 4). All passports issued had to be reported because of the fee received.

[78] No. 270, September 3; No. 272, September 5.

[79] Fish to De Long, April 6, 1874.   [80] No. 293, October 16.

ing abroad, two foreign complications arose which were to have important implications. The first was an attempt to renew relations with Korea. Soyeshima, the Minister for Foreign Affairs, gave De Long this account of the recent developments: Although the Korean Government had steadily refused to receive or confer with any officers sent from Japan, some correspondence had taken place through the officials of Tsushima. Mr. Hanabusa, of the Foreign Office, was to be sent as a Commissioner, with instructions to return the Koreans who were living in Tsushima, to withdraw the clan officials who administered the Japanese trading-post at Fusan, and, if possible, to adjust and settle any accounts which were due. If the Korean Government refused to confer with him, then he should withdraw, leaving some (Imperial) officials in charge of the Fusan post, for he was instructed to submit to any insult rather than commit any act likely to provoke hostilities.[81] His mission, in the opinion of De Long, was practically one to terminate relations between the two countries.[82]

Some weeks later he was able to report the entire success of the mission. Hanabusa had been treated with courtesy, the clan officers had been withdrawn and the Koreans in Tsushima repatriated, and a trade balance due the Japanese had been paid. All danger of any immediate difficulty had been avoided.[83] But the very next day he reported that Japan had resolved to punish Korea for its past offensive conduct, and that, "with characteristic oriental duplicity," the mission of Hanabusa had been planned and executed to mislead Korea into the belief that a satisfactory adjustment had been reached. In fact he interpreted the magnificent welcome accorded the Grand Duke Alexis as designed to further a favor-

[81] The So family were lords of Tsushima, and they monopolized the trade with Korea conducted at Fusan. Hanabusa was to replace the clan officials with Imperial officers.

[82] No. 286, September 30. De Long refers to the clan as Tishu, owing to the use of the Chinese name, Taishu. It will be observed that nothing was said about restoring the old "tributary relations." De Long was incorrect in his estimate of the real purpose of the mission, which was to renew rather than terminate relations. Hanabusa was escorted by a small naval force.

[83] No. 307, November 21.

able adjustment of the Sakhalin question and to obtain Russian nonintervention in the war between Japan and Korea.[84]

The second complication involved the relations between Japan and the Kingdom of Loochoo,[85] in which the United States had an interest, and then developed into a controversy with China, which was to involve American nationals and their Representatives in the Far East.

On his second visit to Loochoo, in 1854, Commodore Perry had negotiated a Treaty, on July 11, which had been proclaimed by the United States on the March 9 following. In October 1872 Soyeshima told De Long that the Kingdom had been formally incorporated into the Empire and the ex-King ordered to reside in Tokyo like any other ex-daimyo. This led to a formal inquiry by De Long as to whether or not Japan would observe the terms of Perry's Treaty with Loochoo, and he was told that it would be respected. This closed any formal interest of the United States in the proceedings.

But in reporting this, De Long went on to say that he had also learned that a number of Loochooans had been slain by Formosan aborigines and on inquiring as to the truth of the report Soyeshima had confirmed it and had intimated that steps would be taken to punish the offenders. At this time De Long was asked for information about Formosa and about the expedition of Rear-Admiral Bell, which had gone there for a similar purpose in 1867.[86] The Japanese also desired to secure copies of maps and charts from the American naval officers, which seemed to indicate an armed expedition.

[84] No. 309, November 22. Receiving these two dispatches on the same day (December 26), the Department must have been puzzled in trying to reconcile them. A reasonable explanation seems to be that the purpose of the first dispatch was to point out the peace and progress which prevailed in Japan, while the second was designed to magnify De Long's efforts for peace in the face of threatened complications with China and Korea, but in any event to estrange Japan from her conservative neighbors. By this time the Department seemed to attach little importance to De Long's interpretations or forecasts.

[85] Also written Lew Chew, Liukiu, Ryukyu.

[86] See *40th Cong., 2d Sess., S. Ex. Doc. No. 52* (April 23, 1868), *Serial Number 1317.*

Just at this time, General L. P. Le Gendre, American Consul at Amoy, arrived in Japan en route to Washington, with a very full set of maps, charts, and photographs of the coast and people of Formosa. He had previously visited the aborigines and obtained guaranties against future attacks upon Americans, which had been made good by their protection of the crews of two wrecked British ships. De Long persuaded Le Gendre to remain a while in Japan in order to consult with the Japanese Government and save it from making an ill-advised effort. De Long, Le Gendre, Soyeshima, and Peshine Smith held a conference, and De Long was assured that he would be kept informed of all developments, which would be in harmony with the wishes of the Legation at Peking and of the Department. He believed that with Le Gendre's aid he would be able to inform Mr. Low at Peking so that he might be able to influence the Chinese Government. But he made it clear that he had asked Le Gendre to come forward, and, should the Department disapprove, he alone was to blame.[87]

But, as we have come to expect, De Long did not wait for instructions before plunging into these troubled waters. Two weeks later he reported his further proceedings in a long dispatch which can hardly be accepted at its face value. He began by saying that in repeated interviews involving himself, Le Gendre, and Soyeshima, the latter had, he believed, "unreservedly developed the latent difficulties disturbing the quiet of this government, and made known its intentions respecting China, Corea and Formosa."

Japan was determined to tolerate no longer the asserted jurisdiction of China over the Loochoo Islands, either nominally or actually. In Formosa, where the people were aborigines, Chinese, and half-castes, the Chinese Government claimed jurisdiction over only a part, which it feebly maintained, and the atrocities committed against the Loochooans had occurred outside the Chinese jurisdiction. A small force sent to Formosa, without previous

[87] No. 302, November 6, *F.R., 1873,* pp. 553–56. De Long's letter to Le Gendre, October 22, asking him to wait over a sailing, was sent to the Department in Bingham's No. 248, August 2, 1875.

notice to the Chinese Government, would be able to seize it, and would be difficult to dislodge.

Its geographical situation gives it a command over the entrance to the China sea and the sea of Japan, which makes its possession an object of great interest to this country.

And, finally, the decision to punish the Koreans also was reported.

Up to this point it is difficult to distinguish between what Soyeshima really said and what De Long inferred. But as he went on, De Long was certainly expressing his own thoughts. He referred to the deceit practiced in the Hanabusa mission to Korea, and to the believed attempt to win Russian nonintervention in the approaching war; he reported the uniform success of the Japanese in their ancient wars with China, which had caused a respectable fear of them in the minds of the Chinese, and an equal opinion of Chinese inferiority; and he pointed out that the Japanese now possessed "a vast body of splendidly armed and well drilled troops, also an efficient and well equipped navy," and that

These people, tired of drilling, are anxious to display their prowess, and the Japanese Government has concluded that it is wiser to allow them to do so in a war with China or Corea, or in a demonstration against the savages of Formosa, than to allow their lingering love of clan-ship to bring about civil disturbances within the empire.

There is no question, but what a foreign war, would be immensely popular with this people, and at once heal all internal dissension.

With China, Japanese relations were already strained. The Treaty of 1871 had not been ratified, and one article had caused misunderstanding. The audience question (which was then being argued by the Western Representatives and the Court of Peking) had been learned of, and the indignation of Japan was kindled by a knowledge that the Chinese Court asserted that the Emperor was the legitimate sovereign of the world.

Japan, inspired by ambition and resentment, has resolved to cut the Gordian Knot by forcing the Chinese Government to receive its ambassador in person by the Emperor, or accept a suspension of the relations which have been commenced, and probable war.

The object of such a war being, to settle the question about Loochoo, obtain Formosa, humiliate China and preserve peace among its own people.

While it is doubtful if a responsible Japanese Minister would express any of the foregoing views, it should be recalled that Soyeshima was an advocate of strong measures against Korea, and he may have dropped some intimations which De Long developed. But Soyeshima was not the "Government."

At this point De Long took up his own actions and his relations with Le Gendre.

General Le Gendre and myself have joined in advising this government to first exhaust all reasonable efforts of a diplomatic and peaceful nature, before resorting to forcible ones. This counsel has prevailed, and this government has resolved to at once send an Embassy to the Court of China which will go instructed not to deliver its letters or ratify the treaty that has been negotiated unless the Sovereign of China admits its members to a personal audience. Secondly, to assert the unconditional and unqualified jurisdiction of Japan over Loochoo, and Thirdly, to obtain from China satisfactory expressions of regret for the massacre of the Loochoo people at Formosa and satisfactory guarantees against repetitions of similar occurrences.

The services of Le Gendre were desired in the conduct of the negotiations, and, in case of war, the benefit of his military experience and his knowledge of the harbors and interior passes of Formosa. Soyeshima repeatedly expressed, to De Long and Le Gendre, the desire of his Government that the latter enter its service. At first the General refused to do so, until he had visited Washington, laid the matters before the President and Mr. Fish, and assured himself that there would be no objections, and that his standing would not be hurt if he desired to enter the American service again. But De Long satisfied himself that the Japanese were not disposed to wait so long, for it would run the serious risk of disturbances within its own armies, "who are clamorous for action, and conscious of the wrongs that at present are unredressed."

He then repeated his expressed fear lest Japan, after it had become Westernized, might relapse into its ancient faith of seclusion and ally itself with China and Korea, thus rendering the Oriental question doubly difficult of solution:[88]

[88] See *supra*, chap. xvii.

. . . . hence I have always believed it to be the true policy of the representatives of the Western Powers to encourage Japan in a course of conduct thoroughly committing its government against this doctrine, and by estranging its Court from those of China & Corea make it an ally of the Western Powers.

In the present situation, I feel convinced that I have discovered an opportunity to execute my plans. Possibly without bloodshed, but, if by war, making that war one such as will place the dreaded territories of Formosa and Corea under the flag of a nation, in sympathy with the Western Powers, relieve the world of the existence of such constant dangers to its commerce as now exists, save Japan from civil disorder and consolidate the present progressive and enlightened rule of its present Emperor.

In order to save Japan from some ill-advised and unfortunate step, De Long agreed with Soyeshima to attempt to induce Le Gendre to resign as Consul at Amoy, by telegraph, and to accept the Japanese offer. This Le Gendre agreed to do, but De Long insisted that, before doing so, a formal offer, designating rank and pay, be received by himself from Soyeshima. This led to an interview between Soyeshima and a Japanese Admiral and De Long and Le Gendre, with their respective interpreters, on November 21. The Foreign Minister stated that, with the Prime Minister Sanjo, he had had a long audience with the Emperor earlier that evening, at which the Emperor had declared his intention of carrying out the project regardless of all opposition. In a private conference, Soyeshima asked De Long for advice as to the terms to be offered Le Gendre.

I replied that it remained for his government to communicate its own offer to the General, and negotiate this matter with him, that I as Minister was precluded by my instructions from recommending any citizen of the United States to this government for any office.

But when Soyeshima asked for his ideas, "in a private and friendly manner," the latter asked for a statement of Soyeshima's. It was proposed to offer Le Gendre the appointment of First Secretary of the Embassy to China, and, in the event of war, a commission as General in the Japanese army. His pay was to be most liberal, and in case of success a liberal pension for life would be granted. De Long replied that he had heard Le Gendre say that, having once been appointed Minister to Buenos Aires by the President, no pecuniary compensation could induce him to enter the service of a foreign Government with lower rank. He could not hope to secure the consent of Le Gendre unless he should be commissioned Assistant Minister to China and promised some rank similar to this, to be continued at that Court, if the mission proved a success.

The Minister then advised me that on the next day or the one following he would address me an official letter formally proposing on the part of his government, after stating its objects, to commission General Le Gendre as Assistant Minister to China, agreeing to leave him in charge of the Japanese Legation at that Court in the event of the success of the Mission, but in the event of its non success, and war should follow, to commission him as General of the land and naval forces to be employed in punishing the barbarians of Formosa, and [if] its possession was obtained and retained by this government, place him in charge as governor of its interests there.

It was arranged that De Long would show such a note to Le Gendre, and if he found it acceptable he would telegraph his resignation, while De Long would send a dispatch asking Mr. Fish to accept the same and reply by telegraph.

The question of compensation then arose, and De Long observed that he had heard Le Gendre remark "that if he engaged in this business, the question of compensation would be of no interest to him." It was finally agreed that Le Gendre should receive a salary equal to De Long's ($12,000).[89]

To this point the dispatch was drafted on November 22. But later in the day, Mr. Ichibashi, an interpreter in the Foreign Office, called to say, on behalf of Soyeshima, that just as the latter was about to sign the promised note the Prime Minister, Sanjo, had called to say that the Grand Council had directed that the matter be further considered, and he asked De Long to meet him that evening in Yokohama. At this conference Soyeshima expressed his profound regret that his Government should have hesitated, after having authorized him to proceed, and he ex-

---

[89] It would be interesting to learn, from Japanese minutes of these conversations, exactly what passed between the several participants.

pressed his entire confidence in his ability to obtain approval of his plan. He desired strongly that Le Gendre wait over for one more steamer.

The opposition in the Emperor's Council, De Long was told, was based on two points:

First, upon the common Oriental objection to granting high civil powers to foreigners, and Secondly, a fear of inviting prejudice in the minds of European Powers, if such marked and distinguished favor should be granted to an American.

Soyeshima also said that the Prime Minister desired to meet and confer with Le Gendre before concluding the matter:

I advised the Minister in reply, that his government must judge for itself, uninfluenced by me, what its policy in this regard should be; that, so far, I had not attempted to influence its conclusions, but upon his making known to me the intention of his government to invade Formosa, and upon his requesting me to place him in possession of such information as I might, relative to its coasts and harbors, and also relative to the object and result of the American expedition against that island led by the late Admiral Bell, I had, in a spirit of courtesy and friendship, introduced General Le Gendre to him, as a person thoroughly competent to give the information which was sought, that beyond this, I had went [sic] no farther than to recommend the employment by Japan of all peaceable means within its power, in the adjustment of this difficulty before force of any kind should be resorted to—that he must bear me witness that I had neither sought nor recommended the engagement of General Le Gendre in this business, that neither had that gentleman expressed any wish or any desire to enter the service of Japan, but that all that had followed had been of his own proposing.

De Long asked that these facts be made known to the Emperor and his Council, to which Soyeshima assented. He then approved the plan of having an interview between Sanjo and Le Gendre. The latter, "with great reluctance, but upon my earnest request to do so," agreed to delay his departure.

Thus this matter stands at present. Should it be productive of no other results, it has at least brought about a much closer intimacy between these Authorities and myself than has ever existed heretofore, and I feel confident that I now understand very fully the secret hopes and fears influencing this government.

Because the Department had approved his views in 1871, in

respect to the Chinese Treaty, he hoped for a similar approval of this action.

P.S. I omitted to state that General Le Gendre and myself concluded and so advised the Minister that in no event could he accept from this government a position as a military officer, but in the event of war, the proper commission for him to accept would be that of Commissioner to accompany the army, to conduct any negotiations that might be necessary, and which would not prevent him from imparting valuable suggestions to their military officers.

This course I deemed advisable in the interest of our relations with China.[90]

This long dispatch, with its representation of Japanese intentions, with its pacific warnings and warlike expectations, with its refusal to commend Le Gendre, and its shrewd bargaining, has been outlined at considerable length because it clarifies several points on which later differences arose. Soyeshima was not able to win the approval of the Council as soon as he had anticipated, for the matter was still in abeyance on December 7, and Le Gendre had then agreed to remain two weeks longer. In the meantime De Long had advised Admiral Jenkins and Minister Low of the situation.[91]

[90] No. 309, November 22. (Part of it was written and dated the twenty-third).

[91] No. 320, December 7. Inclosures: De Long to Rear Admiral Jenkins, November 23; De Long to F. F. Low, November 28. Additional points in these letters were: To Admiral Jenkins—a reference to Korea's refusal to pay the customary tribute, and to the belief of Japan that China was encouraging Korea; a statement that land and naval forces would be mobilized at Kagoshima prepared to invade Formosa if negotiations failed; a statement that he was the only Foreign Representative who had been informed of the secret purposes of the Japanese, on a pledge of profound secrecy, which he enjoined on the Admiral. To Low—transmission of his Nos. 302 and 309 to the Department and his letter to Admiral Jenkins, and enjoining secrecy. Mr. Low at once advised De Long, and the Department, of his regret should an American citizen accompany the Japanese mission as an "Assistant Minister" (Low to Fish, No. 218, December 26, 1872). And he followed this by further cautionary advices. He asked the Department to carefully consider the whole question before assent was given to the employment of American citizens in the diplomatic or military service of Japan, and he referred to the published correspondence dealing with the connection of Generals Ward and Burgevine with the Chinese Imperial Army during the Taiping Rebellion. "If Mr. De Long is correct in supposing that an interruption of friendly relations between Japan and China is probable, the employment of Genl. Le Gendre in a

Two weeks later he reported that the mission to Peking had been decided upon. In the meantime he had held several conferences with the Japanese officials and had never failed to advise them to exhaust all diplomatic efforts before resorting to force. Soyeshima called upon him on the sixteenth and stated that he had been designated Ambassador to the Court of Peking,

charged with the business of bearing an autograph letter from H.M. the Tenno to the Emperor of China congratulating him upon his recent accession to the throne and his late marriage, which letter would be delivered, if a personal audience should be granted the Ambassador by the Emperor. If no audience was granted, a copy of the letter would be delivered.

Also he would be charged with the business of ratifying the recently negotiated treaty between the two states.[92]

Also of making known to the Government of China the assertion of sovereignty of the Empire of Japan over the Lewchew islands.

At the same time calling the attention of the Chinese Government to the recent atrocities committed by the inhabitants of the eastern portion of the island of Formosa, upon Lewchewan people, signifying the intention of this government to at once take steps to punish those barbarians, and prevent a repetition of such occurrences, unless it, the Chinese Government, should grant proper indemnity for the wrongs committed and give satisfactory guarantees against the recurrence of similar events.

He also reported:

That no military or naval preparations would be made, prior to the failure of these diplomatic negotiations, in short, that nothing would be done to give offense to the Chinese provocative of hostilities, but that a sincere and earnest effort had been resolved upon to settle all differences between the two governments by negotiations.

It was still the intention to employ Le Gendre, and a commission as officer of the second rank and appointment as Counsellor to the Embassy would be offered him. De Long was asked to exert his good offices to induce the General to accept this commission. The formal offer came on the eighteenth, and the next day Le Gendre handed in his formal resignation as Consul at Amoy for transmission to the Department and advised De Long of his acceptance of the Japanese offer. This was communicated

diplomatic capacity, as suggested, would, I fear, prove a doubtful, if not hazardous experiment" (Low to Fish, No. 221, January 10, 1873).

[92] The Japanese seem to have abandoned their intention of seeking any modification. Soyeshima's purpose was to *exchange* the ratified texts.

by De Long, in person, to Soyeshima. At this time it was brought out that an officer of the second rank received a salary of 400 yen a month, so that Le Gendre's commission would read "the respect of the second rank." The rank would be more honorary than actual, in view of his enlarged compensation.

De Long then asked what guaranties on the part of China would be considered acceptable, and Soyeshima replied that as China was powerless to restrain the savages of that part of Formosa, the Japanese Government could not accept assurances but must take measures of its own to restrain them. This, thought De Long, was the only feature which now gave any promise of leading to hostilities, and he hoped China would willingly refer this business, in view of its own inability, to Japan.

The Foreign Minister also said that he had been given the rank of Guaimu Daijin, so that he would rank on an equality with Prince Kung.

De Long again reported that he had willingly accepted all responsibility for Le Gendre's proceedings, and he compared the latter's resignation with that of Burlingame from the post of Peking.

> We have both labored earnestly to restrain this government from making any premature and illadvised hostile efforts. Our steady counsel has been to resort first to diplomacy, and exhaust every effort in its power, before applying forcible measures of any kind.
> Our counsel has prevailed and now promises to secure for Japan and the civilized world all that could have resulted from even successful military operations, whilst it quite as fully commits Japan to the policy of Western states and keeps our legations at Pekin and this country most intimately advised of the true relations existing between the two Courts.[93]

We must now turn to the reaction of the Department to these developments. De Long's No. 302 was received on December 7. On the eighteenth Mr. Fish advised him that his proceedings respecting the American Treaty with Loochoo were approved. But as to his conduct in obtaining information about Formosa from Le Gendre, and communicating it to the Japanese government,

[93] No. 323, December 20. De Long's letter to Le Gendre, October 18, stating the terms of appointment was transmitted in Bingham's No. 248, August 2, 1875. The salary was 1,000 yen a month.

not knowing the precise objects for which the Japanese government intend to make the knowledge obtained from you available, I am not prepared to express an opinion whether your action, in this regard, is or is not to be approved. Further information and the use which the Japanese government may make of the information which you furnished may decide this point.[94]

But De Long's No. 309 occasioned more misgivings. His advice to employ peaceful measures before resorting to force could not be too strongly approved, yet his part in arranging for the employment of Le Gendre, with a distinct reference to the use of his services as an adviser in military operations, seemed inconsistent with the policy he recommended.

De Long was then reprimanded for his ignorance of the Act of August 18, 1856, which prohibited diplomatic officers from recommending any person for any employment of trust or profit in the country in which they reside, and from asking for any person any emolument, pecuniary favor, office, or title of any kind from such Government: "The approval of the Department cannot be accorded to proceedings in evasion if not in direct contravention to these terms of the statute."

In regard to Le Gendre's statement that he had been appointed Minister to Buenos Aires, Mr. Fish pointed out that he had been nominated but the Senate had refused to confirm the appointment, so that his civil rank was that of Consul.

It is more than doubtful whether a diplomatic representative can, consistently with the terms of the statute, discuss such matters as these in his conversations with the minister of the government to which he is credited; but it is clear that anything he might feel authorized to state on such subjects should be in precise accordance with the facts.

De Long was to continue, in conversations, to endeavor to induce the Japanese Government to separate themselves as far as possible from the exclusive policy of the Chinese and to adopt the progressive policy of free commercial and social intercourse with other powers.[95]

[94] No. 157, December 18, *F.R., 1873,* p. 564.

[95] No. 164, December 30, *F.R., 1873,* pp. 567–68. An inclosure was a copy of the instructions to Mr. Low, of December 21, on the audience question (*ibid.,* p. 135).

CHAPTER XX

THE CLOSE OF A STORMY CAREER
1873 [1]

Before returning to the later developments of the "Maria Luz" incident, which were to run as an obbligato through the remaining months of De Long's residence, we may pause to consider the surprising proposal which was found in the Minister's first dispatch of any importance in 1873. It read:

> Should an effort be made by the Government of Japan to annex the Hawaiian Islands to itself in a peaceful manner with the consent of the people of those islands would the government of the United States have any objection to such action?
>
> I am led to make this inquiry by the fact that of my knowledge that the idea meets with favor here on the part of some of the authorities to whom it has been mentioned. I do not believe that the business has as yet assumed any actual form, but as it may do so at any time I have thought best to ask advices early so that I might be ready at once to act when called upon. [2]

From many points of view this was an amazing proposal. On its face it intimated that annexation of the Hawaiian Islands was under consideration in Japanese Government circles (although it did not assert that the idea had originated there). This would have meant an expansion across the Pacific at the very time when acquisitions at the expense of China, and perhaps of Korea, were being advocated. And aside from the presence of a few laborers, Japan had no interest in the Hawaiian Kingdom. For a Californian to have discussed such a project so objectively requires some explanation.

---

[1] De Long's dispatches are numbered 327–486 (October 7), and Bingham's, 1–35; of these 195, twelve (eleven dealing with the Peruvian Treaty) were printed in *F.R., 1873* and thirteen in *F.R., 1874*. Instructions to De Long are numbered 165–213, and to Bingham, 1–17; of these sixty-six, three were printed in *F.R., 1873* and five in *F.R., 1874*. [2] No. 331, January 6, 1873.

Mr. Fish replied that the subject had not received the consideration it would, should annexation be probable, and the Government was certainly not prepared to express anything like an assent to the annexation of those islands to any other state.

What opinion it might entertain should it be advised of a wish on the part of the inhabitants of the Islands to become incorporated into another nationality, it will be time enough to express when some indication shall be given of such wish. It will be then considered with a full view of the bearing of such a step upon the important and various American interests in those Islands and in such country as may be contemplated for the object of absorption of their independent nationality.

You will inform me fully of the reasons you have for supposing that the annexation with Japan has been thought of, and you will please to watch carefully every indication of any movement in that direction and to report the same fully and at once to the Department.[3]

In obedience to this instruction, De Long gave the information which should have been included in his original dispatch. The first inkling he had had was from some Honolulu newspapers, which reported a public meeting at which this course was advocated. Then E. M. Van Reed, Consul General for Hawaii, subsequently deceased, had told him that he had received private advices urging him to sound Japanese officials on the subject, and on doing so he had found them strongly inclined to favor the proposal. De Long then mentioned the matter to Soyeshima, unofficially, to discover how far the movement had progressed.

He assured me that he had never heard the subject mentioned before, but seemed strongly inclined to favor the proposal, if one should be made to him officially.

This had all occurred before the election of the then King of Hawaii, and, not knowing how serious the movement might suddenly become, De Long had asked for instructions.

The movement at the time, from what I could learn, was quietly advocated by the capitalists of Hawaii, as a method to enable them to obtain a needed supply of laborers.

At this time De Long was shown official dispatches received by Van Reed directing him to take steps to assist a Commissioner

[3] No. 177, March 3.

who was to visit Japan to obtain an emigration of laborers to Hawaii. Fearing that this movement was really desired to establish a coolie trade, De Long at once asked the Hawaiian Government to release him from further conduct of its business in Japan.[4]

While the United States was distinctly interested in any proposal to extend Japanese sovereignty in the eastern half of the Pacific it had no objection to peaceful annexations nearer home. The question was raised in respect to the Bonin Islands (Ogasawara-jima). They lay about 480 miles south of Yokohama, and had been discovered by Ogasawara Sadayori, of daimyo descent, in 1593. De Long reported that in 1828 Captain Beechey, of H.M.S. "Blossom," had taken formal possession and that (in 1853) one of Perry's captains had raised there the American flag. In 1864 the Shogunate had sent an officer and some colonists to occupy them, but after fourteen months they had all been

[4] No. 389, April 29. In transmitting his correspondence with the Hawaiian Minister for Foreign Affairs De Long considered it a justification of his views and convictions relative to the coolie trade. (He had felt the sting of public criticism of his "Maria Luz" intervention.) In his letter to Minister Hutchinson, January 18, 1873, De Long stated that the information he had received of contemplated efforts to secure Japanese laborers had convinced him of his inability to serve Hawaii longer. As long as the United States was opposed to the coolie trade he could not act for Hawaii. "I sincerely believe that such Japanese as have emigrated to Hawaii have bettered their condition and that others, if they went there, would do the same. I realize the urgent necessity that exists for your government to induce emigration to Hawaii from some source, and also believe that—your climate, soil and productions considered—no other class of emigrants are to be as much desired as Japanese. And in aid of any free labor movement having the knowledge and consent of the Japanese Government I would lend all the influence I could command, but any proposition other than that can obtain nothing but my firm and active opposition."

In reply, C. R. Bishop stated, March 19, that the King would much prefer to have De Long retain his commission; that the proposed emigration would be with the full consent of the Japanese authorities and in all respects honorable and perfectly understood by all parties interested. and that it was unfortunate that all contract labor was called "coolie trade," without respect to the circumstances and conditions of the contracts and their execution. "Japanese men and women can find good employment, fair play and good treatment in this country as laborers on plantations, in mechanic shops, and as house servants, and this government will give them full protection in all their rights the same as it does the native and other subjects of His Majesty, and when they wish to return to their native land they can easily do so, the distance being comparatively short and the expense small."

withdrawn. In the meantime some twenty-seven Americans had established themselves on the three larger islands, as well as seventeen British and four French subjects. The specific query was propounded by Captain Benjamin Pease, who, on his way to Hawaii for cattle, asked De Long under what jurisdiction the islands really lay. He in turn asked the Department if the United States asserted any claim to the islands and, if not, if he should recognize Japanese jurisdiction if still asserted. In the latter case, should he appoint Pease or some other resident as Consular Agent?[5]

Mr. Fish replied that the annexation in 1853 had never been expressly sanctioned by Congress, and he was not aware of any later act which would show a disposition to support such a step. The American citizens who had gone there had done so without any promise, expressed or implied, that the Government would protect them.

By resorting to such remote spots on the globe's surface, under such circumstances, they may fairly be held to have deliberately abandoned the United States without a purpose of returning, and therefore to have relinquished the rights as well as the duties of citizens.[6]

In the last chapter we described the first phase of the "Maria Luz" controversy, in which the Japanese won the acclaim of humanitarians the world over by their intervention to save some 232 Chinese laborers from coolie servitude in Peru. While the strict legality of these proceedings might be questioned, there was no doubt of the humane principles which shaped their actions. The Chinese were well cared for by the Kanagawa officials until a Chinese official arrived to take charge of them, and the cordial reception accorded him and his profuse expression of thanks helped to smooth out some of the difficulties which confronted the two governments.[7]

But between Peru and Japan an issue had been created which

---

[5] No. 380, April 21, *F.R., 1874,* pp. 635–36. De Long did not know that in 1864 the Shogun's Government had paid $1,000 as an indemnity to George Horton, an American citizen, for deporting him from the islands. See *supra.*

[6] No. 200, May 31, *ibid.*

[7] Ariga, in Stead, editor, *Japan by the Japanese,* p. 158.

had to be resolved by diplomacy or force. The Peruvian Government considered that it had been wrongfully treated by Japan and that only an apology and an indemnity could accord satisfaction, while as a guaranty against a repetition of the offense a commercial treaty was essential. Because so much of the record as to this is already available in *Foreign Relations, 1873,* the interest and actions of the United States and its officials can be briefly summarized.

About the middle of January De Long notified the Japanese Government that Peru was about to send a Minister to Japan.[8] Mr. Fish was informed of this *démarche* on the thirtieth by the Peruvian Minister, Mr. Freyre, who said that a Commission would sail from San Francisco the next day; that it sought only an apology to the honor of the flag and a treaty of friendship and commerce; that if this was not obtained it would proceed to China and seek a treaty there, returning to Japan for further negotiations; and that he desired the support of the United States on the question of the indignity to his flag. Mr. Freyre promised to submit a statement of the facts in the case, but, failing to do so, Mr. Fish decided to instruct De Long without further delay as follows:

Should any application be made to you, in behalf of the Peruvian Government in this matter, you will be careful to avoid committing the Government to any sympathy with the infamous trade in which the Maria Luz is represented to have been engaged, or to any implication of censure or criticism of the course pursued by the Japanese Government, unless advised that further development shall have satisfied this Government that an international [intentional] wrong has been done by Japan to the Government of Peru.[9]

This instruction was drafted without reference to a second dispatch from De Long, which had arrived on February 25, in which he stated that there was great excitement in official circles in Japan because of a statement in a Lima newspaper that Cap-

[8] No. 338, January 18.

[9] No. 175, February 26. Freyre pointed out that all the foreign Consuls, except the British, had denounced the action of the Japanese, and stated that he did not wish British influence to prevail in Japan as, so far, the influence and prestige of the United States had been in the ascendant.

tain Garcia y Garcia, who had been appointed Minister, would sail on the ironclad frigate "Independencia," rating sixteen heavy guns, to demand an explanation. Soyeshima asked De Long as to the truth of these reports, and, although the latter did not believe them, he promised to do all that he could to dissuade the envoy if he were disposed to make trouble.[10]

Still smarting under Mr. Fish's rebuke in his instruction of December 5, 1872.[11] De Long defended his conduct as due to his desire to give Japan sound legal advice while always attesting his abhorrence for the coolie trade, and although he was by chance on the unpopular side of the question he felt that events would prove whether he or his British colleague had acted most happily and worthily the part of a Representative at a friendly court.[12]

Captain Garcia y Garcia arrived on the American mail steamer on February 27. He at once sought De Long's good offices, and the latter counseled with the Peruvian and also with Soyeshima. Soyeshima was eager to proceed on his special mission to Peking, which was by far the more important question of the two, and he assured Garcia that nothing could be finished until his return. In this interview, however, he suggested, for the first time, the possibility of arbitration if the negotiations failed. De Long was pleased with the course the events had taken.[13]

From the Minister of Peru, Mr. Fish had learned of the hospitable reception accorded the envoy. And this had been coupled with the request that the United States exert not only its moral influence but its good offices to bring about an amicable settlement of this case in which the Peruvian Government felt that its flag

[10] No. 340, January 22, *F.R.*, *1873*, pp. 568–70. Mr. Fish replied, while approving De Long's conduct, that the Department had no information as to an armed expedition from Peru, and certainly there was no such inference in his conversation with the Peruvian Minister (No. 182, March 10, *ibid.*, p. 582).

[11] See *supra*.

[12] No. 357, March 6. In this dispatch he tried to throw some of the blame on Chargé Shepard.

[13] No. 361, March 9, *F.R.*, *1873*, pp. 572–76. This dispatch covered twelve inclosures. One of them listed eighteen documents forwarded to Garcia by De Long dealing with the municipal government of Yokohama and the validity of the Japanese court at Kanagawa. Garcia was received by the Emperor on March 3.

had been insulted and its honor affected. In reply to Mr. Fish's statement that the United States could do nothing which could be construed as approving the coolie trade, Colonel Freyre affirmed that the Chinese had been engaged by careful and responsible agents at Macao and that the contracts were honest contracts—in fact it cost over $300 before a laborer was landed in Peru. On this statement of the case Mr. Fish consented to authorize the good offices of the United States to effect an amicable settlement of the question.

I have therefore to instruct you that you are authorized to use the good offices of this Government for the settlement of the differences which have unhappily arisen between Japan and Peru. Before doing this officially, you will endeavor unofficially to ascertain whether it will be acceptable to Japan to receive the tender in the spirit in which we desire to proffer it, and whether there is a practicable middle ground on which the acts of Japan and the complaints of Peru can find common foothold and satisfaction. If you become satisfied that the good offices of the United States either will not be acceptable to Japan, or will not prevent a rupture, you will not tender them formally; but you will let both parties understand that we are ready to tender them whenever we can see that they will do any good.

Should you, on the contrary, be satisfied that both parties desire to avail themselves of our good offices, and that amicable relations may be restored through our efforts, you may say that the President, influenced by his strong desire to restore friendly relations and feelings between the two powers, with each of whom the United States are in such relations of entire amity and cordial friendship, has instructed you to tender the good offices of the United States for that purpose.

Whatever may take place you will avoid expressing anything but disapprobation of the coolie trade.[14]

Before this instruction had reached De Long, the negotiations in Japan had taken quite a different turn. The honor of Peru had been satisfied by a statement made by Soyeshima in his interview with Garcia, and the question of an indemnity was now under discussion. De Long reported that in the draft of his formal note (March 31) Garcia had demanded both an indemnity for the owners of the "Maria Luz" and a salute for the flag of Peru, but he had persuaded the envoy not to ask for the latter, as Japan

14 No. 187, March 21, *F.R., 1873*, p. 583.

had intended no insult but only to relieve the coolies. On his part, De Long had asked Uyeno Kagenori,[15] the Second Assistant Minister for Foreign Affairs, when a reply might be expected, and had been told not before Soyeshima returned from China. This De Long regretted, and he suggested that the amount of the indemnity might be left to arbitration, Peru given a treaty like those of other nations, and the whole affair settled. But Soyeshima, he learned, was opposed to entering into any more treaties giving extraterritorial rights. He pointed out that if Peru were refused such a treaty it would be attributed to ill-feeling, and might occasion future difficulties—a better plan would be to offer a treaty like the others, revisable at the same time, and if by then Japan could free herself from extraterritoriality it would apply to Peru; if not, it made little difference, as there were no Peruvian residents in Japan. Both Garcia and Uyeno had asked De Long to suggest an arbiter in case they could not agree, the latter favoring a member of the resident Diplomatic Corps and De Long declining to act—nor seeing how the British Minister could well do so. If they could agree on some other member of the Corps it would be very proper.[16]

Weeks passed, and no reply was forthcoming to the Peruvian note. Garcia was much anoyed, and De Long feared that negotiations might be abruptly broken off. An attempt had been made, indirectly, to get Garcia to accept a treaty without the extraterritorial clause, on the promise that if he would do so the "Maria Luz" case would be settled to his satisfaction; but this he had indignantly rejected.[17]

---

[15] "Mjeno" Kagenori in the printed document.

[16] No. 381, April 21, *F.R., 1873,* pp. 584–85. De Long, as so often happened, failed to transmit the documents which would have clarified this dispatch and sent them on June 2. In his No. 395, May 8, *ibid.,* pp. 585–86, he acknowledged the receipt of Instructions Nos. 175, 182, and 187, and said he had read No. 187 to the Peruvian Minister.

[17] No. 416, June 2, *F.R., 1873,* p. 586. This covered the formal note of Captain Garcia, of March 31, and the many inclosures which accompanied it (pp. 586–602). Garcia explained that a mission had been appointed to seek a commercial treaty, and was about to sail in two warships, when the news of the "Maria Luz" was received. He had then been sent by a mail ship in order

In June, Garcia decided to proceed to China in the hope of
negotiating a treaty there, and at his request De Long gave him
letters to Minister Low and Consul Eli T. Sheppard at Tientsin.[18]
This probably brought the Japanese to resume negotiations, for
it might have been awkward to have the angry Peruvian envoy
appear at Peking. Before handing the reply to Garcia, Uyeno
discussed the matter with De Long at great length. The letter
had been considered twice in the Great Council, before the Emperor, and while it had been adopted, grave doubts had been entertained as to its correctness, and they would welcome an offer
to arbitrate should it be made by the Peruvian Minister. Uyeno
asked De Long to intimate this to the envoy, without letting him
know that the Japanese were ready to discuss the case further.
"There seemed to exist an apprehension," he said, "that the Peruvian government would treat their reply as an end of the discussion and resort to hostilities."

De Long then saw Garcia, warned him that the reply would
be unsatisfactory, and suggested arbitration. But this, Garcia
replied, had already been proposed by Soyeshima when he opened
the case. It was finally agreed that De Long would suggest arbitration to both parties.

The Japanese reply was in the nature of a long legal argument,
without doubt the work of Peshine Smith and perhaps other
foreign advisers. It denied that injustice had been done to the
citizens of Peru, and disclaimed any intention of affronting its
national dignity.

> If any wrong has been done it is because a number of Chinamen chose
> to violate their contracts. It was impossible in this empire to compel them
> to perform those contracts specifically, or to drive them outside of the
> protection to which they were entitled, not only by the laws of humanity

to prevent false representations. (But the Lima press had reported that he
was to sail in an armored frigate to demand explanations.) An indemnity was
demanded because of the illegality of the Kanagawa court and its proceedings.
Some of the documents presented here were mentioned *supra*, chap. xix.

[18] No. 427, June 17, *F.R., 1873*, pp. 605–7. In his No. 418, June 3, De Long
renewed his charges that Chargé Shepard had falsified the records and given
him a misleading oral report.

but by the special obligations which connect this empire with the empire of China.[19]

With De Long exerting his good offices, a protocol was promptly signed, on the nineteenth, to submit the case to the decision of an impartial judge, the chief of a friendly state, and another, on the twenty-second, designating the Emperor of Russia, who was to decide if the claim of Peru was well-founded, and if so, what indemnity should be paid by Japan.[20]

And the case was closed, so far as the American records go, by the transmission of a copy of the Treaty of commerce, signed on behalf of Japan and Peru on August 21.[21]

Although the President of the United States was ready to tender his good offices to restore friendly relations, if both parties desired it, there is no evidence that any request of this nature was made. Mr. Fish had been led to believe, by Colonel Freyre, that the only question was the honor of the flag and that no claim for indemnification would be made. But the former was promptly settled, and the protracted negotiations involved an indemnity and a treaty of commerce. In these the good offices of Mr. De Long sufficed, and no formal reference to the President was necessary.[22]

Paralleling the reports of the Peruvian negotiations were the references to the Japanese mission to China, which was of interest because of the presence there of General Le Gendre, a for-

[19] No. 429, June 19, *F.R., 1873,* pp. 607–8. Japanese reply, June 13, *ibid.,* pp. 609–16. Garcia learned from the Japanese reply that Shepard had supported Watson's demand for an investigation. De Long had not told him, because his own relations with Shepard were unfriendly and he would appear to be involving Shepard in trouble.

[20] No. 433, June 21; No. 440, July 5, *ibid.,* pp. 616–18. At the request of the Japanese and Peruvian Ministers, De Long sold the "Maria Luz." The price obtained was $7,250 (Mexican). After all charges had been paid the balance, $4,713.28, was deposited in the Hong Kong and Shanghai Bank (No. 461, August 20, *ibid.,* pp. 619–29).

[21] No. 470, September 2, *ibid.,* pp. 629–30. For the arbitration decision of the Emperor of Russia, May 29, 1875, which supported the case of Japan, cf. Moore, *History and Digest of International Arbitrations,* V, 5034–36.

[22] The documents contain no answer to the question why the Emperor of Russia was chosen as arbiter. It is probable that Captain Garcia would not accept the President of the United States in view of the national antipathy for the coolie trade.

mer Consul of the United States at Amoy. He had finally been commissioned an officer of the second rank in the Department for Foreign Affairs, and on December 30, 1872, he had been received in audience by the Emperor.[23] The mission set sail on March 11, in two ships of war—one an ironclad—and some alarm was occasioned by the movement of 1,100 troops from Tokyo to Kagoshima, which Soyeshima had explained as the usual shifting of troops between the capital and the provinces. De Long was not satisfied with this answer and he recalled that when the Formosan matter had first come up, Saigo, the comamnder-in-chief of the army, had left suddenly for Kagoshima and had not yet returned. Although he was represented as engaged in restraining the Satsuma soldiery from some premature and ill-advised expedition against Formosa, De Long believed that he was really engaged in organizing a land and naval expedition for any emergency in China, Formosa, or Korea.[24]

The mission reached Tientsin, by way of Shanghai, on April 19. The fact that the Japanese wore European dress, and were accompanied by a foreign adviser, "stung almost to exasperation the proud, stolid Chinese."[25] The Treaty of 1871 had already been ratified and was exchanged on the thirtieth.

[23] No. 350, February 23.

[24] No. 360, March 9. De Long notified the American naval officers of the movement of the little squadron, cf. No. 359, March 8. His own views were reflected in a private letter to General E. O. Babcock, secretary to President Grant, of March 8. "Report says considerable excitement relative to this mission is felt in Chinese official circles, which is all unnecessary however and is mainly promoted by foreigners who wish to arouse a trade in arms and ammunition. However, if the barbarians of Formosa and Corea cannot be stopped by the Chinese government from murdering distressed seamen cast upon their shores you may depend upon it the Japanese will attend to that business for them, and for the life of me I cannot see why we should not sympathize with them when we tend to do the same thing in both places, and meeting in each case with a reverse we left those countries more dreaded scourges in the pathways of commerce than they were before we essayed to punish them."

[25] Consul Eli T. Sheppard to Low, May 7, 1873, *F.R., 1873,* p. 178. De Long reported, on June 6, that the Treaty had been ratified. He was unable to obtain a copy of the revised Text, so he transmitted a draft of the original Treaty. De Long saw in the Treaty a chance to profit in dealing with Japan, "for instance, the right to travel freely throughout the empire. The right to circulate our literature freely, &c., must, it seems to me, flow to us as of right under the most favored nation clause" (No. 423, June 6, *ibid.,* pp. 602–5).

Before proceeding to discuss the other matters intrusted to him, Soyeshima, in his capacity as Ambassador, proceeded to Peking to seek an audience of the Emperor and present his congratulatory letter. His superior rank disturbed the resident Foreign Ministers, while his arrival (May 7), just when the audience question was coming to a head, threatened to reopen it again. Le Gendre made a very unfavorable impression on Minister Low and his colleagues.[26]

During his long delay in Peking, Soyeshima and Low exchanged several calls, and the former spoke with apparent frankness of his mission. His first duty was to inquire if China was responsible for the acts of the Formosan aborigines. If the reply was in the affirmative, Japan would demand redress and indemnity for the murder of the Loochooans; if in the negative, then Japan would send a force to chastise them, first asking permission to land troops at one of the open ports and march them across Chinese territory into the aborigines' country.

The second was to ascertain the precise relations between China and Korea;

whether the former claims to exercise such control over her tributary as to render China responsible for the acts of the Coreans, or whether other nations must look to Corea alike for redress for wrongs and outrages which her people may commit.

In regard to the Loochoo Islands, Soyeshima had nothing to say to China, for Japan would permit neither China nor any other country to question her complete jurisdiction there.

But until he had been received by the Emperor, and recognized as the Japanese Representative, he would take no steps in regard to the other questions. Mr. Low was under the impression that an ultimatum had been delivered, and that if a reply were not received within a certain number of days the Embassy would be

---

[26] No. 264, Low to Fish, June 13, *ibid.*, pp. 188–89. Both Low and De Long reported a Chinese military demonstration. De Long (No. 401, May 21) said that the statement that it threatened the American naval forces was discredited in Japan. Low (No. 259, May 22, *ibid.*, pp. 182–83) believed it was due to alarming reports of the purpose of the Japanese mission, and that offensive operations were not designed against either Japanese or foreigners.

withdrawn and relations cease. China, he understood, had intimated that a reply would be sent within the appointed time.[27]

Two weeks later the long-demanded audience took place. The
Japanese Ambassador was presented first, followed by the Ministers of Russia, the United States, England, France, and Holland.[28] Arriving late in the history of the audience question, the
Japanese, through the superior rank of their envoy and his knowledge of Oriental procedure, won the first reception on June 29.
It required no little tact on Soyeshima's part to quiet the resentment of the other Ministers who had borne the brunt of the battle
before his arrival.[29]

De Long learned of the audience from a Shanghai newspaper,
which alluded to the material aid furnished by Le Gendre; and he
was told by the Acting Minister that all questions between China
and Japan had been satisfactorily concluded. He considered this
a vindication of his conduct and asked credit for

having acted prudently and wisely in intervening to prevent war; in
counseling the sending forth of this embassy, and obtaining its management and direction under American influences.

I feel that if I have ever done anything of actual service to Japan and
to civilization since I have been here it has been in what I have done in
this connection.

I do not nor have felt hurt that you should have felt alarmed and found
I had done what might involve the United States in a misunderstanding
with one or both of these countries, but I beg you to judge of my labors
by results, and by that standard accord me such credit as you consider I
deserve.[30]

The "results" of De Long's labors were not to be appraisable
for several years. Mr. Low, who was close to the negotiations,
gave all the credit to Soyeshima.

The Ambassador proved himself to be a man of no ordinary ability.
In his intercourse with the foreign representatives he was dignified,
courteous and frank; and from my knowledge of his dealings with the

---

[27] No. 264, Low to Fish, June 13, *F.R., 1873*, pp. 188–89.

[28] No. 271, Low to Fish, July 10, *ibid.*, p. 195.

[29] For a Japanese version of this mission, cf. Ariga, in Stead, *op. cit.*, pp.
159–65.

[30] No. 447, July 21.

Chinese officials I feel safe in affirming that he exhibited talent of a high order, combined with rare tact and discretion. It is but justice to say that he fairly earned the respect and confidence of all with whom he came in contact.[31]

De Long reported the return of the Embassy in typical language.

I have the honor to inform you of the return of the Japanese Embassy from China. Unofficially I learn that Mr. Soyeshima obtained the first audience with the Emperor of China and thereby has clothed himself with great renown in Oriental countries. I also learn from unofficial sources that China has disclaimed any jurisdiction over Eastern Formosa and Corea, leaving Japan free to deal with the barbarous inhabitants of each of those countries. I believe that it is also true that China has in effect waived all claim of jurisdiction over the Lew Chew Islands; thus tacitly assenting to the act of incorporating them into this Empire. I believe it to be the intention of this government to soon proceed to the conquest of Eastern Formosa and Corea; and confidently anticipate seeing both of those countries under the flag of Japan within twelve months; with ports opened to the commerce of the world.

Should this take place; it will be observed by you that this empire will then hold the keys to the Pacific over the northern portion of Continental Asia and under her alliance, a matter of great moment, should complications arise between Russia and England.[32]

This dispatch was made up of "unofficial" information and beliefs. The former might have come from minor Japanese officials, but more probably was from the English language press. The latter were probably based on newspaper reports or treaty port gossip. It is interesting to note that Dr. Ariga, who had Japanese sources at his command, reports a conversation between Lord Yanigawara and the Ministers of the Tsungli Yamen on June 24, which he summarizes as disclosing

(1) that China renounced the right of interference with the internal and external affairs of Corea, (2) that she did not object to calling the natives of Liukiu Japanese subjects, and (3) that she had no objection to Japan's sending an expeditionary force against the Formosan savages.

[31] No. 274, Low to Fish, July 14. The Embassy left Peking on July 3, and were to embark in their two warships at Chefoo. Le Gendre returned by mail steamer from Shanghai. Japanese interests were intrusted to the Russian Minister, Doyen of the Corps, until a Minister was designated.

[32] No. 458, August 4.

But a careful reading of the conversation, as reported, does not confirm this epitome. From it we gather that the Chinese held to the definition of their relations with Korea as given to the French Minister in 1866—that the King of Korea received investiture from the Emperor of China, yet the internal administration and the question of war and peace were left to the Koreans themselves. This was the Chinese conception of a protectorate or vassal state, and it did not preclude the intervention of China if she saw fit. Loochoo was asserted to be Chinese territory, although Yanigawara stoutly denied it; and the Yamen Ministers proposed to answer at another time as to what measures had been taken to punish the Formosan aborigines. If the fact that the Chinese did not take exception to the announcement that the Japanese Government intended to punish the Formosans, and had taken this means of notifying China, may be considered a tacit assent, then Ariga is correct. But certainly no formal consent is on record in this conversation as he reports it.[33]

The presence of competent foreign advisers, such as Peshine Smith and M. Boissonade, the French legal adviser, would explain the stiffening of the Japanese attitude toward any extension of treaty rights by foreign interpretation or usage, while the return of Sir Harry Parkes to his post, in April, less well disposed toward the Government which had sought other guidance than his, would account for a stout insistence upon every treaty obligation. Several incidents were to arise which were to form part of the whole Japanese indictment of the old Treaties.

The first was the attempt of the Japanese to establish a court for Kanagawa-ken, which would take over the judicial powers of the Governor and (foreign) Municipal Director in cases involving the nationals of non-treaty Powers. The necessity for such a court had become evident at the time of the "Maria Luz" case. The court was established, and due notice was given the Foreign Representatives. De Long, on his part, challenged the right of the Japanese to amend the Municipal Regulations for Yokohama

[33] Ariga, in Stead, *op. cit.*, pp. 161–63. We shall see later that the informal nature of the Chinese reply involved Japan in serious difficulties.

adopted in 1867,[34] and Soyeshima denied that any such convention existed. Now it happened that neither the Foreign Office nor
any of the Legation files contained a copy of the Japanese assent
to the convention, but De Long was able to produce a letter from
the Japanese Ministers to Van Valkenburgh of December 19,
1869 (two years after the convention was informally agreed to
and put into operation). This rendered a different procedure
necessary, and the Foreign Minister then requested that the new
proposal be incorporated as an amendment to the Municipal Regulations. An acceptable phrasing was finally agreed upon, and De
Long brought it before the assembled Representatives, who gave
their consent. But this procedure delayed the establishment of the
court (which all the Foreign Representatives agreed was very
necessary) from September 12, 1872, when De Long received the
first notice, until February 16, 1873, when he notified the American Consul at Kanagawa to recognize it and transact judicial
business with it.[35]

Then came a request from the Foreign Office that the Ministers call upon their Consuls at Kanagawa to enforce the seventh
article of the Municipal Regulations dealing with the storage of
gunpowder and other explosive materials. This met with no objection at the time, but it was to prove troublesome later.[36]

At about the same time, the German Minister announced that
he would not recognize the newly promulgated marriage law of
Japan because it conflicted with the naturalization laws of Germany. This was, so far as I am aware, the first evidence that the
German Representative would follow the British practice of not
respecting Japanese laws until they had been adopted by him.[37]

---

[34] See *supra*.

[35] No. 346, February 17. Soyeshima told De Long that Peshine Smith was
responsible for the steps taken in the first instance. De Long furnished copies
of the sixteen inclosures which accompanied this dispatch to Captain Garcia,
on March 8, for his information.

[36] No. 370, March 15.

[37] At this time the German Minister made an alleged statement of Peshine
Smith the subject of a formal inquiry. The *Japan Mail,* of January 24, alleged
that Smith had said in a Consular Court: "Not one in ten get their deserts
any more than one person in ten in Japan was murdered that ought to be

This was followed by the Railway Regulations case. As early as June 15, 1872, Chargé Shepard had received a copy of regulations for the line between Yokohama and Shinagawa, which contained penalties for infractions, but he had not made the customary notification. In December the British Chargé called them to De Long's attention and announced that he proposed to enforce them provisionally over British subjects, first framing certain penalties analogous to those in the Japanese code, but had been instructed by Earl Granville to communicate with the other Representatives. De Long was ready to co-operate, but he suggested that it would be more conformable to his instructions if they all proclaimed the Japanese regulations and penalties as applicable to their nationals. A meeting of the Corps was held, and the reasonableness of the regulations was recognized, except certain penalties, which the British Representative was unable to decree. To secure unanimity it was agreed to address an identical note to the Government asking that certain amendments be made. These were agreed to, on both sides, and De Long, in January, gave notice of the regulations and penalties to American residents. His British, French, Russian, and Spanish colleagues did the same, and he acted for Holland. The Italian Representative, however, gave notice of the original penalties, and the German Minister stated that he had no authority to act.

Then arose the question which Government should receive the fines collected in the Consular Courts. De Long had instructed the American Consuls to retain them, until otherwise directed. When Soyeshima asked that they be turned over to the Japanese authorities De Long replied that as arrests would be made by American Marshals, the trials conducted by American Consuls, and the cost of confining prisoners paid by the American Government, it would be inequitable if the United States did not share in the fines or receive some compensation from Japan. Soyeshima admitted the force of this argument, and it was left that the fines should be retained until instructions were received. De Long

murdered" (No. 372, March 16). This is mentioned as indicating the growing resentment to the pugnacious legal adviser of the Foreign Office.

expressed the belief that Japan would be pleased if all the fines were remitted to it after payment of the actual expenses incurred.[38]

The next case to come forward involved the long-discussed game laws, or Hunting Regulations. This issue arose in January 1871;[39] it was to be partly settled in 1873, and then reopened at a later date. Much correspondence between the Representatives and the Foreign Office had taken place, and revised regulations had been offered. To the last draft, De Long, as Doyen of the Corps, proposed detailed amendments, which were substantially accepted. Then Sir Harry Parkes returned and assumed the position of Doyen. He reopened the matter, and proposed a draft, "in which," Soyeshima said, "he could not scarcely observe any of his own remaining." As the members of the Corps (including the British Chargé) had concurred in the amendments proposed by De Long, Soyeshima refused again to revise the regulations, which had been promulgated on January 20. The old question divided the diplomats. Sir Harry insisted that he could issue only a regulation analogous to the Japanese, thus making it British law, while De Long argued for the acceptance of the Japanese version and a notification to his countrymen that it would be enforceable in the American courts. Finding that no agreement could be reached between Sir Harry and Soyeshima, De Long, and his French and German colleagues, on May 30, published the necessary notices to their countrymen. The question of the disposition of the fines collected was left subject to instructions.[40]

[38] No. 374, March 22. No instruction was given in reply.

[39] See *supra*.

[40] No. 411, May 31. An inclosure contains the amendments proposed by De Long on February 23. In No. 415, June 2, De Long transmitted copies of Parkes's correspondence with the Japanese Ministers; of his proposed regulations and of his comments on the Japanese draft; and of regulations promulgated by the British Chargé, August 17, 1871. Parkes accused the Japanese Minister of impropriety in giving notice of their regulations to the Foreign Representatives. De Long had explained to him that the action was an unauthorized move by a local official, which had been promptly corrected by the Foreign Office. The original regulations of January 1873 were submitted to the Foreign Representatives before promulgation (*F.R., 1874*, pp. 637–43). Paragraphs in which De Long criticized Parkes's action are omitted.

The controversy continued, with scarcely a break, on the right of travel in the interior. In part, this grew out of the negotiations for a revised treaty with Italy, which will be discussed later. It began with the dispatch of a letter by von Brandt, the German Minister, to Acting Foreign Minister Uyeno, on July 2, informing him that he would no longer enforce the penalties imposed on German subjects entering the interior without proper passports. This, in effect, would open the country to Germans or involve the Japanese police in endless difficulties in arresting them and returning them to the nearest Consul, who would promptly release them. Von Brandt forwarded a copy of his note to Parkes, asking him to circulate it among his colleagues and to express his own opinion, while intimating that this would be a favorable opportunity for bringing the whole question of access to the interior to an issue.

The argument began when the Japanese denied a passport to a German, and von Brandt, on the ground, as De Long believed, that foreign employes of the Government were allowed free access to the interior and that free access to Kyoto had been granted twice when fairs were held there, demanded free entrance for all his nationals. De Long felt that von Brandt had made a grave mistake in raising this issue before he had conferred with his colleagues.[41]

Sir Harry Parkes, however, considered this a suitable time to bring matters to a conclusion. At a meeting of the Corps on July 24,[42] he read a long memorandum on the subject which met with the approval of his colleagues, and a protocol was drawn up which was to be the basis of an identical note to be drafted by Sir Harry and put into circulation.

The Protocol stated that the only question to be discussed was the right of travel in the interior for any lawful purpose, but not of permanent residence; that all possible guaranties should be offered the Japanese Government in order to avoid collisions or

[41] No. 443, July 6; von Brandt, *Drei und dreissig Jahre in Ost-Asien,* II, 344.

[42] The Representatives of France, Germany, Great Britain, Italy, The Netherlands, Russia, Spain, and the United States were present.

difficulties, such as a system of passports and securities to be deposited by the foreigners; that the right of the Japanese to arrest foreign offenders and send them to the nearest treaty port, and to settle on their own authority all claims between foreigners and Japanese for hotel bills, fares, and similar questions, would be recognized, but on no account would the submission of foreigners to Japanese jurisdiction be admitted. Negotiations might be begun immediately or postponed until the return of Soyeshima, as the Japanese preferred.

On the twenty-sixth De Long dispatched his identical note to Uyeno. It seems that he had been forced to leave the conference on the twenty-fourth, by indisposition, before the Protocol was signed, and had signed the copy the next day. But soon after, he received a copy of the memorandum which Sir Harry had read, and as it did not agree, in some particulars, with his recollection of its phrasing, he ventured to submit certain amendments. Believing the memorandum would form a very important state paper and might become known to the authorities, he considered it

a matter of first consequence that it should be bereft, if possible, of all language calculated to annoy or challenge the contradiction of the Japanese, and certainly it should not be allowed to contain any assertion relative to existing facts that one of us if called upon to prove could not at once do, by plain reference.

His amendments, therefore, were designed to refine some of the brusqueness of Sir Harry's statements.

The Corps met on the twenty-eighth to consider De Long's suggestions. An animated discussion arose, in which some agreed in whole, others in part, and some had amendments of their own to offer. It was finally held, De Long and Parkes dissenting, that the memorandum was not one which the Corps would have to sign and that no action was necessary. So the two discussed the wording, and agreed upon a revised draft (which incorporated most of De Long's suggestions) on the twenty-ninth.

De Long's comment on the whole question was:

What action my other colleagues will take relative to the paper I do not know. I fear that an attempt to unduly force concessions from this government will have a negative effect from the one desired, but governed by your instructions relative to co-operation, I have felt constrained to take this action.[43]

In acknowledging the receipt of the identic notes, Soyeshima, on August 8, requested that the discussion be deferred until the return of Lord Iwakura.[44]

The next move was made by von Brandt, who, in September, drafted a set of regulations to govern the movement of foreigners in the interior and submitted them to his colleagues. They were discussed by the Corps, modified slightly and submitted in a joint note on September 27. Briefly, they called for proper passports, to be issued by the Japanese authorities at the request of the Foreign Ministers or Consuls; a deposit of $200 to cover any expenses incurred by the authorities through the misconduct of foreign travelers; and a fine of $200 or a maximum of thirty days' imprisonment for traveling without a passport. De Long reported that it was generally believed that in a few days' time,

we shall be able to agree with this government upon a plan nearly, if not quite, similar to the one we have proposed, and that Japan in a few weeks will be declared open to foreign trade and residence.[45]

What De Long and his colleagues refused to recognize was that the Japanese Government had firmly resolved not to open the country to foreigners until extraterritoriality had been relinquished.

The first attention which the Department gave to this correspondence was in an instruction to Mr. Bingham which pointed out that the deposits should not be made with the American Consuls, for there was no law authorizing the Government to incur such responsibilities.[46]

And finally, a future *cause célèbre* appeared upon the scene, so inoffensively that its later repercussions could not be foreseen. It was the formulation of Quarantine Regulations. The Diplomatic

[43] No. 454, July 31. The pertinent documents were transmitted.

[44] No. 463, August 20.

[45] No. 482, October 5, *F.R., 1874,* pp. 648–50. The several discussions of 1873 were summarized in the Joint Note of August 14, 1874; see *infra.*

[46] No. 14, November 7, *F.R., 1874,* p. 653.

Corps met and drafted a set of regulations which it proposed to
the Government in a collective note. In a subsequent discussion
at the Foreign Office certain amendments were agreed upon.
These were, in due course, approved by all the Foreign Representatives except Mr. Watson, who could not act in the absence of
Sir Harry Parkes. As it was specified that these regulations were
not to be promulgated nor put in force until some exigency
arose, they remained without official notification by the Foreign
Representatives to their nationals.[47]

The seven incidents thus narrated indicated the difficulties
faced by the Japanese in trying to apply to nationals of the Treaty
Powers the municipal laws which were generally regarded as
desirable. As long as the British Minister would accept no
Japanese law until he approved it and adopted it as a British
regulation, and as long as the American Minister was bound by
the co-operative policy, there was bound to be a three-cornered
friction, involving the Representatives of the other Powers in
turn.[48]

We can now turn back to an individual attempt to secure
access to the interior, on behalf of the nationals of a single power.
On the subject of the Italian negotiations of 1873 many misleading ideas have been current.

Acting on instructions from his Government, in February the
Italian Minister proposed that his nationals be allowed to travel
freely in the interior on condition that they be subjected quali-
fiedly to Japanese jurisdiction when beyond the treaty ports.
Soyeshima admitted to De Long that such a proposal had been
made, and the Italian Minister, at a meeting of the Corps, on
February 23, outlined what he had done. The French Minister,
at this time, reported that he had discussed the *démarche* with

---

[47] No. 467, August 30.

[48] Typical of this situation was the fact that all Trade Regulations had to
be adopted by joint and unanimous consent of the Japanese and foreign officials. In 1873 the amendment to the Customs House Regulations and the
Customs Shed Regulations, at Yokohama, occasioned considerable discussion,
and the presentation of identic notes on February 15 (No. 393, May 7). The
protest was revived in a joint note of February 27, 1874, which Bingham refused to sign. See *infra,* chap. xxi.

Soyeshima and the latter had intimated that Japan would agree to the proposal on condition that offenses involving imprisonment for one year, or a fine of $300, should be subject to Japanese jurisdiction, while greater offenses would involve the arrest of the culprit by the local authorities and his delivery to the nearest Consul for trial and punishment. This statement, it will be observed, was in general terms and might be applied to all foreigners. Soyeshima had also pointed out that the closing of the interior was due not to any risk which the foreigners might run but to the practice of extraterritoriality which permitted the foreigner to carry his own laws wherever he went. De Long believed that the rapid progress of Japan toward civilization would soon result in opening the country, and these changes, he emphasized, were due to their own acts and not in any wise to pressure from foreign sources; and while giving due credit to all that the Foreign Representatives had accomplished, severally and by co-operative effort, he awarded the highest praise to the very able and liberal-minded Soyeshima, "who enjoys the unbounded respect and confidence of us all."[49]

Soon afterward, Mr. Sitta was called to Rome, and the Corps decided to proceed with the discussion for a general agreement. De Long, as Doyen of the Corps, was asked to request Soyeshima to summon a conference to frame a convention. The latter, however, did not wish to open the question until his return from China. But the Russian Minister insisted that the delay would be granted only if in the meantime no special privileges were granted the Italians. To this Soyeshima could not assent, on the ground that the proposal had come from the Italian Minister, that it had been accepted by the Japanese Government, and that it was to become operative as soon as the approval of Italy had been obtained. Other countries agreeing to the same terms would have the same privileges. This reply led to a second meeting of the Corps, at which it was found that the members could not agree as to exactly what had passed when Mr. Sitta had discussed the

---

[49] No. 349, February 23. The Italian Government was motivated by the urgent need of securing silkworm eggs from the interior.

matter with them; so De Long was requested to seek the facts from Soyeshima. From the latter he received, on February 26, a copy of the provisional convention proposed to Italy. The text was in French, and so badly phrased that it was subject to varying translations. A version prepared for Sir Harry Parkes confirmed the previous reports—that Italians in the interior would be subject to Japanese jurisdiction; that cruel punishments would not be imposed, although imprisonment with or without hard labor might be meted out; and that no capital punishment would be inflicted until the case had been referred to Tokyo, as was the usage in respect to Japanese subjects.

So abject a surrender of foreign rights stirred the diplomats to agree to refer the matter at once to their governments for decision before the Italian Government could sanction the proposal. De Long felt that the Japanese considered they had obtained a decided advantage; for, should the Italian Government consent, it was likely that the other Powers must follow in order to prevent the Italian traders from enjoying special advantages, and thus extraterritoriality would be abolished beyond the treaty ports.[50]

The matter was now taken up by the foreign chancelleries. Mr. Fish wrote, on May 7, that the American Minister in Paris had been instructed to make inquiries.[51] But on June 9, the Marquis de Noailles, French Minister in Washington, transmitted to Mr. Fish a copy of an instruction he had recently received from the Count de Rémusat, Minister of Foreign Affairs, with a request for co-operative action. In this dispatch, of May 9, the Count de Rémusat outlined the proceedings in Tokyo exactly as we have described them. The Italian Minister in Japan was about to return home on leave, and he would submit for the approval of his Government an arrangement which he had agreed upon for the free travel of Italians in the interior. M. de Turenne, French Chargé, had sent on two drafts from Tokyo, one supplied by the Italian Legation and the other by the Japanese Minister for Foreign Affairs, and the Count de Rémusat pointed out:

[50] No. 369, March 15.   [51] No. 198.

The difference between the two versions does not change the purport of this document, the sole interest of which for us lies in the provision, in virtue of which Italians, when they have passed the limits assigned by the treaties now in force, as those of the residence of foreigners, are to be subject to the jurisdiction of the Japanese authorities.

The Diplomatic Corps in Tokyo had written their governments urging them to dissuade the Government at Rome from ratifying this arrangement, and the Count de Rémusat could not hesitate to do so. He pleaded for co-operation and argued against the readiness of Japan to exercise jurisdiction over foreigners. And he assumed that when the attention of Mr. Fish was called to this matter he would instruct the American Minister in Rome to endeavor to induce the Italian Government not to sanction an arrangement which might better be secured through co-operative efforts.[52]

The immediate effect of this *démarche* of France was the sending of identical instructions to Schenck in London, Washburne in Paris, Bancroft in Berlin, and Gorham in St. Petersburg, on June 21. These contained the Italian version of the draft (which omitted the reference to imprisonment at hard labor and to capital punishment, said to have been proposed by the Japanese Government). They stated that although Mr. Visconti was not thought to be at present favorably disposed toward it, it was by no means certain that it would not be accepted. Then followed an important statement of the attitude of the American Government toward extraterritoriality.

The President might look without disfavor on efforts in this direction to gratify them [the desires of the Italians]; but it is impossible to shut the eyes to the fact that there is a large party in Japan who regard the ex-territorial right, now possessed by the treaty powers, as a denial of the independence of Japan, and who, availing themselves of aid from any quarter, in shaking them off, will regard the proposed arrangement as a

[52] Marquis de Noailles to Fish, June 9. Inclosure, Count de Rémusat to Marquis de Noailles, May 9 (*F.R., 1873*, pp. 269–70). One of the two drafts is printed: "Draft of a provisional convention relative to the travel of foreigners in the interior of Japan, presented by the minister of Italy to the government of the Tenno." This is the draft which De Long transmitted on March 15. The other draft, which came from the Italian Legation, was incorporated in the identical instructions sent out by Mr. Fish on June 21.

step in that direction. Thus, though it is true that any advantages gained to Italians in this respect must inure, under the provisions of existing treaties, to those of our countrymen who may desire to avail themselves thereof, yet the President is forced to consider the wider question, whether justice is administered in Japan with certainty, equity, firmness, and celerity, and on the basis of such principles of jurisprudence common to Europe and America, as may warrant the surrender of the defensive rights which we now possess.

Japan has no firmer friend than the United States; no one more ready to recognize her rightful autonomy. But, on a candid review of the situation, the President is forced to the conclusion that it is not yet safe to surrender to the local authorities the guaranteed rights of ex-territoriality. We have not such knowledge of the administration of justice in that kingdom, and of the means for the protection of the liberties and rights of foreigners, as would justify such surrender at this time. It appears to us, also, that the welfare, safety, and the interests of all foreigners in Japan are at the present moment dependent, in a large degree, upon the unity of action and of policy of all the treaty powers, and that the acceptance by any one of those powers of privileges for its own citizens, which may be proposed as an inducement to separate that state from the other treaty powers, in the policy which has heretofore been common to all, would tend to the serious discomfort of all the powers in their future relations with Japan, and would weaken their position in the negotiations which must soon be entered into for the revision of the treaties.

Each Minister was instructed to communicate these verbally to the Foreign Minister of the country to which he was accredited, to endeavor to have similar instructions sent to the Representatives at Rome and Tokyo, and to report any suggestions for a different action.[53]

General Schenck reported that he had had a very satisfactory conversation with Lord Granville, who was entirely in accord with Mr. Fish and the President on all points. The latter had already expressed his objections to Mr. Cardona, Italian Minister in London, who was about to go home on leave, and he had given instructions to the British Representatives in harmony with those suggested by Mr. Fish. But Lord Granville understood that the offer from Japan was drawn out by advances first made by Italy,

---

[53] No. 408, Fish to General Schenck, June 21, *F.R., 1873,* pp. 382–83. A copy of this instruction was forwarded to De Long, with directions to apprise the Minister for Foreign Affairs of these views of the President (No. 207, July 22, *F.R., 1874,* p. 645). The delay of a month should be noted.

and he had reason to believe that the proposed arrangement would not be completed. From Mr. Cardona, Earl Granville had received a copy of the arrangement proposed by Japan, which differed from Mr. Fish's text only in the use of the French words for "torture" instead of "corporal punishment."[54]

From Paris, Mr. Wickham Hoffman, Chargé, reported that he had communicated the views of the President to the Duke de Broglie, who had succeeded the Count de Rémusat, and who agreed entirely with them, but he had asked for a few days for reflection before taking action.[55] This must have been read with interest in the State Department because on July 15 a note had been received from the Marquis de Noailles (dated July 12) which covered an instruction from the Duke de Broglie directing him to inform the Secretary of State that the British and Netherlands Governments had joined with France in advising the Italian Government not to sacrifice the right of jurisdiction over its citizens. The Cabinet at Rome, so read the instruction, would refuse to accept the convention.[56]

In other words, before the American *démarche* had been made, the governments of France, Great Britain, and the Netherlands had already brought pressure upon the Government of Italy.

The German Government, so Mr. Bancroft reported, took exactly the same view as the United States, and had communicated its attitude to the Italian Minister in Berlin.[57]

This attempt of Japan to secure an important revision of one of the old Treaties by separate negotiations failed. In the coming years Japan was to try both methods, the joint conference and individual negotiations, until in 1894 the latter method was to gain the desired end. From the point of view of American diplomacy several points should be noticed. First, the statement of policy respecting the relinquishment of extraterritoriality; sec-

[54] No. 455, Schenck to Fish, July 19, *F.R., 1873,* pp. 400–401.

[55] No. 837, Hoffman to Fish, July 24, *ibid.,* p. 261.

[56] Marquis de Noailles to Fish, July 12; inclosure, Duke de Broglie to Marquis de Noailles, June 19, *ibid.,* pp. 271–72. These letters were forwarded to De Long in No. 211, August 14. Another long delay.

[57] No. 501, Bancroft to Fish, July 19, *ibid.,* p. 296.

ondly, the eagerness to advocate the well-established co-operative policy, when France offered the occasion; thirdly, the rejection of De Long's advices from Tokyo and the acceptance of the view that the proposal had come in the first instance from Japan rather than from Italy; and, finally, the fact that effective pressure was brought to bear upon Italy as the result of European agreements before the American proposal was formulated in Washington.[58]

This year saw the settlement, by Japan and in its own way, of a domestic question which had, for years, disturbed the relations between the Empire and the Treaty Powers. In 1873 the Christian religion was tolerated. The last co-operative action of the Powers had occurred in 1870.[59] When the Iwakura mission was in Washington, Mr. Fish had proposed that a clause covering religious freedom be placed in the revised Treaty, and the matter had been the subject of some discussion. It is said that when Ito and Okubo returned to Japan to secure full powers they urged that the article prohibiting the Christian religion be stricken from the official signboards.[60] But even before their arrival, Chargé Shepard had reported signs that the enforcement of the prohibition was going by default. "I *hope,* and there is reason to *believe* that the whole Christian question will thus quietly solve itself," he wrote.[61]

Early in 1873, Soyeshima intimated to the Foreign Representatives that steps would be taken which would satisfy the Treaty Powers, and in February he informed De Long that the objectionable signboards would be removed. When the French Representative asked Soyeshima why the toleration of Christianity was not proclaimed, the latter replied that the masses would misunderstand such an action and would infer that the Govern-

[58] In this year Japan proposed to negotiate a postal treaty with the United States and the other Powers. Mr. S. W. Bryan, formerly of the United States Post Office Department and then an adviser to the Japanese Department, was sent abroad on this mission. The draft of the proposed treaty was forwarded in No. 347, February 18.

[59] See *supra.*   [60] Ariga, in Stead, *op. cit.,* p. 156.

[61] No. 29, April 11, 1872. Black (*Young Japan,* II, 397) states that the Nagasaki Christians were returned to their homes in March 1872.

ment desired them to embrace the Christian faith. He also said that in about a month's time all the Christians who had been banished would return to their homes. The Italian Minister, who was Doyen of the Corps, requested Soyeshima, as a personal favor, to give him some written assurances on this matter before his departure for home on the twenty-fifth, and he was able to present at a meeting of the Corps on February 23 the copy of an edict received from Soyeshima that morning, which read:

Feeling that the measures taken in respect to the professors of the Christian faith have been unjustifiable towards foreigners, We already during the summer of last year instructed the authorities of the Fu and Ken to refrain from arresting them.

In addition to this We are now erasing, from the public tables of the law, the prohibition against Christianity, inscribed on them.[62]

De Long followed up this gratifying development by calling on Soyeshima, in his new capacity as Doyen, and asking for full information. The Foreign Minister gave him a carefully prepared memorandum, which might be laid before the Corps, and then summarized it verbally. The decision was taken for two reasons—the persecution of the native Christians offended the great nations whose good will Japan sought to foster, and its enforcement was futile as a means of eradicating the faith. Education, rather than force, was a better means of restoring the converts to their national faith. The assurance was renewed that the exiles would soon be sent back to their homes, and, in closing his dispatch, De Long gave full credit to the efforts of his honorable colleagues: "We have all united with a will and a steady purpose to succeed, and we all rejoice in the achievement of this triumph."[63]

The tide had turned, but the battle for tolerance had not been completely won. A month later, Mr. Uyeno, Acting Minister for Foreign Affairs, explained frankly to De Long that the laws and

[62] No. 349, February 23. The edict was dated February 19. Black (*op. cit.,* II, 398), states that Chargés Turenne and Watson had pointed out that religious persecution would lessen the cordiality with which Iwakura would be received in Europe.

[63] No. 367, March 14.

edicts had not been repealed and that all the liberal party, which
was in a minority in the Government, could obtain was the removal of the signboards and the return of the exiles. In fact,
when the proclamations were taken down, officials had been sent
from house to house to inform the people that the laws still existed and must be obeyed. De Long replied that all this looked
like an effort to mislead and deceive foreigners, and Uyeno said
that was exactly why he had given this explanation. Although
the advocates of tolerance were, at the moment, in a minority, he
was confident that in a short time they would be in control and
"any attempt to force such reforms any faster than they were
now being accomplished would certainly lead to defeat."[64]

The restoration of the converts to their homes and property
promptly began. On May 9 De Long was able to report that
about fifty who had been confined in Kaga had been sent home,[65]
and soon the several groups were quietly and safely repatriated.

This brought to a close the renewal of the anti-Christian pro-
scriptions which had begun in the last years of the Shogunate.
It will be remembered that Japan had never accepted a treaty
provision for the toleration of the alien faith, and thus she
escaped the endless difficulties in which China was embroiled after
1858.[66] So long as she did not interfere with the religious practices of the nationals of the Treaty Powers, the Foreign Representatives could do no more than protest or counsel in respect to
the treatment of her own subjects. In the early phases of the

[64] No. 379, April 20. In this dispatch De Long paraphrased Uyeno as saying
that he (De Long) had never thrust his views upon the Government or evinced
any impatience, and, believing that he had given the Government more credit
than it now deserved, Uyeno had sought this opportunity to give him the real
facts.

[65] No. 397.

[66] While the Legation dispatches from Peking were largely made up of
correspondence dealing with missionary and convert cases, Tokyo rarely had
occasion to refer to them. A case in 1871, involving the arrest of a native
teacher, which led to an unofficial intervention in his behalf by Mr. De Long,
was not even mentioned in a dispatch (Greene, E. B., *A New-Englander in
Japan,* pp. 110–12). A similar case in 1873 was successfully handled (No. 479,
October 1, *F.R., 1874,* pp. 646–47). The application of Rev. D. G. Greene for
permission to circulate the Scriptures throughout the Empire was refused by
the Government, and De Long asked for instructions (No. 437, July 2).

discussion there was a readiness in certain foreign circles to do more than protest, but against this the British Minister and his Government stood firm. The Japanese understood their treaty obligations, and in this respect, at least, they would not permit them to be enlarged under foreign pressure. In due season, tolerance came in the most satisfactory way, by recognition from within rather than pressure from without. The Foreign Representatives and their governments could have learned much about the spirit and purpose of New Japan from the way it handled the question of religious tolerance.

Passing from these questions of larger significance we come to a number of incidents involving Americans and their interests in Japan. These involved trade regulations, claims, concessions, and personal rights.

From Kobe came the question as to whether or not gold leaf should be considered on the free list as bullion,[67] an interpretation which the Department did not sustain.[68] And to the advantage of foreign traders was the removal of the prohibition of the export of saltpeter.[69]

Illegal port charges at Kobe were protested by the Pacific Mail Steamship Company, and promptly removed on De Long's representation.[70] A request for instructions on a complaint against customs charges at Nagasaki met with no attention.[71] And a charge that obstacles had been created to the shipment of American freight at Niigata was referred to Mr. Bingham for investigation.[72]

A prospect of better handling of claims in the future was held out by the draft of a code of rules and regulations for the new courts, which De Long received from Soyeshima in February, and which he described as being "in all respects so far as they go, similar to the rules prevailing in the courts of California."[73] He promptly inquired if this would not modify the instruction not to

---

[67] No. 414, May 31.   [68] No. 208, August 2.   [69] No. 344, February 7.

[70] No. 368, March 15; No. 383, April 22.

[71] No. 438, July 2.   [72] No. 2, September 1.   [73] No. 349, February 23.

present a claim until it had been referred to the Department;[74] but as Mr. Fish had repeatedly urged the settlement of all claims in Japanese courts, so far as possible, he should not have been disappointed when his query was ignored.

Notwithstanding repeated disapprovals, De Long could not resist trying to secure advantages, direct or indirect, for his countrymen. Thus, he asked the Japanese Government to remit the ground rent on a Bluff lot at Yokohama where Miss Mary Pruyn had a school, and he received a favorable reply.[75] But the application of D. W. Ap Jones, on behalf of a Californian company for the exclusive right to catch seals and otters in Japanese waters was refused.[76] This brought down the disapproval of the Department for failing to submit the application to the Department before presenting it to the Japanese Government.[77] The immediate result was that when W. H. Doyle asked his assistance in obtaining land for a paper-mill, De Long applied for instructions.[78] His successor was directed to render such aid as he properly could.[79] On the other hand, De Long did not hesitate to ask permission for Mr. Jones to visit the wild lands of Japan and report on their adaptability for sheep culture.[80]

[74] No. 355, March 5. Claims which were the subject of correspondence were: (1) the Hozier claim, which the Department again pressed. The Japanese Government had insisted that Dr. Hozier and the clan officer, who had made the contract, be confronted; the Department insisted upon the award made by Mr. Alt (but which, it admitted, was an arbitration arranged by the Tosa Government, and not by the Imperial Government, which was called upon to pay the award) (No. 174, February 22). (2) The claims of Schultze, Reiss & Company and Smith, Baker & Company, which Japan refused to settle (No. 382, April 21), and which the Department asked be reconsidered (No. 202, June 12). (3) The counterclaims of Japan *versus* Rice (No. 351, March 2). (4) And the old claim against the United States for services rendered by the "Aroostook" (No. 467, August 30). Japan continued to press for the payment of rents for lots used by the United States (No. 426, June 17). On the lot at Yokohama, Bluff, No. 27, De Long paid $662, to June 1 (No. 469, September 2).

[75] No. 364, March 13.   [76] No. 365, March 13.

[77] No. 195, April 22. This instruction also applied to De Long's presentation of a small model of the ironclad "Monitor," in April 1872 (but reported on March 13, 1873, No. 366), and his request for permission for an American to execute an engraving of the Emperor, which the Government refused (No. 371, March 16).   [78] No. 432, June 20.   [79] No. 11, Fish to Bingham, October 16.

[80] No. 480, October 1. An abstract of Jones's report was transmitted by Mr. Bingham, and printed (No. 24, December 5, *F.R., 1874,* pp. 655–58).

Several interesting cases arose involving the personal rights of Americans. The first concerned the validity of a regulation issued by De Long directing American citizens to register in one of the Consulates. It began with a dispute between De Long and Consul Shepard, at Yokohama, because the latter had not ordered all Americans in Japanese employ to register, and had placed on the list of assessors, to be employed in the Consular Court, a number of these employees, while he had omitted the names of other resident citizens. De Long held that an American employed by Japan should not serve as an assessor.[81] In carrying out De Long's instructions, Shepard ordered Peshine Smith to register. The latter refused to do so, and he was brought into Court and fined. His defense, it should be observed, was that he was a naturalized Japanese subject.[82]

This trial of the American legal adviser to the Foreign Office before the American Consul was a choice topic of conversation in the treaty ports. But the Department did not consider it so lightly. In a pointed instruction De Long was informed that the regulation in question was without validity. The plain language of the Act of 1860 was pointed out, and the power of the Minister to issue regulations was limited to the exercise of his judicial authority, and in order to provide suitable and appropriate remedies where the laws of the United States were ill adapted or deficient.

I am therefore constrained to disapprove of your action in counselling Consul Shepard in support of your (his) jurisdictional right to compel all American citizens in Japan within your (his) consular jurisdiction, whether in the employ of the Japanese Government, or otherwise, to enroll their names upon your Consular Register.[83]

By the time this instruction reached De Long he knew that he had been recalled, so he did not hesitate to argue the question with the Secretary of State. There was much which could be said in his favor. He summed up the whole record of his regulations of 1870, as we have narrated it.[84] Once promulgated by the Min-

---

[81] No. 339, January 20. [82] No. 341, January 22.
[83] No. 176, February 26, *F.R., 1873*, pp. 570–72. The paragraph quoted above is omitted from the printed instruction. [84] See *supra*.

ister, they were binding and obligatory until annulled or modified by Congress. His draft had been criticized by Mr. Fish, but it had been referred to Congress and no action had subsequently been taken. At about the same time, when the question of the registration of firms came up, he had been instructed that individual citizens only were to be registered, and he issued the regulations in question in November 1870. These, also, had not been set aside by Congress, nor had Mr. Fish commented adversely upon them. So when, during the trial, Peshine Smith stated that these regulations had been disapproved by the Department and De Long had been so notified, the Minister replied in terms which he admitted were "unnecessarily harsh and abrupt." He then defended the system of registration as a basis for the selection of assessors, by lot, and he asserted that the system had worked well in the past.[85]

While we cannot overlook the fundamental error of the Minister in drafting regulations which went far beyond his authority, in this and in other cases, we cannot fail to sympathize with him in view of the failure of Congress to pass upon his code and of the Department to reply to his repeated requests for instructions.

Then the question of the validity of deportation as a punishment for American criminals was raised anew.[86] The Department had disapproved of this practice in 1870, but it had reversed itself the next year, on condition that the offender be allowed one year to arrange his affairs after leaving jail. This had happened when Shepard was Chargé, and De Long was not familiar with the case.[87] So when in March 1873 he received the complaint of John Rogers that he had been sentenced to deportation, he acted with unusual promptness, for this would be another count in his growing indictment of Consul Shepard. He found that the sentence had been handed down on December 7, 1871, just a year after Shepard had been instructed that deportations were not to be enforced.[88] At the time, Rogers was given one month to close his

---

[85] No. 387, April 28.   [86] See *supra,* chap. xxvi.   [87] See *supra,* chap. xxvii.
[88] The ban against deportations had been called to Shepard's attention in the correspondence over registration, No. 341, January 22.

affairs (which violated the Department's ruling of 1871), but this had been allowed to run for over a year. Finally, when De Long went aboard the mail steamer he found the United States Marshal there, with four Americans whom he had brought off for deportation. As De Long was not satisfied with Shepard's explanations he placed the whole matter before the Department.[89]

The reply gave him some satisfaction. In the case of Rogers, Shepard's proceedings were correct, because the assessors who sat with him had concurred in the judgment and there was no appeal to the Minister. In the other three cases the Consul was called upon to explain his action.[90] Now, in defiance of the retiring Minister, Shepard ordered eight more Americans returned to their home land, which caused De Long to ask if the approval mentioned above set aside the disapproval of 1870.[91] To this query the Department did not deign to reply.

The next question was one which was to come up many times in the Far East, and most frequently in China. It involved the right of American citizens to waive their extraterritorial privileges and submit themselves to the laws of Japan. The advantages accruing from such a proceeding, in the days when alien rights were confined to treaty stipulations, were obvious. De Long, in agreement with his colleagues, took the position that foreigners were subject to the jurisdiction of their national laws and officers.[92] The Department approved his position, pointing out that an American could expatriate himself if he chose.[93]

On the other hand, the question was raised as to whether Americans in the employ of the Japanese Government were subject to consular jurisdiction, which De Long answered in the affirmative.[94]

[89] No. 358, March 7.

[90] No. 193, April 16. They proved to be destitute seamen, and, like the eight mentioned above, were properly repatriated. Cf. *F.R., 1878*, p. 519.

[91] No. 410, May 27.   [92] No. 439, July 5, *F.R., 1874*, pp. 643–44.

[93] No. 212, August 21, *ibid.*, p. 645. The question was raised by W. H. Doyle, who wanted to operate a paper-mill in the interior. On another occasion, De Long refused to accept a declaration of intentions as proof of American citizenship (No. 391, April 29).

[94] No. 430, June 20. De Long had previously asked the Department what

And, finally, De Long extended the theory of American protection on the basis of precedents which had no standing in the treaty stipulations. When the Japanese servant of an American was arrested by local officers, De Long held that no arrest could be made on American premises without the intervention of American authorities, and, on the ground that the charge in this case was baseless, he secured the release of the accused.[95]

A few incidents may be cited to show the undercurrent of good will which prevailed in these days. In a single mail De Long reported two cases. On the one hand, some of the crew of the wrecked brigantine "Admiral" had been rescued and kindly treated by the villagers, for which he had expressed the thanks of his Government,[96] while Japan, for her part, had presented 300 *rio* to Captain Cobb, of the "China," for the rescue of Japanese sailors who had been helplessly adrift for seven months.[97] And when the "Golden Age" ran down a fishing-junk, $300 was promptly paid.[98] Permission sought by the Navy Department for a party of astronomers to be accorded facilities to observe the transit of Venus was gladly accorded.[99] And some correspondence occurred on the request of Admiral Jenkins for permission to establish a temporary naval storehouse at Nagasaki.[100]

Before turning to the less pleasant incidents of the year we can note that on January 16 the Emperor received in audience Mr. De Long and Mr. Butzow, the Russian Minister, while at the same time the Empress received their wives, the first foreign ladies to be admitted to the Palace.[101] With the departure of the Italian Minister, on February 25, De Long became Doyen, a position which he held until Sir Harry Parkes returned in April.[102] And when Lord Iwakura returned, on September 13, from his far-extended travels, he heard him express

---

recognition he should accord such Americans (No. 406, May 22). His relations with Peshine Smith, and some of the other Japanese employees, had long been strained.

[95] No. 468, September 1.   [96] No. 475, September 18.
[97] No. 476, September 18.   [98] No. 392, May 7.
[99] No. 199, May 20; No. 465, August 27.   [100] No. 459, August 4.
[101] No. 342, January 23; Black, *op. cit.,* II, 389.   [102] No. 353, March 2.

in a heartfelt manner his deep sense of obligation to the government and people of the United States for the extreme courtesy which marked his reception and treatment while there. He also honored me by expressing his warm personal and official regards.[103]

De Long had refused to remove the Legation to Tokyo, despite all the suggestions from the Department. In September 1872 the *bettos,* or guards, had been withdrawn from all the foreign Legations, but no danger had been incurred.[104] A further inducement to establish himself in Tokyo was offered when the Department gave him permission to rent a courthouse and jail in Yedo for two years, subject to renewal for the same term, at an annual rental of $5,000.[105] But De Long passed this responsibility over to his successor.[106]

Of the bitter controversies which filled up so many pages of De Long's dispatches little need now be said. They serve, however, to help delineate the figure of this American diplomat. His quarrels with Portman, Shepard, and Peshine Smith have been touched upon. In the last months of his service his one thought seemed to be to wreak vengeance upon Colonel Shepard, against whom he had many grievances. In one of the longest dispatches which he prepared, on May 7, he poured out his complaints, based upon a minor clash between Shepard and the Japanese customs officials at Yokohama, and asked for the views of Mr. Fish on all the matters of controversy.[107] Although both the Minister and the Consul resided at Yokohama, all personal intercourse between them had ceased and an angry correspondence had taken its place.

In this and in other dispatches, De Long had accused Shepard of carelessness and deception in the handling of the Legation files, and he returned to the charge with papers dealing with the audience of Admiral Jenkins in 1872.[108] New charges on this score were found in Shepard's handling of a case involv-

---

[103] No. 477, September 22, *F.R., 1874,* p. 646.   [104] No. 419, June 3.

[105] No. 196, May 3.   [106] No. 484, October 5.

[107] No. 393, May 7. Also No. 402, May 22; No. 413, May 31.

[108] No. 445, July 7; No. 451, July 17. See *supra.* Shepard was dismissed, as he believed, on this charge, and he later submitted a vindication and demand that his good name be restored. Shepard to Fish, December 20, 1874.

ing the mate of an American merchant ship who had been discharged by Shepard and promptly reinstated by De Long.[109] Then
he hurled a bombshell by charging the Consul with high crimes
and misdemeanors in the management of the postal agency at
Yokohama,[110] and followed this up with charges of ill treatment
of the crew of the ship just mentioned.[111] Further charges arising
from the operations of the postal agency implicated Marshal
Denison (who was receiving additional pay as a postal clerk),
and Vice-Consul Mitchell. The "high crimes" consisted of removing excess stamps from mail matter and selling them! So
infuriated was De Long by this time that he telegraphed this dispatch—one of the few instances of his use of this medium.[112]
This shocking expenditure of Government funds jarred the Department into action. It had ignored all the previous complaints.
Now the Minister was reminded that he had jurisdiction in such
a case and that the Department could give no instructions.

> But knowing that the relations between you and that officer [Shepard]
> are not altogether pleasant and amicable, it appreciates the delicacy which
> prompted you to ask instructions,

Happily Mr. Bingham would, at an early date, relieve him from
sitting as judge in a case which must be disagreeable to him.[113]

Finally, Shepard was accused of wrongfully withdrawing
American protection from the firm of Schultze, Reiss & Company.[114]

To conclude this unpleasant story we need only say that Mr.
Bingham was instructed to investigate the charges involving the
postal agency and the withdrawal of American protection, and in
both cases he reported them unfounded.[115]

---

[109] No. 446, July 17.   [110] No. 448, July 21.   [111] No. 450, July 21.
[112] No. 460, August 4. Also a telegram of the same date.
[113] No. 209, August 6. The Secretary had before him a memorandum, by
Mr. O'Connor, attached to No. 448, to the effect that in his opinion the charge
was trumped-up.   [114] No. 455, July 31.
[115] Nos. 6 and 7, September 18; No. 6, Bingham to Fish, October 18; No.
12, October 29. De Long himself was reprimanded for failing to send pertinent information to the Department. When the Pacific Mail steamship
"America" was burned in the harbor of Yokohama, on August 24, 1872, some
sixty lives were lost. Some of the victims were Chinese, returning from Cali-

De Long, as we have intimated, was recalled from his post. This was not simply the customary retirement of a Minister at the close of a political administration in Washington. President Grant had been re-elected in 1872, and De Long confidently expected to remain in Japan for the new term. But about March 1, 1873, he received a private note from Mr. Fish advising him that the President desired him to submit his resignation, to take effect four years from the date of his original appointment. He was not a little surprised, and he drafted his resignation, intending to send it forward; but instead he wrote a personal letter to General E. O. Babcock, secretary to the President. He had heard, at the Foreign Office, that the Japanese officials had learned of the President's action as soon as he had, and that they accounted for it on the ground that De Long's action in obtaining permission for Dr. Hepburn to present a Bible to the Emperor had incurred severe disapproval and that for that reason he would be called upon to resign. They also told him that the appointment had been offered to Judge Bingham, of Ohio, who had declined it on account of ill health, and that it was then under consideration by a gentleman in New York. After further discussion the Japanese begged De Long not to submit his resignation until they could forward a request that he be allowed to remain. De Long finally consented to do so, and he was able to inclose a copy of an instruction from Soyeshima to Mr. Mori, in Washington, expressing the earnest hope of the Emperor that Mr. De Long's resignation should not be accepted and that he might be allowed to remain at his post, permanently if possible. Mr. Mori was directed to read this dispatch to the Secretary of State.[116]

fornia, with their savings in gold. The money which was recovered was placed in the Consulate. A correspondence then took place between De Long and Low, in Peking, and the first word the Department received of the matter came from the latter. A request for a full report was at once sent to De Long (No. 191, April 15). He sent in the required report on May 27 (No. 408), and later reported that the amount, some $8,000 to $9,000, including gold dust, would be sent to Reverend Dr. Kerr, at Canton, to be distributed among the heirs (No. 420, June 4; No. 422, June 6). De Long's course was approved (No. 205, July 14).

[116] This private letter, of March 8, was forwarded by General Babcock to the State Department. Soyeshima's letter stated that the disapproval of the

Although De Long had received the Department's disapproval of the presentation of the Bible more than a month before, he now hastened to explain his conduct on the grounds of good intention and ignorance of any standing rule, and he reported what he had learned at the Foreign Office of the reason for his recall.[117]

So his resignation was not forthcoming, until on April 5 he cabled his compliance; but not until the twenty-third was the formal document sent forward.[118] Judge Bingham was advised of his appointment on June 3, and De Long's letter of recall was dated June 16; but, as we shall see, it was not sent forward. Months passed, and although De Long knew from private advices that his successor had been appointed and had accepted the post, he had received no acknowledgment of his resignation nor the customary letter of recall. On September 18 he telegraphed directly to the President, asking for permission to return in a naval vessel; the President indorsed the message laconically, "No objection that I know of," and referred it to the Secretary of the Navy. Judge Bingham arrived on September 27, and De Long not only refused to welcome him, but demanded that he show his credentials. His papers being in good order, he at once took over the Legation, but when he presented his letter of credence, at an audience on October 7, De Long was unable to present his letter of recall. This embarrassment was due to the fact that the instruction of June 16 covering the letter of recall, had not actually been posted until after September 6.[119] De Long wrote a letter

Bible incident had been learned from Mori. It is quite probable that Peshine Smith also was kept informed of developments in Washington.

[117] No. 354, March 5. He also reported that the Japanese had known promptly of the Department's disapproval in No. 151 of his conduct in the "Maria Luz" affair. "These things convince me that through some agency this government possesses itself of a perfect and immediate knowledge of all correspondence between your Department and this Legation." This was rather late in his service for De Long to have come to this conviction. Whether the leak was in Washington, and the news came to Peshine Smith, or in the Legation at Yokohama, it is a safe inference that the Japanese were well informed of all important matters of correspondence.

[118] No. 386, April 23. A written copy of the resignation should have been sent on the fifth at the time his telegram was dispatched.

[119] See its position in Volume II, Japan, Instructions (State Department).

of protest at this inexcusable oversight, and asked for some explanation.[120]

Although De Long ascribed his recall to the disapproval occasioned by his presentation of a Bible to the Emperor, there is no good reason for accepting this explanation. That incident was only one of many, and a trifling one at most, in which he had incurred the disapprobation of the Department. No other American Minister to Japan received censure so frequently and praise so seldom as this shirt-sleeves diplomat, and it would be surprising if the records showed any comparable record of a Minister who was permitted to serve a full term. In the first place, he was unqualified for the position by either education or experience. His temperament was lacking in the first requisites of diplomacy, and he commenced his career by bullying the Japanese and ended it by quarreling with his countrymen. The improvement of his relations with Soyeshima and the Foreign Office in his last year may be placed to his credit. In his relations with the Department he succeeded in forfeiting all confidence. His early reports were so inadequate and at times so misleading that he involved the Department in ill-advised instructions. After his return from leave in 1872, during which he had visited Washington and become known to Mr. Fish and his associates, his dispatches were given only the slightest consideration. His conduct in the "Maria Luz" affair, in the recommendation of Le Gendre, in the prosecution of certain claims and the request for certain concessions, all annoyed the Department, while his habit of arguing with the Secretary of State and even of requesting new instructions in place of those at hand, and his inattention to standing regulations, would have irritated any executive. In addition, he never forgot that his appointment was a reward for political services, and he did not hesitate to go over the head of the Secretary, to Senator Stewart, of Nevada, to General Babcock, to the President himself, when he sought some favor. Hamilton Fish, on the other hand, was an aristocrat. It must have more than irked him to have to accept in

[120] October 20. The original is missing from the files. De Long sailed for home on November 20.

such a post a political appointee so ill prepared for its responsibilities. And when De Long's dispatches were placed before him,
with their shocking spelling and grammatical constructions, he
must have writhed in his office chair.[121]

On the other side of the account we can give him credit for
doing as well as he did with the meager advantages he possessed.
While he was quick to protect American interests and to further
the aims of his countrymen, he gradually gained a respect for the
Japanese and for their rights which made him, in the latter part
of his service, one of the most sympathetic of the Foreign Representatives. Although he plunged into bitter controversies and
made many enemies, he also made friends, in both the foreign and
the Japanese communities, and there is reason to believe that the
Japanese officials valued his direct but well-meant suggestions. No
other Minister of the United States was to have so colorful a
career in Japan; nor was his period of service lacking in events
of importance, in those days when the new régime was finding
itself and when the Japanese began their long struggle to regain
the rights which they had in ignorance yielded up in the early
Treaties.

[121] As has been pointed out, where quotations from De Long's dispatches
have been used in this book, they have been edited. The purpose of the quotations has been to convey the thought, not to reproduce the immaterial deficiencies. Some of the originals have been corrected, with a blue pencil, in the files.
Berry, whom De Long brought out with him as Secretary, in 1872, was lacking
in education, and after several reprimands he was suspended on August 6, 1873.

CHAPTER XXI

JOHN A. BINGHAM: A NEW POINT OF VIEW
1873-74 [1]

FROM almost every point of view the contrast between the fourth and fifth Ministers of the United States to Japan was marked. De Long had possessed almost no qualifications for such a post; his successor was unusually well equipped in comparison with the other non-career diplomats who made up the American foreign service. John Armor Bingham was born in Mercer, Pennsylvania, on January 21, 1815. He had the advantage of two years of higher education, at Franklin College, and, later studying law, began to practice in Cadiz, Ohio, in 1840. The law was but a stepping-stone to politics, where his flowery and forceful oratory made him a popular speaker. In 1854 he was elected to Congress, and was re-elected, with the exception of one term, until 1872. In 1864 he served for a time as Judge Advocate of the Army, which brought him into prominence during the trial of the assassins of President Lincoln, and later as Solicitor of the Court of Claims. Returning to Congress, he was prominent in the reconstruction debates, and was one of the seven managers chosen by the House to conduct the impeachment of President Johnson. He took credit for framing part of the famous Fourteenth Amendment of the Constitution. His last term would expire on March 4, 1873, and, when it was decided to recall De Long, Bingham's availability was considered. The final decision was not reached until May (De Long was informed that at first Bingham declined

[1] The dispatches for 1874 are numbered 36–166; of these one hundred and thirty-one, seventeen were printed in *F.R., 1874,* eight in *F.R., 1875,* II, one in *F.R., 1875,* I, and No. 162 was later printed in *48th Cong., 2d Sess., H. Ex. Doc. No. 195 (Serial Number 2303),* 1885. The instructions are numbered 18–109 (but one number is repeated); of these ninety-three, twelve were printed in *F.R., 1874,* and three in *F.R., 1875,* II.

the offer), and on June 3 he was advised of his appointment. His commission was dated May 31.[2]

Judge Bingham (for this title was usually applied to him) had for eighteen years been an important figure in the national politics of his country, and for thirty-four years he had been a successful lawyer. During his long service in Japan, when the interpretation and revision of treaties were the outstanding diplomatic questions, Bingham was well prepared for his duties. And when we remember that he rose to political prominence through his advocacy and defense of human rights, we can understand the line of conduct which he adopted in Japan. His great protagonist there was Sir Harry Parkes, already Minister of Great Britain for eight years and Doyen of the Diplomatic Corps. But in years (Bingham was fifty-eight and Parkes was forty-five), in formal education, in knowledge of law, and in experience in large affairs, Bingham was the superior of the two. In the practice of diplomacy, especially in dealing with semi-subject nations such as China and Japan, Parkes had the advantage of long experience. That the two men should clash from the very first was inevitable.

A few details will show how Bingham prepared for his work. His first letter to the Department was a request for a number of reference works for the Legation library, which were supplied him, and he later asked for the *Congressional Record* and two American newspapers.[3] Immediately on his arrival he recommended that the old temple Legation in Tokyo be given up and a suitable residence leased, which was also approved.[4] He had se-

---

[2] *Dictionary of American Biography,* II, 277–78.

[3] July 3; October 20; Fish to Bingham, December 17, 1873.

[4] October 7; No. 15, October 31; Fish to Bingham, December 18, 1873. A building was leased from J. M. Batchelder, an American citizen (No. 58, February 23; Instruction No. 38, April 28, in which Mr. Fish points out that the appropriation is for a courthouse and jail, subject to renewals for two years; No. 86, May 29, covering the amended lease.) As there was little use for such specified buildings in Tokyo the leased property really was used for Legation purposes. Bingham was instructed to surrender the lease of the temple Zempukuji, in No. 90, December 2. And he was authorized to draw $3,700 for rent and $716.18 for furnishings of the courthouse and jail (under the Act of March 3, 1873) in No. 89, December 2.

cured a competent secretary to the Legation in Durham White Stevens[5] before he left the United States, and within a few months he had preferred charges against the interpreter, Nathan E. Rice, and secured his removal. In his place, David Thompson was commissioned on November 18, 1874.[6] There had been a clean sweep in the Legation staff.

As we have seen, Mr. Bingham arrived at Yokohama on September 27, 1873, and presented his credentials to the Emperor on October 7.[7] His first duties were to carry out certain special instructions, notably to examine and report on the charges preferred by his predecessor against Consul Shepard at Yokohama. But soon arose a number of incidents of far greater significance. If we were to accept the survey of American relations with Japan presented in the annual address of the President to Congress on December 7, 1874, we should consider the Formosan incident the most important, with the Shimonoseki indemnity and the opening of the interior as the only other questions. But with the advantage of a longer perspective the Formosan controversy sinks into a very minor position.

The oldest question at issue was the Shimonoseki indemnity. On the one hand Sir Harry Parkes was seeking joint pressure for the payment of the balance due, while Bingham was familiar with the efforts of the administration to secure the passage of a bill for the remission of the American share. He asked for instructions, for he felt that this proposed gesture would confirm Japan in the belief of the good intentions of the United States.[8] As the bill had failed in one House, Mr. Fish could not set aside the obligation, but he advised that it be not unduly pressed.[9] Bingham, therefore, did not sign the joint note, which was presented

[5] Berry was suspended by Presidential Executive Order on August 6, 1873, and Stevens was commissioned the same day. His salary was $2,500.

[6] Bingham to Fish, July 31; Fish to Rice, September 15; Fish to Bingham, September 15; Dispatch No. 134, October 9; Instruction No. 87, November 20, 1874.

[7] No. 3, October 7, *F.R., 1874,* pp. 651–52.

[8] No. 18, November 18, 1873, *ibid.,* p. 654.

[9] No. 19, January 8, 1874, *ibid.,* p. 659.

by his colleagues of Great Britain, France, and Holland, and which secured to each of their countries the payment of one-third of the balance due, $125,000. But in reporting this development he intimated that this demand was made because of the refusal of Japan to accept the Protocol for the opening of the interior which had been proposed in a joint note of September 27, 1873, and that an offer had been made to postpone or remit the balance due if Japan would accept those regulations.[10] This was but one of many attempts to use the very questionable Shimonoseki indemnity to force new concessions from the Japanese.

The next move was the offer of Parkes to remit to Bingham $5,833.33, which had been overpaid to Great Britain and which belonged to the United States (and an equal amount to France and Holland, because their shares of the original indemnity exceeded that of Great Britain).[11] Mr. Bingham refused to accept the amount, and again asked for instructions.[12] He was told to accept the tender. If the other Powers had refrained from collecting their portions, the United States would not have pressed for its share; but as they had been paid, the United States must expect similar consideration. And the instruction then developed and stressed the desirability of co-operation.[13]

Before this instruction reached Mr. Bingham, Parkes had offered a second similar sum (derived from a second instalment paid by the Japanese). Again Bingham declined to receive it, and he suggested to Mr. Fish that if the United States decided to demand its share it should receive it from Japan, and not from time to time from the British Minister.[14] This brought a direction to follow Instruction No. 35, which by this time was in Bingham's hands.[15] This he did, and at the same time informed

[10] No. 55, February 18, 1874.   [11] See Appendix in Vol. II.

[12] No. 57, February 23, 1874, *F.R., 1874,* pp. 669–70.

[13] No. 35, April 20, *ibid.,* pp. 674–75.

[14] No. 84, May 20, 1874, *F.R., 1874,* pp. 682–83. It will be recalled that Japan was obligated to pay equal shares to the four Powers. The decision to award larger shares to three of them had been arrived at among themselves, after a proposal by the British Secretary of State for Foreign Affairs.

[15] No. 50, July 3.

the Japanese Minister that the United States would expect a payment equal to that made to the other Powers.[16] The Japanese Government paid two instalments, $250,000, in one sum on June 29, and the balance on August 1.[17] In due time Mr. Bingham was instructed to give a receipt in full for the share due the United States.[18] The next problem was to find some way of returning this unwanted indemnity to the Japanese.

Another unsettled issue was that of the Hunting Regulations. Bingham had been instructed to examine them and report if anything therein conflicted with the treaty privileges of Americans in Japan.[19] This furnished an opportunity for the new Minister to set forth his views on extraterritoriality, and, as he was to follow them tenaciously during his long term of service, they may well be quoted *in extenso*.

I am of the opinion that nothing therein contained when construed according to the manifest intent thereof, conflicts with the privileges secured by treaty to American citizens in Japan. It may not be improper for me to add in support of this opinion that I find nothing in the treaty of 1858 which in anywise denies to Japan the general power to legislate over all persons within her territorial limits by general laws, while article 6 of that treaty does, by necessary implication, in my judgment, declare that the government of Japan may by law define and prohibit offenses within her territorial limits, and that no person resident therein is privileged by any treaty to disregard and violate such general law. It is no answer to this to say that because there are certain privileges secured by treaty to the government and citizens of the United States, Japan may not, therefore, rightfully exercise general legislative power over all persons within her limits in all matters not expressly provided for in the text of the treaty. I am not unmindful, in considering this question, that by the sixth article of the treaty Americans committing offenses against Japanese are to be tried in American consular courts, and, when guilty, punished according to American law; but I submit that it does not result from this that the government of Japan may not by general law define and

[16] No. 94, June 17, *F.R., 1874,* pp. 686–87. His action was approved (No. 57, July 23).

[17] No. 97, July 7; No. 108, August 12, *F.R., 1874,* pp. 694–97. For the third payment, Parkes simply informed Bingham that $5,833.33 would be paid to his order by the Oriental Bank.

[18] No. 72, September 12, *ibid.,* p. 699; Dispatch No. 144, November 2; No. 163, December 17.

[19] No. 5, September 6, 1873, *F.R., 1874,* p. 645.

prohibit all crimes and misdemeanors against person and property within her limits. There is nothing in the "hunting regulations" that I can discover which can be construed to deny to American citizens the right to be tried for any breaches thereof before the American consular courts, and to be punished, upon conviction, according to American law. The penalties prescribed by the regulations can only be held to apply to Japanese subjects, while the prohibitions therein are obligatory upon all. This seems to me to be their intent, and so I understand they have been uniformly administered. If, however, the manifest intent of these regulations be disregarded in their construction, and the letter alone, so imperfectly expressed, be followed, it might properly be said that articles 18 and 21, and the specific penalties annexed, do conflict with the provisions of the treaty of 1858.[20]

This was a restatement of the American position, already laid down by Mr. Fish, that the extraterritorial privilege covered only the right of trial and punishment according to American law. And Mr. Fish expressed the entire approval of the Department in the views expressed above.[21]

Here the matter rested until on November 10, 1874, Terashima sent to Bingham, and the other Representatives, a draft of revised Hunting Regulations and a protocol. Sir Harry Parkes called upon Bingham and explained that, under the Orders in Council, such regulations would have to be adopted and promulgated by him, and that the Government of Japan could not enact laws applicable to British subjects. Bingham pointed out that he possessed no such general legislative authority, interpreting his ministerial authority to make rules of procedure, orders, and decrees in the strict sense, and that the only objection he saw in the proposed regulations was that the penalties and mode of procedure could not be applied to American citizens.[22]

A meeting of the Foreign Representatives was called, and they all seemed to agree that there was nothing in the revised regula-

---

[20] No. 17, November 17, 1873, *ibid.,* pp. 653–54.

[21] No. 18, January 7, 1874, *ibid.,* pp. 658–59.

[22] The Protocol, which was submitted for the signature of the Japanese officials and the Foreign Representatives, exempted foreign nationals from all the penal regulations, and from some other details, but provided for small fines, in Consular Courts, to be paid to the Japanese Government, and for civil suits in the case of damages to crops or property.

tions and protocol to object to, except that the penalties and the mode of trial could not apply to Treaty-Power subjects. They desired that a collective note be sent in, advising the Foreign Minister of their views and that each Minister should consult his Government in regard to a uniform system. To this Bingham assented, reserving the right to qualify his approval of the note so as to accord with his expressed views.[23]

Instead of a collective note, individual notes were submitted, along the lines of the general agreement. The Minister for Foreign Affairs was advised that further discussion of the subject would be postponed pending instructions from their respective governments. While the proposed regulations were deemed just and reasonable, "the proposed changes in existing treaties as to the tribunal, and penalties in cases arising under the regulations" rendered this course inadvisable.[24]

The next subject for joint consideration was the opening of the interior, and this became so involved with the broader question of Treaty revision that the two must be discussed together. On November 8, 1873, the Foreign Representatives were invited to meet with Mr. Terashima to receive an "oral reply" to the identical notes submitted on July 26 relative to travel in the interior. The discussion promptly turned to the joint note covering a set of regulations which had been submitted on September 27.[25] Bingham's contribution was an intimation that foreigners must be subject to the laws of Japan while subject to answer in their own judicial tribunals. And Terashima avowed that Japan would be willing to admit trade and travel throughout the Empire if the Treaty Powers would surrender their extraterritorial jurisdiction. This led Parkes to ask Bingham if the United States would be willing to surrender this treaty right, and the latter,

[23] No. 151, November 19, 1874, *F.R., 1875,* II, 773–76. In this dispatch Bingham repeats his arguments as to the right of Japan to legislate, and as to the interpretation of the Minister's powers under the Act of 1860. The Department withheld further comment until it might receive a copy of the collective note (No. 109, December 30).

[24] No. 164, December 18, 1874, *F.R., 1875,* II, 779–80.

[25] See *supra,* chap. xx.

having in mind Mr. Fish's instruction to General Schenck just previously, replied that he was advised it would not.[26] And he added, for the information of the Secretary of State, that this view was fully justified by conditions in Japan.

A second interview took place on the fifteenth, and at this time Bingham read to the Foreign Minister a memorandum in which he stated that he was under instructions to ascertain what changes the Japanese Government desired to make in the existing Treaties and suggested that the Treaties be so revised as to secure liberty of travel and trade, the right to work mines and cultivate or stock lands throughout the Empire under a passport system and subject to such police regulations as might be made and published in advance by Japan and approved by the Foreign Powers, a right answerable for all crimes and offenses to person or property only to the judicial authorities of their respective governments.[27]

This led to a private interview between Bingham and Iwakura and Terashima on December 22 on the subject of the revision of the Treaties. Throughout, Bingham adhered to his instructions that extraterritorial jurisdiction should be continued but that violations of Japanese law and offenses against the Government or people of Japan should be subject to the penalties prescribed by the respective countries or by the common law. At their re-

---

[26] *Ibid.*

[27] No. 19, November 18, 1873. His course was approved. Further instruction would be given after Japan's desires were known (No. 20, January 8, 1874). After the events narrated in No. 19, above, Bingham received Instruction No. 14, November 7, 1873, which disapproved of making the Consuls the depositaries of the deposits (*F.R., 1874,* p. 653). He, also, did not approve of this (No. 30, December 18, *ibid.,* p. 658). A concrete case was presented when an American set out from Hakodate and was brought back from a point two hundred and fifty miles in the interior. The authorities presented a bill for $93.62 expenses, to the American Consul, and the offender was fined $51.27 in the Consular Court (No. 43, January 14, 1874, *ibid.,* p. 660). While Mr. Fish avoided expressing an opinion as to the legality of this action, he did defend it under De Long's regulations as a misdemeanor at common law: "The American policy in Japan has been the strict observance of our treaty obligations towards that power as a ground for insisting upon a similar observance towards us. Good policy, therefore, as well as good faith call upon us to maintain the consular jurisdiction over such cases . . . . unless we violate well-settled principles of law by doing so" (No. 26, February 23, 1874, *ibid.,* pp. 668–69).

quest he formulated his views in a memorandum, which was to be considered strictly unofficial.

In this he developed his proposal for opening the country under a passport system, with the obligation to obey the laws of Japan, enforceable in the Consular Courts. Six advantages of such a revision he set forth. First, the country would not be over-run by irresponsible persons. Second, it would result in a rapid increase of productions and wealth, and permit a reduction of taxes. Third, it would insure a large increase of revenue. Fourth, it would diversify the industries of the country and give new and profitable employment to all the people of Japan, and largely increase its commerce. Fifth, it would add strength and stability to the existing Government by reason of the new treaty obligations of the Western Powers to maintain the laws and regulations of Japan, and because of the new material interests they would have in upholding the Government and its laws. Sixth, it would work a speedy development of the almost untouched resources of the country—railways constructed by private enterprise and private capital would make Japan independent in peace and impregnable in war. In time the Japanese would become so skilled in the judicial administration of their own laws that the Treaty Powers would be willing to surrender their extraterritorial rights. And he suggested that even Western states labored under certain limitations of their sovereignty, as found in extradition treaties and the most-favored-nation clause of commercial conventions.

In the covering dispatch Bingham pointed out that the European Powers sought the opening of the country for transient trade and travel, which would be in the interests of their capitalists, while the broader provisions would benefit both Japan and the United States.[28]

Two days before this interview took place, Terashima had

[28] No. 45, January 17, 1874. Bingham pointed out the fact that all railroad, telegraph, and lighthouse contracts had been obtained by English firms, while the French controlled the naval and military schools and navy yards. He believed German, French, and English advisers would supplant Americans in the Educational and Agricultural Departments as soon as their contracts expired.

given his reply to the Regulations proposed in September. It was addressed to Parkes, as Doyen, and he sent a copy and the accompanying memorandum, of December 20, to Bingham. The latter was a long and well-reasoned argument as to why the country could not be opened to permanent residence and the acquisition of real estate as long as extraterritoriality was enforced, and due stress was laid upon the abuses of the system. In transmitting this correspondence, Bingham again expressed the belief that Japan would be satisfied if foreigners were made subject to Japanese law, enforceable in their own courts under penalties prescribed by statute or common law.[29] The Representatives replied to the memorandum by a joint note of January 17, which stated that they did not desire such wide privileges but only the right of travel and trade.

Mr. Fish expressed his approval of the general views advanced by Bingham in the last two dispatches. Further instructions would follow should a definite proposition be made.[30] This crossed a request from Bingham for these very instructions:

> I am fully persuaded that the immediate and pressing want of Japan is capital and skilled labor, and that she cannot obtain these without a revision of existing treaties. It is very desirable that whatever may be the purposes of our Government in this direction should be made known to the Japanese officials, as I am assured it is their desire to effect a revision of the existing Treaty first with the United States.[31]

Two very interesting developments are suggested by this extract. The American Minister had returned to the Townsend Harris policy of thinking in terms of Japan's interests, and he had freed himself from the limitations of the co-operative policy.

The latter possibility was not viewed with unconcern by the Department. In a temperate but firm instruction, Mr. Fish directed him to act in harmony with his European colleagues and to adopt the proposal they had advanced for freedom of access to

[29] No. 46, January 19, 1874, *F.R., 1874*, pp. 662–64. The omitted paragraph refers to his No. 45, discussed above.

[30] No. 27, February 27, *ibid.*, pp. 670–71.

[31] No. 56, February 19, 1874, *ibid.*, pp. 664–65. The last sentence above is omitted.

the interior, with the only modification that deposits must not be made with the American Consuls. Bingham's "more extended and wiser scheme" for permanent residence with permission to engage in permanent occupations, the President was convinced could be accomplished only by co-operative action.[32]

Bingham carried out this instruction and was advised by the Foreign Office, on July 28, that the matter would be taken up when the whole subject of Treaty revision was entered into.[33] The immediate objection, was, of course, the repeated inconvenience arising from extraterritoriality. But the Foreign Representatives, led by Sir Harry Parkes, were unwilling to have this desired extension of treaty rights postponed to some later day. On August 14 another collective note, which reviewed the whole discussion since July 1873, was signed, and Mr. Bingham attached his signature, noting, however, that he had forwarded a separate note in which he referred to his proposal for residence in the interior.[34]

The position taken by Mr. Bingham on each of the four matters just considered was consistently assumed in the other cases involving joint action. One was as to the right of the Japanese Government to make general customs regulations. The matter

[32] No. 35, April 20, *F.R., 1874,* pp. 674–76.

[33] No. 106, July 29. Soyeshima had informed the Representatives, at a conference on June 20 that the Government declined to accept their proposals, and he gave the pertinent reasons. At that time 422 foreigners were in Government employ, and 244 in the service of Japanese individuals. They had freedom of travel under a passport, and the Representatives saw no danger involved in extending this system to all foreigners. Soyeshima restated his views in a note of July 13.

[34] No. 114, August 31. With the two notes mentioned above, Bingham transmitted a copy of a memorandum made by Mr. Marshall, an Englishman attached to the Japanese Legation in Paris, which purported to relate his conversation with Lord Derby, British Foreign Minister, in which he suggested that England and France modify their policy in Japan in order to destroy the influence which the American Minister was regaining there (see also No. 131, October 6). Mr. Fish forwarded this report to General Schenck with a request that he secure some confirmation. Lord Derby remembered the interview, but had attached no importance to it, and assured General Schenck of his adherence to the co-operative policy. Fish interpreted the move as an attempt to play off Great Britain against the United States, just as the British Government had been told at times of similar moves on the part of the United States (Instruction No. 103, December 22, covering No. 656, Schenck to Fish, November 5, 1874).

had been argued at some length in 1873,[35] and identic notes had been presented on February 15. Replies from Terashima were forthcoming just a year later. They denied that in issuing such regulations the Commissioner of Customs had done anything in conflict with treaty stipulations, and the provision of the Austro-Hungarian Treaty of 1869, which had been relied upon by the Foreign Representatives, was interpreted to relate to consultation with the Consuls when regulations for the removal of [existing] inconveniences were to be issued. A meeting of the Foreign Representatives was called to consider this reply, and a joint note was drafted by Sir Harry Parkes, which Bingham refused to sign. The language of the note was needlessly strong. It held that the promulgation of regulations or measures

referring to the transaction of business at the custom-house, to the lading and shipping of goods, and to the hiring of boats, coolies, servants, &c., without previous consultation with the foreign consuls, does constitute a violation of the previous aforesaid treaties.

It argued that the provisions of the Treaties referred to the correction from *time to time* of abuses and inconveniences, and it asserted that the proper procedure had been followed until 1872, when the Japanese assumed the power of issuing notifications and regulations affecting the rights and interests of foreigners. A protest of May 22 had been left unanswered, and on November 6 a new notification respecting the refund of duties had been issued. Finally, it opposed the interpretation given by the Foreign Minister, requested the observance of the distinct stipulation in the Austrian Treaty, and repeated that if regulations continued to be published without previous consultation with the foreign Consuls they would not be considered binding on their subjects and citizens.

On three grounds Judge Bingham refused to sign such a note. First, it assumed that the Treaty provisions took from Japan the right to make any general customs regulations without the consent and concurrence of the several foreign Consuls. Second, it as-

[35] See *supra*.

sumed that the Consuls had a right to determine upon all means and measures for the correction of any abuses and inconveniences. And, third, he supported the regulation which had led to the joint note, namely, that a limit of ten days would be placed for filing applications for the refund of duties overpaid in error. But, in addition, the note assumed that the co-operation of all the Consuls was necessary for the enforcement of such regulations, an assumption far beyond any stipulation of the Treaties and which would, in fact, prevent an American Consul from agreeing upon other regulations with the local authorities. While local co-operation among the foreign Consuls was desirable, where it could be obtained, it would be most inconvenient if an American Consul could not agree to proper regulations as long as any other foreign Consul chose to disagree. He asked for instructions.[36]

While no attention was given to this dispatch by the Department, the new developments in Japan were soon to be brought to its attention from other quarters. On July 14 Mr. Marshall Jewell, American Minister to Russia, advised Mr. Fish that he had often been questioned of late as to American policy in Japan and that very day three of his colleagues had spoken to him on the subject. Whether they had been advised by their own governments or the Russian Foreign Office had talked freely with them he did not know. But his colleagues of Britain, France, and Germany had asked if Mr. Bingham was acting under instructions or was carrying out a policy of his own which might place the American Government in antagonism to all the European Powers in its intercourse with the Japanese Empire. The French Ambassador was able to assure him that the Russian Foreign Office was very angry at the course pursued by Mr. Bingham, while, on the other hand, the newly arrived Japanese Minister believed that the policy was not a chance one but one which would tend to strengthen the bond of friendship between Japan and the United States. "The Minister spoke as though he valued the friendship of the United States more than that of any of the other Powers." Mr. Jewell

---

[36] No. 65, March 9, 1874, *F.R., 1874*, pp. 671–74. The joint note of February 27 was signed by the other five Representatives.

asked for instructions as to what he should reply when asked as to American policy in Japan.[37]

Soon after this dispatch arrived, the British Chargé in Washington left with Mr. Fish a copy of the correspondence between Sir Harry Parkes and Lord Derby in relation to the arrest of the servant of one of the secretaries of the British Legation, and asked whether Bingham had communicated the occurrence to the Department, remarking that the absence of his name from the joint note signed by all the other Representatives had been a source of regret.

Mr. Fish thereupon sent to Bingham a copy of Jewell's dispatch, and called to his attention Instruction No. 35, April 20, in which the importance of co-operation had been laid down. He also reported the British complaint, and regretted that Bingham had not seen fit to report a matter which had called for a collective note. While Mr. Fish was not prepared to criticize an advanced assertion of immunity from local jurisdiction, he did stress the necessity for co-operative action.

The President therefore relies upon your prudent efficiency to carry out the policy which has been indicated to you, and which has been announced to other powers as that which is to govern our intercourse with Japan, unless in cases where you may see the interests of this Government to be so clearly in a different direction that you may feel it your duty to withhold concert of action until you shall have had opportunity to lay the case before your Government.[38]

Mr. Bingham, in reply, asked for a statement of the exact reasons for the alarm of the Russian Foreign Office, and he defended his conduct in Japan as in accord with approval given from time to time. But in regard to the joint note at the time of the arrest of the Japanese servant, he stated that he had never seen such a note or been consulted thereto. He had learned of the incident later, from Mr. Terashima. As Mr. Bingham was now living in Tokyo, and Sir Harry was calling regular meetings of the Diplomatic Corps in Yokohama, it was possible that this had been

[37] No. 104, Jewell to Fish, July 14, 1874.
[38] No. 65, August 26, *F.R., 1874,* pp. 697–98.

discussed at such a conference, but he certainly had never seen a copy of the joint note in question.[39]

In order to reassure the Powers, Mr. Fish sent copies of his pertinent instructions to Bingham, Nos. 35 and 65, to the American Ministers in Europe, with a statement of the importance of continued concert between the Treaty Powers in Japan, at least until the revision of the Treaties. He also was impressed with the importance that they should be informed of the determination of each other to adhere to the policy of co-operation.[40]

Mr. Marsh reported from Rome, which had been the danger spot in 1873, that the Italian Government was not inclined to encourage separate action. The motive which had led to the *démarche* of the Italian Minister, the year before, was much diminished by the success of the Pasteur method for combating the disease of the silkworm, and the importation of eggs had been greatly reduced.[41]

General Schenck carried out his instruction and found that Lord Derby considered the views of Mr. Fish "exceedingly satisfactory." He seemed to distinguish between the common general policy and any doubt which might arise as to a specific case, such as that involving the Japanese servant.[42] But when Mr. Fish received Bingham's statement, he forwarded an extract to General Schenck to be brought to the attention of Lord Derby.[43] In the latter's absence, the statement was read to Lord Tenterden, who made a note of the substance, "with a view, I suppose, of asking some explanation from Sir Harry Parkes."[44]

As we are well aware, the co-operative policy was the corner stone of Seward's Far Eastern diplomacy, and he had carried it so far as to recommend a joint demonstration against Japan in

[39] No. 131, October 6. An extract is printed in *F.R., 1875,* I, 584.

[40] No. 703, Fish to Nicholas Fish, September 2, *F.R., 1874,* p. 460.

[41] No. 515, March to Fish, September 27, *F.R., 1875,* II, 754–55.

[42] No. 620, Schenck to Fish, October 9, *F.R., 1875,* I, 580–81.

[43] No. 641, Fish to Schenck, December 1, *ibid.,* p. 583.

[44] No. 669, Schenck to Fish, December 19, *ibid.,* p. 584. Mr. Fish kept Mr. Bingham informed of this correspondence with London (No. 91, December 2, *F.R., 1875,* II, 776; No. 113, January 5, 1875).

1861 and a Franco-American intervention in Korea in 1867. And Mr. Fish, who was primarily interested in European and Caribbean questions, saw no reason for displacing this established principle. But it may be observed that co-operation could only be defensible, and could only appeal to Americans alive to the national traditions, if it were carried through on a high plane of conduct. Such co-operation would not only protect treaty rights but would respect the interests of the Oriental nation. And, for the most part, such was the nature of co-operation in China when Mr. Burlingame was the master personality in the Diplomatic Corps. But it requires little thought to realize that the co-operation of the Great Powers (and the small ones as well) could work inestimable damage if it were applied against a weak state in an unreasonable or selfish way. The situation in Japan was not favorable for the co-operation envisaged by Mr. Seward, for the Doyen of the Diplomatic Corps and the most experienced of the Foreign Representatives in Japan was a man who thought first of all in terms of his country's advantage, then of the other Treaty Powers', and last of all of Japan's. We have said that it was inevitable that Sir Harry Parkes and Mr. Bingham should clash. And we may, at this point, look ahead to the time when the State Department finally recognized that co-operation in Japan, under the conditions which prevailed there, could not be uniformly followed. Within a few months after Mr. Bingham's arrival, an English officer in the Japanese foreign service warned Lord Derby that the American Minister "is rapidly regaining the position and the influence which the United States used to possess in Japan, but which they had recently altogether lost."[45]

All these conflicting forces were involved in the *cause célèbre* of 1874, the Formosan expedition. On the surface it finds a place in American diplomatic history as an episode in its relations with Japan and China, but underneath was a desire, in certain quarters, to crush the rising power of Japan and to destroy the influence of the American Minister at its Court.

From time to time De Long had reported on the disposition of

[45] The Marshall Memorandum, see *supra,* footnote 34.

high Japanese officials to resolve their disputes with Korea and China by force. There can be no doubt of the correctness of his general observations, for he was in intimate contact with Soyeshima, then Minister for Foreign Affairs and a leader of the so-called "War Party." What encouragement De Long may have given to these plans we do not know, but that they appealed to his vigorous nature is probable. On the other hand, Mr. Bingham never lost a chance to advocate the cultivation of peace, as the first duty of nations as of men. The issue of peace or war had been postponed until the return of the Iwakura mission in September 1873, and then it had been fought out in the Grand Council with great bitterness. Mr. Bingham believed that some of the pressure was brought by Russian and English intrigue; but we can discount this assumption. The decision was finally reached at the end of October. Iwakura, Kido, and Okubo, who had been members of the mission, opposed the proposition as sheer madness, and insisted that the policy of the Empire should be peace. They carried a majority of the Grand Council with them, with the result that Soyeshima and all the heads of departments resigned and the Ministry was reconstituted. Iwakura assumed more power as Junior Prime Minister, Kido and Okubo became Advisers, Katsu Awa, Minister of Marine, Ito, Minister of Public Works, and Terashima, Minister for Foreign Affairs. The other four departments were less important. This was, therefore, a "Peace Ministry." In spite of all the anti-Korean and anti-Chinese intrigues in high and low places, the decision of the Government, and that was what really counted, was for peace.[46]

The statesmen of New Japan were realists, and that explains

---

[46] No. 16, November 1, 1873. Bingham explained his reference to British and Russian intrigue by saying that he had been informed that both Powers had tried to induce Japan to make war on Korea: Russia, in order to come to the help of Korea and then possess the country, with perhaps Hokkaido and Sakhalin as well; England, in order to acquire, or secure control of, Honshiu, the main island of Japan. Ariga (in Stead, editor, *Japan by the Japanese,* pp. 165–67) describes "The Great Cabinet Crisis of 1873" and states that the final decision for peace was made by the young Emperor. Saigo, Commander-in-Chief, with Soyeshima, Goto, Itagaki, and Eto, led the war party. The question was one of war with Korea, not with China. Sanjo, the Senior Prime Minister, retained the title, but Iwakura assumed more responsibility.

in good part the success they achieved. Having gained the adoption of their broad policy, they were willing to concede some part of the contentions of their opponents. Of the two foreign issues, the one in which the Japanese case was best founded was that of the Formosan outrages. Being well aware that European maritime Powers had never failed to inflict reprisals upon offending savages, and that an American naval force had also descended upon the Formosan aborigines, it believed its position was sound should it decide to follow such precedents. The annoying thing about the Japanese was their ability to find and apply European precedents. But, in addition, the new Cabinet believed that Soyeshima, in 1873, had received oral permission from the Tsungli Yamen to take direct measures. We have many reasons for believing that Soyeshima left Peking with such an impression, but the Japanese Foreign Office was to learn that in dealing with those past-masters of Oriental diplomacy, the Tsungli Yamen, only a written, signed, and sealed statement was to have any weight. An expedition against the Formosan savages would not only vindicate the national dignity of Japan, support its claim to the Loochoo Islands, and appease in some measure the advocates of a strong policy, but would also give employment to some of the restless samurai of the western provinces, whose cup of grief was overflowing because of the passing of feudalism and the dubious reforms of the new régime.

The decision to send a punitive expedition to Formosa was reached early in April 1874.[47] Sir Harry Parkes at once, April 10, telegraphed to Mr. Wade, at Peking, advising him that colonization was the real object but the chastisement of the aborigines on the eastern (*sic*) shore of Formosa the pretense. This was brought to the attention of the Tsungli Yamen on the nineteenth, and they were asked by Mr. Wade whether or not China considered that region a part of its domain and whether or not the Japanese had consulted with them and obtained permission to punish the savages. A prompt reply was given on the twentieth, as follows:

[47] Stead, *op. cit.,* p. 168.

When the Japanese Minister was in Peking last year he never consulted with the members of the Foreign Office in relation to taking troops
to Formosa and landing them on the east side of that island to chastise
the aborigines; nor have we received any despatches (from him) giving
the reasons why Japan is mustering her forces. But all aboriginal tribes,
which, like these unsubdued people, are included within the territory of
China, are under her jurisdiction. Although we do not attempt to interfere
with their peculiar usages, or bring them under the strict restraint of our
laws, still the regions they occupy all form a part of this empire. All this
is doubtless fully known to Your Excellency, and we shall be obliged if
you will discuss it in your reply to Sir H. Parkes, so that he may know
our sentiments.[48]

The comment of S. Wells Williams, the American Chargé,
on this statement was:

With this characteristic reply, these officials received the announcement of a threatened descent upon their borders, and apparently expected
that other nations are to do what is necessary to ward it off.

Chargé Williams also reported that Mr. Wade had shown him
an extract from a dispatch of Terashima to Parkes of April 14,
stating:

The present expedition being despatched in order to accomplish the
object of punishing the persons in that territory who were guilty of
murdering or plundering our subjects, of putting a stop to such evil
practices, and of preventing them in future, and also of insuring the
safety of our subjects' navigation, of course nothing will be done of such
a nature as to draw upon us the hostility of the Chinese Government.
Besides, the territory in question, is, as you are aware, beyond the jurisdiction of the Chinese Government, and therefore, even if our Government engages British ships and subjects, I do not see that the said
Government can regard us as enemies, and object (to our employment of
them).

To this Sir Harry replied that he had lived in China for twenty
years and had always understood that the whole island of Formosa was Chinese territory.[49]

Mr. Bingham had picked up rumors of the intended expedi-

[48] Compare this statement with Ariga's report of Yanigawara's conversation in 1873, *supra*. The Japanese Government repeatedly asserted that China
did not claim the territory of the aborigines.

[49] These details of the early phases of the expedition were transmitted by
Williams, from Peking, No. 33, May 26. The dispatch was not received until
July 20, almost two months after Bingham's first dispatch.

tion, but the first definite news reached him through the press. On April 17, the *Japan Daily Herald* stated that the expedition was designed to occupy the "eastern" side of the Island, and charged that Bingham had tacitly, if not expressly, authorized it, and that his Government had given leave to officers in its service to join it. Mr. Bingham at once asked Terashima for information; denied that he had ever been consulted about employing American ships or officers; advised him that two American citizens who had been invited to take part in the expedition had assured him that they were not to engage in hostilities against any Power whatever; and while not assuming that the purposes entertained by the Japanese Government were of a hostile nature, he protested against the employment of any American ships or officers in any expedition hostile to the Government of China or to any portion of her people.[50]

In an interview the same day, Terashima denied that the expedition was designed to commit any hostile act against China, its purpose being to send a high commission to Formosa, with the knowledge and consent of China, under the protection of an armed force, to demand satisfaction and to obtain amicably from the aboriginal chiefs a convention, which would prevent cruelty to shipwrecked Japanese in the future. The formal reply, on the nineteenth, covered these points, and was accompanied by a memorandum which summarized the Japanese grievances (fifty-four Loochooans murdered in 1871, and four Japanese plundered in 1873), stated that retribution had been inflicted by naval forces of Holland, 1654, of Great Britain, 1867, and the United States, 1867, and asserted that the Tsungli Yamen had, in 1873, stated that that region did not belong to China. It further expressed the hope that satisfaction and assurances for the future might be obtained without the shedding of blood.

To this Bingham immediately replied, with a protest against the expedition "until the written consent of China be first obtained," and he pointed out that although Japan might intend no hostile act, China might think differently and resist by force. Al-

[50] Bingham to Terashima, April 18. Inclosure in No. 76.

though he had been told that the consent of China had been obtained, he could find no evidence of it in the information given him, and he requested that the steamship "New York" and the three American citizens be detained until this written consent of China was obtained.

In reporting all this to the Department, Mr. Bingham stated that he had acted under the Act of June 22, 1860, (Section 24) and his recommendations had been so effective that Terashima assured him verbally that the expedition would not proceed to Formosa or any other port of the Chinese Empire without the written and authenticated consent and approval of the Chinese Government, and that the proclamation of April 17 (announcing the expedition) had been recalled. Bingham had asked Terashima to transmit, for him, notices to the three Americans that they should not proceed with the expedition "until they have received further official orders and authority for so doing." These had been immediately delivered to Lieutenant Commander Cassel, U.S.N., and Mr. Wasson (formerly Lieutenant, U.S.A) while the notice to Le Gendre had been forwarded to Nagasaki. Although some of the vessels of the expedition had already sailed from Nagasaki, Bingham assured the Department that no hostile acts would be committed or attempted upon any foreign Power with which the United States was at peace.[51]

In all these proceedings, Mr. Bingham stated that he had tried to discharge his duty and maintain the rights of the United States while avoiding the appearance of unwarranted interference with rights which pertained to Japan as a sovereignty. In other words, he had protested against the expedition because it might involve Japan in a needless war with China, and he had protested against the employment of American ships and men because it might involve his country as well. But in doing so he ran the risk of jeopardizing the influence which he possessed in Japanese Government circles. So sure were they of his sympathetic understanding that, as we have seen, they took pains to assure Sir Harry Parkes of the pacific purposes of the expedition before they even

[51] No. 76, April 22, 1874, *F.R., 1874*, pp. 675–81.

mentioned it to Bingham. And so anxious was Bingham to do the right thing that he brought down upon himself the disapproval of the Department for going beyond his proper duties in the circumstances.

Two days later Mr. Bingham reported his pleasure on being advised that the "New York" and the three Americans had been detached from the expedition. He believed the measure would be abandoned unless China should give a formal consent, in which case he did not see how he could forbid American citizens from taking part.[52]

The scene now shifts to Peking. Dr. Williams had received a telegram from Le Gendre, at Nagasaki, of April 19, saying:

Don't allow Formosan matters to be so misrepresented by interested parties as to change friendly feelings between China and Japan.

But before this, he had learned of the warning sent by Sir Harry Parkes. In reporting to Mr. Bingham this move of Le Gendre, Williams advised him of the Yamen's reply to Wade, and argued against the right of the Japanese to take up the cause of the Loochooans as long as the latter continued to send their own envoys to Peking.[53]

Williams' dispatch of April 24 did not reach Bingham until May 17, and it brought the first official statement that China had never authorized the expedition. On the nineteenth, he reported this to Terashima, who said that although three Japanese ships had sailed from Amoy to Formosa, they were under instructions not to attempt to land if China objected, and in that case to return to Japan.

General Le Gendre had been detached from the expedition, and he returned to Tokyo, where he argued with Bingham as to the constitutionality of the Act of 1860, a matter which the latter did not consider he had any authority to settle. It is surprising to us that these two trained lawyers should not have realized that the Act operated only when a state of war existed. Bingham was still of the opinion that this unwise adventure would be so man-

[52] No. 78, April 24, *ibid.,* pp. 681–82.

[53] Williams to Bingham, April 24, 1874, in Bingham's No. 82, May 19.

aged as to avoid any serious difficulty with China, and he was assured by Terashima that the Commander had been given orders to confer with the Chinese Governor at Amoy before setting out for Formosa.[54]

In Peking, the Chinese had heard rumors of the employment of American ships and citizens (they first thought they were naval vessels and personnel), and they asked Williams, on May 15, for information, citing the first article of the American Treaty of 1858, and counting upon American support. Their position involved the rendering of the Chinese and English texts of the Treaty, which Williams explained to them. And in reporting the gossip of the capital, he said that the Russian Minister, who knew Japan well, believed the *démarche* was primarily due to a desire to give employment to the samurai, that others thought Japan was only reasserting old claims to the east coast of Formosa, while he himself felt that they were following the American precedent of 1867.[55]

The first Japanese ship reached Formosa on May 6, and some marines were landed on the eighth. The occupation had begun.[56] In Tokyo a second notification was issued on May 19, very similar in terms to the one withdrawn in April. On the twenty-second the first skirmish occurred, and that day General Saigo Yorimichi, Commander-in-Chief, and brother of Field Marshal Saigo, arrived. The Tokyo authorities now hoped a settlement would be reached by the Japanese Minister who was returning to Peking, while Bingham more resolutely acted to withhold the "New York" from the expedition.[57]

---

[54] No. 82, May 19.

[55] No. 33, Williams to Fish, May 26. Prince Kung to Williams, May 17, is printed in *F.R., 1874,* p. 689.

[56] Edward H. House, *The Japanese Expedition to Formosa,* is the account of an American journalist who accompanied the expedition. Cassel and Wasson were with the first party. The camps were established at Liang Kiao Bay on the west coast near the southern tip of the island.

[57] No. 89, June 3, *F.R., 1874,* pp. 684–85. Yung Wing, Chinese Commissioner of Education in the United States, passed through Tokyo and told Bingham that if the Japanese did not speedily withdraw or give assurances that their occupation was only temporary, there would be hostilities.

Williams had kept Bingham informed of developments in Peking, and the latter now feared open hostilities. From Amoy, Commander Kautz telegraphed to naval headquarters in Yokohama, on June 4, that the Viceroy had ordered the Japanese to leave Formosa, and had asked the American Consul to prevent American citizens from assisting the Japanese. The Consul had called upon him for assistance. He was instructed by Rear-Admiral Pennock to

notify and command all American citizens to abstain and withdraw from all enterprises unfriendly to the Chinese government, and to avoid all acts which are inconsistent with treaty obligations, on pain of forfeiting all claim to American protection.[58]

By this time, Williams had decided that some steps should be taken on his part, and he first reported the grounds for his action, and then instructed Consul Henderson to warn the two American officers to leave the expedition. The action of the latter was very gratifying to the Chinese.[59]

Up to this time neither Bingham nor Williams had received any instructions—so parsimonious was the Department that it would not make use of the cable. On July 16 the former sent in a further justification of his proceedings, and reported that, having detached the "New York" from the expedition, the Japanese Government proceeded to file a civil suit for $10,250 damages for failing to obey orders. This suit was dismissed in the Consular Court at Kanagawa, but notice of an appeal to the United States Circuit Court of California was filed.[60]

On July 24 Bingham received his first reply from Mr. Fish. It was in the form of a telegram:

[58] For this correspondence see No. 95, June 28, ibid., pp. 687–91. For the correspondence at Amoy, and the notification of Consul Henderson, on June 6, see *ibid.,* pp. 311–18.

[59] No. 34, Williams to Fish, May 29; No. 39, same to same, June 15.

[60] No. 98, July 16. This includes correspondence with Williams, and between Williams and Seward and Henderson. The suit was dismissed by the Federal Court in 1878 (No. 868, September 19, 1878). Other pertinent dispatches are Williams' No. 39, June 15; No. 40, June 24; No. 41, June 27; No. 51, August 3; No. 55, August 22.

Caution American citizens against hostile proceedings against China. See Article twenty-six Treaty of Tientsin.[61]

He at once instructed the Consuls in Japan, who issued the proper notifications. And when he sought information of the present situation he was informed that China had made two proposals to Japan: one, that the Japanese forces should withdraw; and the other, that, having punished the savages, they should now withdraw and China would build a lighthouse on the northeast coast of Formosa and furnish a land and naval force for the protection of foreign commerce on that coast. He was surprised to learn that neither proposal had been accepted, and he assumed it was because Japan proposed to retain possession of that area. China had then withdrawn the second proposal, and was actively preparing for war. But with the arrival of the Japanese Ambassador in Peking, negotiations had been resumed.[62]

The first written instruction of the Department was dated June 6, and it did not reach Mr. Bingham until July 27. It was in reply to Bingham's Nos. 76 and 78, and it intimated that the Act of 1860 was doubtless intended to confer on Ministers in extra-territorial countries the powers of the President under the neutrality Act of 1818. But it warned him that to constitute an offense under either act there must be a purpose of carrying on war against a country with which the United States was at peace and the offender must contemplate taking part as a belligerent. Engaging in the transportation of troops or dealing in arms or munitions of war did not come within the penal provisions of the Act of 1818.[63]

This was followed by an instruction which approved Mr. Bingham's proceedings in the case of the "New York" and the three American citizens, but it was evidently based on the assumption that the purpose of the engagement was to make war upon China. Mr. Wasson, it added, had not been in the service of the United States since July 1, 1872.[64]

---

[61] Telegram, July 21.   [62] No. 105, July 29, *F.R., 1874,* pp. 693–94.
[63] No. 43, June 6, *ibid.,* p. 686.   [64] No. 60, July 29, *ibid.,* pp. 692–93.

The next development was the arrest of General Le Gendre by the American Consul at Amoy, on August 6. He was sent to Shanghai, for trial, but Consul General Seward recognized that it would be difficult to bring in witnesses to any overt acts, and for a moment he thought of sending him on to Nagasaki for examination there. He finally resolved so doubtful a case by sending his Marshal to meet Le Gendre on arrival and to inform him that he was at liberty.[65]

Terashima at once demanded some explanation from Mr. Bingham, which the latter was unable to give. Yet Bingham certainly approved the arrest, for he advised the Department that the expedition was beyond doubt an act of war upon China. But he then added that "war seems inevitable between China and Japan." He had endeavored to avert it, and he had advised the authorities that, having inflicted punishment on the savages, they should withdraw their troops.[66]

This ended the American interest in the expedition, but not in the diplomatic settlement. That war was threatened was evident from an enlightened notification issued by the Japanese Government to Chinese resident in the Empire, assuring them that they would be neither imprisoned nor plundered if they pursued their lawful occupations in peace.[67]

Then, in due time, the views of the Department reached the astonished diplomats in Eastern Asia. The two previous instructions might have prepared them. A third, on September 1, to Bingham, warned him to be vigilant

in the exercise of all the powers of your official position for the protection of the rights of American citizens, and for the strict maintenance of the neutrality of the United States and of its citizens, and the observance of all treaty and international duties, in the event of war between Japan and China.[68]

Consul General Seward had been instructed, on August 26, that there must be some actual violation of law to justify an inter-

---

[65] For this correspondence see *ibid.*, pp. 328–31, 340–44.
[66] No. 112, August 18.   [67] No. 132, October 8, *F.R., 1875,* II, 768–70.
[68] No. 67, September 1, *F.R., 1874,* pp. 698–99.

ference, and Henderson's notification was disapproved as an exercise of a prerogative of the Minister.[69]

Henderson was instructed in similar terms, on September 4. If a state of war existed, of which the Department was not advised, and a notice or proclamation was called for, it must be impartial and warn against unlawful aid to either belligerent party.[70] A copy of this instruction was sent to Chargé Williams.[71]

When the arrest of Le Gendre was reported, the Department at once asked Seward for information, and withheld its approval as it was not aware a state of war existed.[72] And when it had the facts before it, it condemned Seward's proceedings throughout. Such judicial proceedings should not have been commenced without grave cause; the charge was indefinite; American Consuls could try offenders only for acts committed in China; the accused must be charged with an offense known to the law and should be informed of the particular offense; and no Consul in China had the right to send a prisoner to Japan for trial. The arrest of Le Gendre was held to be without warrant of law and such as could not receive approval. If it had been the act of a foreign Power, it would have been the ground for energetic action on the part of the United States.[73]

And, finally, the Department advised Mr. Bingham that it was not necessary to discuss the general question suggested by the employment of Mr. Wasson.[74]

The correspondence dealing with the Formosan expedition was the most extensive of all the incidents of 1874, in both Japan and China. A more careful analysis than could be given above indicates that Mr. Bingham was interested primarily in the maintenance of peace, even to the extent of a most liberal interpretation

---

[69] No. 409, Fish to Seward, August 26, *F.R., 1874,* pp. 332–34. It was pointed out that China, which then and in the past had employed so many foreigners in its military forces, was in no position to complain; while the United States, during the Civil War, had not protested the services of foreigners in the insurgent army.

[70] *Ibid.,* pp. 344–45.   [71] *Ibid.,* p. 345.

[72] No. 416, Cadwalader to Seward, October 9, *ibid.,* p. 346.

[73] No. 425, Cadwalader to Seward, November 2, *ibid.,* pp. 348–50.

[74] No. 92, December 3, *F.R., 1875,* II, 776–77.

of his powers, but had no special sympathy with China.[75] But Dr. Williams and the American Consuls in China saw in the complications a chance to show their good will and they were outspoken advocates of her cause. It is doubtful if Dr. Williams would have ordered the arrest of Le Gendre, but Consul General Seward had to decide quickly, and on afterthought he withdrew from his first position. The Department left no doubt in their minds that, in the future, only an enlistment in time of war, or with the purpose of war in view, could come within the meaning of the Acts of 1818 and 1860.

With the settlement of the controversy, the United States was not directly concerned. To the first direct protest of the Tsungli Yamen, the Japanese Government replied that the matter would be handled by Yanagiwara, recently appointed Minister to Peking. His departure from Tokyo was delayed because of the complications occasioned by the attitude of the Foreign Representatives, and it was July 31 before he reached Peking. While he was en route a basis of settlement had been arrived at in Formosa, between Pan Wi and General Saigo, the Chinese agreeing to reimburse Japan for the cost of the expedition and to guarantee such effective control of the savages' territory as would prevent the recurrence of similar outrages, and the Japanese agreeing to withdraw on these terms. The arrangement was to be confirmed by the Tsungli Yamen and the Japanese Minister.[76]

The Japanese now determined to send to China Okubo, one of their ablest statesmen, who had already acted as Special Commissioner in charge of the expedition. His appointment was announced on August 5, and on September 10 he reached Peking. Pending his arrival, Yanagiwara had engaged in fruitless discussion with the Chinese Ministers. From the first interview, on September 14, until October 5, Okubo could accomplish nothing.

---

[75] House (*op. cit.*, p. 84) believes Bingham took his unexpected stand because of annoyance at not being consulted in advance. But (on p. 23) he avers that Bingham was informed of the project early in March! House was very critical of Bingham and the other Foreign Representatives.

[76] House, *op. cit.*, pp. 160–70, 192–93. The agreement in Formosa was reached on June 25, and the punitive measures of the Japanese at once ceased.

The most they would do was to offer arbitration by a Foreign Representative, but this was not acceptable to Okubo. As a starting-point for the negotiations, Okubo insisted upon an acknowledgment of the truth of Soyeshima's statements, that in 1873 the Yamen had denied that China had any authority over the savages, and also that the Japanese had acted rightly in view of such a statement. On October 10, Okubo gave the Chinese five days in which to reply to his questions, and at the last moment a statement, not satisfactory but encouraging, was received. On the eighteenth the Chinese offered a sum of money as compensation, but the next day they refused to place the promise in writing, to stipulate the amount, or to pay it before the Japanese force left the island. To Okubo's repeated request for a written engagement, the Chinese stood firm. On the twenty-fifth he announced that he was returning to Japan, and that afternoon Le Gendre, and some of the suite, left the capital. At this point Mr. Wade, the British Minister, who had been following the negotiations carefully, took an active part. Chargé Williams reported that Wade took the initiative and urged one of the Chinese Ministers to make a definite offer to Okubo before he left the next morning. House was informed that Prince Kung had hurriedly asked for Wade's good offices. In any event he was able to assure Okubo that the Chinese would give a written assurance to pay 100,000 taels immediately for the relief of the sufferers, and 400,000 taels as reimbursement for the expenditures made by the Japanese, after they had left. Negotiations were resumed on the twenty-sixth, a draft of the terms was prepared by the Yamen the next day, accepted by Okubo on the thirtieth, and signed on the thirty-first.

The preamble not only was a justification of the Japanese action, but in its recognition of the right of protection it laid down a very useful precedent in Chinese diplomacy.[77] The first article

[77] When, early in the discussions, Okubo had referred to international law, the Yamen officials said that such codes had only recently been compiled by Europeans, and that "there being no mention of China in them, they intended to negotiate without adopting any of the opinions therein contained" (House, *op. cit.,* p. 195).

stated that the enterprise was "a just and rightful proceeding, to protect her own subjects, and China does not designate it as a wrong action." The second article said that a sum of money would be paid for the relief of the maltreated subjects, and a further payment for the roads and houses constructed by Japan. All the official correspondence would be mutually returned, and China engaged to establish her authority over the savages and promised that navigators should be protected from injury by them.

Annexed to this agreement was a contract, which incorporated the name of Mr. Wade as the virtual guarantor. It fixed the sum of 100,000 taels for the sufferers and that of 400,000 taels for the roads and houses. Japan was to withdraw her troops, and China would pay the whole sum by December 20. If Japan did not withdraw her troops, China should not pay the amount.[78]

The long delay had cost many Japanese lives. If the agreement reached in Formosa, on June 25, had been promptly ratified, the expeditionary force could have been withdrawn in a few weeks. As the months passed, fever swept through the camp, and several hundred lives were lost. Aside from the long refusal of the Chinese to admit the correctness of the Japanese action, the amount of the reimbursement was subject to long discussion, also whether or not it was to be an indemnity or a compensation—for injuries and expenditures. Okubo was reported as having demanded 2,000,000 taels as an indemnity, which the Chinese flatly refused to pay. He was broad-minded enough to accept a more moderate figure and enable the Chinese to "save their face" by dropping the objectionable term. But even then the negotiations almost failed because of the refusal of the Chinese to give a written evidence of the promise. After Soyeshima's experience in 1873, Okubo

[78] The preamble defined the duty and right of protection in terms similar to those held by the United States today. If a country failed to protect aliens and undertake the duty of reparation, then the other party had the right to take effective measures for the security of its own subjects. In connection with the insistence of Okubo that Wade guarantee the promise of the Chinese, we note that in 1901 the Powers insisted that every possible provision of the Boxer Protocol be carried out *before* the Protocol was signed.

not only insisted on a written statement but on the guaranty of Mr. Wade. China paid the "indemnity" on December 1, and the Japanese embarked on the third, seventeen days before the time agreed upon.

During the negotiations in Peking, Mr. Wade, as Doyen, played a decisive rôle, for which he received the thanks of both governments and the recognition of his colleagues.[79] Chargé Williams used his personal influence with Okubo to counsel moderation, and Mr. Bingham had steadily worked for peace. Williams considered Okubo a man of more than ordinary ability and prudence, while he gave Wensiang credit for bringing his colleagues to accept a peaceful settlement.[80]

In addition to the major diplomatic incidents which have been discussed, the fifteen months brought their usual assortment of claims and concessions, consular problems, and trade regulations. Mr. Bingham adopted a correct attitude toward the claims, reporting them for instructions, using his personal good offices when directed, and pressing them only under specific advices. Some of them were easily handled; that is, were referred to the Japanese courts for adjudication. Such was the claim of William H. Doyle against Japan for alleged breach of contract involving a mill site at Yokohama.[81] Also two new claims of Walsh, Hall & Company; one for the detention of a shipment of gold leaf at Kobe while its duty classification was under consideration, and another for goods sold to the Uki Han in 1870.[82] And the Pacific Mail Steamship

[79] *China. No. 2 (1875)*.

[80] No. 70, Williams to Fish, October 29; No. 6, Avery to Fish, November 12, *F.R., 1875*, I, 221–23; No. 147, Bingham to Fish, November 6; No. 149, November 8; No. 152, November 19.

[81] No. 20, November 19, 1873. The Department considered he had no "just grounds" for a claim, and would not support it (No. 22, January 9, 1874).

[82] See *supra*. The gold leaf was detained from April to the end of December, 1873, and then released as duty free. Damages of $638.67 were claimed. Bingham thought the claim should be for the amount of the loss actually sustained (No. 72, April 8, 1874). The Department did not think it a good claim, but asked for information as to the long detention (No. 69, September 3). The claim against the Uki Han was for $23,220 (No. 74, April 16). Bingham was instructed to use his good offices unofficially with a view to

Company demanded $1,000 (Mexican) because the steamer "New York" had been detained two days at Kobe through the refusal of the customs authorities to grant the sailing permit. Bingham protested against the detention, and reported the claim.[83]

One case, however, holds attention because of its human interest. It was pressed by Peter K. L. Cole, and it called for $2,500 (Mexican) with interest at six per cent from 1862. Cole was a free-born Negro whose parents had been slaves of Governor R. R. Livingston, of New York. He had come to the attention of Rev. Francis L. Hawks, later the historian of Perry's expedition, and through his aid had gone out to China. At Hong Kong he joined the "Mississippi," of Perry's fleet, and visited Japan. In 1860 he was a sailor on the "Powhatan," which brought the first Japanese mission to the United States. Returning to China he served with Ward and Burgevine in the "Ever Victorious Army," and in 1862 he found his way back to Japan. Settling down outside the treaty limits at Yokohama, he was evicted by the local authorities and deprived of his Japanese housekeeper. He at once claimed damages, and he alleged that he placed in Consul Fisher's hands a receipt for $2,500 in case the sum were paid. The Japanese officials stated, when the claim was renewed, that the amount had been turned over to Fisher.[84] With these conflicting statements before it, the Department held that the claim in the first instance was excessive, as the actual property loss was small, and it instructed Bingham to investigate the charge against Fisher.[85]

Four claims, on the other hand, were to cause considerable discussion. The first was the "Valetta" claim arising from the sale of this bark to a Japanese daimyo.[86] The Department considered this a private contract, properly enforceable in the Japanese courts, but Bingham was instructed to use his good offices personally to

securing an impartial investigation and adjustment. The Department considered it a private contract (No. 68, September 2). Bingham's requests for instructions in these two cases were received early in June—the replies went forward three months later.

[83] No. 39, January 9, 1874.   [84] No. 137, October 27, 1874.

[85] No. 116, January 14, 1875. He reported that he could obtain no satisfactory information (No. 354, March 8, 1876).   [86] No. 28, December 12, 1873.

promote a settlement.[87] The second and third arose during the Japanese Civil War. Captain J. M. Batchelder claimed damages for the wrongful seizure and detention of the steamer "Peiho," at Aomori, in 1869. Minister Van Valkenburgh had promptly demanded the release of the steamer, which had been granted.[88] But two years later De Long had pressed a claim for damages, which had led to some correspondence between the Legation and the Foreign Office but which had not been reported to the Department. The affair first came to Bingham's attention when Terashima sent him a note, on December 27, 1873, summarizing the previous discussion. Bingham then reported the matter and asked for instructions.[89]

The Japanese statement averred that the "Peiho" had been "stolen away" from Yokohama when the Tokugawa fleet absconded in 1868. It had been sold by Enomoto, the Commander-in-Chief, to a French firm at Hakodate, and by it transferred to Captain Batchelder, both transactions being made without the approval of the respective Consuls. When it put into Aomori, with rebels on board, it was seized as an "illegal vessel," and the subsequent detention was held to be "indisputably our right, for which no indemnity is recoverable."[90]

At the same time Batchelder was pressing a claim for breach of contract. Four wrecked men-of-war of the late insurgent fleet, at Hakodate, had been sold to him by Van Reed, who acted as agent for the Imperial navy, but the guns and other property were removed before Batchelder could start his wrecking operations.[91]

The Department was inclined to support the "Peiho" claim. It suggested arbitration, and instructed Bingham, if both parties agreed, to draw up a protocol, naming such person as arbitrator as might be agreed upon with Mr. Batchelder, and consulting him as to the terms of submission;[92] and, if both parties consented, the second claim might be included in the arbitration.[93]

---

[87] No. 31, March 23, 1874.   [88] See *supra.*   [89] No. 49, January 22, 1874.
[90] Terashima to Bingham, December 27, in No. 49.
[91] No. 54, February 18.   [92] No. 32, April 6.   [93] No. 34, April 16.

Finally, the Department returned for the third time to the Dr. Hozier claim.[94] Bingham promptly presented the case to the Ministers, but without effect.[95] His efforts were approved, and he was told to continue his good offices, urging the peculiar demands of justice and equity in favor of this claim.[96] In the course of later discussions, Terashima desired the claim to be presented in the court, holding that Alt and Goto had acted as "mediators" and not as "arbitrators," while Bingham advocated the payment of their award of $10,000.[97] This delay was considered a matter of regret, and the Minister was instructed to continue his efforts.[98]

During the year some progress was made in meeting the claim for arrears of rent due Japan. An appropriation was made by the Act of March 3, 1873. The lot involved was No. 178, Bluff, Yokohama, which had been rented as the site of a naval hospital. The Municipal Director of Yokohama (Benson, an American citizen), claimed three years rent, June 1, 1871, to June 1, 1874, the sum of $415.08. The Japanese Legation claimed only two years, or $278.72. The result was that the latter sum was paid twice, in Washington and in Tokyo, while Japan still asked for an adjustment which would cover the extra year. This settlement did not cover all the claims for rent, but it did provide for the relinquishment of lot No. 178.[99]

Another claim brought by Japan involved a question of treaty interpretation. Under the Perry Treaty each country was to be reimbursed for the cost of succoring shipwrecked seamen. When the "Cygnet" was wrecked in the far north, and her crew finally reached Nemuro, they were transported to Hakodate, the nearest treaty port, and a bill for $82.86 was presented. On the ground that the "Cygnet" was a British ship, Bingham denied this claim, and his decision was approved.[100]

---

[94] No. 21, January 10, 1874. Dr. Hozier had died in February 1873.

[95] No. 67, March 21.   [96] No. 74, September 15.

[97] No. 133, October 8.   [98] No. 99, December 11.

[99] No. 13, October 30, 1873; No. 63, March 6, 1874; No. 81, May 19; No. 120, September 9; Instruction No. 23, January 13, 1874; No. 88, December 1.

[100] No. 70, April 1; Instruction No. 41, May 9.

Finally, the Japanese pressed the claim of Nagai Jiuske (Jiusuke) for the loss of his ship, in 1869, through collision with U.S.S. "Ashuelot." The claim was transmitted to the Navy Department for a report.[101]

The correspondence for the year does not record any concessions sought by Mr. Bingham. At his request Commander George E. Belknap, of the U.S.S. "Tuscarora," was afforded every facility for examining the coast to ascertain a suitable place for landing a submarine cable.[102] But, like De Long, he recognized the advantages which flowed from the employment of Americans by Japan. Early in 1874 he reported that efforts were being made by certain of the Foreign Representatives to bring about the dismissal of the Americans in Japanese employ, and he recommended that the Act of August 18, 1856, be so amended that diplomatic and consular officers might recommend their nationals for appointment.[103]

The Department promptly followed up this suggestion and Congress passed an amendment on June 17 which permitted such recommendations, the approval of the Secretary of State having been previously obtained. An instruction was then sent Mr. Bingham authorizing him to make such proposals "whenever in your opinion the interests of your Government will be promoted by the appointment of Americans to office in Japan." He was still expected to report each case to the Department.[104]

Soon after this instruction arrived there came to Japan two American army officers, Brevet Brigadier General William Myers

[101] No. 162, December 16, 1874, and see *48th Cong., 2d Sess., H. Ex. Doc. No. 195 (Serial Number 2303)*; Instruction No. 130, March 18, 1875.

[102] No. 83, May 19, *F.R., 1874,* p. 682.   [103] No. 53, February 17.

[104] No. 47, June 27. During the debate on this Bill in the House, Mr. Banning quoted from Bingham's No. 53 as to the activities of certain Foreign Representatives. This came to the attention of Sir Harry Parkes, in the *Congressional Record,* and he took occasion to inform Bingham that he had never made such a move as had been reported to the latter by a Japanese official. Bingham was obviously annoyed that his statement had been made public (No. 102, July 17). Mr. Fish, on his part, denied that a statement in the House could be the subject of official interrogation, and certainly not by any Representative of a foreign government (No. 64, August 18).

and Brevet Lieutenant Colonel S. C. Lyford, apparently commissioned by the President to present to Japan certain arms and military stores and to examine the Japanese army and defenses. Mr. Bingham arranged for the execution of their mission.[105] We can imagine his surprise when he learned that his dispatch had been the first intimation the Department had received of such a mission. He was told:

> The commissioning of agents of this Government to other Powers, and the direction of all intercourse with such Powers, is by law and usage entrusted to the Department of State.

It was regretted that he did not report so unusual an occurrence to the Department and await instructions, for the delay and inconvenience involved would have been "of entire insignificance in view of the departure from law and usage in their mission," and of the possible complications which might arise in the present excited state of feelings in China and the jealousy of the latter of the relations of the United States toward Japan.[106] The mission, it seemed, had really been promoted by the War Department, and the official letter of the Secretary of War had seemed to Bingham to give it proper standing.[107]

The first specific case to come under the recent instruction, and the first recommendation he had made since his arrival, was that of Dr. J. C. Berry, who applied for an appointment to examine and report on the condition of the prisons of Japan, at the expense of the Japanese Government.[108] This application was refused, and the Department was not surprised at the answer; in fact it would have hesitated to approve such a request if its advice had been sought.[109] The next was the recommendation of Passed Assistant Paymaster J. Q. Barton for appointment as paymaster in the Japanese navy. This recommendation was accepted.[110]

---

[105] No. 110, August 13.   [106] No. 75, September 30.

[107] No. 153, November 20.

[108] No. 143, October 23. The cost would be trifling, only 280 yen for expenses.   [109] No. 98, December 10.

[110] No. 145, November 3. The contract was for three years; at $4,000 gold and $300 for house rent. At this time Bingham was attacked by House in the

Typical of the sensitive attitude of the Department was its reaction to the presentation, by Bingham, of six copies of the California Code, in appreciation of which two porcelain vases were presented to the compilers. Bingham was advised that while no harm was done in this case, it was a settled rule of the Government that presents should not be offered or given to foreign governments through diplomatic officers of the United States, and particularly not without the direction of the Department.[111] On the other hand, his services in procuring facilities for the American and Mexican expeditions sent out to observe the transit of Venus met with approval,[112] and the facilities afforded by the Japanese were deeply appreciated.[113] And Mr. Bingham was under instruction to further the participation of Japan in the approaching Centennial Exposition in Philadelphia.[114]

With one exception the cases involving the Consulates were of minor importance. Portugal asked that the United States Consul at Hakodate act as Consul for Portugal, and Peru made the same request in the case of Kobe. In both cases Bingham held that the appointment could not be accepted but good offices might be tendered, and his decision was approved.[115]

Judicial cases involved an appeal to his Court by a Japanese plaintiff in Yokohama, which Bingham could not grant, as the case involved more than $2,500 and it should go to the Circuit Court for the District of California.[116] This, we should point out, was a substantial impediment to the prosecution of appeals from American Consular Courts by Japanese litigants. On the other hand, the Japanese Court at Kanagawa refused to compel the

Japan Gazette as being opposed to the appointment of Americans, a backwash of the Formosan affair (No. 146, November 5).

[111] No. 142, October 30, 1874; Instruction No. 95, December 10.

[112] No. 127, September 26, *F.R., 1875,* II, 767–68; No. 165, December 18, *ibid.,* pp. 780–81.

[113] Instruction No. 84, November 6, *ibid.,* p. 772; No. 121, February 6, 1875.

[114] Four instructions and three dispatches deal with these matters.

[115] No. 27, December 8, 1873; No. 33, December 20; No. 71, April 4, 1874; Instruction No. 25, February 19, 1875; No. 40, May 8.

[116] No. 38, January 8, 1875.

attendance of witnesses in a suit brought by an American. This seemed to Bingham to be a violation of the Treaty of 1858, and a denial of justice, but he was careful to await instruction.[117] Mr. Fish, however, recognized that the procedure in Japanese courts might be different from that in American, and the only question was as to whether or not the American plaintiff had been accorded the same facilities and opportunities to obtain testimony as were allowed to Japanese suitors. If he had not, then Bingham was to make suitable representations.[118] The Department had been concerned with the procedure in the Consular Courts, and it later instructed Bingham to ascertain on what law or regulations the practice of charging a fee for the Judge (Consul) was based, and whether or not all fees were reported, as provided by the Act of 1860.[119]

The one troublesome case came up from Yokohama, and it involved the old question of the legislative power of American diplomatic officers. The problem was created by the lawless acts of American citizens at that port. The remedy proposed by Consul General Thomas B. Van Buren was the adoption by him of a code of regulations issued by the British Minister, dealing with the licensing of public houses, with penal provisions for violation of the same. Bingham took the position that American Consuls, or even the Minister, had no such authority, although it was conferred upon the British Minister by Orders in Council, and he asked for instructions.[120]

While the Department recognized the soundness of Bingham's views, it now perceived that something would have to be done to remedy this defect in the American procedure. It believed that Congress should either legislate for American citizens in Japan or delegate the power to do so. In the meantime it desired information as to the power claimed by the Consular Board, whether or not it was claimed by the Consuls to have been conferred by their

---

[117] No. 88, June 3, 1874, *F.R., 1874,* p. 683.
[118] No. 60, July 29, *ibid.,* pp. 692–93.   [119] No. 104, December 22.
[120] No. 158, December 4, 1874, *F.R., 1875,* II, 777–79.

governments; on what authority it existed; and what authority on these questions had been conferred by the other Treaty Powers upon their Ministers in Japan.

The Department further desires to be informed by what authority the general, municipal, and police regulations of Yokohama, or other towns, are adopted and made binding, and what difference there may be in this respect in the towns occupied by foreigners.[121]

For the first time the Department had faced the realities of the situation. Laws were needed, but who was to supply them?

Only a few matters came up affecting American trade. The free export of rice and wheat flour was permitted in November 1873 and suspended in June following.[122] The restrictive regulations of the Silk Guild were set aside by the Government, following a protest.[123] And the only charge of treaty violation was the trifling one that a clearance fee of $20 had been charged the "New York" when it went to the Yokosuka docks for repairs. The Department considered this a breach of the Treaty and approved Bingham's protest.[124]

Of immediate benefit to commercial relations was the Postal Convention between the two countries, the ratification of which was exchanged at Washington on April 18, 1874. It provided for the abolition of the American postal agencies in Japan on January 1, 1875. But it was found that its terms conflicted with the convention between the United States and Hong Kong, and the postmaster of the latter colony refused to accept American mails from the Japanese. This caused the appointment of Van Buren, at Yokohama, as postal agent to handle the mail forwarded from that port to Hong Kong.[125]

The pressure of other matters prevented Mr. Bingham from

[121] No. 115, January 7, 1875, *F.R., 1875,* pp. 782–83.

[122] No. 21, December 1, 1873; No. 90, June 4, 1874.

[123] No. 47, January 20, 1874. This was the Kiito Aratame Kaisho. No non-member could deal in raw silk.

[124] No. 42, January 14, 1874; Instruction No. 28, March 16.

[125] No. 154, November 23, 1874; No. 156, December 3, and telegram; telegram to Bingham, December 28; No. 112, January 4, 1875.

preparing such dispatches on domestic affairs as were to be features of his later correspondence. We have already referred to his report on the Cabinet crisis of 1873, and the determination to follow a program of peace with Korea. A little later he was able to report that the troublesome fractional paper currency had been withdrawn from circulation.[126] In January he wrote of the attempt to assassinate Iwakura, on the fourteenth, the only motive being a desire to overthrow the present Ministry.[127] This was followed by a report of the memorial presented by Soyeshima and other prominent Japanese asking for the establishment of a parliament or popular assembly. The proposal was believed by Bingham to be intended to excite hostility to the newly organized government, as it emanated from men who advocated war with Korea. He linked it with the outbreak of samurai in Hizen, which soon followed.[128]

And, finally, he described his own unofficial efforts to bring about the abolition of torture, which had resulted in a notification of August 25 to the effect that torture was abolished but that "for a short period" it might be employed in certain cases where difficulty occurred in the examination.[129] While the Department viewed the prospect with satisfaction, it felt that Bingham's interposition was a delicate one and that it was fortunate that it had been well received.[130] This caused Bingham to explain that he had refused to join in a protest, as desired by some of the Consuls at Yokohama, and had acted personally and unofficially.[131]

---

[126] No. 22, December 2, 1873.

[127] No. 44, January 17, *F.R., 1874,* p. 661; Instruction No. 29, March 20, *ibid.,* p. 674. For this outrage nine Tosa samurai were degraded and executed on July 10 (No. 100, July 16).

[128] No. 56, February 19, *F.R., 1874,* pp. 664–65.

[129] No. 125, September 26, *F.R., 1875,* II, 766–77.   [130] No. 81, November 3.

[131] No. 171, January 4, 1875. *F.R., 1874,* pp. 659–60, contains Bingham's No. 41, January 12, 1874, dealing with the reception to the Diplomatic Corps on New Year's Day. A sporadic instance of the old anti-foreign feeling was found in the murder of Mr. L. Haber, Acting German Consul at Hakodate, by a samurai. The assassin was promptly tried, found guilty, degraded, and beheaded. A notification of the crime and punishment was published throughout the country (No. 124, September 26, 1874, *F.R., 1875,* II, 765). Consul Hawes attended the execution (No. 140, October 28).

AFTER the frequent squalls of the preceding year, the American Legation in 1875 entered comparatively smooth water. The firm but, as it seemed, inconsistent attitude of Mr. Bingham on several of the matters before him left certain reactions which were to annoy him later. On the one hand, there was a temporary coolness on the part of the Japanese Government and its foreign advisers because of his unexpected actions in the Formosan expedition affair; and, on the other, Sir Harry Parkes and some of his colleagues resented the independent course which Mr. Bingham had adopted in other matters before he received strict instructions to continue the co-operative policy as far as possible. And less important, but far more annoying, was the enmity aroused in Mr. House, the American teacher-journalist, who, at this time, was the most vigorous advocate of the sovereign rights of the Japanese. In those days of national rivalries in the Far East the hostility of the foreign press was to be expected, but Mr. House could reach an American constituency. [2]

One of the first dispatches of the year reported an outburst of criticism in a British-owned paper, this time of the President's proposal to return the Shimonoseki indemnity to Japan for educational purposes, a suggestion which Bingham warmly approved.

---

[1] The dispatches are numbered 167–314; of these one hundred and forty-eight, twenty-one are printed in *F.R., 1875,* II, and five in *F.R., 1876,* and No. 227 is printed in *United States Commercial Relations, 1875,* pp. 1081–84. The instructions are numbered 110–194; of these eighty-five, only five are found in *F.R., 1875,* II, and one in *F.R., 1876.* Mr. Bingham usually designated the dispatches which he would like to have printed.

[2] No. 256, August 19.

The dispatch as printed in *Foreign Relations* seems to be complete, but in the manuscript it reads, in part:

nothing is to my mind clearer than that the application, as suggested by the President, of the increase of this fund to educational purposes in Japan would [be greatly deplored by these journalists because such action would] strengthen American influence. . . . .[3]

The words in brackets are marked "omit," "no stars," and with this editing the dispatch appears in print.

This was the first instance the writer observed in the Japanese correspondence of such a regrettable practice. The pencil notations were, most probably, the work of Alvey A. Adee, then Chief of the Diplomatic Bureau and later Assistant Secretary of State for many years. Up to this point the printed correspondence had been compared with the manuscripts merely to check excusable errors in transcribing strange and badly written Japanese names, and in filling out omissions which were properly defined by asterisks ("stars"). But after this editorial comment was noted, the process became one of trying to discover what had been omitted without proper warning. While it may be said that few instances of this practice were observed, and the significant ones will be duly mentioned, it seems hardly necessary to say that the very fact that such editing was employed must lessen the confidence with which scholars can use the *Foreign Relations* in this long period.

We have already observed that during the incumbency of Secretary of State Seward, 1861–69, the diplomatic correspondence was printed in great fullness. At least the writer can vouch for it in the case of Japan. In 1869–70 no volume appeared, and after that year the annual compilation was not only small in amount but of less than ordinary significance. With few exceptions, the important dispatches and instructions were not disclosed. While the writer is quite prepared to attach certain reservations to open diplomacy, he does not recall any serious inconvenience occasioned by the enlightened policy adopted by Mr. Seward.

The Formosan controversy flared up for a moment when the

---

[3] No. 173, January 19, 1875, *F.R., 1875,* II, 783.

report of Okuma Shigenobu, President of the Formosan Commission, to the Emperor was published. In it this statement appeared: "After our troops had started and were on their way, foreign public servants remonstrated." While this was a correct statement of the case, its implications did not please the Foreign Representatives. It might create the assumption that they had protested against the expedition itself, whereas at most they had only publicly protested against the use of their men and ships. To be sure this was a refinement of terms which had not occurred to Okuma, for if they had not objected to the expedition itself they would not have refused to allow their nationals to take part. But as the German Acting Consul had recently been murdered at Hakodate as an anti-foreign demonstration, the Representatives determined to make a protest. The result was an explanation on Okuma's part that the remonstrance was only against the employment of their national ships and subjects or citizens "until it was known whether such employment would or would not be regarded as hostile by China."[4]

Although according to the accepted principles of international law the very fact that China paid a sum of money to Japan for the relatives of the murdered Loochooans would have constituted a recognition of Japanese sovereignty over their islands, neither

[4] No. 179, January 29, *F.R., 1875,* II, 784–86; No. 183, February 9, *ibid.,* pp. 786–87. In his report Okuma said: "I humbly pray that His Majesty the Tenno will eagerly carry on the work . . . . and that he will not stop with the chastisement of the savages." No explanation was given for this cryptic utterance. The Department awaited further information before giving instructions (No. 129, March 8). In the winter of 1874–75, the Chinese sent a small force to occupy a position near the seat of the Japanese operations. Mr. Bingham reported that three hundred Chinese soldiers were massacred by the aborigines on February 16 (No. 203, March 20). House (*The Japanese Expedition to Formosa,* p. 222) gives the number as more than ninety, and the date as February 13. In July, Bingham received a request from Le Gendre for copies of certain documents in the Legation files. The purpose was to substantiate his claim for salary due. While De Long had proposed a salary of 12,000 yen a year, the actual offer was 1,000 yen a month (which meant a month-to-month tenure). Mr. Bingham refused to furnish such records without instructions from the Department, and his action was approved, leaving Le Gendre free to apply directly to the Department (No. 248, August 2, 1875; Instruction No. 173, September 16). Bingham's dispatch transmitted two letters of De Long to Le Gendre which were not sent to the Department at the time (October 22 and December 18, 1872).

the Chinese nor the Loochooans so interpreted it. The officials of
the Tsungli Yamen had told Okubo that they would not be guided
by the Western code. And while China had never interfered in
the local administration of the Kingdom of Loochoo, and Japan
had recently incorporated it into the Empire, still the old assumption was maintained. Early in 1875 the customary embassy from
Loochoo arrived in Peking, bearing gifts or tribute, and it was received with the usual ceremony, although it occasioned a protest
by the Japanese Minister.[5] And in May, Mr. Avery reported that
Japan intended to assume complete jurisdiction over the islands
and make them an integral part of the Empire.[6] Copies of these
dispatches were forwarded to Bingham, with instructions to see to
it that if Japan took the islands the American Treaty with Loochoo was maintained, unless it was more advantageous to apply
the Treaty with Japan or such parts as might be applicable to the
territory involved.[7]

In one of his conversations with Okubo, on October 24, 1874,
Chargé Williams had cited the Bonin Islands as an example of the
revival of an old claim to territory which had not been administered for many years, and just as Great Britain, so he understood,
had accepted the prior claim of Japan, so he thought Japan should
recognize the generally acknowledged rights of China in all parts
of Formosa.[8] The Department had decided against the assertion
of any American claim in the Bonin Islands, in 1873, but when
Sir Harry Parkes proposed to send the British Consul at Yokohama to visit them, Mr. Bingham reported the action and suggested that, if any of the islands was to be appropriated by Great
Britain in the absence of any claim by any other Power, Bailey
Island, annexed in 1854, might not be retained. As Sir Harry had
offered to investigate any matters there which Bingham might
suggest, the latter availed himself of the opportunity to secure

[5] No. 47, Avery to Fish, April 8, 1875, *F.R., 1875,* I, 313.

[6] No. 58, May 30, *ibid.,* p. 331.

[7] No. 164, July 29. The Department had forgotten that this matter had
been satisfactorily settled in 1872; see *supra.*

[8] No. 70, Williams to Fish, October 29, 1874.

information concerning the recent murder of Captain Pease and as to the number of resident Americans.[9] On the strength of the reports he received he recommended that no further steps were needful for the protection of American citizens or interests in those isolated islands.[10]

Two questions, concerning all the Treaty Powers in Japan, were carried over from previous years. The most troublesome of these involved the general right of legislation and especially the status of Municipal Regulations. In accordance with his instructions Mr. Bingham requested Consul General Van Buren to gather all the information he could obtain. Pending the submission of his report Bingham made a statement as to the legislative authority of the British Minister, who seemed to be the only Foreign Representative in Japan invested with such powers. These powers, as we are aware, were based on the Order in Council of March 9, 1865, which in turn was based on the acts of 6/7 Vict. ch. 80 and ch. 94.[11] When Van Buren made his report it was found that only the Consuls of Germany and the Netherlands had any authority to make local regulations for their nationals having the force of law. The Municipal Regulations for Yokohama had been adopted by the Japanese Government on the recommendation of the Foreign Representatives, while those for Nagasaki seemed to have no authority of law. Bingham was of the opinion that local Municipal and Police Regulations should be made by the Japanese authorities, violations of them being punishable in the Consular Courts in accordance with the laws of the respective governments. He questioned the expediency of intrusting this legislative power to the local Consuls, and he was not sure that Congress could delegate it to either the Consuls or the Minister. In fact he intimated that the Congressional power extended only to the establishment of the necessary courts, in which Americans might be tried,

[9] No. 293, November 18.

[10] No. 312, December 29, *F.R., 1876,* pp. 354–57. It was doubtful if Captain Benjamin Pease was an American citizen.

[11] No. 217, April 17, *F.R., 1875,* II, 791–93.

for every infraction by them, in Japan, of the treaty, of our statutes, or of the laws of Japan not inconsistent with our laws or with the rights guaranteed by treaty.[12]

This was followed by a dispatch in which the authority of the British Minister to issue notifications, under the Order in Council of March 9, 1865, was examined. A list of such notifications showed that Sir Harry Parkes had issued ten, between 1866 and 1870, and the Chargé two, in 1871 and 1873; of the entire twelve, only three might be considered still in force—one dealing with the registration of mortgages, of bills of sale, and of agencies, 1866, one with the Hunting Regulations of 1871, and one with the Railway Regulations of 1873.[13]

The Department took these two dispatches under consideration and no action was taken until, in November, Mr. Bingham presented a concrete case which called for an instruction. The Municipal Council at Nagasaki had levied certain taxes and license fees on property holders, which were to be enforced against delinquents by the several foreign Consuls. When Consul Mangum refused to force payment from an American citizen the matter was reported to Bingham, and in turn to the Department. He indicated his own views in the matter by the statement:

I am not prepared to say that laws can be enacted in Japan to affect the rights of American citizens resident here either by the Municipal Council of Nagasaki or by the joint action of the Foreign Consuls stationed for the time being in that city.

[12] No. 228, May 20, *ibid.,* pp. 798–99. Consul General Van Buren, who had collected the information from the several American Consuls, transmitted a considerable body of correspondence to Bingham. He described the anomalous conditions which had grown up at Yokahama, without definite laws or powers, and apparently without relative legal duties or obligations. He reported having asked the British Consul to arrest a British subject charged with assisting two notorious convicts to escape from the American jail, only to be told that no British law applied to such an offense; and on another occasion he refused a subpoena to bring a British subject into his court as a witness. The German Consul had the right to issue police rules, with a maximum fine of ten thalers ($7.00), but these had to be transmitted to the Minister or the Minister for Foreign Affairs, who could annul the same. The German law was that of June 29, 1865 (No. 812, Van Buren to Bingham, May 11, *ibid.,* pp. 800–809).

[13] No. 229, May 21.

And he repeated his opinion that the Nagasaki Municipal Regulations were agreed upon without the authority of law.[14]

The instruction which was now adopted was the most carefully reasoned of the year's series. The Department repeated its former views, and was in complete accord with Mr. Bingham as to the lack of authority in the American Minister to decree general legislation. "The question now presented, however, is conceived to be different." And then followed a long argument for the necessity of the informal municipal bodies in Japan and for the expediency of supporting their proceedings. A distinction, therefore, had to be made between the power of general legislation and that of municipal regulation. The fact that these municipal bodies lacked adequate sanction was dismissed.

But instances are not wanting in the history of this Government in which similar powers have been exercised by inchoate communities suddenly formed within the jurisdiction of the United States, and who, for the time being, finding themselves situated outside of any organized State or Territory, have been led by the dictates of prudence and necessity to form themselves into a volunteer political organization, frame codes of laws for the preservation of order and good government and the protection of the lives and property of the individuals composing such communities, and to establish tribunals for the administration and enforcement of such laws; and the laws enacted, administered, and executed under such conditions have, so far as is now known, been respected and sanctioned by both the executive and judicial branches of the Government of the United States, as it is believed they have been by the judicial tribunals of the several States of the Union.

This extension to Japan, where a stable government existed, able and willing both to enact and administer municipal laws subject only to the limitations imposed by extraterritoriality, of a system which grew up on the frontier or in the mining camps among citizens of the territorial sovereign, was almost naïve. But, the instruction continued:

If, in the case of the residents of what is known as the "foreign quarter" of Nagasaki, the Government of Japan, in its concession of the territory for that purpose, conferred upon the foreigners residing within such territory the right of such local municipal legislation, or if, in the

[14] No. 291, November 18.

absence of any direct grant, that Government offered no objection to such local arrangement, and cast upon the inhabitants the duty of providing for the general police of the "quarter," such as lighting, paving, sanitary arrangements, and the preservation of the public peace and good order, it would seem to follow that regulations and ordinances enacted and promulgated by a council, selected by the people in such manner as they had mutually agreed upon, should be accepted as the municipal law of the community, have the force and effect of law, and that their observance might be enforced by proper proceedings in the consular courts, subject to the ordinary conditions governing the jurisdiction of these tribunals; and if the correctness of this proposition is admitted, there cannot, it is believed, be any doubt of the right of the municipal council to maintain an action in the consular court for the recovery of a penalty incurred by a failure to pay a public-house license imposed by these regulations.

This argument, however, was qualified by a request for full information

as to the precise nature and extent of the powers granted or conceded by the Japanese government to the residents of the "foreign quarter" at Nagasaki.

Mr. Fish was on firmer ground in developing his next point:

But even in the absence of any such express grant from the authorities of Japan, I am unable to concur in the opinion expressed by you that the regulations or ordinances of the municipal council should not be recognized as binding upon citizens of the United States residing in that community. American citizens, in common with the citizens and subjects of other foreign powers composing the population, enjoy all the rights and privileges pertaining to such residence or domicile, and they share in the common protection afforded to persons and property in the advantages and conveniences resulting from such regulations as provide for the lighting, paving, cleansing, and other sanitary measures for the general welfare of the municipality. They are there voluntarily, it is to be presumed, for the advancement of their own interests; while they share the benefits of a regulated police, they should not be free from the charges of its support, or from its control.

But in any event the Consular Court should have been open to such an action as was contemplated against the American citizen cited. He could offer any kind of defense, he might plead against the competence of the parties bringing suit, he might even question the validity of the license tax, but the Court certainly had no right to refuse to entertain the action on the presupposition that the plaintiff's right was unfounded. Such a refusal on the part of the Consular Court would amount to a practical denial of justice.

Having discussed the whole matter at such length, and in what seemed to be no uncertain terms, the Department refrained from giving Mr. Bingham any definite and final instructions in view of its imperfect information as to the source and origin of the powers claimed by the Municipal Council, and until additional information should have been received.[15]

After a year's delay, the Hunting Regulations again came up for discussion. In November 1874 the revised regulations had been referred to the home governments, but none would accept them in their existing form. The question at issue was over the payment into the Japanese treasury of fines collected in the Consular Courts. Bingham tried to persuade Terashima that this was a small matter in comparison with the acceptance of the regulations and the readiness to enforce them in the foreign courts, but the Minister for Foreign Affairs was unyielding. As the amount involved was so small, Bingham suggested to Mr. Fish that they might well be turned over to the Japanese Government. "Something, it seems to me, should be accorded to these people."[16]

Two questions of treaty interpretation came up during the year, in each of which Mr. Bingham adopted the Japanese point of view. The first arose from a proposal to regulate the opium trade, with a view to the importation of medicinal opium. This had been the subject of a joint recommendation, in which Mr. De Long had joined with some of his colleagues in 1873.[17] On January 19 of that year the Representatives had pointed out the serious inconvenience occasioned by the sudden refusal to permit the importation of medicinal opium, and they had renewed the

[15] No. 200, January 20, 1876, *F.R., 1876,* pp. 350–53.

[16] No. 304, December 7, *ibid.,* p. 350. Just at this time an American was charged in the Yokohama Consular Court with unlawfully shooting and wounding a Japanese with intent to kill. This was a hunting accident, and the accused was acquitted, as no malicious intent was proved. Bingham repeated his recommendation about the paying over of fines collected, believing that they would not exceed $100 a year (No. 313, December 29).

[17] He failed to report this proceeding.

protest on May 12. The next day Mr. Uyeno forwarded a draft
of regulations under which the importation might be provisionally
allowed. This led to the drafting of an agreement, incorporating
the views of the Diplomatic Corps, which they requested the Government to adopt in place of the rules submitted by Uyeno. But
no action was taken in 1873. Sir Harry Parkes now sought Bingham's support in 1875. The latter took the position that Japan
had the right to make such regulations as she pleased for the
importation of medicinal opium, while if all forms of opium were
prohibited by the Treaty, then a joint regulation was equally inadmissible without a revision of the treaty provisions.[18]

Mr. Fish held that a reasonable quantity, such as might actually be required for medicinal purposes, might be admitted under
proper restrictions and without change or violation of the Treaty.
He did not approve the wording of the counter regulations, as
suggesting that the Foreign Representatives and the Japanese authorities had the right to modify the Treaty, and felt that both
proposals seemed to contemplate a larger importation than would
appear necessary for the purposes alleged.

> While a reasonable importation may be necessary for medicinal pur-
> poses, we should see that no such necessity be taken advantage of to per-
> mit a trade which is specially prohibited by the Treaty.[19]

The other instance afforded Mr. Bingham an opportunity to
develop for the first time the view which he was so often to express, that Japan should be relieved of the conventional tariff
imposed in 1866. In transmitting a trade report for 1874, in
which the balance was strongly against Japan, and additional figures for the first six months of 1875, in which her imports were
valued at $15,046,008 and her exports at $6,969,313, in addition
to gold exported to the amount of $9,455,274 and gold imports of
only $86,544, he said that this was largely, if not exclusively,

---

[18] No. 227, May 18, *United States Commercial Relations, 1875,* pp. 1081–84.
The counter regulations proposed by the Japanese are found here.

[19] No. 160, July 12. By refraining from any reference to the right of the
Japanese to make their own regulations, Mr. Fish intimated that joint regulation was preferable or proper.

attributable to the Convention of 1866, which subjected Japan to large importations, chiefly from Europe, "without the right, supposed to be inherent in nations, to check them by impost duties, or to derive large revenues from them."

And in this connection he forwarded a copy of a Protocol signed by Terashima, Parkes, and von Brandt, on May 10, 1874, which was designed to clarify the meaning of "iron manufactured" in the Convention, and fix specific duties on certain categories.

It has occurred to me that if Great Britain and Germany may thus reform the tariff Convention of 1866, it might be proper for the United States to reform it so as to relieve Japan from its oppressive limitations.[20]

While failing to comment on this *démarche* of the two Ministers, the Department did request Bingham to inform it fully as to the effect of his suggested revision upon American trade and of his reasons for thinking it might be proper to reform the tariff Convention.[21]

Before this request could be received, Bingham had returned to his proposal, this time reporting the Russian Minister as having recently declared the Convention a great injustice. He himself believed that if it were proposed to abrogate the Convention, and all other commercial restrictions, and to allow Japan to regulate her own foreign commerce by reasonable revenue laws, she would gladly open Shimonoseki, and perhaps other ports, to each Treaty Power that would grant a release.

I do not think anyone of the treaty powers would venture long to reject so just a measure of relief to Japan if it were proposed by the United States alone or jointly with one or two of the other treaty powers. Inasmuch as Japan is the natural gate of commercial communication for all Eastern Asia with the United States, and through the United States with all Western Europe, it concerns the United States quite as much as it does any State in Europe to observe and insist upon a policy of justice toward Japan.[22]

[20] No. 276, October 8. It is surprising that this Protocol which was designed to benefit British and German importers, and was applicable only to them—unless the most-favored-nation clause was invoked—had not come to Bingham's attention earlier.   [21] No. 199, January 15, 1876.

[22] No. 298, November 22. The dispatch covered a reprint of an article in

These were the first expressions of Mr. Bingham's belief in the justice and wisdom of granting tariff autonomy to Japan, a belief which he voiced with increasing emphasis until, in 1878, it was approved by his Government. But that could not be until after the stout advocate of the co-operative policy had retired from the Department of State.

Ten claims were reported by Mr. Bingham as coming to his attention. Seven were old or new ones brought against Japan, three were claims against the United States or one of its officers. With the old claims little progress was made. The Hozier claim was pressed without result, to the regret of the Department, which urged the continuance of Bingham's efforts. In reporting on the defense put forward by Japan, Bingham blamed the "legal adviser whoever that may be." We need not assume that Judge Bingham did not know who he was. He was unquestionably Peshine Smith, former Examiner of Claims in the United States Department of State, who was well versed in the methods of handling claims and whose devotion to the cause of his present employers brought down upon him the wrath and the ridicule of a considerable portion of the foreign community. While other foreigners were employed as legal advisers in some of the departments, it is most probable that Mr. Smith handled all claims which came up to the Ministry of Foreign Affairs.[23]

Nor did the "Peiho" claim make any progress. Japan at first evaded the proposal for arbitration, and then made it conditional on Captain Batchelder's presentation of his proofs in advance. In this claim, also, the Department directed Bingham to continue his efforts.[24]

Four new claims were brought forward. Captain Alfred Ever-

the London *Spectator* which purported to give the plans of Great Britain for securing the support of China and Japan in her threatened complications with Russia. It even went so far as to envisage the making of San Francisco a British port. The friendliness of Russia to Japan just at this time was a repercussion of the Anglo-Russian situation. Bingham was instructed to report any further indication along the lines suggested by the article (No. 194, December 30).

[23] No. 181, February 8; No. 222, May 6; Instruction No. 149, June 7.
[24] No. 182, February 8; No. 200, March 3; Instruction No. 148, June 7.

son, of the Japanese ship "Capron," was dismissed before the expiration of his contract. His claim for $1,083.33 seemed to Bingham to be just. The Department directed him to use his good offices unofficially if he considered the dismissal arbitrary and without sufficient cause.[25] The very active firm of Walsh, Hall & Company, whose claims had been pressed by both De Long and Bingham, now sought support for a claim for $474,000 for money loaned to Japanese contractors who engaged in filling up a swamp and building a canal at Yokohama. Bingham referred it to the Department without comment. While this fell within the category of voluntary contracts, he was directed to use his unofficial good offices.[26]

The claim of the estate of R. G. Carlyle, against the Minister of Public Works, brought up a question of procedure within the American foreign service. The claim was presented directly to the Ministry through Consular channels, from Hawes, at Hakodate, to Van Buren, at Yokohama. This caused a protest by Bingham and a reprimand from the Department to the offending Consular officers. The case was a simple one, and required no intervention, for Carlyle had died during the term of his contract.[27] And another question of procedure was raised when George E. Rice asked for copies of certain papers in the Legation files in order to support the old claim of his father, E. E. Rice, against Japan, which had arisen in 1858–59. Mr. Bingham would not open the archives except on instruction, and the Department held that such papers could be supplied only in special cases, and then only at the request of an interested party or his legally authorized agent.[28]

[25] No. 213, April 8; Instruction No. 147, June 7. The "Capron" was one of two ships built in New York for the Yezo Colonization Commission, in 1872. Everson had a two-year contract but was dismissed within four months of its expiration. On further investigation Bingham considered the claim not well founded (No. 352, March 7, 1876).

[26] No. 240, June 23; Instruction No. 182, October 24. In February 1876 this claim was settled for $300,000 (No. 338, February 8, 1876).

[27] No. 269, September 20; No. 296, November 22; Instruction No. 185, November 1.

[28] No. 279, October 8; Instruction No. 186, November 10. Bingham sent a copy of the desired deed to the Department (No. 411, June 5, 1876).

The most interesting of the claims was that of Joseph Heco, the first Japanese to travel extensively in the United States, who has given us an account of his many adventures in *The Narrative of a Japanese*. Returning to Japan as an American citizen he had engaged in business and in journalism, and for a time was attached to the Yokohama Consulate as an interpreter. He now brought forward a "Daimyo claim," for money loaned in 1871 to carry on a coal mine in Hizen. The amount was small, $1,000, plus two per cent interest a month from August 24, 1871. Bingham considered the claim well founded.[29]

The Department took this instance as an occasion for warning Bingham against receiving such claims and recommending them to its consideration. If persons holding such petty claims could count upon diplomatic intervention, both the Legation and the Department would be seriously inconvenienced and possibly the Government itself might be involved. But the unfavorable attitude was, in part, adduced by the intimation that Heco was not eligible for naturalization in the first place.[30]

This led Mr. Bingham to write the first dispatch dealing with Japanese naturalization which may be found in the Legation files. He proceeded to say:

> How white the alien must be to constitute him "a white person" within the Act of 1824, or, in other words, whether the applicant is "a white person" within the meaning of the Act is a judicial question, the decision of which by the United States Court in this case is, I suppose, conclusive upon me.

Heco had been naturalized by Honorable William F. Gill, Judge of the District Court of the United States for the Maryland District, on June 30, 1858, and a copy of his naturalization papers was forwarded for the information of the Department.[31]

The United States continued to be a negligent tenant, and Bingham reported that $1,621.09 was due Japan for the Zempu-

---

[29] No. 225, May 14.   [30] No. 153, July 2.

[31] No. 265, September 8. Mr. Bingham, the experienced lawyer and legislator, was not ready to accept a criticism of his recognition of Heco, as an American citizen, without comment.

kuji, the former temple Legation in Tokyo, from July 1, 1872, to June 8, 1874. These quarters were surrendered to the Japanese early in the year as Bingham had removed to a more convenient and habitable residence. The back rent was finally paid in October, while the overpayment of rents for Lot 178 at Yokohama was settled by the return of $276.72 by Japan.[32]

Japan also continued to press its claim against E. E. Rice for supplies furnished three American vessels at Hakodate when he was Consul there, in 1857–58,[33] and Bingham reported, in 1876, that he thought the claim was just.[34]

The "Aroostook" claim, which had been before the Legation and the Department since 1870, was settled in a surprising way. The claim was now pressed on behalf of A. Vermede, for $10,000, and Bingham reported it with a favorable recommendation. The Department decided to transmit it to the Navy Department for a report, and it found that the claim had already been paid to the administrator of J. O. P. Stearns, who was considered to have been the real owner of the vessel.[35]

While, as we have seen, Bingham's request for authority to recommend Americans for appointment in Japan had been granted, his recommendations were subject to the careful scrutiny of the Department. To clarify the record he stated that he had made only three such recommendations; one of Dr. Berry and Paymaster Barton, which he had reported at the time; and one for G. J. Rockwell, who had been appointed a teacher in the Agricultural Department.[36] But so careful was he not to overstep his authority that he asked the approval of the Department in advance before recommending General Horace Capron for appointment to the Japanese Commission for the Philadelphia Exposition and

[32] No. 175, January 19; No. 176, January 19; No. 223, May 10; No. 288, October 30; Instruction No. 125, February 27.

[33] Instruction 151, June 17, 1875.   [34] No. 468, November 24, 1876.

[35] No. 271, September 22; Instruction No. 184, October 29, and No. 195, January 3, 1876. With the dispute which then arose between the two claimants we are not concerned (No. 344, February 20; Instruction No. 245, August 12, 1876).

[36] No. 185, February 9.

Dr. H. L. Latham for a civil appointment.[37] On the promotion of Mr. Rockwell, Bingham recommended William R. Corwin to succeed him. The instruction to recommend General Capron arrived after he had left Japan, but Dr. Latham was appointed in the Agricultural Department, Dr. J. G. Ayres was recommended and appointed as a surgeon but declined the post, while George L. Harris and Charles F. Powell were recommended for other positions.[38]

These were the only recommendations which were made during the year, but Mr. Bingham was able to report the entire satisfaction which had been given by General Capron, Dr. David Murray, and Mr. George B. Williams, who were leaving Japan, the last named on a Government mission.[39] He also transmitted two reports by American advisers, one by Thomas Hogg, on the flora of Yesso (Hokkaido) and Niphon (Honshiu), which was published in *Foreign Relations,* and the other an additional report by D. W. Ap Jones, on grazing lands.[40]

Bingham's cautiousness, in comparison with De Long's impetuousness, was well founded. It would be hard to imagine a less harmful procedure than the presentation to the Japanese Government of a set of charts from the Coast Survey Office on behalf of Professor George Davidson, of the astronomical party at Nagasaki. But he was promptly reminded of previous instructions that such gifts should not be presented without the specific direction of the Department.[41] And, mindful of his experience with a military mission in the previous year, we may assume that he scrutinized

[37] No. 187, February 12. The Department approved the recommendation of Rockwell, and instructed him to make the recommendation of Capron and Latham (No. 138, April 22; No. 139, April 22). The Department made clear that it had objected only to the proposal of Dr. Berry.

[38] No. 246, July 17; No. 260, September 6.

[39] For the farewell audience of General Capron, and the tribute paid him by Governor Kuroda, see No. 220, April 21, *F.R., 1875,* II, 795–96. Dr. Murray was returning on leave, from his great service as adviser to the Department of Education. Mr. Williams was an adviser in the Department of Finance (No. 287, October 25).

[40] No. 193, February 22, *F.R., 1875,* II, 789–90; No. 208, March 24.

[41] No. 177, January 20; Instruction No. 124, February 26.

with care the credentials of Major General Upton, Brigadier General Forsyth, and Major Sanger, who had been commissioned to report on military service in Asia and Europe. He presented them to the Minister of War, and they were honored by a review of troops.[42]

On the other hand, he was active in furthering an adequate participation of Japan in the Philadelphia Exposition, and he was happy to report that Okubo had been appointed President, and General Saigo Yorimichi, Vice-President of the Japanese Commissioners. The anticipated public and private expenditure for Japanese exhibits was estimated at 600,000 yen.[43]

Several interesting cases involving extraterritoriality arose during the year. From Yokohama came one of the troublesome deportation cases. Rappeport, an American citizen, who had several times been convicted of assault, and who had spent the greater part of the previous year in the Consular jail, would be released on May 30. Van Buren had notified the local governor that he would withdraw his protection, leaving the man to be deported or punished by the Japanese authorities for future offenses. The latter, in reply, asked the Consul General to deport him under the seventh article of the Treaty, which Van Buren said he had no authority to do. Bingham approved this reply, but he did not approve the original statement that Van Buren could withdraw American protection from a citizen, even after his second conviction for a misdemeanor. He held that the Japanese could make their own law for such a contingency, to be enforced in the Consular Courts and according to American procedure and penalties.[44]

[42] No. 264, September 8, *F.R., 1875,* II, 828; No. 267, September 15, *ibid.*
[43] Seven dispatches deal with these details.
[44] No. 232, June 7, *F.R., 1875,* II, 809–12. In the John Rogers case, in 1873, the original sentence in the Consular Court was imprisonment for one year and deportation, which the Department approved. The seventh article of the Treaty of 1858 read: ". . . . Americans who have been convicted of felony, or twice convicted of misdemeanors, shall not go more than one Japanese ri inland from the places of their respective residences, and all persons so convicted shall lose their right to permanent residence in Japan, and the Japanese authorities may require them to leave the country. A reasonable time shall be allowed to all

In other words, the penalty of deportation could not be enforced. The Japanese could not lay hands upon an American offender and send him away, and the Consuls had no authority to do so. While the treaty provision was designed to protect the Japanese, the practice of extraterritoriality denied the remedy. A very simple and honorable solution of the problem would have been for Congress to have conferred this authority on American Consuls in order to carry out the plain intent of the Treaty. Mr. Bingham's solution, which was the only one open to him, would have incurred continual expense to the American authorities through the repeated confinement of recalcitrant citizens.

From Yokohama came the case of a British subject, McCondrill, serving on U.S.S. "Lackawanna." When he was arrested on shore for drunkenness and assault Van Buren turned him over to the British Consul. This action was disapproved by the Minister.[45] But just at the same time there came a complaint from Sir Harry Parkes that British subjects who had been discharged from American naval and merchant ships had become a charge on the British Consul for relief.[46] The distinction here was, in the mind of Mr. Bingham, that as long as British subjects were serving on an American ship they were subject to American law and extraterritorial jurisdiction, while on severing that connection they resumed their national status. The Department approved Bingham's views in the first instance. The matter, however, became the subject of a protest by the British Minister in Washington.[47]

The issue was again raised in the case of an Italian subject who committed a murderous assault upon the mate of an American vessel on the high seas. Van Buren held that he had authority to try only American citizens, and he asked if he should turn the

---

such persons to settle their affairs, and the American Consular authority shall, after an examination into the circumstances of each case, determine the time to be allowed, but such time shall not in any case exceed one year, to be calculated from the time the person shall be free to attend to his affairs."

[45] No. 204, March 20.   [46] No. 205, March 23.

[47] No. 144, June 5. The problem of destitute American citizens was also present, and there was no provision for their relief, unless they were seamen (No. 212, April 6; Instruction No. 143, May 11).

man over to the Italian Consul. After a further exchange of letters, Bingham ruled that the man was subject to American law, and should be tried in the United States by an American Court.[48] The question here was one not of extraterritoriality, for Van Buren could only try a person accused of an offense in Japan, but of the supremacy of American laws on American ships on the high seas. Bingham's advice to Van Buren was approved as "in strict accordance with law, precedent, and the invariable ruling of the department."[49]

The third case involved the law of extradition. A British subject, accused of embezzlement in Japan, had fled to the United States. Both Van Buren and Bingham held that he could not be returned there, under the American extradition Treaty with Great Britain. The Department sustained their views, on the ground that embezzlement was not an extraditable offense under the Treaty of August 9, 1842, and that an offense committed in Japan was not within the jurisdiction of Great Britain.[50]

The right of an American Consul to prosecute private claims before Japanese courts was questioned by Mr. Bingham. It grew out of Van Buren's request for information which the former had received from Japanese officials and which the latter needed for his private practice. The Department was not quite sure of its position in this matter, for much would depend upon the rules and mode of procedure in the Japanese courts, but it "was not prepared to assert that circumstances may not arise when it may be necessary for the Consul to appear in Court in behalf of a citizen of the United States." As for the furnishing or withholding of papers, the Minister must be governed by his own knowledge of the circumstances and his own judgment.[51]

The Consular jail at Yokohama had been a continual source

---

[48] No. 270, September 22, 1875, *F.R., 1876*, pp. 344–48.

[49] No. 183, October 28, *ibid.,* p. 348.

[50] No. 245, July 17, *F.R., 1875*, II, 817–18; No. 170, August 18, *ibid.,* p. 821.

[51] No. 309, December 27; Instruction No. 207, February 21, 1876. The only other reported complaint against a Consular officer was one of E. E. Rice against Vice-Consul Denison, which Bingham refused to entertain (No. 262, September 8).

of complaint. It had been built by the Japanese authorities for the use of the United States, and the rent was based on the capital expenditure. Within two years considerable repairs were necessary, and the whole matter was referred to Bingham for investigation and report. He ascertained that the necessary repairs would cost $1,000, while the Japanese would sell the building for $5,000 and charge $175.40 ground rent. But he also believed that the cost of the building, $5,956, was exorbitant and should not have been more than $3,000. Van Buren alleged that the Japanese contractors had defrauded their own authorities. The Department was quite distressed to learn that the United States had been paying a rental of ten per cent on an excessive cost. It held that the Japanese should make the repairs, and directed Bingham to report whether or not the rent was excessive and should be reduced.[52]

The Postal Convention of 1874 had broken down, in part, through the attitude of Hong Kong, and Japan sought a new agreement, but the difficulty was removed, for the time at least, by the willingness of the Hong Kong Postmaster to permit the transfer of American mails through the British post office at Yokohama. The American Postal Agency there would be closed on January 1, 1876, a year after the agreed date.[53]

On only one occasion did Mr. Bingham have to protest against the wrong treatment of his nationals, and the outcome was a most gratifying one. On August 14 two American visitors, Hon. William A. Richardson and Commander R. F. R. Lewis, U.S.N., were arrested some eighteen miles from Yokohama, but within the treaty limits of travel. They were returned to Yokohama the next day, under guard, and released under the promise of an officer of the Consulate General that they would appear to answer any complaint against them. Bingham at once reported the matter to Terashima and asked for investigation and the punishment of the guilty. The fault was found to lie with ignorant local officials,

---

[52] Instruction No. 118, January 16, No. 123, February 20, No. 154, July 2; Dispatch No. 206, March 23.

[53] No. 167, January 2; No. 286, October 25; Instruction No. 169, August 17.

two of whom were promptly dismissed, and the sincere regret of the Government was expressed. While this action was considered satisfactory, Bingham suggested that it be made the subject of a public notification as was done in 1874, when a member of Sir Harry's escort was assaulted in the British Legation. This recommendation was also promptly acceded to, and a statement of the offense and the punishment was sent out to all local functionaries. While Mr. Bingham and the gentlemen involved were entirely satisfied with the prompt action of the Japanese authorities, some of the Yokohama residents clamored for sterner measures. The Minister was of the opinion,

that no further satisfaction than has been so promptly given in this case could be demanded, save upon the hypothesis that a government is to be punished for every lawless act of its petty officials, committed in ignorance of duty and in violation of express instructions. The adoption of any such rule would surely imperil the peace of nations and insult the enlightened judgment of mankind.[54]

Over against this prompt satisfaction for the lawless conduct of petty Japanese officials stands a Japanese protest of a more serious nature.

The incident developed out of the settlement of the Sakhalin controversy with Russia. After the failure of the attempt to secure the good offices of the President, in 1870, the Japanese had dealt directly with Russia. In 1872 Japan tried to buy the island from Russia; the next year it was decided to abandon the territory as worthless, but this decision was soon reversed, and Vice-Admiral Enomoto, the Hakodate "pirate" of 1869, was sent to St. Petersburg as Minister, with instructions to settle the boundary. For a time Russia refused to make the slightest concession, but when the war clouds gathered in the Balkans she accepted the Japanese terms. Sakhalin would be recognized as Russian territory, while all the Kurile Islands would pass to Japan. The Treaty was signed on May 7, 1875.[55]

[54] No. 257, August 23, *F.R., 1875*, II, 821–25; No. 261, September 7, *ibid.*, pp. 825–27.

[55] Ariga, in Stead, editor, *Japan by the Japanese*, pp. 173–75. Ariga states that in August 1873 De Long told Soyeshima, privately, that Russia was willing

At the end of July the Japanese Government published regulations to govern fishing and hunting off the coasts and on the shores of Hokkaido and the adjacent islands, and the Foreign Representatives were asked to promulgate them to their countrymen. Foreign vessels were prohibited from hunting or fishing within a cannon's range of the shores. Japanese officers could warn a vessel to leave the neighborhood if they believed her preparing to violate the regulations, and if she did violate them they could board her and examine her cargo. Failure to withdraw, or to permit the examination of cargo, would result in the bringing of the ship to the nearest port and her delivery to the Consul, where if found guilty she would be condemned.

Bingham was not prepared to promulgate such regulations without instruction. He had not been officially informed of the new territorial claims of Japan, and he was not sure about the validity of the articles providing for the search and seizure of foreign vessels on the high seas.[56]

But in an accompanying dispatch he reported some very pertinent information which Sir Harry Parkes had given him. The latter had been informed that American vessels were engaged in sea-otter hunting along the coasts of the northern islands. Recently local officers had brought to the American Consul at Hakodate four American citizens who had been left on Iturup over the winter to hunt sea otters. Consul Hawes had fined the leader $100 for entering an open port and had discharged the others, but he was holding some fifty-three sea-otter pelts, worth $100 to $150 each, for the return of their ship.

Parkes also told him that the tiny American sloop "Dolphin," ten tons, had cruised all winter hunting sea otters, until it was lost with its crew of three. This was the fifth fatal wreck which had come to Bingham's attention in the last eighteen months, and he thought it would be well to issue some proclamations to warn

to sell her claims to Japan. De Long did not report this to the Department. Bingham was not able to transmit a copy of the Treaty until his No. 297, November 22. Schuyler reported the signature from St. Petersburg on May 15 (*F.R., 1875*, II, 1065).

[56] No. 253, August 4, *ibid.*, pp. 819–20.

American vessels not to violate the regulations, for if the hunters could not land on the islands they could not transact their business very successfully.[57]

This was in keeping with Bingham's views that the Japanese had the right to legislate and the Treaty Powers the right to try and punish. The Department would not go all the way with him. Instead of a proclamation of warning, he was told, a semi-official notice of caution might be published.[58] But the regulations proposed by Japan, the Department wrote, were by no means acceptable. A marine league should be substituted for a cannon's shot. The power to warn and arrest should be confined strictly to waters over which Japan had exclusive jurisdiction, and the power to warn might be abused. In fact the whole regulation was loosely drawn, and might be improved after proper representation.[59]

At this point the Japanese Government formally protested against the acquittal of the four sea-otter hunters at Hakodate. There seemed to be nothing that Bingham could do in the matter, except report it to the Department, and while Mr. Fish thought that, on Terashima's statement of the facts, there was some reasonable ground for complaint, he could suggest no remedy.[60]

A number of dispatches dealt with matters of political interest. In April the Imperial decrees for the establishment of the Genro-in (Senate) and the Daishin-in (Supreme Court) were transmitted, and the working regulations soon followed.[61] The new badges of merit and of military service, in eight classes, were described.[62]

[57] No. 254, August 4, *F.R., 1875*, II, 820–21.

[58] No. 174, September 20, *ibid.*, p. 829.

[59] No. 178, September 28, *ibid.*, pp. 829–30.

[60] No. 193, December 3. Up to that date Consul Hawes had not reported his action. If the facts were as reported by both Parkes and Terashima, Hawes could have found them guilty of misdemeanors in going beyond the treaty limits, irrespective of the applicability of the new regulations which were not, of course, known to them. He certainly should not have returned the illegally taken pelts.

[61] No. 219, April 20, *F.R., 1875*, II, 794; No. 224, May 11. The publication of so many Japanese Government documents in *Foreign Relations* made the series a very useful source book until the publication of McLaren, *Japanese Government Documents*, 1914.

[62] No. 226, May 15, *F.R., 1875*, II, 797–98.

The proclamation, and regulations, for the Assembly of Prefectural Governors,[63] and for the new courts, from the Supreme Court to the District Court, were sent forward.[64] Some months later the regulations for appeals to superior courts were submitted,[65] then the proclamation of November 5 modifying the system of conscription,[66] and, finally, an account of the opening of a normal school for girls in Tokyo by Her Majesty the Empress.

The establishment of this institution, at the instance and largely by patronage, as I am advised, of Her Majesty, may be considered an event of great significance in the East, and, if maintained, will doubtless contribute most effectively to the moral and intellectual elevation of the women of this empire.[67]

Cabinet dissensions were reported in November, which involved the withdrawal of the Satsuma statesman, Shimadzu Saburo. At this time General Le Gendre withdrew from Japanese employ.[68]

Because of the quicker mail service, especially during the winter months, American Ministers in Japan occasionally reported news from China, and later from Korea. Thus Mr. Bingham sent in a report of the death of the Emperor, of the regency established for his adopted heir, and of the apprehension regarding an antiforeign attitude in the Court.[69] He also reported the murder of Mr. Margary, which was to have important implications the next year.[70] Mr. Avery, from Peking, told of the arrival of a Japanese Commission to inspect agricultural, military, customs, and internal affairs.[71] The Japanese who had sent such missions to the West were not unmindful of their old teacher.

When the Japanese Government, in 1873, decided against hostilities with Korea, it assumed the responsibility for the establishment of friendly relations through diplomacy. Its efforts in

---

[63] No. 238, June 22, *ibid.*, pp. 812–13. The regulations are not given in McLaren.

[64] No. 239, June 22, *ibid.*, pp. 814–17. These are not found in McLaren.

[65] No. 292, November 18. [66] No. 300, November 22.

[67] No. 303, December 4, *F.R., 1876*, p. 349. [68] No. 294, November 18.

[69] No. 195, February 22. [70] No. 216, April 16.

[71] No. 90, Avery to Fish, August 17, *F.R., 1875*, I, 401–2.

this direction either escaped the attention of Mr. Bingham or were not considered worthy of transmission. But Mr. Avery, in Peking, furnished the Department with a helpful summary of these developments, which he had obtained from the Japanese Chargé there:

> It would seem that during the five or six years prior to 1874, the Mikado of Japan sent several deputations to the Corean Government, seeking, generally, to cultivate more intimate relations with his neighbor upon the Northwest, and, particularly, to arrange for the more friendly treatment by the Coreans of certain Japanese merchants and sailors who go thither in the interests of commerce. These deputations, without exception, failed of both the general and particular objects of their mission, being in no case allowed access to His Majesty, the King, and in one or two instances—so my informant stated—the lower members of the deputation had been seized on pretext of some crime, and been beaten and cast into prison, where some had died and others were believed to be still incarcerated.[72]

In the summer of 1874, a Korean Embassy visited Japan with a letter from the King expressing his regret at the treatment accorded the previous Japanese emissaries and giving assurance of his desire for friendly intercourse. This encouraged the Japanese to send a high official, with a large retinue, to deliver a letter from the Emperor. But on his arrival he was denied an audience because of the Western uniform which was prescribed for Japanese diplomatic officers. All he could do was to report the situation and await instructions. In the meantime he wrote to the Japanese Chargé in Peking asking him to inquire, either from the Korean tribute mission or from the Tsungli Yamen itself, whether or not China was interfering to thwart the Embassy. The Chargé felt unable to enter upon this discussion lest it bring about the very result which was feared. But he gave Mr. Avery this very useful piece of information: When the Japanese Commission passed through Tientsin, in August, Li Hung-Chang asked one of its members,

[72] Observe that the Japanese had not forgotten that the alleged *raison d'être* of Commodore Perry's mission was the protection of shipwrecked American seamen and their property. The negotiations described above had taken place at Fusan. The 1874 attempt secured a promise to send a letter to Japan and receive an envoy in return.

in a brusque manner, for which the Viceroy is somewhat noted:—"What, after all, was the real desire and purpose of Japan regarding Corea?" The answer was given that the Japanese only desired to establish and cultivate the relations of intimacy and friendly intercourse proper between two independent Powers, lying in such close proximity. The Viceroy responded: "That is right. If the Coreans fail to respond to your friendly overtures, let me know, and I will advise them in your behalf."[73]

On the very day that this dispatch was received, the mail brought a dispatch from Bingham reporting a current rumor that Japan might declare war upon Korea. The explanation was found in the attack by Korean forts upon a small Japanese warship engaged in soundings off the coast. The fire was returned and the fort captured, with some loss of life. As Mr. Bingham thought war was a possibility he asked for instructions as to declaring strict neutrality, which would have to assume that both Powers were at peace with the United States, although no treaty was in existence with Korea.[74]

Mr. Avery was able to report additional details, although his dispatch did not arrive until much later. The attack occurred very near the scene of Admiral Rodger's engagement in 1871 (and on this occasion also the Americans were engaged in making soundings). The Japanese did not attack the batteries until the third day, and after a boat, under a flag of truce sent to inquire into the first attack, had been fired upon. When the retaliatory measures did take place, the Japanese destroyed the fort, killed thirty Koreans and captured thirty, and took seventeen cannon and many small arms. When the Japanese Chargé informed Prince Kung of the occurrence the latter made no comment, and whether or not this was due to China's existing complications with Great Britain over the Margary murder was doubtful. But, said Mr. Avery,

I am of opinion that, in any event, China would manifest no interest in this question of Corea versus Japan, except in case of actual war; and it is doubtful whether even then she would interfere in any positive manner.[75]

[73] No. 98, Avery to Fish, September 7 (received November 9).
[74] No. 274, October 6, *F.R., 1876*, p. 348.
[75] No. 111, Avery to Fish, October 26 (received December 27).

The Department approved Bingham's view of considering both Powers as at peace with the United States, but preferred to consider the issuance of a proclamation of neutrality only after active hostilities might be commenced.[76]

But before this instruction reached him, Bingham had altered his views somewhat. On December 9, he had discussed the whole matter with Terashima.[77] The latter gave him a résumé of Japan's relations with Korea and said that the Government "has determined to send thither a Commissioner duly authorized to request the negotiation of a treaty of commerce and friendship as was agreed upon [in 1874]." Bingham's views on this proposal were requested. He promptly stressed the importance of avoiding war and the duty of seeking an amicable settlement by the peaceful negotiation, if possible, of a treaty of friendship and commerce. But as this had already been decided upon, what Terashima sought was an opinion as to the best way to approach Korea and as to the propriety of sending the Commissioner in a Japanese man-of-war. Bingham said such a ship might be employed, if it lay outside the harbor and the Commissioner went ashore in a small boat, but it would avoid complaint on the part of the Foreign Powers if Japan would abstain from employing foreign vessels or nationals in the matter. He was assured that Japan would not use either in this service. He had nothing more to offer, except to add that should the Commissioner be rejected it seemed to him that the conquest of Korea was hardly "worth the candle." And while Terashima disclaimed any purpose of conquest, he intimated that Korea must respect the rights of Japan and the general rights of nations. From this conversation Bingham inferred that at no very distant day Japan would make war upon Korea, unless the friendly intervention of other Powers brought about an amicable treaty relation between the two countries. "While war upon Corea should be avoided, it also seems needful that by some means Corea should be made amenable to reason and justice."

[76] No. 187, November 10.

[77] For conversation of Terashima with British Chargé Plunkett the same day see *Japan. No. 1 (1876)*, p. 1.

Since sending his last dispatch he had examined *Foreign Relations, 1871,* which covered the Low-Rodgers expedition to Korea, and had found that Korea was held to be independent and that the reprisals inflicted at that time were approved.

This . . . . inclines me to the opinion that Japan but follows our example in seeking reparation for the alleged unprovoked assault by Corea upon her vessel and flag.

He therefore renewed his request for instructions as to a neutrality proclamation in case of war.[78]

---

[78] No. 306, December 13. The Department merely referred him to its vague instruction of November 10 (No. 205, February 14, 1876). The writer has been told, by an intimate friend of Mr. Bingham, that at Terashima's request he supplied the latter with the *Narrative* of Perry's expedition.